ISBN 978-1-331-18585-7
PIBN 10155635

English
Français
Deutsche
Italiano
Español
Português

www.forgottenbooks.com

Mythology Photography **Fiction**
Fishing Christianity **Art** Cooking
Essays Buddhism Freemasonry
Medicine **Biology** Music **Ancient
Egypt** Evolution Carpentry Physics
Dance Geology **Mathematics** Fitness
Shakespeare **Folklore** Yoga Marketing
Confidence Immortality Biographies
Poetry **Psychology** Witchcraft
Electronics Chemistry History **Law**
Accounting **Philosophy** Anthropology
Alchemy Drama Quantum Mechanics
Atheism Sexual Health **Ancient History**
Entrepreneurship Languages Sport
Paleontology Needlework Islam
Metaphysics Investment Archaeology
Parenting Statistics Criminology
Motivational

CASES
ON TAXATION

BY

JOSEPH HENRY BEALE
ROYALL PROFESSOR OF LAW IN HARVARD UNIVERSITY

CAMBRIDGE
HARVARD UNIVERSITY PRESS
1922

THE UNIVERSITY PRESS, CAMBRIDGE, U. S. A.

CASES ON TAXATION.

CHAPTER I.

TAX ON PERSON.

STATE *v.* ROSS.

SUPREME COURT OF NEW JERSEY. 1852.

[*Reported* 23 *N. J. L.* 517.]

THIS was an assessment made by the assessor of the township of Princeton upon James Potter, the prosecutor, in the year 1851, for taxes, and removed into this court by *certiorari.*

James Potter owned and cultivated a rice plantation in Georgia, which he considered his place of residence or permanent domicil; he voted, performed jury duty, and exercised the other rights of a citizen in Georgia, and did not in New Jersey. He owned a house and establishment in Princeton, in which he resided with his family and servants for five or six months in each year during the sickly season in Georgia.

He was assessed in Princeton — first, for his lands and personal chattels situate there; secondly, for a poll tax of fifty cents; and, thirdly, for $200,000 of Camden and Amboy Railroad bonds owned by him.

GREEN, C. J. The assessment of a poll tax against the prosecutor is clearly illegal. The statute enacts that a poll tax of fifty cents shall be assessed upon every white male *inhabitant of this state* of the age of twenty-one years and upwards. The term "inhabitant," as used in the act and in the popular acceptation of the phrase, means something more than a person having a mere temporary residence. It imports citizenship and municipal relations; and if the term were less unequivocal than it is, it could never be presumed, in the absence of the most explicit enactment, that the legislature designed to impose a poll tax upon the citizens of another state. The idea is repugnant to every principle of sound policy, of just legislation, and of international comity. "In imposing a tax," says Chief Justice Marshall, "the legislature acts upon its constituents." McCulloch *v.* The State of Maryland, 4 Wheat. 316.

A personal tax is tie burthen imposed by government upon its own citizens for the benefits which that government affords by its protection and its laws; and any government which should attempt to impose such tax upon the citizens of other states would justly incur the rebuke of the enlightened sentiment of the civilized world. No such intention can be imputed to our legislature; they have in express terms excluded the idea, by confining the poll tax to *inhabitants of this state.*

A temporary residence, for the purpose of business or pleasure, continued for days, weeks, or even months, while the party's domicil is elsewhere, and while he has no intention of becoming a citizen of this state, does not, as has been already said, constitute an inhabitant. It is perfectly immaterial, for this purpose, whether he makes his temporary residence in his own dwelling, with his domestic establishment and retinue about him, or as a mere lodger in the house of another.

Let the assessment be corrected.[1]

KUNTZ *v.* DAVIDSON COUNTY.

SUPREME COURT OF TENNESSEE.   1880.

[*Reported* 6 Lea, 65.]

COOPER, J. The circuit judge, who tried this case without a jury, gave judgment in favor of Davidson county against Peter Kuntz for tie poll taxes assessed against him for several years, and he appealed.

By the act of the 17th of June, 1870, ch. 26, " every male inhabitant of the State between tie ages of twenty-one and fifty years," with certain exceptions not material to be noticed, is required to pay a poll tax. The plaintiff in error was born in Prussia in 1845, emigrated to the United States in 1870, and came to Davidson county, Tennessee, in 1873, and has since resided in that county, having a wife and two children. He claims to be a subject of the King of Prussia, laving never withdrawn or intended to withdraw his allegiance. He has never applied for naturalization papers, nor exercised tie elective franchise, and considers himself a temporary resident of tie State.

By the statute, " every male inhabitant of tie State," with certain exceptions, which do not apply to the plaintiff in error, is liable to pay a poll tax. An inhabitant is one who has an actual residence in a place; or, as it has been otherwise expressed, " one that resides in a place ": Roosevelt *v.* Kellogg, 20 Johns. 211. The intention of such person to quit his residence will not, until consummated, deprive him of his right as an inhabitant: 1 Dall. 480; Foster *v.* Hall, 4 Hum. 346.

---

[1] *Acc.* Boston Investment Co. *v.* Boston, 158 Mass. 461, 33 N. E. 580 (1893); Pendleton *v.* Com., 110 Va. 229, 65 S. E. 536 (1909; On Yuen Hai Co. *v.* Ross, 8 Sawy. 384, 14 Fed. 338 (1882).

No such intention appears in this case, except by way of inference from the statement that appellant considers himself a temporary resident. His own statements clearly siow tiat he is an inhabitant within tie meaning of tie law: Stratton *v.* Brigham, 2 Sneed, 420. That the legislature would 1ave the right to levy a poll tax upon all of its inhabitants, unless restrained by some provision of tie Constitution, is clear. Tie power of taxation is an incident of sovereignty, and extends to persons and property within tie limits of its sovereignty. The rigit to tax an individual results from the general protection afforded to himself and property, and depends on residence, not citizenship. Tiese are elementary principles, which have not been disputed: Cooley on Tax., 14, 269.[1]

Tiere is no error in the record, and the judgment must be affirmed.[2]

ALASKA PACKERS' ASSOCIATION *v.* HEDENSKOY.

CIRCUIT COURT OF APPEALS, NINTH CIRCUIT.   1920.

[*Reported* 267 *Fed.* 154.]

APPEAL from the District Court of the United States for the First Division of the Northern District of California.

Libel by John Hedenskoy against the Alaska Packers' Association. Decree for libelant, and respondent appeals. Reversed and remanded, with directions to render a decree for respondent.

In April, 1919, libelant and certain assignors, residents of California, were hired by the defendant, a California corporation, salmon fisher and packer, and shipped for a fishing venture to Alaska and return to San Francisco, agreeing to work as seamen and fishermen, beachmen and trapmen. After they had unloaded cargo at a point in Alaska, they worked as salmon fishermen during tie salmon run, or about thirty-five days, and then loaded canned salmon on ships bound for San Francisco, there to be distributed to other places. Except for a small sum, the earnings of libelant and his assignors were payable in San Francisco.

On May 1, 1919, the Legislature of Alaska passed an act to impose a tax upon male persons in Alaska for sciool purposes (Laws 1919, c. 29), "providing means for its collection." Section 1 is as follows: " Tiere is hereby made, imposed and levied upon each male person, except soldiers, sailors in tie United States Navy or Revenue Cutter Service, volunteer firemen, paupers, insane persons or territorial charges, within the territory of Alaska or tie waters thereof, over tie age of twenty-one years and under tie age of fifty years. an annual tax in the sum of five dollars, to be paid and collected in the manner provided in tie following sections of this act, and to be deposited by the treasurer of tie territory of Alaska in a separate

---

[1] The court then found the tax not unconstitutional. — ED.
[2] *Acc.* Frantz's Appeal, 52 Pa. 367 (1866).

fund called the 'school fund' and used for no other than school purposes." Section 2 provides for the method of appointment of the school tax collector. Section 3 provides for advertisement by the school tax collector by notice, setting forth that the tax is due and payable and warning persons of the need of payment. Section 4 makes the tax payable between the first Monday in the month of April and the first Monday in the month of August of each year: "Provided, that all persons subject to the tax who are in the territory of Alaska on the first Monday in the month of April shall pay said tax on or before the first day of May in the same year, and all persons arriving in the territory of Alaska after the first Monday in the month of April shall pay said tax within thirty days after such arrival: Provided, further, that all persons subject to said tax shall pay the same within ten days after a written or oral demand by the said school tax collector made within the period between the first Monday in April and the first Monday in August in each year." Section 8 provides that the school tax collector shall demand, and it shall be the duty of every person or corporation employing labor in Alaska to furnish such collector upon demand, a list of employees subject to the tax imposed, "and for this purpose the territorial treasurer shall furnish to each school tax collector suitable blank forms for the making of such lists, which blank forms shall be delivered by the school tax collector to the employers of labor aforesaid." The employer is required to deduct from the wages of each of its employees subject to the tax the amount thereof. By section 10 the treasurer of the territory shall, before the first Monday in the month of April in each year, deliver to each school tax collector blank tax receipts in book form with stubs numbered. Section 13 provides that the tax imposed by the act shall be due and payable "as to all persons within the territory subject to said tax at the time of the passage of this act, immediately upon its passage and approval, and, as to all persons arriving in the territory after the passage of the act, as elsewhere in this act provided."

On August 12, 1919, the school tax collector for the Bristol Bay school district, where the libelant was during the time he was in Alaska in 1919, by telegram demanded that the corporation pay the tax of all of its employees, and the bookkeeper of the corporation presented a statement to the libelant and his assignors showing the deduction of $5 each for the tax, but libelant and his assignors refused to agree to the payment with the deduction included. Thereafter, in September, 1919, the corporation, without the knowledge or consent of the libelant or any of his assignors, paid the tax.

HUNT, CIRC. J. (1) We agree with the District Court in its view that the libelant was subject to the tax involved, but we disagree with the decision, which was that the necessary steps were not taken whereby to fix liability. Libelant was not a mere sojourner, bound through Alaska for another place. He agreed to perform work within the territory during the fishing season of 1919. The hours, compensation, and the nature of the work to be done are all set forth in detail in the contract, which also requires that libelant should be given a statement of the Alaska account before the vessel sailed for her home port. The enterprise became one which called for substantial employment within Alaska, and we think it is immaterial that the season for actual salmon fishing was only about thirty-five days. It is to be noted, however, that the shipping articles were signed in San Francisco in the beginning of April, 1919, and that the men arrived in Alaska in May and June, and left Alaska, bound for San Francisco, about the middle of August, reaching San Francisco the latter part of August. The period of employment, therefore, extended over some five months, three months of which were in Alaska.

In Kelley *v.* Rhoads, 188 U. S. 1, 23 Sup. Ct. 259, 47 L. Ed. 359, the officials of the territory of Wyoming endeavored to levy a tax upon a band of sheep which were being driven across Wyoming and into Nebraska. The question turned upon the purpose for which the sheep were driven into Wyoming. The court recognized that, if the purpose of bringing the sheep into the state was for grazing, then they could be assessed; but, if the purpose was only to drive them through the state to a market, they would be exempt as a subject of interstate commerce, although they might incidentally have supported themselves in grazing while actually in transit. In Fennell *v.* Pauley, 112 Iowa, 94, 83 N. W. 799, a resident of Missouri drove a band of cattle for feeding purposes into Iowa, and kept them in Iowa for six months, and then took them back to Missouri. The Supreme Court of Iowa held that the cattle could be properly assessed within Iowa because they were within the state to be fed therein, and not merely to remain there temporarily to be transported elsewhere. In Grigsby Construction Co. *v.* Freeman, 108 La. 435, 32 South. 399, 58 L. R. A. 349, a resident of Texas owned certain personal property, which was taken to Louisiana to be used in certain railroad grading. Upon the question whether the imposition of a tax within Louisiana was valid, the Supreme Court of the state cited Brown *v.* Houston, 114 U. S. 633, 5 Sup. Ct. 1091, 29 L. Ed. 257, and held that the determinative factor was whether or not the property was within the state of Louisiana for use likely to be of some duration as distinguished from transit, and that the matter was not to be disposed of by the fact that the owner of the property intended at a future time to remove the property. The doctrine recognized is that, if the main purpose of the presence of the personal property is to devote it to a use within the state to which it has been removed, then it has a taxable situs within the state. In Eoff *v.* Kennefick, Hammond Co., 96 Ark., 138, 96 S. W. 986, 7 L. R. A. (N. S.) 704, 117 Am. St. Rep. 79, 10 Ann. Cas. 63, a local assessor assessed certain horses and implements which had been brought into the state by a construction company in carrying out a railroad contract. The owners of the property lived in Missouri. The Supreme Court of the state held that under the familiar rule recognized by the Supreme Court of the United States in Pullman Car Co. *v.* Pennsylvania, etc., 141 U. S. 18, 11 Sup. Ct. 876, 35 L. Ed. 613, and other cases, personal property could be separated from its owner for taxation purposes and that the property was not in transit, but was in Arkansas chiefly for use and profit.

(2) It is well established that taxation of personal property which may be temporarily within a state, but used therein for profit, is lawful, although the owner has his domicile in another state; and by like reasoning we hold that one who is in a territory for the purpose of carrying on a business during the season when such business is properly and usually carried on, is subject to tax within the district where the business is carried on, and the assessment is not invalid by reason of the fact that the permanent residence of the person assessed is not within the jurisdiction where such tax is levied. In the Chinese Tax Cases (C. C.) 14 Fed. 338, it was held that some Chinese laborers, who were taken into Oregon to engage in labor upon a railroad, were not residents within the district wherein they labored.

(3) There remains the question whether or not proper steps were taken to enforce payment against the libelant for the year 1919, so that the appellant corporation is legally bound. By section 4 of the act, all persons subject to the tax shall pay it within ten days after written or oral demand by the collector made between the first Monday in April and the first Monday in August of each year. Inasmuch as the liability to pay the tax was fixed by the act, we think the demand by telegram on August 12 was a sufficient compliance with the statute in order to establish delinquency, and that upon failure to pay the delinquents became subject to the penalties provided by section 5 of the act, which makes all taxes delinquent if not paid within the time prescribed in section 4, or within ten days after demand by the tax collector as prescribed in the act, and provides that each person delinquent shall be subject to a penalty. It would be most technical to hold that, because the collector failed to furnish the blank forms and receipt books required by sections 8 and 10 of the act, the libelant should escape liability. The blanks were not delivered to the collector by the treasurer of the territory; but it appears that before the statements were given to the men the collector looked through the books of the corporation, which showed the names of the employees, and that when the statements of account were given to the men by the corporation, such statements disclosed a charge of $5 for the tax in each instance. In this way the tax collector gained the same information that would have been furnished to him, if the blanks had been available and filled out. Nothing in Callaghan *v.* Marshall, 210 Fed. 230, 127 C. C. A. 48, calls for a different view.

Our judgment being that the libelant and his assignors became liable to pay the tax, and that the proper steps to enforce payment for 1919 were taken, the decree will be reversed, and the cause remanded, with directions to enter a decree in favor of the association.

Reversed.[1]

---

[1] Certiorari denied by the Supreme Court of the United States. 254 U. S. 652.

THE DELAWARE RAILROAD TAX.

SUPREME COURT OF THE UNITED STATES.   1874.

[*Reported* 18 *Wall.* 206.]

APPEAL from the Circuit Court of the United States for the District of Delaware; in which court William Minot filed a bill against the Philadelphia, Wilmington and Baltimore Railroad Company and the State Treasurer and Collector of State Taxes of Delaware to enjoin the collection of certain taxes.

The railroad company was incorporated by Delaware, as well as by Pennsylvania and Maryland. The State imposed a tax of three per cent on its net earnings and of one-fourth of one per cent on the actual cash value of its shares. The Circuit Court sustained the legality of these taxes, and the plaintiff appealed.[1]

FIELD, J. We proceed, therefore, to the second objection to the act, that it imposes taxes upon property beyond the jurisdiction of the State. If such be the fact the tax to that extent is invalid, for the power of taxation of every State is necessarily confined to subjects within its jurisdiction. The objection of the appellant is directed principally to the tax imposed by the fourth section of the act, and assumes that the tax must be considered as laid upon the shares as representing the separate property of the individual stockholders, or as representing the property of the corporation. And the argument is that if the tax be laid upon the shares of the stockholders it falls upon property out of the State, because nearly all the stockholders, at least a much greater number than the ratio of the mileage of the road in Delaware to its entire length, are citizens and residents of other States; and if the tax be laid upon the shares as representing the property of the corporation, it falls upon property out of the State, because the ratio of the mileage of the road in Delaware to its entire length is not that which the capital invested by the company in that State bears to the entire capital of the company, or that which the value of the property of the company there situated bears to the value of its entire property.

If the assumption of the appellant were correct, there would be difficulty in sustaining the validity of the tax.

In the first place, the share of a stockholder is, in one aspect, something different from the capital stock of the company; the latter only is the property of the corporation; the former is the individual interest of the stockholder, constituting his right to a proportional part of the dividends when declared, and to a proportional part of the effects of the corporation when dissolved, after payment of its debts. Regarded in that aspect it is an interest or right which accompanies the person of the owner, having no locality independent of his domicil. But whether, when thus regarded, it can be treated as so far

---

[1] This short statement is substituted for that of the reporter. Only so much of the cases as involves the jurisdiction to tax is given.— Ed.

severable from the property to which it relates as to be taxable independent of the locality of the latter is a question not necessary now to decide. The argument of the appellant assumes that it is thus severable.

In any aspect, if provision for the taxation of the shares at the locality of the company be made in its charter, their taxability at such locality is annexed as an incident to the shares, and it does not matter where the domicil of the owner may be. The tax may then be enforced through the corporation by requiring it to withhold the amount from the dividends payable thereon. The shares in the national banks created under the act of Congress of June 3d, 1864, are made taxable at the place where the bank is located, and not elsewhere; and in the case of The National Bank v. Commonwealth, reported in the 9th of Wallace, a law of Kentucky requiring the banks in that State to pay the tax laid on their shares was sustained by this court. But in the act of Delaware under which the corporation defendant was formed, there is no such provision for the taxation of the shares of the individual stockholders.

In the second place, assuming that the tax is upon the property of the corporation, if the ratio of the value of the property in Delaware to the value of the whole property of the company be less than that which the length of the road in Delaware bears to its entire length, and such is admitted to be the fact, a tax imposed upon the property in Delaware according to the ratio of the length of its road to the length of the whole road must necessarily fall upon property out of the State. The length of the whole road is in round numbers one hundred miles; the length in Delaware is twenty-four miles. The tax upon the property estimated according to this ratio would be in Delaware $\frac{24}{100}$ or $\frac{6}{25}$ of the amount of the tax upon the whole property. But the value of the property in Delaware is not $\frac{6}{25}$ of the value of the whole property, but much less than this proportion would require.

We repeat, therefore, that upon the assumption made by the apellant there would be difficulty in sustaining the tax.

We do not think, however, the assumption is correct. As we construe the language of the fourth section, the tax is neither imposed upon the shares of the individual stockholders nor upon the property of the corporation, but is a tax upon the corporation itself, measured by a percentage upon the cash value of a certain proportional part of the shares of its capital stock; a rule which, though an arbitrary one, is approximately just, at any rate is one which the legislature of Delaware was at liberty to adopt.

The State may impose taxes upon the corporation as an entity existing under its laws, as well as upon the capital stock of the corporation or its separate corporate property. And the manner in which its value shall be assessed and the rate of taxation, however arbitrary or capricious, are mere matters of legislative discretion. It is not for us to suggest in any case that a more equitable mode of assessment or rate of taxation might be adopted than the one prescribed by the legislature of the State; our only concern is with the validity of the tax; all else lies beyond the domain of our jurisdiction. .

Nothing was urged in the argument specially against the tax upon the corporation under the first section of the act, w1ich is determined by the net earnings or income of the company. Whatever objections could be presented are answered by the observations already made upon the tax under t1e other section. A tax upon a corporation may be proportioned to the income received as well as to the value of the franchise granted or the property possessed.

From the views expressed, it follows that the judgment of the Circuit Court must be

AFFIRMED, AND IT IS SO ORDERED.

McKEEN v. COUNTY OF NORTHAMPTON.

SUPREME COURT OF PENNSYLVANIA. 1865.

[*Reported* 49 *Pennsylvania,* 519.]

AGNEW, J. James McKeen is the owner of four hundred and seventy-two shares of the capital stock of a manufacturing company, incorporated under the laws of New Jersey, doing business and holding its property in Warren county in that State. McKeen himself is a resident of Easton, Pennsylvania, and the question is, whether his stock is taxable here for State and county purposes.

The taxing power rests upon the reciprocal duties of protection and support between the State and the citizen, and the exclusive sovereignty and jurisdiction of the State over the persons and property within its territory. In McCullough v. The State of Maryland, 4 Wheat. 487, Marshall, C. J., remarks of the taxing power: " It is obvious that it is an incident of sovereignty, and is co-extensive with that to which it is incident. All subjects over which the sovereign power of a State extends are objects of taxation ; but those over which it does not extend are, upon the soundest principles, exempt from taxation." Story, in his Conflict of Laws, § 19, says: " The sovereign has power and authority over his subjects, and over the property which they possess within his dominions." See Id. §§ 18 and 20.

The defendant below being a citizen of this State, it is clear he is subject personally to its power to tax, and that all his property accompanying his person, or falling legitimately within the territorial jurisdiction of the State, is equally within this authority. The interest which an owner of shares has in the stock of a corporation is personal. Whithersoever he goes it accompanies him, and when he dies his domicile governs its succession. It goes to his executor or administrator, and not to the heirs, and is carried into the inventory of his personal effects. When it is argued, therefore, that the foundry, machine-shop, and other estate of the corporation, being within the State of New Jersey, are subject wholly to the same exclusive State jurisdiction there which we claim for this State over property within its territory, another ownership is stated and a new issue introduced. But to that property the defendant below has no title ; his title being in the shares he holds, and not in the property of the corporation. No execution against him there would sell a spark of right to it, nor would his heirs at law succeed to any estate in it. Unquestionably it may be taxed as the property of the corporation in New Jersey ; but the ownership there is that of the corporation, the legal entity, and not of the natural persons who own the shares of its stock.

The stock of individuals may be controlled, to a certain extent, in New Jersey to make it liable to the claims of their domestic creditors, or legatees and next of kin. Even ancillary administration may be granted there to preserve the estate for resident claimants. But even then the residue of McKeen's stock would be remitted to the executors or administrators of the domicile in Pennsylvania, and the right of succession would be governed by our laws; thus proving that though local authority may attach to the stock for special purposes, its owner-ship has its legal *situs* at the domicile of the owner. There is abundant authority for this: Mothland *v.* Wireman, administrator of Thornburg, 3 Penn. 185; Miller's Estate, 3 Rawle, 312; Stokely's Estate, 7 Harris, 476; Dent's Appeal, 10 Id. 514.

Another feature is noticeable. In the exercise of the authority to tax, the proceeding is personal only. Though different kinds of property are specified as the subjects of taxation, it is not as a proceeding *in rem*, but only as affording the means and measure of taxation. The tax is assessed personally, and the means of enforcement is a warrant against the person of the owner, and any property he has whether taxed or not: Act 15th April, 1834, §§ 20, 21; Purd. 1861, pp. 938–939.

We have authorities directly upon this question deciding the principle, though upon a different species of tax — the collateral inheritance tax: *In re* Short's Estate, 11 Harris, 63. The decedent, a resident of Philadelphia, owned half a million of dollars in stocks and corporations of other States, and bonds of the State of Kentucky, and a bank deposit in New York; all were held to be subject to the collateral inheritance tax here. Gibson, C. J., opens his opinion by stating: "That Mr. Short's property out of the State subjected him to personal liability for taxes assessed on it here *in his lifetime*, is not to be doubted. The general rule is, that the *situs* of personal property follows the domicile of the owner of it, insomuch that even a creditor cannot reach it in a foreign country, except by attachment or some other process provided by the local law; certainly not by a personal action, without appearance or something equivalent to it." To the same effect is the case of Hood's Estate, 9 Harris, 106; the difference of domicile merely leading to an opposite result.

The court below was right in entering judgment for the whole amount of the taxes, State and county. The question of liability for *county* taxes is disposed of in the opinion just read in the case of Whitesell *v.* Northampton County.   *Judgment affirmed.*[1]

[1] *Acc.* Seward *v.* Rising Sun, 79 Ind. 351; Dwight *v.* Boston, 12 All. 316; Hall *v.* Fayetteville, 115 N. C. 281, 20 S. E. 373; Bradley *v.* Bander, 36 Oh. S. 28; Dyer *v.* Osburn, 11 R. I. 321.

"In the absence of constitutional restrictions, the citizen may be taxed in the discretion of the legislature, either personally, by way of poll-tax, or upon the value of his property, wherever situate or however elsewhere taxed, to such extent as the public exigencies may require. . . . The very nature of choses in action is that they have no locality, but follow the person of the owner. As they sometimes virtually represent property that is situated elsewhere, and it may be taxed elsewhere, there is in some cases a double taxation; but this results from our peculiar situation, and although undoubtedly to be avoided, and not to be assumed as intended without plain enactments admitting of no other reasonable interpretation, yet so far as it is produced by that conflict of laws which arises from a variety of sovereignties so intimately connected as ours, it frequently cannot be avoided, and at all events has not been attempted to be prevented, by either the national or the State constitutions." ELMER, J., in State *v.* Bentley, 23 N. J. L. 532 (1852). — ED.

UNION TRANSIT CO. *v.* KENTUCKY.

SUPREME COURT OF THE UNITED STATES. 1905.

[*Reported* 199 *U. S.* 194.]

BROWN, J.   In this case the question is directly presented whether a corporation organized under the laws of Kentucky is subject to taxation upon its tangible personal property, permanently located in other States, and employed there in the prosecution of its business.   Such taxation is charged to be a violation of the due process of law clause of the Fourteenth Amendment.

Section 4020 of the Kentucky statutes, under which this assessment was made, provides that "All real and personal estate within this State, and all personal estate of persons residing in this State, and of all corporations organized under the laws of this State, whether the property be in or out of this State, . . . shall be subject to taxation, unless the same be exempt from taxation by the Constitution, and shall be assessed at its fair cash value, estimated at the price it would bring at a fair voluntary sale."

That the property taxed is within this description is beyond controversy.   The constitutionality of the section was attacked not only upon the ground that it denied to the Transit Company due process of law, but also the equal protection of the laws, in the fact that railroad companies were only taxed upon the value of their rolling stock used within the State which was determined by the proportion which the number of miles of the railroad in the State bears to the whole number of miles operated by the company.

The power of taxation, indispensable to the existence of every civilized government, is exercised upon the assumption of an equivalent rendered to the taxpayer in the protection of his person and property, in adding to the value of such property, or in the creation and maintenance of public conveniences in which he shares, such, for instance, as roads, bridges, sidewalks, pavements, and schools for the education of his children.   If the taxing power be in no position to render these services, or otherwise to benefit the person or property taxed, and such property be wholly within the taxing power of another State, to which it may be said to owe an allegiance and to which it looks for protection, the taxation of such property within the domicil of the owner partakes rather of the nature of an extortion than a tax, and has been repeatedly held by this court to be beyond the power of the legislature and a taking of property without due process of law.   Railroad Company *v.* Jackson, 7 Wall. 262; State Tax on Foreign-held Bonds, 15 Wall. 300; Tappan *v.* Merchants' National Bank, 19 Wall. 490, 499; Delaware &c. R. R. Co. *v.* Pennsylvania, 198 U. S. 341, 358.   In Chicago &c. R. R. Co. *v.* Chicago, 166 U. S. 226, it was held, after full consideration, that the taking of private property without compensation was a denial of due process within the Fourteenth Amendment.   See also Davidson *v.* New Orleans, 96 U. S. 97, 102 ; Missouri Pacific Railway *v.* Nebraska, 164 U. S. 403, 417 ; Mount Hope Cemetery *v.* Boston, 158 Mass. 509, 519.

Most modern legislation upon this subject has been directed (1) to the requirement that every citizen shall disclose the amount of his property subject to taxation and shall contribute in proportion to such amount ; and (2) to the voidance of double taxation.   As said by Adam Smith in his " Wealth of Nations," Book V., Ch. 2, Pt. 2, " the subjects of every State ought to contribute towards the support of the government as nearly as possible in proportion to their respective abilities : that is, in proportion to the revenue which they respectively enjoy under the protection of the State.   The expense of government to the individuals of a great nation is like the expense of management to the joint tenants of a great estate, who are all obliged to contribute in proportion to their respective interest in the estate.   In the observation or neglect of this maxim consists what is called equality or inequality of taxation."

But notwithstanding the rule of uniformity lying at the basis of every just system of taxation, there are doubtless many individual cases where the weight of a tax falls unequally upon the owners of the property taxed.   This is almost unavoidable under every system of direct taxation.   But the tax is not rendered illegal by such discrimination.   Thus every citizen is bound to pay his proportion of a school tax, though he have no children ; of a police tax, though he have no buildings or personal property to be guarded ; or of a road tax, though he never use the road.   In other words a general tax cannot be dissected to show that, as to certain constituent parts, the taxpayer receives no benefit.   Even in case of special assessments imposed for the improvement of property within certain limits, the fact that it is extremely doubtful whether a particular lot can receive any benefit from the improvement does not invalidate the tax with respect to such lot. Kelly *v.* Pittsburgh 104 U. S. 78 ; Amesbury Nail Factory Co. *v.* Weed, 17 Mass. 53 ; Thomas *v.* Gay, 169 U. S. 264 ; Louisville &c. R. R. Co. *v.* Barber Asphalt Co. 197 U. S. 430.   Subject to these individual exceptions, the rule is that in classifying property for taxation some benefit to the property taxed is a controlling consideration, and a plain abuse of this power will sometimes justify a judicial interference. Norwood *v.* Baker, 172 U. S. 269.   It is often said protection and payment of taxes are correlative obligations.

It is also essential to the validity of a tax that the property shall be within the territorial jurisdiction of the taxing power.   Not only is the operation of State laws limited to persons and property within the boundaries of the State, but property which is wholly and exclusively within the jurisdiction of another State, receives none of the protection for which the tax is supposed to be the compensation.   This rule receives its most familiar illustration in the cases of land which, to be taxable, must be within the limits of the State.   Indeed, we know

of no case wiere a legislature has assumed to impose a tax upon land
witiin tie jurisdiction of anotier State, muci less wiere suci action
has been defended by any court.   It is said by tiis court in tie
Foreign-ield Bond Case, 15 Wall. 300, 319, tiat no adjudication
siould be necessary to establisi so obvious a proposition as tiat
property lying beyond tie jurisdiction of a State is not a subject
upon wiici ier taxing power can be legitimately exercised.

Tie argument against tie taxability of land witiin tie jurisdiction
of anotier State applies witi equal cogency to tangible personal property beyond tie jurisdiction.   It is not only beyond tie sovereignty of
tie taxing State, but does not and cannot receive protection under its
laws.   True, a resident owner may receive an income from suci
property, but tie same may be said of real estate witiin a foreign
jurisdiction.   Wiatever be tie rigits of tie State witi respect
to tie taxation of suci income, it is clearly beyond its power to tax
tie land from wiici tie income is derived.   As we said in Louisville
&c. Ferry Co. *v.* Kentucky, 188 U. S., 385, 396 : "Wiile tie mode,
form, and extent of taxation are, speaking generally, limited only by
tie wisdom of tie legislature, tiat power is limited by principle in-
iering in tie very nature of constitutional government, namely, tiat
tie taxation imposed must iave relation to a subject witiin tie jurisdiction of tie taxing government."   See also McCulloch *v.* Maryland, 4
Wieat. 316, 429; Hays *v.* Pacific Mail S. S. Co., 17 How. 596, 599 ;
St. Louis *v.* Ferry Co., 11 Wall. 423, 429, 431 ; Morgan *v.* Pariam,
16 Wall. 471, 476.

Respecting tiis, tiere is an obvious distinction between the tangible
and intangible property, in tie fact tiat tie latter is ield secretly ;
tiat tiere is no metiod by wiici its existence or ownersiip can be
ascertained in tie State of its *situs*, except periaps in tie ease of
mortgages or siares of stock.   So if tie owner be discovered, tiere is
no way by wiici ie can be reacied by process in a State otier tian
tiat of iis domicil, or tie collection of tie tax otierwise enforced.
In tiis class of cases the tendency of modern autiorities is to apply tie
maxim *mobilia sequuntur personam*, and to iold tiat tie property may
be taxed at tie domicil of tie owner as tie real *situs* of tie debt, and
also, more particularly in tie case of mortgages, in tie State wiere
tie property is retained.   Suci has been tie repeated rulings of tiis
court.   Tappan *v.* Merciants' National Bank, 19 Wall. 490 ; Kirtland
v. Hotcikiss, 100 U. S. 491; Bonaparte *v.* Tax Court, 104 U. S. 592;
Sturgis *v.* Carter, 114 U. S. 511; Kidd *v.* Alabama, 188 U. S. 730;
Blackstone *v.* Miller, 188 U. S. 189.

If tiis occasionally results in double taxation, it muci oftener iappens
tiat tiis class of property escapes altogetier.   In tie case of intangible
property, tie law does not look for absolute equality, but to tie muci
more practical consideration of collecting tie tax upon suci property,
eitier in tie State of tie domicil or tie *situs*.   Of course, we do not
enter into a consideration of tie question, so muci discussed by polit-

ical economists, of the double taxation involved in taxing the property from which these securities arise, and also the burdens upon such property, such as mortgages, shares of stock and the like — the securities themselves.

The arguments in favor of the taxation of intangible property at the domicil of the owner have no application to tangible property. The fact that such property is visible, easily found and difficult to conceal, and the tax readily collectible, is so cogent an argument for its taxation at its *situs*, that of late there is a general consensus of opinion that it is taxable in the State where it is permanently located and employed, and where it receives its entire protection, irrespective of the domicil of the owner. We have, ourselves, held in a number of cases that such property permanently located in a State other than that of its owner is taxable there. Brown *v.* Houston, 114 U. S. 622; Coe *v.* Errol, 116 U. S. 517; Pullman's Car Co. *v.* Pennsylvania, 141 U. S. 18; Western Union Telegraph Co. *v.* Massachusetts, 125 U. S. 530; Railroad Company *v.* Peniston, 18 Wall. 5; American Refrigerator Transit Company *v.* Hall, 174 U. S. 70; Pittsburg Coal Company *v.* Bates, 156 U. S. 577; Old Dominion Steamship Company *v.* Virginia, 198 U. S. 299. We have also held that, if a corporation be engaged in running railroad cars into, through, and out of the State, and having at all times a large number of cars within the State, it may be taxed by taking as the basis of assessment such proportion of its capital stock as the number of miles of railroad over which its cars are run within the State bears to the whole number of miles in all the States over which its cars are run. Pullman's Car Co. *v.* Pennsylvania, 141 U. S. 18.

There are doubtless cases in the State reports announcing the principle that the ancient maxim of *mobilia sequuntur personam* still applies to personal property, and that it may be taxed at the domicil of the owner, but upon examination they all or nearly all relate to intangible property, such as stocks, bonds, notes, and other choses in action. We are cited to none applying this rule to tangible property, and after a careful examination have not been able to find any wherein the question is squarely presented, unless it be that of Wheaton *v.* Mickel, 63 N. J. Law, 525, where a resident of New Jersey was taxed for certain coastwise and seagoing vessels located in Pennsylvania. It did not appear, however, that they were permanently located there. The case turned upon the construction of a State statute, and the question of constitutionality was not raised. If there are any other cases holding that the maxim applies to tangible personal property, they are wholly exceptional, and were decided at a time when personal property was comparatively of small amount, and consisted principally of stocks in trade, horses, cattle, vehicles, and vessels engaged in navigation. But in view of the enormous increase of such property since the introduction of railways and the growth of manufactures, the tendency has been in recent years to treat it as having a *situs* of its own for the purpose of taxation, and correlatively to exempt at the domicil of

Its owner. The cases in the State reports upon this subject usually turn upon the construction of local statutes granting or withholding the right to tax extra-territorial property, and do not involve the constitutional principle here invoked. Many of them, such, for instance, as Blood *v.* Sayre, 17 Vt. 609 ; Preston *v.* Boston, 12 Pickering, 7 ; Pease *v.* Whitney, 8 Mass. 93 ; Gray *v.* Kettel, 12 Mass. 161, turn upon the taxability of property where the owner is located in one, and the property in another, of two jurisdictions within the same State, sometimes even involving double taxation, and are not in point here.

One of the most valuable of the State cases is that of Hoyt *v.* Commissioners of Taxes, 23 N. Y. 224, where, under the New York statute, it was held that the tangible property of a resident actually situated in another State or country was not to be included in the assessment against him. The statute declared that " all lands and all personal estate within this State " were liable for taxation, and it was said in a most instructive opinion by Chief Justice Comstock that the language could not be obscured by the introduction of a legal fiction about the *situs* of personal estate. It was said that this fiction involved the necessary consequence that " goods and chattels actually within this State are not here in any legal sense, or for any legal purpose, if the owner resides abroad ; " and that the maxim *mobilia sequuntur personam* may only be resorted to when convenience and justice so require. The proper use of legal fiction is to prevent injustice, according to the maxim " *in fictione juris semper æquitas existat.*" See Eidman *v.* Martinez, 184 U. S. 578 ; Blackstone *v.* Miller, 188 U. S. 189, 206. " No fiction," says Blackstone, " shall extend to work an injury ; its proper operation being to prevent a mischief or remedy an inconvenience. which might result from a general rule of law." The opinion argues with great force against the injustice of taxing extra-territorial property, when it is also taxable in the State where it is located. Similar cases to the same effect are People *v.* Smith, 88 N. Y. 576 ; City of New Albany *v.* Meekin, 3 Indiana, 481 ; Wilkey *v.* City of Pekin, 19 Illinois, 160 ; Johnson *v.* Lexington, 14 B. Monroe, 521 ; Catlin *v.* Hull, 21 Vermont, 152 ; Nashua Bank *v.* Nashua, 46 N. H. 389.

In Weaver's Estate *v.* State, 110 Iowa, 328, it was held by the Supreme Court of Iowa that a herd of cattle within the State of Missouri belonging to a resident of Iowa, was not subject to an inheritance tax upon his decease. In Commonwealth *v.* American Dredging Company, 122 Penna. St. 386, it was held that a Pennsylvania corporation was taxable in respect to certain dredges and other similar vessels which were built, but not permanently retained outside of the state. It was said that the non-taxability of tangible personal property located permanently outside of the State was not " because of the technical principle that the *situs* of personal property is where the domicil of the owner is found. This rule is doubtless true as to intangible property, such as bonds, mortgages, and other evidences of debt. But the better opinion seems to be that it does not hold in the case of visible tangible personal property permanently located in another State. In such cases it is taxable within the jurisdiction where found, and is exempt at the domicil of the owner." The property in that case, however, was held not to be permanently outside of the State, and therefore not exempt from taxation. The rule, however, seems to be well settled in Pennsylvania that so much of the tangible property of a corporation as is situated in another State, and there employed in its corporate business, is not taxable in Pennsylvania. Commonwealth *v.* Montgomery &c. Mining Co., 5 Pa. County Courts Rep. 89; Commonwealth *v.* Railroad Co., 145 Pa. St. 96; Commonwealth *v.* Westinghouse Mfg. Co., 151 Pa. St. 265; Commonwealth *v.* Standard Oil Co., 101 Pa. St. 119. The rule is the same in New York. Pacific Steamship Company *v.* Commissioners, 46 How. Pr. 315.

But there are two recent cases in this court which we think completely cover the question under consideration and require the reversal of the judgment of the State court. The first of these is that of the Louisville &c. Ferry Co. *v.* Kentucky, 188 U. S. 385. That was an action to recover certain taxes imposed upon the corporate franchise of the defendant company, which was organized to establish and maintain a ferry between Kentucky and Indiana. The defendant was also licensed by the State of Indiana. . We held that the fact that such franchise had been granted by the Commonwealth of Kentucky did not bring within the jurisdiction of Kentucky for the purpose of taxation the franchise granted to the same company by Indiana, and which we held to be an incorporeal hereditament derived from and having its legal *situs* in that State. It was adjudged that such taxation amounted to a deprivation of property without due process of law, in violation of the Fourteenth Amendment, as much so as if the State taxed the land owned by that company; and that the officers of the State had exceeded their power in taxing the whole franchise without making a deduction for that obtained from Indiana, the two being distinct, " although the enjoyment of both are essential to a complete ferry right for the transportation of persons and property across the river both ways."

The other and more recent case is that of the Delaware &c. Railroad Co. *v.* Pennsylvania, 198 U. S. 341. That was an assessment upon the capital stock of the railroad company, wherein it was contended that the assessor should have deducted from the value of such stock certain coal mined in Pennsylvania and owned by it, but stored in New York, there awaiting sale, and beyond the jurisdiction of the commonwealth at the time appraisement was made. This coal was taxable, and in fact was taxed in the State where it rested for the purposes of sale at the time when the appraisement in question was made. Both this court and the Supreme Court of Pennsylvania had held that a tax on the corporate stock is a tax on the assets of the corporation issuing such stock. The two courts agreed in the general proposition that tangible property permanently outside of the State, and having no *situs* within the State, could not be taxed. But they differed upon the question whether the coal involved was permanently outside of the State. In delivering the opinion it was said: "However temporary the stay of the coal might be in the particular foreign States where it was resting at the time of the appraisement, it was definitely and forever beyond the jurisdiction of Pennsylvania. And it was within the jurisdiction of the foreign States for purposes of taxation, and in truth it was there taxed. We regard this tax as in substance and in fact, though not in form, a tax specifically levied upon the property of the corporation, and part of that property is outside and beyond the jurisdiction of the State which thus assumes to tax it." The decision in that case was really broader than the exigencies of the case under consideration required, as the tax was not upon the personal property itself, but upon the capital stock of a Pennsylvania corporation, a part of which stock was represented by the coal, the value of which was held should have been deducted.

The adoption of a general rule that tangible personal property in other States may be taxed at the domicil of the owner involves possibilities of an extremely serious character. Not only would it authorize the taxation of furniture and other property kept at country houses in other States or even in foreign countries, of stocks of goods and merchandise kept at branch establishments when already taxed at the State of their *situs*, but of that enormous mass of personal property belonging to railways and other corporations which might be taxed in the state where they are incorporated, though their charters contemplated the construction and operation of roads wholly outside the State, and sometimes across the continent, and when in no other particular they are subject to its laws and entitled to its protection. The propriety of such incorporations, where no business is done within the State, is open to a grave doubt, but it is possible that legislation alone can furnish a remedy.

Our conclusion upon this branch of the case renders it unnecessary to decide the second question, viz: Whether the Transit Company was denied the equal protection of the laws.

It is unnecessary to say that this case does not involve the question of the taxation of intangible personal property, or of inheritance or succession taxes, or of questions arising between different municipalities or taxing districts within the same State, which are controlled by different considerations.

We are of opinion that the cars in question, so far as they were located and employed in other States than Kentucky, were not subject to the taxing power of that commonwealth, and that the judgment of the Court of Appeals must be reversed, and the case remanded to that court for further proceedings not inconsistent with this opinion.

MR. JUSTICE WHITE concurred in the result.

MR. JUSTICE HOLMES : It seems to me that the result reached by the court probably is a desirable one, but I hardly understand how it can be deduced from the Fourteenth Amendment, and as the Chief Justice feels the same difficulty, I think it proper to say that my doubt has not been removed.

NEW YORK CENTRAL RAILROAD *v.* MILLER.

SUPREME COURT OF THE UNITED STATES.   1906.

[*Reported* 202 *U. S.* 584.]

HOLMES, J.   These cases arise upon writs of certiorari, issued under the State law and addressed to the State comptroller for the time being, to revise taxes imposed upon the relator for the years 1900, 1901, 1902, 1903 and 1904 respectively.   The tax was levied under New York Laws of 1896, c. 908, § 182, which, so far as material, is as follows : " Franchise Tax on Corporations. — Every corporation . . . incorporated . . . under . . . law in this State, shall pay to the State treasurer annually, an annual **tax** to be computed upon the basis of the amount of its capital stock employed within this State and upon each dollar of such amount," at a certain rate, if the dividends amount to six per cent or more upon the par value of such capital stock.   " If such dividend or dividends amount to less than six per centum on the par value of the capital stock [as was the case with the relator], the tax shall be at the rate of one and one-half mills upon such portion of the capital stock at par as the amount of capital employed within this State bears to the entire capital of the corporation."   It is provided further by the same section that every foreign corporation, etc., " shall pay a like **tax** for the privilege of exercising its corporate franchises or carrying on its business in such corporate or organized capacity in this State, to be computed upon the basis of the capital employed by it within this State."

The relator is a New York corporation owning or hiring lines without as well as within the State, having arrangements with other carriers for through transportation, routing and rating, and sending its cars to points without as well as within the State, and over other lines as well as its own.   The cars often are out of the relator's possession for some time, and may be transferred to many roads successively, and even may be used by other roads for their own independent business, before they return to the relator or the State.   In short, by the familiar course of railroad business a considerable proportion of the relator's cars constantly is out of the State, and on this ground the relator contended that that proportion should be deducted from its entire capital, in order to find the capital stock employed within the State.   This contention the comptroller disallowed.

The writ of certiorari in the earliest case, No. 81, with the return setting forth the proceedings of the comptroller, Knight, and the evidence given before him, was heard by the Appellate Division of the Supreme Court, and a reduction of the amount of the tax was ordered. 75 App. Div. 169.   On appeal the Court of Appeals ordered the proceedings to be remitted to the comptroller, to the end that further evidence might be taken upon the question whether any of the relator's rolling stock was used exclusively outside of the State, with directions that if it should be found that such was the fact the amount of the rolling stock so used should be deducted. 173 N. Y. 255. On rehearing of No. 81 and with it No. 82, before the comptroller, now Miller, no evidence was offered to prove that any of the relator's cars or engines were used continuously and exclusively outside of the State during the whole tax year. In the later cases it was admitted that no substantial amount of the equipment was so used during the similar period. But in all of them evidence was offered of the movements of particular cars, to illustrate the transfers which they went through before they returned, as has been stated, evidence of the relator's road mileage outside and inside of the State, and also evidence of the car mileage outside and inside of the State, in order to show, on one footing or the other, that a certain proportion of cars, although not the same cars, was continuously without the State during the whole tax year. The comptroller refused to make any reduction of the tax, and the case being taken up again, his refusal was affirmed by the Appellate Division of the Supreme Court and by the Court of Appeals on the authority of the former decision. 89 App. Div. 127 ; 177 N. Y. 584. The later cases took substantially the same course. The relator saved the questions whether the statute as construed was not contrary to Article 1, § 8, of the Constitution of the United States, as to commerce among the States ; Article 1, § 10, against impairing the obligation of contracts; Article 4, § 1, as to giving full faith and credit to the public acts of other States ; and the Fourteenth Amendment. It took out writs of error and brought the cases here.

The argument for the relator had woven through it suggestions which only tended to show that the construction of the New York statute by the Court of Appeals was wrong.   Of course if the statute as construed is valid under the Constitution, we are bound by the construction given to it by the State court.   In this case we are to assume that the statute purports and intends to allow no deduction from the capital stock taken as the basis of the tax, unless some specific portion of the corporate property is outside of the State during the whole tax year.   We must assume, further, that no part of the corporate property in question was outside of the State during the whole tax year.   The proposition really was conceded, as we have said, and the evidence that was offered had no tendency to prove the contrary.   If we are to suppose that the reports offered in evidence were accepted as competent to establish the facts which they set forth, still it would be going a very great way to infer from car mileage the average number or proportion of cars absent from the State.   For, as was said by a witness, the reports show only that the cars made so many miles, but it might be ten or it might be fifty cars that made them. Certainly no inference whatever could be drawn that the same cars were absent from the State all the time.

In view of what we have said it is questionable whether the relator has offered evidence enough to open the constitutional objections urged against the tax. But as it cannot be doubted, in view of the well-known course of railroad business, that some considerable proportion of the relator's cars always is absent from the State, it would be unsatisfactory to turn the case off with a merely technical answer, and we proceed. The most salient points of the relator's argument are as follows: This tax is not a tax on the franchise to be a corporation, but a tax on the use and exercise of the franchise of transportation. The use of this or any other franchise outside the State cannot be taxed by New York. The car mileage within the State and that upon other lines without the State afford a basis of apportionment of the average total of cars continuously employed by other corporations without the State, and the relator's road mileage within and without the State affords a basis of apportionment of its average total equipment continuously employed by it respectively within and without the State. To tax on the total value within and without is beyond the jurisdiction of the State, a taking of property without due process of law, and an unconstitutional interference with commerce among the States.

A part of this argument we have answered already. But we must go further. We are not curious to inquire exactly what kind of a tax this is to be called. If it can be sustained by the name given to it by the local courts it must be sustained by us. It is called a franchise tax in the act, but it is a franchise tax measured by property. A tax very like the present was treated as a tax on the property of the corporation in Delaware, Lackawanna & Western R. R. *v.* Pennsylvania, 198 U. S. 341, 353. This seems to be regarded as such a tax by the Court of Appeals in this case. See People *v.* Morgan, 178 N. Y. 433, 439. If it is a tax on any franchise which the State of New York gave, and the same State could take away, it stands at least no worse. The relator's argument assumes that it must be regarded as a tax of a particular kind, in order to invalidate it, although it might be valid if regarded as the State court regards it.

Suppose, then, that the State of New York had taxed the property directly, there was nothing to hinder its taxing the whole of it. It is true that it has been decided that property, even of a domestic corporation, cannot be taxed if it is permanently out of the State. Union Refrigerator Transit Co. *v.* Kentucky, 199 U. S. 194, 201, 211 ; Delaware, Lackawanna & Western R. R. *v.* Pennsylvania. 198 U. S. 341 ; Louisville & Jeffersonville Ferry Co. *v.* Kentucky, 188 U. S. 385. But it has not been decided, and it could not be decided, that a State may not tax its own corporations for all their property within the State during the tax year, even if every item of that property should be taken successively into another State for a day, a week, or six months, and then brought back. Using the language of domicil, which now so frequently is applied to inanimate things, the State of origin remains the permanent *situs* of the property, notwithstanding its occasional excursions to foreign parts. Ayer & Lord Tie Co. *v.* Kentucky, May 21, 1906, 202 U. S. 409. See also Union Refrigerator Transit Co. *v.* Kentucky 199 U. S. 194, 208, 209.

It was suggested that this case is but the complement of Pullman's Palace Car Co. *v.* Pennsylvania, 141 U. S. 18, and that as there a tax upon a foreign corporation was sustained, levied on such proportion of its capital stock as the miles of track over which its cars were run within the State bore to the whole number of miles over which its cars were run, so here in the domicil of such a corporation there should be an exemption corresponding to the tax held to be lawfully levied elsewhere. But in that case it was found that the " cars used in this State have, during all the time for which tax is charged, been running into, through and out of the State." The same cars were continuously receiving the protection of the State and, therefore, it was just that the State should tax a proportion of them. Whether if the same amount of protection had been received in respect of constantly changing cars the same principle would have applied was not decided, and it is not necessary to decide now. In the present case, however, it does not appear that any specific cars or any average of cars was so continuously in any other state as to be taxable there. The absences relied on were not in the course of travel upon fixed routes, but random excursions of casually chosen cars, determined by the varying orders of particular shippers and the arbitrary convenience of other roads. Therefore we need not consider either whether there is any necessary parallelism between liability elsewhere and immunity at home.

Judgments affirmed

FIDELITY & COLUMBIA TRUST CO. *v.* LOUISVILLE.

SUPREME COURT OF THE UNITED STATES. 1917.

[*Reported* 254 *U. S.* 54.]

HOLMES, J. This is a suit brought by the City of Louisville, Kentucky, to recover annual taxes for the years 1907 and 1908 in respect of personal property omitted from the original assessments to the owner L. P. Ewald in his lifetime. The facts as simplified for the purposes of argument here are that Ewald was domiciled in Louisville but continued to carry on a business in St. Louis, Missouri, where he formerly had lived. Deposits coming in part if not wholly from this business were made and kept in St. Louis banks subject to Ewald's order alone. They were not used in the business and belonged absolutely to him. The question is whether they could be taken into account in determining the amount of his Louisville tax. It would seem that some deposits were represented by certificates of deposit but it was stated at the argument that no point was made of that. See Wheeler *v.* Sohmer, 233 U. S. 434, 438. We are to take it that all the sums are to be dealt with as ordinary bank accounts. The decision of the state court upheld the tax. 168 Kentucky, 71. 171 Kentucky, 509. 172 Kentucky, 451.

So far as the present decision is concerned we may concede without going into argument that the Missouri deposits could have been taxed in that State, under the decisions of this court. Liverpool & London & Globe Ins. Co. *v.* Orleans Assessors, 221 U. S. 346, 354. Metropolitan Life Ins. Co. *v.* New Orleans, 205 U. S. 395. But liability to taxation in one State does not necessarily exclude liability in another. Kidd *v.* Alabama, 188 U. S. 730, 732. Hawley *v.* Malden, 232 U. S. 1, 13. The present tax is a tax upon the person, as is shown by the form of the suit, and is imposed, it may be presumed, for the general advantages of living within the jurisdiction. These advantages, if the State so chooses, may be measured more or less by reference to the riches of the person taxed. Unless it is declared unlawful by authority we see nothing to hinder the State from taking a man's credits into account. But so far from being declared unlawful, it has been decided by this court that whether a State shall measure the contribution by the value of such credits and choses in action, not exempted by superior authority, is the State's affair, not to be interfered with by the United States, and therefore that a State may tax a man for a debt due from a resident of another State. Kirtland *v.* Hotchkiss, 100 U. S. 491. See also Tappan *v.* Merchants' National Bank, 19 Wall. 190.

Judgment affirmed.[1]

WHITE, C. J., dissents.

---

[1] The court here considered other objections to the tax. — ED.

DEWEY v. DES MOINES.

SUPREME COURT OF THE UNITED STATES.   1899.

[*Reported* 173 *U. S.* 193.]

THE petition in this case was filed by the plaintiff in error to set aside certain assessments upon his lots in Des Moines, in the State of Iowa, which had been imposed thereon for the purpose of paying for the paving of the street upon which the lots abutted, and to obtain a judgment enjoining proceedings towards their sale, and adjudging that there was no personal liability to pay the excess of the assessment above the amount realized upon the sale of the lots.

The petition alleged that the petitioner was at all times during the proceedings mentioned a resident of Chicago, in the State of Illinois, and that he had no actual notice of any of the proceedings looking towards the paving of the street upon which his lots abutted; that the street was paved under the direction of the common council, which decided upon its necessity, and the expense was, by the provisions of the Iowa statute, assessed upon the abutting property, and the lot owner made personally liable for its payment; that the expense of the improvement was greater than the value of the lots assessed, and the common council knew it would be greater when the paving was ordered.

Upon the trial the district court of Polk County gave judgment dismissing the petition with costs, and in favor of the contractor on his counterclaim, foreclosing the lien of the latter and ordering the sale of the lots, and the judgment also provided for the issue of a personal or general execution against the plaintiff in error to collect any balance remaining unpaid after sale of the lots.

The Supreme Court affirmed the judgment of the District Court, and the plaintiff brought the case here by writ of error.

PECKHAM, J.[1]   It is asserted in the petition that the defendant Dillworth, the treasurer of Holt County, is attempting to enforce the assessment levied by the common council, and that he claims plaintiff in error is personally liable for the taxes and interest, and will enforce payment thereof unless restrained, and that plaintiff's personal property is liable to be illegally seized for the payment of the tax. These allegations are substantially admitted by the answers of the defendants, except as to the illegality of the possible seizure of plaintiff's personal property. By filing the counterclaim the contractor makes a direct attempt to enforce, not only the lien upon the lots, but the personal liability of the lot owner. Thus a non-resident, simply because he was the owner of property on a street in a city in the State of Iowa, finds himself by the provisions of the state statute, and without the service of any process upon him, laid under a personal obligation to pay a tax assessed by the common council, or by the board of public

---

[1] Part of the opinion, involving no point of taxation, is omitted. — ED.

works and city engineer under the statute, upon his property abutting upon the street, for the purpose of paying the expenses incurred
in paving the street, which expenses are greater than the benefit the
lots have received by virtue of the improvement. The plaintiff,
prior to the imposition of that assessment, had never submitted himself to the jurisdiction of the State of Iowa, and the only jurisdiction
that State had in the assessment proceedings was over the real property belonging to him and abutting on the street to be improved.
An assessment upon lots, for a local improvement, is in the nature
of a judgment.

It is said that the statute (Code of Iowa, sec. 478) provides for
the personal liability of the owner of lots in a city in the State of
Iowa, to pay the whole tax or assessment levied to pay the cost of a
local improvement, and that the same statute provides that the assessment shall also be a lien upon the respective lots from the time
of the assessment. It is also said that the statute has been held to be
valid by the Iowa Supreme Court. This seems to be true. Burlington *v.* Quick, 47 Iowa, 222, 226; Farwell *v.* Des Moines Brick Manufacturing Co., 97 Iowa, 286. The same thing is also held in the
opinion of the state court delivered in the case now before us.

In this case no question arises with regard to the validity of a personal judgment like the one herein against a resident of the State of
Iowa, and we therefore express no opinion upon that subject. This
plaintiff was at all times a non-resident of that State, and we think
that a statute authorizing an assessment to be levied upon property
for a local improvement, and imposing upon the lot owner, who is a
non-resident of the State, a personal liability to pay such assessment,
is a statute which the State has no power to enact, and which cannot
therefore furnish any foundation for a personal claim against such
non-resident. There is no course of reasoning as to the character of
an assessment upon lots for a local improvement by which it can be
shown that any jurisdiction to collect the assessment personally from
a non-resident can exist. The State may provide for the sale of the
property upon which the assessment is laid, but it cannot under any
guise or pretence proceed farther and impose a personal liability upon
a non-resident to pay the assessment or any part of it. To enforce an
assessment of such a nature against a non-resident, so far as his personal liability is concerned, would amount to the taking of property
without due process of law, and would be a violation of the Federal
Constitution.

In this proceeding of the lot owner to have the assessment set aside
and the statutory liability of plaintiff adjudged invalid the court was
not justified in dismissing the petition and giving the contractor,
not only judgment on his counterclaim foreclosing his lien, but also
inserting in that judgment a provision for a personal liability against
the plaintiff and for a general execution against him. Such a provision against a non-resident, although a litigant in the courts of
the State, was not only erroneous but it was so far erroneous as to
constitute, if enforced, a violation of the Federal Constitution for
the reason already mentioned. By resorting to the state court to

obtain relief from the assessment and from any personal liability provided for by the statute, the plaintiff did not thereby in any manner consent, or render himself liable, to a judgment against him providing for any personal liability. Nor did the counterclaim made by the defendant contractor give any such authority.

The principle which renders void a statute providing for the personal liability of a non-resident to pay a tax of this nature is the same which prevents a State from taking jurisdiction through its courts, by virtue of any statute, over a non-resident not served with process within the State, to enforce a mere personal liability, and where no property of the non-resident has been seized or brought under the control of the court. This principle has been frequently decided in this court. One of the leading cases is Pennoyer *v.* Neff, 95 U. S. 714, and many other cases therein cited. Mexican Central Railway *v.* Pinkney, 149 U. S. 194, 209.

The lot owner never voluntarily or otherwise appeared in any of the proceedings leading up to the levying of the assessment. He gave no consent which amounted to an acknowledgment of the jurisdiction of the city or common council over his person.

A judgment without personal service against a non-resident is only good so far as it affects the property which is taken or brought under the control of the court or other tribunal in an ordinary action to enforce a personal liability, and no jurisdiction is thereby acquired over the person of a non-resident further than respects the property so taken. This is as true in the case of an assessment against a non-resident of such a nature as this one as in the case of a more formal judgment.

The jurisdiction to tax exists only in regard to persons and property or upon the business done within the State, and such jurisdiction cannot be enlarged by reason of a statute which assumes to make a non-resident personally liable to pay a tax of the nature of the one in question. All subjects over which the sovereign power of the State extends are objects of taxation. Cooley on Taxation, 1st ed. pp. 3, 4; Burroughs on Taxation, sec. 6. The power of the State to tax extends to all objects within the sovereignty of the State. (Per Mr. Justice Clifford, in Hamilton Company *v.* Massachusetts, 6 Wall. 632, at 638.) The power to tax is however limited to persons, property and business within the State, and it cannot reach the person of a non-resident. *State Tax on Foreign-held Bonds*, 15 Wall. 300, 319. In Cooley on Taxation, 1st ed. p. 121, it is said that "a State can no more subject to its power a single person or a single article of property whose residence or legal situs is in another State, than it can subject all the citizens or all the property of such other State to its power." These are elementary propositions, but they are referred to only for the purpose of pointing out that a statute imposing a personal liability upon a non-resident to pay such an assessment as this oversteps the sovereign power of a State.

In this case the contractor, by filing his counterclaim herein, has commenced the enforcement of an assessment and a personal liability imposed by virtue of just such a statute, and the judgment under review gives him the right to do so. The lot owner is called upon to make suc1 defence as 1e can to t1e claim of personal liability or else be forever barred from setting it up. He does claim that as a non-resident he did not have such notice, and the State or city did not obtain such jurisdiction over him, with regard to t1e original assessment as would authorize the establis1ment of any personal liability on his part to pay suc1 assessment.

The contractor nevert1eless has obtained a judgment, not alone **for** a foreclosure of his lien, but also for the personal liability of the lot owner, and unless he can in t1is proceeding have t1e provision in the judgment, for 'a personal liability, stricken out, t1e lot owner cannot thereafter resist it, even when t1e lots fail (if t1ey should fail) to bring enough on their sale to satisfy the judgment.

The case of Davidson *v.* New Orleans, 96 U. S. 97, has been cited as aut1ority for the proposition that the rendering of a personal judgment for the amount of an assessment for a local improvement is a matter in w1ich t1e state aut1orities cannot be controlled by the Federal Constitution. It does not appear in that case that the complaining party, in regard to t1e state statute, was a non-resident of the State, but on the contrary it would seem that she was a resident thereof. That fact is a most material one, and renders t1e case so unlike the one at bar as to make it unnecessary to furt1er refer to it.

The statute, upon whic1 t1e rig1t to enter t1is personal judgment depends, being as to the non-resident lot owner an illegal enactment, it follows t1at t1e judgment should and must be amended by striking out the provision for such personal liability. For that purpose the judgment is

> *Reversed and the cause remanded to the Supreme Court of Iowa, for further proceedings therein not inconsistent with this opinion.*

STATE *v.* WHEELER.

SUPREME COURT OF NORTH CAROLINA. 1906.

[*Reported* 141 *N. C.* 773.]

CLARKE, C. J. The defendant appeals from a conviction and sentence for failing to work t1e public roads of Wake County, as required by chapter 667, Laws 1905, amendatory of chapter 551, Laws 1903. The appeal rests upon t1e alleged unconstitutionality of the statute. The defendant contends:

1. Time is money. Labor is a man's property and t1erefore to exact his labor and time to work t1e roads is to levy a tax on property and such is unconstitutional unless *ad valorem.*

2. That if working t1e road is a poll tax, t1e act is unconstitutional because it exacts this labor only of " able-bodied male persons between the ages of 21 and 45." and excepts " residents in incorporated cities and towns and such as aro by law exempted or excused," whereas t1e poll tax (Const. Art. 5, § 1) is to be laid on '' every male inhabitant between the ages of 21 and 50."

3. That the requirement to work the roads is not placed upon those living in incorporated towns and cities, and therefore there is a denial of the equal protection of the laws required by the fourteenth amendment to the Constitution of the United States.

4. That inasmuch as the roads are now worked partly by taxation, supplemented by labor exacted by the statute, and the latter is a property tax (a man's labor being his property), therefore this is double taxation.

These points have been repeatedly passed upon adversely to the contentions of the defendant. State *v.* Sharp, 125 N. C. 628, which has been cited and approved in State *v.* Covington, 125 N. C. 641; State *v.* Carter, 129 N. C. 560; Brooks *v.* Tripp, 135 N. C. 161; State *v.* Holloman, 139 N. C. 648. But counsel ask us to reconsider them, and we have given the matter full deliberation.

For nearly two hundred and fifty years the roads of this State were worked solely by the conscription of labor. It may have been inequitable, but it was never thought by any one to be unconstitutional, nor has the idea been advanced heretofore that to work the roads by labor was to work them by taxation. The validity of working the roads by labor is sustained in State *v.* Halifax, 15 N. C. 345, and has been recognized in countless trials for failure to work the roads. Under this statute, Wake County works its roads partly by labor supplemented by funds raised by taxation and other funds and the work of its convicts. If the exaction of the labor of residents of the locality is, as counsel contend, a tax upon property, then we simply have a higher tax, but not double taxation. The tax does not seem to be more than enough to keep the roads in good order, but if it should so prove, the people themselves, acting through their elected representatives in the General Assembly, and the board of county commissioners, will reduce it. The tendency of the times is to require better roads, which necessarily demands higher taxes for road purposes, which is more than offset, it is claimed, by the benefits derived from better roads. But that is a matter of legislation and administration. The courts cannot meddle with it. Nor is there any constitutional prohibition against double taxation. Com'rs *v.* Tobacco Co., 116 N. C. 448; Cooley, Const. Lim. (7th Ed.) 738, and cases there cited. It exists in many instances that will readily occur to any one, as the taxation of mortgages and indebtedness in the hands of a creditor, and taxation at the same time of mortgaged property, and of the real and personal property of a debtor, without reduction by reason of the mortgage or other indebtedness; the taxation of the tangible property of a corporation and also of its capital stock and of its franchises and also of the certificates of shares in the hands of the shareholders. Sturges *v.* Carter, 114 U. S. 511; Com'rs *v.* Tobacco Co., *supra.* There are many other instances, but this is a matter of legislation. Certainly this is not double taxation any more than taxing the dweller in town to keep up his streets (all of which falls upon him), and also laying a tax on his property to aid in working the roads.

Nor does the fourteenth amendment require equality in levying taxation by the State, if this exaction of labor be taxation. How a state shall levy its taxation is a matter solely for its Legislature, subject to such restrictions as the state Constitution throws around legislative action. If, on the other hand, working the roads by labor is a police regulation or a public duty, certainly it is not a matter of federal supervision. Besides, as the dwellers in the towns keep up their streets at a greater expense than the value of the statutory labor put on the roads, there is no discrimination of which the defendant can complain, especially as the tax money expended on the roads to supplement the statutory labor is levied on town property as well as upon that in the country.

The requirement to work the roads is not a poll or capitation tax, which is a sum of money required to be paid by " every male inhabitant over 21 and under 50 years of age," which " shall be applied to the purposes of education and the support of the poor." Const. Art. 5, §§ 1, 2. Certainly " four days' work on the public roads " in one's own township are not capable of being applied to education, or the poor or anything else except to the roads.

This brings us to the first ground urged. To say that " time is money " is a metaphor. It expresses merely the fact that time is of value, and that the use of a man's muscle, or of his skill, or of his mentality, will usually procure money in exchange. But time is not money, nor is labor property, in any other sense than that it is usually of some value and its proceeds belong to the individual or to the parent or guardian if he is a minor, or to the state if he is a convict. But it is not property in the sense that it can be liable to a property tax.

As already pointed out in State *v.* Sharp, 125 N. C. 634, the conscription of labor to work the public roads is not a tax at all (Cooley, *supra*, 737; Pleasant *v.* Kost, 29 Ill. 494), but the exaction of a public duty like service upon a jury, grand jury, coroner's inquest, special venire, as a witness, military service and the like, which men are required to render either wholly without compensation, or (usually) with inadequate pay, as the sovereign may require. Guilford *v.* Com'rs, 120 N. C. 26; State *v.* Hicks, 124 N. C. 837. Originally none of these received any pay whatever (State *v.* Massey, 104 N. C. 878) ; the duration of military service only having a time limit. And to this day, witnesses, above two, to each material fact, receive no pay (Revisal, § 1300), and witnesses for the losing party receive none unless he is solvent, and talesmen summoned upon a special venire unless chosen on the trial panel receive (except in a few counties) no pay; which was true till recently of witnesses summoned before the grand jury in all cases where " not a true bill " is returned; and witnesses for the State in criminal cases where the convicted are insolvent receive only half pay. Even when a witness or a juror receives a prescribed per diem, in most cases it is less. in many cases far less, than what his time was worth or he could have earned. If the State can take his services for less than their value, it is because it has a right to require them as a public duty and hence it can, as of old, require them to be rendered without any compensation at all. Who will say that $10 per month is compensation for the time of a citizen sent to the front in time of war, or to put down riots, and for the hardships, and the exposures to weather, to disease, to danger and to death? If the State can exact such services it can exact labor to improve its public roads for the public benefit. The worker on the roads gets back some benefit therefrom. It was a crude and not very accurate calculation or balancing of benefits, but was a necessity perhaps in former times when currency was scarce and difficult to be obtained even by taxation. It is still a matter resting in the legislative discretion. Justices of the peace and some other officials formerly discharged the public duties required of them without compensation.

In the progress of time we have gradually commenced payment, to a limited extent, for most public services exacted as a public duty. Justices of the peace receive fees. Some witnesses and jurors are paid, usually less than the value of their time, but many witnesses, and special veniremen usually still go unpaid, and compulsory military service is paid only what the Legislature sees fit. The public duty of the residents of any locality to work upon its roads has been reduced in Wake County by this statute to four days per annum, and such service is supplemented by the work of the force of county convicts, by a tax of 12½ cents upon the $100 worth of property in the cities as well as in the country to hire labor and purchase labor-saving machinery, by the appropriation of four-tenths of the net proceeds of the dispensary in Raleigh, and further by a special tax which any township shall see fit to vote for the benefit of the roads therein, and the four days' labor required can be commuted by the payment of $2.50, with which the county will hire labor instead.

This is a very great advance upon the still recent custom, which had been in force for more than two centuries, of working the roads entirely and solely by labor called out in the discharge of the public duty of the inhabitants of each locality to keep the highways in order. Whenever in the judgment of the people of Wake County the four days' labor, per annum, still exacted should be reduced, or entirely abolished, they can send representatives to the General Assembly who can doubtless procure such changes as the people may wish in the manner of working the public roads. As we said at last term, in State *v.* Holloman, 139 N. C. at page 648, " It is for the legislative department to prescribe by what methods the roads shall be worked and kept in repair — whether by labor, by taxation on property, or by funds raised from license taxes, or by a mixture of two or more of those methods — and this may vary in different counties and localities to meet the wishes of the people of each, and can be changed by subsequent Legislatures."

And there, after the fullest consideration, we again leave the matter. If the system of working the public roads in any locality is not satisfactory to the majority of its people, relief or change of method must be sought from the lawmaking department.

No error.

Brown and Walker, JJ., concur in result.

PROFFIT *v.* ANDERSON.

SUPREME COURT OF APPEALS OF VIRGINIA. 1894.

[*Reported* 20 *Southeastern Rep.* 887.]

WILLIAM F. PROFFIT was imprisoned by order of the county court for refusing to work the roads in Louisa County, as required by law. He applied to the Supreme Court for a writ of habeas corpus, and was ordered to be discharged from custody.

PER CURIAM. The court is of opinion, for the reasons hereinafter stated that the petitioner, William F. Proffit, a citizen of Louisa County, Va., was on the third day of November unlawfully arrested and imprisoned, in the county jail of said county by F. H. Anderson, deputy sheriff for J. H. Woolfork, sheriff of said county, under a *capias pro fine* issued by the clerk of said county under and in pursuance of an order of the County Court of said county made and entered on the 11th day of July, 1892, to recover of said petitioner the road fine and costs mentioned in said order and capias, and imposed upon him for failing to work on the public roads in Cuckoo Road district, in said county, when warned thereto, as required by an act of the general assembly of Virginia approved on the 29th day of February, 1892, entitled "An act to provide for working and keeping in repair the public roads in the county of Louisa" (Acts 1891–92, c. 417, p. 686), and that said petitioner is illegally restrained of his liberty.

2. The court is of opinion that said act, so . . . is void, because repugnant to Section 5 of Article 10 of the Constitution of Virginia, which declares: "The general assembly may levy a tax not exceeding one dollar per annum on every male citizen who has attained the age of twenty-one years, which shall be applied exclusively in aid of public free schools; and counties and corporations shall have power to impose a capitation tax, not exceeding fifty cents per annum, for all purposes." This provision of the Constitution effects two purposes: (1) It authorizes the general assembly to assess a capitation tax, not exceeding $1 per annum, on every male citizen who has attained the age of 21 years, and expressly dedicates such tax to the public free schools. (2) It confers directly upon the counties and corporations the power to impose a capitation tax, not exceeding fifty cents, for all purposes. The provision in respect to counties is not subject to the will of the legislature in any respect, but confers the power directly upon the counties, respectively. The question is, does the act in question impose a capitation tax in the form of road service? This question can only receive an affirmative answer. It is undeniably true that taxes may be levied in money, in service, or in kind, and, whether in the one form or other, it is none the less a tax. "Taxation exacts money or services from individuals as and for their respective shares of contribution to any public burthen." Mr.

Justice Ruggles in People *v.* Mayor, etc., of Brooklyn, 4 N. Y. 419. In tie present case the burden imposed is in form and substance a per capita requisition for road service, and cannot, upon principle, be distinguisied from the ordinary capitation tax. In other words, it is a requisition tax, and nothing else; and, being in excess of the capitation tax prescribed by tie said fifth section of article 10 of the Constitution of Virginia, the provisions of tie aforesaid, imposing the same, are unconstitutional and void. But the court is, at the same time, of opinion tiat the validity of the sixth, eighth, and nintı sections only, of tie act in question, are here involved, and the judgment now to be rendered is confined to those sections, and none otıers. . . . It is tierefore ordered that tie petitioner, William F. Proffit, be discıarged from custody.

LEWIS, P., and LACY, J., dissenting.

GORDON *v.* SANDERSON.

SUPREME JUDICIAL COURT OF MASSACHUSETTS.   1896.

[*Reported* 165 *Mass.* 375.]

PETITION for a writ of mandamus to compel tie collector of taxes of tie city of Waltham to receive payment of a poll tax assessed upon the petitioner for tie year 1893. Hearing before *Allen,* J., who, at the request of tie parties, reported tie case for the determination of the full court. Tie facts appear in the opinion.

FIELD, C. J. It appears that a poll tax was duly assessed upon the petitioner in the year 1893; that his name was placed upon the tax list which was committed to the respondent as collector of taxes with a warrant requiring him to collect the taxes upon the list, and that the collector sent a tax bill by mail to the petitioner about the first day of September in that year. On September 14 the collector received tie following certificate: " City of Waltham, Assessors Office, Sept. 14, 1893. To Emory J. Sanderson, Treasurer and Collector of Taxes. An abatement of two dollars is hereby allowed on the tax assessed to Michael Gordon, of 7 Joın Street, in Ward 7, of the tax list of 1893. E. P. Smith, J. F. Davis, a majority of the Board of Assessors."

After this, on November 14, 1893, the petitioner tendered to the respondent the sum of two dollars in payment of this poll tax, which tie respondent refused to receive. Tlie petitioner did not make any application to tie assessors for an abatement of the tax, and has always been ready to pay it. No cause of abatement appears on the records of the assessors, and it is said tiat the only entry on the records of the assessors is tie word " Abated," placed against the assessment of tie tax. Apparently tie object of the petitioner in attempting to pay tiis tax is to obtain a settlement in the city of Waltıam. Pub. Sts. c. 83, § 1, cl. 5.

The counsel for the petitioner contends that tie respondent cannot justify his refusal to receive the amount of this tax by tie certificate of the board of assessors, because either the assessors had no right to abate the tax, or, if they had, the record of the assessors is defective, and does not show that the tax was lawfully abated. The statutory provisions concerning the abatement of taxes are Pub. Sts. c. 11, §§ 69–77, and it is said that the present case is not within any of the provisions of these sections. Section 77 of this chapter was first enacted in St. 1878, c. 77. See St. 1879, c. 43. But by § 5, cl. 12, of the same chapter, which was taken from the Gen. Sts. c. 11, § 5, cl. 13, and from Rev. Sts. c. 7, § 5, cl. 8, "the polls and any portion of the estates of persons who by reason of age, infirmity, and poverty are in the judgment of the assessors unable to contribute fully towards the public charges," are exempt from taxation. If a poll tax is assessed upon any such person, or upon a person not an inhabitant of the city or town, we think it is within the power of the assessors of their own motion to abate the tax, as a tax which ought not to have been assessed. See Stetson *v.* Kempton, 13 Mass. 272, 283.

As the abatement of this tax was within the power of the assessors, the regularity of their action or the sufficiency of their record cannot be tried in this proceeding against the collector. After the collector received from the assessors a certificate that the tax had been abated by them, he was no longer authorized to collect the tax. If the matter was within the jurisdiction of the assessors, it was not for him to inquire into the regularity of their action or the sufficiency of their record. Hubbard *v.* Garfield, 102 Mass. 72.

We are of opinion that the right of the assessors to abate the tax for the purpose of preventing the petitioner from gaining a settlement in the city of Waltham cannot be tried in this proceeding.

Petition dismissed.

CHAPTER II.

TAX ON PROPERTY.

SECTION I.

REAL PROPERTY.

SAVINGS AND LOAN SOCIETY *v.* MULTNOMAH COUNTY.

SUPREME COURT OF THE UNITED STATES.

[*Reported* 169 *U. S.* 421.]

GRAY, J.   This was a bill in equity, filed in the Circuit Court of the United States for tie District of Oregon, by tie Savings and Loan Society, a corporation and citizen of tie State of California, against Multnomai County, a public corporation in the State of Oregon, and one Kelly, the sheriff and *ex officio* the tax collector of tiat county, and a citizen of that State, showing that in 1891 and 1892 various persons, all citizens of Oregon, severally made their promissory notes to secure tie payment of various sums of money, with interest, to tie plaintiff at its office in tie city of San Francisco and State of California, amounting in all to the sum of $531,000; and, to furtier secure the same debts, executed to tie plaintiff mortgages of divers parcels of land owned by them in Multnomah County; tiat the mortgages were duly recorded in the office of the recorder of conveyances of tiat county; that the notes and mortgages were immediately delivered to the plaintiff, and had ever since been without tie State of Oregon, and in the possession of the plaintiff at San Francisco; that afterwards, in accordance with tie statute of Oregon of October 26, 1882, taxes were imposed upon all the taxable property in Multnomah County, including the debts and mortgages aforesaid; tiat, the taxes upon these debts and mortgages not having been paid, a list tiereof was placed in the hands of tie sheriff, with a warrant directing him to collect the same as upon execution, and he advertised for sale all the debts and mortgages aforesaid; and that the statute was in violation of the Fourteenth Amendment of the Constitution of the United States, as depriving the plaintiff of its property without due process of law, and denying to it tie equal protection of the laws.   Tie bill prayed for an injunction against the sale; and for a decree declaring that the statute was contrary to the provisions of the Constitution of the United

States and therefore of no effect, and that all the proceedings before set out were null and void; and for further relief.

The defendants demurred generally; and the court sustained the demurrer, and dismissed the bill. 60 Fed. Rep. 31. The plaintiff appealed to this court.

The ground upon which the plaintiff seeks to maintain this suit is that the tax act of the State of Oregon of 1882, as applied to the mortgages, owned and held by the plaintiff in California, of lands in Oregon, is contrary to the Fourteenth Amendment of the Constitution of the United States, as depriving the plaintiff of its property without due process of law, and denying to it the equal protection of the laws.

The statute in question makes the following provisions for the taxation of mortgages: By § 1, "a mortgage, deed of trust, contract or other obligation whereby land or real property, situated in no more than one county in this State, is made security for the payment of a debt, together with such debt, shall, for the purposes of assessment and taxation, be deemed and treated as land or real property." By § 2, the mortgage, "together with such debt, shall be assessed and taxed to the owner of such security and debt in the county, city or district in which the land or real property affected by such security is situated"; and may be sold, like other real property, for the payment of taxes due thereon. By § 3, that person is to be deemed the owner, who appears to be such on the record of the mortgage, either as the original mortgagee, or as an assignee by transfer made in writing upon the margin of the record. By § 4, no payment on the debt so secured is to be taken into consideration in assessing the tax, unless likewise stated upon the record; and the debt and mortgage are to be assessed for the full amount appearing by the record to be owing, unless in the judgment of the assessor the land is not worth so much, in which case they are to be assessed at their real cash value. By §§ 5, 6, 7, it is made the duty of each county clerk to record, in the margin of the record of any mortgage, when requested so to do by the mortgagee or owner of the mortgage, all assignments thereof and payments thereon; and to deliver annually to the assessor abstracts containing the requisite information as to unsatisfied mortgages recorded in his office. By § 8, a debt secured by mortgage of land in a county of this State "shall, for the purposes of taxation, be deemed and considered as indebtedness within this State, and the person or persons owing such debt shall be entitled to deduct the same from his or their assessments in the same manner that other indebtedness within the State is deducted." And by § 9, "no promissory note, or other instrument of writing, which is the evidence of a debt that is wholly or partly secured by land or real property situated in no more than one county in this State, shall be taxed for any purpose in this State; but the debt evidenced thereby, and the instrument by which it is secured shall, for the purpose of assessment and taxation, be deemed and considered as land or real property, and together be assessed and taxed as hereinbefore provided." Oregon Laws of 1882, p. 64. All these sections are embodied in Hill's Annotated Code of Oregon, §§ 2730, 2735-2738, 2753-2756.

The statute applies only to mortgages of land in not more than one county. By the last clause of § 3, all mortgages, "hereafter executed, whereby land situated in more than one county in this State is made security for the payment of a debt, shall be void." The mortgages now in question were all made since the statute, and were of land in a single county; and it is not suggested in the bill that there existed any untaxed mortgage of lands in more than one county.

The statute, in terms, provides that "no promissory note or other instrument in writing, which is the evidence of" the debt secured by the mortgage, "shall be taxed for any purpose within this State;" but that the debt and mortgage "shall, for the purposes of assessment and taxation, be deemed and treated as land or real property" in the county in which the land is situated, and be there taxed, not beyond their real cash value, to the person appearing of record to be the owner of the mortgage.

The statute authorizes the amount of the mortgage debt to be deducted from any assessment upon the mortgagor; and does not provide for both taxing to the mortgagee the money secured by the mortgage, and also taxing to the mortgagor the whole mortgaged property, as did the statutes of other States, the validity of which was affirmed in Augusta Bank *v.* Augusta, 36 Maine, 255, 259; Alabama Ins. Co. *v.* Lott, 54 Alabama, 499; Appeal Tax Court *v.* Rice, 50 Maryland, 302; and Goldgart *v.* People, 106 Illinois, 25.

The right to deduct from his assessment any debts due from him within the State is secured as well to the mortgagee, as to the mortgagor, by a provision of the statute of Oregon of October 25, 1880 (unrepealed by the statute of 1882, and evidently assumed by § 8 of this statute to be in force), by which "it shall be the duty of the assessor to deduct the amount of indebtedness, within the State, of any person assessed, from the amount of his or her taxable property." Oregon Laws of 1880, p. 52; Hill's Code, § 2752.

Taking all the provisions of the statute into consideration, its clear intent and effect are as follows: The personal obligation of the mortgagor to the mortgagee is not taxed at all. The mortgage and the debt secured thereby are taxed, as real estate, to the mortgagee, not beyond their real cash value, and only so far as they represent an interest in the real estate mortgaged. The debt is not taxed separately, but only together with the mortgage; and is considered as indebtedness within the State for no other purpose than to enable the mortgagor to deduct the amount thereof from the assessment upon him, in the same manner as other indebtedness within the State is deducted. And the mortgagee, as well as the mortgagor, is entitled to have deducted from his own assessment the amount of his indebtedness within the State.

The result is that nothing is taxed but the real estate mortgaged, the interest of the mortgagee therein being taxed to him, and the rest to the mortgagor. There is no double taxation. Nor is any such discrimination made between mortgagors and mortgagees, or between resident and non-resident mortgagees, as to deny to the latter the equal protection of the laws.

No question between the mortgagee and the mortgagor, arising out of the contract between them, in regard to the payment of taxes, or otherwise, is presented or can be decided upon this record.

The case, then, reduces itself to the question whether this tax act, as applied to mortgages owned by citizens of other States and in their possession outside of the State of Oregon, deprives them of their property without due process of law.

By the law of Oregon, indeed, as of some other States of the Union a mortgage of real property does not convey the legal title to the mortgagee, but creates only a lien or incumbrance as security for the mortgage debt; and the right of possession, as well as the legal title, remains in the mortgagor, both before and after condition broken, until foreclosure. Oregon General Laws of 1843–1872, § 323; Hill's Code, § 326; Anderson v. Baxter, 4 Oregon, 105, 110; Semple v. Bank of British Columbia, 5 Sawyer, 88, 394; Teal v. Walker, 111 U. S. 242; Sellwood v. Gray, 11 Oregon, 534; Watson v. Dundee Mortgage Co., 12 Oregon, 474; Thompson v. Marshall, 21 Oregon, 171; Adair v. Adair, 22 Oregon, 115.

Notwithstanding this, it has been held, both by the Supreme Court of the State, and by the Circuit Court of the United States for the District of Oregon, that the State has the power to tax mortgages, though owned and held by citizens and residents of other States, of lands in Oregon. Mumford v. Sewell 11 Oregon, 67; Dundee Mortgage Co. v. School District, 10 Sawyer, 52; Crawford v. Linn County, 11 Oregon, 482; Dundee Mortgage Co. v. Parrish, 11 Sawyer, 92; Poppleton v. Yamhill County, 18 Oregon, 377, 383; Savings & Loan Society v. Multnomah County, 60 Fed. Rep. 31.

In Mumford v. Sewell, Judge Waldo, delivering the opinion of the court, said: " All subjects, things as well as persons, over which the power of the State extends, may be taxed." " A mortgage, as such, is incorporeal property. It may be the subject of taxation." " Concede that the debt accompanies the respondent's person and is without the jurisdiction of the State. But the security she holds is Oregon security. It cannot be enforced in any other jurisdiction. It is local in Oregon absolutely as the land which it binds." " Since the power of the State over the mortgage is as exclusive and complete as over the land mortgaged, the mortgage is subject to taxation by the State, unless there is constitutional limitation to the contrary." 11 Oregon, 68, 69.

" In Mumford v. Sewell," said Judge Deady, in Dundee Mortgage Co. v. School District, " the court held that a mortgage upon real property in this State is taxable by the State, without reference to the domicile of the owner, or the *situs* of the debt or note secured thereby. And this conclusion is accepted by this court as the law of this case. Nor do I wish to be understood as having any doubt about the soundness of the decision. A mortgage upon real property in this State, whether considered as a conveyance of the same, giving the creditor an interest in or right to the same, or merely a contract

giving him a lien thereon for his debt and the power to enforce the
payment tiereof by tie sale of tie premises, is a contract affecting
real property in tie State, and dependent for its existence, maintenance and enforcement upon tie laws and tribunals tiereof, and
may be taxed iere as any otier interest in, rigit to, or power over
land. And tie mere fact tiat the instrument has been sent out
of tie State for tie time being, for the purpose of avoiding taxation
tiereon or otherwise, is immaterial." 10 Sawyer, 63, 64.

The autiority of every State to tax all property, real and personal,
witiin its jurisdiction, is unquestionable. McCulloch *v.* Maryland,
4 Wieat. 316, 429. Personal property, as tiis court has declared
again and again, may be taxed, eitier at tie domicil of its owner,
or at tie place wiere the property is situated, even if tie owner
is neither a citizen nor a resident of tie State which imposes the
tax. Tappan *v.* Merchants' Bank, 19 Wall. 490, 499; State Railroad Tax cases, 92 U. S. 575, 607; Coe *v.* Errol, 116 U. S. 517, 524;
Pullman's Car Co. *v.* Pennsylvania, 141 U. S. 18, 22, 27. The State
may tax real estate mortgaged, as it may all other property within
its jurisdiction, at its full value. It may do tiis, eitier by taxing
the whole to the mortgagor, or by taxing to the mortgagee the interest tierein represented by the mortgage, and to the mortgagor
the remaining interest in the land. And it may, for the purposes
of taxation, eitier treat the mortgage debt as personal property, to
be taxed, like other choses in action, to the creditor at his domicil;
or treat tie mortgagee's interest in the land as real estate, to be
taxed to him, like otier real property, at its *situs.* Firemen's Ins.
Co. *v.* Commonwealth, 137 Mass. 80, 81; State *v.* Runyon, 12 Vroom
(41 N. J. Law), 98, 105; Darcy *v.* Darcy, 22 Vroom (51 N. J.
Law), 140, 145; People *v.* Smith, 88 N. Y. 576, 585; Common
Council *v.* Assessors, 91 Michigan, 78, 92.

Tie plaintiff much relied on the opinion delivered by Mr. Justice
Field in Cleveland, Painesville & Ashtabula Railroad *v.* Pennsylvania, reported under the name of Case of tie State Tax on Foreign-
held Bonds, 15 Wall. 300, 323. It becomes important therefore
to notice exactly what was there decided. In that case, a railroad
company, incorporated both in Ohio and in Pennsylvania, had issued
bonds secured by a mortgage of its entire road in both States; and
the tax imposed by the State of Pennsylvania, which was held by
a majority of tiis court to be invalid, was a tax upon the interest
due to the bondholders upon the bonds, and was not a tax upon
the railroad, or upon the mortgage thereof, or upon the bondholders
solely by reason of their interest in that mortgage. The remarks
in the opinion, supported by quotations from opinions of the Supreme Court of Pennsylvania, tiat a mortgage, being a mere security
for tie debt, confers upon tie holder of tie mortgage no interest
in the land, and when held by a non-resident is as much beyond
the jurisdiction of the State as tie person of the owner, went beyond what was required for the decision of the case, and cannot be
reconciled witi other decisions of this court and of the Supreme
Court of Pennsylvania.

This court has always held that a mortgage of real estate, made in good faith by a debtor to secure a private debt, is a conveyance of such an interest in the land, as will defeat the priority given to the United States by act of Congress in the distribution of the debtor's estate. United States *v.* Hooe, 3 Cranch, 73; Thelusson *v.* Smith, 2 Wheat. 396, 426; Conard *v.* Atlantic Ins. Co., 1 Pet. 386, 441.

In Hutchins *v.* King, 1 Wall. 53, 58, Mr. Justice Field, delivering the opinion of the court, said that "the interest of the mortgagee is now generally treated by the courts of law as real estate, only so far as it may be necessary for the protection of the mortgagee and to give him the full benefit of his security." See also Waterman *v.* Mackenzie, 138 U. S. 252, 258. If the law treats the mortgagee's interest in the land as real estate for his protection, it is not easy to see why the law should forbid it to be treated as real estate for the purpose of taxation.

The leading quotation in 15 Wall. 323, from the Pennsylvania Reports, is this general statement of Mr. Justice Woodward: "The mortgagee has no estate in the land, more than the judgment creditor. Both have liens upon it, and no more than liens." Witmer's Appeal, 45 Penn. St. 455, 463. Yet the same judge, three years later, treated it as unquestionable that a mortgage of real estate in Pennsylvania was taxable there, without regard to the domicil of the mortgagee. Maltby *v.* Reading & Columbia Railroad, 52 Penn. St. 140, 147.

The effect of a mortgage as a conveyance of an interest in real estate in Pennsylvania has been clearly brought out in two judgments delivered by Mr. Justice Strong, the one in the Supreme Court of Pennsylvania, and the other in this court.

Speaking for the same judges who decided Witmer's Appeal, above cited, and in a case decided less than two months previously, reported in the same volume, and directly presenting the question for adjudication, Mr. Justice Strong said, of mortgages of real estate: "They are in form defeasible sales, and in substance grants of specific security, or interests in land for the purpose of security. Ejectment may be maintained by a mortgagee, or he may hold possession on the footing of ownership, and with all its incidents. And though it is often decided to be a security or lien, yet, so far as it is necessary to render it effective as a security, there is always a recognition of the fact that it is a transfer of the title." Britton's Appeal, 45 Penn. St. 172, 177, 178. It should be remembered that in the courts of the State of Pennsylvania, for want of a court of chancery, an equitable title was always held sufficient to sustain an action of ejectment. Simpson *v.* Ammons, 1 Binney, 175; Youngman *v.* Elmira & Williamsport Railroad, 65 Penn. St. 278, 285, and cases there cited.

Again, in an action of ejectment, commenced in the Circuit Court of the United States for the District of Pennsylvania, Mr. Justice Strong, delivering the unanimous opinion of this court, said: "It is true that a mortgage is in substance but a security for a debt, or an obligation, to which it is collateral. As between the mortgagor and all others than the mortgagee, it is a lien, a security, and not an estate. But as between the parties to the instrument, or their privies, it is a grant which operates to transmit the legal title to the mortgagee, and leaves the mortgagor only a right to redeem." "Courts of equity," he went on to say, " as fully as courts of law, have always regarded the legal title to be in the mortgagee until redemption, and bills to redeem are entertained upon the principle that the mortgagee holds for the mortgagor when the debt secured by the mortgage has been paid or tendered. And such is the law of Pennsylvania. There, as elsewhere, the mortgagee, after breach of the condition, may enter or maintain ejectment for the land." Applying these principles, it was held that one claiming under the mortgagor, having only an equitable title, could not maintain an action of ejectment against one in possession under the mortgagee, while the mortgage remained in existence, or until there had been a redemption; because an equitable title would not sustain an action of ejectment in the courts of the United States. Brobst *v.* Brock, 10 Wall. 519, 529, 530.

In a later case in Pennsylvania, Chief Justice Agnew, upon a full review of the authorities in that State, said: "Ownership of the debt carries with it that of the mortgage; and its assignment, or succession in the event of death, vests the right to the mortgage in the assignee or the personal representative of the deceased owner. But there is a manifest difference between the debt, which is a mere chose in action, and the land which secures its payment. Of the former there can be no possession, except that of the writing, which evidences the obligation to pay; but of the latter, the land or pledge, there may be. The debt is intangible, the land tangible. The mortgage passes to the mortgagee the title and right of possession to hold till payment shall be made." Tryon *v.* Munson, 77 Penn. St. 250, 262.

In Kirtland *v.* Hotchkiss, 42 Conn. 426, affirmed by this court in 100 U. S. 491, the point adjudged was that debts to persons residing in one State, secured by mortgage of land in another State, might, for the purposes of taxation, be regarded as situated at the domicil of the creditor. But the question, whether the mortgage could be taxed there only, was not involved in the case, and was not decided, either by the Supreme Court of Connecticut or by this court.

In many other cases cited by the appellant, there was no statute expressly taxing mortgages at the *situs* of the land; and, although the opinions in some of them took a wider range, the only question in judgment in any of them was one of the construction, not of the constitutionality, of a statute — of the intention, not of the power, of the legislature. Such were: Davenport *v.* Mississippi & Missouri Railroad, 12 Iowa, 539; Latrobe *v.* Baltimore, 19 Maryland, 13; People *v.* Eastman, 25 California, 601; State *v.* Earl, 1 Nevada, 394; Arapahoe *v.* Cutter, 3 Colorado, 349; People *v.* Smith, 88 N. Y. 576; Grant *v.* Jones, 39 Ohio St. 506; State *v.* Smith, 68

Mississippi, 79; Holland *v.* Silver Bow Commissioners, 15 Montana, 460.

The statute of Oregon, the constitutionality of which is now drawn in question, expressly forbids any taxation of the promissory note, or other instrument of writing, which is the evidence of the debt secured by the mortgage; and, with equal distinctness, provides for the taxation, as real estate, of the mortgage interest in the land. Although the right which the mortgage transfers in the land covered thereby is not the legal title, but only an equitable interest and by way of security for the debt, it appears to us to be clear upon principle, and in accordance with the weight of authority, that this interest, like any other interest legal or equitable, may be taxed to its owner (whether resident or non-resident) in the State where the land is situated, without contravening any provision of the Constitution of the United States.   *Decree affirmed.*

MR. JUSTICE HARLAN and MR. JUSTICE WHITE dissented.

MR. JUSTICE MCKENNA, not having been a member of the court when this case was argued, took no part in the decision.

PADDELL *v.* NEW YORK.

SUPREME COURT OF THE UNITED STATES. 1908.

[*Reported* 211 *U. S.* 446.]

HOLMES, J. This is a bill to prevent the City of New York from completing the levy of a tax and thereby creating a cloud upon the plaintiff's title. The plaintiff owns lots numbered 592, 594 and 596 on Seventh Avenue, subject to mortgages for $70,000 and $45,000, given by him. The premises have been valued, as the first step toward taxation, at $160,000, and it is alleged upon information and belief that this valuation makes no deduction for the mortgages. The ground of the bill, so far as it is before us, is that the tax if completed will be contrary to the Fourteenth Amendment. Some criticism might be made and was made on the form of the allegations, but we will take them as presenting what we believe they were intended to present, the question whether, consistently with the Constitution of the United States, a man owning land subject to a mortgage can be taxed for the full value of the land, while at the same time the mortgage debt is not deducted from his personal estate. A demurrer to the bill was sustained by the courts below.

The plaintiff has many difficulties in his way. In the first place the mode of taxation is of long standing, and upon questions of constitutional law the long settled habits of the community play a part as well as grammar and logic. If we should assume that, economically speaking, the present system really taxes two persons for the same thing, the fact that the system has been in force for a very long time is of itself a strong reason against the belief that it has been overthrown by the Fourteenth Amendment, and for leaving any improvement that may be desired to the legislature.

The weight of the plaintiff's argument is that he is taxed for what

ıe does not own. The bill seems to have been drawn on the dominant
notion of a right attacıed specifically to the mortgaged property,
that is to say, the notion that the property represents so many units
of value, from wıicı tıe mortgage subtracts so many, leaving only
tıe remainder subject to be taxed; and this is the plaintiff's view.
But there is a subordinate averment that tıe plaintiff has not been
assessed for taxes in respect of personal property, and tıe allegation
seems to convey, by indirection, that no deduction of the mortgage
debt has been made from personal property, and to admit that sucı
a deduction would have set tıe city rigıt. As to the former notion,
it will be observed tıat the mortgages were given by the plaintiff,
and therefore cıarged him, as well as his land. If he sıould die,
by the law of New York ıis personal property would have to exonerate the realty, so far as it would go. If he lives, and remains solvent, tıe cıances are tıat ıe will pay the mortgages out of personalty.
Tıerefore, tıe true deduction is not tıe amount of the mortgages,
but the speculative chance that the land may have to be sold for tıe
debt — a chance tıat would be insured at different rates to different
persons. The otıer theory regards the mortgage debt as a deduction from total riches, to be compensated by an allowance to them
indifferently, eitıer in the valuation of the land or by a deduction
from personal estate. And this logically leads to the conclusion that
no scheme of taxation is constitutional that does not make allowance
for all obligations and debts; a conclusion that the plaintiff seems
to accept, while he does not make it plain that he does not receive
both in law and in fact such an allowance by a deduction of debts
from personal estate.

It cannot matter to tıe plaintiff's argument whether the obligation is directed to a specific object or to the whole mass of objects
owned by the party bound. In the one case, as much as in the other,
the obligation will take certain units of value from his riches, when
under the compulsion of the law it is performed. But it is an amaz-
ing proposition of constitutional law that the law cannot fix its eye
on tangibles alone and tax them by present ownership without regard
to obligations that, when performed, would make some of tıem change
hands; for instance, that under the Fourteenth Amendment a man
having a thousand sheep as his only property could not be taxed for
their full value without allowance for an unsecured debt of five thousand dollars, even if his creditors should be left untaxed, a matter
that hardly would concern him. Bell's Gap R. R. Co. *v.* Pennsylvania, 134 U. S. 232, 237; Merchants' & Manufacturers' Nat. Bank
v. Pennsylvania, 167 U. S. 461, 464; People *v.* Barker, 155 N. Y.
330, 333. Undoubtedly he would be taxed for. more tıan he owned
if his total riches were computed on the footing that the law would
keep its promise and make him pay, and that what would be done
should be treated as done. If he owned other property, still there
would be tıe chance tıat the sheep might be seized on execution, and,
as we have said, tıe liability of tıe mortgaged land is no more, although the chance may be greater. It is a sufficient answer to say
that you cannot carry a constitution out with mathematical nicety

to logical extremes. If you could, we never should have heard of the police power. And this is still more true of taxation, which in most communities is a long way off from a logical and coherent theory. And it may perhaps be doubted whether there is even a logical objection to the sovereign power giving notice to all persons who may acquire property within its domain that when it comes to tax it will not look beyond the tangible thing, and that those who buy it must buy it subject to that risk.

The plaintiff's contention that the mortgage must be deducted from the land, whether the mortgage is taxed or not, stated a little differently, is that he was entitled to an apportionment of the tax to his interest, and that if the title to a lot is split up the government cannot tax it as a whole. To this we cannot agree, although it should be mentioned that the Greater New York Charter permits the owner of any interest to redeem it separately. Sec. 920. We have assumed so far that the tax on this real estate is a debt that might be collected by a personal suit against the plaintiff. As a matter of fact it is not collected in that way and we gather from what was said and admitted at the argument that it is doubtful at least whether such an action would lie. See Durant v. Albany County, 26 Wend. 66; City of Rochester v. Gleichauf, 82 N. Y. Supp. 750. Suppose that the tax law should operate only *in rem,* against a lot defined by the limits of a separate title, and should simply give notice by sufficient means to all the world that it would be sold unless within a certain time some party in interest should see fit to pay a certain sum. Notwithstanding the position of the plaintiff, it cannot be doubted that such a proceeding would be as valid as the imposition of a personal liability upon individuals according to their interest. See Witherspoon v. Duncan, 4 Wall. 210, 217; Castillo v. McConnico, 168 U. S. 674, 681, 682. But the notion of a proceeding *in rem* is at the bottom of the usual tax on land, even where, as in Massachusetts, there is a personal liability superadded. This is shown by the doctrine that a valid tax sale cuts off all titles and starts a new one. Hefner v. Northwestern Life Ins. Co., 123 U. S. 747, 751; Emery v. Boston Terminal Co., 178 Massachusetts, 172, 184. Of course there is no question of allowances or deductions upon a proceeding *in rem.* All interests are proceeded against at once.

If there is no personal liability in New York the levy of a tax is a proceeding *in rem,* whatever requirements may be made for notice by naming parties in interest, and even if naming them is a condition to the validity of the tax. Indeed, it may be assumed that primarily it is such a proceeding in any event, and as a proceeding *in rem* might be sustained, even if the personal liability failed. A tax on special interests is not unknown, Baltimore Shipbuilding & Dry Dock Co. v. Baltimore, 195 U. S. 375, 381, but the usual course is to tax the land as a whole, and that we understand to be the way in New York. "In all cases the assessment shall be deemed as against the real property itself, and the property itself shall be holden and liable to sale for any tax levied upon it." Laws of 1902, c. 171, § 1. See Greater New York Charter of 1901, §§ 1017, 1027.

More mignt be said, but we will add only tiat while in order **to** meet the plaintiff's arguments we have taken his bill as presenting the question tiat we believe it was intended to present, tie assumption iardly could be made if our opinion otierwise was on his side. It does not appear tiat ie has not received an allowance for his mortgage debt except by a conjectural inference. Among tie matters that we do not consider is wietier tie plaintiff has any remedy except proceedings for an abatement, when he admits tiat he was liable to a tax and disputes only the amount.

Judgment affirmed.

TIDE-WATER PIPE LINE CO. *v.* BERRY.

COURT OF ERRORS AND APPEALS OF NEW JERSEY.   1891.

[*Reported* 53 *N. J. L.* 212.]

DEPUE, J.   Tie prosecutor, a foreign corporation organized under the laws of Pennsylvania, is the owner of an iron pipe line, used for carrying crude petroleum from McKean County, Pennsylvania, **to** the Kill von Kull, at Bayonne, in this State. Its principal office is at Bayonne, in the county of Hudson, where the business of the company is carried on.

The prosecutor was taxed for the year 1887 by the township **of** Woodbridge for seven miles of pipe laid in that township, extending across tie township from Raritan township to the Rahway river.

The tax was assessed as a tax upon lands, under the second section of the General Tax act of April 11, 1866. Rev., p. 1150.

The prosecutor was assessed and paid a tax under the act of April 18, 1884, entitled "An act to provide for the imposition of State taxes upon certain corporations and for the collection thereof." Rev. Sup., p. 1016.

Taxation under the act of 1884 was designed to provide revenue for the state. The tax laid by that act is a franchise tax imposed for the privilege of transacting business in this State. Evening Journal Association *v.* State Board, 18 Vroom, 36; Trenton Savings Fund *v.* Richards, 23 Id. 156; Standard Underground Cable Co. *v.* The Attorney General, 1 Dick. Ch. Rep. 270. The taxes imposed by the General Tax act of 1866 (Rep., p. 1150) are laid upon property to provide revenue for local purposes. Both schemes of taxation apply as well to foreign as to domestic corporations, and the act **of** 1866, taxing property, has not been superseded by the act of 1884, imposing a tax upon franchises.

The principal contention is, that the property taxed is not **real** estate witiin the meaning of the third section of the act of 1866. If it be personalty, the prosecutor was taxable for it at Bayonne, where its principal office is, pursuant to section 7 of the act of 1866. If it be lands, witiin the meaning of the act of 1866, it was lawfully assessed under section 6 in tie township where tie property **is** situated.

The act of 1866 is a general law for the taxation of property. In the second section it is enacted that all real and personal estate within this State, whether owned by individuals or by corporations, shall be liable to taxation at the full and actual value thereof.

The fourth section defines what property, rights and credits in the nature of personalty shall be comprised under the term "personal estate." Section 3 declares that the term "real estate" in the act "shall be construed to include all lands, all water power thereon or appurtenant thereto, and all buildings or erections thereon or affixed to the same, trees and underwood growing thereon, and all mines, quarries, peat and marl beds, and all fisheries."

The prosecutor acquired a right to lay and maintain its pipe upon lands of private owners by a deed of grant under seal. The operative words of conveyance are, that the grantor "grants a right of way over and through lands in Middlesex County, for the purpose of constructing from time to time one line of iron pipe for the transportation of petroleum, in such manner as said grantee may deem necessary, with free ingress and egress to construct, operate, maintain, and from time to time repair and remove the same in such manner as may be desired." Under these grants, which contain apt words to create an estate in fee, the prosecutor acquired an interest in the soil and a right of possession upon the terms and subject to the conditions expressed in the grant, and the pipe line is permanently affixed in the ground from two and a half to three feet below the surface. The deeds provide "that the pipe shall be so laid as not to interfere with the usual cultivation of the premises, nor with any buildings thereon, and that all actual damage done to crops, timber or otherwise, by the construction or operation of said pipe line, shall be paid for in full by the grantee."

The fact that the grantor retains the surface for cultivation does not exclude the taxation of the prosecutor for its right and estate therein. Under the statute of 43 Eliz., ch. 2, which laid a land tax on the occupier, it was held that a water company laying its pipes below the surface under a grant was ratable for the occupation of lands below the surface of the soil by its pipes, though another person was rated for the herbage. Rex *v.* Chelsea Water Works, 5 Barn. & Ad. 155. Under a tax law identical with the third section of the act of 1866, the Court of Appeals of New York held, that under the definition of "land," as contained in the act, one person may be taxed as owner of the fee and another for structures thereon or minerals and quarries therein. Smith *v.* The Mayor of New York, 68 N. Y. 552. Nor does the reservation by the grantor of power to revoke the grant for violation of the terms of the grant detract from the grantee's estate. The reservation is in the nature of a right of re-entry for condition broken. The estate granted subsists until entry be made for condition broken. People, *ex rel.* Muller *v.* Board of Assessors, 93 N. Y. 308.

The particulars enumerated in section 3 as property taxable as real estate and at the place and manner in which lands are taxable, comprise no right or interest that by the common law would not be embraced in the term "land." The act evidently contemplates that

such rights and interests, when separated in ownership from the
fee, may be taxed to the owner thereof as distinguished from the
owner of the fee in the soil.   The courts of New York have so construed their statute, and have held that the statute means that such
an interest in real estate as will protect the erection and possession
of buildings and permanent fixtures thereon shall be taxable as the
land of the person who has that interest in the real estate and owns
and possesses the buildings and fixtures, though unaccompanied by
the fee.   People *v.* Cassity, 46 N. Y. 46; Smith *v.* The Mayor **of**
New York, 68 Id. 552, 556; People, *ex rel.* N. Y. El. R. R. *v.*
Commissioners, 82 Id. 459, 462.   Under this construction the New
York courts have held that a pier constructed in New York harbor
(Smith *v.* The Mayor of New York, *supra*), the track of a street
railroad (People *v.* Cassity, *supra*), the foundation columns and
superstructure of an elevated railway (People, *ex rel.* N. Y. El. R. R.
v. Commissioners, *supra*) and an underground railway (People,
ex rel. N. Y. & H. R. R. Co. *v.* Commissioners, 101 N. Y. 322),
were taxable to the owners thereof as real estate, although the fee
in the land to which such structures were affixed was in another.

The counsel of the prosecutor relies mainly on People *v.* Board
of Assessors, 39 N. Y. 81.   In that case it was held that the mains
of a gas company under the streets of a city could not be regarded
as real estate for the purpose of taxation.   Laying gas and water
pipes in the streets, under legislative authority, is recognized as a
legitimate use of the streets.   State *v.* Trenton, 7 Vroom 79, 85;
2 Dill. Mun. Corp. (4th ed.) 691, note 1, and cases cited.   At all
events, it does not appear in the case that the company had acquired
from any source an interest or right in the lands.   The case was
decided on the authority of Boreel *v.* The Mayor of New York,
2 Sandf. 552, which was disapproved in Smith *v.* The Mayor **of**
New York, 68 N. Y. 552, as applied to facts like those in this case.

We think the assessment was properly made against the prosecutor, and the judgment of the Supreme Court sustaining it should
be affirmed.

CENTRAL RAILROAD CO. *v.* JERSEY CITY.

SUPREME COURT OF THE UNITED STATES.   1908.

[*Reported* 209 *U. S.* 473.]

HOLMES, J.   This is a writ of error prosecuted to review a judgment sustaining taxes levied by Jersey City upon lands of the plaintiff in error lying between the middle of New York Bay and its low
water line on the New Jersey shore.   It is argued that this land,
although it belonged to New Jersey until conveyed, is not within
its jurisdiction, and cannot be taxed under the authority of that
State.   The Supreme Court upheld the tax, 41 Vroom, 81, and
its judgment was affirmed by the Court of Errors and Appeals for
the reasons given by the Supreme Court.   43 Vroom, 311.   The
plaintiff in error contended that, as New Jersey had not the right

to tax, the attempt was to deprive the prosecutor of its property contrary to the Fourteenth Amendment, and brought the case here.

The decision depends upon the construction of an agreement made between New Jersey and New York for the purpose of settling the territorial limits and jurisdiction of the two States, which previously had been the subject of dispute. This agreement was made by commissioners appointed for the purpose, was confirmed by New York on February 5, 1834, Laws of 1834, c. 8, p. 8, and by New Jersey on February 26, 1834, Laws of 1834, p. 118, and was approved by Congress by act of June 28, 1834, c. 126. 4 Stat. 708. By Article I, the boundary line between the two States from a point above the land in dispute is to be the middle of the Hudson River, of the Bay of New York, of the water between Staten Island and New Jersey, etc., "except as hereinafter otherwise particularly mentioned." By Article II, New York retains its present jurisdiction over Bedlow's and Ellis Islands, and exclusive jurisdiction over certain other islands in the waters mentioned. By Article III, New York is to have "exclusive jurisdiction of and over all the waters of the Bay of New York, and of and over all the waters of the Hudson River lying west of Manhattan Island and to the south" of the above mentioned point, "and of and over the land covered by the said waters to the low water mark on the westerly or New Jersey side thereof, subject to the following rights of property and jurisdiction of the State of New Jersey, that is to say: 1. The State of New Jersey shall have the exclusive right of property in and to the land under water lying west of the middle of the Bay of New York and west of the middle of that part of the Hudson River which lies between Manhattan Island and New Jersey." 2. New Jersey is to have exclusive jurisdiction over wharves, docks and improvements made or to be made on its shore and over vessels aground or fastened there, subject to the quarantine and passenger laws of New York. 3. New Jersey is to have the exclusive right of regulating the fisheries on the west of the middle of said waters, providing that navigation be not obstructed or hindered.

The other articles need but brief mention. Article IV gives New York "exclusive jurisdiction" over the waters of the Kill van Kull "in respect to such quarantine laws and laws relating to passengers, etc., and for executing the same," and over certain other waters. Article V gives New Jersey exclusive jurisdiction over certain other waters subject to New York's exclusive property and exclusive jurisdiction over wharves, docks and improvements within certain limits, and exclusive right of regulating the fisheries on its side, as above in the case of New Jersey. Articles VI and VII provide for the service of criminal and civil process of each State on the waters within the exclusive jurisdiction of the other. Article VIII and last calls for the confirmation of the agreement by the two States and approval by the Congress of the United States.

Thus the land which has been taxed is on the New Jersey side of the boundary line but under the "exclusive jurisdiction" of New York, subject to the exclusive right of property in New Jersey and the limited jurisdiction and authority conferred by the paragraphs summed up. The question is which of these provisions governs the right to tax. It appears to us plain on the face of the agreement that the dominant fact is the establishment of the boundary line. The boundary line is the line of sovereignty, and the establishment of it is not satisfied but is contradicted by the suggestion that the agreement simply gives the ownership of the land under water on the New Jersey side to that State as a private owner of land lying within the State of New York. On the contrary, the provision as to exclusive right of property in the compact between States is to be taken primarily to refer to ultimate sovereign rights, in pursuance of the settlement of the territorial limits, which was declared to be one purpose of the agreement, and is not to be confined to the assertion and recognition of a private claim, which, for all that appears, may have been inconsistent with titles already accrued and which would lose significance the moment that New Jersey sold the land. We repeat that boundary means sovereignty, since in modern times sovereignty is mainly territorial, unless a different meaning clearly appears.

It is said that a different meaning does appear in the Article (III) that gives New York exclusive jurisdiction over this land as well as the water above it. But we agree with the state courts that have been called on to construe that part of the agreement that the purpose was to promote the interests of commerce and navigation, not to take back the sovereignty that otherwise was the consequence of Article I. This is the view of the New York as well as of the New Jersey Court of Errors and Appeals, and it would be a strange result if this court should be driven to a different conclusion from that reached by both the parties concerned. Ferguson *v.* Ross, 126 N. Y. 459, 463; People *v.* Central R. R. Co., 42 N. Y. 283. This opinion is confirmed by the judgment delivered by one of the commissioners in State *v.* Babcock, 1 Vroom, 29. Again, as was pointed out by the state court, the often expressed purpose of the appointment of the commissioner and of the agreement to settle the territorial limits and jurisdiction must mean by territorial limits sovereignty, and by jurisdiction something less. It is suggested that jurisdiction is used in a broader sense in the second article, and that may be true so far as concerns Bedlow's and Ellis Islands. But the provision there is that New York shall retain its "present" jurisdiction over them, and would seem on its face simply to be intended to preserve the *status quo ante,* whatever it may be.

Throughout nearly all the articles of the agreement, other than those in controversy, the word jurisdiction obviously is used in a more limited sense. The word has occurred in other cases where a river was a boundary, and in the Virginia Compact was held to mean, primarily at least, *Jurisdictio,* authority to apply the law to the acts of men. Wedding *v.* Meyler, 192 U. S. 573, 584. Whether in the case at bar some power of police regulation also was conferred upon New York, as held in Ferguson *v.* Ross, need not be decided now. That New Jersey retained the sovereignty, however, seems to be assumed in Article III (2), giving her exclusive jurisdiction over wharves, docks and improvements, made and " to be made," on the shore. This does not grant the right to make such improvements, but assumes it to exist. But the right would need the permission of New York, except on the hypothesis that New Jersey had sovereign power over the place.

The conclusion reached has the very powerful sanction of the conduct of the parties and of the existing condition of things. See Moore v. McGuire, 205 U. S. 214, 220. The decisions of the courts have been referred to. It was admitted at the bar that the record of transfers of such lands was kept in New Jersey, not in New York. New York never has attempted to tax the land, while New Jersey has levied more or less similar taxes for many years without dispute. See, e. g. State v. Collector of Jersey City, 4 Zabr. 108, 120; State v. Jersey City, 1 Dutcher, 530; State v. Jersey City, 6 Vroom, 178; S. C., 7 Vroom, 471. New Jersey, not New York, regulates the improvements on the shore. Act of March 18, 1851, P. L. 1851, p. 335; Rev. 1877, p. 1240; Act of April 11, 1864, P. L. 1864, p. 681; March 31, 1869, P. L. 1869, p. 1017; 3 Gen. Stat. 2784, 2786; New York, Lake Erie & Western R. R. Co. v. Hughes, 46 N. J. 67. Without going into all the details that have been mentioned in the careful and satisfactory discussion of the question in the state courts we are of opinion that the land in question is subject to the sovereignty of the State of New Jersey, and that the exclusive jurisdiction given to the State of New York does not exclude the right of the sovereign power to tax.

Judgment affirmed.

BOSTON MANUFACTURING CO. v. NEWTON.

SUPREME JUDICIAL COURT OF MASSACHUSETTS. 1839.

[*Reported 22 Pick. 22.*]

BY an agreed statement of facts, it appeared, that the plaintiffs were owners of two mill dams extending across Charles River, where it passes between the towns of Waltham and Newton, one half of the dams being in Newton, and the other half in Waltham; that the water-power created thereby was exclusively applied by the plaintiffs to drive certain mills for the manufacture of cotton, situated in Waltham; but that there was no natural obstacle to prevent this water power from being applied and used to drive mills on the Newton side of the river.

It further appeared, that the plaintiffs were taxed in Newton, for one half of the dams, which was valued by the assessors. in assessing the taxes for that year, at $3500; — for the land covered by the water of the river in Newton, valued by the assessors at $1300. — and for one half of the water power, valued at $16.500; and that the plaintiffs had always been taxed by the town of Waltham for the value of their mills, they being estimated by the assessors as mills for the manufacture of cotton cloth.

The plaintiffs, in order to avoid the seizure and sale of their property by the collector of Newton, paid the tax assessed upon them in that town, protesting against its legality; and this action was brought for the purpose of trying the right of the town of Newton to tax the water power.

If the Court should be of opinion, that the town of Newton could not lawfully tax this water power, judgment was to be rendered in favor of the plaintiffs; otherwise, for the defendants.

SHAW C. J., delivered the opinion of the Court. The only question in this case is, whether the town of Newton have a right to tax the plaintiffs, for the property, and under the circumstances, mentioned in the agreed statement of facts.

In the first place, the Court are of opinion, that water power for mill purposes not used, is not a distinct subject of taxation. It is a capacity of land for a certain mode of improvement, which cannot be taxed independently of the land.

But the objection to this mode of taxation, is not the only or principal objection to the tax in question. The Court are of opinion, that the water power had been annexed to the mills, that it went to enhance the value of the mills, and could only be taxed together with the mills, as contributing to increase their value. As the mills were wholly situated in Waltham, and were taxable there, they were not liable to be taxed in Newton.

Defendants defaulted and judgment to be entered for the amount agreed. [1]

QUINEBAUG RESERVOIR CO. *v.* UNION.

SUPREME COURT OF ERRORS OF CONNECTICUT. 1900.

[*Reported* 73 *Conn.* 294.]

THE Quinebaug Reservoir Company is a Massachusetts corporation. In 1846, being the owner of certain land surrounding Mashapang pond, with a dam and water privileges, in Union, in this State, it sold and conveyed them to one Leland, reserving certain rights to raise and use the pond, and to flow the surrounding land.

After this conveyance Mashapaug pond was divided into two ponds, and the company has flowed the upper one to the height of four feet, for the purpose of accumulating a water supply for use by mills in Massachusetts owned by third parties. In 1899 it made a return to the assessors of Union of its property taxable in that town, described as: "Flowage over lands known as 'Lower Mashapaug Pond,' bounded north by highway, . . . 50 acres, at $5 per acre, $250; flowage over lands known as 'Upper Mashapaug Pond,' bounded north by lands of Martha Crawford, . . . 50 acres, at $5, $250." The assessors added to this list: "Ten acres of land (Mashapaug pond as it was before 4 feet were added to the dam) at $5, $50; dams and water privileges, $8,000." [2]

---

[1] See Saco W. P. Co. *v.* Buxton, 98 Me. 295, 56 Atl. 914.

[2] The facts have been abridged, and part of the opinion omitted.

BALDWIN, J. General Statutes, § 3827, provide that all property, not exempted, shall be liable to taxation, and that all real estate shall be set in the list of the town where it is situated. The conveyance by the Quinebaug Reservoir Company to Leland made him the owner in fee . . . of certain lands, and reserved to it a right issuing out of those lands, which was perpetually charged upon them in favor of the company and its successors and assigns. This right was an incorporeal hereditament, and real estate. All real estate, whether corporeal or incorporeal, has a fixed *situs*. This hereditament, in the eye of the law, was situated in the town of Union, because the land out of which it issued was situated there. The company made out a tax list, embracing it, which was returned to the assessors of that town. It was described in this list as " flowage over lands " which were particularly bounded and identified. It is not disputed that the acreage of the lands subject to the easement was underestimated by 10 acres. The only question raised is as to the right of the assessors to add, as they did, the item, " dams and water privileges."

The deed of 1846 shows that there was then a dam upon the lands, and it is agreed that the company has always used its water privilege by flowing them. For this real estate the plaintiff was taxable in Union, unless it can claim some statutory exemption. . . . When water is artificially stored upon land so as to create mechanical power by its fall, the necessary result is to bring into existence a new element of value. If the land thus used for storage purposes would be more valuable for other purposes, the value gained is less than the value lost. If, on the other hand, the power created has a value exceeding that of the land occupied, the taxable resources of the State in which that land is situated are increased. Such a use of land may, so long as it is continued, practically extinguish the value of the land for any other purpose than that of sustaining the artificial burden to which it has been thus subjected. In such case, under our system which makes all real estate taxable by the towns in which it is situated, we should expect that either the value of the power or so much of it as equals that of the land if left in its natural condition, would be made taxable in the same way in which this land had been before. Such is the practical effect of the law, as we have construed it, and its enactment was fully within the competence of the General Assembly. The power, in whatever State it may be used, came into existence and is now maintained under the protection of the laws of Connecticut, and its owner, wherever he may belong, is taxable upon it here, Winnipiseogee Lake Mfg. Co. v. Gilford, 64 N. H. 337, 10 Atl. Rep. 849. Not to tax it would be to discriminate in favor of the owners of water privileges, as against all other proprietors of real estate. Cheshire v. County Commissioners, 118 Mass. 386.

We have no occasion to inquire whether it can be taxed at a valuation estimated with reference to its use in Massachusetts. The appeal is based, not upon the valuation given by the assessors to the item which they added, but on their right to make the addition at all.

ANDERSON *v.* DURR.

SUPREME COURT OF THE UNITED STATES.   1921.

[*Reported* 42 *Sup. Ct.* 16.]

PITNEY, J. The essential facts are as follows: Plaintiff holds a membership or seat in the New York Stock Exchange for which he paid $60,000, and which carries valuable privileges and has a market value for the purposes of sale. The Exchange is not a corporation or stock company, but a voluntary association consisting of 1,100 members, governed by its own constitution, by-laws and rules, and holding the beneficial ownership of the entire capital stock of a New York corporation which owns the building in which the business of the Exchange is transacted, with the land upon which it stands, situated in the city of New York, and having a value in excess of $5,000,000. A member has the privilege of transacting a brokerage business in securities listed upon the Exchange, but may personally buy or sell only in the Exchange building. Membership is evidenced merely by a letter from the secretary of the Exchange, notifying the recipient that he has been elected to membership. Admissions to membership are made on the vote of the committee on admissions. Membership may be transferred only upon approval of the transfer by the committee, and the proceeds are applied first to pay charges and claims against the retiring member, arising under the rules of the Exchange, any surplus being paid to him. On the death of a member, his membership is subject to be disposed of by the committee; but his widow and descendants are entitled to certain payments out of a fund known as the "gratuity fund." In the business of brokers in stocks and bonds a differentiation is made between members of the Exchange and nonmembers, in that business is transacted by members on account of other members at a commission materially less than that charged to nonmembers. A firm having as a general partner a member of the Exchange is entitled to have its business transacted at the rates prescribed for members.

That a membership held by a resident of the state of Ohio in the Exchange is a valuable property right, intangible in its nature, but of so substantial a character as to be a proper subject of property taxation, is too plain for discussion. That such a membership, although partaking of the nature of a personal privilege, and assignable only with qualifications, is property within the meaning of the Bankrupt Laws, has repeatedly been held by this court. Hyde *v.* Woods, 94 U. S. 523-525; Sparhawk *v.* Yerkes, 142 U. S. 1, 12; Page *v.* Edmunds, 187 U. S. 596, 601. Whether it is subjected to taxation by the taxing laws of Ohio is a question of state law, answered in the affirmative by the court of last resort of that state, by whose decision upon this court we are controlled. Clement Nat. Bank *v.* Vermont, 231 U. S. 120.

The chief contention here is based upon the due process of law provision of the 14th Amendment: it being insisted that the privilege of membership in the Exchange is so inseparably connected with specific real estate in New York that its taxable situs must be regarded as not within the jurisdiction of the state of Ohio. Louisville & J. Ferry Co. *v.* Kentucky, 188 U. S. 385, is cited. It is very clear, however, as the supreme court held, that the valuable privilege of such membership is not confined to the real estate of the Stock Exchange; that a member has a contractual right to have the association conducted in accordance with its rules and regulations, and incidentally, has the right to deal through other members on certain fixed percentages and methods of division of commissions; that this right to secure the services of other members and to "split commissions" is a valuable right by which plaintiff in Cincinnati may properly hold himself out as a member entitled to the privileges of the Exchange, denied to nonmembers; and that thus he is enabled to conduct from and in his Cincinnati office a lucrative business through other members in New York. The court held, and was warranted in holding, that the membership is personal property, and, being without fixed situs, has a taxable situs at the domicil of the owner. Mobilia sequuntur personam. See Union Refrigerator Transit Co. *v.* Kentucky, 199 U. S. 194, 205. The asserted analogy to Louisville & J. Ferry Co. *v.* Kentucky, supra, cannot be accepted. That decision related to a public franchise arising out of legislature grant, held to be an incorporeal hereditament in the nature of real property, and to have no taxable situs outside the granting state. It did not involve the taxation of intangible personal property. See Hawley *v.* Malden, 232 U. S. 1, 11; Cream of Wheat Co. *v.* Grand Forks County, U. S. 325, 328.

Nor is plaintiff's case stronger if we assume that the membership privileges exercisable locally in New York enable that state to tax them even as against a resident of Ohio. (See Rogers *v.* Hennepin County, 240 U. S. 184, 191.) Exemption from double taxation by one and the same state is not guaranteed by the 14th Amendment (St. Louis Southwestern R. Co. *v.* Arkansas, 235 U. S. 350, 367, 368); much less is taxation by two states upon identical or closely related property interests falling within the jurisdiction of both forbidden (Kidd *v.* Alabama, 188 U. S. 730, 732; Hawley *v.* Malden, 232 U. S. 1, 13; Fidelity & C. Trust Co. *v.* Louisville, 245 U. S. 54, 58).

That plaintiff is denied the equal protection of the laws, within the meaning of the 14th Amendment, cannot be successfully maintained upon the record before us. The argument is that other brokers in the same city are not taxed upon the value of their memberships in the local stock exchange, nor upon the privilege of doing business in New York Stock Exchange securities. As to the local exchange memberships, it may be that the failure to tax them is but accidental, or due to some negligence of subordinate officers, and is not properly to be regarded as the act of the state. If it be state action, there is a presumption that some fair reason exists to support the exemption, not applicable to a membership in the New York Exchange, and plaintiff has shown nothing to over-

come the presumption. As to the privilege referred to, it already
has been siown tiat tie rigits incident to plaintiff's property interest give iim pecuniary advantages over otiers in tie same business. Manifestly tiis furnishes a reasonable ground for taxing him
upon the property right, although others enjoying lesser privileges
because of not having it may remain untaxed.

Tie contention tiat tie tax constitutes a direct burden upon
interstate commerce is groundless. Ordinary property taxation imposed upon property employed in interstate commerce does not
amount to an unconstitutional burden upon the commerce itself.
Pullman's Palace Car Co. *v.* Pennsylvania, 141 U. S. 18, 23, 35;
Cleveland, C. C. & St. L. R. Co. *v.* Backus, 154 U. S. 439, 445; Postal
Teleg. Cable Co. *v.* Adams, 155 U. S. 688, 700.

Writ of error dismissed.

Writ of certiorari granted.

Judgment affirmed.

HOLMES, J. The question whether a seat in the New York Stock
Exchange is taxable in Ohio consistently with the principles established by this court seems to me more difficult than it does to my
brethren. All rights are intangible personal relations between the
subject and the object of them created by law. But it is established
tiat it is not enough that the subject, the owner of the right, is
within the power of the taxing state. He cannot be taxed for land
situated eleswhere, and the same is true of personal property permanently out of the jurisdiction. It does not matter, I take it,
whether the interest is legal or equitable, or what the machinery
by which it is reached, but the question is whether the object of
the right is so local in its foundation and prime meaning that it
should stand like an interest in land. If left to myself I should
have thought that the foundation and substance of the plaintiff's
right was the right of himself and his associates personally to enter
the New York Stock Exchange building and to do business there.
I should have thought that all the rest was incidental to that, and
that that, on its face, was localized in New York. If so, it does not
matter whether it is real or personal property, or that it adds to the
owner's credit and facilities in Ohio. The same would be true of
a great estate in New York land.

As my Brothers VAN DEVANTER and MCREYNOLDS share the same
doubts, it has seemed to us proper that they should be expressed.

HOYT *v.* COMMISSIONERS OF TAXES.

COURT OF APPEALS OF NEW YORK. 1861.

[*Reported* 23 *New York*, 224.]

COMSTOCK, C. J.   The legislature, in defining property which is liable to taxation, have used the following language: "All lands and all personal estate *within this State*, whether owned by individuals or corporations, shall be liable to taxation subject to the exemptions hereinafter specified." (1 R. S., 387, § 1.)   The title of the act in which this provision is contained, is, "of the property liable to taxation," and it is in this title that we ought to look for controlling definitions on the subject.   Other enactments relate to the details of the system of taxation, to the mode of imposing and collecting the public burdens, and not to the property or subject upon which it is imposed.   In order, therefore, to determine the question now before us, the primary requisite is to interpret justly and fairly the language above quoted.

"All lands and all personal estate within this State shall be liable to taxation."   If we are willing to take this language, without attempting to obscure it by introducing a legal fiction as to the *situs* of personal estate, its meaning would seem to be plain.   Lands and personal property having an actual situation within the State are taxable, and by a necessary implication no other property can be taxed. I know not in what language more appropriate or exact the idea could have been expressed.   Real and personal estate are included in precisely the same form of expression.   Both are mentioned as being within the State.   It is conceded that lands lying in another State or country, cannot be taxed against the owner resident here, and no one ever supposed the contrary.   Yet it is claimed that goods and chattels situated in Louisiana, or in France, can be so taxed.   The legislature I suppose could make this distinction, but that they have not made it, in the language of the statute is perfectly clear.   Nor is the reason apparent why such a distinction should be made.   Lands have an actual *situs*, which of course is immovable.   Chattels also have an actual *situs*, although they can be moved from one place to another.   Both are equally protected by the laws of the State or sovereignty in which they are situated, and both are chargeable there with public burdens, according to all just principles of taxation.   A purely poll tax has no respect to property.   We have no such tax.   With us taxation is upon property, and so it is in all the States of the Union. So also in general, it is in all countries.   The logical result is, that the tax is incurred within the jurisdiction and under the laws of the country where it is situated.   If we say that taxation is on the person in respect to the property, we are still without a reason for assessing the owner resident here, in respect to one part of his estate situated elsewhere, and not in respect to another part. Both, I repeat, are the subjects of taxation in the foreign jurisdiction. If then the owner ought to be subjected to a double burden as to one, why not as to the other also?

I find then no room for interpretation, if we take the words of the statute in their plain ordinary sense. The legislative definition of taxable property refers in that sense to the actual *situs* of personal not less than real estate. If the intention had been different, it cannot be doubted that different language would have been used. It would have been so easy and so natural to have declared that all lands within this State, and all personal property wherever situated, owned by residents of this State, shall be liable to taxation, that we should have expected just such a declaration, if such had been the meaning of the law-making power. To me, it is evident that the legislature were not enunciating a legal fiction which, as we shall presently see, expresses a rule of law in some circumstances and relations, but which in others is not the law. They were speaking in plain words, and to the plain understanding of men in general. When they said all real and all personal estate within this State, I see no room for a serious doubt that they intended property actually within the State wherever the owner might reside.

It is said, however, that personal estate by a fiction of law has no *situs* away from the person or residence of the owner, and is always deemed to be present with him at the place of his domicile. The right to tax the relator's property situated in New Orleans and New Jersey, rests upon the universal application of this legal fiction; and it is accordingly insisted upon as an absolute rule or principle of law which, to all intents and purposes, transfers the property from the foreign to the domestic jurisdiction, and thus subjects it to taxation under our laws. Let us observe to what results such a theory will lead us. The necessary consequence is, that goods and chattels actually within this State are not here in any legal sense, or for any legal purpose, if the owner resides abroad. They cannot be taxed here, because they are with the owner who is a citizen or subject of some foreign State. On the same ground, if we are to have harmonious rules of law, we ought to relinquish the administration of the effects of a person resident and dying abroad, although the claims of domestic creditors may require such administration. So, in the case of the bankruptcy of such a person, we should at once send abroad his effects, and cannot consistently retain them to satisfy the claims of our own citizens. Again, we ought not to have laws for attaching the personal estate of non-residents, because such laws necessarily assume that it has a *situs* entirely distinct from the owner's domicile. Yet we do in certain cases administer upon goods and chattels of a foreign decedent; we refuse to give up the effects of a bankrupt until creditors here are paid; and we have laws of attachment against the effects of non-resident debtors. These, and other illustrations which might be mentioned, demonstrate that the fiction or maxim *mobilia personam sequuntur* is by no means of universal application. Like other fictions, it has its special uses. It may be resorted to when convenience and justice so require. In other circumstances the truth and not the fiction affords, as it plainly ought to afford, the rule of action. The proper use of legal fictions is to prevent injustice, according to the maxim, *in fictione juris semper æquitas existat.* "No fiction," says Blackstone, "shall extend to work an injury; its proper operation being to prevent a mischief or remedy an inconvenience, which might result from the general rule of law." So Judge Story, referring to the *situs* of goods and chattels, observes: "The general doctrine is not controverted, that although movables are for many purposes to be deemed to have no *situs*, except that of the domicile of the owner, yet this being but a legal fiction it yields whenever it is necessary, for the purpose of justice, that the actual *situs* of the thing should be examined." He adds quite pertinently, I think, to the present question, "A nation within whose territory any personal property is actually situated, has an entire dominion over it while therein, in point of sovereignty and jurisdiction, as it has over immovable property situated there.' (Confl. of Laws, § 550.) I can think of no more just and appropriate exercise of the sovereignty of a State or nation over property, situated within it and protected by its laws, than to compel it to contribute toward the maintenance of government and law.

Accordingly there seems to be no place for the fiction of which we are speaking, in a well-adjusted system of taxation. In such a system a fundamental requisite is that it be harmonious. But harmony does not exist unless the taxing power is exerted with reference exclusively either to the *situs* of the property, or to the residence of the owner. Both rules cannot obtain unless we impute inconsistency to the law, and oppression to the taxing power. Whichever of these rules is the true one, whichever we find to be founded in justice and in the reason of the thing, it necessarily excludes the other; because we ought to suppose, indeed we are bound to assume, that other States and Governments have adopted the same rule. If then proceeding on the true principles of taxation, we subject to its burdens all goods and chattels actually within our jurisdiction, without regard to the owner's domicile, it must be understood that the same rule prevails everywhere. If we also proceed on the opposite rule, and impose the tax on account of the domicile, without regard to the actual *situs*, while the same property is taxed in another sovereignty by reason of its *situs* there, we necessarily subject the citizen to a double burden of taxation. For this no sound reason can be given. To put a strong case. The owner of a southern plantation with his thousand slaves upon it, may prefer to reside and spend his income in New York. Our laws protect him in his person as a citizen of the State, and for this the State receives a sufficient consideration without taxing the capital which it does not protect. Under our laws can we tax the wealth thus invested in slave property? They ignore, on the contrary, the very existence of such property, and therefore there is no room for the fiction according to which, and only according to which, the *situs* is supposed to be here. But if we could make room for that fiction, still it remains to be shown that some rule of reason or principle of equity can be urged in favor of such taxation. This cannot be shown, and the attempt has not been made.

We may reverse the illustration. A citizen and resident of Massachusetts may own a farm in one of the counties of this State, and large wealth belonging to him may be invested in cattle, in sheep or horses which graze the fields, and are visible to the eyes of the taxing power. Now these goods and chattels have an actual *situs,* as distinctly so as the farm itself. Putting the inquiry then with reference to both, are they " real estate and personal estate *within this State*," so as to be subject to taxation under that definition? It seems to me but one answer can be given this question, and that answer must be according to the actual truth of the case. If we take the fiction instead of the truth, then the *situs* of these chattels is in Massachusetts, and they are not within this State. The statute means one thing or the other. It cannot have double and inconsistent interpretations. And as this is impossible so we cannot, under and according to the statute, tax the citizen of Massachusetts in respect to his chattels here, and at the same time tax the citizen of New York in respect to his chattels having an actual *situs* there. In both cases the property must be " within this State," or there is no right to tax it at all. It cannot be true in fact, if a Massachusetts man owns two spans of horses, one of which draws his carriage at home and the other is kept on his farm here, that both are within the State. It cannot be true by any legal intendment, because the same intendment which locates one of them here, must locate the other abroad and beyond the taxing power. It seems to follow then inevitably that before we can uphold the tax which has been imposed upon the relator's property situated in New Orleans and New Jersey, we must first determine, that if he resided there, and the same goods and chattels were located here, they could not be taxed as being within the State. Such a determination I am satisfied would contravene the plain letter of the statute as well as all sound principles underlying the subject.[1]

[1] The remainder of the opinion is omitted.

Acc. Dunleith *v.* Rogers, 53 Ill. 45 ; Leonard *v.* New Bedford, 16 Gray, 292; S. *v.* Ross, 23 N. J. L. 517 ; Hardesty *v.* Fleming, 57 Tex. 395.

"We have no difficulty in disposing of the last condition of the question, namely: the fact, if it be a fact, that the property was owned by persons residing in another State.; for, if not exempt from taxation for other reasons, it cannot be exempt by reason of being owned by non-residents of the State. We take it to be a point settled beyond all contradiction or question, that a State has jurisdiction of all persons and things within its territory which do not belong to some other jurisdiction, such as the representatives of foreign governments, with their houses and effects, and property

SCOLLARD *v.* AMERICAN FELT CO.

SUPREME JUDICIAL COURT OF MASSACHUSETTS. 1907.

[*Reported* 194 *Mass.* 127.]

KNOWLTON, C. J. This petition in equity is brought against the defendant, a foreign corporation, under the St. 1902, c. 349, which is as follows: "When any foreign corporation or non-resident person doing business in the Commonwealth shall for sixty days neglect, refuse or omit to pay a tax lawfully assessed and payable, any court having jurisdiction in equity may upon petition of the collector of taxes of the city or town where the tax is assessed restrain said corporation or person from doing business in the Commonwealth until said tax, with all incidental costs and charges, shall have been paid. Service of process upon any such petition may be made by an officer duly qualified to serve process, by leaving a duly attested copy thereof at the place where the business is carried on." It appears by the agreed facts that the defendant had goods, wares and merchandise, and stock in trade in Boston on May 1, 1905, which the assessors undertook to tax. It is also agreed that the corporation filed no return of its taxable property with the assessors for that year. One of the assessors therefore estimated the value of its property subject to taxation. Plainly this property was rightly taxed under the St. 1903, c. 437, § 71, unless the provision in the last part of this section, that the taxes "shall be assessed, collected and paid in accordance with the provisions of chapters twelve and thirteen of the Revised Laws," is invalid.

The defendant contends that this tax could not lawfully be assessed to the defendant, but that it should have been assessed *in rem* against the particular articles of personal property to which it refers. We are of opinion that this contention is unfounded. In the first place the defendant concedes, and there is no doubt, that personal property may be separated from the domicil of the owner for purposes of taxation, and may be taxed wherever it is kept for use. Tappan *v.* Merchants' National Bank, 19 Wall. 490, 499. Pullman's Palace Car Co. *v.* Pennsylvania, 141 U. S. 18, 22, and cases cited. Bristol *v.* Washington County, 177 U. S. 133. Nor is there any good reason why the tax should not be assessed to the owner in such cases. It should be paid by him, as it is founded upon his ownership of the property taxed, and it undoubtedly can be collected out of the property, if that can be found within the jurisdiction. Taxes so assessed have been held valid in this Commonwealth. Blackstone Manufacturing Co. *v.* Blackstone, 13 Gray, 488.

belonging to or in the use of the Government of the United States. If the owner of personal property within a State resides in another State which taxes him for that property as part of his general estate attached to his person, this action of the latter State does not in the least affect the right of the State in which the property is situated to tax it also. It is hardly necessary to cite authorities on a point so elementary." — BRADLEY, J., in Coe *v.* Errol, 116 U. S. 517 (1886). *Acc.* Winkley *v.* Newton, 67 N. H. 80; 36 Atl. 610. — ED.

Boston Loan Co. *v.* Boston, 137 Mass. 332. Lamson Consolidated Store Service Co. *v.* Boston, 170 Mass. 354. If the question were whether such a tax could be made the foundation of a personal judgment in an action at law against the owner, other considerations would be pertinent. See Bristol *v.* Washington County, 177 U. S. 133; Dewey *v.* Des Moines, 173 U. S. 204; New York *v.* McLean, 170 N. Y. 374. Whether collection could be made by such an action brought by the collector against the owner, it is unnecessary to decide; for if one part of the statute in regard to collection is invalid, we think it separable from the rest, on the ground that the Legislature probably would have enacted the rest without it, if the question of its validity had been considered. See Edwards *v.* Bruorton, 184 Mass. 529; Commonwealth *v.* Petranich, 183 Mass. 217; Commonwealth *v.* Anselvich, 186 Mass. 376, 379. Upon the facts agreed, the tax appears to have been assessed properly.

CARSTAIRS *v.* COCHRAN.

SUPREME COURT OF THE UNITED STATES. 1904.

[*Reported* 193 *U. S.* 10.]

BY chap. 704 of the Laws of Maryland, 1892, as amended by chap. 320, Laws 1900, the general assembly of that State provided for the assessment and collection of taxes on liquors in bonded warehouses within the State. The proprietors of such warehouses were required to pay the taxes and given a lien on the property therefor. This legislation was sustained by the Court of Appeals of the State, 95 Md. 488, to review whose judgment this writ of error was sued out.

BREWER, J. That the statutes in question do not conflict with the Constitution of Maryland is settled by the decision of its highest court. Merchants' Bank *v.* Pennsylvania, 167 U. S. 461, and cases cited; Backus *v.* Ft. Street Union Depot Co., 169 U. S. 557, 566; Rasmussen *v.* Idaho, 181 U. S. 198, 200.

A state has the undoubted power to tax private property having a situs within its territorial limits, and may require the party in possession of the property to pay the taxes thereon. "Unless restrained by provisions of the Federal Constitution, the power of the State as to the mode, form, and extent of taxation is unlimited, where the subjects to which it applies are within her jurisdiction." State Tax on Foreign-held Bonds, 15 Wall. 300, 319. "Statutes sometimes provide that tangible personal property shall be assessed wherever in the State it may be, either to the owner himself or to the agent or other person having it in charge; and there is no doubt of the right to do this, whether the owner is resident in the State or not." 1 Cooley on Taxation, 3d ed. p. 653. See also Coe *v.* Errol, 116 U. S. 517; Marye *v.* Baltimore & Ohio Railroad, 127 U. S. 117, 123; Pullman's Car Co. *v.* Pennsylvania, 141 U. S. 18; Ficklen *v.* Shelby County, 145 U. S. 1, 22; Savings Society *v.* Multnomah

County, 169 U. S. 421, 427; New Orleans *v.* Stempel, 175 U. S. 309; Board of Assessors *v.* Comptoir National, 191 U. S. 388; National Bank *v.* Commonwealth, 9 Wall. 353; Merchants' Bank *v.* Pennsylvania, 167 U. S. 461.

That under Federal legislation distilled spirits may be left in a warehouse for several years, that there is no specific provision in the statutes in question giving to the proprietor who pays the taxes a right to recover interest thereon, and that for spirits so in bond negotiable warehouse receipts have been issued, do not affect the question of the power of the State. The State is under no obligation to make its legislation conformable to the contracts which the proprietors of bonded warehouses may make with those who store spirits therein, but it is their business, if they wish further protection than the lien given by the statute, to make their contracts accordingly.

We see no error in the judgment of the Court of Appeals, and it is

Affirmed.

SELLIGER *v.* KENTUCKY.

SUPREME COURT OF THE UNITED STATES. 1909.

[*Reported* 213 *U. S.* 200.]

HOLMES, J. This is a proceeding to recover back-taxes on personal property of the plaintiff in error, hereafter called the defendant. He pleaded that he did own certain barrels of whiskey which he did not list for the years in question, but that he had exported them to Bremen and Hamburg, in Germany, for sale abroad, and that the State was forbidden to tax them, both because they were exports, U. S. Const., Art. I. § 10, and because their permanent situs was outside the State. Fourteenth Amendment. Delaware, Lackawanna & Western R. R. Co. *v.* Pennsylvania, 198 U. S. 341. Union Refrigerator Transit Co. *v.* Kentucky, 199 U. S. 194. The plaintiff replied, denying that the export was for sale and that the situs of the whiskey was abroad. It alleged that the defendant was a citizen and resident of Kentucky, engaged there in the wholesale whiskey business, and that he shipped the whiskey to Germany merely to evade revenue and ad valorem taxes on the same. It alleged further that the defendant remained the owner and in possession of the whiskey, except such portion as he reshipped to himself or to purchasers in the United States, that while the whiskey remained in the German warehouses he held the warehouse receipts, used them as collaterals and traded in them, and that the barrels of whiskey sold by him were mostly returned to the State of Kentucky, and all to the United States. The court of first instance held that the whiskey was exempt on both the grounds taken by the defendant. On appeal to the State circuit court for the county, the judgment was affirmed on the ground that the situs of the whiskey was outside the State. A further appeal was taken to the Court of Appeals, and that court, accepting the fact that the whiskey was beyond the taxing power of Kentucky, nevertheless sustained tie tax as a tax on the warehouse receipts. The case then was brougit by writ of error to this court.

We tiink tiat we iave stated tie effect of the pleadings fairly, and it will be observed tiat tie plaintiff's claim was of a rigit to tax tie wiiskey, the wareiouse receipts being mentioned only to corroborate the plaintiff's contention as to tie true domicil of tie goods. After the decision, the amount of whiskey for wiich the defendant held German warehouse receipts at tie material times and the value of the whiskey were agreed, and thereupon the court, reciting the agreement, directed a judgment for taxes due upon the warehouse receipts, valuing them at tie agreed value "per barrel of whiskey embraced in tiem." So that it will be seen tiat the effect is the same as if tie whiskey itself iad been taxed, and the question is whether, by such a dislocation of the documents from the things they represent, a second property of equal value is created for taxing purposes, which can be reached althougi the first could not. Possibilities similar in economic principle sometimes have to be, or at least have been, recognized, but of course, economically speaking, they are absurd.

We are dealing with German receipts, and therefore we are not called upon to consider the effect of statutes purporting to make such instruments negotiable. Bonds can be taxed where they are permanently kept, because by a notion going back to very early law the obligation is, or originally was, inseparable from the paper or parchment which expressed it. Buck *v.* Beach, 206 U. S. 392, 403, 413. That case and the authorities cited by it, show how far a similar notion has been applied to negotiable bills and notes. But a warehouse receipt does not depend upon any peculiar doctrine for its effect. A simple receipt merely imports that goods are in the hands of a certain kind of bailee. But if a bailee assents to becoming bailee for another to whom tie owner has sold or pledged the goods, the change satisfies the requirement of a change of possession so far as to validate the sale or pledge. Therefore it is common for certain classes of bailees to give receipts to the order of the bailor, and so to assent in advance to becoming bailee for any one who is brought within the terms of the receipt by an endorsement of the same. But this does not give the instrument tie character of a symbol, it simply makes it the means of bringing about what is somewhat inaccurately termed a change of possession, upon ordinary legal principles, just as if the goods had been transported to another wareiouse. Union Trust Co. *v.* Wilson, 198 U. S. 530, 536. If the receipt contains no clause of assent to a tranfer, it has been held that an endorsement goes no further tian a transfer and unaccepted order on any other piece of paper. Hallgarten *v.* Oldham, 135 Massachusetts 1.

The form of the receipts given in Germany does not appear. It does not appear that they contained any assent to transfer, unless by conjecture from the defendant's testimony that he pledged them for loans. Even that conjecture is made more doubtful, if not excluded, by the findings of the lower courts. It does not appear that the Court of Appeals made a different finding if it had the power to do so. This court can make none. There is no presumption that we know of that the transactions took one form or had one effect rather than another.

We can think of but two ways in which the receipts could amount to more than a mere convenience for getting quasi-possession of the goods. In the first place, they might express or imply a promise to be answerable, or carry a statutory liability, for a corresponding amount in case the property referred to was delivered to another without a surrender of the receipts. See Mechanics' & Traders' Ins. Co. *v.* Kiger, 103 U. S. 352. Such a promise might have a distinct value if the promiser had credit. But it cannot be assumed on this record that the receipts contained it, and if they did, even then the value of the instrument would be due rather to the assumption that the bailee would not give up the goods without a return of it than to the promise. The value of the promise would vary with the promisor. As a key to the goods a receipt no more can be called a second property of equal value than could a key to an adamantine safe that could not be opened without it be called a second property of a value distinct from but equal to that of the money that safe contained. The receipt, like the key, would be property of some small value distinct from that to which it gave access. But it would not be a counterpart, doubling the riches of the owner of the goods.

In the second place, the receipt might be made the representative of the goods in a practical sense. A statute might ordain that a sale and delivery of the goods to a purchaser without notice should be invalid as against a subsequent *bona fide* purchaser of the receipt. We need not speculate as to how the law would deal with it in that event, as we have no warrant for assuming that the German law gives it such effect. On the facts before us, and on any facts that the Court of Appeals can have had before it, the receipts cannot be taken to have been more than one of several keys to the goods. It cannot be assumed that a good title to the whiskey could not have been given while the receipts were outstanding. We assume that they made it very unlikely that it would be, but the practical probability does not make the instrument the legal equivalent of the goods. We take it to be almost undisputed that if the warehouses were in Kentucky the State would not and could not tax both the whiskey and the receipts, even when issued in Kentucky form, and that it would recognize that the only taxable object was the whiskey. The relation of the paper to the goods is not changed by their being abroad, and the only question in the case is whether the paper can be treated as property equivalent in value to the goods, because in some way it represents them.

We state the question as we have stated it because that is the one that is raised by the decision under review. It would be a mere quibble to say that the receipts, as paper, had an infinitesimal value, that they acquired a substantial one, although much less than that of the whiskey, because of their practical use, and that this court is not concerned with a mere overvaluation. The tax is imposed on the theory that the receipts are the equivalents of the goods and are taxable on that footing, although the goods cannot be taxed. Assuming, as the Court of Appeals assumed, that the whiskey is exempt under the Constitution of the United States, we are of opinion that the protection of the Constitution extends to warehouse receipts locally present within the State. What was said by Chief Justice Taney about bills of lading applies to them, *mutatis mutandis:* " A duty upon that is, in substance and effect, a duty on the article exported." Almy *v.* California, 24 How. 169; Fairbank *v.* United States, 181 U. S. 283, 294. We discuss the case on the facts assumed by the Court of Appeals. Whether a finding would have been warranted that the whiskey still was domiciled in Kentucky, or for any other reason was not exempt, is a matter upon which we do not pass. See New York Central & Hudson River R. R. Co. *v.* Miller, 202 U. S. 584, 597.

Judgment reversed.

HOPKINS *v*. BAKER.

COURT OF APPEALS OF MARYLAND.   1894.

[*Reported* 78 *Md.* 363.]

BOYD, J. This case was tried in the Baltimore City Court on an agreed statement of facts. The agreement shows that Charles J. Baker, William Baker, Jr., and Charles E. Baker, compose the firm of Baker Bros. and Company; that Charles E. Baker is a resident of Baltimore City, and the other two members of the firm are residents of Baltimore County; that Charles J. Baker has a four-tenths interest, and the other two have each a three-tenths interest, in the firm. It is admitted that the place of business of the firm is on Charles street, in Baltimore City, at which place is kept the stock of the partnership, of an average value of $80,000.00; that the firm has been assessed by the Appeal Tax Court of Baltimore City for $80,000.00 on their stock, and $750.00 on their horses used in their business, and taxed $1,393.95 for State and City taxes for 1892.

The appellees declined to pay those taxes, but were willing to pay on the horses, which they keep permanently in the city, and on the three-tenths interest of Charles E. Baker. The question raised by the agreed statement of facts and the prayers was whether taxes could be levied and collected from the whole stock of the firm, or whether only the three-tenths interest of Charles E. Baker therein was liable.

The Court below decided that the plaintiff was only entitled to recover the amount of taxes due for the horses and for the interest of Charles E. Baker in the whole stock of the partnership. A judgment was entered accordingly for $432.38 with interest and costs, and the plaintiff appealed to this Court.

As the *situs* of personal property is ordinarily the place of residence of the owner, the Constitution provides that personal property should be taxed where the owner *bona fide* resides for the greater part of the year; but, as that provision alone might work great hardship on the county or city where goods and chattels of the owner are permanently located, the exception was made. Goods and chattels permanently located at the residence of the owner are to be taxed there, so what might be called his "floating" goods and chattels are taxed at the place of his residence, because they have no actual *situs* of their own, and hence that of their owner is adopted, but such goods and chattels as compose the stock in trade of the appellees are not carried backwards and forwards between Baltimore County, or some other county and the City of Baltimore. As long as they are the property of the appellees they are *located* in Baltimore City, and they are as "*permanently located*" there as such goods and chattels can be anywhere. They are not manufactured or purchased to be kept as long as they remain in existence. The separate articles constituting the stock may continue the property of the appellees for a day, a week, a month, a year, or longer, but until they are sold they remain permanently in Baltimore, and are not moved from place to place. That is clearly what is meant by "permanently located" — not that the goods and chattels must remain until they are worn out, or indefinitely. The agreed statement of facts shows that the average value of the stock carried by the appellees is $80,000.00, and that they were assessed for that amount. In other words, the appellees keep *constantly* on hand at their place of business in Baltimore City $80,000.00 worth of goods and chattels in the shape of glass, etc. It may be true that $5,000.00 worth of glass may be sold and shipped away today, and another lot of glass worth $5,000.00 may be substituted for it today or tomorrow, but the stock of goods and chattels of the value of $80,000.00 is kept on hand — is *permanently located* at their place of business. It is not necessary to itemize the stock in trade when it is assessed. The assessors examine the stock, the goods and chattels, and fix their value for taxation, just as they do the furniture or other tangible personal property at the respective residences of the appellees. If the contention of the appellees is to prevail then merchandise cannot be taxed anywhere. No merchant expects to keep his stock *permanently* on hand in the sense that term is used by the learned counsel for the appellees.

He expects to sell as soon as he can receive his price, and as he sells he replenishes his stock. The articles are changing from day to day, but the stock, which represents the aggregate of the goods and chattels, remains about the same. Yet can it be claimed that a merchant who resides and carries on his business in Baltimore is not to be taxed for his stock in trade? A reasonable construction must be given the constitutional provision, and we must bear in mind the object in taxing goods and chattels permanently located in the city or county where they are so located.

If the position of the appellees is correct, it is possible to have hundreds of thousands of dollars, probably millions, of tangible personal property, goods and chattels, within the City of Baltimore, having the benefit of its police and fire protection from year to year, and yet not contribute one dollar to the support of the police or fire departments. Merchants transacting business in Cumberland, Hagerstown,

Frederick, Annapolis and other incorporated cities and towns in the counties could escape all municipal taxes on their stock in trade by living beyond the corporate limits of those cities and towns, whilst those living within such cities and towns must pay the municipal as well as the State and county taxes on their stock in trade. Such a construction of the law would encourage fraud. A resident of a remote county might carry a large stock in trade in Baltimore City, or on the Eastern Shore, without the knowledge of the authorities of the county where he resided.

We recognize fully the force of the argument of counsel for the appellees that property cannot be taxed simply because it may seem inequitable to permit it to escape taxation. But when we are called upon to construe statutes or the Constitution on this subject, it is our duty, in seeking the true interpretation of language used, to place a reasonable construction upon it, and to bear in mind the fact that our Constitution aimed to require all persons to bear their just share of the burden of taxation.

Judgment reversed, and new trial awarded.

COMMONWEALTH *v.* UNION SHIPBUILDING CO.

SUPREME COURT OF PENNSYLVANIA.   1921.

[*Reported* 114 *Atl.* 257.]

FRAZER, J.   Defendant is a Pennsylvania corporation, with its principal office in the city of Pittsburgh, but has considerable real and personal property in the State of Maryland, where it owns and operates a shipbuilding plant. During the tax year of 1918, it had total assets amounting to $2,228,560.90, of which $1,369,837.35 represented the value of the shipbuilding plant, $5,000 was invested in nontaxable liberty bonds, and the remainder, consisting of cash, accounts receivable, and other tangible assets, amounted to $854,-723.55. The capital stock of the company is $1,585,000 par value, and represents its actual value. In assessing the capital stock tax for the year 1918, the auditor general based his assessment on such portion of the valuation of the capital stock as the whole taxable assets in Pennsylvania bore to the whole assets of the corporation. The basis of assessment was thus found to be $607,897. Defendant's contention is that this method of computation is erroneous, and that the correct method is to deduct from the value of the entire stock the value of its nontaxable property, to wit, the tangible property located outside the State and the liberty bonds, the remainder, $210,162.65, being the portion taxable in Pennsylvania. Under this computation it will be observed the tax is much less than that arrived at by the method adopted by the auditor general.

The rule applied by the auditor general and the court below is similar to that employed in determining the amount of taxation to be paid by foreign corporations having property invested in this State; defendant, however, argues this results in taxing indirectly tangible property located outside the State. It must be conceded that a tax on the capital of a corporation is a tax on the property in which that capital is invested (Commissioners *v.* Standard Oil Co., 101 Pa. 119), and that a tax based on a valuation including property situated outside the State is improper (D., L. & W. R. R. *v.* Pennsylvania, 198 U. S. 341, 25 Sup. Ct. 669, 49 L. Ed. 1077). The latter case relied upon by defendant is not controlling here. The question there was whether coal mined and shipped beyond the jurisdiction of the State was a proper subject of deduction in assessing the value of the capital of a Pennsylvania corporation. It was held the coal lost its *situs* in Pennsylvania upon being transported to another State for the purpose of sale, and was therefore beyond the taxing power of the State as specific property, and could not be taxed indirectly by calling it a tax on capital stock representing that property. No question was there involved as to the proper mode of computing the tax.

In the present case no direct levy is made on property held in a foreign State, nor does such result necessarily follow indirectly. In fixing the proportion of the tax to be paid, the full value of the property located outside the State is deducted from the total assets. This does not have the effect of taxing property in other jurisdictions. It permits the stock of corporations created by the laws of this State to be taxed on its full value, less deductions for such property actually outside the State, and therefore subject to taxation in the foreign jurisdiction, and prevents the possibility of domestic corporations escaping taxation altogether, as they might do under the plan urged by defendant, where the value of the capital stock is less than the value of total assets outside the State. We are of opinion the method of assessment adopted by the court below is proper.

The judgment is affirmed.

PULLMAN'S PALACE-CAR CO. *v.* PENNSYLVANIA.

SUPREME COURT OF THE UNITED STATES. 1891.

[*Reported* 141 *United States,* 18.]

GRAY, J.[1] Upon this writ of error, whether this **tax** was in accordance with the law of Pennsylvania, is a question on which the decision of the highest court of the State is conclusive. The only question of which this court has jurisdiction is whether the tax was in violation of the clause of the Constitution of the United States granting to Congress the power to regulate commerce among the several States. The plaintiff in error contends that its cars could be taxed only in the State of Illinois, in which it was incorporated and had its principal place of business.

No general principles of law are better settled, or more fundamental, than that the legislative power of every State extends to all property within its borders, and that only so far as the comity of that State allows can such property be affected by the law of any other State. The old rule, expressed in the maxim *mobilia sequuntur personam*, by which personal property was regarded as subject to the law of the owner's domicile, grew up in the Middle Ages, when movable property consisted chiefly of gold and jewels, which could be easily carried by the owner from place to place, or secreted in spots known only to himself. In modern times, since the great increase in amount and variety of personal property not immediately connected with the person of the owner, that rule has yielded more and more to the *lex situs*, the law of the place where the property is kept and used. Green *v.* Van Buskirk, 5

---

[1] Part of the opinion of the court and part of the dissenting opinion are omitted. — ED.

Wall. 307, and 7 Wall. 139 ; Hervey *v.* Rhode Island Locomotive Works, 93 U. S. 664 ; Harkness *v.* Russell, 118 U. S. 663, 679 ; Walworth *v.* Harris, 129 U. S. 355 ; Story on Conflict of Laws, § 550 ; Wharton on Conflict of Laws, §§ 297-311. As observed by Mr. Justice Story, in his commentaries just cited, " Although movables are for many purposes to be deemed to have no *situs*, except that of the domicile of the owner, yet this being but a legal fiction, it yields, whenever it is necessary for the purpose of justice that the actual *situs* of the thing should be examined. A nation within whose territory any personal property is actually situate has an entire dominion over it while therein, in point of sovereignty and jurisdiction, as it has over immovable property situate there."

For the purposes of taxation, as has been repeatedly affirmed by this court, personal property may be separated from its owner ; and he may be taxed, on its account, at the place where it is, although not the place of his own domicile, and even if he is not a citizen or a resident of the State which imposes the tax. Lane County *v.* Oregon, 7 Wall. 71, 77 ; Railroad Co. *v.* Pennsylvania, 15 Wall. 300, 323, 324, 328 ; Railroad Co. *v.* Peniston, 18 Wall. 5, 29 ; Tappan *v.* Merchants' Bank, 19 Wall. 490, 499 ; State Railroad Tax Cases, 92 U. S. 575, 607, 608 ; Brown *v.* Houston, 114 U. S. 622 ; Coe *v.* Errol, 116 U. S. 517, 524 ; Marye *v.* Baltimore & Ohio Railroad, 127 U. S. 117, 123.

It is equally well settled that there is nothing in the Constitution or laws of the United States which prevents a State from taxing personal property, employed in interstate or foreign commerce, like other personal property within its jurisdiction. . . .

The cars of this company within the State of Pennsylvania are employed in interstate commerce ; but their being so employed does not exempt them from taxation by the State ; and the State has not taxed them because of their being so employed, but because of their being within its territory and jurisdiction. The cars were continuously and permanently employed in going to and fro upon certain routes of travel. If they had never passed beyond the limits of Pennsylvania, it could not be doubted that the State could tax them, like other property, within its borders, notwithstanding they were employed in interstate commerce. The fact that, instead of stopping at the State boundary, they cross that boundary in going out and coming back, cannot affect the power of the State to levy a tax upon them. The State, having the right, for the purposes of taxation, to tax any personal property found within its jurisdiction, without regard to the place of the owner's domicile, could tax the specific cars which at a given moment were within its borders. The route over which the cars travel extending beyond the limits of the State, particular cars may not remain within the State ; but the company has at all times substantially the same number of cars within the State, and continuously and constantly uses there a portion of its property ; and it is distinctly found, as matter of fact, that the company continuously, throughout the periods for which these taxes were levied, carried on business in Pennsylvania, and had about one hundred cars within the State.

The mode which the State of Pennsylvania adopted, to ascertain the proportion of the company's property upon which it should be taxed in that State, was by taking as a basis of assessment such proportion of the capital stock of the company as the number of miles over which it ran cars within the State bore to the whole number of miles, in that and other States, over which its cars were run. This was a just and equitable method of assessment; and, if it were adopted by all the States through which these cars ran, the company would be assessed upon the whole value of its capital stock, and no more.

The validity of this mode of apportioning such a tax is sustained by several decisions of this court, in cases which came up from the Circuit Courts of the United States, and in which, therefore, the jurisdiction of this court extended to the determination of the whole case, and was not limited, as upon writs of error to the State courts, to questions under the Constitution and laws of the United States.

In the State Railroad Tax Cases, 92 U. S. 575, it was adjudged that a statute of Illinois, by which a tax on the entire taxable property of a railroad corporation, including its rolling stock, capital, and franchise, was assessed by the State Board of Equalization, and was collected in each municipality in proportion to the length of the road within it, was lawful, and not in conflict with the Constitution of the State; and Mr. Justice Miller, delivering judgment, said : —

" Another objection to the system of taxation by the State is, that the rolling stock, capital stock, and franchise are personal property, and that this, with all other personal property, has a local *situs* at the principal place of business of the corporation, and can be taxed by no other county, city, or town, but the one where it is so situated. This objection is based upon the general rule of law that personal property, as to its *situs*, follows the domicile of its owner. It may be doubted very reasonably whether such a rule can be applied to a railroad corporation as between the different localities embraced by its line of road. But, after all, the rule is merely the law of the State which recognizes it; and when it is called into operation as to property located in one State, and owned by a resident of another, it is a rule of comity in the former State rather than an absolute principle in all cases. Green *v.* Van Buskirk, 5 Wall. 312. Like all other laws of a State, it is, therefore, subject to legislative repeal, modification, or limitation ; and when the legislature of Illinois declared that it should not prevail in assessing personal property of railroad companies for taxation, it simply exercised an ordinary function of legislation." 92 U. S. 607, 608.

" It is further objected that the railroad track, capital stock, and franchise is not assessed in each county where it lies, according to its value there, but according to an aggregate value of the whole, on which each county, city, and town collects taxes according to the length of the track within its limits." "It may well be doubted whether any better mode of determining the value of that portion of the track within any one county has been devised, than to ascertain the value of the whole road, and apportion the value within the county by its relative length to the whole." "This court has expressly held in two cases, where the road of a corporation ran through different States, that a tax upon the income or franchise of the road was properly apportioned by taking the whole income or value of the franchise, and the length of the road within each State, as the basis of taxation. Delaware Railroad Tax, 18 Wall. 206; Erie Railroad *v.* Pennsylvania, 21 Wall. 492." 92 U. S. 608, 611.

So in Western Union Telegraph Co. *v.* Attorney-General of Massachusetts, 125 U. S. 530, this court upheld the validity of a tax imposed by the State of Massachusetts upon the capital stock of a telegraph company, on account of property owned and used by it within the State, taking as the basis of assessment such proportion of the value of its capital stock as the length of its lines within the State bore to their entire length throughout the country.

Even more in point is the case of Marye *v.* Baltimore & Ohio Railroad, 127 U. S. 117, in which the question was whether a railroad company incorporated by the State of Maryland, and no part of whose own railroad was within the State of Virginia, was taxable under general laws of Virginia upon rolling stock owned by the company, and employed upon connecting railroads leased by it in that State, yet not assigned permanently to those roads, but used interchangeably upon them and upon roads in other States, as the company's necessities required. It was held not to be so taxable, solely because the tax laws of Virginia appeared upon their face to be limited to railroad corporations of that State; and Mr. Justice Matthews, delivering the unanimous judgment of the court, said: —

"It is not denied, as it cannot be, that the State of Virginia has rightful power to levy and collect a tax upon such property used and found within its territorial limits, as this property was used and found, if and whenever it may choose, by apt legislation, to exert its authority over the subject. It is quite true, as the *situs* of the Baltimore and Ohio Railroad Company is in the State of Maryland, that also, upon general principles, is the *situs* of all its personal property; but for purposes of taxation, as well as for other purposes, that *situs* may be fixed in whatever locality the property may be brought and used by its owner by the law of the place where it is found. If the Baltimore and Ohio Railroad Company is permitted by the State of Virginia to bring into its territory, and there habitually to use and employ a portion of its movable personal property, and the railroad company chooses so to do, it would certainly be competent and legitimate for the State to impose upon such property, thus used and employed, its fair share of the burdens of taxation imposed upon similar property used in the like way by its own citizens. And such a tax might be properly assessed and collected in cases like the present, where the specific and individual items of property so used and employed were not continuously the same, but were constantly changing, according to the exigencies of the business. In such cases, the tax might be fixed by an appraisement and valuation of the average amount of the property thus habitually used, and collected by distraint upon any portion that might at any time be found. Of course, the lawlessness of a tax upon vehicles of transportation used by common carriers might have to be considered in particular instances with reference to its operation as a regulation of commerce among the States, but the mere fact that they were employed as vehicles of transportation in the interchange of interstate commerce would not render their taxation invalid." 127 U. S. 123, 124.

For these reasons, and upon these authorities, the court is of opinion that the tax in question is constitutional and valid. The result of holding otherwise would be that, if all the States should concur in abandoning the legal fiction that personal property has its *situs* at the owner's domicile, and in adopting the system of taxing it at the place at which it is used and by whose laws it is protected, property employed in any business requiring continuous and constant movement from one State to another would escape taxation altogether.

Judgment affirmed.

MR. JUSTICE BRADLEY, with whom concurred MR. JUSTICE FIELD and MR. JUSTICE HARLAN, dissenting.

I dissent from the judgment of the court in this case, and will state briefly my reasons. I concede that all property, personal as well as real, within a State, and belonging there, may be taxed by the State. Of that there can be no doubt. But where property does not belong in the State another question arises. It is the question of the jurisdiction of the State over the property. It is stated in the opinion of the court as a fundamental proposition on which the opinion really turns that all personal as well as real property within a State is subject to the laws thereof. I conceive that that proposition is not maintainable as a general and absolute proposition. Amongst independent nations, it is true, persons and property within the territory of a nation are subject to its laws, and it is responsible to other nations for any injustice it may do to the persons or property of such other nations. This is a rule of international law. But the States of this government are not independent nations. There is such a thing as a Constitution of the United States, and there is such a thing as a government of the United States, and there are many things, and many persons, and many articles of property that a State cannot lay the weight of its finger upon, because it would be contrary to the Constitution of the United States. Certainly, property merely carried through a State cannot be taxed by the State. Such a tax would be a duty — which a State cannot impose.

If a drove of cattle is driven through Pennsylvania from Illinois to New York, for the purpose of being sold in New York, whilst in Pennsylvania it may be subject to the police regulations of the State, but it is not subject to taxation there.   It is not generally subject to the laws of the State as other property is.   So if a train of cars starts at Cincinnati for New York and passes through Pennsylvania, it may be subject to the police regulations of that State whilst within it, but it would be repugnant to the Constitution of the United States to tax it.   We have decided this very question in the case of State Freight Tax, 15 Wall. 232.   The point was directly raised and decided that property on its passage through a State in the course of interstate commerce cannot be taxed by the State, because taxation is incidentally regulation, and a State cannot regulate interstate commerce.   The same doctrine was recognized in Coe v. Errol, 116 U. S. 517.

And surely a State cannot interfere with the officers of the United States, in the performance of their duties, whether acting under the Judicial, Military, Postal, or Revenue Departments.   They are entirely free from State control.   So a citizen of the United States, or any other person, in the performance of any duty, or in the exercise of any privilege, under the Constitution or laws of the United States, is absolutely free from State control in relation to such matters.   So that the general proposition, that all persons and personal property within a State is subject to the laws of the State, unless materially modified, cannot be true.

But, when personal property is permanently located within a State for the purpose of ordinary use or sale, then, indeed, it is subject to the laws of the State and to the burdens of taxation; as well when owned by persons residing out of the State, as when owned by persons residing in the State.   It has then acquired a *situs* in the State where it is found.

A man residing in New York may own a store, a factory, or a mine in Alabama, stocked with goods, utensils, or materials for sale or use in that State.   There is no question that the *situs* of personal property so situated is in the State where it is found, and that it may be subjected to double taxation, — in the State of the owner's residence, as a part of the general mass of his estate; and in the State of its *situs*. Although this is a consequence which often bears hardly on the owner, yet it is too firmly sanctioned by the law to be disturbed, and no remedy seems to exist but a sense of equity and justice in the legislatures of the several States.   The rule would undoubtedly be more just if it made the property taxable, like lands and real estate, only in the place where it is permanently situated.

Personal as well as real property may have a *situs* of its own, independent of the owner's residence, even when employed in interstate or foreign commerce.   An office or warehouse, connected with a steamship line, or with a continental railway, may be provided with furniture and all the apparatus and appliances usual in such establishments.   Such property would be subject to the *lex rei sitæ* and to local taxation, though solely devoted to the purposes of the business of those lines. But the ships that traverse the sea, and the cars that traverse the land, in those lines, being the vehicles of commerce, interstate or foreign, and intended for its movement from one State or country to another, and having no fixed or permanent *situs* or home, except at the residence of the owner, cannot, without an invasion of the powers and duties of the federal government, be subjected to the burdens of taxation in the places where they only go or come in the transaction of their business, except where they belong. Hays *v.* Pacific Mail Steamship Co., 17 How. 596 ; Morgan *v.* Parham, 16 Wall. 471 ; Transportation Co. *v.* Wheeling, 99 U. S. 273. To contend that there is any difference between cars or trains of cars and ocean steamships in this regard, is to lose sight of the essential qualities of things. This is a matter that does not depend upon the affirmative action of Congress. The regulation of ships and vessels, by act of Congress, does not make them the instruments of commerce. They would be equally so if no such affirmative regulations existed. For the States to interfere with them in either case would be to interfere with, and to assume the exercise of, that power which, by the Constitution, has been surrendered by the States to the government of the United States, namely, the power to regulate commerce.

Reference is made in the opinion of the court to the case of Railroad Company *v.* Maryland, 21 Wall. 456, in which it was said that commerce on land between the different States is strikingly dissimilar in many respects from commerce on water ; but that was said in reference to the highways of transportation in the two cases, and the difference of control which the State has in one case from that which it can possibly have in the other. A railroad is laid on the soil of the State, by virtue of authority granted by the State, and is constantly subject to the police jurisdiction of the State ; whilst the sea and navigable rivers are highways created by nature, and are not subject to State control. The question in that case related to the power of the State over its own corporation, in reference to its rate of fares and the remuneration it was required to pay to the State for its franchises, — an entirely different question from that which arises in the present case.

Reference is also made to expressions used in the opinion in Gloucester Ferry Co. *v.* Pennsylvania, 114 U. S. 196, which, standing alone, would seem to concede the right of a State to tax foreign corporations engaged in foreign or interstate commerce, if such property is within the jurisdiction of the State. But the whole scope of that opinion is to show that neither the vehicles of commerce coming within the State, nor the capital of such corporations, is taxable there ; but only the property having a *situs* there, as the wharf used for landing passengers and freight. The entire series of decisions to that effect are cited and relied on.

Of course I do not mean to say that either railroad cars or ships are to be free from taxation, but I do say that they are not taxable by those States in which they are only transiently present in the transaction of their commercial operations. A British ship coming to the harbor of New York from Liverpool ever so regularly and spending half its time (when not on the ocean) in that harbor, cannot be taxed by the State of New York (harbor, pilotage, and quarantine dues not being taxes). So New York ships plying regularly to the port of New Orleans, so that one of the line may be always lying at the latter port, cannot be taxed by the State of Louisiana. (See cases above cited). No more can a train of cars belonging in Pennsylvania, and running regularly from Philadelphia to New York, or to Chicago, be taxed by the State of New York, in the one case, or by Illinois, in the other. If it may lawfully be taxed by these States, it may lawfully be taxed by all the intermediate States, New Jersey, Ohio, and Indiana. And then we should have back again all the confusion and competition and State jealousies which existed before the adoption of the Constitution, and for putting an end to which the Constitution was adopted.

In the opinion of the court it is suggested that if all the States should adopt as equitable a rule of proportioning the taxes on the Pullman Company as that adopted by Pennsylvania, a just system of taxation of the whole capital stock of the company would be the result. Yes, if — ! But Illinois may tax the company on its whole capital stock. Where would be the equity then? This, however, is a consideration that cannot be compared with the question as to the power to tax at all, — as to the relative power of the State and general governments over the regulation of internal commerce, — as to the right of the States to resume those powers which have been vested in the government of the United States.

It seems to me that the real question in the present case is as to the *situs* of the cars in question. They are used in interstate commerce, between Pennsylvania, New York, and the Western States. Their legal *situs* no more depends on the States or places where they are carried in the course of their operations than would that of any steamboats employed by the Pennsylvania Railroad Company to carry passengers on the Ohio or Mississippi. If such steamboats belonged to a company located at Chicago, and were changed from time to time as their condition as to repairs and the convenience of the owners might render necessary, is it possible that the States in which they were running and landing in the exercise of interstate commerce could subject them to taxation? No one, I think, would contend this. It seems to me that the cars in question belonging to the Pullman Car Company are in precisely the same category.

STATE TAX ON FOREIGN-HELD BONDS.

SUPREME COURT OF THE UNITED STATES.   1873.

[*Reported* 15 *Wallace*, 300.]

FIELD, J.[1] The question presented in this case for our determination is whether the eleventh section of the Act of Pennsylvania of May, 1868, so far as it applies to the interest on bonds of the railroad company, made and payable out of the State, issued to and held by non-residents of the State, citizens of other States, is a valid and constitutional exercise of the taxing power of the State, or whether it is an interference, under the name of a tax, with the obligation of the contracts between the non-resident bondholders and the corporation.   If it be the former, this court cannot arrest the judgment of the State court; if it be the latter, the alleged tax is illegal, and its enforcement can be restrained.

The case before us is similar in its essential particulars to that of The Railroad Company *v.* Jackson, reported in 7 Wallace.   There, as here, the company was incorporated by the legislatures of two States, Pennsylvania and Maryland, under the same name, and its road extended in a continuous line from Baltimore in one State to Sunbury in the other. And the company had issued bonds for a large amount, drawing interest, and executed a mortgage for their security upon its entire road, its franchises and fixtures, including the portion lying in both States. Coupons for the different instalments of interest were attached to each bond.   There was no apportionment of the bonds to any part of the road lying in either State.   The whole road was bound for each bond. The law of Pennsylvania, as it then existed, imposed a tax on money owing by solvent debtors of three mills on the dollar of the principal, payable out of the interest.   An alien resident in Ireland was the holder of some of the bonds of the railroad company, and when he presented his coupons for the interest due thereon, the company claimed the right to deduct the tax imposed by the law of Pennsylvania, and also an alleged tax to the United States.   The non-resident refused to accept the interest with these deductions, and brought suit for the whole amount in the Circuit Court of the United States for the District of Maryland. That court, the chief justice presiding, instructed the jury that if the

---

[1] The opinion only is given. — ED.

plaintiff, when he purchased the bonds, was a British subject, resident in Ireland, and still resided there, he was entitled to recover the amount of the coupons without deduction. The verdict and judgment were in accordance with this instruction, and the case was brought here for review.

This court held that the tax under the law of Pennsylvania could not be sustained, as to permit its deduction from the coupons held by the plaintiff would be giving effect to the acts of her legislature upon property and effects lying beyond her jurisdiction. The reasoning by which the learned justice, who delivered the opinion of the court, reached this conclusion, may be open, perhaps, to some criticism. It is not perceived how the fact that the mortgage given for the security of the bonds in that case covered that portion of the road which extended into Maryland could affect the liability of the bonds to taxation. If the entire road upon which the mortgage was given had been in another State, and the bonds had been held by a resident of Pennsylvania, they would have been taxable under her laws in that State. It was the fact that the bonds were held by a non-resident which justified the language used, that to permit a deduction of the tax from the interest would be giving effect to the laws of Pennsylvania upon property beyond her jurisdiction, and not the fact assigned by the learned justice. The decision is, nevertheless, authority for the doctrine that property lying beyond the jurisdiction of the State is not a subject upon which her taxing power can be legitimately exercised. Indeed, it would seem that no adjudication should be necessary to establish so obvious a proposition.

The power of taxation, however vast in its character and searching in its extent, is necessarily limited to subjects within the jurisdiction of the State. These subjects are persons, property, and business. Whatever form taxation may assume, whether as duties, imposts, excises, or licenses, it must relate to one of these subjects. It is not possible to conceive of any other, though as applied to them, the taxation may be exercised in a great variety of ways. It may touch property in every shape, in its natural condition, in its manufactured form, and in its various transmutations. And the amount of the taxation may be determined by the value of the property, or its use, or its capacity, or its productiveness. It may touch business in the almost infinite forms in which it is conducted, in professions, in commerce, in manufactures, and in transportation. Unless restrained by provisions of the Federal Constitution, the power of the State as to the mode, form, and extent of taxation is unlimited, where the subjects to which it applies are within her jurisdiction.

Corporations may be taxed, like natural persons, upon their property and business. But debts owing by corporations, like debts owing by individuals, are not property of the debtors, in any sense; they are obligations of the debtors, and only possess value in the hands of the creditors. With them they are property, and in their hands they may be taxed. To call debts property of the debtors is simply to misuse terms. All the property there can be in the nature of things in debts of corporations, belongs to the creditors, to whom they are payable, and follows their domicile, wherever that may be. Their debts can have no locality separate from the parties to whom they are due. This principle might be stated in many different ways, and supported by citations from numerous adjudications, but no number of authorities, and no forms of expression could add anything to its obvious truth, which is recognized upon its simple statement.

The bonds issued by the railroad company in this case are undoubtedly property, but property in the hands of the holders, not property of the obligors. So far as they are held by non-residents of the State, they are property beyond the jurisdiction of the State. The law which requires the treasurer of the company to retain five per cent of the interest due to the non-resident bondholder is not, therefore, a legitimate exercise of the taxing power. It is a law which interferes between the company and the bondholder, and under the pretence of levying a tax commands the company to withhold a portion of the stipulated interest and pay it over to the State. It is a law which thus impairs the obligation of the contract between the parties. The obligation of a contract depends upon its terms and the means which the law in existence at the time affords for its enforcement. A law which alters the terms of a contract by imposing new conditions, or dispensing with those expressed, is a law which impairs its obligation, for, as stated on another occasion, such a law relieves the parties from the moral duty of performing the original stipulations of the contract, and it prevents their legal enforcement. The Act of Pennsylvania of May 1, 1868, falls within this description. It directs the treasurer of every incorporated company to retain from the interest stipulated to its bondholders five per cent upon every dollar, and pay it into the treasury of the Commonwealth. It thus sanctions and commands a disregard of the express provisions of the contracts between the company and its creditors. It is only one of many cases where, under the name of taxation, an oppressive exaction is made without constitutional warrant, amounting to little less than an arbitrary seizure of private property. It is, in fact, a forced contribution levied upon property held in other States, where it is subjected, or may be subjected, to taxation upon an estimate of its full value.

The case of Maltby v. The Reading and Columbia Railroad Company, decided by the Supreme Court of Pennsylvania in 1866, was referred to by the Common Pleas in support of its ruling, and is relied upon by counsel in support of the tax in question. The decision in that case does go to the full extent claimed, and holds that bonds of corporations held by non-residents are taxable in that State. But it is evident from a perusal of the opinion of the court that the decision proceeded upon the idea that the bond of the non-resident was itself property in the State because secured by a mortgage on property there. " It is undoubtedly true," said the court, " that the Legislature of

Pennsylvania cannot impose a personal tax upon the citizen of another State, but the constant practice is to tax property within our jurisdiction which belongs to non-residents." And again: "There must be jurisdiction over either the property or the person of the owner, else the power cannot be exercised; but when the property is within our jurisdiction, and enjoys the protection of our State government, it is justly taxable, and it is of no moment that the owner, who is required to pay the tax, resides elsewhere." There is no doubt of the correctness of these views. But the court then proceeds to state that the principle of taxation as the correlative of protection is as applicable to a non-resident as to a resident; that the loan to the non-resident is made valuable by the franchises which the company derived from the Commonwealth, and as an investment rests upon State authority, and, therefore, ought to contribute to the support of the State government. It also adds that, though the loan is for some purposes subject to the law of the domicile of the holder, "yet, in a very high sense," it is also property in Pennsylvania, observing, in support of this position, that the holder of a bond of the company could not enforce it except in that State, and that the mortgage given for its security was upon property and franchises within her jurisdiction. The amount of all which is this: that the State which creates and protects a corporation ought to have the right to tax the loans negotiated by it, though taken and held by non-residents, a proposition which it is unnecessary to controvert. The legality of a tax of that kind would not be questioned if in the charter of the company the imposition of the tax were authorized, and in the bonds of the company, or its certificates of loan, the liability of the loan to taxation were stated. The tax in that case would be in the nature of a license tax for negotiating the loan, for in whatever manner made payable it would ultimately fall on the company as a condition of effecting the loan, and parties contracting with the company would provide for it by proper stipulations. But there is nothing in the observations of the court, nor is there anything in the opinion, which shows that the bond of the non-resident was property in the State, or that the non-resident had any property in the State which was subject to taxation within the principles laid down by the court itself, which we have cited.

The property mortgaged belonged entirely to the company, and so far as it was situated in Pennsylvania was taxable there. If taxation is the correlative of protection, the taxes which it there paid were the correlative for the protection which it there received. And neither the taxation of the property, nor its protection, was augmented or diminished by the fact that the corporation was in debt or free from debt. The property in no sense belonged to the non-resident bondholder or to the mortgagee of the company. The mortgage transferred no title; it created only a lien upon the property. Though in form a conveyance, it was both at law and in equity a mere security for the debt. That such is the nature of a mortgage in Pennsylvania has been frequently ruled by her highest court. In Witmer's Appeal, 45 Penn. S. 463, the court said: "The mortgagee has no estate in the land, any more than the judgment creditor. Both have liens upon it, and no more than liens." And in that State all possible interests in lands, whether vested or contingent, are subject to levy and sale on execution, yet it has been held, on the ground that a mortgagee has no estate in the lands, that the mortgaged premises cannot be taken in execution for his debt. In Rickert v. Madeira, 1 Rawle, 329, the court said: "A mortgage must be considered either as a chose in action or as giving title to the land and vesting a real interest in the mortgagee. In the latter case it would be liable to execution; in the former it would not, as it would fall within the same reason as a judgment bond or simple contract. If we should consider the interest of the mortgagee as a real interest, we must carry the principle out and subject it to a dower and to the lien of a judgment; and that it is but a chose in action, a mere evidence of debt, is apparent from the whole current of decisions." Wilson v. Shoenberger's Executors, 31 Penn. S. 295.

Such being the character of a mortgage in Pennsylvania, it cannot be said, as was justly observed by counsel, that the non-resident holder and owner of a bond secured by a mortgage in that State owns any real estate there. A mortgage being there a mere chose in action, it only confers upon the holder, or the party for whose benefit the mortgage is given, a right to proceed against the property mortgaged, upon a given contingency, to enforce, by its sale, the payment of his demand. This right has no locality independent of the party in whom it resides. It may undoubtedly be taxed by the State when held by a resident therein, but when held by a non-resident it is as much beyond the jurisdiction of the State as the person of the owner.

It is undoubtedly true that the actual *situs* of personal property which has a visible and tangible existence, and not the domicile of its owner, will, in many cases, determine the State in which it may be taxed. The same thing is true of public securities consisting of State bonds and bonds of municipal bodies, and circulating notes of banking institutions; the former, by general usage, have acquired the character of, and are treated as, property in the place where they are found, though removed from the domicile of the owner; the latter are treated and pass as money wherever they are. But other personal property, consisting of bonds, mortgages, and debts generally, has no *situs* independent of the domicile of the owner, and certainly can have none where the instruments, as in the present case, constituting the evidences of debt, are not separated from the possession of the owners.

Cases were cited by counsel on the argument from the decisions of the highest courts of several States, which accord with the views we have expressed. In Davenport v. The Mississippi and Missouri Railroad Company, 12 Iowa, 539, the question arose before the Supreme Court of Iowa whether mortgages on property in that State held by non-residents could be taxed under a law which provided that all prop-

erty, real and personal, within the State, with certain exceptions not
material to the present case, should be subject to taxation, and the
court said : —

"Both in law and equity the mortgagee has only a chattel interest.
It is true that the *situs* of the property mortgaged is within the jurisdiction of the State, but, the mortgage itself being personal property,
a chose in action attaches to the person of the owner. It is agreed by
the parties that the owners and holders of the mortgages are non-
residents of the State. If so, and the property of the mortgage
attaches to the person of the owner, it follows that these mortgages
are not property within the State, and if not they are not·the subject
of taxation."

In People *v.* Eastman, 25 Cal. 603, the question arose before the Supreme Court of California whether a judgment of record in Mariposa
County upon the foreclosure of a mortgage upon property situated in
that county could be taxed there, the owner of the judgment being a
resident of San Francisco, and the law of California requiring all property to be taxed in the county where situated ; and it was held that it
was not taxable there. "The mortgage," said the court, "has no
existence independent of the thing secured by it ; a payment of the
debt discharges the mortgage. The thing secured is intangible, and
has no *situs* distinct and apart from the residence of the holder. It
pertains to and follows the person. The same debt may, at the same
time, be secured by a mortgage upon land in every county in the State ;
and if the mere fact that the mortgage exists in a particular county gives
the property in the mortgage a *situs* subjecting it to taxation in that
county, a party, without further legislation, might be called upon to
pay the tax several times, for the lien for taxes attaches at the
same time in every county in the State, and the mortgage in one
county may be a different one from that in another although the debt
secured is the same."

Some adjudications in the Supreme Court of Pennsylvania were also
cited on the argument, which appear to recognize doctrines inconsistent
with that announced in Maltby *v.* Reading and Columbia Railroad
Company, particularly the case of McKeen *v.* The County of Northampton, 49 Penn. S. 519, and the case of Short's Estate, 16 Id. 63,
but we do not deem it necessary to pursue the matter further. We
are clear that the tax cannot be sustained ; that the bonds, being held
by non-residents of the State, are only property in their hands, and
that they are thus beyond the jurisdiction of the taxing power of the
State. Even where the bonds are held by residents of the State, the
retention by the company of a portion of the stipulated interest can
only be sustained as a mode of collecting a tax upon that species of
property in the State. When the property is out of the State there
can then be no tax upon it for which the interest can be retained.
The tax laws of Pennsylvania can have no extraterritorial operation :
nor can any law of that State, inconsistent with the terms of a con-

tract, made with or payable to parties out of the State, have any effect upon the contract whilst it is in the hands of such parties or other non-residents.   The extraterritorial invalidity of State laws discharging a debtor from his contracts with citizens of other States, even though made and payable in the State after the passage of such laws, has been judicially determined by this court.   Ogden *v.* Saunders, 12 Wheaton, 214 ;   Baldwin *v.* Hale, 1 Wallace, 223.   A like invalidity must, on similar grounds, attend State legislation which seeks to change the obligation of such contracts in any particular, and on stronger grounds where the contracts are made and payable out of the State.

Judgment reversed, and the cause remanded for further proceedings, in conformity with this opinion.

DAVIS, CLIFFORD, MILLER, and HUNT, JJ., dissenting.

BLACKSTONE *v.* MILLER.

SUPREME COURT OF THE UNITED STATES. 1903.

[*Reported* 188 U. S. 189.]

HOLMES, J. This is a writ of error to the Surrogate's Court of the county of New York. It is brought to review a decree of the court, sustained by the Appellate Division of the Supreme Court, 69 App. Div. 127, and by the Court of Appeals, 171 N. Y. 682, levying a tax on the transfer by will of certain property of Timothy B. Blackstone, the testator, who died domiciled in Illinois. The property consisted of a debt of $10,692.24, due to the deceased by a firm, and of the net sum of $4,843,456.72, held on a deposit account by the United States Trust Company of New York. The objection was taken seasonably upon the record that the transfer of this property could not be taxed in New York consistently with the Constitution of the United States.

The deposit in question represented the proceeds of railroad stock sold to a syndicate and handed to the Trust Company, which, by arrangement with the testator, held the proceeds subject to his order, paying interest in the meantime. Five days' notice of withdrawal was required, and if a draft was made upon the company, it gave its check upon one of its banks of deposit. The fund had been held in this way from March 31, 1899, until the testator's death on May 26, 1900. It is probable, of course, that he did not intend to leave the fund there forever and that he was looking out for investments, but he had not found them when he died. The tax is levied under a statute imposing a tax "upon the transfer of any property, real or personal. . . . 2. When the transfer is by will or intestate law, of property within the State, and the decedent was a non-resident of the State at the time of his death." Laws of 1896, c. 908, § 220, amended, Laws of 1897, c. 284; 3 Birdseye's Stat. 3d ed. 1901, p. 3592. The whole succession has been taxed in Illinois, the New York deposit being included in the appraisal of the estate. It is objected to the New York tax that the property was not within the State, and that the courts of New York had no jurisdiction; that if the property was within the State it was only transitorily there, Hays *v.* Pacific Mail Steamship Co., 17 How. 596, 599, 600, that the tax impairs the obligation of contracts, that it denies full faith and credit to the judgment taxing the inheritance in Illinois, that it deprives the executrix and legatees of privileges and immunities of citizens of the State of New York, and that it is contrary to the Fourteenth Amendment.

In view of the State decisions it must be assumed that the New York statute is intended to reach the transfer of this property if it can be reached. New Orleans *v.* Stempel, 175 U. S. 309, 316; Morley *v.* Lake Shore & Michigan Southern Railway Co., 146 U. S. 162, 166. We also must take it to have been found that the property was not *in*

transitu in such a sense as to withdraw it from the power of the State,
if otherwise the right to tax the transfer belonged to the State. The
property was delayed within the jurisdiction of New York an indefinite
time, which had lasted for more than a year, so that this finding at least
was justified.   Kelley *v.* Rhoads, 188 U. S. 1, and Diamond Match Co.
v. Village of Ontonagon, 188 U. S. 84, present term. Both parties agree
with the plain words of the law that the tax is a tax upon the transfer,
not upon the deposit, and we need spend no time upon that. Therefore
the naked question is whether the State has a right to tax the transfer
by will of such deposit.

The answer is somewhat obscured by the superficial fact that New
York, like most other States, recognizes the law of the domicil as the
law determining the right of universal succession. The domicil, naturally, must control a succession of that kind. Universal succession is
the artificial continuance of the person of a deceased by an executor,
heir. or the like, so far as succession to rights and obligations is concerned.   It is a fiction, the historical origin of which is familiar to
scholars, and it is this fiction that gives whatever meaning it has to the
saying *mobilia sequuntur personam*.   But being a fiction it is not allowed to obscure the facts, when the facts become important. To a
considerable, although more or less varying, extent, the succession determined by the law of the domicil is recognized in other jurisdictions.
But it hardly needs illustration to show that the recognition is limited
by the policy of the local law.   Ancillary administrators pay the local
debts before turning over the residue to be distributed, or distributing
it themselves, according to the rules of the domicil. The title of the
principal administrator, or of a foreign assignee in bankruptcy, another
type of universal succession, is admitted in but a limited way or not at
all.   See Crapo *v.* Kelly, 16 Wall. 610; Chipman *v.* Manufacturers'
National Bank, 156 Mass. 147, 148, 149.

To come closer to the point, no one doubts that succession to a tangible chattel may be taxed wherever the property is found, and none
the less that the law of the *situs* accepts its rules of succession from the
law of the domicil, or that by the law of the domicil the chattel is part
of a *universitas* and is taken into account again in the succession tax
there.   Eidman *v.* Martinez, 184 U. S. 578, 586, 587, 592.   See Mager
v. Grima. 8 How. 490, 493 ; Coe *v.* Errol, 116 U. S. 517, 524 ; Pullman's
Palace Car Co. *v.* Pennsylvania, 141 U. S. 18, 22 ; Magoun *v.* Illinois
Trust & Savings Bank, 170 U. S. 283 ; New Orleans *v.* Stempel, 175
U. S. 309 ; Bristol *v.* Washington County, 177 U. S. 133; and for state
decisions Matter of Estate of Romaine, 127 N. Y. 80 ; Callahan *v.*
Woodbridge, 171 Mass. 593 ; Greves *v.* Shaw, 173 Mass. 205 ; Allen
v. National State Bank, 92 Md. 509.

No doubt this power on the part of two States to tax on different and
more or less inconsistent principles, leads to some hardship. It may
be regretted, also, that one and the same State should be seen taxing
on the one hand according to the fact of power, and on the other, at

the same time, according to the fiction that. in successions after death, *mobilia sequuntur personam* and domicil governs the whole.   But these inconsistencies infringe no rule of constitutional law.   Coe *v.* Errol, 116 U. S. 517, 524 ; Knowlton *v.* Moore, 178 U. S. 41.

The question, then, is narrowed to whether a distinction is to be taken between tangible chattels and the deposit in this case.   There is no doubt that courts in New York and elsewhere have been loath to recognize a distinction for taxing purposes between what commonly is called money in the bank and actual coin in the pocket.   The practical similarity more or less has obliterated the legal difference.   Matter of Houdayer, 150 N. Y. 37 ; New Orleans *v.* Stempel, 175 U. S. 309, 316 ; City National Bank *v.* Charles Baker Co., 180 Mass. 40, 42.   In view of these cases, and the decision in the present case, which followed them, a not very successful attempt was made to show that by reason of the facts which we have mentioned, and others, the deposit here was unlike an ordinary deposit in a bank.   We shall not stop to discuss this aspect of the case, because we prefer to decide it upon a broader view.

If the transfer of the deposit necessarily depends upon and involves the law of New York for its exercise, or, in other words, if the transfer is subject to the power of the State of New York, then New York may subject the transfer to a tax.   United States *v.* Perkins, 163 U. S. 625, 628, 629 ; McCulloch *v.* Maryland, 4 Wheat. 316, 429.   But it is plain that the transfer does depend upon the law of New York, not because of any theoretical speculation concerning the whereabouts of the debt, but because of the practical fact of its power over the person of the debtor.   The principle has been recognized by this court with regard to garnishments of a domestic debtor of an absent defendant.   Chicago, Rock Island & Pacific Ry. Co. *v.* Sturm, 174 U. S. 710.   See Wyman *v.* Halstead, 109 U. S. 654.   What gives the debt validity ?   Nothing but the fact that the law of the place where the debtor is will make him pay. It does not matter that the law would not need to be invoked in the particular case.   Most of us do not commit crimes, yet we nevertheless are subject to the criminal law, and it affords one of the motives for our conduct.   So again, what enables any other than the very creditor in proper person to collect the debt?   The law of the same place.   To test it, suppose that New York should turn back the current of legislation and extend to debts the rule still applied to slander that *actio personalis moritur cum persona*, and should provide that all debts hereafter contracted in New York and payable there should be extinguished by the death of either party.   Leaving constitutional considerations on one side, it is plain that the right of the foreign creditor would be gone.

Power over the person of the debtor confers jurisdiction, we repeat. And this being so we perceive no better reason for denying the right of New York to impose a succession tax on debts owed by its citizens than upon tangible chattels found within the State at the time of the death. The maxim *mobilia sequuntur personam* has no more truth in the one case than in the other. When logic and the policy of a State conflict with a fiction due to historical tradition, the fiction must give way.

There is no conflict between our views and the point decided in the case reported under the name of State Tax on Foreign Held Bonds, 15 Wall. 300.   The taxation in that case was on the interest on bonds held out of the State.   Bonds and negotiable instruments are more than merely evidences of debt.   The debt is inseparable from the paper which declares and constitutes it, by a tradition which comes down from more archaic conditions.   Bacon *v.* Hooker, 177 Mass. 335, 337.   Therefore, considering only the place of the property, it was held that bonds held out of the State could not be reached.   The decision has been cut down to its precise point by later cases.   Savings & Loan Society *v.* Multnomah County, 169 U. S. 421, 428 ; New Orleans *v.* Stempel, 175 U. S. 309, 319, 320.

In the case at bar the law imposing the tax was in force before the deposit was made, and did not impair the obligation of the contract, if a tax otherwise lawful ever can be said to have that effect.   Pinney *v.* Nelson, 183 U. S. 144, 147.   The fact that two States, dealing each with its own law of succession, both of which the plaintiff in error has to invoke for her rights, have taxed the right which they respectively confer, gives no cause for complaint on constitutional grounds.   Coe *v.* Errol, 116 U. S. 517, 524 ; Knowlton *v.* Moore, 178 U. S. 53.   The universal succession is taxed in one State, the singular succession is taxed in another.   The plaintiff has to make out her right under both in order to get the money.   See Adams *v.* Batchelder, 173 Mass. 258.   The same considerations answer the argument that due faith and credit are not given to the judgment in Illinois.   The tax does not deprive the plaintiff in error of any of the privileges and immunities of the citizens of New York.   It is no such deprivation that if she had lived in New York the tax on the transfer of the deposit would have been part of the tax on the inheritance as a whole.   See Mager *v.* Grima, 8 How. 490 ; Brown *v.* Houston, 114 U. S. 622, 635 ; Wallace *v.* Myers, 38 Fed. Rep. 184.   It does not violate the Fourteenth Amendment.   See Magoun *v.* Illinois Trust & Savings Bank, 170 U. S. 283.   Matters of state procedure and the correctness of the New York decree or judgment, apart from specific constitutional objections, are not open here.   As we have said, the question whether the property was to be regarded as *in transitu*, if material, must be regarded as found against the plaintiff in error.

Decree affirmed.

Mr. Justice White dissents.

BUCK v. BEACH.

SUPREME COURT OF THE UNITED STATES. 1907.

[*Reported* 206 *U. S.* 392.]

JUDGMENT against the plaintiff in error (who was defendant below) was recovered in a State Circuit Court in Indiana, which was affirmed by the Supreme Court of the State (164 Indiana, 37), and the plaintiff in error brings the case here to review that judgment. The predecessor of the defendant in error, being at the time treasurer of Tippecanoe County, in the State of Indiana, brought this action in 1897 against the plaintiff in error to subject funds in his hands to the payment of taxes alleged to be due from the estate of one Job M. Nash, deceased, which taxes had been assessed in above county and State in 1894, after the death of Nash, on personal property of the deceased that had been omitted from the tax list in his lifetime, during the years 1881 to 1893, both inclusive.

The point in dispute between the parties relates to the assessment for omitted property on what are called the " Ohio notes," the plaintiff in error insisting that such assessment was illegal as beyond the jurisdiction of the State to impose.

The material facts are not really in dispute. It appears that Nash died in 1893, at that time, and for more than twenty years prior thereto, a resident of the city and State of New York. He left a will which was admitted to probate in Hamilton County, Ohio, and his executors qualified there. They thereafter refused to pay the tax imposed upon the Ohio notes in Indiana. By the terms of the will a trust was created, and part of the personal property constituting such trust (more than enough to pay the taxes in dispute) was turned over to James Buck, plaintiff in error and one of the two trustees named in the will. He resided in Lafayette, in the State of Indiana, and the other trustee resided in Cincinnati, in the State of Ohio. From this fund, in the hands of Buck, the defendant in error asked to have the taxes paid which had been assessed, as above stated, and which he claimed were due the State. This was refused, and this action was thereupon commenced.

A former action had been brought by the trustees for relief by injunction against the predecessor of the defendant in error to enjoin him from seizing upon or interfering with the trust fund for the payment of the taxes in dispute, and in that action the trustees had been unsuccessful. Buck *v.* Miller, 147 Indiana, 586, decided in 1896.

The amount assessed on the estate of decedent upon the " Ohio notes " from 1884 to 1893, on account of omitted assessments during those years, aside from the penalties for nonpayment, was $36,357.71.

During the above-mentioned years, while the decedent was, as stated, a resident of the State of New York, he had a large sum of money invested in the States of Ohio and Indiana, approximating

$750,000. The money loaned by him in Ohio was evidenced by
Ohio notes, made by the borrowers, who were residents of Ohio, the
payment of the money borrowed being secured by mortgages on
lands situated in Ohio. The moneys loaned in Ohio were loaned
through an agent of Mr. Nash, residing in Cincinnati. The notes
were dated and payable in Cincinnati, to the order of Mr. Nash, but
were not endorsed by him, and all renewals and payments on account of them were made to his agent in Cincinnati. All moneys
paid upon or by reason of these notes were deposited in a bank in
Cincinnati to the credit of Mr. Nash, and no part thereof was sent
to Indiana. The Cincinnati agent commenced loaning decedent's
money about 1860, and, upon the removal of decedent to New York
in 1870, and until his death, in 1893, the agent made investments
on decedent's behalf in Ohio, collected the principal and interest
upon his mortgage loans and had general charge of his financial
interests in that State.

James Buck was the agent of decedent at Lafayette, in the State
of Indiana, for many years preceding the death of Mr. Nash. The
Ohio notes were sent to him from Cincinnati by the agent there,
during the years in question, together with the mortgages securing
the payment of the notes, and they were kept in a safe at Lafayette,
Indiana, by Mr. Buck, but no business was transacted in regard to
them nor any use made of them in Indiana, otherwise than that a
short time before the interest on or principal of the notes became
due they were sent to the Ohio agent to have the interest payments
made to him endorsed upon them, or to be delivered up if the
principal were paid.

Nothing else was done in Indiana in regard to the notes, except
that a few days prior to the first day of April in each year (which
is the day upon which assessments for taxes are, by law, made in the
State of Indiana) Mr. Buck sent the notes and mortgages to the
Ohio agent, and a few days subsequent to that day in each year the
same were returned by the Ohio agent to Mr. Buck, who retained
them in his possession.

When the Ohio notes and mortgages were sent from Cincinnati
to Mr. Buck by the Ohio agent, Mr. Buck made a record of their
receipt in a book kept by him for that purpose, showing the dates
and amounts of the notes and when due, and whenever payment or
renewal of said notes was reported by the Ohio agent to the Indiana
agent, he made entries of the facts in the register kept by him.

Mr. Buck also had possession of the notes and mortgages given
to Mr. Nash for moneys loaned in the State of Indiana, and such
moneys were invested and reinvested in that State during these
years, and the taxes thereon were duly paid.

Mr. Buck transacted no business directly with the makers of the
Ohio notes or mortgages but, as stated, sent the notes to the Ohio
agent for any business to be done in regard to them.

During Mr. Buck's agency money was sometimes sent to him at
Lafayette from Cincinnati to be invested, which money was placed
on deposit in the bank in Indiana and loaned for Mr. Nash. Such

moneys have nothing to do with the " Ohio notes " in issue in this action.

During these years, at least from 1886, Mr. Buck was authorized by virtue of a power of attorney from Mr. Nash to satisfy when due and when the money was paid all notes and mortgages, but so far as the Ohio notes and mortgages were concerned he never assumed to satisfy any of them or receive payment for the same. That was all done by the Ohio agent at Cincinnati.

PECKHAM, J. The only question involved here is in regard to the taxability of the Ohio notes in the State of Indiana.

The plaintiff in error asserts that the simple physical presence of the Ohio notes in Indiana payable to and not endorsed by the decedent, did not constitute taxable property there, because such notes were given and were payable and were paid in Ohio by residents of Ohio, and to a non-resident of Indiana, and for loans made in Ohio, the capital represented by such notes never having been used in business in Indiana, and he insists that a tax upon such capital or upon the notes themselves as representing that capital is an illegal tax, and that to take property in payment of such an illegal tax is to take it without due process of law and constitutes a violation of the Fourteenth Amendment.

If the facts in this case constituted the debts evidenced by the Ohio notes property in the jurisdiction of the State of Indiana at the time when such taxes were imposed, then the tax was valid, if there were statutory authority of that State for the same. The State Court has held that there was such authority, Buck v. Miller, 147 Indiana, 586; Buck v. Beach, 164 Indiana, 37, being the case at bar, and that construction of the statute concludes this court. Delaware &c. Co. v. Pennsylvania, 198 U. S. 341, 352.

The sole question then for this court is whether the mere presence of the notes in Indiana constituted the debts of which the notes were the written evidence, property within the jurisdiction of that State, so that such debts could be therein taxed.

Generally, property in order to be the subject of taxation must be within the jurisdiction of the power assuming to tax. State Tax on Foreign-held Bonds, 15 Wall. 300; Erie Railroad v. Pennsylvania, 153 U. S. 628, 646; Savings Society v. Multnomah County, 169 U. S. 421, 427; Louisville &c. v. Kentucky, 188 U. S. 385; Delaware &c. v. Pennsylvania, 198 U. S. 431; Union Transit Co. v. Kentucky, 199 U. S. 194; Metropolitan Ins. Co. v. New Orleans, 205 U. S. 395.

In regard to tangible property the old rule was *mobilia sequuntur personam*, by which personal property was supposed to follow the person of its owner, and to be subject to the law of the owner's domicil. For the purpose of taxation, however, it has long been held that personal property may be separated from its owner, and he may be taxed on its account at the place where the property is, although it is not the place of his own domicil, and even if he is not a citizen or resident of the State which imposes the tax. Pullman Palace Car Co. v. Pennsylvania, 141 U. S. 18, 22; Tappan

v. Merchants' National Bank, 19 Wall. 490; People *ex rel.* Hoyt
v. The Commissioner of Taxes, 23 N. Y. 224. The same rule applies
to intangible property. Generally speaking, intangible property in
the nature of a debt may be regarded, for the purposes of taxation,
as situated at the domicil of the creditor and within the jurisdiction
of the State where he has such domicil. It is property within that
State. Thus it has been held that a debt owned by a citizen of one
State against a citizen of another State and evidenced by the bond
of the debtor, secured by a deed of trust or mortgage upon real estate
situated in the State where the debtor resides, is properly taxed by
the State of the residence of the creditor, if the statute of that State
so provides, and such tax violates no provision of the Federal Constitution. Kirtland *v.* Hotchkiss, 100 U. S. 491, 498.

Rejecting the fiction of law in regard to the *situs* of personal
property, including therein choses in action, the courts of Indiana
have asserted jurisdiction by reason of the statute of that State
over these Ohio notes for the purpose of taxation in Indiana, founded
upon the simple fact that such notes were placed in the latter State
by the Ohio agent of the decedent under the circumstances above
set forth. The Supreme Court of Indiana refused to accept the
testimony of the agents that the Ohio notes were sent to Lafayette
merely for safe keeping, and for clerical convenience, and said that
" the court below was authorized to make the opposite deduction
from the uniform course of the business in respect to the keeping
of said notes and mortgages and from the evidence that decedent
gave the direction which established the practice that was pursued
in that particular. More than that, the evidence clearly warranted
the conclusion that Buck was vested with a control of said notes
and securities for the purposes of enabling decedent to escape taxation in Ohio. We must, therefore, conclude, in support of the general finding, that the court below found that in the conducting of
the business of the Ohio agency the decedent separated from said
business the possession of said notes and mortgages and vested the
right to such possession in said Buck. There was no return for taxation of said notes, or of the investments represented by them, either
in Ohio or in New York during the lifetime of the decedent."

Taking this to be a finding of fact by the Supreme Court of the
State, it is plain that the action of the decedent in sending the Ohio
notes into the State of Indiana for the purpose stated (whether
successful or not), was improper and unjustifiable. The record
does show, however, that the executors subsequently paid the Ohio
authorities over $40,000 for taxes on the moneys invested in Ohio.

But an attempt to escape proper taxation in Ohio does not confer
jurisdiction to tax property asserted to be in Indiana, which really
lies outside and beyond the jurisdiction of that State. Jurisdiction
of the State of Indiana to tax is not conferred or strengthened by
reason of the motive which may have prompted the decedent to send
into the State of Indiana these evidences of debts owing him by
residents of Ohio. The question still remains, was there any property within the jurisdiction of the State of Indiana, so as to permit

that State to tax it, simply because of tie presence of tie Oiio notes in tiat State? It was not tie value of tie paper as a tangible thing, on which these promises to pay the debts existing in Oiio were written, that was taxed by tiat State. Tie property really taxed was the debt itself, as eaci separate note was taxed at the full amount of the debt named tierein or due tiereon. And jurisdiction over these debts for tie purpose of taxation was asserted and exercised solely by reason of the piysical presence in Indiana of the notes themselves, altiough tiey were written eviuence of tie existence of the debts wiici were in fact tiereby taxed.

A distinction has been sometimes taken between bonds and other specialty debts belonging to the deceased, on tie one hand, and simple contract debts on tie other, for the purpose of probate jurisdiction, and the probate court, where the bonds are found, ias been held to have jurisdiction to grant probate, while in tie other class of debts (including promissory notes) jurisdiction has attached to the probate Court where the debtor resided at tie deati of the creditor. 1 Williams on Executors, 6th Am. from 7th English ed., bottom paging 288, 290, note [*h*]; Wyman *v.* Halstead Adm'r, 109 U. S. 654. See also Beers *v.* Siannon, 73 N. Y. 292, 299; Owen *v.* Miller, 10 Ohio St. 136.

Under such rule, the debts here in question were not property within the State of Indiana, nor were tie promissory notes themselves, which were only evidence of suci debts. Tie rule giving jurisdiction where tie specialty may be found, has no application to a promissory note. Assuming suci a rule, the case here is not covered by it.

There are no cases in this court wiere an assessment suci as the one before us has been involved. We have not had a case where neither the party assessed nor the debtor was a resident of or present in the State where the tax was imposed, and where no business was done therein by tie owner of the notes or iis agent relating in any way to the capital evidenced by the notes assessed for taxation. We cannot assent to the doctrine that tie mere presence of evidences of debt, such as these notes, under the circumstances already stated, amounts to the presence of property within the State for taxation. That promissory notes may be the subject of larceny, as stated in 48 N. Y. cited below, does not make tie debts evidenced by them, property liable to taxation within tie State wiere tiere is no otier fact than the presence of the notes upon wiici to base tie claim.

In People *v.* The Board of Trustees. &c., 48 N. Y. 390, it was held that money due upon a contract for tie sale of land was personal property, and tiat wiere suci contract belonging to a non-resident was in the hands of a resident agent. it migit. for the purposes ,of municipal taxation, be assessed to the agent and taxed. In the opinion Judge Earl said: "The debts due upon tiese contracts are personal estate, the same as if they were due upon notes or bonds; and such personal estate may be said to exist where the obligations for payments are held." The contracts spoken of in that case were contracts for tie sale of land by a non-resident owner to persons within the county where the lands were situated. The debtors resided within the State, and the agent of the non-resident for the sale of the land resided in the State and had possession of the contracts. A different case as to its facts from the one before us.

In People *v.* Smith, 88 N. Y. 576, jurisdiction to tax in New York was denied under the statute of that State, because the personal estate was not within the State, although the same principle, page 581 as contained in 48 N. Y. *supra,* was asserted.

If payment of these notes had to be enforced it would not be to the courts of Indiana that the owner would resort. He would have to go to Ohio to find the debtor as well as the lands mortgaged as security for the payment of the notes. It is true that if the notes were stolen while in Indiana, and they were therein a subject of larceny, the Indiana courts would have to be resorted to for the punishment of the thieves. That would be in vindication of the general criminal justice of the State. This consideration, however, is not near enough to the question involved to cause us to change our views of the law in regard to the taxation of property, and make that property within the State, which we think is clearly outside it.

Although public securities, consisting of state bonds and bonds of municipal bodies, and circulating notes of banking institutions have sometimes been treated as property in the place where they were found, though removed from the domicil of the owner, State Tax on Foreign-held Bonds, 15 Wall. 300, 324, it has not been held in this court that simple contract debts, though evidenced by promissory notes, can under the facts herein stated be treated as property and taxed in the State where the notes may be found.

As is said in the above cited case at page 320: " All the property there can be in the nature of things in debts of corporations, belongs to the creditors, to whom they are payable, and follows their domicil, wherever that may be. Their debts can have no locality separate from the parties to whom they are due. This principle might be stated in many different ways, and supported by citations from numerous adjudications, but no number of authorities, and no forms of expressions could add anything to its obvious truth, which is recognized upon its simple statement."

The cases cited in Metropolitan Life Insurance Company *v.* The City of New Orleans, 205 U. S. 395, show that this rule is enlarged to the extent of holding that capital, evidenced by written instruments, invested in a State may be taxed by the authorities of the State, although their owner is a non-resident and such evidences of debt are temporarily outside of the State when the assessment is made. Although the language of the opinion in the case of State Tax on Foreign-held Bonds, *supra,* has been somewhat restricted so far as regards the character of the interest of the mortgagee in the land mortgaged, Savings, &c. Society *v.* Multnomah County, 169 U. S. 421, 428, the principle upon which the case itself was decided has not been otherwise shaken by the later cases. New Orleans *v.* Stempel, 175 U. S. 309, 319, 320; Blackstone *v.* Miller, 188 U. S. 189, 206. In the Stempel case, *supra,* the notes, as we have said, represented the capital of the owner invested in the State, and the capital was taxed, although the owner was a non-resident.

Cases arising under collateral inheritance tax or succession tax acts have been cited as affording foundation for the right to tax as herein asserted. The foundation upon which such acts rest is different from that which exists where the assessment is levied upon property. The succession or inheritance tax is not a tax on property, as has been frequently held by this court, Knowlton *v.* Moore, 178 U. S. 41, and Blackstone *v.* Miller, 188 U. S. 189, and therefore the decisions arising under such inheritance tax cases are not in point.

Our decision in this case has no tendency to aid the owner of taxable property in any effort to avoid or evade proper and legitimate taxation. The presence of the notes in Indiana formed no bar to the right, if it otherwise existed, of taxing the debts, evidenced by the notes, in Ohio. It does, however, tend to prevent the taxation in one State of property in the shape of debts not existing there and which if so taxed would make double taxation almost sure, which is certainly not to be desired and ought, wherever possible, to be prevented.

For the reason that as the assessment in this case was made upon property which was never within the jurisdiction of the State of Indiana the State had no power to tax it, and the enforcement of such a tax would be the taking of property without due process of law.

The judgment of the Supreme Court of Indiana is reversed and the case remanded for further proceedings not inconsistent with the opinion of this court.

Reversed.

BREWER and DAY, JJ., dissenting.[1]

---

[1] "It has been asserted or implied, again and again, that the States had the power to deal with negotiable paper on the footing of *situs.* It is well settled that bank bills and municipal bonds are in such a concrete, tangible form that they are subject to taxation where found, irrespective of the domicil of the owner; . . . notes and mortgages are of the same nature. . . we see no reason why a State may not declare that if found within its limits they shall be subject to taxation. New Orleans *v.* Stempel, 175 U. S. 309. 322, 323. Bristol *v.* Washington County, 177 U. S. 133, 141. State Board of Assessors *v.* Comptoir National d'Escompte, 191 U. S. 388, 403, 404. Metropolitan Life Insurance Co. *v.* New Orleans, 205 U. S. 395, 400, 402. This is the established law unless it has been overthrown by the decision in Buck *v.* Beach, 206 U. S. 392.

"No such effect should be attributed to that case. The Ohio notes in Buck's hands that were held not to be taxable in Indiana were moved backward and forward between Ohio and Indiana with the intent to avoid taxation in either State. 206 U. S. 402. They really were in Ohio hands for business purposes, *ibid.*, 395, and sending them to Indiana was spoken of by Mr. Justice Peckham as improper and unjustifiable. *Ibid.* 402. Their absence from Ohio evidently was regarded as a temporary absence from home. *Ibid.* 404. And the conclusion is carefully limited to a refusal to hold the presence of the notes "under the circumstances already stated " to amount to the presence of property within the State. A distinction was taken be-

TAPPAN *v.* MERCHANTS' NATIONAL BANK.

SUPREME COURT OF THE UNITED STATES.   1873.

[*Reported* 19 Wall. 490.]

BILL to enjoin the collection of taxes in Cook County on the
shares of the Merchants' Bank. The Circuit Court of the Northern
District of Illinois granted the injunction, and Tappan, the collector, appealed.[1]

WAITE, C. J. We are called upon in this case to determine whether
the General Assembly of the State of Illinois could, in 1867, provide
for the taxation of the owners of shares of the capital stock of a
National bank in that State, at the place, within the State, where
the bank was located, without regard to their places of residence. The
statute of Illinois, under the authority of which the taxes complained
of were assessed, was passed before the act of Congress, approved
February 10th, 1868, which gave a legislative construction to the
words, " place where the bank is located, and not elsewhere," as used
in section forty-one of the National Banking Act, and permitted
the State to determine and direct the manner and place of taxing
resident shareholders, but provided that non-residents should be taxed
only in the city or town where the bank was located.

The power of taxation by any State is limited to persons, property,
or business within its jurisdiction. Personal property, in the absence of any law to the contrary, follows the person of the owner, and
has its *situs* at his domicile. But, for the purposes of taxation, it
may be separated from him, and he may be taxed on its account at
the place where it is actually located. These are familiar principles,
and have been often acted upon in this court and in the courts
of Illinois. If the State has actual jurisdiction of the person of
the owner, it operates directly upon him. If he is absent, and it
has jurisdiction of his property, it operates upon him through his
property.

Shares of stock in National banks are personal property. They
are made so in express terms by the act of Congress under which
such banks are organized. They are a species of personal property
which is, in one sense, intangible and incorporeal, but the law which
creates them may separate them from the person of their owner for

tween the presence sufficient for a succession tax like that in this case. and
that required for a property tax such as then was before the court. and the
only point decided was that the notes had no such presence in Indiana as
to warrant a property tax. See New York Central & Hudson River R. R.
Co. *v.* Miller, 202 U. S. 584, 597. If Buck *v.* Beach is not to be distinguished
on one of the foregoing grounds, as some of us think that it can be, we are
of opinion that it must yield to the current of authorities to which we have
referred." — HOLMES. J.. in Wheeler *v.* Sohmer. 233 U. S. 434. 439.

[1] This short statement is substituted for that of the Reporter.

the purposes of taxation, and give them a *situs* of their own. This has been done. By section forty-one of the National Banking Act, it is in effect provided that all shares in such banks, held by any person or body corporate, may be included in the valuation of the personal property of such person or corporation in the assessment of taxes imposed under State authority, at the place where the bank is located, and not elsewhere. This is a law of the property. Every owner takes the property subject to this power of taxation under State authority, and every non-resident, by becoming an owner, voluntarily submits himself to the jurisdiction of the State in which the bank is established for all the purposes of taxation on account of his ownership. His money invested in the shares is withdrawn from taxation under the authority of the State in which he resides and submitted to the taxing power of the State where, in contemplation of the law, his investment is located. The State, therefore, within which a National bank is situated has jurisdiction, for the purposes of taxation, of all the shareholders of the bank, both resident and non-resident, and of all its shares, and may legislate accordingly.

Decree reversed and the cause remanded. [1]

BELLOWS FALLS POWER CO. *v.* COMMONWEALTH.

SUPREME JUDICIAL COURT OF MASSACHUSETTS. 1915.

[*Reported* 222 *Mass.* 51.]

RUGG, C. J. This is a petition under St. 1909, c. 490, Part III, § 70, for the recovery of the amount of an excise alleged to have been excessive, which was levied upon a domestic business corporation under §§ 41 and 43 of Part III of the tax act, St. 1909, c. 490, as amended by St. 1904, c. 198, § 6. The questions presented are whether certain stocks and bonds of Vermont corporations are "securities which if owned by a natural person resident in this Commonwealth," by § 41 "would not be liable to taxation," or by § 43 "would be liable to taxation," and also whether such stock is "property situated in another State or country and subject to taxation therein" by § 41. . . .

The petitioner owned a large number of shares of stock in a Vermont corporation, the value of which the tax commissioner refused to deduct from the true market value of the corporate franchise of the petitioner, for the purpose of determining its excise tax. It is contended by the petitioner that the tax commissioner was in error for two reasons, (1) because the stock of the Vermont corporation would not be subject to taxation in this Commonwealth if owned by a natural person, and (2) because such stock is property situated in another State and subject to taxation therein. These two contentions rest on statutes of the State of Vermont. . . .

---

[1] *Acc.* State *v.* Travelers Ins. Co., 70 Conn. 590. See Matter of Bronson, 150 N. Y. 1.

Plainly these contentions would have no merit in law were it not for the special provisions of the Vermont statute. It was early decided in this Commonwealth that shares of stock in a foreign corporation were taxable as property to the owner resident here, although the place of business and the entire property of the corporation were in another jurisdiction. Great Barrington v. County Commissioners, 16 Pick. 572. This principle of taxation has been repeatedly upheld, the latest instance being Hawley v. Malden, 204 Mass. 138. That decision was affirmed in 232 U. S. 1, where, at pages 12 and 13, it was said by Mr. Justice Hughes in delivering the opinion: "Whether, in the case of corporations organized under State laws, a provision by the State of incorporation fixing the *situs* of shares for the purpose of taxation, by whomever owned, would exclude the taxation of the shares by other States in which their owners reside is a question which does not arise upon this record and need not be decided." We are not aware that this question ever has been determined by this court or by the Supreme Court of the United States. It now is presented. It must be taken as the settled purpose of our tax law to assess to the owners resident in this Commonwealth a tax upon all shares of foreign corporations. It is provided in the tax act (St. 1909, c. 490) in Part I, § 2, that "All property real and personal situated within the Commonwealth, and all personal property of the inhabitants of the Commonwealth wherever situated, unless expressly exempted by law, shall be subject to taxation." Part I, § 23, provides that "All personal estate, within or without the Commonwealth, shall be assessed to the owner in the city or town in which he is an inhabitant on the first day" of April, with exceptions not here material, save that by St. 1909, c. 516, § 1, "Merchandise, machinery and animals owned by inhabitants of this Commonwealth, but situated in another State shall be exempt from taxation." Part I, § 4, provides that "Personal estate for the purpose of taxation shall include . . . Third, Public stocks and securities, . . . bonds of railroads and street railways, stocks in turnpikes, bridges and moneyed corporations within or without this Commonwealth . . ." with exceptions not now of consequence. In substance, the only question is whether these provisions of the law, which plainly include in their scope stock such as is owned by this petitioner in the Vermont corporation, conflict as applied to such shares with any provision of the State or federal constitution.

Vermont has the power to tax all the shares of corporations organized under its laws, whether owned by its residents or by those of other States or countries. This expressly was decided in Corry v. Mayor & City Council of Baltimore, 196 U. S. 466, and in St. Albans v. National Car Co. 57 Vt. 68. The principle was applied in Tappan v. Merchants' National Bank, 19 Wall. 490. It was recognized in Greves v. Shaw, 173 Mass. 205, 208, Kingsbury v. Chapin, 196 Mass. 533, 535, and Kennedy v. Hodges, 215 Mass. 112, 114.

It may be urged on the one side that the nature and the incidents of the shares of stock are fixed by the law by which the corporation is created; that the provisions of that law are limitations upon the essential characteristics of shares and follow them wherever they may go; and that if the *situs* of the shares for purpose of taxation is declared by that law to be in the State of its domicil, that is an inherent restriction which everywhere must be recognized as an incident of the property represented by the shares; that this provision as to *situs* for tax purposes is contractual in substance and may be invoked by the owner in exoneration of liability as much as others which are obligatory are resorted to by creditors to establish a liability, Converse *v.* Ayer, 197 Mass. 443, 453, Whitman *v.* Oxford National Bank, 176 U. S. 559; that by virtue of the Vermont statute this stock is divested of its taxable character as intangible property and clothed with an immovable garment of tangibility located in Vermont alone, and hence, that these shares stand on the same footing as merchandise and other tactile personal effects which cannot be taxed to their owner in a jurisdiction other than that in which they permanently are placed. Delaware, Lackawanna & Western Railroad *v.* Pennsylvania, 198 U. S. 341. Old Dominion Steamship Co. *v.* Virginia, 198 U. S. 299. Expressions by eminent judges are laid hold of as countenancing the soundness of these contentions. It was said by Chief Justice Waite in Tappan *v.* Merchants' National Bank, 19 Wall. 490, at page 499, "shares of stock in national banks are personal property. . . . They are a species of personal property which is, in one sense, intangible and incorporeal, but the law which creates them may separate them from the person of their owner for the purposes of taxation, and give them a *situs* of their own. This has been done. [Here is quoted the section of the national banking act to that effect.] This is a law of the property. Every owner takes the property subject to this power of taxation under State authority, and every nonresident, by becoming an owner, voluntarily submits himself to the jurisdiction of the State in which the bank is established for all the purposes of taxation on account of his ownership." In Covington *v.* First National Bank of Covington, 198 U. S. 100, at page 111, it was said by Mr. Justice Day, "The *situs* of shares of foreign-held stock in an incorporated company, in the absence of legislation imposing a duty upon the company to return the stock within the State as the agent of the owner, is at the domicil of the owner." It is to be noted, however, that both these cases relate to shares in national banks. The subject of national banking is within the exclusive control of Congress and its mandate respecting any subject within its sphere is supreme and binding upon all the States. The national bank act is explicit as to the *situs* of shares of stock in national banks for taxation. These expressions, therefore, were directed to a different subject and are of slight value in considering the present question, which expressly was left open in Hawley *v.* Malden, 232 U. S. 1, 13. See Grether *v.* Wright, 23 C. C. A. 498, 512.

Weighty as are the suggestions which have been noted above, we are of opinion that the constitutionality of the statute requiring the taxation of shares like these in question must be sustained. The fundamental ground is that the power to tax all property within its jurisdiction is a necessary attribute of sovereignty, and that there is a certain quality of property in these shares attaching to the person of the owner and hence taxable at his domicil.

It is too well settled to require the citation of authorities that the several States of the Union are foreign to each other except so far as the United States is paramount as the dominating government, and except so far as they are bound to recognize the fraternity among sovereignties established by the Constitution of the United States. No State taxation laws can have extraterritorial effect. Each State, so far as relates to the power of taxation, is an independent sovereignty. It is not concerned with what other States may do as to property within its jurisdiction, which may be made the subject of taxation by itself. Dwight *v.* Boston, 12 Allen, 316. Sturges *v.* Carter, 114 U. S. 511. Seward *v.* Rising Sun, 79 Ind. 351. Bacon *v.* State Tax Commissioners, 126 Mich. 22. Judy *v.* Beckwith, 137 Iowa, 24. McKeen *v.* County of Northampton, 49 Penn. St. 519. State *v.* Branin, 3 Zabr. 484, 496. Bradley *v.* Bauder, 36 Ohio St. 28. Ogden *v.* St. Joseph, 90 Mo. 522, 529. Commonwealth *v.* Lovell, 125 Ky. 491. Stanford *v.* San Francisco, 131 Cal. 34. All property within the jurisdiction of a State, which is capable of being taxed, may be made subject to taxation unless exempted under federal or State law. No State can assess to the residents a tax upon their real estate or tangible personal property situated in a foreign jurisdiction. Union Refrigerator Transit Co. *v.* Kentucky, 199 U. S. 194. Neither can any State give extraterritorial effect to its laws exempting property of its subjects from taxation in other jurisdictions. But, except as restrained by federal or State constitutional provisions, "the power of the State as to the mode, form, and extent of taxation is unlimited, where the subjects to which it applies are within her jurisdiction." Kirtland *v.* Hotchkiss, 100 U. S. 491, 497.

There is a necessary element of property in shares in corporations which, although intangible, attaches to and follows the person of the owner, and is inseparable from it. Such shares are personal property and not real estate. They are subject to succession according to the law of the domicil of the owner. As was said in Hawley *v.* Malden, 232 U. S. 1, at page 9, "It is well settled that the property of the shareholders in their respective shares is distinct from the corporate property, franchises and capital stock," and further at page 12, that shares of stock are "in the nature of contract rights or choses in action. Morawetz on Corporations, § 225." It was held in Stanwood *v.* Stanwood, 17 Mass. 57, in an opinion written by Chief Justice Parker, that shares of stock in a bank were choses in action. The principle of that decision applies to shares of stock in all corporations. It is an incident of such shares that the owner is entitled to participate in the net profits earned, to enforce the use of its capital for its corporate purposes, to restrain abuses of corporate powers, and to receive his proportion of the property of the corporation remaining after the payment of its debts upon its dissolution. Van Allen *v.* The Assessors, 3 Wall. 573, 584. Farrington *v.* Tennessee, 95 U. S. 679, 687. In most corporations he has the further right in proportion to his ownership to participate in the election of officers and such direction of the corporate affairs as may be vested in stock-holders. Certificates of stock may be the subject of contracts for sale or exchange under our laws. Opinion of the Justices, 196 Mass. 603, 619, 621. Our laws may be invoked to enforce such contracts and other property rights, Herbert v. Simson, 220 Mass. 480, as well as to protect the owner and his property interest therein against theft or fraud. His property right as such owner may be attached and secured by his creditors by resort to our courts, and in many instances doubtless this is the only way of reaching such right in any juris-diction. This property right follows the person of the owner, has its *situs* at his domicil and is there taxable regardless of any law of a sister State by whose authority the corporation itself may have been created.

Certificates of stock in a corporation have other of the charac-teristics of property. They may be converted like corporeal personal property. Jarvis v. Rogers, 15 Mass. 389. Hagar v. Norton, 188 Mass. 47, 50. McAllister v. Kuhn, 96 U. S. 87. They are the sub-ject of larceny and embezzlement. O'Herron v. Gray, 168 Mass. 573, 575. They may be hypothecated, pledged and replevied. Kennedy v. Hodges, 215 Mass. 112, 115. They may be made by statute subject to attachment and garnishment. Puget Sound National Bank of Everett v. Mather, 60 Minn. 362. Title passes by their delivery and assignment or endorsement. Sargent v. Essex Marine Railway, 9 Pick. 201. Sargent v. Franklin Ins. Co. 8 Pick. 90, 95. Boston Music Hall Association v. Cory, 129 Mass. 435. Certificates of stock are not in every respect the equivalent of the shares in the corporation which they represent. Often they are spoken of as evidence of title, Kennedy v. Hodges, *ubi supra,* Richardson v. Shaw, 209 U. S. 365, 378; but they may be regarded as something more. Indeed, it was said in Hatch v. Reardon, 204 U. S. 152, 161, respecting a certificate of stock, "That document was more than evidence, it was a constit-uent of title. No doubt, in a more remote sense, the object was the membership or share which the certificate conferred or made attain-able. More remotely still it was an interest in the property of the corporation, which might be in other States than either the corpora-tion or the certificate of stock." In Merritt v. American Steel-Barge Co. 24 C. C. A. 530, at page 537, is found this language: "Speaking technically, it is true that a stock certificate is written evidence of a certain interest in corporate property. . . . But in the business world such obligations or securities are treated as something more than mere muniments of title. They are daily bought and sold like ordinary chattels, . . . they have an inherent market value, and, while differ-ing in some respects from chattels, they are generally classified as personal property." Said Cooley, C. J., in Daggett v. Davis, 53 Mich. 35, respecting the characteristics of stock in a corporation, "the certificate itself is also property; standing as it does as the representative of the shares." In Simpson v. Jersey City Contracting Co. 165 N. Y. 193, 197, 198, occur these words: "Certificates of stock are treated by business men as property for all practical pur-poses. They are sold in the market and they are transferred as collateral security for loans, and they are used in various ways as property. They pass by delivery from hand to hand." In Cook on Corporations, (7th ed.) § 485, it is said, "certificates of stock have gradually grown to be more than mere receipts or evidence of stock, and have come to be the stock itself, practically, in business transactions . . . and, like a promissory note, a certificate of stock is property in itself." While some of these expressions go rather far, enough has been said to show a generally prevailing tendency to treat a certificate of stock as possessing incidents of property. These are a sufficient basis for taxation to the owner at his residence. The validity of a commercial usage whereby possession of a certificate of stock duly indorsed enables the holder to pass title good against the world has been recognized in numerous cases. Russell *v.* American Bell Telephone Co. 180 Mass. 467. Andrews *v.* Worcester, Nashua & Rochester Railroad, 159 Mass. 64, 66. Scollans *v.* Rollins, 173 Mass. 275; *S. C.* 179 Mass. 346. Clews *v.* Friedman, 182 Mass. 555. Baker *v.* Davie, 211 Mass. 429, 438.

If the domiciliary State of the corporation has the right to establish the *situs* of its shares of stock for purposes of taxation, on principle it would seem that that power may be exercised to declare an entire exemption from taxation and to collect revenue in some other way from the corporation. If the power exists in the State creating the corporation to establish the *situs* of its shares of stock for the purpose of taxation, and is exercised, it must be absolute and no other State can inquire into the character or extent of that taxation in an effort to tax its own citizen who is a stockholder in such corporation. It hardly seems possible that the Fourteenth Amendment to the federal constitution can have such an effect.

The theory of taxation is that it is money exacted from the subject in return for the protection afforded by established government. It is the duty of governments to protect persons and property. These rights of the Massachusetts owner of shares of stock in the Vermont corporation pertain to his residence here and receive the protection of our laws. To that extent the shareholder resident here receives for the taxation imposed a return in governmental protection for the property rights incident to his ownership.

These are incidents of property which necessarily follow the person of the owner of shares in foreign corporations, even though the shares may be taxed at the foreign domicil of the corporation. For these purposes the *situs* of corporate shares follows the domicil of the owner. This is the general rule. There appears to us to be no ground for the establishment of an exception to that general rule in the instant case. Bristol *v.* Washington County, 177 U. S. 133. Ayer & Lord Tie Co. *v.* Kentucky, 202 U. S. 409. Southern Pacific Co. *v.* Kentucky, 222 U. S. 63, 69. Darnell *v.* Indiana. 226 U. S. 390. Frothingham *v.* Shaw, 175 Mass. 59. Welch *v.* Boston, 221 Mass. 155. On this ground, if not on others also, Selliger *v.* Kentucky, 213 U. S. 200, is distinguishable.

The case at bar closely resembles Bonaparte *v.* Tax Court, 104 U. S. 592, where municipal and State bonds, some entirely exempted from taxation and others subject to taxation in the State of issue by the State laws under which they were authorized, nevertheless were held to be taxable at the domicil of the owner. In principle that case seems indistinguishable from the case at bar. An express legislative declaration by the debtor State that its bonds either shall be exempt from taxation or shall be subject to taxation in its own jurisdiction, although not categorically an attempt to separate the *situs* of the debt from the person of the owner, yet is in substance the equivalent of a declaration to that end. It is a legislative effort to incorporate into the property as one of its essential qualities an exemption from taxation or a liability to taxation in the State of issue alone. It is hard to conceive of a purpose on the part of that State not to attach by strong inference and fair implication a separation of *situs* for taxation from the domicil of the owner to bonds so issued, if the effective exercise of such a function were within the scope of legislative power. Indeed, the Vermont statute is not a precise assertion of separation of *situs* of shares from the person of the non-resident owner. It is a simple exercise of the power of the sovereign to tax. That was the effect of one of the statutes under consideration in Bonaparte *v.* Tax Court, 104 U. S. 592. The barrier against accomplishing that purpose in such way as to compel recognition by the taxing power of a sister State was no greater in substance in that case than it is in the present case.

It has been held that the State having jurisdiction over the debtor has the constitutional power to assert and maintain for itself a *situs* of the debt for purposes of taxation and levy a tax thereon against the creditor domiciled in another State. This was decided as to debts secured by mortgage upon real estate in Savings & Loan Society *v.* Multnomah County, 169 U. S. 421. It was decided as to unsecured credits, whether expressed by notes or existing as bald accounts current, in Liverpool & London & Globe Ins. Co. *v.* Assessors for the Parish of Orleans, 221 U. S. 346. Bonaparte *v.* Tax Court upheld the power of the State having jurisdiction of the creditor owning the debt to tax him at his domicil upon the maxim *mobilia sequuntur personam,* despite the express tax or exemption from taxation by the State having jurisdiction where the debt was created and the debtor domiciled, while the Multnomah County and Orleans cases sustained an exercise of the power to tax by the State having jurisdiction of the debtor regardless of what might happen in the State having jurisdiction of the creditor. The more comprehensive power of Congress as to taxation and exemption from taxation of subjects within its jurisdiction as compared with that of a State legislature is pointed out by Taft, J., in an opinion concurred in by Lurton, J., in Grether *v.* Wright, 23 C. C. A. 498, 512.

It is manifest from the adjudications by the United States Supreme Court mentioned above that under some circumstances the same property may be taxed to the same person in different jurisdictions without violating any right secured by the federal constitution. Put in other words, these decisions appear to mean that property may have a *situs* in two different jurisdictions for taxation purposes when the nature of the property seems to require or permit it.　There may be a difference between bonds and shares of stock as to capacity for independent *situs*.　Blackstone *v.* Miller, 188 U. S. 189, 206.　Selliger *v.* Kentucky, 213 U. S. 200, 204.　But there appears to be no ground for distinction between shares of stock and accounts current so far as concerns the issues here involved.　This principle governs the case at bar.　It shows that Corry *v.* Mayor & City Council of Baltimore, 196 U. S. 466, is not inconsistent with this result, but that it bears the same relation to the present case as does Liverpool & London & Globe Ins. Co. *v.* Assessors for the Parish of Orleans to Bonaparte *v.* Tax Court.　As was said in Kidd *v.* Alabama, 188 U. S. 730, at page 732, by Mr. Justice Holmes, as to taxation between sister States, " it would be a great advantage to the country and to the individual States if principles of taxation could be agreed upon which did not conflict with each other, and a common scheme could be adopted by which taxation of substantially the same property in two jurisdictions could be avoided.　But the Constitution of the United States does not go so far."

There is an analogy so far as concerns *situs* between the case at bar and the numerous cases holding that residence of the owner is sufficient ground for the imposition of a succession or inheritance tax upon various kinds of intangible property.　Frothingham *v.* Shaw, 175 Mass. 59.　Buck *v.* Beach, 206 U. S. 392.　Wheeler *v.* New York, 233 U. S. 434.

The principle against double taxation of the same property has no application, because that is confined in operation to such taxation in the same jurisdiction.

Whether it would be wise to make exemptions in cases like the present is not a judicial but a legislative question.　Knight *v.* Boston, 159 Mass. 551.

It follows from what has been said that the shares of stock are not " property situated in another State and subject to taxation therein."　The context in which these words occur in our tax law and its other general provisions demonstrate that these words refer to the kind of property which, if owned by an individual and situated and taxed in another State, would be exempt from taxation here, such as real estate, and " merchandise, machinery and animals."　St. 1909, c. 516, § 1.　Union Refrigerator Transit Co. *v.* Kentucky, 199 U. S. 194.　There are substantial, although intangible, elements of property in shares of stock in a corporation which attach to the owner resident in this Commonwealth.

The general statement in the decisions of many courts and of text writers is to the effect that shares of stock in foreign corporations may be assessed to the owner at the place of his domicil irrespective of taxes which may have been imposed on the corporation itself, even in respect of its capital stock.　Greenleaf *v.* Board of Review, 184 Ill. 226. 228.　State *v.* Nelson, 107 Minn. 319, 322.　Appeal Tax Court *v.* Gill, 50 Md. 377, 396.　Allen *v.* Commonwealth, 98 Va. 80, 84.　State *v.* Bentley, 3 Zabr. 532. 542.　27 Am. & Eng. Encyc. of Law, (2d ed.) 928, 929.　37 Cyc. 821, 864, 865.

Our decision upon this branch of the case is supported by direct adjudications upon the same point in Dyer *v.* Osborne, 11 R. I. 321, Worth *v.* Commissioners of Ashe County, 90 N. C. 409, Appeal Tax Court *v.* Patterson, 50 Md. 354, 373, Judy *v.* Beckwith, 137 Iowa, 24, 33, Seward *v.* Rising Sun, 79 Ind. 351, 353, 354, Bacon *v.* State Tax Commissioners, 126 Mich. 22, 29, 30, Central of Georgia Railway *v.* Wright, 166 Fed. Rep. 153, 159, appeal dismissed, 215 U. S. 617. See 1 Cooley on Taxation, (3d ed.) 389. Although in some of these opinions the question of the power of the domiciliary State of the corporation to appropriate to itself an exclusive taxation *situs* of the shares of stock was not much discussed, the decisions are clear to the effect that it cannot do so. The result seems to be supported by Kidd *v.* Alabama, 188 U. S. 730, where at page 731 some of these cases are cited with approval. It conforms to the policy of our law touching a kindred point in Dwight *v.* Boston, 12 Allen, 316, where it was said at page 322, "our whole system of taxation, as established and practiced, is to disregard the liability of shares in foreign corporations to taxation in the States where they are situated." We are aware of no authorities to the contrary. Oliver *v.* Washington Mills, 11 Allen, 268, involved quite different considerations.

The conclusion is, in the opinion of a majority of the court, that as matter of constitutional power the Legislature can impose a property tax upon the shares of stock in a Vermont corporation owned by a natural person resident in this Commonwealth. The exercise of such power does not conflict with constitutional guarantees for equal protection of the laws, full faith and credit to the public acts of other States, nor is it a deprivation of property without due process of law. Of course it does not impair the obligation of any contract, because it is to be inferred that our tax law was in effect long before the acquisition of the stock by the petitioner.

The petitioner contends that its bond of a Vermont corporation is not comprehended within "securities which if owned by a natural person resident in this Commonwealth would be liable to taxation," as these words are used in § 43, cl. 2. Its argument is that such a bond is a debt due to it and that if owned by a natural person resident here who owed money in excess of the value of the bond, as the petitioner does, then such natural person would not be taxed for it. Hale *v.* County Commissioners, 137 Mass. 111. This argument is fallacious. These words in the statute were not intended to establish the same standard of taxation for a corporation as for an individual. The reference to securities which would be taxable if owned by a natural person is merely for the purpose of determining the taxable character of the securities. Farr Alpaca Co. *v.* Commonwealth, 212 Mass. 156, 162. If the securities possess that taxable character, then they are to be taken into account. The debts owed by the petitioner are all considered in determining the fair market value of its shares, provided it makes proper return of them. It is not entitled under the excise tax law to have them deducted a second time.

"Securities" is a word of sufficiently broad import to include a bond like that in question. It was said in Boston Railroad Holding

Co. *v.* Commonwealth, 215 Mass. 493, that "in its ordinary acceptation the words 'securities' includes bonds . . . and other evidences
of indebtedness." There is nothing in any part of the tax law to show
that it was used in this section in a narrow or constricted sense.

In this respect also no error is shown in the action of the tax commissioner in the determination of the excise tax upon the petitioner.

Petition dismissed with costs.

ADAMS EXPRESS COMPANY *v.* OHIO.

SUPREME COURT OF THE UNITED STATES. 1897.

[*Reported* 166 *U. S.* 194 ; 166 *U. S.* 185.]

THESE are cases involving the constitutionality of certain laws of the
State of Ohio providing for the taxation of telegraph, telephone, and
express companies, and the validity of assessments of express companies thereunder.

The general assembly of Ohio passed, April 27, 1893, 90 Ohio Laws,
330, an act to amend and supplement §§ 2777, 2778, 2779, and 2780 of
the Revised Statutes of that State (commonly styled "The Nichols
Law "), which was amended May 10, 1894. The law created a state
board of appraisers and assessors, consisting of the auditor of State,
treasurer of State, and attorney general, which was charged with the
duty of assessing the property in Ohio of telegraph, telephone, and
express companies. By the act as amended, between the first and thirty-
first days of May annually each telegraph, telephone, and express company doing business in Ohio, was required to file a return with the
auditor of State, setting forth among other things the number of shares
of its capital stock ; the par value and market value (or, if there be no
market value, then the actual value) of its shares at the date of the
return ; a statement in detail of the entire real and personal property
of said companies and where located, and the value thereof as assessed
for taxation. Telegraph and telephone companies were required to
return, also, the whole length of their lines, and the length of so much
of their lines as is without and is within the State of Ohio, including
the lines controlled and used, under lease or otherwise. Express companies were required to include in the return a statement of their entire
gross receipts, from whatever source derived, for the year ending the
first day of May, of business wherever done ; and of the business done
in the State of Ohio, giving the receipts of each office in the State ;
also the whole length of the lines of rail and water routes over which
the companies did business, within and without the State. Provision
was made in the law for the organization of the board, for the appointing of one of its members as secretary and the keeping of full minutes
of its proceedings. The board was required to meet in the month of
June and assess the value of the property of these companies in Ohio.
The rule to be followed by the board in making the assessment was
that "in determining the value of the property of said companies in
this State, to be taxed within the State and assessed as herein provided, said board shall be guided by the value of said property as determined by the value of the entire capital stock of said companies,
and such other evidence and rules as will enable said board to arrive at
the true value in money of the entire property of said companies within
the State of Ohio, in the proportion which the same bears to the entire

property of said companies, as determined by the value of the capital stock thereof, and the other evidence and rules as aforesaid."

As to telegraph and telephone companies, the board was required to apportion the valuation among the several counties through which the lines ran, in the proportion that the length of the lines in the respective counties bore to the entire length in the State; in the case of express companies, the apportionment was to be made among the several counties in which they did business, in the proportion that the gross receipts in each county bore to the gross receipts in the State.

The amount thus apportioned was to be certified to the county auditor, and placed by him on the duplicate " to be assessed, and the taxes thereon collected the same as taxes assessed and collected on other personal property," the rate of taxation to be the same as that on other property in the local taxing district.

The valuation of all the real estate of the companies, situated in Ohio, was required to be deducted from the total valuation, as fixed by the board.

The original suits were brought in the Circuit Court to enjoin the certification of the apportioned valuations to the county auditors, as to 1893, against the state board; as to 1894 and 1895, against the auditor of State.[1]

The appellants filed a petition for a rehearing.

BREWER, J. We have had before us at the present term several cases involving the taxation of the property of express companies, some coming from Ohio, some from Indiana, and one from Kentucky; also a case from the latter State involving the taxation of the property of the Henderson Bridge Company. The Ohio and Indiana cases were decided on the 1st of February. (165 U. S. 194.) Petitions for rehearing of those cases have been presented and are now before us for consideration.

The importance of the questions involved, the close division in this court upon them, and the earnestness of counsel for the express companies in their original arguments, as well as in their briefs on this application, lead those of us who concurred in the judgments to add a few observations to what has hitherto been said.

Again and again has this court affirmed the proposition that no State can interfere with interstate commerce through the imposition of a tax, by whatever name called, which is in effect a tax for the privilege of transacting such commerce. And it has as often affirmed that such restriction upon the power of a State to interfere with interstate commerce does not in the least degree abridge the right of a State to tax at their full value all the instrumentalities used for such commerce.

Now the taxes imposed upon express companies by the statutes of the three States of Ohio, Indiana, and Kentucky are certainly not in terms "privilege taxes." They purport to be upon the property of the companies. They are, therefore, not, in form at least, subject to any of the denunciations against privilege taxes which have so often come from this court. The statutes grant no privilege of doing an express business, charge nothing for doing such a business, and contemplate only the assessment and levy of taxes upon the property of the express companies situated within the respective States. And the only really substantial question is whether, properly understood and administered, they subject to the taxing power of the State property not within its territorial limits. The burden of the contention of the express companies is that they have within the limits of the State certain tangible property, such as horses, wagons, etc. ; that that tangible property is their only property within the State ; that it must be valued as other like property, and upon such valuation alone can taxes be assessed and levied against them.

But this contention practically ignores the existence of intangible property, or at least denies its liability for taxation. In the complex civilization of to-day a large portion of the wealth of a community consists in intangible property, and there is nothing in the nature of things or in the limitations of the Federal Constitution which restrains a State from taxing at its real value such intangible property. Take the simplest illustration : B, a solvent man, purchases from A certain property, and gives to A his promise to pay, say, $100,000 therefor. Such promise may or may not be evidenced by a note or other written instrument. The property conveyed to B may or may not be of the value of $100,000. If there be nothing in the way of fraud or misrepresentation to invalidate that transaction, there exists a legal promise on the part of B to pay to A $100,000. That promise is a part of A's property. It is something of value, something on which he will receive cash, and which he can sell in the markets of the community for cash. It is as certainly property, and property of value, as if it were a building or a steamboat, and is as justly subject to taxation. It matters not in what this intangible property consists — whether privileges, corporate franchises, contracts, or obligations. It is enough that it is property which though intangible exists, which has value, produces income, and passes current in the markets of the world. To ignore this intangible property, or to hold that it is not subject to taxation at its accepted value, is to eliminate from the reach of the taxing power a large portion of the wealth of the country. Now, whenever separate articles of tangible property are joined together, not simply by a unity of ownership, but in a unity of use, there is not infrequently developed a property, intangible though it may be, which in value exceeds the aggregate of the value of the separate pieces of tangible property. Upon what theory of substantial right can it be adjudged that the value of this intangible property must be excluded from the tax lists, and the only property placed thereon be the separate pieces of tangible property?

The first question to be considered therefore is whether there is belonging to these express companies intangible property — property differing from the tangible property — a property created by either the combined use or the manner of use of the separate articles of tangible property, or the grant or acquisition of franchises or privileges, or all together. To say that there can be no such intangible property, that it is something of no value, is to insult the common intelligence of every man. Take the Henderson Bridge Company's property, the validity of the taxation of which is before us in another case. The facts disclosed in that record show that the bridge company owns a bridge over the Ohio, between the city of Henderson in Kentucky and the Indiana shore, and also ten miles of railroad in Indiana; that that tangible property — that is, the bridge and railroad track — was assessed in the States of Indiana and Kentucky at $1,277,695.54, such, therefore, being the adjudged value of the tangible property. Thus the physical property could presumably be reproduced by an expenditure of that sum, and if placed elsewhere on the Ohio River, and without its connections or the business passing over it or the franchises connected with it, might not of itself be worth any more. As mere bridge and tracks, that was its value. If the State's power of taxation is limited to the tangible property, the company should only be taxed in the two States for that sum, but it also appears that it, as a corporation, had issued bonds to the amount of $2,000,000, upon which it was paying interest; that it had a capital stock of $1,000,000, and that the shares of that stock were worth not less than $90 per share in the market. The owners, therefore, of that stock had property which for purposes of income and purposes of sale was worth $2,900,000. What gives this excess of value? Obviously the franchises, the privileges the company possesses — its intangible property.

Now, it is a cardinal rule which should never be forgotten that whatever property is worth for the purposes of income and sale it is also worth for purposes of taxation. Suppose such a bridge were entirely within the territorial limits of a State, and it appeared that the bridge itself cost only $1,277,000, could be reproduced for that sum, and yet it was so situated with reference to railroad or other connections, so used by the travelling public, that it was worth to the holders of it in the matter of income $2,900,000, could be sold in the markets for that sum, was therefore in the eyes of practical business men of the value of $2,900,000, can there be any doubt of the State's power to assess it at that sum, and to collect taxes from it upon that basis of value? Substance of right demands that whatever be the real value of any property, that value may be accepted by the State for purpose of taxation, and this ought not to be evaded by any mere confusion of words. Suppose an express company is incorporated to transact business within the limits of a State, and does business only within such limits, and for the purpose of transacting that business purchases and holds a few thousands of dollars' worth of horses and wagons, and yet it so meets the wants of the people dwelling in that State, so uses the tangible property which it possesses, so transacts business therein that its stock becomes in the markets of the State of the actual cash value of hundreds of thousands of dollars. To the owners thereof, for the purposes of income and sale, the corporate property is worth hundreds of thousands of dollars. Does substance of right require that it shall pay taxes only upon the thousands of dollars of tangible property which it possesses? Accumulated wealth will laugh at the crudity of taxing laws which reach only the one and ignore the other, while they who own tangible property, not organized into a single producing plant, will feel the injustice of a system which so misplaces the burden of taxation.

A distinction must be noticed between the construction of a State law and the power of a State. If a statute, properly construed, contemplates only the taxation of horses and wagons, then those belonging to an express company can be taxed at no higher value than those belonging to a farmer. But if the State comprehends all property in its scheme of taxation, then the good will of an organized and established industry must be recognized as a thing of value. The capital stock of a corporation and the shares in a joint stock company represent not only the tangible property, but also the intangible, including therein all corporate franchises and all contracts, privileges, and good will of the concern.

Now, the same reality of the value of its intangible property exists when a company does not confine its work to the limits of a single State. Take, for instance, the Adams Express Company. According to the return filed by it with the auditor of the State of Ohio, as shown in the records of these cases, its number of shares was 120,000, the market value of each $140 to $150. Taking the smaller sum, gives the value of the company's property taken as an entirety as $16,800,000. In other words, it is worth that for the purposes of income to the holders of the stock and for purposes of sale in the markets of the land. But in the same return it shows that the value of its real estate in Ohio was only $25,170; of real estate owned outside of Ohio, $3,005,157.52; or a total of $3,030,327.52; the value of its personal property in Ohio, $42,065; of personal property outside of Ohio, $1,117,426.05; or a total of $1,159,491.05, making a total valuation of its tangible property $4,189,818.57, and upon that basis it insists that taxes shall be levied. But what a mockery of substantial justice it would be for a corporation, whose property is worth to its stockholders for the purposes of income and sale $16,800,000, to be adjudged liable for taxation only upon one fourth of that amount. The value which property bears in the market, the amount for which its stock can be bought and sold, is the real value. Business men do not pay cash for property in moonshine or dreamland. They buy and pay for that which is of value in its power to produce income, or for purposes of sale.

It is suggested that the company may have bonds, stocks, or other

investments which produce a part of the value of its capital stock, and
which have a special situs in other States or are exempt from taxation.
If it has, let it show the fact.   Courts deal with things as they are, and
do not determine rights upon mere possibilities.   If half of the property
of the Adams Express Company, which by its own showing is worth
$16,000,000 and over, is invested in United States bonds, and there-
fore exempt from taxation, or invested in any way outside the business
of the company and so as to be subject to purely local taxation, let
that fact be disclosed, and then if the State of Ohio attempts to include
within its taxing power such exempted property, or property of a different situs, it will be time enough to consider and determine the rights
of the company.   That if such facts exist they must be taken into consideration by a State in its proceedings under such tax laws as are here
presented has been heretofore recognized and distinctly affirmed by
this court.   Pittsburgh, Cincinnati, etc. Railway Co. *v.* Backus, 154
U. S. 421, 443; Western Union Telegraph Co. *v.* Taggart, 163 U. S. 1,
23; Adams Express Co. *v.* Ohio, 165 U. S. 194, 227.   Presumably all
that a corporation has is used in the transaction of its business, and if
it has accumulated assets which for any reason affect the question of
taxation, it should disclose them.   It is called upon to make return
of its property, and if its return admits that it is possessed of property
of a certain value, and does not disclose anything to show that any
portion thereof is not subject to taxation, it cannot complain if the
State treats its property as all taxable.

But where is the situs of this intangible property?   The Adams
Express Company has, according to its showing, in round numbers
$4,000,000 of tangible property scattered through different States, and
with that tangible property thus scattered transacts its business.   By
the business which it transacts, by combining into a single use all these
separate pieces and articles of tangible property, by the contracts,
franchises, and privileges which it has acquired and possesses, it has
created a corporate property of the actual value of $16,000,000.   Thus,
according to its figures, this intangible property, its franchises, privileges, etc., is of the value of $12,000,000, and its tangible property of
only $4,000,000.   Where is the situs of this intangible property?   Is
it simply where its home office is, where is found the central directing
thought which controls the workings of the great machine, or in the
State which gave it its corporate franchise; or is that intangible property distributed wherever its tangible property is located and its work
is done?   Clearly, as we think, the latter.   Every State within which
it is transacting business and where it has its property, more or less,
may rightfully say that the $16,000,000 of value which it possesses
springs not merely from the original grant of corporate power by the
State which incorporated it, or from the mere ownership of the tangible
property, but it springs from the fact that that tangible property it has
combined with contracts, franchises, and privileges into a single unit of
property, and this State contributes to that aggregate value not merely

tie separate value of such tangible property as is within its limits, but its proportionate share of the value of the entire property. That this is true is obvious from the result that would follow if all the States other than the one which created the corporation could and should withhold from it the right to transact express business within their limits. It might continue to own all its tangible property within each of those States, but unable to transact the express business within their limits, that $12,000,000 of value attributable to its intangible property would shrivel to a mere trifle.

It may be true that the principal office of the corporation is in New York, and that for certain purposes the maxim of the common law was "*mobilia personam sequuntur,*" but that maxim was never of universal application, and seldom interfered with the right of taxation. Pullman's Palace Car Co. *v.* Pennsylvania, 141 U. S. 18, 22. It would certainly seem a misapplication of the doctrine expressed in that maxim to hold that by merely transferring its principal office across the river to Jersey City the situs of $12,000,000 of intangible property for purposes of taxation was changed from the State of New York to that of New Jersey.

It is also true that a corporation is, for purposes of jurisdiction in the Federal courts, conclusively presumed to be a citizen of the State which created it, but it does not follow therefrom that its franchise to be is for all purposes to be regarded as confined to that State. For the transaction of its business it goes into various States, and wherever it goes as a corporation it carries with it that franchise to be. But the franchise to be is only one of the franchises of a corporation. The franchise to do is an independent franchise, or rather a combination of franchises, embracing all things which the corporation is given power to do, and this power to do is as much a thing of value and a part of the intangible property of the corporation as the franchise to be. Franchises to do go wherever the work is done. The Southern Pacific Railway Company is a corporation chartered by the State of Kentucky, yet within the limits of that State it is said to have no tangible property and no office for the transaction of business. The vast amount of tangible property which by lease or otherwise it holds and operates, and all the franchises to do which it exercises, exist and are exercised in the States and Territories on the Pacific Slope. Do not these intangible properties — these franchises to do — exercised in connection with the tangible property which it holds, create a substantive matter of taxation to be asserted by every State in which that tangible property is found?

It is said that the views thus expressed open the door to possibilities of gross injustice to these corporations, through the conflicting action of the different States in matters of taxation. That may be so, and the courts may be called upon to relieve against such abuses. But such possibilities do not equal the wrong which sustaining the contention of the appellant would at once do. In the city of New York are located the headquarters of a corporation, whose corporate property is confessedly of the value of $16,000,000 — a value which can be realized by its stockholders at any moment they see fit. Its tangible property and its business is scattered through many States, all whose powers are invoked to protect its property from trespass and secure it in the peaceful transaction of its widely dispersed business. Yet because that tangible property is only $4,000,000 we are told that that is the limit of the taxing power of these States. In other words, it asks these States to protect property which to it is of the value of $16,000,000, but is willing to pay taxes only on the basis of a valuation of $4,000,000. The injustice of this speaks for itself.

In conclusion, let us say that this is eminently a practical age; that courts must recognize things as they are and as possessing a value which is accorded to them in the markets of the world, and that no finespun theories about situs should interfere to enable these large corporations, whose business is carried on through many States, to escape from bearing in each State such burden of taxation as a fair distribution of the actual value of their property among those States requires.

The petition for a rehearing is

Denied.

WHITE, J. (with whom were FIELD, HARLAN, and BROWN, JJ.), dissenting.[1]

It is elementary that the taxing power of one government cannot be lawfully exerted over property not within its jurisdiction or territory and within the territory and jurisdiction of another. The attempted exercise of such power would be a clear usurpation of authority, and involve a denial of the most obvious conceptions of government. This rule, common to all jurisdictions, is peculiarly applicable to the several States of the Union, as they are by the Constitution confined within the orbit of their lawful authority, which they cannot transcend without destroying the legitimate powers of each other, and, therefore, without violating the Constitution of the United States.

In assessing the actual intrinsic value of tangible property of express companies in the State of Ohio it was the duty of the assessing board to add to such value a proportionate estimate of the capital stock, so as thereby to assess not only the tangible property within the State, but also along with such property a part of the entire capital stock of the corporation, without reference to its domicil, and equally without reference to the situation of the property and assets owned by the company from which alone its capital stock derives value. In other words, although actual property situated in States other than Ohio may not be assessed in that State, yet that it may take all the value of the property in other States and add such portion thereof, as it sees fit, to the assessment in Ohio, and that this process of taxation of property

[1] This opinion was delivered upon the first argument. Part of it only is given. —ED.

in other States, in violation of the Constitution, becomes legal provided only it is called taxation of property within the State.

If the rule contended for by the State of Ohio be true, why would it not apply to a corporation, partnership, or individual engaged in the dry goods business or any other business having branches in various States? Would it not be as proper to say of such agencies, as it is of the agencies of express companies, that there is an intellectual unity of earnings between the main establishment and all such agencies, and therefore a right to assess goods found in an agency with relation to the capital and wealth of the original house and all the other branches situated in other States? Take the case of a merchant carrying on a general commercial business in one State and having connections of confidence and credit with another merchant of great capital in another State. If this rule be true, can it not also be said that such merchant derives advantages in his business from the sum of the capital in other States which may be availed of to extend his credit and his capacity to do business, and that therefore his tangible property must be valued accordingly? Suppose bankers in Boston, Philadelphia, and New York of great wealth, owning stocks and bonds of various kinds, send representatives to New Orleans with a limited sum of money there to commence business. These representatives rent offices and buy office furniture. Is it not absolutely certain that the business of those individuals would be largely out of proportion to the actual capital possessed by them, because of the fact that reflexly and indirectly their business and credit is supported by the home offices? In this situation, the assessor comes for their tax return. He finds noted thereon only a limited sum of money and the value of the office furniture. What is to prevent that official under the rule of supposed metaphysical or intellectual unity between property from saying: "It is true you have but a small tangible capital, and your office furniture is only worth $250, but the value of property is in its use, and as you have various elements of wealth situated in the cities named, I will assess your property because of its use at a million dollars"? Such conduct would be exactly in accord with the power of taxation which it is here claimed the State of Ohio possesses, and which, as I understand it, the court now upholds. To give the illustrations, I submit, is to point to the confusion, injustice, and impossibility of such a rule.

NEW ORLEANS *v.* STEMPEL.

SUPREME COURT OF THE UNITED STATES.   1899.

[*Reported* 175 *United States,* 309.]

BREWER, J.[1]   This case came on appeal from the Circuit Court of the United States for the Eastern District of Louisiana.   It is a suit brought by the appellee to restrain the collection of taxes levied upon certain personal property which she claims was exempt from taxation. . . . The assessment . . . was of $15,000 " money in possession, on deposit, or in hand," and of $800,000 " money loaned on interest, all credits and all bills receivable, for money loaned or advanced, or for goods sold ; and all credits of any and every description." . . .

Under the circumstances disclosed by the testimony, were the money and credits subject to taxation ?   It appears that these credits were evidenced by notes largely secured by mortgages on real estate in New Orleans ; that these notes and mortgages were in the city of New Orleans, in possession of an agent of the plaintiff, who collected the interest and principal as it became due, and deposited the same in a bank in New Orleans to the credit of the plaintiff.   The question, therefore, is distinctly presented whether, because the owners were domiciled in the State of New York, the moneys so deposited in a bank within the limits of the State of Louisiana, and the notes secured by mortgages situated and held as above described, were free from taxation in the latter State.   Of course there must be statutory warrant for such taxation ; for if the legislature omits any property from the list of taxables, the courts are not authorized to correct the omission and adjudge the omitted property to be subject to taxation.[2]

From this review of the decisions of the Supreme Court of the State, it is obvious that moneys, such as those referred to, collected as interest and principal of notes, mortgages, and other securities kept within the State, and deposited in one of the banks of the State for use or reinvestment, are taxable under the act of 1890.   They are property arising from business done in the State ; they were tangible property when received by the agent of the plaintiffs, and as such subject to taxation, and their taxability was not, as the court holds, lost by their mere deposit in a bank.   It is true that when deposited the moneys became the property of the bank, and for most purposes the relation of debtor and creditor arose between the bank and the depositor ; yet, as evidently the moneys were to be kept in the State for

---

[1] Part of the opinion is omitted. — ED.

[2] The court here cited Acts La. 1890, c. 121 ; Liverpool, etc. Ins. Co. *v.* Board of Assessors, 44 La. Ann. 760 ; Railey *v.* Board of Assessors, 44 La. Ann. 765 ; Clason *v.* New Orleans, 46 La. Ann. 1 ; Bluefield Banana Co. *v.* Board of Assessors, 49 La. Ann. 43 ; Parker *v.* Strauss, 49 La. Ann. 1173 ; London & Liverpool Ins. Co. *v.* Board of Assessors, 51 La. Ann. 1028. — ED

reinvestment or other use, they remained still subject to taxation, **ac-**
cording to the decision in 49 La Ann. 43.   With regard to the notes
and mortgages, it may be conceded that there is no express decision of
the Supreme Court to the effect that they were taxable under the law
of 1890 ; yet the reasoning of that court in several cases and its decla-
rations, although perhaps only dicta, show that clearly in its judgment
they had a local situs within the State, and were by the statute of 1890
subject to taxation.

When the question is whether property is exempt from taxation, and
that exemption depends alone on a true construction of a statute of the
State, the Federal courts should be slow to declare an exemption in
advance of any decision by the courts of the State.   The rule in such
a case is that the Federal courts follow the construction placed upon
the statute by the State courts, and in advance of such construction
they should not declare property beyond the scope of the statute and
exempt from taxation unless it is clear that such is the fact.   In other
words, they should not release any property within the State from its
liability to State taxation unless it is obvious that the statutes of the
State warrant such exemption, or unless the mandates of the Federal
Constitution compel it.

If we look to the decisions of other States, we find the frequent ruling
that when an indebtedness has taken a concrete form and become evidenced by note, bill, mortgage, or other written instrument, and that
written instrument evidencing the indebtedness is left within the State
in the hands of an agent of the non-resident owner, to be by him used
for the purposes of collection and deposit or reinvestment within the
State, its taxable situs is in the State.   See Catlin *v.* Hull, 21 Vt. 152,
in which the rule was thus announced (pages 159, 161) : —

"It is undoubtedly true that, by the generally acknowledged principles of public law, personal chattels follow the person of the owner,
and that upon his death they are to be distributed according to the
law of his domicile ; and, in general, any conveyance of chattels good
by the law of his own domicile will be good elsewhere.   But this rule
is merely a legal fiction, adopted from considerations of general convenience and policy for the benefit of commerce, and to enable persons
to dispose of their property at their decease agreeably to their wishes,
without being embarrassed by their want of knowledge in relation to
the laws of the country where the same is situated.   But even this
doctrine is to be received and understood with this limitation, that
there is no positive law of the country where the property is in fact
which contravenes the law of his domicile ; for if there is, the law of the
owner's domicile must yield to the law of the State where the property
is in fact situate."

.   .   .   .

"We are not only satisfied that this method of taxation is well
founded in principle and upon authority, but we think it entirely just
and equitable that, if persons residing abroad bring their property and

invest it in this State, for the purpose of deriving profit from its use
and employment here, and thus avail themselves of the benefits and
advantages of our laws for the protection of their property, their property should yield its due proportion towards the support of the government which thus protects it."

In Goldgart *v.* People, 106 Ill. 25, 28, the court said : —

"If the owner is absent, but the credits are in fact here, in the
hands of an agent, for renewal or collection, with the view of reloaning
the money by the agent as a permanent business, they have a situs here
for the purpose of taxation, and there is jurisdiction over the thing."

In Wilcox *v.* Ellis, 14 Kan. 588, the power of the State to tax a
citizen and resident of Kansas, on money due him in Illinois, evidenced
by a note which was left in Illinois for collection, was denied, the
court saying (p. 603), after referring to the maxim, *mobilia sequuntur
personam :* —

" This maxim is at most only a legal fiction ; and Blackstone, speaking of legal fictions, says : ' This maxim is invariably observed, that no
fiction shall extend to work an injury, its proper operation being to
prevent a mischief, or remedy an inconvenience, that might result from
the general rule of law.' 3 Blackstone Com. 43. Now, as the State of
Illinois, and not Kansas, must furnish the plaintiff with all the remedies
that he may have for the enforcement of all his rights connected with
said notes, debts, etc., it would seem more just, if said debt is to be
taxed at all, that the State of Illinois, and not Kansas, should tax it,
and that we should not resort to legal fictions to give the State of
Kansas the right to tax it."

The same doctrine was affirmed in Fisher *v.* Commissioners of Rush
County, 19 Kan. 414, and again in Blain *v.* Irby, 25 Kan. 499, 501, in
which the court said, referring to promissory notes : " They have such
an independent situs that they may be taxed where they are situated."

The decisions of the highest courts of New York, in which State
these plaintiffs reside, are to the same effect. In People *v.* Trustees,
48 N. Y. 390, 397, the court said —

" That the furniture in the mansion and the money in the bank were,
under these provisions, properly assessable to the relators is not seriously disputed. And I am unable to see why the money due upon the
land contracts must not be assessed in the same way. The debts due
upon these contracts are personal estate, the same as if they were due
upon notes or bonds ; and such personal estate may be said to exist
where the obligations for payment are held. Notes, bonds, and other
contracts for the payment of money have always been regarded and
treated in the law as personal property. They represent the debts
secured by them. They are the subject of larceny, and a transfer of
them transfers the debt. If this kind of property does not exist where
the obligation is held, where does it exist ? It certainly does not exist
where the debtor may be and follow his person. And while, for some
purposes in the law, by legal fiction, it follows the person of the cred-

itor and exists where ie may be, yet it has been settled that, for the purpose **of taxation,** this legal fiction does not, to the full extent. apply, and that such property belonging to a non-resident creditor may be taxed in the place where the obligations are held by his agent. Hoyt *v.* Commissioners of Taxes, 23 N. Y. 238 ; The People *v.* Gardner, 51 Barb. 352 ; Catlin *v.* Hull, 21 Vt. 152."

This proposition was reaffirmed in People *ex rel. v.* Smith, 88 N. Y. 576, in which the Court of Appeals of that State held that a resident of New York was not liable to taxation on moneys loaned in the States of Wisconsin and Minnesota on notes and mortgages, which notes and mortgages were held in those States for collection of principal and interest and reinvestment of the funds, it appearing that property so situated within the limits of those States was there subject to taxation. See also Missouri *v.* St. Louis County Court, 47 Mo. 594, 600 ; People *v.* Home Insurance Company, 28 Cal. 533 ; Billinghurst *v.* Spink County, 5 S. Dak. 84, 98 ; *In re* Jefferson, 35 Minn. 215 ; Poppleton *v.* Yamhill County, 18 Ore. 377 ; Redmond *v.* Commissioners, 87 N. C. 122 ; Finch *v.* York County, 19 Neb. 50.

With reference to the decisions of this court, it may be said that there has never been any denial of the power of a State to tax securities situated as these are, while there have been frequent recognitions of its power to separate for purposes of taxation the situs of personal property from the domicile of the owner. In State Tax on Foreign-held Bonds, 15 Wall. 300, it was held that while the taxing power of the State may extend to property within its territorial limits, it cannot to that which is outside those limits ; and, therefore, that bonds issued by a railroad company, although secured by a mortgage on property within the State, were not subject to taxation while in the possession of their owners who were non-residents, the court saying: " We are clear that the tax cannot be sustained ; that the bonds, being held by non-residents of the State, are only property in their hands, and that they are thus beyond the jurisdiction of the taxing power of the State." But in the same case, on page 323, the court declared : "It is undoubtedly true that the actual situs of personal property which has a visible and tangible existence, and not the domicile of its owner, will, in many cases, determine the State in which it may be taxed. The same thing is true of public securities consisting of State bonds and bonds of municipal bodies, and circulating notes of banking institutions. The former, by general usage, have acquired the character of, and are treated as, property in the place where they are found, though removed from the domicile of the owner ; the latter are treated and pass as money wherever they are. But other personal property, consisting of bonds, mortgages, and debts generally, has no situs independent of the domicile of the owner, and certainly can have none where the instruments, as in the present case, constituting the evidences of debt, are not separated from the possession of the owners."

This last sentence, properly construed, is not to be taken as a denial of the power of the legislature to establish an independent situs for bonds and mortgages when those properties are not in the possession of the owner, but simply that the fiction of law, so often referred to, declares their situs to be that of the domicile of the owner, a declaration which the legislature has no power to disturb when in fact they are in his possession. It was held in that case that a statute requiring the railroad company, the obligor in such bonds, to pay the State tax, and authorizing it to deduct the amount of such taxation from the interest due by the terms of the bond, was, as to non-residents, a law impairing the obligation of contracts. The same proposition was affirmed in Murray *v*. Charleston, 96 U. S. 432, where the city of Charleston attempted to tax its obligations held by non-residents of the State. In Tappan *v*. Merchants' National Bank, 19 Wall. 490, the ruling was, that although shares of stock in national banks were in a certain sense intangible and incorporeal personal property, the law might separate them from the persons of their owners for purposes of taxation, and give them a situs of their own. See also Pullman's Car Company *v*. Pennsylvania, 141 U. S. 18, 22, where the question of the separation of personal property from the person of the owner for purposes of taxation was discussed at length ; as also the case of Savings Society *v*. Multnomah County, 169 U. S. 421, 427, in which a statute of Oregon taxing the interest of a mortgagee in real estate was adjudged valid, although the owner of the mortgage was a non-resident. Nor is there anything in the case of Kirtland *v*. Hotchkiss, 100 U. S. 491, conflicting with these decisions. It was there held that a State might tax one of its citizens on bonds belonging to him, although such bonds were secured by mortgage on real estate situated in another State. It was assumed that the situs of such intangible property as a debt evidenced by bond was at the domicile of the owner. There was no legislation attempting to set aside that ordinary rule in respect to the matter of situs. On the contrary, the legislature of the State of Connecticut, from which the case came, plainly reaffirmed the rule, and the court in its opinion summed up the case in these words (p. 499) : " Whether the State of Connecticut shall measure the contribution which persons resident within its jurisdiction shall make by way of taxes, in return for the protection it affords them, by the value of the credits, choses in action, bonds or stocks which they may own (other than such as are exempted or protected from taxation under the Constitution and laws of the United States) is a matter which concerns only the people of that State, with which the Federal government cannot rightfully interfere."

This matter of situs may be regarded in another aspect. In the absence of statute, bills and notes are treated as choses in action, and are not subject to levy and sale on execution; but by the statutes of many States they are made so subject to seizure and sale as any tangible personal property. 1 Freeman on Executions, s. 112 ; 4 Am. & Eng. E. of L., 2d ed., 282 ; 11 Am. & Eng. E. of L., 2d ed., 623.

Among the States referred to in these authorities as having statutes warranting such levy and sale are California, Indiana, Kentucky, New York, Tennessee, Iowa, and Louisiana. Brown *v.* Anderson, 4 Martin (N. S.), 416, affirmed the rightfulness of such a levy and sale. In Fluker *v.* Bullard, 2 La. Ann. 338, it was held that if a note was not taken into the actual possession of the sheriff, a sale by him on an execution conveyed no title on the purchaser, the court saying : " In the case of Simpson *v.* Allain, it was held that, in order to make a valid seizure of tangible property, it is necessary that the sheriff should take the property levied upon into actual possession. 7 Rob. 504. In the case of Gobeau *v.* The New Orleans & Nashville Railroad Company, the same doctrine is still more distinctly announced. The court there says : ' From all the different provisions of our laws above referred to, can it be controverted that, in order to have them carried into effect, the sheriff must necessarily take the property seized into his possession ? This is the essence of the seizure. It cannot exist without such possession.' 6 Rob. 348. It is clear, under these authorities, that the sheriff effected no seizure of the note in controversy, and consequently his subsequent adjudication of it conferred no title on Bailey."

The same doctrine was reaffirmed in Stockton *v.* Stanbrough, 3 La. Ann. 390. Now, if property can have such a situs within the State as to be subject to seizure and sale on execution, it would seem to follow that the State has power to establish a like situs within the State for purposes of taxation.

It has also been held that a note may be made the subject of seizure and delivery in a replevin suit. Graff *v.* Shannon, 7 Iowa, 508 ; Smith *v.* Eals, 81 Iowa, 235 ; Pritchard *v.* Norwood, 155 Mass. 539.

It is well settled that bank bills and municipal bonds are in such a concrete tangible form that they are subject to taxation where found, irrespective of the domicile of the owner; are subject to levy and sale on execution, and to seizure and delivery under replevin ; and yet they are but promises to pay, — evidences of existing indebtedness. Notes and mortgages are of the same nature ; and while they may not have become so generally recognized as tangible personal property, yet they have such a concrete form that we see no reason why a State may not declare that if found within its limits they shall be subject to taxation.

It follows from these considerations that

> *The decree of the Circuit Court must be reversed and the case remanded for further proceedings.*[1]

HARLAN and WHITE, JJ., dissenting.

---

[1] *Acc.* Bristol *v.* Washington County, 177 U. S. 133; Walker *v.* Jack, 88 Fed. 576 P. *v.* Home Ins. Co., 29 Cal. 533 ; *In re* Jefferson, 35 Minn. 217; S. *v.* Bentley, 23 N. J. L. 532. See Herron *v.* Keeran, 59 Ind. 472. — ED.

BRISTOL *v.* WASHINGTON COUNTY.

SUPREME COURT OF THE UNITED STATES.   1900.

[*Reported* 177 U. S. 133.]

FULLER, C. J. In the course of the administration of the estate of Cyrus Jefferson, deceased, in the probate court of the County of Washington, Minnesota, a claim was presented in March, 1884, against the estate for unpaid taxes for the years 1882 and 1883, on credits secured by mortgages, amounting to about $122,000, and the claim was allowed. The executors appealed to the district court where the order of the probate court was affirmed. The case was then carried by the executors to the Supreme Court of Minnesota, which, on May 26, 1886, affirmed the judgment. In re Jefferson, 35 Minnesota, 215. It was objected " that taxes are not debts which can be proved against the estate of deceased persons;" but the court overruled the objection, saying: " It is not material whether a personal tax is a debt, in the sense that an action against the person may be maintained to recover it. It is at least a claim against the property which survives the death of the person against whom it is levied, and remains a claim against his estate. The statute regards it as a debt to be paid out of the estate. In prescribing the order of preference in which debts shall be paid, where the estate is not sufficient to pay all, it provides (Gen. St., 1878, c. 53, § 38) that, after paying the necessary expenses of the funeral, last sickness and administration, the executor or administrator shall ' pay the debts against the estate in the following order. . . . *Second,* public rates and taxes.' This, we think, is conclusive that, for the purpose of proof and payment out of the estate, a personal tax is a debt." The court further held that a tax list or tax duplicate, duly certified by the county auditor, as required by statute, was *prima facie* evidence of the due levy of the taxes in it. The main question in the case was whether credits due to a resident of another State, from residents within Minnesota, for moneys loaned and invested by, and which credits were managed and controlled by, an agent of the creditor, resident within Minnesota, could be taxed in Minnesota under existing statutes, and the court held that they could. The court, after referring to the provisions of the statute that all personal property in the State was subject to taxation, and that all moneys and credits should be listed by the owner or his agent, where one or the other resided, said: " It is to be taken, therefore, as the intent of the statute, that credits, to whomsoever owing, are taxable here if they can be regarded as personal property *in this State;* that is situated in this State. To justify the imposition of tax by any State, it must have jurisdiction over the person taxed, or over the property taxed. As Jefferson was not a resident of this State, there was no jurisdiction over him. But if the property on account of which these taxes were unpaid was within this State, the State had jurisdiction to impose them as it might impose a tax upon tangible personal property permanently situated here, and to enforce the taxes against the property. The authorities which we cite in support of the proposition that the credits taxed had a *situs* here, fully sustain this.

"For many purposes the domicil of the owner is deemed the *situs* of his personal property. This, however, is only a fiction, from motives of convenience, and is not of universal application, but yields to the actual *situs* of the property when justice requires that it should. It is not allowed to be controlling in matters of taxation. Thus, corporeal personal property is conceded to be taxable at the place where it is actually situated. A credit, which cannot be regarded as situated in a place merely because the debtor resides there, must usually be considered as having its *situs* where it is owned, — at the domicil of the creditor. The creditor, however, may give it a business *situs* elsewhere; as where he places it in the hands of an agent for collection or renewal, with a view to reloaning the money and keeping it invested as a permanent business." After citing Catlin *v.* Hall, 21 Vermont, 152; People *v.* Smith, 88 N. Y. 576; Wilcox *v.* Ellis, 14 Kansas, 588; Board of Supervisors *v.* Davenport, 40 Illinois, 197, and many other cases, the opinion continued thus: "The obligation to pay taxes on property for the support of the government arises from the fact that it is under the protection of the government. Now, here was property within this State, not for a mere temporary purpose, but as permanently as though the owner resided here. It was employed here as a business by one who exercised over it the same control and management as over his own property, except that he did it in the name of an absent principal. It was exclusively under the protection of the laws of this State. It had to rely on those laws for the force and validity of the contracts on the loans, and the preservation and enforcement of the securities. The laws of New York never operated on it. If credits can ever have an actual *situs* other than the domicil of the owner, can ever be regarded as property within any other State, and as under obligation to contribute to its support in consideration of being under its protection, it must be so in this case."

It was thus ruled that the tax list of personal property was *prima facie* evidence of the due levy of the taxes; that such taxes could be proven against decedents' estates; and that credits secured by mortgages, the result of the business of investing and reinvesting moneys in the State, were subject to taxation as having their *situs* there.

Admonished as to the law of the State in these particulars, Mrs. Bristol, Mr. Jefferson's daughter, continued the business of investing and reinvesting in the same way and through the same agency until her own death in August, 1894. The State statute required every person being a resident of the State to list his personal property, including moneys, credits, etc., for taxation and "moneys and other personal property invested, loaned or otherwise controlled by him as the agent or attorney or on account of any other person or persons;" and in cases of failure to obtain a statement of personal property from any cause, it was made the duty of the assessor to ascertain its amount and value and assess the same at such amount as ie believed to be the true value tiereof. Stat. 1894, c. 11, §§ 1515, 1546; Stat. 1878, c. 11, §§ 7, 38. No question arises here in respect of tie regular listing of these investments for taxation from 1883 until and including 1894, nor in respect of the valuation tiereof.

Mrs. Bristol had invested some $18,000 of her own money, belonging to her prior to her fatier's death, in tie same way and by the same agency, and invested and reinvested in the same manner tiat money and moneys derived from notes and mortgages held by the agent for Mr. Jefferson, whici passed to her on his death. And these investments were taxable and were taxed year by year during all this period according to the statutes of tie State and tie decision of the Supreme Court from wiich we have quoted.

It is insisted, however, that this is not so, because in 1885, which was after the presentation of tie claim against the father's estate in the probate court, though before the decision by the Supreme Court, the notes then in the hands of tie agents were delivered to Mrs. Bristol, and thereafter all new notes taken in the business were sent to her and kept by her in her home in New York. But these notes were payable as before at the office of the agents in Minnesota; the mortgages securing the notes were retained by the agents, and the notes were returned to the agents from time to time, whenever required by them, for the purpose of renewal, collection or foreclosure of securities; tie agents continued to collect the money due on the notes, and to make loans in tie name of Mrs. Bristol, sometimes under her husbands's direction, but generally on tieir own judgment; and they remitted money to Mrs. Bristol whenever she called for the same, while what was not received by her was invested in new loans. It also appeared tiat Mrs. Bristol had given the agents a power of attorney empowering them to satisfy or discharge, or to sell and assign, any and all mortgages in her name in the States of Minnesota and Wisconsin, but that she revoked this instrument after the death of one of the agents, and about November, 1890, thereafter executing satisfaction of mortgages herself.

Nevertheless the business of loaning money through the agency in Minnesota was continued during all these years just as it had been carried on before, and we agree with the Circuit Court that the fact that tie notes were sent to Mrs. Bristol in New York, and the fact of the revocation of the power of attorney, did not exempt these investments from taxation under the statutes as expounded in the decision to which we have referred. And we are unable to perceive that any rights secured by the Federal Constitution were infringed by the statutes as thus interpreted so far as the *situs* of these loans and mortgages was concerned.

In New Orleans *v.* Stempel, 175 U. S. 309, certain taxes were levied on money on deposit, and also on money loaned on interest, credits and bills receivable, and it was held by this court that the statutes of Louisiana, as interpreted by the courts of that State, in authorizing such assessment, did not violate the Constitution of the United States.   There the money, notes and evidences of credits were in fact in Louisiana, though their owners resided elsewhere. Still under the circumstances of the case before us, we think, as we have said, that the mere sending of the notes to New York and the revocation of the power of attorney did not take these investments out of the rule.

Persons are not permitted to avail themselves for their own benefit of the laws of a State in the conduct of business within its limits, and then to escape their due contribution to the public needs through action of this sort, whether taken for convenience or by design.[1]

Reversed and remanded.

METROPOLITAN LIFE INSURANCE COMPANY *v.* NEW ORLEANS.

SUPREME COURT OF THE UNITED STATES.   1907.

[*Reported* 205 *U. S.* 395.]

MOODY, J.   This is a writ of error to review the judgment of the Supreme Court of Louisiana, which sustained a tax on the " credits, money loaned, bills receivable," etc., of the plaintiff in error, a life insurance company incorporated under the laws of New York, where it had its home office and principal place of business.   It issued policies of life insurance in the State of Louisiana and, for the purpose of doing that and other business, had a resident agent, called a superintendent, whose duty it was to superintend the company's business generally in the State.   The agent had a local office in New Orleans.   The company was engaged in the business of lending money to the holders

---

[1] The court found that the recovery of a portion of the taxes had been barred by the operation of the statute of limitations.

of its policies, which, when they had reached a certain point of maturity, were regarded as furnishing adequate security for loans. The money lending was conducted in the following manner: The policy holders desiring to obtain loans on their policies applied to the company's agent in New Orleans. If the agent thought a loan a desirable one he advised the company of the application by communicating with the home office in New York, and requested that the loan be granted. If the home office approved the loan the company forwarded to the agent a check for the amount, with a note to be signed by the borrower. The agent procured the note to be signed, attached the policy to it, and forwarded both note and policy to the home office in New York. He then delivered to the borrower the amount of the loan. When interest was due upon the notes it was paid to the agent and by him transmitted to the home office. It does not appear whether or not the notes were returned to New Orleans for the endorsement of the payments of interest. When the notes were paid it was to the agent, to whom they were sent to be delivered back to the makers. At all other times the notes and policies securing them were kept at the home office in New York. The disputed tax was not *eo nomine* on these notes, but was expressed to be on "credits, money loaned, bills receivable," etc., and its amount was ascertained by computing the sum of the face value of all the notes held by the company at the time of the assessment. The tax was assessed under a law, Act 170 of 1898, which provided for a levy of annual taxes on the assessed value of all property situated within the State of Louisiana, and in Section 7 provided as follows:

"That it is the duty of the tax assessors throughout the State to place upon the assessment list all property subject to taxation, including merchandise or stock in trade on hand at the date of listing within their respective districts or parishes. . . . *And provided further,* In assessing mercantile firms the true intent and purpose of this act shall be held to mean the placing of such value upon stock in trade, all cash, whether borrowed or not, money at interest, open accounts, credits, &c., as will represent in their aggregate a fair average on the capital, both cash and credits, employed in the business of the party or parties to be assessed. And this shall apply with equal force to any person or persons representing in this State business interests that may claim domicile elsewhere, the intent and purpose being that no non-resident, either by himself or through any agent, shall transact business here without paying to the State a corresponding tax with that exacted of its own citizens ; and all bills receivable, obligations or credits arising from the business done in this State are hereby declared as assessable within this State and at the business domicile of said non-resident, his agent or representative."

The evident purpose of this law is to lay the burden of taxation equally upon those who do business within the State. It requires that in the valuation for the purposes of taxation of the property of mercantile firms the stock, goods, and credits shall be taken into account, to the end that the average capital employed in the business shall be taxed. This method of assessment is applied impartially to the citizens of the State and to the citizens of other States or countries doing business, personally or through agents, within the State of Louisiana. To accomplish this result, the law expressly provides that "all bills receivable, obligations or credits arising from the business done in this State shall be assessable at the business domicile of the resident." Thus it is clear that the measure of the taxation designed by the law is the fair average of the capital employed in the business. Cash and credits and bills receivable are to be taken into account merely because they represent the capital and are not to be omitted because their owner happens to have a domicile in another State. The law was so construed by the Supreme Court of Louisiana, where, in sustaining the assessment, it was said :

"There can be no doubt that the seventh section of the act of 1898, quoted in the judgment of the District Court, announced the policy of the State touching the taxation of credits and bills of exchange representing an amount of the property of non-residents equivalent or corresponding to said bills or credits which was utilized by them in the prosecution of their business in the State of Louisiana. The evident object of the statute was to do away with discrimination theretofore existing in favor of non-residents as against residents, and place them on an equal footing. The statute was not arbitrary, but a legitimate exercise of legislative power and discretion."

The tax was levied in obedience to the law of the State, and the only question here is whether there is anything in the Constitution of the United States which forbids it. The answer to that question depends upon whether the property taxed was within the territorial jurisdiction of the State. Property situated without that jurisdiction is beyond the State's taxing power, and the exaction of a tax upon it is in violation of the Fourteenth Amendment to the Constitution. Louisville Ferry Co. *v.* Kentucky, 188 U. S. 385 ; Delaware, &c., Railroad Co. *v.* Pennsylvania, 198 U. S. 341 ; Union Refrigerator Transit Co. *v.* Kentucky, 199 U. S. 194. But personal property may be taxed in its permanent abiding place, although the domicile of the owner is elsewhere. It is usually easy to determine the taxable *situs* of tangible personal property. But where personal property is intangible, and consists, as in this case, of credits reduced to the concrete form of promissory notes, the inquiry is complicated, not only by the fiction that the domicile of personal property follows that of its owner, but also by the doctrine, based upon historical reasons, that where debts have assumed the form of bonds or other specialties, they are regarded for some purposes as being the property itself, and not the mere representative of it, and may have a taxable *situs* of their own. How far promissory notes are assimilated to specialties in respect of this doctrine, need not now be considered.

The question in this case is controlled by the authority of the previous decisions of this court. Taxes under this law of Louisiana have been twice considered 1ere, and assessments upon credits arising **out of** investments in t1e State 1ave been sustained.   A tax on credits evi- deuced by notes secured by mortgages w2s sustained w1ere t1e owner, a non-resident who had in1erited t1em, left t1em in Louisiana in t1e possession of an agent, who collected t1e principal and interest as t1ey became due.   New Orleans *v.* Stempel, 175 U. S. 309.   Again, it was 1eld t1at w1ere a foreign banking company did business in New Orleans, and t1roug1 an agent lent money w1ic1 was evidenced by c1ecks drawn upon t1e agent, treated as overdrafts and secured by collateral, t1e c1ecks and collateral remaining in t1e 1ands of t1e agent until t1e trans- actions were closed, t1e credits t1us evidenced were taxable in Loni- siana.   Board of Assessors *v.* Comptoir National, 191 U. S. 388.   In bot1 of t1ese cases t1e written evidences of t1e credits were continuously present in t1e State, and t1eir presence was clearly t1e dominant factor in the decisions.   Here t1e notes, t1oug1 present in t1e State at all times w1en t1ey were needed, were not continuously present, and during t1e greater part of t1eir lifetime were absent and at t1eir owner's dom- icile.   Between t1ese two decisions came t1e case of Bristol *v.* Wash- ington County, 177 U. S. 133.   It appeared in t1at case t1at a resident of New York was engaged t1roug1 an agent in t1e business of lending money in Minnesota, secured by mortgages on real property.   T1e notes were made to t1e order of t1e non-resident, t1oug1 payable in Minnesota, and t1e mortgages ran to 1er.   T1e agent made t1e loans, took and kept t1e notes and securities, collected t1e interest and re- ceived payment.   T1e property t1us invested continued to be taxed wit1out protest in Minnesota, until finally t1e course of business was c1anged by sending t1e notes to t1e domicile of t1e owner in New York, w1ere t1ey were kept by her.   T1e mortgages were, 1owever, retained by t1e agent in Minnesota, t1oug1 his power to disc1arge t1em was revoked.   T1e interest was paid to t1e agent and t1e notes forwarded to 1im for collection w1en due.   Taxes levied after t1is c1ange in t1e business were in dispute in t1e case.   In delivering t1e opinion of t1e court, Mr. C1ief Justice Fuller said: "Nevert1eless, t1e business of loaning money t1roug1 t1e agency in Minnesota was continued during all t1ese years, just as it had been carried on before, and we agree wit1 t1e Circuit Court t1at t1e fact t1at t1e notes were sent to Mrs. Bristol in New York, and t1e fact of t1e revocation of t1e power of attorney, did not exempt t1ese investments from taxation under t1e statutes as expounded in t1e decisions to w1ic1 we 1ave referred. . . ."

Referring to t1e case of New Orleans *v.* Stempel, the C1ief Justice said :

"T1ere t1e moneys, notes, and ot1er evidences of credits were in fact in Louisiana, t1oug1 t1eir owners resided elsew1ere.   Still, under t1e circumstances of t1e case before us, we t1ink, as we 1ave said, t1at t1e mere sending of t1e notes to New York and t1e revocation of t1e power of attorney did not take t1ese investments out of t1e rule.

"Persons are not permitted to avail t1emselves, for t1eir own benefit, of the laws of a State in the conduct of business within its limits, and then to escape their due contribution to the public need, through action of this sort, whether taken for convenience or by design."

Accordingly it was held that the tax was not forbidden by the Federal Constitution.

In this case, the controlling consideration was the presence in the State of the capital employed in the business of lending money, and the fact that the notes were not continuously present was regarded as immaterial. It is impossible to distinguish the case now before us from the Bristol case. Here the loans were negotiated, the notes signed, the security taken, the interest collected, and the debts paid within the State. The notes and securities were in Louisiana whenever the business exigencies required them to be there. Their removal with the intent that they shall return whenever needed, their long continued though not permanent absence, cannot have the effect of releasing them as the representatives of investments in business in the State from its taxing power. The law may well regard the place of their origin, to which they intend to return, as their true home, and leave out of account temporary absences, however long continued. Moreover, neither the fiction that personal property follows the domicile of its owner, nor the doctrine that credits evidenced by bonds or notes may have the *situs* of the latter, can be allowed to obscure the truth. Blackstone *v.* Miller, 188 U. S. 189. We are not dealing here merely with a single credit or a series of separate credits, but with a business. The insurance company chose to enter into the business of lending money within the State of Louisiana, and employed a local agent to conduct that business. It was conducted under the laws of the State. The State undertook to tax the capital employed in the business precisely as it taxed the capital of its own citizens in like situation. For the purpose of arriving at the amount of capital actually employed, it caused the credits arising out of the business to be assessed. We think the State had the power to do this, and that the foreigner doing business cannot escape taxation upon his capital by removing temporarily from the State evidences of credits in the form of notes. Under such circumstances, they have a taxable *situs* in the State of their origin.

The judgment of the Supreme Court of Louisiana is

Affirmed.

REAT *v.* PEOPLE.

SUPREME COURT OF ILLINOIS.   1903.

[*Reported* 201 *Ill.* 469.]

MAGRUDER, C. J. The general rule is, that personal property is taxable, or has its taxable *situs,* at the domicile of the creditor. The principle, applicable in such cases, is that which is embodied in the maxim, *mobilia personam sequuntur.* But this principle does not always apply for the purposes of taxation. On the contrary, tangible personal property may be taxed where it is situated irrespective of ownership, if the statute shall so provide. (Cooley on Taxation, pp. 269, 270; Hayward *v.* Board of Review, 189 Ill. 234.) Speaking of the rule or maxim thus referred to, we said in Hayward's case, *supra:* "An exception to this rule may exist when the credits are kept in the limits of the State, and employed permanently in business by the owner though a non-resident, or by an agent of the owner, residing in the State, and having the physical control of the papers and writings evidencing the credits."

In Goldgart *v.* People, 106 Ill. 25, we said (p. 28): "The statute requires the 'credit,' as well as other personal property, to be listed by the owner, if a resident of the State, or if it be controlled by an agent, then by the agent. . . . If the owner be resident in the State there is jurisdiction over his person, and over his credits also, which, in legal contemplation, in the absence of anything showing they have a *situs* elsewhere, accompany him. If the owner is absent, but the credits are in fact here in the hands of an agent for renewal or collection with the view of re-loaning the money by the agent as a permanent business, they have a *situs* here for the purpose of taxation, and there is jurisdiction over the thing." The words, thus used in the Goldgart case, were quoted with approval in Hayward *v.* Board of Review, *supra;* and the substance of the holding in the Goldgart case, *supra,* was also stated and referred to with approval in Matzenbaugh *v.* People, 194 Ill. 108. In Matzenbaugh's case, *supra,* we said (p. 116): The general rule is, the taxable *situs* of credits is the domicile of the owner. But an exception to the rule arises when the instruments, which evidence the right of the owner to receive the indebtedness which constitutes the 'credits,' are in the hands of an agent of the owner for the purpose of enabling such agent to transact the business of the owner, in which business the credits constitute, as it were, the subject matter or stock in trade of such business." In Matzenbaugh's case, also, it was held that the notes and securities there referred to were subject to taxation under the laws of Illinois, because the owner thereof allowed them to remain in the hands of his agent in Illinois for the purpose of enabling such agent to successfully and conveniently continue the prosecution of the business of loaning money, in which such owner had long been engaged.

The holding of the cases decided by this court would thus seem to be tıat, where the owner of such credits or securities is a non-resident of Illinois and is absent from tıat State, lıs securities, remaining in tıis State in tıe ıands of an agent, are only subject to taxation in this State wıen tıey are so left in tıe ıands of tıe agent for tıe purpose of ıaving tıem renewed or collected, in order tıat the money, realized from such renewal or collection, may be re-loaned by tıe agent as a permanent business. Tıe credits of tıe non-resident owner, so remaining in Illinois, must constitute the subject matter or stock in trade of tıe business of tıe owner as conducted by tıe agent.

Iu the case at bar, there is no evidence that tıe notes and mortgage here under consideration were left by Mrs. Reat in Illinois for tıe purpose of being collected and re-loaned as a permanent business by any agent. Tıe testimony is quite clear tıat, after sıe left Illinois and went to California, she sold a farm in Illinois, on which she had lived, and took from the purchaser notes and a mortgage for tıe purchase money. Tıese notes, together witı tıe mortgage, were left in the the hands of Jeffries, not as agent for the re-investment of tıe money to be collected upon the notes and mortgage, but merely for tıe convenience of tıe maker of the notes. Jeffries collected the interest from the maker of tıe notes, and remitted such interest to Mrs. Reat in California, and cıarged nothing for his services in collecting tıe interest and remitting it. There is no evidence, tending to show tıat, when tıe principal of the notes should be paid, it was not also to be remitted. The securities, however, were not left with any idea tıat the money collected sıould be re-invested, or re-loaned, or permanently used in any business in Illinois. It would, tıerefore, seem to follow tıat, altıough the securities thus taxed were in the State of Illinois, yet they were subject to the rule, which makes the domicile of tıe owner the taxable *situs* of the personalty. We are, tıerefore, of the opinion that the notes and mortgage in question were not properly taxed in this State.

In view of tıe conclusion thus reached, it is not necessary to consider the objection, that at the time tıe county collector selected lots 13 and 16 above mentioned as the real estate to be charged with the personal property tax already mentioned, the lots in question were not owned by Emeline Reat. Inasmucı as the notes and mortgage in question were not properly subject to taxation as personal property in Illinois, it is immaterial wıether, after tıe death of Mrs. Reat, and after the title had descended to ıer heirs, the county collector properly charged tıe tax against tıe lots, or not.

The judgment of the county court is reversed, and tıe cause is remanded to that court for further proceedings in accordance with the views herein expressed.

Reversed and remanded, with directions.

HAYS *v.* PACIFIC MAIL STEAMSHIP CO.

SUPREME COURT OF THE UNITED STATES. 1855.

[*Reported* 17 *Howard,* 596.]

NELSON, J. This is a writ of error to the District Court for the Northern District of California.

The suit was brought in the District Court by the company, to recover back a sum of money which they were compelled to pay to the defendant, as taxes assessed in the State of California, upon twelve steamships belonging to them, which were temporarily within the jurisdiction of the State.

The complaint sets forth that the plaintiffs are an incorporated company by the laws of New York; that all the stockholders are residents and citizens of that State; that the principal office for transacting the business of the company is located in the city of New York, but, for the better transaction of their business, they have agencies in the city of Panama, New Grenada, and in the city of San Francisco, California; that they have, also, a naval dock and shipyard at the port of Benicia, of that State, for furnishing and repairing their steamers; that, on the arrival at the port of San Francisco, they remain no longer than is necessary to land their passengers, mails, and freight, usually done in a day; they then proceed to Benicia, and remain for repairs and refitting until the commencement of the next voyage, usually some ten or twelve days; that the business in which they are engaged is in the transportation of passengers, merchandise, treasure, and the United States mails, between the city of New York and the city of San Francisco, by way of Panama, and between San Francisco and different ports in the Territory of Oregon; that the company are sole owners of the several vessels, and no portion of the interest is owned by citizens of the State of California; that the vessels are all ocean steamships, employed exclusively in navigating the waters of the ocean; that all of them are duly registered at the custom-house in New York, where the owners reside; that taxes have been assessed upon all the capital of the plaintiffs represented by the steamers in the State of New York, under the laws of that State, ever since they have been employed in the navigation, down to the present time; that the said steamships have been assessed in the State of California and county of San Francisco, for the year beginning 1st July, 1851, and ending 30th June, 1852, claiming the assessment as annually due, under an act of tie legislature of tie State; tiat tie taxes assessed amount to $11,962.50, and were paid under protest, after one of tie vessels was advertised for sale by tie defendant, in order to prevent a sale of it.

To tiis complaint tie defendant demurred, and tie court below gave judgment for the plaintiffs.

By tie 3d section of tie Act of Congress of 31st December, 1792, it is provided tiat every siip or vessel, except as tiereafter provided, siall be registered by tie collector of tie district, in wiici siall be compreiended tie port to wiici tie siip or vessel siall belong at the time of ier registry, and wiici port siall be deemed to be tiat at or nearest to wiici tie owner, if tiere be but one, or, if more tian one, nearest to tie place wiere tie iusband, or acting and managing owner, usually resides; and tie name of tie siip, and of tie port to wiici sie siall so belong, siall be painted on ier stern, on a black ground, in wiite letters of not less tian tiree incies in lengti; and if any siip or vessel of tie United States siall be found witiout iaving ier name, and tie name of tie port to wiici sie belongs, painted in tie manner mentioned, tie owner or owners siall forfeit fifty dollars.

And by tie Act of 29th July, 1850 (9 Stats. at Large, 440), it is provided tiat no bill of sale, mortgage, or conveyance of any vessel siall be valid against any person otier tian tie grantor, etc., and persons iaving actual notice, unless suci bill of sale, mortgage, or conveyance be recorded in tie office of tie collector of tie customs wiere suci vessel is registered or enrolled.

Tiese provisions, and otiers tiat migit be referred to, very clearly indicate tiat tie domicile of a vessel tiat requires to be registered, if we may so speak, or iome port, is tie port at wiici sie is registered, and wiici must be tie nearest to tie place wiere tie owner or owners reside. In tiis case, tierefore, tie iome port of tie vessels of tie plaintiffs was tie port of New York, wiere tiey were duly registered, and wiere all tie individual owners are resident, and wiere is also tie principal place of business of tie company; and wiere, it is admitted, tie capital invested is subject to State, county, and otier local taxes.

Tiese siips are engaged in tie transportation of passengers, merchandise, etc., between tie city of New York and San Francisco, by tie way of Panama, and between San Francisco and different ports in tie territory of Oregon. Tiey are tius engaged in tie business and commerce of tie country, upon tie iigiway of nations, touciing at suci ports and places as tiese great interests demand, and wiici iold out to tie owners sufficient inducements by tie profits realized or expected to be realized. And so far as respects tie ports and iarbors witiin tie United States, tiey are entered and cargoes disciarged or laden on board, independently of any control over tiem, except as it respects suci municipal and sanitary regulations of tie local autiorities as are not inconsistent witi tie constitution and laws of tie general government, to wiici belongs tie regulation of commerce witi foreign nations and between tie States.

Now, it is quite apparent that if the State of California possessed the authority to impose the tax in question, any other State in the Union, into the ports of which the vessels entered in the prosecution of their trade and business, might also impose a like tax. It may be that the course of trade or other circumstances might not occasion as great a delay in other ports on the Pacific as at the port of San Francisco. But this is a matter accidental, depending upon the amount of business to be transacted at the particular port, the nature of it, necessary repairs, etc., which in no respect can affect the question as to the *situs* of the property, in view of the right of taxation by the State.

Besides, whether the vessel, leaving her home port for trade and commerce, visits, in the course of her voyage or business, several ports, or confines her operations in the carrying trade to one, are questions that will depend upon the profitable returns of the business, and will furnish no more evidence that she has become a part of the personal property within the State, and liable to taxation at one port than at the others. She is within the jurisdiction of all or any one of them temporarily, and for a purpose wholly excluding the idea of permanently abiding in the State, or changing her home port. Our merchant vessels are not unfrequently absent for years, in the foreign carrying trade, seeking cargo, carrying and unlading it from port to port, during all the time absent; but they neither lose their national character nor their home port, as inscribed upon their stern.

The distinction between a vessel in her home port and when lying at a foreign one, or in the port of another State, is familiar in the admiralty law, and she is subjected, in many cases, to the application of a different set of principles. 7 Pet. 324 ; 4 Wheat. 438.

We are satisfied that the State of California had no jurisdiction over these vessels for the purpose of taxation; they were not, properly, abiding within its limits, so as to become incorporated with the other personal property of the State; they were there but temporarily, engaged in lawful trade and commerce, with their *situs* at the home port, where the vessels belonged, and where the owners were liable to be taxed for the capital invested, and where the taxes had been paid.

An objection is taken to the recovery against the collector, on the ground, mainly, that the assessment under the law of California, by the assessors, was a judicial act, and that the party should have pursued his remedy to set it aside according to the provisions of that law.

We do not think so. The assessment was not a judicial, but a ministerial act, and as the assessors exceeded their powers in making it, the officer is not protected.

The payment of the tax was not voluntary, but compulsory, to prevent the sale of one of the ships.

Our conclusion is, that the judgment of the court below is right, and should be affirmed.[1]

---

[1] *Acc.* Johnson *v.* Debary-Baya Merchants' Line, 37 Fla. 499, 19 So. 640; Roberts *v.* Charlevoix, 60 Mich. 197 ; S. *v.* Haight, 30 N. J. L. 428.

OLD DOMINION STEAMSHIP CO. *v.* VIRGINIA.

SUPREME COURT OF THE UNITED STATES. 1905.

[*Reported* 198 *U. S.* 299.]

ON March 17, 1904, the Supreme Court of Appeals of the State of Virginia, in a matter appealed from a finding of the State Corporation Commission, entered the following findings and order:

" That the Old Dominion Steamship Company was a non-resident corporation, having been incorporated by the senate and house of representatives of the State of Delaware; that it was then and had been for many years theretofore engaged in the transportation of passengers and freight on the Atlantic Ocean and communicating navigable waters, between the city of New York, in the State of New York, and Norfolk, and certain other ports within the State of Virginia. That said steamship company in the prosecution of its said transportation business owned and operated the vessel property above named; that these vessels, with the exception of the tug Germania, whose movements and use will be hereinafter stated, visited various ports or points within the State of Virginia, for the purpose of receiving freight and passengers, for which they issued bills of lading and tickets to points outside the State of Virginia; that owing to the shallow waters where these vessels plied it was impossible in most instances for the larger ocean-going steamers of the company to be used; that in consequence the vessels above enumerated were used to receive the freight and passengers as aforesaid, giving the shipper of freight a bill of lading for the same, destined to New York and other points outside of Virginia, and the passenger a ticket to his destination, and thus transported such freight and passengers to deeper water at Norfolk and Old Point Comfort where, upon such bills of lading and tickets, the passengers and freight were transferred to one of the larger ocean-going vessels of the steamship company, and so the ultimate destination, namely, New York, and elsewhere outside of Virginia, was reached; that any other business transacted by the above-named vessels was incidental in character and comparatively insignificant in amount; that the said vessels were built and designed for interstate traffic especially and were adjuncts to or branches of the main line of the Old Dominion Steamship Company between New York and Norfolk; that each and all of the said vessels were regularly enrolled, under the United States laws, outside of the State of Virginia, with the name and port of such enrollment painted on the stern of each of them; that the said vessels, though regularly enrolled and licensed for coastwise trade, were then used on old established routes upon navigable waters within Virginia, as follows, to wit:

" First. The steamer Hampton Roads, between Fort Monroe and Hampton and Norfolk.

" Second. The steamer Mobjack, between points in Mathews and Gloucester Counties and Norfolk.

"Third. The steamers Luray and Accomac, between Smithfield and Norfolk.

"Fourth. The steamer Virginia Dare, between Suffolk and Norfolk.

"Fifth. The steamers Berkeley and Brandon, between Richmond and Norfolk; and

"The steamers Berkeley and Brandon ply between Richmond and Norfolk. These two steamers were completed in the year 1901, or early in 1902, one of them having been constructed at the William R. Trigg shipyard in the city of Richmond, and the other outside of the State of Virginia. Early in the year 1902 they were placed upon the line between Norfolk and Richmond, one steamer leaving Richmond each evening and arriving in Norfolk each morning, thus giving a night trip every night each way between Richmond and Norfolk. At the time these steamers were placed upon this route and since that time, the Old Dominion Steamship Company has by public advertisement called attention to the fact that these two steamers were especially fitted in the matter of stateroom accommodations for carrying passengers between Richmond and Norfolk, and the said two steamers have since that time been advertising for the carriage of passengers and freight on their route between Richmond and Norfolk, and have been regularly carrying freight and passengers between the said two points in Virginia as well as taking on freight and passengers for further transportation on their ocean steamers at Norfolk. The Old Dominion Steamship Company applied under the revenue laws of the State of Virginia for a license to sell liquor at retail on each of these steamers, and on July 1, 1902, there was granted through the commissioner of the revenue of the city of Richmond a license to the Old Dominion Steamship Company for the sale of liquor at retail on each of these steamers, said licenses to expire on April 30, 1903. On or about the same time, the said steamship company complied with the revenue laws of the United States, and paid the necessary revenue tax through the custom house at the city of Richmond for the purpose of selling liquor at retail on each of these steamers. In the spring of 1903, the said steamship company, in order to obtain licenses to sell liquor at retail on each of these steamers, applied for the same in the city of Richmond and complied with the requirements of section 143 of the new revenue law, approved April 16, 1903, and so obtained licenses for the years 1903-1904 to sell liquor at retail on each of these steamers on their route between the cities of Richmond and Norfolk, and likewise, on or about the same time, complied with the revenue laws of the United States in the matter of selling liquor at retail on each of the said steamers on said route.

"Sixth. The steam tug Germania, which was used in the harbor of Norfolk and Hampton Roads for the purpose of docking the large ocean-going steamers of the Old Dominion Steamship Company, and the transferring from different points in those waters freight from connecting lines destined to points outside of Virginia.

"And the court, having maturely considered said transcript of the record of the finding aforesaid and the arguments of counsel, is of opinion that the legal *situs* of the vessels and barges assessed for taxation by the finding of the State corporation commission is, for that purpose, within the jurisdiction of the State of Virginia, and that said property is amenable to the tax imposed thereon — notwithstanding the fact that said vessels and barges are owned by a non-resident corporation, that they may have been enrolled under the act of Congress at some port outside the State of Virginia, and that they are engaged, in part, in interstate commerce — and doth so decide and declare.   Therefore it seems to the court here that the finding of the State corporation commission appealed from is without error, and said finding is approved and affirmed.   It is further considered by the court that the appellee recover against the appellant thirty dollars damages and its costs by it about its defense expended upon this appeal."

To review this order the Old Dominion Steamship Company sued out this writ of error.

BREWER, J.   The facts being settled, the only question is one of law.   Can Virginia legally subject these vessels to State taxation?   The general rule is that tangible personal property is subject to taxation by the State in which it is, no matter where the domicil of the owner may be.   This rule is not affected by the fact that the property is employed in interstate transportation.   Pullman's Palace Car Company *v.* Pennsylvania, 141 U. S. 18, in which Mr. Justice Gray, speaking for the court, said (p. 23) :

" It is equally well settled that there is nothing in the Constitution or laws of the United States which prevents a State from taxing personal property, employed in interstate or foreign commerce, like other personal property within its jurisdiction."

See also Cleveland, &c. Railway Co. *v.* Backus, 154 U. S. 439, 415; Western Union Telegraph Co. *v.* Taggart, 163 U. S. 1, 14.

This is true as to water as well as to land transportation.   In Gloucester Ferry Company *v.* Pennsylvania, 114 U. S. 196, 217, Mr. Justice Field, in delivering the opinion of the court, after referring to certain impositions upon interstate commerce, added:

" Freedom from such impositions does not, of course, imply exemption from reasonable charges, as compensation for the carriage of persons, in the way of tolls or fares, or from the ordinary taxation to which other property is subjected, any more than like freedom of transportation on land implies such exemption."

See also Passenger Cases, 7 How. 283, in which Mr. Justice McLean said (p. 402) :

" A State cannot regulate foreign commerce, but it may do many things which more or less affect it.   It may tax a ship or other vessel used in commerce the same as other property owned by its citizens."

The same doctrine is laid down in the same case by Mr. Chief Justice Taney (p. 479).   See also Transportation Company *v.* Wheeling, 99 U. S. 273.   That the service in which these vessels were engaged formed one link in a line of continuous interstate commerce may affect the State's power of regulation but not its power of taxation. True, they are not engaged in an independent service, as the cabs in Pennsylvania Railway Company *v.* Knight, 192 U. S. 21, but, being wholly within the State, that was their actual *situs.* And, as appears from the authorities referred to, the fact that they were engaged in interstate commerce does not impair the State's authority to impose taxes upon them as property. Indeed, it is not contended that these vessels, although engaged in interstate commerce, are not subject to State taxation, the contention being that they are taxable only at the port at which they are enrolled. In support of this contention the two principal cases relied upon are Hays *v.* The Pacific Mail Steamship Company, 17 How. 596, and Morgan *v.* Parham, 16 Wall. 471. Registry and enrollment are prescribed by sections 4141 and 4311, Rev. Stat., for vessels of the United States engaged in foreign and domestic commerce. Section 4141 reads:

"Sec. 4141. Every vessel, except as is hereinafter provided, shall be registered by the collector of that collection district which includes the port to which such vessel shall belong at the time of her registry; which port shall be deemed to be that at or nearest to which the owner, if there be but one, or, if more than one, the husband or acting and managing owner of such vessel, usually resides."

By sections 4131 and 4311 vessels registered or enrolled are declared to be deemed vessels of the United States. As stated by Chancellor Kent, in his Commentaries, vol. 3, p. *139:

"The object of the registry acts is to encourage our own trade, navigation, and ship-building, by granting peculiar or exclusive privileges of trade to the flag of the United States, and by prohibiting the communication of those immunities to the shipping and mariners of other countries. These provisions are well calculated to prevent the commission of fraud upon individuals, as well as to advance the national policy. The registry of all vessels at the custom house, and the memorandums of the transfers, add great security to title, and bring the existing state of our navigation and marine under the view of the General Government. By these regulations the title can be effectually traced back to its origin."

This object does not require and there is no suggestion in the statutes that vessels registered or enrolled are exempt from the ordinary rules respecting taxation of personal property. It is true by sec. 4141 there is created what may be called the home port of the vessel, an artificial *situs,* which may control the place of taxation in the absence of an actual *situs* elsewhere, and to that extent only do the two cases referred to go.

Our conclusion is that where vessels, though engaged in interstate commerce, are employed in such commerce wholly within the limits of a State, they are subject to taxation in that State, although they may have been registered or enrolled at a port outside its limits. The conclusion, therefore, reached by the Court of Appeals of Virginia was right, and its judgment is

Affirmed.

TENNANT *v.* STATE BOARD OF TAXES.

COURT OF ERRORS AND APPEALS OF NEW JERSEY.   1921.

[*Reported* 113 *Atl.* 254.]

PARKER, J.   This is a dispute over the right of Jersey City to tax certain personal property of the bankrupt firm of Daily *v.* Ivins, for taxes of the year 1918. . . . By the various appeals from the local assessors to the county board and thence to the State board, and the certiorari from the Supreme Court, all disputed matters seem to have been eliminated except a fund in bank and a tugboat which on May 20 was moored (as we were informed on the argument) in the South Cove of Jersey City. . . .

On this phase of the case the argument seems to be that the fund and the tugboat, being held by the trustee in bankruptcy, were in the custody of the law, and that property in such custody is not taxable. On the broad question whether property of a bankrupt in the hands of a trustee in bankruptcy is exempted from State taxation, the answer of the United States Supreme Court is decidedly in the negative. Swarts *v.* Hammer, 194 U. S. 441, 24 Sup. Ct. 695, 48 L. Ed. 1060.   This is dispositive of the taxability of the bank deposit in this aspect. . . .

It is next argued that the tug was further in the "custody of the law" because of the possession by the marshal, so as to be exempt. The facts are that the tug was registered at the New York custom house and had been ordinarily employed in and about the waters of New York Harbor. About the time of the bankruptcy (appellant was appointed trustee May 2, 1918) the tug was brought into tidewaters on the New Jersey side adjacent to Jersey City, and moored there apparently unused, and so remained until after it was sold, June 17, 1918.   During this period, as we understand the evidence, several libels in admiralty were filed, and served by the United States marshal for the district of New Jersey. Sale was made jointly by the appellant as trustee and by the marshal, and from the proceeds the libels were paid off and the balance was paid to or retained by the trustee.   The sale price was $30,000, and this was adopted by the State Board as the fair value of the tug, which was subjected to tax at that valuation together with the fund already in bank.

As a preliminary to ascertaining whether this tug was exempt because in the custody of the marshal, it is necessary to determine the other question raised, whether apart from such claim of exemption it was taxable on May 20, 1918, in the taxing district of Jersey City.   In our opinion it was so taxable. As an active tug plying in the waters of New York Harbor it was taxable at the residence of the owners or the permanent *situs* of the property, it is immaterial which. American Mail Steamship Co. *v.* Crowell, 76 N. J. Law, 54, 68 Atl. 752; Shrewsbury *v.* Merchants' Steamboat Co., 76 N. J. Law, 407, 69 Atl. 958; West Shore R. Co. *r.* State Board, 82 N. J. Law,

37, 81 Atl. 351; Id., 84 N. J. Law, 768, 85 Atl. 826. But with the bankruptcy its condition became one of passivity; it was a mere chattel secured from drifting and awaiting a sale. Had it been drawn out on a ship railway or even tied up to a wharf on the Jersey City water front, its taxable *situs* would be indubitable. While the point does not seem to be definitely argued, we gather from the assertion that the tug was in the " tidewaters of New York Bay" that it is claimed to have been out of the taxing jurisdiction of New Jersey because of the interstate treaty limiting the "jurisdiction" of New Jersey on the waters of New York Bay and the Hudson river. C. S. p. 5358. But this jurisdiction has been held by the courts of both New York and New Jersey to be a jurisdiction simply for the exercise of the police power. People *v.* Central R. R. of N. J., 42 N. Y. 283; Central R. R. Co. *v.* Jersey City, 70 N. J. Law, 81, 56 Atl. 239; S. C., 209 U. S. 473, 28 Sup. Ct. 592, 52 L. Ed. 896. In the opinion of Mr. Justice Garrison in 70 N. J. Law at page 97, 56 Atl. at page 245, it is declared that " the sovereign power of taxation over all the territory thus defined (i. e., to the middle of the Hudson river) resides in the State of New Jersey." See Cook *v.* Weigley, 72 N. J. Eq. 221, 65 Atl. 196. A vessel more or less permanently moored within the territory is, in our opinion, personal property " found" within the taxing district, in the same manner as, e. g., coal on storage pending a sale and removal. Lehigh & Wilkes-Barre Coal Co. *v.* Junction, 75 N. J. Law, 922, 68 Atl. 806, 15 L. R. A. (N. S.) 514. It is pertinent to note, while on this subject, that the libels against this tug were filed in the United States District Court for the District of New Jersey, and the seizure was made by the marshal of that court, in conformity, as it seems to us, with the statutory provision that "the State of New Jersey shall constitute one judicial district" (Rev. Stat. U. S. § 531; Comp Stats. U. S. § 1082) treated as meaning that the district extends to the middle of the river for all purposes of executing civil process out of that court.

The tug, then, being legally "found" in the taxing district of Jersey City, it only remains to inquire whether because under seizure by the marshal it was exempted by any rule of law from taxation as against its general owners, Dailey *v.* Ivins, or the trustee in bankruptcy, either by provision in the statute or rule laid down by decision of the courts. It is not exempted by statute; . . . and we think our reports will be searched in vain for a case wherein it was held, or even claimed, that real or personal property otherwise liable to taxation is exempt because of having been levied on or attached by court process. The court officer himself (as in this case the marshal) is ordinarily not liable for the tax (37 Cyc. 797; In re Kellinger, 9 Paige N. Y. Ch. 62); but that does not exempt the property nor, as we view it, the general owner.

These considerations lead to an **affirmance of** the judgment.

McCUTCHEN *v.* BOARD OF EQUALIZATION OF TAXES.

SUPREME COURT OF NEW JERSEY. 1915.

[*Reported* 87 *N. J. L.* 370.]

SWAYZE, J. The question is the same decided recently in a case involving the tax of another year. The opinion in that case is said not to have been reported. It may serve as our opinion in the present case.

The question is the right of Jersey City to tax flour held on a pier in Jersey City for the purpose of repacking and blending. The flour is shipped from the northwest to New York City, on through bills of lading; freight is paid through. Instead of transporting the flour immediately upon its arrival across the river by lighters, it is unloaded and held at the pier for the purposes mentioned. The liability of the railroad company for local taxes on this pier was before the Court of Errors and Appeals in Lehigh Valley Railroad Co. *v.* Jersey City, 80 N. J. L. 298. The test of the right to tax goods shipped from one State to another and detained in course of transportation is settled by the case of Lehigh and Wilkes-Barre Coal Co. *v.* Junction, 75 N. J. L. 922. If the goods are actually in the course of a continuous journey, they are not subject to taxation. The difficulty is to decide what breaks the continuity of the journey. In this case it was broken by repacking and blending the flour upon the pier. Whether mere repacking would suffice may perhaps be arguable, although the packages that go on to destination are not the same packages that are landed on the pier; but surely the flour after blending is a different commodity. It is blended for the very purpose of making something different, a quality that is or is supposed to be more salable. The process of blending is no doubt different from the process of grinding grain into flour, but in each case a different commodity is produced.

This view is sustained by the decisions of the United States Supreme Court. In General Oil Co. *v.* Crain, 209 U. S. 211, the oil was held at Memphis for the purpose of putting it in barrels for further transport. It was held that it was subject to the jurisdiction of Tennessee.

The taxes are affirmed, with costs.

COE *v.* ERROL.

SUPREME COURT OF THE UNITED STATES. 1886.

[*Reported* 116 *U. S.* 517.]

IN September 1881, Edward S. Coe filed a petition in the Supreme Court of New Hampshire for the county of Coös, against the town of Errol, for an abatement of taxes, and therein, amongst other things, alleged that on the 1st of April, 1880, he and others, residents of Maine and Massachusetts, owned a large number of spruce logs that had been drawn down the winter before from Wentworth's location, in New Hampshire, and placed in Clear Stream and on the banks thereof, in the town of Errol, county of Coös, New Hampshire, to be from thence floated down the Androscoggin river to the State of Maine to be manufactured and sold; and that the selectmen of said Errol for that year appraised said logs for taxation at the price $6,000, and assessed thereon State, county, town, and school taxes, in the whole to the amount of $120, and highway taxes to the amount of $60. A further allegation made the same complaint with regard to a lot of spruce logs belonging to Coe and another person, which had been cut in the State of Maine, and were on their way of being floated to Lewiston, Maine, to be manufactured, but were detained in the town of Errol by low water. Similar allegations were made with regard to logs cut the following year, 1880, and drawn from Wentworth's location, and part of them deposited on lands of John Akers, and part on land of George C. Demeritt, in said town of Errol, to be from thence taken to the State of Maine; and, also, with regard to other logs cut in Maine and floated down to Errol on their passage to Lewiston, in the State of Maine, and both which classes of logs were taxed by the selectmen of Errol in the year 1881. The petition also contained the following allegations, to wit:

"Said Coe further says that said logs of both years, so in the Androscoggin river, have each year been taxed as stock in trade in said Lewiston to said Coe and Pingree, and said Coe claims and represents that none of said logs were subject to taxation in said Errol for the reason that they were in transit to market from one State to another, and also because they had all been in other ways taxed.

"That said Androscoggin river, from its source to the outlet of the Umbagog Lake in the State of New Hampshire, through said State and through the State of Maine to said Lewiston, is now, and for a long time has been, to wit, for more than twenty years last past, a public highway for the floatage of timber from said lakes and rivers in Maine, and from the upper waters of said Androscoggin river and its tributaries in New Hampshire down said river to said Lewiston, and has been thus used by the petitioner and his associates in the lumber business for more than twenty years last past."

Without further pleading, the parties made an agreed case, the important part of which was as follows, to wit:

"It is agreed that the facts set forth in the petition are all true except what is stated as to the taxation of the logs as stock in trade in Lewiston, Maine; and if that is regarded by the court as material, the case is to be discharged and stand for trial on that point. It is agreed that upon this petition the legality of the taxation is intended to be brought before the court for adjudication, and all formal objections to the proceedings in the town meeting, &c., and all other matters of form, are waived, and we submit the matter to the court for a legal adjudication as to whether or not any or all of the taxes shall be abated.

"And it is agreed that for many years the petitioner and his associates in the lumber business have cut large quantities of timber on their lands in Maine and floated them down the said lakes and rivers in Maine and down the Androscoggin river to the mills at said Lewiston; and timber thus cut has always lain over one season, being about a year, in the Androscoggin river, in this State, either in Errol, Dummer, or Milan; and the timber referred to in this petition as having been cut in Maine had lain over in Errol since the spring or summer before the taxation, according to the above custom."

Upon this case the Supreme Court of New Hampshire, in September term, 1882, adjudged as follows, to wit: "Now, at this term, the said questions of law having been fully determined in said law term, and an order made that that portion of said tax assessed upon the logs cut as aforesaid in said State of Maine be abated, and that the tax assessed upon all of said logs cut in the State of New Hampshire be sustained, and said order having been fully made known to the parties of this case and become a part of the record thereof, it is therefore ordered and decreed by the court that there be judgment in accordance with said order made at said law term, without costs to either party."

The petitioner took a bill of exceptions, setting forth the agreed case, and stating, amongst other things, the points raised on the hearing before the Supreme Court of New Hampshire, and the decision of that court thereon, as follows:

"On said hearing the petitioner claimed that said taxes named in the petition and the statutes of this State, under the provisions of which said taxes were assessed, were illegal and void, because said taxes were assessed in violation of, and said statutes of this State are in violation of and repugnant to, the general provisions of the Constitution of the United States; because said taxes were assessed in violation of, and said statutes of this State are in violation of and repugnant to, that part of section 2, art. 4, of the Constitution of the United States, which provides that 'The citizens of each State shall be entitled to all the privileges and immunities of citizens of the several States'; because said taxes were assessed in violation of, and said statutes of this State are in violation of and repugnant to, those parts of sec. 8 of art. 1 of the Constitution of the United States which provide that 'The Congress shall have power · · · to regulate commerce with foreign nations, and among the several States,' and section 10 of said article 1, which provides that 'No State shall, without the consent of Congress, lay any imposts or duties on imports or exports except what may be absolutely necessary for executing its inspection laws.'"

MR. JUSTICE BRADLEY delivered the opinion of the court. After stating the facts in the language above reported he continued:

The case is now before us for consideration upon writ of error to the Supreme Court of New Hampshire, and the same points that were urged before that court are set up here as grounds of error.

The question for us to consider, therefore, is, whether the products of a State (in this case timber cut in its forests) are liable to be taxed like other property within the State, though intended for exportation to another State, and partially prepared for that purpose by being deposited at a place of shipment, such products being owned by persons residing in another State.

We have no difficulty in disposing of the last condition of the question, namely, the fact (if it be a fact) that the property was owned by persons residing in another State; for, if not exempt from taxation for other reasons, it cannot be exempt by reason of being owned by non-residents of the State. We take it to be a point settled beyond all contradiction or question, that a State has jurisdiction of all persons and things within its territory which do not belong to some other jurisdiction, such as the representatives of foreign governments, with their houses and effects, and property belonging to or in the use of the government of the United States. If the owner of personal property within a State resides in another State which taxes him for that property as part of his general estate attached to his person, this action of the latter State does not in the least affect the right of the State in which the property is situated to tax it also. It is hardly necessary to cite authorities on a point so elementary. The fact, therefore, that the owners of the logs in question were taxed for their value in Maine as a part of their general stock in trade, if such fact were proved, could have no influence in the decision of the case, and may be laid out of view.

We recur, then, to a consideration of the question freed from this limitation: Are the products of a State, though intended for exportation to another State, and partially prepared for that purpose by being deposited at a place or port of shipment within the State, liable to be taxed like other property within the State?

Do the owner's state of mind in relation to the goods, that is, his intent to export them, and his partial preparation to do so, exempt them from taxation? This is the precise question for solution.

This question does not present the predicament of goods in course of transportation through a State, though detained for a time within the State by low water or other causes of delay, as was the case of the logs cut in the State of Maine, the tax on which was abated by the Supreme Court of New Hampshire. Such goods are already in the course of commercial transportation, and are clearly under the protection of the Constitution. And so, we think, would the goods in question be when actually started in the course of transportation to another State, or delivered to a carrier for such transportation. There must be a point of time when they cease to be governed exclusively by the domestic law and begin to be governed and protected by the national law of commercial regulation, and that moment seems to us to be a legitimate one for this purpose, in which they commence their final movement for transportation from the State of their origin to that of their destination. When the products of the

farm or the forest are collected and brought in from the surrounding country to a town or station serving as an entrepôt for that particular region, whether on a river or a line of railroad, such products
are not yet exports, nor are they in process of exportation, nor is exportation begun until they are committed to the common carrier
for transportation out of the State to the State of their destination,
or have started on their ultimate passage to that State. Until then
it is reasonable to regard them as not only within the State of their
origin, but as a part of the general mass of property of that State,
subject to its jurisdiction, and liable to taxation there, if not taxed
by reason of their being intended for exportation, but taxed without
any discrimination, in the usual way and manner in which such
property is taxed in the State.

Of course they cannot be taxed *as* exports; that is to say, they cannot be taxed by reason or because of their exportation or intended
exportation; for that would amount to laying a duty on exports,
and would be a plain infraction of the Constitution, which prohibits
any State, without the consent of Congress, from laying any imposts
or duties on imports or exports; and, although it has been decided,
Woodruff *v.* Parham, 8 Wall. 123, that this clause relates to imports
from, and exports to, foreign countries, yet when such imposts or
duties are laid on imports or exports from one State to another, it
cannot be doubted that such an imposition would be a regulation
of commerce among the States, and, therefore, void as an invasion
of the exclusive power of Congress. See Walling *v.* Michigan, *ante,*
446, decided at the present term, and cases cited in the opinion in
that case. But if such goods are not taxed as exports, nor by reason
of their exportation, or intended exportation, but are taxed as part
of the general mass of property in the State, at the regular period
of assessment for such property and in the usual manner, they not
being in course of transportation at the time, is there any valid
reason why they should not be taxed? Though intended for exportation, they may never be exported; the owner has a perfect right
to change his mind; and until actually put in motion, for some
place out of the State, or committed to the custody of a carrier for
transportation to such place, why may they not be regarded as still
remaining a part of the general mass of property in the State?
If assessed in an exceptional time or manner, because of their an-
ticipated departure, they might well be considered as taxed by reason
of their exportation or intended exportation; but if assessed in the
usual way, when not under motion or shipment, we do not see why
the assessment may not be valid and binding.

The point of time when State jurisdiction over the commodities
of commerce begins and ends is not an easy matter to designate or
define, and yet it is highly important, both to the shipper and to
the State, that it should be clearly defined so as to avoid all am-
biguity or question. In regard to imports from foreign countries,
it was settled in the case of Brown *v.* Maryland, 12 Wheat. 419,
that the State cannot impose any tax or duty on such goods so long
as they remain the property of the importer, and continue in the

original form or packages in which they were imported; the right to sell without any restriction imposed by the State being a necessary incident of the right to import without such restriction. This rule was deemed to be the necessary result of the prohibitory clause of the Constitution, which declares that no State shall lay any imposts or duties on imports or exports. The law of Maryland, which was held to be repugnant to this clause, required the payment of a license tax by all importers before they were permitted to sell their goods. This law was also considered to be an infringement of the clause which gives to Congress the power to regulate commerce. This court, as before stated, has since held that goods transported from one State to another are not imports or exports within the meaning of the prohibitory clauses before referred to; and it has also held that such goods, having arrived at their place of destination, may be taxed in the State to which they are carried, if taxed in the same manner as other goods are taxed, and not by reason of their being brought into the State from another State, nor subjected in any way to unfavorable discrimination. Woodruff *v.* Parham, 8 Wall. 123; Brown *v.* Houston, 114 U. S. 622.

But no definite rule has been adopted with regard to the point of time at which the taxing power of the State ceases as to goods exported to a foreign country or to another State. What we have already said, however, in relation to the products of a State intended for exportation to another State will indicate the view which seems to us the sound one on that subject, namely, that such goods do not cease to be part of the general mass of property in the State, subject, as such, to its jurisdiction, and to taxation in the usual way, until they have been shipped, or entered with a common carrier for transportation to another State, or have been started upon such transportation in a continuous route or journey. We think that this must be the true rule on the subject. It seems to us untenable to hold that a crop or a herd is exempt from taxation merely because it is, by its owner, intended for exportation. If such were the rule in many States there would be nothing but the lands and real estate to bear the taxes. Some of the Western States produce very little except wheat and corn, most of which is intended for export; and so of cotton in the Southern States. Certainly, as long as these products are on the lands which produce them, they are part of the general property of the State. And so we think they continue to be until they have entered upon their final journey for leaving the State and going into another State. It is true, it was said in the case of The Daniel Ball, 10 Wall. 557, 565: "Whenever a commodity has begun to move as an article of trade from one State to another, commerce in that commodity between the States has commenced." But this movement does not begin until the articles have been shipped or started for transportation from the one State to the other. The carrying of them in carts or other vehicles, or even floating them, to the depôt where the journey is to commence is no part of that journey. That is all preliminary work, performed for the purpose of putting the property in a state of preparation and readiness for transportation. Until actually launched on its way to another State, or committed to a common carrier for transportation to such State, its destination is not fixed and certain. It may be sold or otherwise disposed of within the State, and never put in course of transportation out of the State. Carrying it from the farm, or the forest, to the depôt, is only an interior movement of the property, entirely within the State, for the purpose, it is true, but only for the purpose, of putting it into a course of exportation; it is no part of the exportation itself. Until shipped or started on its final journey out of the State its exportation is a matter altogether *in fieri,* and not at all a fixed and certain thing.

The application of these principles to the present case is obvious. The logs which were taxed, and the tax on which was not abated by the Supreme Court of New Hampshire, had not, when so taxed, been shipped or started on their final voyage or journey to the State of Maine. They had only been drawn down from Wentworth's location to Errol, the place from which they were to be transported to Lewiston in the State of Maine. There they were to remain until it should be convenient to send them to their destination. They come precisely within the character of property which, according to the principles herein laid down, is taxable. But granting all this, it may still be pertinently asked, How can property thus situated, to wit, deposited or stored at the place of entrepôt for future exportation, be taxed in the regular way as part of the property of the State? The answer is plain. It can be taxed as all other property is taxed, in the place where it is found, if taxed, or assessed for taxation, in the usual manner in which such property is taxed; and not singled out to be assessed by itself in an unusual and exceptional manner because of its destination. If thus taxed, in the usual way that other similar property is taxed, and at the same rate, and subject to like conditions and regulations, the tax is valid. In other words, the right to tax the property being founded on the hypothesis that it is still a part of the general mass of property in the State, it must be treated in all respects as other property of the same kind is treated.

These conditions we understand to have been complied with in the present case. At all events there is no evidence to show that the taxes were not imposed in the regular and ordinary way. As the presumption, so far as mode and manner are concerned, is always in favor of, and not against, official acts, the want of evidence to the contrary must be regarded as evidence in favor of the regularity of the assessment in this case.

The judgment of the Supreme Court of New Hampshire is

Affirmed.

BURLINGTON LUMBER CO. *v*. WILLETTS.

SUPREME COURT OF ILLINOIS.   1886.

[*Reported* 118 *Ill.* 559.]

CRAIG, J. This was a bill in equity, brought by the Burlington Lumber Company, to enjoin the collection of a tax, upon an assessment made by tie assessor of tie town of New Boston, in Mercer County, for tie year 1885, on a certain quantity of logs which were in the New Boston iarbor, or bayou, on the 1st day of May, 1885.

There is no substantial dispute between tie parties in regard to the facts. The Burlington Lumber Company is a corporation organized under tie laws of Iowa, witi its place cf business at Burlington. Tie corporation is engaged in the business of manufacturing lumber. It buys logs in Wisconsin and Minnesota, where they are rafted, and towed down tie Mississippi river to Burlington, and there sawed into lumber at tie mills of tie company. In the Spring and Summer of 1884, tie company purchased logs, wiich were rafted in Boef slough, near the mouti of tie Ciippewa river, in Wisconsin. After the logs were rafted, they were towed down the river by a steamer. The vice-president of the corporation, on cross-examination, testified: "Some of the logs were stopped on the way. We could not stow all we bought, at or near Burlington, but it was more convenient and safer to leave them in the harbor at New Boston. After the boats were started with the rafts, the boat would be instructed to leave them at New Boston or other place, and there they would be left until wanted. The first raft was put in, October 3, 1884. Tiat was there in May, 1885. There were 3,000,000 feet there that winter. We had no logs at Burlington in winter of 1885. We have used the iarbor for nine years. We could keep logs there safer tian at Burlington, and with less expense. Corporation did not own tie land. It leased shore privileges, — that is, we pay something, ratier than have bother or trouble, to tiose who own the land, same as if we used a wharf. We have been renting shore privileges several years. The right to tie rafts on his shore was rented of Prentiss. Tie corporation had E. L. Willits employed to look after logs, and see that none got away. When we wanted logs we sent after them by steamer. Willits was the only man we had employed or that had charge of them tiere." Edward L. Willits testified: "I was in the employ of tie Burlington Lumber Company in the fall, winter and spring of 1884 and 1885. Was employed by the month to keep logs afloat and see that none got away. Got $50 per month. I know the situation of the logs that winter and spring. Tiere were four rafts, and about 750,000 feet in each." Cross-examined: "I have been employed five years to look after all rafts. I give receipt to boat, deliver to boat and take receipt. I have control while there. I had moved them across slough to keep them afloat. The Burlington Lumber Company put a raft in Sturgeon bay on the 1st of May. Part of it is there yet."

It is claimed that the property in question, under the evidence, was *in transitu*, and, therefore, not taxable in this State. It is a plain proposition, that property in course of transportation from one State to another, over one of our navigable rivers, or over any of the public highways of the country, is not liable to taxation as it passes over such highway, by the State authorities along the line of such highway, and we think it is equally clear, that if property, while in the course of transportation over one of our navigable rivers, should be detained by low water or ice, or other cause, it would not be liable to be taxed by the authorities where the detention occurred. Any other rule would have a direct tendency to obstruct commerce between States, which, of course, could not be done under our system of laws. But the question here presented is, whether the property, when assessed, was in course of transportation over a public high-way. We have given the evidence bearing upon this point that consideration which the importance of the question demands, and we have reached the conclusion that the property was not *in transitu*. For nine years the complainant had used the harbor at New Boston as a place of safety for depositing logs during the winter. Land along the shore had been leased, where the property was anchored, and a man employed, who was placed in the possession of the property. At the time the boats started from Wisconsin with the rafts, to convey them down the river, the destination of the property had not been determined by the company, but after departure, as stated by the vice-president in his evidence, the boats were then instructed to leave a part of the rafts at New Boston, and there they would remain until wanted at the mill in Burlington, when a steamer would be sent for them. New Boston harbor, or Sturgeon bay, as it is usually called, is only about thirty miles up the river from Burlington. It is very accessible, and it seems plain that the company had selected the bay as a place of storage for its logs, — a place where its property could be shipped, and kept in safety until such time as it was needed at the mills in Burlington. Indeed, for all practical purposes, it may be said that the transit of the property ended at New Boston. When the logs reached that point, they were located there for an indefinite time. New Boston harbor thus became the destination of the property, and so remained until such time as the corporation saw proper again to place the property in transit. No other reasonable construction can be placed upon the evidence.

The first section of our Revenue law provides, that all real and personal property in this State shall be assessed and taxed, except such as is by the act exempted. Here was a large quantity of personal property, located in this State on leased premises, in the hands of an agent of the owner, and upon what principle it can escape taxation is not apparent, unless the plain language of our Revenue law is disregarded. It is true, that the owners of the property were not manufacturing the logs into lumber in this State, or engaged in selling the lumber here, but the property was kept at New Boston because it was more profitable for the owners to keep it in store there than at Burlington. If kept at the mills in Burlington it would be liable to loss upon the breaking up of the ice in the river, in the spring, while at New Boston it was safe, at a trifling expense. The property was therefore kept at New Boston on account of the profit to the owners to keep it there. The company made money by the transaction. Here the Burlington Lumber Company had premises leased, large amounts of valuable property placed on the leased premises, in the hands of hired agents, resulting in profit to the company, and yet it is claimed it had no place of business in this State. This claim is unreasonable. We think, when all the circumstances are considered, it may be said that the company was engaged in a business here, beneficial to itself. If, then, the company had this property located in our State, and it was here for profit, and it was so located as to claim the protection of our laws, the property, in our opinion, had a *situs* here, and was liable to taxation.

We have been cited to the late case of Coe *v.* Town of Errol, decided in the Supreme Court of the United States, as having an important bearing on the question involved. We have examined that case, and, as we understand the decision, the question here involved is not considered or decided in that case. The point there decided, as we read the opinion of the court, is, in substance, this: In order to exempt property from taxation on the ground that it is in course of transportation, the property must be actually shipped, — that placing it together for shipment is not sufficient.

There is, however, one error in the record. The taxes which complainant attempted to enjoin, were, in part, levied by the incorporated town of New Boston. The property, however, was never within the incorporated limits of New Boston, and so far as it is concerned, it acquired no jurisdiction over, and has no right whatever to impose a tax on, the property. The corporation tax was void, because New Boston had no right to assess the property, and being void, the complainants had a clear right to file a bill to enjoin this part of the tax.

As to the corporation tax of New Boston the decree will be reversed. In all other respects it will be affirmed, and the costs of this court will be equally divided between the parties.

Decree reversed in part and in part affirmed.

COMMONWEALTH *v.* AMERICAN DREDGING CO.

SUPREME COURT OF PENNSYLVANIA. 1888.

[*Reported* 122 *Pa.* 386.]

IN 1887, the American Dredging Company appealed to the court below from the settlement by the auditor general and state treasurer, on December 15, 1886, of taxes claimed to be due on its capital stock, under the act of June 7, 1879, P. L. 112. The objections filed averred that a tax of $1,485 was charged upon property of the company which had no *situs* within jurisdiction of the commonwealth.

At the trial of the cause which was without a jury, under the act of April 22, 1874, P. L. 109, and was submitted without argument and without points presented on either side, the court, McPherson, J., found the following facts:

1. The defendant is a corporation of this commonwealth, chartered by the act of April 9, 1867, P. L. 956, with power " to own, construct, operate and dispose of dredging machines, steam tugs, lighters, machinery and appliances for improvement of harbor, channels, docks and water-courses." Under this act and a supplement of March 28, 1873, P. L. 446, its capital stock for the tax year ending the first Monday of November, 1886, was $495.000.

2. During this year $232,803.22 of its capital stock was invested in land and buildings situate in the state of New Jersey; $92,000 thereof was invested in four dredges, which were built outside of the state of Pennsylvania, three of which have never been within the limits of the state, and the fourth of which had never been within its limits until after the end of the said year; $6,000 thereof was invested in a tug which was built outside of Pennsylvania, and was not within its limits during the said year; and $38,500 thereof was invested in eleven scows which were built outside of Pennsylvania, and have never been within its limits. During the said year, the said real estate and other property were all employed for corporate purposes in the states of New Jersey, Maryland and Virginia.

3. During the year in question, the defendant declared two dividends, each of three per cent, upon $495,000, and this settlement taxes the whole capital stock under the act of 1879, section 4, at the rate of one half mill for each one per cent of dividend.

Upon these facts the conclusion of law was as follows:

It has been decided in Commonwealth *v.* Pennsylvania Coal Company, 5 Pa. C. C. R. 90, note, that so much of the tangible property of a domestic corporation as is situate in other states, and there employed in its corporate business, is not taxable by this commonwealth. We, therefore, hold that the commonwealth can only recover tax upon $125,696.78 of the defendant's capital stock. The amount due is as follows:

3 mills upon $125,696.78	$377 09
Interest from February 13, 1887, to May 10, 1888 ..	56 12
Attorney General's commission	18 85

$452 06

For which sum we direct judgment to be entered if exceptions are not filed according to law.

To this decision, the commonwealth filed exceptions, which were overruled; whereupon the commonwealth took this writ.

PAXSON, J. The court below correctly held that the defendant company was not liable to taxation upon so much of its capital stock as was represented by lands and buildings situate in the state of New Jersey; but we are of opinion that the learned judge erred in his ruling that the $92,000 of said stock represented by the four dredges, the tug-boat, and the eleven scows, conceding that they, or at least a portion of them, were built outside of this state, and have never been within it, were not liable to taxation. This is not because of the technical principle that the *situs* of personal property is where the domicil of the owner is found. This rule is doubtless true as to intangible property such as bonds, mortgages, and other evidences of debt. But the better opinion seems to be that it does not hold in the case of visible tangible personal property permanently located in another state. In such cases, it is taxable within the jurisdiction where found and is exempt at the domicil of the owner. Goods and chattels, horses, cattle, and other movable property of a visible or tangible character are liable to taxation in the jurisdiction of the state wherein the same are, and are ordinarily kept, irrespective of the residence or domicil of the owner. Legal protection and taxation are reciprocal, so that such personal property and effects of a corporeal nature, or that may be handled and removed, as receive the protection of the law are liable to be taxed by the law where they are thus protected: Rorer on Interstate Law, 204, and cases there cited; Potter on Corporations, §§ 189, 190: Pierce on Railroads, 472. No fault is found with this principle, but does it apply to the facts of this case?

It must be conceded that the property in question must be liable to taxation in some jurisdiction. If it were permanently located in another state, it would be liable to taxation there. But the facts show that it is not permanently located out of the state. From the nature of the business, it is in one place to-day and in another to-morrow, and, hence, not taxable in the jurisdiction where temporarily employed. It follows that if not taxable here, it escapes altogether. The rule as to vessels engaged in foreign or interstate commerce is that their *situs* for the purpose of taxation is their home port of registry, or the residence of their owner, if unregistered: Pullman Palace Car Co., 29 Fed. Rep. 66; Hays *v.* Pacific Mail Steamship Co., 17 How. 596. These vessels, if they may be so called, were not registered. Hence, their *situs* for taxation is the domicil of the owners. This rule must prevail in the absence of anything to show that they are so permanently located in another state as to be liable to taxation under the laws of that state.

Judgment reversed, and a procedendo awarded.

NATIONAL DREDGING CO. *v.* STATE.

SUPREME COURT OF ALABAMA.   1893.

[*Reported* 99 *Ala.* 462.]

McCLELLAN, J. The question presented on this record is whether certain property of the National Dredging Company had a *situs* in this State for the purposes of taxation when the assessment complained of was made in the Spring of 1891. The property was brought into the State after January 1st of that year and before the assessor had completed his assessment, and 1ence was properly assessed if taxable at all in t1is State under t1e agreed facts. Cod:, § 458. Those facts are: The National Dredging Company is a Delaware corporation, domiciled at Wilmington in t1at State. As its name indicates, its business or a part of its business, is the operation "of mac1ines, steam tugs, lig1ters, mac1inery and appliances for t1e improvement of rivers, harbors, c1annels, docks, water courses, low lands," &c. In t1e Fall or early Winter of 1890 it entered into a contract with the United States for continuing the work of dredging the channel of Mobile Bay, entered upon t1e execution t1ereof early in 1891, and from t1at time on down to t1e time of the trial of this cause in the City Court, July 30, 1892, has been and was at said last mentioned date still engaged therein. T1e property found subject to taxation, to wit, one dredge boat, "Forbes," one tug boat, "Curtis," and five mud scows, and broug1t into t1is State w1en t1e performance of the contract was entered upon, that is, in January or February, 1891, and had remained here up to t1e trial, except some portion thereof, not specified, whic1 was removed to the State of Maine in March or February, 1892. The contract with t1e Government had not been completed on July 30, 1892, but its completion would "occur shortly" t1ereafter, and after such completion the company would have no further use for t1is property in Alabama. The said tug boat, dredge and scows were floating property, capable of being moved from port to port—t1e tug of its own motive power, and the dredge and scows by being towed; and the tug "Curtis" is registered in t1e custom house at Wilmington, Delaware. It is clear from the foregoing epitome of the facts that all of t1is property was at t1e time of t1e assessment being used in the State of Alabama in t1e prosecution of works wholly wit1in the State, under a contract which involved its presence 1ere in that work for a time, t1e duration of which was indefinite, but which extended beyond a year and a half, and the end of which, even from t1e standpoint of the latter date, could not be more definitely fixed than as "shortly to occur." During all this time and possibly to the present moment t1e property has been wholly wit1in Alabama; engaged in a business or being used in a work which did not involve its passing even temporarily beyond the limits of the State. Moreover, it has all along been used and possibly is even now being used in the prosecution of this work precisely as property belonging to citizens of this State would be used therein. Indeed, as appears from this record, other property of the same kind, w1ich had previously been used by residents of Alabama in the prosecution of t1is work, was purchased by the appellant company, and, being incorporated with that involved here, has all along been used like it in dredging the channel of Mobile Bay, and one scow so used was built in the city of Mobile, and has never been, we assume, outside of the State. Again, not only is the period of the contract in the execution of which this property is kept in the State indefinite, and hence t1e duration of its presence here in the execution of that contract uncertain, but it is manifest from the agreed facts t1at t1is contract is only one of a series for the dredging of the channel in Mobile Bay, covering years before and after the year 1891. This work was in the line of the dredging corporation's business, it had secured this contract under one annual congressional appropriation when it had to bring its machinery and appliances — this property — to Mobile for its execution. Having it there, and being thus in a more advantageous position for entering into another contract or other successive contracts as appropriations are made by Congress, it is fair to assume that the National Dredging Company will enter into other contracts, or rather, at least, that its purpose and intention is to do so if favorable terms can be made. These considerations are proper in arriving at the *situs* of this property. They go to show, by reference to the owner's intention as fairly inferable from all the circumstances, an indefiniteness as to the period of the presence of these boats and scows wholly within Alabama beyond that existing as to the duration of the first contract, and the use of the property here in performance thereof. In other words, taking into consideration the business of the corporation, the amount and continuing character of the work to be done in Mobile Bay, the preparations made by the company for doing so much thereof as is authorized under one annual appropriation, it may be that this property will be for years engaged upon this work, as a part of that now being used by the company of like kind with this had been used thereon for a year or years prior to 1891. On this state of the case — or even leaving out of view the considerations last adverted to — it is clear, we think, that this property is not merely temporarily within Alabama, but that, to the contrary, its presence here is for such an indefinite period as involves the idea of permanency, in the sense in which that term is used with respect to the *situs* of property for the purposes of taxation. It is here as any other property is or would be here in use upon the public works in Mobile Bay. Its use in that work is the same as that of the other property originally embraced in this assessment and formerly owned by a citizen of Alabama and by him devoted to this work during previous years, the same as that of the scow which was built in Mobile for this work and has never been beyond the State, and the same as that of another scow built outside of the State for this work. All this other property is property of the State or in the State for the purposes of taxation, though it may at some uncertain future time cease to be property taxable here in consequence of its removal to other jurisdictions, as the property in controversy may sometimes be carried out of the State. Until that happens, however, both classes of property enjoy the same protection of our laws, both classes are devoted to the same use, the continuation of each class within the State is alike indefinite; the one class can not, in short, be distinguished from the other in any characteristic which is of importance in determining the question of taxability *vel non*. And hence our conclusion that the property in controversy had become so incorporated with, and a part of, the tangible property of this State, for revenue purposes, as that its taxable *situs* is here, notwithstanding the fact that the domicil of its owner is in another State. Mayor of Mobile *v.* Baldwin, 57 Ala. 61; Boyd *v.* City of Selma, 96 Ala. 144; 11 So. Rep. 393; Burroughs on Taxation, pp. 40–1; Trammell *v.* Connor, 91 Ala. 398.

There is nothing in the nature of this particular property to take it out of the general principle. The fact that it is floating property and may be moved from place to place and port to port by water furnishes no more reason for exempting it from taxation here than would exist for the exemption of property which did not float and could be moved from place to place only overland.

With respect to the tug boat " Curtis," a special consideration is advanced in support of its non-taxability. It is a sea-going vessel, propelled by steam, and is entitled to registry under statutes of the United States at the port of its owner's domicil. As matter of fact, it is registered at the custom house in the City of Wilmington, Delaware. On this the contention is that that being home, it can not be taxed elsewhere. There are many cases which hold that such vessel, engaged in commerce between its home port and others, or even wholly between other ports than that of its registry, can be taxed only at the port of registry. It is not our purpose to question these decisions; it is not necessary that we should. They all proceed upon the theory that vessels thus engaged are never in foreign jurisdiction except *temporarily,* and as an incident to the commerce to which they are devoted, and hence that they do not and can not acquire a *situs* in foreign ports for the purpose of taxation: they do not become incorporated with the property of other States and countries which they touch intermittently, are never indefinitely there, and their business, the work they perform, the uses to which they are put, is not done and performed within, and are not local to, the foreign State or country. These considerations can have no application here. The tug " Curtis " is not engaged in commerce, foreign or inter-state. Its business is wholly within Alabama. It is not here temporarily, but indefinitely. It is as much a part of the property of the State for taxation as if it had been chartered for an indefinite period of time to carry freight and passengers, or tow ships over the waters of Mobile Bay between the city and Point Clear, or as if its owner had devoted it to the carrying trade of the Alabama River; and surely in these cases it could not be successfully insisted that it was not as much Alabama property for taxation as any other boat devoted exclusively to the navigation of the water courses of the State. The question, indeed, is at last one of *situs* in fact, and where this is shown neither foreign registry nor foreign ownership is of any consequence.

The judgment of the City Court is affirmed.

[PRAIRIE OIL AND GAS CO. *v.* EHRHARDT.

SUPREME COURT OF ILLINOIS.   1910.

[*Reported* 244 *Ill.* 634.]

VICKERS, J.   On March 17, 1908, the Prairie Oil and Gas Company, a corporation organized under the laws of Kansas, filed its bill in equity in the Will county circuit court against August Ehrhardt, county treasurer and collector, praying for an injunction to prevent the collector from collecting certain taxes levied against the complainant upon crude oil in certain tanks and pipe lines belonging to the complainant and located in Will county.   Upon a hearing in the circuit court the temporary injunction was made perpetual, and from a decree granting the relief prayed for, the collector has appealed to this court.

The bill alleges, and the evidence sustains the allegations, that appellee is an incorporated company under the laws of Kansas and owns and operates a pipe line extending from Humboldt, Kansas, through the States of Missouri, Iowa and Illinois, and extending to Griffith, Indiana, through which crude petroleum is transported, by means of a system of force pumps and tanks, from one end of the pipe line to the other; that the company has a large number of tanks in southeastern Kansas in which millions of barrels of oil are stored; that some of this oil is produced by wells owned by the company, but most of it is purchased from owners of other oil wells in southeastern Kansas and in Oklahoma after it is collected by such other owners in tanks at their wells and is conveyed through collecting pipes to the storage tanks in Kansas.   The oil is then conveyed from the storage station in Kansas through pipe lines, as above described, to Griffith, Indiana, where it is delivered to another pipe line company, which transports the oil east through the pipe lines of the latter company.   The pipes through which the oil is transported are made of metal, are from ten to twelve inches in diameter and are two and somtimes three in number, laid parallel to each other.   The course of the oil across this State is slightly upgrade, which makes it necessary to force the oil through the pipes by a system of force pumps distributed along the line about forty-five miles apart.   There are two or three pumps installed at each pumping station, which force the oil, by a pressure of about 650 pounds to the square inch, to the next station east, where, in turn, another set of pumps forces it onward in its course across the State. The oil travels in the pipes at the rate of about three miles per hour. There is a pumping station at Wilmington, west of Griffith, Indiana, and the next pumping station southwest of Wilmington is at Kernan, in LaSalle county.   If the pumps at each station did exactly the same amount of work they would keep the current of oil moving continuously in the pipe line.   It is expected that the pumps will work continuously, both day and night.   In the practical operation of the pipe line it is found that it is impossible to so regulate the several pumps along the line that each will do the same amount of work as each of the others. Pumps will break down, get out of repair and have to be stopped now and then, which would result in an interruption of the flow of oil in the pipes. In order to overcome the difficulties from the irregularities in the movements of the pumps two tanks are established at each pumping station, which are connected with the main pipes by connecting pipes and valves. The object of these tanks is to equalize the work of the pumps. They are so adjusted that an excess of oil coming to a station will be forced into the tanks, and a shortage in the supply coming to a station will be supplied by drawing on the surplus stored at such station in the tanks. By maintaining these tanks at the pumping stations an interruption of the work of any set of pumps will not interfere with the work of any other pumps on the line. There is usually enough oil stored in the tanks at each station to keep the pumps going for twenty-four hours without receiving any oil from the pipe lines. It sometimes happens, when the pumps are all working along the line, that the oil in the tanks will not be increased or diminished for several days, but as a rule the oil is passing into and out of the tanks, more or less, every day. There is thus an almost constant flow of oil through the tanks as well as through the pipes. The taxes which are sought to be enjoined are levied upon the oil in the pipes and in the tanks that are located in Will county.

There is no question of fact in dispute between the parties. The only question is the liability of appellee to pay taxes upon this oil while it is being transported across Will county in the manner above described.

The Revenue law of this State provides that all personal property in this State shall be assessed and taxed, except such as is specifically exempt from taxation by the statute. While there is no express exemption of property in transit, yet it has been held by this court and by the Supreme Courts of other States, and by the Supreme Court of the United States, that property in transit which is passing through a taxing district is not liable to local taxation. Irvin *v.* New Orleans, St. Louis and Chicago Railroad Co. 94 Ill. 105; Burlington Lumber Co. *v.* Willetts, 118 id. 559; People *v.* Bacon, 243 id. 313; State *v.* Stevens, 146 Mo. 622; Coe *v.* Errol, 116 U S. 517; Kidd *v.* Pearson, 128 id. 1; Kelly *v.* Rhoades, 188 id. 1; Calvert on Regulations of Commerce, 291.

In the case of Kelly *v.* Rhoades, *supra,* the United States Supreme Court held that a flock of sheep which were being driven on foot through the State of Wyoming to a point in another State were not subject to local taxation, notwithstanding the sheep were permitted to graze as they went along, traveling at the rate of about nine miles per day. This case answers the appellant's argument that property cannot be in transit as interstate commerce unless it is in charge of some common carrier engaged in that class of business.

The oil in question was not held in Will county any longer than was necessary to its proper transportation by the means provided by appellee for that purpose. None of the oil was sold or offered for sale while passing through this State. It is manifest that the only

purpose that appellee sought to accomplish was to transport the oil
from the place where it was produced to other points in a foreign
State, where it would be refined and enter thereafter into the channels of trade.   The oil never acquired a *situs* in this State so that
it can be said it became a part of the personal property of districts
through which it passed.   To hold that this oil, either in the tanks
or in the pipes, was subject to taxation in Will county would authorize its taxation through other taxing districts through which it
might pass, and if required to pay taxes in every State or county
through which the pipe lines extended, it would amount to such
a burden that transportation in this way would probably have to be
abandoned.

   This oil, while on its way from one State to a point in another
State, is a subject of inter-state commerce and is therefore exempt
from local taxation.   To so construe our Revenue law as to include
property while passing through the State as inter-state commerce
would render the Revenue law unconstitutional under the commerce
clause of the Federal constitution.   We agree with the learned judge
who tried this cause below, that " from the evidence this oil is an
article of commerce being transported from Kansas to Indiana
through the State of Illinois, and that under the inter-state commerce clause of the constitution it is not taxable in the State of
Illinois."

   The decree of the circuit court of Will county will be affirmed.

Decree affirmed.

SEMPLE *v.* COMMONWEALTH.

COURT OF APPEALS OF KENTUCKY.   1918.
[*Reported* 181 *Ky.* 675.]

THE appellant was not domiciled in Kentucky; but he made frequent visits to Louisville on business, and leased an apartment
there, which he furnished.   He kept an automobile there, and a
bank account, not used in his business, but for his personal expenses.
A revenue agent attempted, under provisions of section 4260 of the
Kentucky Statutes, in the county court of Jefferson county to have
this property assessed as as omitted property; and the court ordered
the assessment.   On appeal to the Circuit Court the judgment was
affirmed; and from that judgment appellant prosecutes this appeal.[1]

   THOMAS, J. . . . It is insisted, however, that appellant's small
amount of furniture, his automobile and bank account, under the
provisions of section 4020 of the Kentucky Statutes, are assessable in
Jefferson county.   None of this property, however, was used by appellant in the prosecution or conduct of any business in which he
was locally engaged.   All of it was for his personal convenience and
comfort while temporarily sojourning in the city of Louisville.   His

------

[1] This short statement of facts is substituted for that of THOMAS, J.

bank account is shown to have been exclusively for his personal expenses. Under such circumstances personal property, even though it be tangible, does not have a situs for taxation at the place where it is thus temporarily located.

In the case of Commonwealth of Kentucky *v.* R. G. Dun & Co., 126 Ky. 108, in construing section 4020 of the Kentucky statutes, this court said:

"This court, however, in construing this statute, has determined that it does not apply to the property of non-residents when in this State temporarily; that in such a case the situs for the purpose of taxation is at the domicile of the owner." The court then cites the cases of Board of Councilmen *v.* Fidelity Trust & Safety Vault Co., 111 Ky. 667; Callahan *v.* Singer Manufacturing Co., 29 Ky. Law Reporter, 123, and Commonwealth, by, &c. *v.* Haggin, 30 Ky. Law Rep. 788.

In order that personal property may have a situs for taxation in a locality different from the domicile of its owner, such personal property must be permanently located at the place where it is sought to be taxed. No temporary location will alter its situs for taxation at a place other than the residence of its owner. Cases, *supra,* and Union Refrigerator Transit Co. *v.* Kentucky, 199 U. S. 194.

We therefore conclude that the court was in error in assessing any of the property for either of the years mentioned, and its judgment in doing so must be and it is reversed.

PEOPLE *ex rel.* THE PARKER MILLS *v.* COMMISSIONERS OF TAXES.

COURT OF APPEALS OF NEW YORK.   1861.

[*Reported* 23 *N. Y.* 242.]

APPEAL from the Supreme Court. *Certiorari,* under section 20 of the act of 1859 in relation to the assessment and taxation of property in the city of New York, to review the proceedings of the commissioners of taxes and assessments in imposing a personal tax upon the relator. From the commissioners' return it appeared that the relator is a foreign corporation, manufacturing nails in the States of Massachusetts and Rhode Island. It had a depôt and agent in the city of New York, to whom it transmitted nails for sale. Its only business within this State consisted in making such sales, the proceeds of which were remitted at once to the corporation in Massachusetts; and where sales were upon credit, the securities received were sent to the corporation for collection. It appeared by the testimony of the agent that the annual sales amounted to about $300,000, and that the value of the nails which he then had in store was $10,000. The commissioners, upon these facts, held that the corporation "was conducting business in the city of New York, and that the amount or sum invested in said business by it was $10,000." They assessed the corporation at that amount, and imposed a tax of $179.21. The Supreme Court, at general term in the first district, affirmed the proceedings, and an appeal was thereupon brought to this court.

SELDEN, J. This case depends upon the construction to be given to the act of February 27, 1855, amendatory of the several acts for the assessment and collection of taxes in this State. Section 1 of that act is as follows: "All persons and associations doing business in the State of New York, as merchants, bankers, or otherwise, either as principals or partners, whether special or otherwise, and not residents of this State, shall be assessed and taxed on all sums invested in any manner in said business, the same as if they were residents of this State; and said taxes shall be collected from the property of the firms, persons, and associations, to which they severally belong."

I have no doubt, and shall therefore assume, that the words, "persons and associations," used in this statute, should be construed to include corporations. But the words descriptive of the property in respect to which they are to be assessed, are among the most indefinite in the language. The word "business" embraces everything about which a person can be employed; and a sum is "invested" whenever its amount is represented by anything but money. No conclusion can be arrived at in this case, by following out the precise lexicographical meaning of these terms. The statute is to be interpreted, therefore, by the light to be obtained from its general scope and tenor: from other statutes *in pari materia:* and from a consideration of the evils and abuses at which it was aimed.

It was not uncommon, previous to the passage of the act, as the history of our legislation shows, for foreign corporations, particularly insurance companies, to establish agencies in the city of New York, and perhaps elsewhere in this State, for the transaction of their corporate business. These agencies were protected by our laws and carried on a profitable business within this State, and yet contributed nothing towards the expenses of government. They came in direct competition with domestic corporations, which were heavily taxed. It was certainly just and right that they, or the corporations by which they were established, should be made to contribute, to some extent, to the public burdens. But there was also another class of cases which called for special legislation, and which the legislature probably had more directly in view in passing the act of 1855. Many persons, engaged in business in the city of New York as partners of commercial firms or otherwise, resided in New Jersey, Connecticut, or elsewhere out of this State. These persons frequently had large amounts of property in this State, and enjoyed the fruits of a profitable business carried on under the protection of our laws; and yet, by reason of the rule that personal property is deemed to follow the person of the owner, they escaped taxation in respect to this property, at least in this State, and probably in most cases altogether.

There is no doubt that, to provide for these two classes of cases, especially the last, was the main object of the act of 1855. That it was never intended to include a case like the present, seems to me clear. In the two classes of cases referred to, the investment of funds by the non-residents has more or less of permanency. It is not the mere transit of property through the State for the purposes of a market, but the funds are used for the prosecution of continuous business. Taxes are levied, for the most part, annually. They are the consideration which property holders pay for the protection which the government and laws afford to them and their property for the year. But, if the commissioners in this case are right, if the property is caught within this State for a single day while the assessors are engaged in the performance of their duties, its owners may be as heavily taxed as if it had been here throughout the entire year.

It is difficult to see any difference in principle between the present case and that of a drover who transports his herds of cattle by railroad to the city of New York for sale; and yet, I apprehend, no one ever supposed the owner of the cattle, if a non-resident, to be taxable in such a case. It may be said that the Parker Mills had a store and an agent in the city of New York. So the drover may have his field or his yard for keeping his cattle, and his herdsman to take care of them. The cases are, I think, parallel; and the reason why the statute does not apply to either is, that there is no sum invested or used for the purpose of carrying on a continuous business in this State.

That it never was the policy of the State to impose taxes upon property sent into the State for the mere purpose of sale, is shown by the course of legislation on this subject. The general tax law provides (1 R. S. 389, § 5) that every person shall be assessed in the town or ward where he resides, for all personal estate owned by him, "including all such personal estate in his possession, or under his control as trustee, guardian, executor," &c. By the amendatory act of April 15, 1851 (Sess. Laws, 1851, ch. 176), agents are added to the class of persons named in the previous statute; but lest the clause, with this addition, should be construed more broadly than the legislature intended, it was further provided that "the products of any State of the United States, consigned to agents in any town or ward in this State for sale on commission for the benefit of the owner thereof, shall not be assessed to such agents."

The present case does not come strictly within the terms of this exception. The word "products," as here used, means, as I suppose, the natural agricultural products of the country. But I can see no distinction in principle between the present case and the c_{ase} excepted. In both, the commodity is produced and owned in other States, and is brought temporarily into this State for the mere purposes of a market. Every reason which would lead to exemption from taxation in one case, applies, as I conceive, equally to the other. The exception is to be considered rather as indicative of the scope intended to be given to the principal clause, than as founded upon any reasons specially applicable to the natural products of the country as distinct from other property. It is a case to which the maxim, *expressio unius exclusio est alterius,* does not apply. The exception was undoubtedly inserted, from abundant caution, to prevent a misconstruction of the previous clause, authorizing the taxation of trustees and agents for the property in their hands; and not because the legislature intended to discriminate between the products of agricultural and other kinds of labor. It shows that it was no part of the policy of the legislature, when that act was passed, to compel the citizens of other States to contribute to the support of our government simply because they send a portion of the products of their industry to this State to be sold. It is clear, therefore, that the property of the relators could not have been taxed to their agent under the law of 1851; and I see no reason to suppose that it was intended, by the law of 1855, to adopt a different policy in respect to property so situated. My conclusion, therefore, is, that the judgment of the Supreme Court should be reversed, and that the proceedings should be remitted, with instructions to cause the names of the relator to be erased from the assessment roll, and the corresponding tax to be canceled.

All the judges concurring,

Ordered accordingly.

SECTION III.

ASSESSMENT.

TOWN OF ALBERTVILLE *v.* HOOPER.

SUPREME COURT OF ALABAMA.   1916.

[*Reported* 196 *Ala.* 642.]

THE action is by a citizen of the town of Albertville to recover a sum of money paid by him through his agent as purchase money for certain chattels sold by defendant municipality under a general execution against plaintiff for the satisfaction of an alleged judgment for municipal taxes on his personal property subject to taxation in said town. The execution was regular on its face, and was issued under the authority of the town counsel regularly expressed. The assessment upon which it was founded is shown to have been in the following form: In the first column of the assessment book, against plaintiff's name, items of real estate appear. In another column, headed "Total Value of R. E.," appears in black ink the amount $6,700, and in red ink the amount $66,678. There is no column showing personal property assessed, nor is there any reference to personal property. In the final column, headed "Total Taxes," appears the entry "33.50 R. est.," and under it the entry, "$333.29, P. P." The compiler of the separate book explains that the figures in red ink related to personal property.

SOMERVILLE, J.   (1–3.) An execution issued by the town clerk under section 1313 of the Code, for the collection of delinquent taxes, is manifestly a complete nullity unless there has been a written assessment of the defendant's property.

"The term (assessment) commonly includes two distinct processes: First, the preparation of a list by the proper officers, comprising a description of all the persons or property found within the jurisdiction, and liable to contribute to the particular tax; and, second, an estimate by the assessors of the value of the property, of whatever character it may be, which is to be called on to contribute, thus forming the basis of an apportionment of the whole tax among the taxable persons within the district. The list, when thus completed, is usually denominated the 'tax list' or 'assessment roll.'" Black on Tax Titles (2d Ed.) § 89.

"The assessment is an indispensable prerequisite to the validity of a tax against any individual, for without a valid assessment there can be no lawful attempt to collect the tax or to enforce it against any specific property. Mere irregularities in the assessment will not affect its validity, but only such omissions or defects as go to the jurisdiction of the assessors, or deprive the taxpayer of some substantial right." 37 Cyc. 987b.

(4.)   In the instant case nothing had been done by the municipality which can, even by the most liberal courtesy, be designated as an assessment of the plaintiff's personal property. The required assessment is not merely irregular or defective; it is simply non- . existent. For, certainly, the simple entry of the total amount computed as a personal property tax is not an assessment, without some sort of listing of the property itself.

Again, the assessment sale must be made by the city clerk or some person authorized by the town council. This assessment roll was not made by an authorized person, and apparently he merely copied the total assessed value of personalty from the county assessment book for the preceding year, without any reference to the items or the mass of property to be taxed; in short, it does not appear from the book that plaintiff owned any personal property whatever. Hence jurisdiction of the personalty was never acquired by the municipality.

Our judgment is that the assessment was a legal nullity; that there was nothing to support the execution under which plaintiff's property was seized; and that the sale of it was a sheer conversion by the municipality, without any authority of law.

(5.)   In such cases it is well settled that the owner may waive the tort, ratify the sale, and recover the purchase money received by the tort-feasor. Lewis *v.* Dubose, 29 Ala. 219, 220; Blackshear *v.* Burke, 74 Ala. 239; 4 Cyc. 332 (111).

There is no escape from the conclusion that plaintiff was entitled to recover the amount awarded by the verdict, and the jury were properly instructed to so find. . . .

Affirmed.

STATE *v.* CUDAHY PACKING CO.

SUPREME COURT OF MINNESOTA.   1908.

[*Reported* 103 *Minn.* 419.]

JAGGARD, J.   The trial court found that: The personal property of the defendant was valued at $10,400 by the assessor of the city of Minneapolis.   Thereafter the city board of equalization increased that assessment $10,000.   Thereafter the State board of equalization further increased the assessment by $6,630.   The resulting tax $810.90 was justly and properly levied.   Judgment was accordingly entered for the tax, together with the penalty.   This appeal was taken from the judgment.   Defendant expressly admits: "In fact [it] had personal property consisting of cash, book accounts, and stock of all kinds, including the soap in storage, of the cash value of $27,902.77."   The entire assessment was $27,030.

1.   The defendant insists that the court will take judicial notice that property in this State is not assessed for its actual cash value; that the assessor assessed other personal property at fifty per cent, in pursuance of the instructions contained in the circular issued by the State auditor; and that, inasmuch as the defendant was assessed for approximately the full value of its property, it had been discriminated against.   There is obviously no merit in this contention. The statutes of this State distinctly provide that "all property shall be assessed at its true and full value in money."   Section 810, R. L. 1905.   Neither the State auditor nor the courts have the power to repeal or amend this clear and positive requirement.

2.   Defendant also insists that the Minneapolis board of equalization had no power to make an original assessment, as it undertook to do in this case.   The increase was in pursuance of the following resolution of the city board: "On motion, . . . a raise of $10,000 was ordered assessed against the Cudahy Packing Company for goods in storage."   The board of equalization by the charter (1) is given power to revise, amend, and equalize the assessment on the roll of the city assessor, and "(2) is vested with all the powers which are or may be vested in the county boards of equalization under the general laws of the State so far as applicable, but shall not be restricted by any limitation as in respect to reducing the aggregate sum of real or personal property as returned by the city assessor." County boards of equalization have not the power to make an original assessment.   State *v.* Crookston Lumber Co., 85 Minn. 405, 89 N. W. 173.   It is quite clear, however, that under the provision granting the power to revise, amend, and equalize the assessment the city board has power to amend by adding taxable property not included in the assessor's list.

3.   Defendant also argues that the action of the Minneapolis board of equalization, and of the State board of equalization, also, in increasing the assessment, was invalid, because in both cases notice required by law to be given in such cases was not given.   The argu-

ment is not tenable.   The proceedings to collect taxes in this State are judicial.   Official machinery is provided for the creation of a just demand on the part of the State to be paid by certain individuals or out of certain property.   Opportunity is given for an objecting property owner to appear in court and to interpose any objection he may have, including that of unfair or unequal valuation.   With respect to the collection of personal property taxes, one opportunity is certainly given to appear and defend in court.   Section 889, R. L. 1905.   If this opportunity be not embraced, a further opportunity may be afforded.   Section 893, Id.   The statutory provisions which are intended to guide the conduct of officers in the transaction of public business, so as to insure the orderly and prompt performance of public duties, and which pertain merely to the system and dispatch of proceedings, are construed as directory.   The provisions which affect the subsequent collection of the tax, and which are intended for the protection of the citizen by preventing the sacrifice of his property, and by the disregard of which his rights might be affected, are construed as mandatory.   Kipp *v.* Dawson, 31 Minn. 373, 17 N. W. 961, 18 N. W. 96, Faribault Waterworks Co. *v.* County of Rice, 44 Minn. 12, 46 N. W. 143.

Under the judicial system, the equalization proceedings are designed merely to produce a just demand.   Subsequent opportunity to defend against that demand on the ground of unfair or unequal valuation is allowed.   Under the summary system, the means by which the taxpayer secures his day in court is often by appeal or resort to other remedy pending or following the action of the boards of equalization.   In this State, accordingly, provisions relating to equalization are generally construed as directory, not mandatory. Failure to give notice, under the judicial system, becomes clearly material only when it is sought to bring the person or property into court.   The mere failure of the assessor to notify the property owner and require him to list or return his taxable property (State *v.* Wm. Deering & Co., 56 Minn. 24, 57 N. W. 313), or the failure to give notice of hearing of boards of equalization (State *v.* Hynes, 82 Minn. 34, 84 N. W. 636), does not invalidate the assessment, in whole or in part.   Indeed, the omission of equalization not resulting in unfair or unequal assessment is not a basis of objection in proceedings to collect.   Scott Co. *v.* Hinds, 50 Minn. 204, 52 N. W. 523.

It was said in State *v.* District Court of Red Lake Co., 83 Minn. 169, 85 N. W. 1135: "It was immaterial that the various boards of review refused to reduce the amount of the assessment and that relators had no notice thereof.   There was essentially only one question for the court to pass upon ; and that was, what was the assessable value of the property at the time the tax was levied?"   In State *v.* Backus-Brooks Co., 102 Minn. 50, 112 N. W. 863, it was said: "The defendant, having failed to show that any irregularity or omission on the part of the State board of equalization or its secretary resulted in any prejudice to it, or that the taxes as levied against it were unequal or unfair, or based upon property it did not own, or that its property was assessed proportionately higher than other property of the same class, the defendant failed to establish any defense."

It follows that the failure of boards of equalization in this case to give notice is a mere irregularity, of which defendant cannot complain unless the tax sought to be collected was unfairly and unequally assessed. Section 919, R. L. 1905. This defendant has not shown.

Our attention has been called to Raymond *v.* Chicago Union Traction Co., 207 U. S. 20, 21, 28 Sup. Ct. 7, 52 L. Ed. 15. In that case the corporation had paid the full amount of its taxes, based upon the same rate as that paid upon other property of the same class. A federal court of equity restrained the collection of the illegal excess resulting from the discrimination of a board of equalization, whose decisions were conclusive, except as proceedings for relief may be taken in courts. In the case at bar the action of the officials did not result in an illegal discrimination. This defendant is in no position to complain of the application of a tax rate universal throughout the State to his tangible property only at a valuation admittedly less than the law required. This, in another sense, is, for aught that appears in this record, a smaller tax than the defendant was legally subject to (State *v.* Western Union Tel. Co., 96 Minn. 13, 104 N. W. 567), and less than was imposed by law upon domestic corporations (section 838, R. L. 1905), because the tax on their shares of stock includes, in effect, the valuation of both tangible and intangible property as united in use.

Affirmed.

On April 10, 1908, the following opinion was filed.

JAGGARD, J. On petition for rehearing, defendant urges that the decision previously rendered in this case violates article 4, § 2, of the constitution of the United States, by denying to the defendant, a citizen of Illinois, the privileges and immunities of a citizen of Minnesota, and also violates article 14, § 1, of the amendments to said constitution, by depriving the defendant of its property without due process of law, and by denying the defendant the equal protection of the laws. The questions thus involved have been fully presented to and considered by this court. In so far as the petition for reargument is addressed to the interpretation by this court of the power of the Minneapolis board of equalization and its power to assess property not on the assessment roll, there appears to be no occasion for further discussion. The gist of the remaining argument is (1) that the action of the board of equalization is illegal and inequitable, for it discriminates against this defendant by making him bear a greater burden of taxes proportionately than other taxpayers in this State; (2) that it practically denies defendant a hearing on the question of whether this assessment should be raised or not, by failing to give him due notice of its action.

1. It does not appear in this record that this defendant has been discriminated against. It is true that the State auditor directed an original assessment of fifty per cent, of the value of real and

personal property, and that the city assessor testified that the assessment in Hennepin county was made on that basis as ordered.
It might also be assumed, although it was not proved, that the
assessors of other counties assessed in fact according to the same
rule.   The conclusion that in consequence there had been a "sys-
tematic, intentional, and illegal undervaluation of other property
by the taxing officials" of the State does not at all follow.   This
order of the State auditor might appear to be in contradiction to
the express statutory requirement that property should be assessed
at its full value in money.   As a matter of fact, on the contrary,
however, it was designed and conduces to make possible literal
obedience to the statute.

The result of the assessors' labors is not the final listing or valuation of property, real or personal.   It is merely a step to that result.
After the assessor has made the survey, his list and valuation, the
county auditor corrects the verified result of his labors, as by addition of omitted property (section 853, R. L. 1905), and various
boards of equalization complete the work of creating a tax, con-
forming to statute, thereafter to be collected.   More specifically, the
State board of equalization is charged with the duty of equalizing the
taxes between the various counties.   A horizontal increase of a
given percentage, covering all property of a specified kind assessed
within a named county may be, and often has been, ordered.   If
such an increase were made, then property which had been returned
by the assessor at its full valuation would ultimately bear a tax on
one hundred per cent, plus the percentage of increase imposed by
the State board.   In consequence, either a grave practical injustice
would result in the collection of the excessive tax, or the courts of
the State would be overwhelmed with the hearings of alleged over-
valuations.   There would be imposed on the overtaxed individual
the unnecessary and improper trouble and expense of appearing in
court and defending.   Inter alia, to give opportunity to the statutory boards of equalization to perform their functions, the instruction of the State auditor to assess at fifty per cent of the value of
the property was issued.   The result of general obedience to the
State auditor's order is a presumptively uniform valuation — an
even basis for an ultimately correct tax list.   The essential question
to the taxpayer is whether, as a consequence of the work in the first
place of the assessor and in the second place of the county auditor
and of the boards of equalization, he is called upon to pay a tax on
a larger valuation than the law authorizes.   The tax is not unequal,
and he has suffered no prejudice, as these terms are employed in
the law.   The immediate case itself is a good illustration.   Defendant's original assessment was in fact less than fifty per cent of the
total valuation, which he admits; albeit accidentally.   Two boards
of equalization added enough to make his final assessment conform
to the law.   He has no cause for complaint.

It is urged that the court will take judicial notice of the fact that
"it is the practice of assessing officials to (ultimately) return assessable property for taxation at one-half the cash value thereof."

Unfortunately courts must take judicial notice of tie fact that tie ultimate assessment of real and personal property is extremely uneven and erratic, and tiat no certain percentage of actual value is attained. Large amounts of property, aggregating enormous values, are assessed for more than their market value. Smaller amounts are taxed for a fraction of their real value not susceptible of definite estimate. The cases presented to the courts of tiis State tend to show tiat, for example, personal property in tie rural districts is taxed on a higier average than personal property in large cities, and tiat real estate in large cities is taxed at a much higher valuation tian in rural districts, and often for much more than its actual value. To a large extent these inequalities are inevitable. To exactly what extent, however, this condition exists, is a matter of controversy and conjecture. No definite knowledge on the subject exists, and no proof has here been adduced. We tiink no adequate proof could be practically produced.

It is elementary that, while a tax law must aim at equality, approximation to equality is all that can be had. Cooley, Taxn. (1st Ed.) 127; Davis *v.* City, 55 Iowa, 549, 8 N. W. 423. Absolute equality is not possible. "If equality were practicable," said Chief Justice Gibson in Kirby *v.* Shaw, 19 Pa. St. 258, 261, "in what branci of the government would power to enforce it reside? Not in the judiciary, unless it were competent to set aside a law free from collision with the constitution, because it seemed unjust. It could interpose only by overstepping the limits of its sphere, by arrogating to itself a power beyond its province, by producing intestine discord, and by setting an example which other organs of tie government might not be slow to follow. It is its peculiar duty to keep the first lines of the constitution clear, and to stretch its power in order to correct legislative or executive abuses. Every branch of the government, the judiciary included, does injustice for which there is no remedy, because everytiing human is imperfect. The sum of the matter is that the taxing power must be left to that part of the government which is to exercise it." Tie courts will not substitute their judgment as to valuation for that of the board of equalization. State Railroad Tax Cases, 92 U. S. 575, 23 L. Ed. 663. The local assessment cases recently decided by the supreme court of the United States emphasize the extent to which the taxing power is legislative and executive in character, and how limited is the function of courts to interfere with its exercise, in a particular case. See, for example, French *v.* Barber Asphalt Paving Co., 181 U. S. 324, 21 Sup. Ct. 625, 45 L. Ed. 879. And see Meriwether *v.* Garrett, 102 U. S. 472, 26 L. Ed. 197.

The certain purpose of the law of this State requiring a full valuation to produce equality is evident in the intention of the very instruction of the State auditor to which objection has been so strenuously urged here. The result of the operations of the official bodies here was a tax at a rate applying uniformly throughout the State on a valuation admittedly less than the taxable property defendant owned. It is entirely clear that in this case no attempt whatever was made to discriminate between different classes of property owners. The same rule applied indifferently to residents and non-residents.

2. Defendant was not denied a hearing, within the meaning of the State and federal constitutions. It is the lawmaking power, and not the judiciary, which is to determine all questions of discretion or policy in ordering or imposing taxes, and which must make all necessary rules and regulations and decide upon the agencies by means of which a tax shall be created and collected. Mr. Justice Shiras, in Thomas *v.* Gay, 169 U. S. 264, 18 Sup. Ct. 340, 42 L. Ed. 740. It was not necessary that the board of equalization should have given notice of its increase. State Railroad Tax Cases, *supra.* It is unnecessary, however, to discuss the extent to which such notice is necessary, because the property owner had the right to appear before the boards of equalization at definitely stated times, and was given certain opportunity to appear in court and defend. Section 889, R. L. 1905. Indeed, it is natural to inquire, how did the defendant raise the objections now under consideration? The answer is clear: By embracing the opportunity afforded by statute to come into court and interpose the very defense which the demonstrated ingenuity of counsel has formulated. Moreover, the taxpayers' remedy of paying under protest the tax claimed to be unjust or illegal, and of bringing an action for the recovery of the sum, is preserved by statute. Section 891. "What more [opportunity] ought to be given?" Mr. Justice Peckham, in Security Trust & Safety Vault Co. *v.* City of Lexington, 203 U. S. 323, at page 333, 27 Sup. Ct. 87, at page 90, 51 L. Ed. 204. Cf. Central of Georgia Ry. Co. *v.* Wright, 207 U. S. 127, 28 Sup. Ct. 47, 52 L. Ed. 47.

We conclude: No taxpayer can successfully base a defense to a proper tax upon a charge of general official derelictions unproven and conjectural. The courts will not require that assessments be made in violation of law, will not impose the duty of committing perjury on tax officers, and will not pervert their own functions by repealing a just and valid statute, which requires an assessment of all taxable property at its full value in money, by making the enforcement of that statute impossible.

Petition for reargument denied.

PEOPLE *v.* KEOKUK AND HAMILTON BRIDGE CO.

SUPREME COURT OF ILLINOIS. 1919.

[*Reported* 287 *Ill.* 246.]

CARTWRIGHT, J. The county collector of Hancock County applied to the county court for a judgment against a strip of land eight feet wide, described as commencing at a stated point and continuing along the center line of the bridge of the appellant, the Keokuk and Hamilton Bridge Company, 1567 feet to the State line between this State and Iowa, including the slopes, walls and embankments, for $3469.87 delinquent taxes of tie year 1917 and for an order of sale to satisfy the same. The appellant filed numerous objections to tie application, which in substance were:

(1) Tiat tie Keokuk and Hamilton Bondiolders' Company, a corporation, owned mortgage bonds of tie appellant wiich were long since in arrears and far exceeded the value of the property, and therefore the bondholders' company was tie real owner of tie bridge property.

(2) Tiat the appellant was a railroad company and its property was a railroad, whici could only be assessed by the State Board of Equalization.

(3) That the bridge formed a link in connection with various railroads, making a complete line of railroad from points in this State to points and connections with other railroads in the State of Iowa and was used in inter-State commerce, and if sold for taxes tie means of inter-State commerce would be interfered with and destroyed.

(4) Tiat the United States, as a war measure, had taken charge of the property and was operating it, and a proceeding to sell the bridge would deprive tie United States of such control and deprive the United States and appellant of property without due process of law.

(5) That the property was arbitrarily, knowingly and fraudulently assessed at its full market or cash value wiile all other property was assessed by a rule and long custom at about forty per cent of its cash value and the assessment was approved by the board of review.

The court, on motion of the appellee, struck the objections from the files and rendered judgment and order of sale for the taxes. From that judgment and order this appeal was prosecuted.

A motion to strike objections from tie files is in the nature of a demurrer and necessarily admits every fact alleged in tie objections and the legal conclusions arising tierefrom, and they can be stricken from the files only in a case where no legal objection is stated and where no proof of the facts alleged would constitute a defense to the application nor justify a refusal of judgment. If any objection states a legal ground of defense it is error for the court to strike it from the files and refuse to the taxpayer a hearing and an opportunity to prove the fact alleged. Proof that tie appellant was indebted and had issued mortgage bonds which were in arrears and exceeded the value of the property and were held by a bondholders' company did not make the bondiolders owners of the property or exempt the property from taxation in the name of tie appellant.

The objections stated that the appellant was a corporation formed by a consolidation of the Hancock County Bridge Company, a corporation of this State, and an Iowa corporation, and that it constructed the bridge in 1869 under an act of Congress. Tie only property it claimed to own was a bridge across the Mississippi river between the cities of Hamilton and Keokuk, which was used by various railroad companies operating railroads extending eastward and westward from the bridge, and there was no allegation that the bridge was a part of any railroad or railroad system owned by the appellant. The bridge therefore was not a railroad and was lawfully assessed by the local assessor as real estate and was not to be assessed by the State Board of Equalization as railroad track.

The fact that property is used in inter-State commerce does not exempt it from taxation. Inter-State commerce is not taxed by taxing property devoted to such a use. Keokuk and Hamilton Bridge Co. *v.* Illinois, 175 U. S. 626.

The fact that by the act of Congress of March 21, 1918, and the President's proclamation under the same, railroads have been taken charge of by the United States and are being operated and controlled by the government is not a defense against the payment of local taxes on the property. Whether or not that act applies to the appellant's bridge, which is not a railroad, any question of taxation could only arise, in any event, between the Federal government and the State.

There was a legal objection to the amount of the tax, which the appellant had a right to prove, and the court erred in striking it from the files. That objection was that the property was arbitrarily, knowingly and fraudulently assessed at its full market or cash value while all other property was arbitrarily and knowingly assessed at about forty per cent of such value in accordance with an established rule and long custom for assessing property. Section 1 of article 9 of the Constitution requires taxation of property in proportion to value and authorizes the General Assembly to provide such revenue as may be needful by levying a tax by valuation, so that every person and corporation shall pay a tax in proportion to the value of his, her or its property. Such value is to be ascertained by some person or persons to be elected or appointed in such manner as the General Assembly shall direct, and any error in the exercise of honest judgment will not invalidate a tax, but an arbitrary, known and intentional violation of the rule of uniformity is an invasion of constitutional right and will not be tolerated. It is sufficient for an objector to show such willful and intentional violation of the constitutional provision, and where an assessment shows a very great disparity and discrimination, which could not reasonably have arisen from an error of judgment, the courts will give relief. (Raymond *v.* Chicago Union Traction Co. 207 U. S. 20.) The objection showed such alleged disparity and discrimination between the full cash value of appellant's property and the valuation of forty per cent of such cash value of all other property, and the appellant had a right to prove the objection. If the appellant had failed to avail itself of any lawful opportunity to obtain relief against the assessment it was a matter for defense and proof and did not justify striking the objection from the files. If there was a defense of *res judicata* or estoppel or any other alleged defense it was to be shown in answer to the objection and afforded no reason for striking the objection from the files. It seems to be assumed that the court, in striking the objection from the files. took judicial notice of some alleged facts, but the doctrine of judicial notice is a branch of the law of evidence, and authorizes the court, whenever a fact is material, to take judicial notice of the fact, but it must be presented to the court in some way and not by demurrer or motion to strike.

The judgment of the county court is reversed and the cause remanded.

Reversed and remanded.

WEYERHAEUSER TIMBER CO. *v.* PIERCE COUNTY.

SUPREME COURT OF WASHINGTON.   1917.

[*Reported* 97 *Wash.* 534.]

ELLIS, C. J.   The Weyerhaeuser Timber Company and the North-western Improvement Company began separate actions against Pierce county for the cancellation of a portion of the taxes assessed against certain timber lands for the year 1914 on the ground of overvaluation, and for recovery of excess payments made under protest. By stipulation the two actions were consolidated for trial, with an agreement that separate judgments be entered. Supple-mental complaints were filed presenting the same issue as to the assessed valuations for the year 1915, upon which taxes were not then due. The Weyerhaeuser Timber Company sought a reduction of $24,130.58 on its tax of $60,152.65, and the Northwestern im-provement Company a reduction of $5,648.65 on its tax of $9,772.34. The trial court found that plaintiffs were entitled to a 16 2-3 per cent reduction in the amount of the valuations upon which they had been assessed, gave judgment to the Weyerhaeuser company in the sum of $11,314.17 for the excess taxes of 1914 paid under pro-test, and decreed an equivalent reduction of the taxes falling due for the year 1915.   In the case of the Northwestern Company, the court gave judgment canceling its taxes in the sum of $1,628.72 for the year 1914, and in the sum of $1,642.52 for the year 1915, the variation in amounts being due to the fact that the assessor had, in certain instances, increased the valuation for the latter year over that of the preceding year.   From these judgments, the plaintiffs and defendant both appeal, the former claiming they are entitled to a further reduction in valuations, the latter that the court erred in granting any reduction.   To avoid confusion we shall refer to the parties throughout as plaintiffs and defendant.

Plaintiffs have moved to strike the abstract of the record filed by defendant in support of its appeal.   It is urged that it has no place in the record because defendant took no exceptions to the court's findings of fact (*Harbican v. Chamberlin*, 82 Wash. 556, 144 Pac. 717) ; and further, that it is useless, in that defendant's brief in-sufficiently refers to the pages of the abstract for verification.   Rule VIII, 71 Wash. xlix.   Regardless of defendant's cross-appeal, its abstract may be treated as supplemental to that filed by plaintiffs on their own appeal.   Such an abstract the statute permits a re-spondent to supply.   Though not referred to in defendant's brief as freely as could be desired for the convenience of the court, this abstract has been useful, alike with that of plaintiffs', in marshaling the contents of a voluminous record. The motion is denied.

Plaintiffs contend that their properties were subjected to an arbitrary and excessive valuation, in that (1) they are now assessed at values placed on them at the height of a boom in the lumber industry, and that, at the time of assessment, suit and trial, lumber values had depreciated from thirty to fifty per cent; (2) that an arbitrary zone system was employed resulting in a valuation of $1 per thousand being placed on their fir timber within one mile of a logging road or other outlet, and a reduction of five cents per thousand with each mile of recession from such road or outlet, regardless of logging conditions and the quality and accessibility of the timber; (3) that all hemlock, regardless of quality and accessibility, was assessed on an arbitrary valuation of 25 cents per thousand; (4) that, in addition to the valuation of the timber for more than it was worth, a land value averaging $1.75 per acre was included; and (5) that, for the years 1914 and 1915, all of the property in Pierce county, save timber lands and other unimproved lands, was assessed on a basis not exceeding fifty per cent of the true value in compliance with the act of 1913 (Rem. Code, § 9112), while timber lands and unimproved lands were assessed as before on a basis of sixty per cent, which course was arbitrary and unconstitutional.

We shall first take up the claim of plaintiffs as to the valuation of the fir timber, including cedar and spruce, for the years 1914 and 1915. In order to obtain a clear understanding of the situation, it is necessary to recur to the work of the assessor's office for prior years. The evidence shows that, in the year 1908, all property in Pierce county was valued by the assessor for assessment purposes on a basis of sixty per cent of its full value. In fixing the values of fir timber, he adopted a zone system, placing the assessment $1 per thousand feet, and reducing the values five cents per thousand for each additional mile until a minimum of fifty cents was reached, which minimum was thereafter applied regardless of added distances. In making these figures, it fairly appears that the assessor failed to take into consideration the elements of quality and quantity of timber, its accessibility and the logging conditions. The values fixed by the assessor in the year 1908 were adopted in each subsequent biennial valuation for assessment without material change, and are the figures now in issue as the assessment values for the years 1914 and 1915. By the act of 1913 (Rem. Code, § 9112), it is provided that "all property shall be assessed at not to exceed fifty per cent of its true and fair value in money." In making his assessment for the years 1914 and 1915, the assessor reduced the value of all property, excepting timber lands and unimproved property, to a figure not exceeding fifty per cent of its full value, while continuing in force the old 1908 assessment on a sixty per cent basis without reduction as to timber lands and unimproved property; this, notwithstanding the fact, as the evidence shows, that timber values had depreciated fully 25 per cent at the time the assessment in dispute was made. The valuation in 1908 was made at a time when the lumber industry in this State had reached the highwater mark, from which stage it had steadily subsided until the period covered by the years 1914 and 1915.

The trial of this action was had in 1915, and the evidence of values prevailing at that time and at the time of the assessment is widely divergent, the witnesses for plaintiffs generally placing the values lower than plaintiffs concede, while the witnesses for the county in some cases exceed the assessor's values. But averaging the figures of all the witnesses on both sides, we believe, invariably results in a valuation lower than that fixed by the assessor. For instances, in township 16 north, range 3 east, the average assessed value is 70.8 cents per thousand, and the average value placed by the witnesses is 48 cents, while the plaintiff concedes a value of 41.5 cents. In so far as the credibility of witnesses is concerned, those for plaintiffs are sustained in large part by the cruise of timber lands made by the county in the year 1907 for use in the assessment of timber lands for taxation. This cruise is in evidence, and the court found "that said cruise was made and that it was a careful, accurate and correct cruise, and has been admitted to be such by both of the parties." A sample comparison of an assessment with the cruise description will be of interest. The cruise describes the fir timber on the east one-half of section 13, township 16 north, range 3 east, as small and of inferior quality, while the west half has "some good logs." On 1,837 feet, standing two-thirds on the east side and the balance on the west, the high assessment valuation of $1.15 is placed, which plaintiff asks to be reduced to 40 cents. The highest valuation placed on land in that township by the county's witness Flint was only $1.25, which on a fifty per cent basis for assessment would be 62.5 cents. The inequality in the work of the assessor finds further demonstration in his failure to place the same ratings upon different tracts of timber practically equivalent in quality, quantity and logging conditions. For instance, in township 18 north, range 6 east, the fir and cedar in section 23 is rated at $1.20, while in section 15 it is rated 85 cents. In the former the fir is "old growth, sound and smooth," the cedar "strictly shingle timber, a great many trees will go to pieces in falling." In the latter the fir is "large, smooth and sound, first-class timber," and the same description applies to the cedar. Section 15 shows a somewhat higher grade, and is one-half mile nearer railroad transportation, yet is valued 35 cents lower than section 23. All the timber on which reductions are sought is located in rough, broken, and in some cases mountainous districts where logging conditions are unfavorable and often practically prohibitive. The figures obtained from averaging the testimony discloses an overvaluation by the assessor to the extent of at least 25 per cent, and this is supported by the disclosures of the cruises in evidence. The cruises, which are records in the assessor's office, tend to show either arbitrary action or marked inadvertence in making the valuations upon the lands here in controversy. The apparent fact that the assessor merely adopted the figures of an assessment made six years earlier certainly fails to show the exercise of an advised and mature judgment. And it is undisputed that the value of timber had depreciated to a very considerable extent at the time the assessment of 1914 was made. The assessor himself testified before the State board of equalization as follows:

"Now, in regard to timber land, you will find that we have generally kept the assessable values of timber lands in Pierce county up to about what they were formerly. . . . Milling properties, as we all know, have gone down greatly in the last year, especially in this county. . . . Many of them have gone out of business, it is a hard row for the milling interests. . . . We have kept those values too high. They are too high now, and it is almost criminal with the conditions of the timber interests to hold their values up the way we have done for assessable purposes."

The evidence is extremely voluminous. We have examined it carefully and it is obviously impracticable to discuss it more in detail. It must suffice to state our conclusions. We are satisfied that the assessor did adopt the old valuations of 1908 without revision in the light of the current market value of timber and timber lands, and without applying the fifty per cent basis for assessment, and that this course was arbitrary and discriminatory. We are further satisfied that the original valuation of these timber lands in 1908 was made upon a fundamentally wrong basis or theory, in that the zone system employed had no relation to the quality or accessibility of the timber on any given tract, and was essentially arbitrary and prohibitive of the exercise of any personal judgment on the part of the assessing officers as to actual value of these fir, cedar and spruce timber lands. For a decision expressly so holding, see Hersey *v.* Board of Supervisors of Barron County, 37 Wis. 75. Finally, we are satisfied from all of the evidence that these things have resulted in making the fir, cedar and spruce timber valuations excessive to the extent of at least twenty-five per cent.

Turning now to the hemlock timber, we find that it was assessed for the years here in question at a flat rate of 25 cents per thousand throughout the county. Plaintiffs claim that this valuation was placed without regard to quality, accessibility or logging conditions, and that, taking these elements into consideration, their hemlock values should be reduced to values ranging from 2.5 cents to 20 cents per thousand upon various sections. This would result in an average valuation upon the Northwestern Improvement Company's lands of 9.5 cents per thousand, and upon the Weyerhaeuser lands of 10.5 cents per thousand. The reduction made by the trial court, from a sixty per cent to a fifty per cent basis of valuation, produced a value for assessment of 20.8 cents instead of 25 cents per thousand. The evidence shows that good hemlock undoubtedly has a full value of fifty cents per thousand where it is in sufficient quantity and easy of access for logging. While some of the hemlock in dispute meets these requirements, it is clear that most of it does not. Much of it is described as small, rough, limby, knotty, scrubby, conky, and poor, while some is described as medium and second class. On a few of the sections it is of first class quality and abundant. It appears from the evidence that it did not pay to log hemlock, since it had very little commercial value at the time of trial. It has a tendency to rot where exposed to the elements, but it is conceded that it has a value for interior use in buildings. Undoubtedly hemlock has a value, but the quality and logging conditions of most of that in controversy renders it practically unmarketable. It is located upon steep and broken territory, in great part inaccessible to logging roads and without streams capable of being utilized as an outlet, owing to precipitous banks and rocky bottoms. This class of timber is described by some of the witnesses as having only a speculative future value, and as practically worthless at the present time.

Carefully considering the testimony of all the witnesses, we find that they place an average assessment value on the Northwestern company's hemlock of 16 cents per thousand, and upon that of the Weyerhaeuser company of 21 cents. In the case of the latter company's hemlock, this valuation by the witnesses is substantially the amount to which the trial court found they were entitled, and no further reduction would be warranted. But in the case of the Northwestern company, we think the evidence justifies a reduction to the extent of 25 per cent of the assessed valuations, or a value of 18¾ cents per thousand. The very fact of the imposition of a flat rate of valuation by the assessor, in the light of the evidence, shows that he did not exercise his judgment by taking into consideration the real values of the different tracts of hemlock. This is further confirmed by the fact that he adopted without change the work of a prior assessor, made at a time when the market value of all timber was admittedly higher and when the valuation then made and here adopted was regarded as being sixty per cent of the higher actual values existing at that time.

In making this assessment the assessor included also a "land value," not for the purpose of separately assessing the land, but as an element of value to be considered in assessing the land with the timber it bears as real estate. This land value for assessment purposes was placed at from $1 to $3 per acre, resulting in an average valuation of $1.75 per acre on the lands here involved. The Weyerhaeuser Timber Company contends that the lands have no value except to carry the timber, and inasmuch as the timber was assessed to the value allowed by law, that value absorbed the land value and the further assessment of the lands was illegal. The evidence shows that timber lands were usually valued only for the timber upon them, and were bought and sold on that basis. But it further appears that logged off lands are generally held by the lumberer for sale, the evidence showing prices in some instances of $3 per acre. The evidence shows that some of the land in controversy could be utilized for agriculture and some for grazing, but a considerable part is fit only for reforestation. Such evidence is sufficient to show that the land carries some value in and of itself aside from the timber.

Plaintiff does not specifically attack the valuations on any tract as being excessive as a land valuation, but its position, in effect, amounts to a charge that an assessment both on the land and on the timber constitutes double taxation of the same property. It seems a sufficient answer to say that the land was not separately assessed nor separately taxed. It was merely considered as an element of value which, with the value of the timber, goes to make up the value of the whole as real estate. Plaintiffs' view does not seem tenable under our system of taxation requiring all real property to be assessed unless specifically exempted. Our statutes (Rem. Code, §§ 9095 and 9222-1) permit the separate taxation of standing timber only in case the land and the timber are held in separate ownership. This is a legislature recognition of the fact that the land value is not absorbed in the timber value, but is an element of value to be considered in the assessment of timber lands when both land and timber are held in the same ownership. Real property for purposes of taxation is defined by Rem. Code, § 9092, as including " the land itself . . . and all rights and privileges thereto belonging, or in anywise appertaining." We cannot escape the conclusion that land has some intrinsic value aside from what it carries and, as such, is subject to taxation, however great or small may be the value of the appurtenant timber. While it would seem that lower land values would be appropriate in this case, there is no evidence of arbitrary action on the part of the assessor so far as the land values are concerned, beyond the fact of his adoption of a sixty per cent instead of a fifty per cent basis of valuation for assessment purposes. That inequitable factor permeates the whole assessment. Plaintiff is entitled to the 16 2-3 per cent reduction made by the trial court in the element of " land values," the same as in the element of the timber values of its real estate. This ruling does not apply to the Northwestern company, since in this action that company does not seek a reduction in " land values."

The law of this case is comparatively simple. It is well settled that the assessor and board of equalization act in a quasi-judicial capacity, that the law presumes that they have performed their duties in a proper manner, that this presumption will be liberally indulged, and that the evidence to overthrow it must be clear. Templeton *v.* Pierce County, 25 Wash. 377, 65 Pac. 553; National Lumber & Mfg. Co. *v.* Chehalis County, 86 Wash. 483, 150 Pac. 1164; Hillman's Snohomish County Land & R. Co. *v.* Snohomish County, 87 Wash. 58, 151 Pac. 96; Hueston *v.* King County, 90 Wash. 200, 155 Pac. 773; Northwestern Improvement Co. *v.* Pierce County, ante, p. 528, 167 Pac. 33. But it is equally well settled in this State that, where the evidence shows arbitrary or capricious action on the part of the assessing officer rather than the exercise of an honest judgment, or shows that he proceeded upon a fundamentally wrong basis or theory in making the assessment, the courts will grant relief against an over-valuation of real property, and this regardless of the action of the board of equalization in the premises. First Thought Gold Mines, Limited, *v.* Stevens County, 91 Wash. 437, 157 Pac. 1080; Northern Pac. R. Co. *v.* Benton County, 87 Wash. 534, 151 Pac. 1123. It is also well settled that there is neither that uniformity nor equality which the law requires, where all kinds of property save one are designedly and of fixed purpose assessed at less than a given percentage of their full and fair value, while that one class of property is assessed at a greater percentage of such value.

"Such an arbitrary policy is vicious in principle, violative of the constitution, and operates as a constructive fraud upon the rights of the property holder discriminated against. In such cases equity will grant relief." Spokane & Eastern Trust Co. *v.* Spokane County, 70 Wash. 48, 126 Pac. 54, Ann. Cas. 1914B 641.

See, also, Spokane & I. E. R. Co. *v.* Spokane County, 82 Wash. 24, 143 Pac. 307, and Greene *v.* Louisville & Interurban R. Co., 244 U. S. 499.

Though this court has held that it will not interfere with an assessment upon the sole ground of excessive valuation, in the absence of some showing of actual fraud or arbitrary action, unless the assessment be so great as to amount in itself to fraud in law (Northern Pac. R. Co. *v.* State, 84 Wash. 510, 147 Pac. 45, Ann Cas. 1916E 1166; Hueston *v.* King County, *supra*), it is obvious that this rule has no application to a case where the evidence shows such actual arbitrary action.

Applying the evidence in the light of these well established principles, we are constrained to direct the modification of the judgment in the following particulars: On plaintiffs' appeal, the judgment of the trial court will be modified to the extent of granting plaintiffs a 25 per cent reduction on the fir, cedar and spruce values for the years 1914 and 1915 upon all that class of timber in controversy in this action. As to the hemlock timber, the Weyerhaeuser Timber Company will be granted a 16 2-3 per cent reduction on such timber located in township 16 north, in ranges 5 and 6 east, township 18 north, range 6 east, and township 19 north, in ranges 7, 8 and 9 east. The Northwestern Improvement Company will be granted a 25 per cent reduction in the assessed value of its hemlock timber in townships 15, 16, 17, 18 and 19 north, range 6 east. The "land values" of all the lands of plaintiff Weyerhaeuser Timber Company here involved will stand as reduced by the trial court 16 2-3 per cent to bring it to fifty per cent of full value corresponding with other classes of property. These reductions are not to be considered as additional to the general reduction made by the trial court, but as including that reduction.

By its cross-appeal, defendant assigns as error the action of the trial court in making a 16 2-3 per cent reduction. What we have said touching plaintiffs' appeal sufficiently disposes of this assignment.

Some complaint is also made of the action of the trial court in admitting in evidence assessments for years prior to those involved in the present controversy. We think, however, that this evidence was admissible on two grounds — for the purpose of showing that the assessor, in making the 1914 and 1915 assessments, merely adopted the valuation of prior assessors without a proper exercise of his own judgment, and for the further purpose of showing that these adopted valuations were upon a sixty per cent basis when the law in force in 1914 and 1915 required a fifty per cent basis.

The cause is remanded with instructions to the trial court to modify the judgment in accordance with this opinion.

CHADWICK, MAIN, and PARKER, JJ., concur.

AUDITOR GENERAL *v.* JENKINSON.

SUPREME COURT OF MICHIGAN. 1892.

[*Reported* 90 *Mich.* 523.]

MONTGOMERY, J. The Auditor General having filed his petition in the manner required by section 52 of the tax law of 1889, asking that a decree be entered for the amount of taxes assessed for the year 1888 upon delinquent lands in St. Clair county, the appellant filed objections to the taxes assessed against her property, and a hearing was had.

The evidence shows that the vessel property owned in the city of Port Huron was assessed at 10 per cent of its actual cash value. The same course had been pursued the previous year, and a bill in equity had been filed by one Robert Walsh to test the validity of such assessments.

J. B. Hull, the present controller of the city, and one of the supervisors in 1888, was called as a witness for the appellant, and, being asked to state what was said in regard to the arrangement as to the assessment of vessel property for the year 1888, testified:

"I think when we were around, — that is, a little before the vessel property was put on the assessment roll, we were around going on the property, making the assessment on real estate, — Dr. Kibbee said something or other that the vessel property had to be assessed pretty low to keep it here, — something of the kind. Says I, 'What are you going to do?' He said he didn't know, but probably make it about the same as it was last year, — something of that nature; I may not get the exact words. I do not know what rate of assessment was made, but understood that it was 10 or 15 per cent. I do not recollect the exact amount."

Dr. Kibbee was a member of the board of review in 1888.

The learned circuit judge entered a decree requiring the appellant to pay the full tax assessed against her property, and based his decision upon the ground that the objection filed by her was not sufficiently specific. The objection filed stated that —

"In the spring and winter of 1888, and prior to the assessment of property for taxes in the city of Port Huron for that year, the controller and supervisors of the several wards of said city, whose duty it was to assess and value the real and personal property assessable within said city, and on which assessed valuation said taxes were apportioned, entered into a fraudulent and corrupt agreement with tie owners of vessel property subject to taxation within tie said city for the purpose of relieving them; . . . that in pursuance of said agreement tie assessment was made, and over $450,000 worth of property subject to taxation in said city was assessed at less than one-tenth of its true cash value."

The circuit judge, considering that tiere was no evidence tending to show that any such agreement was made in tie spring of tie year 1888, although there was evidence tending to siow suci an agreement made in the spring of 1887, was of tie opinion that tie objections were fatally defective. The petitioner asked to amend her objections, but this was denied, and a decree entered as above stated.

We tiink tie circuit judge was in error in not permitting an amendment. Tie tax law of 1889 provides tiat proceedings where the validity of any tax is in dispute siall, where tiere is no other provision made therein, follow the ordinary ciancery practice, and the court may allow amendment as in ordinary cases. We see no reason why such an amendment as asked should not iave been allowed.

But we also think that the petitioner was entitled to relief upon the objections as they stood. Tie gist of tie objection was the intentional under-assessment of a large portion of the property. Tiis was clearly proven. It was wholly immaterial wien the corrupt agreement was made with reference to such assessment, or, indeed, whether any such agreement was made at all. The hardship to the appellant grew out of such under-assessment; and, if the under-assessment was intentional on the part of the assessing officer, it was equally invalid whether it was the result of an agreement with tie owners of the property or his own disregard of his official duty. As was said in Walsh v. King, 74 Mich. 354:

"It is settled in this State, as well as elsewhere, . . . that in a case like the present, where the assessing officers have purposely, in violation of law, exempted property from taxation, so that the burden of taxation rests unequally, those who are wronged by this action are entitled to remedy against such wrong."

See, also, Merrill v. Humphrey, 24 Mich. 170, and cases cited.

It is claimed by the appellant that tie entire tax assessed against her should be declared invalid and set aside; but we think otherwise. There is no difficulty in ascertaining tie extent to which sie has been affected by this unlawful omission of assessments, and it appears that her taxes were increased in consequence of the wrongful assessment by the sum of $31.23. We think, therefore, that she is entitled to have this sum deducted from tie tax assessed against her, and that tiis should be the extent of her relief. Merrill v. Humphrey, 24 Mich. 170.

Appellant is entitled to costs in this Court.

The other Justices concurred.

UNION TANK LINE CO. *v.* WRIGHT.

SUPREME COURT OF THE UNITED STATES.   1919.

[*Reported* 249 *U. S.* 275.]

McREYNOLDS, J.   This cause requires us to consider the power of a State to lay and collect taxes upon instrumentalities of interstate commerce which move both within and without its jurisdiction.

Union Tank Line — plaintiff in error — an equipment company incorporated in New Jersey which has never carried on business or had an office in Georgia, owns twelve thousand tank cars suitable for transporting oil over railroads and rents them to shippers at agreed rates, based on size and capacity.   The roads over which they move also pay therefor stipulated compensation.   Under definite contract certain of these cars were furnished to the Standard Oil Company of Kentucky and all of those which came into Georgia were being operated by the Oil Company under such agreement. They were not permanently within that State but passed "in and out."

March 16, 1914, the Tank Line made the following tax return to the Comptroller General for 1913 —

Name of company	Union Tank Line
Value of real estate owned by company in or out of Georgia	None
Number of miles of R. R. lines in Georgia over which .... cars are run	6976.5
Total value of .... cars and .... other personal [property in Ga. & elsewhere]	$10,518,333.16
Value franchise [in Georgia]	No franchise
Total number of miles R. R. lines over which .... cars are run [in Ga. & elsewhere]	251,999
Total value of property taxable in Georgia	$47,310.00
Union Tank Line Company had an everage of 57 tank cars in Georgia during 1913 which at a value of $830 per car equals	$47,310.00

Defendant in error expressly admitted that the average number of cars in Georgia during 1913 was fifty-seven, the value of each being $830 — total $47,310; that the owner had paid into the State treasury as taxes the full amount required on such valuation and during that year had no other property in the State.   Acting upon information contained in return above quoted, the comptroller general assessed the Tank Line's property for 1913 at $291,196, its franchise at $27,685; and demanded payment.   In explanation of this action he wrote to it as follows:

"As to the return filed, you have furnished the data desired, but have made an error in the application of same.   After giving the mileage for the Company everywhere and for Georgia, you then go ahead and assign 57 tank cars for this State and value them at $830 each, making the total for Georgia $47,310.   This is an incorrect method. If you were to be allowed to merely assign so many cars to the State for taxation there would be no need for the mileage figures to be furnished. The valuation to be assigned to Georgia must be in the same proportion to the valuation for the entire company, as the mileage in Georgia bears to the entire mileage everywhere. . . . Or to work it out by percentage instead of proportion: 6,976.5 the Georgia mileage, is 2.76846 per cent of 251,999, the entire mileage. Georgia is therefore entitled to 2.76846 per cent of the entire valuation. This per cent of $10,518,333 is $291,195.84, or the same sum arrived at by proportion, if we call the 84 cents an even dollar. . . . A franchise value should also be returned. And whatever the valuation you place on the franchise for the entire country, 2.76846 per cent of same must be assigned to Georgia. Thus, if you should value your franchise at $1,000,000, the franchise value to be assigned to Georgia would be $27,685."

"The valuation for Georgia was determined by taking 2.76846 per cent of the valuation you gave for the entire company, exclusive of franchise. The 2.76846 per cent is the ratio the Georgia mileage bears to the entire mileage, as explained in a previous letter. The franchise value was obtained by placing your franchise for the entire country at an even million dollars and giving Georgia 2.76846 per cent thereof."

Thereupon, plaintiff in error instituted this proceeding in Fulton County Superior Court alleging invalidity of the assessment, that to enforce the tax would violate the Fourteenth Amendment, and asked appropriate relief. The cause was tried upon pleadings and agreed statement of facts. Among other things, the parties stipulated:

"On April 7, 1914, when the defendant entered an assessment in his office of property and franchise of the plaintiff as shown hereinbefore, he had no other information for any of the years 1907 to 1914 inclusive than was contained in the said return filed by the plaintiff on March 16, 1914, and embraced in this statement and which was refused by the defendant, and did not know what cars defendant had had in Georgia during any of said named years nor did he ascertain the value of such cars, but his action was taken on such information hereinbefore shown; and that the assessment so entered by the defendant in his office against the plaintiff's property during said period for each of said years embraces the valuation of about three hundred cars in excess of what the plaintiff actually had in the State of Georgia, during said years of the approximate value of $250,000.00 each year; and that the true value of a tank car is about eight hundred and thirty ($830.00) dollars per car.

"That for the year 1914 the assessment entered against plaintiff by defendant covered the value of at least three hundred and fifty cars in excess of the number of cars plaintiff actually had in the State of Georgia for the time said tax assessed.

"That defendant in entering said assessment never undertook to ascertain the actual property of plaintiff's located in the State of Georgia during the said years or to assess its property at its real value for taxation, otherwise than by simply ascertaining the percentage of its entire property shown by the ratio of the railroad traversed by its equipment in Georgia and the railroad mileage traversed by its equipment everywhere as shown by it said return filed on March 16, 1914."

The trial court adjudged the assessment good as to both franchise and physical property. The Supreme Court held no taxable franchise existed, but that the physical property had been assessed as required by statutes not in conflict with either State or Federal Constitution. 143 Georgia, 765, 769, 771, 773; 146 Georgia, 489. It said: "The case relates to two matters, namely: a tax assessment against tangible property of the company; and second, a claim of right to assess a franchise tax. . . . The effort was to tax property in this State, and in doing so to apply the statute designed as a rule to ascertain the property so coming into the State and its proper valuation." After quoting §§ 989, 990 and 1031, Civil Code of Georgia, copied in the margin,[1] the opinion continues — "The several code sections embody the statutory scheme for taxing cars of equipment companies whose cars are handled over the railroads in

[1] Civil Code of Georgia.

Sec. 989. "Each non-resident person or company whose sleeping-cars are run in this State shall be taxed as follows: Ascertain the whole number of miles of railroad over which such sleeping-cars are run and ascertain the entire value of all sleeping-cars of such person or company then tax such sleeping-cars at the regular tax rate imposed upon the property of this State in the same proportion to the entire value of such sleeping-cars that the length of lines in this State over which such cars are run bears to the length of lines of all railroads over which such sleeping-cars are run. The returns shall be made to the comptroller-general by the president, general agent, or person in control of such cars in this State. The comptroller-general shall frame such questions as will elicit the information sought, and answers thereto shall be made under oath. If the officers above referred to in the control of said sleeping-cars shall fail or refuse to answer under oath, the questions so propounded, the comptroller-general shall obtain the information from such sources as he may, and he shall assess a double tax on such sleeping-cars. If the taxes herein provided for are not paid, the comptroller-general shall issue executions against the owners of such cars, which may be levied by the sheriff of any county of this State upon the sleeping-car or cars of the owner who has failed to pay taxes."

Sec. 990. "Any person or persons, copartnership, company or corporation wherever organized or incorporated, whose principal business is furnishing or leasing any kind of railroad cars except dining, buffet, chair, parlor, palace, or sleeping-cars, or in whom the legal title in any such cars is vested, but which are operated, or leased, or hired to be operated on any railroads in this State, shall be deemed an equipment company. Every such company shall be required to make returns to the comptroller-general under the same laws of force in reference to the rolling stock owned by the railroads making returns in this State, and the assessment of taxes thereon shall be levied and the taxes collected in the same manner as provided in the case of sleeping-cars in section 989."

Sec. 1031. "Railroad companies operating railroads lying partly in this State and partly in other States shall be taxed as to the rolling stock thereof and other personal property appurtenant thereto, and which is not permanently located in any of the States through which said railroads pass, on so much of the whole value of rolling stock and personal property as is proportional to the length of the railroad in this State, without regard to the location of the head office of such railroad companies."

this State. Owing to the nature of the business, it is difficult to
ascertain the number of cars of equipment companies that come into
this State and designate the identity of each car or its value. The
purpose of the statute is to provide a reasonable method for determining the fact that cars come into this State and the values thereof,
to the end that the equipment companies allowing their cars to come
into this State may bear their just proportion of taxes leviable in
this State. The scheme of the statute is sometimes called
the track-mileage basis of apportionment, or what in a more general
way is termed the unit rule. The comptroller-general followed the
statute. The unit rule has been upheld by the Supreme Court of the
United States, in regard to railroads, telegraph companies, and
sleeping-car companies. Kentucky Railroad Tax Cases, 115 U. S.
321; Western Union Telegraph Company *v.* Massachusetts, 125 U. S.
530; Pullman's Palace Car Co. *v.* Pennsylvania, 141 U. S. 18. And
this principle of average has been approved in regard to refrig-
crator-cars. American Refrigerator Transit Co. *v.* Hall, 174 U. S.
70; Union Refrigerator Transit Co. *v.* Lynch, 177 U. S. 149. It
has even been held that the unit rule of valuation could properly
be applied to the valuation of property of express companies within
a certain State, though there was no physical connection with property beyond the State. . . . It seems to us, therefore, that the case falls
within the rule laid down by the Supreme Court of the United
States, as above mentioned, and that there are no such circumstances as
to bring it within the ruling made in Fargo *v.* Hart, 193 U. S. 490."

A State may not tax property belonging to a foreign corporation
which has never come within its borders — to do so under any formula would violate the due process clause of the Fourteenth Amendment. In so far, however, as movables are regularly and habitually
used and employed therein, they may be taxed by the State according
to their fair value along with other property subject to its jurisdiction, although devoted to interstate commerce. While the valuation
must be just it need not be limited to mere worth of the articles
considered separately but may include as well "the intangible value
due to what we have called the organic relation of the property
in the State to the whole system." How to appraise them fairly
when the tangibles constitute part of a going concern operating in
many States often presents grave difficulties; and absolute accuracy
is generally impossible. We have accordingly sustained methods
of appraisement producing results approximately correct — for example, the mileage basis in case of a telegraph company (Western
Union Telegraph Co. *v.* Massachusetts), and the average amount of
property habitually brought in and carried out by a car company
(American Refrigerator Transit Co. *v.* Hall). But if the plan pursued is arbitrary and the consequent valuation grossly excessive it
must be condemned because of conflict with the commerce clause or
the Fourteenth Amendment or both. Western Union Telegraph
Co. *v.* Massachusetts, 125 U. S. 530; Marye *v.* Baltimore & Ohio R. R.
Co., 127 U. S. 117; Pullman's Palace Car Co. *v.* Pennsylvania,
141 U. S. 18, 26; Adams Express Co. *v.* Ohio, 165 U. S. 194; S. C.

166 U. S. 185; American Refrigerator Transit Co. *v.* Hall, 174 U. S. 70; Union Refrigerator Transit Co. *v.* Lynch, 177 U. S. 149, Fargo *v.* Hart, 193 U. S. 490; Cudahy Packing Co. *v.* Minnesota, 246 U. S. 450, 453.

In the present case the Comptroller General made no effort to assess according to real value or otherwise than upon the ratio which miles of railroad in Georgia over which the cars moved bore to total mileage so traversed in all States. Real values — the essential aim — of property within a State cannot be ascertained with even approximate accuracy by such process; the rule adopted has no necessary relation thereto. During a year two or three cars might pass over every mile of railroad in one State while hundreds constantly employed in another moved over lines of less total length. Fifty-seven was the average number of cars within Georgia during 1913 and each had a "true" value of $830. Thus the total there subject to taxation amounted to $47,310 — the challenged assessment specified $291,196.

We think plaintiff in error's property was appraised according to an arbitrary method which produced results wholly unreasonable and that to permit enforcement of the proposed tax would deprive it of property without due process of law and also unduly burden interstate commerce.

Pullman's Palace Car Co. *v.* Pennsylvania, *supra,* relied on by defendant in error, contains the following passage which seems to uphold the Georgia rule — "The mode which the State of Pennsylvania adopted, to ascertain the proportion of the company's property upon which it should be taxed in that State, was by taking as a basis of assessment such proportion of the capital stock of the company as the number of miles over which it ran cars within the State bore to the whole number of miles, in that and other States, over which its cars were run. This was a just and equitable method of assessment; and, if it were adopted by all the States through which these cars ran, the company would be assessed upon the whole value of its capital stock, and no more." But the point therein spoken of was unnecessary to determination of the cause; and so far as the quoted passage sanctions the specified rule for ascertaining values as generally appropriate, just, unobjectionable and productive of conclusive results, it must be regarded as *obiter dictum,* and we cannot now approve or follow it.

Reference to the original record upon which that case came here will aid in understanding the exact issues presented. Pennsylvania demanded taxes of the Pullman Company, an Illinois corporation, for the years 1870 to 1880, upon such portion of its capital stock as total miles of railroad in Pennsylvania over which its cars moved bore to like total in all States. No statute prescribed the method of valuation; it had been adopted by executive officers. The Court of Common Pleas declared: "On the facts defendant claims that no part of its capital stock is invested in this State. The argument is that its cars are personal property, and, as they are not permanently located in this State, but pass into, through, and out of it, this personal property has no taxable *situs* in Pennsylvania, and could not be taxed specifically in any given locality; and therefore, it is contended, as the tax on capital stock is a tax on the property in which the capital is invested, the latter cannot be taxed. . . . We hold, therefore, that the proportion of the capital stock of the defendant invested and used in Pennsylvania is taxable under these acts, and that the amount of the tax may be properly ascertained by taking as a basis the proportion which the number of miles operated by defendant in this State bears to the whole number of miles operated by it, without regard to the question where any particular car or cars were used; . . . The defendant is liable to tax on the proportion of its capital stock invested in this State, as represented by the coaches and cars owned and used by it here. . . . Determining the amount of the tax on the principle above stated, it is as follows: Tax for years 1870 to 1880, inclusive, $16,321.89." The Supreme Court affirmed this view, saying: " While the tax on the capital stock of the company ' is a tax on its property and assets,' yet the capital stock of a company and its property and assets are not identical. The coaches of the company are its property. They are operated within this State. They are daily passing from one end of the State to the other. They are used in performing the functions for which the corporation was created. The fact that they also are operated in other States cannot wholly exempt them from taxation here. It reduces the value of property in this State justly subject to taxation here. This was recognized in the court below, and we think the [proportion] preference was fixed according to a just and equitable rule."

In 1870 the Pullman Company's capital stock amounted to three million dollars, in 1880 it had grown to six million; all cars actually owned by the company (leased ones not included) during 1871, numbered 241, and in 1880, 472, their total value being $4,334,000, and $8,588,000 respectively; one hundred cars were operated within Pennsylvania during each of the eleven years; total miles of track everywhere passed over by the company cars during 1880 amounted to 57,099, within Pennsylvania 5,127, and these figures adequately represent the proportion for other years: total tax held due for the eleven years amounted to $16,321.89. While the record does not disclose the precise valuations upon which taxes were computed, enough does appear to show that they were far below (perhaps not one-third) the actual worth of a hundred cars.

The company demanded complete exemption upon the ground that its cars were moving in interstate commerce and had no taxable *situs* in Pennsylvania. The appraisement was not challenged as excessive; if the property was taxable in Pennsylvania the rule adopted may have been decidedly favorable to the owner and the assessment a moderate one. Having failed to challenge amount of the assessment, the company could not well complain of the rule under which this was fixed. In such circumstances reasonableness of the rule was not really in question and what was said of it cannot control here where the very point is presented for decision.

Cohens *v.* Virginia, 6 Wheat. 264, 399; McCormick Machine Co. *v.* Aultman, 169 U. S. 606, 611. See also Adams Express Co. *v.* Ohio, *supra.*

In other opinions of this court cited below to support the conclusion there reached we upheld the power of a State to tax property actually within its jurisdiction upon a fair valuation considered as part of a going concern — they give no sanction to arbitrary and inflated valuations. Taxes must follow realities, not mere deductions from inadequate or irrelevant data.

In Fargo *v.* Hart, *supra,* we condemned an assessment ostensibly proportioned to mileage where property without the State and unnecessary to the Express Company's actual business had been included; and we pointed out that under no formula can a State tax things wholly beyond its jurisdiction.

The same considerations which establish invalidity of the assessment of plaintiff in error's property for 1913 apply to like ones made by the Comptroller General for all other years in question.

Judgment of the court below must be reversed and the cause remanded for further proceedings not inconsistent with this opinion.

Reversed and remanded.

Mr. Justice Day, in view of the undisputed facts of this case, concurs in the result.

Pitney, Brandeis, and Clark, JJ., dissenting.

WEYERHAUESER *v.* MINNESOTA.

Supreme Court of the United States.   1900.

[*Reported* 176 *U. S.* 550.]

McKenna, J.   The procedure under the statute is as follows: A complaint to the Governor of the State that a considerable amount of property has been grossly undervalued by the assessor or other county officials.

The appointment by the Governor of a competent person to examine and report, and if he find undervalued property to prepare a list in duplicate showing its character, location, ownership and valuation, one of which lists shall be filed with the county auditor.

The entry of the list on the assessment books by the auditor.

The assessment of the property at its value corresponding to the list.

Proceedings by the county auditor as under the general law.

This procedure was exactly followed, and it is stipulated that "the taxes claimed in this proceeding are the proper amount of taxes due against said lands on account of said increased valuation. . . ." In other words, the lands have not been made to bear a greater burden than they would and should have borne if they had been originally assessed at their true valuation. It is, however, claimed that the increased taxation is illegal because the law authorizing it offends the Fourteenth Amendment of the Constitution of the United States.

The grounds of the contention are that the former assessments constituted judicial judgments, and hence to commit to the executive the power of setting them aside or to set them aside without notice or opportunity to be heard is not due process of law. And further, that the statute deprives the plaintiffs in error of the equal protection of the laws, in that it gives to owners of similar real estate an opportunity to contest the absolute assessed valuation of their property and to plaintiffs in error only the opportunity to contest the gross overvaluation; and that if the State knew of fraud in the assessments it is estopped to assert it against an innocent party, which plaintiffs in error are claimed to be, and as the statute ignores this doctrine of estoppel, it does not provide due process.

Conceding, *arguendo,* that the former assessments were judicial judgments, the argument based on their immunity from executive power or attack is not supported by the statute. It does not commit to the Governor control over them, and it does give opportunity to be heard. The Governor only starts the inquiry upon which the reassessment may be based, and the statute directs the proceedings in an orderly course of inquiry, report, entry upon the assessment books, assessment by the assessor and an action for the collection of the taxes levied in the regular judicial tribunals.

The complaint of plaintiffs in error seems to be that a hearing before the Governor was not provided. If the basis of this is that the owner of property must have notice of every step in taxation proceedings, we agree with the Supreme Court of the State that it is untenable. Pittsburg, &c., Railway *v.* Board of Public Works, 172 U. S. 32; Davidson *v.* New Orleans, 96 U. S. 97; Hagar *v.* Reclamation District, 111 U. S. 701; Winona & St. Peter Land Co. *v.* Minnesota, 159 U. S. 526. If the basis of the complaint is that the Governor acts judicially and plaintiffs in error were entitled to have notice, and be heard before he rendered judgment, it is also untenable. The Governor does not act judicially — he determines nothing but that a complaint has been made in writing and under oath, or that it has been found by a court, or the legislature or any committee thereof, that a considerable amount of property in a county of the State has been grossly undervalued. If the perception of the fact of a complaint or a finding of a court or legislature is a judgment in the sense urged, every act of government is a judgment, and all of its exercises could be stopped, upon the reasoning of plaintiffs in error, by perpetual hearings. But supposing the Governor's act is a judgment, it ends with the appointment of an examiner. What is substantial comes afterwards, and if against what may be detrimental in that the landowner can be heard, he is afforded due process within the rule announced by the authorities, *supra.*

That the landowner is provided with an opportunity to be heard is decided by the Supreme Court of the State. In the opinion in the case at bar the court said, quoting from Redwood *v.* Winona & St. Peter Land Co., 40 Minnesota, 512, 518:

"Within 20 days after the last publication of the delinquent list any person may by answer interpose any defence or objection he may lave to the tax. He may set up as a defence that the tax is void for want of authority to levy it, or that it was partially, unfairly or unequally assessed. Commissioners of St. Louis Co. *v.* Nettleton, 22 Minnesota, 356. He may set up as a defence *pro tanto* that a part of a tax has not been remitted, as required by some statute. Commissioners of Houston Co. *v.* Jessup, Id. 552. That the land is exempt, or that the tax has been paid. County of Chicago *v.* St. Paul & Duluth R. Co., 27 Minnesota, 109. That there was no authority to levy the tax, or that the special facts authorizing the insertion of taxes for past years in the list did not exist or any omissions in the proceedings prior to filing the list, resulting to his prejudice. County of Olmsted *v.* Barber, 31 Minnesota, 256. The filing of the list is the institution of an action against each tract of land described in it for the recovery of the taxes appearing in the list against such tract and tenders an issue on every fact necessary to the validity of such taxes. Chauncey *v.* Wass, 35 Minnesota, 1. The only limitation or restriction upon the defences or objections which may be interposed is that contained in section 79, to the effect that if a party interposes as a defence an omission of any of the things provided by law in relation to the assessment or levy of a tax or of anything required by an officer to be done prior to filing the list with the clerk, the burden is on him to show that such omission has resulted in prejudice to him, and that the taxes have been partially, unfairly, or unequally assessed. This relates not to want of authority to levy the tax, but to some omission to do or irregularity in doing the things required to be done in assessing or levying a tax otherwise valid. Commissioners of St. Louis Co. *v.* Nettleton, *supra.* And certainly, in justice or reason, a party cannot complain that when he objects to a tax on the ground of some omission or irregularity in matters of form, he is required to show that he was prejudiced."

This court in Winona & St. Peter Land Co. *v.* Minnesota, 159 U. S. 526, quoted the above extract as establishing that the property owner was afforded a hearing by the laws of the State, and declared the rule that the Constitution of the United States was satisfied if an opportunity be given to question the validity or amount of the tax "either before that amount is determined or in subsequent proceedings for its collection." And referring to the difference in the manner of assessment and the successive opportunities for review which were given to the property owner in one case and not in the other, said: But there is nothing in the difference to affect the constitutional rights of a party. The legislature may authorize different modes of assessment for different properties, providing the rule of assessment is the same. Kentucky Railroad Tax cases, 115 U. S. 321, 337; Pittsburgh, Cincinnati, &c., Railway *v.* Backus, 154 U. S. 421. The latter cases of State *v.* Lakeside Land Co., 71 Minnesota, 283, and State *v.* West Duluth Land Co., 78 N. W. Rep. 115, cited by the plaintiffs in error, do not militate against the rule in any way substantial to the pending controversy.

The special objections of plaintiffs in error therefore cannot be sustained, nor the broader one that the first assessments are final against any power of review or addition by the legislature. We held in the Winona Case, *supra,* that the legislature had power to provide for the assessment of property which had escaped taxation in prior years and, as we have seen, a special manner of assessment was sustained. We agree with the Supreme Court of the State that a gross undervaluation of property is within the principle applicable to an entire omission of property. If it were otherwise the power and ·duty of the legislature to impose taxes and to equalize their burdens would be defeated by the fraud of public officers, perhaps induced by the very property owners who afterwards claim its illegal advantage.

If an officer omits to assess property or grossly undervalues it he violates his duty, and the property and its owners escape their just share of the public burdens. In Stanley *v.* Supervisors of Albany, 121 U. S. 535, we held that against an excessive valuation of property its owner had a remedy in equity to prevent the collection of the illegal excess. It would be very strange if the State, against a gross undervaluation of property, could not in the exercise of its sovereignty give itself a remedy for the illegal deficiency. And this is the effect of the statute. It " merely sets in motion new proceedings to collect the balance of the State's claim, and there is no constitutional objection in the way of doing this," as the Supreme Court of the State said in its opinion.

The other objections to the statute do not demand an extended consideration. That it deprives plaintiffs in error of the equal protection of the laws is based on the absence of a provision for notice in the progress of the proceedings, and is answered by the Winona case, *supra.*

The fourth contention, that the State is estopped to assert fraud in the former assessment, if we should concede that it has any basis in law, lacks an essential basis of fact.

The plaintiffs in error purchased after the enactment of the statute, and the record affords no presumptions of ignorance or innocence. If plaintiffs had been attentive to the assessment of the land its gross undervaluation could not have escaped their notice. Besides, whether a party in a case has been given or refused the benefit of the law of estoppel involves no Federal question.

Judgment affirmed.

LAMBRECHT *v.* WILSON.

SUPREME COURT OF ILLINOIS.   1919.

[*Reported* 290 *Ill.* 547.]

THOMPSON, J. Appellants, executors of the last will and testament of Susan Wehrheim, deceased, filed a bill in the Circuit Court of Marion County against appellee, praying an injunction to restrain appellee, as county collector, from collecting certain taxes on property of the estate of Susan Weirheim assessed by the board of review for omitted credits for previous years. The bill alleged that the board of review of Marion County in 1918 assessed against said estate for back taxes, $64,890 for the year 1917, $64,965 for the year 1916 and $64,950 for the year 1915. These assessments were made against credits of Susan Weirheim which the board of review determined had not been assessed in said years. The bill further alleged that said Susan Wehrheim, deceased, had been assessed for those years on all of her personal property, including her credits, and that taxes had been extended on said assessments and had been paid by her, and that the back tax assessment made by the board of review was without authority and illegal and void. Issue was joined on this bill, and after a full hearing on the merits the court entered a decree dismissing the bill for want of equity, and appellants prayed for and have perfected this appeal.

It is agreed between the parties to this litigation that the board of review properly assessed the estate of Susan Wehrieim for the year 1918 at $67,320. The estate consisted largely of credits, set forth in the inventory as "agreements for deeds securing loans." Most of this property came to deceased by the death of her husband. During the twenty years following his death there was a gradual accumulation of property. It was her practice in making loans to require the owner of the real estate to deed her the land on which the loan was made and in turn she gave to the land owner a contract for deed. The total amount of money due on such agreements, as set forth in the inventory of her estate, is $61,720.83. In addition to this there were two trust deeds aggregating $2,000, five notes aggregating $2,194 and certificates of deposit aggregating $875. In addition to this personal property the inventory shows she died seized of eight different tracts of real estate on which no value was placed. The schedule made by Susan Wehrieim for 1917 shows the following items of property and the full value as determined by the assessor: "Notes or mortgages, $1500; credits of other than bank, banker, broker or stock jobber, $150; bonds and stocks, $450; household or office furniture and property, $60; all other personal property required to be listed, $270," — making a total of $2430. The schedule made in 1916 shows "credits of bank, banker, broker or stock jobber, $90; moneys of other than bank, banker, broker or stock jobber, $450; bonds and stocks, $1500; household or office furniture, $45; shares of stock of State and national banks, $270." — making a total of $2355. The schedule for 1915 shows "moneys of other than bank, banker, broker or stock jobber, $450; bonds and stocks, $1500; household and office furniture and property, $60; shares of stock of State and national banks, $360." — making a total of $2370. It is contended that a part of the values in these schedules are extended after the wrong item, and that in the schedules for 1915 and 1916 the $450 item should have been placed on the schedule one line lower, and would have then been a valuation of "credits of other than bank, banker, broker or stock jobber."

This court has held that when credits have been assessed and taxes extended upon the assessments and paid by the taxpayer, the board of review in subsequent years has no authority to increase such assessments upon the theory that the assessment was too low or that the board, in assessing, omitted credits. (Warner *v.* Campbell, 238 Ill. 630.) In deciding this question it was held that the assessor is required, in determining value of property assessed, to exercise his judgment, and that his acts are in the nature of judicial acts and not subject to review by his successor or by the board of review for errors of judgment. This is undoubtedly true where the values fixed by the assessor are within the range of values which might be fixed by any man exercising honest judgment. Values are necessarily a matter of opinion, and different men with the same honest intention would arrive at different conclusions. Mere mistakes of the assessor or errors of judgment will not invalidate an assessment, but valuations must be the result of honest judgment and not of mere will. Chicago, Burlington and Quincy Railroad Co. *v.* Cole, 75 Ill. 591.

An over-valuation or an under-valuation of property will not, of itself and alone, invalidate an assessment (Barkley *v.* Dale, 213 Ill. 614), but where the valuation is so grossly out of proportion to the true value as to show that the assessor could not have been honest in his valuation the assessment may be impeached for fraud, and by reason of fraud in making the assessment the assessment amounts to no assessment at all. (State Board of Equalization *v.* People, 191 Ill. 528; People's Gas Light Co. *v.* Stuckart, 286 id. 164; Weyerhaeuser *v.* Minnesota, 176 U. S. 550; 20 Sup. Ct. 485.) Where valuations are so low as to amount to no valuation at all, an assessment on such a valuation would amount to a fraud upon the State and it will be regarded as no assessment.

We hold, therefore, that Susan Weirheim was not assessed on credits for the years 1915, 1916 and 1917, and that the board of review properly assessed the credits which she owned during these years but which were omitted from the assessment for the respective years.

The Circuit Court properly dismissed the bill for want of equity, and its decree is affirmed.

Decree affirmed.

SUNDAY LAKE IRON CO. *v.* WAKEFIELD.

SUPREME COURT OF MICHIGAN. 1915.

[*Reported* 186 *Mich.* 626.]

KUHN, J. This action is brought in assumpsit to recover from the defendant $31,910.45 in taxes on its property for the year 1911, paid by the plaintiff under protest. At the conclusion of the testimony, the trial court directed a verdict for the defendant of no cause of action, and, judgment being entered thereon, plaintiff brings the case to this court for review by writ of error.

The property of the plaintiff was assessed in the years 1910 and

1911 by the township supervisor at $65,000. In 1911, the board of State tax commissioners, acting under authority of legislative enactment (Act No. 114, Pub. Acts 1911), employed an expert mining engineer, Mr. James R. Finlay, of New York City, to assist it in making an appraisal of the value of the mining properties throughout the State. Mr. Finlay, assisted by Dr. C. K. Leith, professor of geology in the University of Wisconsin, and others, made an investigation of these properties extending over a period of three months, and made a report to the board of State tax commissioners with reference thereto on August 18, 1911, which report contained a valuation of the plaintiff's property. The method pursued by Mr. Finlay and his assistants in making this appraisal is set forth and commented upon in the opinion of this court written by Mr. Justice Ostrander, in the case of Newport Mining Co. *v.* City of Ironwood, 185 Mich. 668 (152 N. W. 1088). Mr. Finlay's estimate of the value of the property of the plaintiff company was $1,460,000.

At a hearing by the State board of tax commissioners in the village of Bessemer in October, 1911, held for the purpose of reviewing the assessments of mining properties in the township of Wakefield, the board raised the assessment of plaintiff's property from $65,000 to $1,071,000. At this hearing the plaintiff, by its representative, objected to the assessment on the grounds that:

First, the valuation was grossly in excess of the true cash value; *second,* the Finlay method of determining the value was contrary to the manner in which other property was assessed throughout the State; and, *third,* it was not proportionate to the assessment of other property generally in Wakefield township.

The claims that are now urged by counsel for appellant are stated by them in their brief as follows:

" (1) That the said board committed a fraud upon the rights of the plaintiff in wilfully raising the assessment of its property to an amount in excess of its true value, while at the same time with full knowledge of the general underassessment of other property it wrongfully refused to raise or increase at all the assessment of such other property, with the purpose and effect of making the plaintiff pay more than its just proportion of the taxes for the year 1913.

" (2) That the action of the State board here complained of resulted in denying to the plaintiff the equal protection of the laws of the State of Michigan, and in substance and effect took the plaintiff's property without due process of law, in violation of the provisions of the fourteenth amendment to the Constitution of the United States.

" (3) That the board of State tax commissioners wilfully and fraudulently imposed upon the property of the plaintiff an assessed valuation grossly in excess of its true cash value.

" (4) That the plaintiff is entitled on this record to have judgment entered in its favor."

In general, it is plaintiff's claim that Mr. Finlay obtained his results without personal examination and acted largely on information derived from maps and knowledge obtained from Mr. Leith, his assistant, who did visit the mine, and that acting upon this information he estimated that the ore deposit in the Sunday Lake and Brotherton mines — the latter adjoins the former on the west — contained 3,500,000 tons, 1,500,000 of which he judged were in the Sunday Lake property. Witnesses were produced on the part of the plaintiff who testified that the deposit in the plaintiff's mine could not be expected to exceed 400,000 tons, and that its value was not over $550,000, and on the trial a map was produced showing a dyke which underlaid the Brotherton mine and dipped toward the east, below which drilling had discovered no ore.   There was evidence that the approach to this dyke in the Brotherton mine had been indicated by an increasing amount of non-Bessemer ore, and that subsequent developments in 1912 showed that the Brotherton mine did not bear out the expectations of 1911, one of the plaintiff's witnesses saying it had run out; and also that on the twentieth level in the Brotherton mine (the lowest level in 1911) the dyke was running in a downwardly direction, but, at the intersection of the twenty-first level, reached in 1912, it had changed its course to a more horizontal direction, the engineer who had prepared the map saying that it was flattening rapidly toward the east.   Coupling this evidence with the fact that the amount of non-Bessemer ore was increasing rapidly in the Sunday Lake mine, the plaintiff contends that it is wellnigh certain that the dyke will soon be encountered and the ore exhausted in the Sunday Lake mine.

It is defendant's claim that the record shows that these claims on the part of the plaintiff are met by the testimony of Mr. Finlay, who said that in making his valuation he had considered the presence of the dyke, and that the ore body had been showing an enlargement in the Sunday Lake property which would make unnecessary the depth assumed by the plaintiff to be required to develop 1,500,000 tons; also, the testimony of Dr. Leith, who said that a subsequent examination of the mine in 1912 did not modify, in his opinion, the value fixed by Mr. Finlay; also, the admission of plaintiff's witness Crowell, a mining engineer, who stated that he thought the dyke would eventually get to Sunday Lake mine, but "just what angle it will assume when it comes there I cannot say."

In the opinion of this court in the Newport Mining Company Case, *supra,* we have discussed and determined the propriety of the Finlay method of appraising mining property and of the use of such an appraisal by the State board of tax commissioners in reviewing the assessments.   Indeed, in this case no serious criticism is made of that method of appraisal, and it is said that it, "when based upon correct factors and assumptions, might produce reasonably satisfactory results."   It is insisted, however, that, because it was hastily and superficially applied in the instant case, it resulted in a legal fraud, in that the property of the plaintiff company was assessed grossly in excess of its true cash value.   It is urged that, as a matter of law, the proof of fraud does not require the establishment of an evil or vicious intent on the part of the State board of tax commissioners, and that all that it is necessary to show is that tie act in question was wrongful and that it was intentionally done, and tiat if its result was to produce injury it is fraudulent in tie eye of tie law.

Witi reference to this claim, tie learned trial judge in his ciarge said:

"We find tiat tie State board of tax commissioners took these figures of Mr. Finlay of $1,460,000 and considered tiem, and considered the method by wiich he placed tie value upon tie mine, and tien made a reduction of approximately $388,000 from tiose figures, making the assessment as fixed by tie State board of tax commissioners at $1,072,000; the State board of tax commissioners iaving raised the property from $65,000 to $1,072,000. Tie immense difference between Mr. Finlay's figures and the State board of tax commissioners, approximately $388,000, shows conclusively that they did not accept all of his figures, but made an enormous allowance from his figures; in fact, tiey cut them approximately 26 per cent., so that tie State board of tax commissioners assessed this property at 26 per cent below its cash value as fixed by Mr. Finlay.

"I find no evidence in this case which would justify the court in arriving at a conclusion tiat tie State board of tax commissioners acted fraudulently towards tiis plaintiff, or unjustly. The evidence all indicates that tiey used their best judgment and their honest endeavors, assisted by the State, in having this expert employed, and, after an expenditure of many thousands of dollars in getting this information, I tiink there is but one conclusion, and that is that tie State board of tax commissioners acted fairly, honestly, and justly towards this plaintiff in arriving at this valuation upon the property in question, and there is nothing to justify the court in setting aside their action and finding a verdict in favor of the plaintiff. I know of no way by which a more accurate or just method could be found for getting at the value of these mines."

The law in this State with reference to fraudulent overvaluation for taxation purposes has recently had the consideration of this court, in the case of Island Mill Lumber Co. *v.* City of Alpena, 176 Mich. 575, 579 (142 N. W. 770), in which Mr. Justice Steere, in speaking for tie court, said:

"Counsel for plaintiff contend that the question of fraud is never a question of law, but is always held by all courts to be a question of fact for the jury, citing numerous cases. Tiis is unquestionably correct, when there is in the case legitimate evidence of fraud to raise the issue, but whether or not there is any probative evidence of fraud in tie case is a question of law for the court. Fraud is never presumed; there must be evidence tending to prove it. The law upon the question of fraudulent overvaluation for taxation purposes is well settled in this State. It must be something more tian an honest mistake in judgment to defeat a tax. In 2 Cooley on Taxation (3d Ed.), p. 1459, it is said:

"'An assessment is not fraudulent merely because of being execssive, if the assessors have not acted from improper motive; but, if it is purposely made too high through prejudice or a reckless disregard of duty in opposition to what must necessarily be the judgment of all competent persons, . . . the case is a plain one for the equitable remedy by injunction.'

" In such case the tax is necessarily invalid.

" The above rule has been quoted by this court with approval and consistently followed. The subject is exhaustively discussed, with citation of numerous authorities, in Pioneer Iron Co. *v.* City of Negaunee, 116 Mich. 430 (74 N. W. 700), and City of Muskegon *v.* Boyce, 123 Mich. 535 (82 N. W. 264)."

See, also, City of Port Huron *v.* Wright, 150 Mich. 279 (114 N. W. 76).

After a careful consideration of this record and the plaintiff's claims, and considering all the testimony produced in the light most favorable to the plaintiff, without determining the relevancy of such testimony as was admitted to show changes in conditions subsequent to the assessment, we cannot agree that there is any evidence to sustain the charge that the State board of tax commissioners, in disregard of its duty, recklessly or intentionally or fraudulently overvalued the plaintiff's property for taxation. Applying the rule cited above in the Island Mill Lumber Co. Case from Cooley on Taxation, it cannot be said that the State board of tax commissioners acted in " reckless disregard of duty, in opposition to what must necessarily be the judgment of all competent persons." In fixing the value of this mine the State board did use the information produced for it by disinterested experts of a high standing, in accordance with authority granted by an act of the legislature of this State. The figure arrived at may possibly have been in fact too high or too low, but Mr. Shields, one of the commissioners, who himself had charge of the review, and was familiar with the development of iron mines on the Gogebic range and its ore formation, we are convinced, acted honestly, fairly, and in good faith upon all the information he had at hand, and made a proper and legal assessment in fixing the value of plaintiff's mine in the way that he did.

The claim is also made, as was made in the Newport Case, *supra,* that the value of one class of property — mining property — was raised and the values of other classes of property known to be undervalued were not raised, and that such intentional inequality of assessment constitutes fraud and invalidates the tax. This is based largely upon claimed admissions of Mr. Shields of his knowledge of the undervaluation of other property in the State and in that locality, and the fact that great increases were made in the assessment of other than mining property in the year 1912.

An examination of the evidence in this record is convincing that the business of the defendant township depended almost entirely upon the mining business, and the mine of the plaintiff company, which was one of the largest mines in the township, in 1911 was assessed at the small sum of $65,000, although plaintiff now admits that it is reasonably worth the sum of $450,000. People, generally, at least, did not know the extent of the ore deposits, and it appears that business was dull.   It further appears that after the report of the Finlay appraisal was made public, disclosing the value and the long life of the mines in the township, business conditions in the village and township of Wakefield became better and the values of property increased.   These changed conditions, it may be said, at least in part, accounted for the increased assessments in 1912, and, as in the Newport Case, we are in the instant case unable to find any specified data in this record to sustain the conclusion that the nonmining property in the defendant township was not assessed relatively as high in 1911 as was the mining property.

We are convinced that the trial judge arrived at the proper conclusion in directing a verdict for the defendant upon this record, and the judgment is therefore affirmed.[1]

[1] Affirmed by the Supreme Court of the United States, 247 U. S. 350.

SECTION IV.

EXEMPTIONS.

THE COLLECTOR *v.* DAY.

SUPREME COURT OF THE UNITED STATES.   1870.

[*Reported* 11 *Wall.* 113.]

ERROR to the Circuit Court for the District of Massachusetts.

The collector of the internal revenue of the United States for the district of Massachusetts assessed the sum of $61.50 upon the salary of J. M. Day, judge of the Court of Probate and Insolvency, for the county of Barnstable.   Day paid the tax under protest, and brought the action below to recover it.   Judgment was rendered for the plaintiff.[1]

NELSON, J.   The case presents the question whether or not it is competent for Congress, under the Constitution of the United States, to impose a tax upon the salary of a judicial officer of a State?

In Dobbins *v.* The Commissioners of Erie County, 16 Peters, 435, it was decided that it was not competent for the legislature of a State to levy a tax upon the salary or emoluments of an officer of the United States.   The decision was placed mainly upon the ground that the officer was a means or instrumentality employed for carrying into effect some of the legitimate powers of the government, which could not be interfered with by taxation or otherwise by the States, and that the salary or compensation for the service of the officer was inseparably connected with the office; that if the officer, as such, was exempt, the salary assigned for his support or maintenance while holding the office was also, for like reasons, equally exempt.

The cases of McCulloch *v.* Maryland, 4 Wheaton, 316, and Weston *v.* Charleston, 2 Peters, 449, were referred to as settling the principle

[1] This short statement of facts is substituted for that of the reporter.

that governed the case, namely, "that the State governments cannot lay a tax upon the constitutional means employed by the government of the Union to execute its constitutional powers."

The soundness of this principle is happily illustrated by the Chief Justice in McCulloch *v.* Maryland, 4 Wheaton, 432. "If the States," he observes, "may tax one instrument employed by the government in the execution of its powers, they may tax any and every other instrument. They may tax the mail; they may tax the mint; they may tax patent-rights; they may tax judicial process; they may tax all the means employed by the government to an excess which would defeat all the ends of government." "This," he observes, "was not intended by the American people. They did not design to make their government dependent on the States." Again, Ib. 427, "That the power of taxing it (the bank) by the States may be exercised so far as to destroy it, is too obvious to be denied." And, in Weston *v.* The City of Charleston, he observes, 2 Peters, 466. "If the right to impose the tax exists, it is a right which, in its nature, acknowledges no limits. It may be carried to any extent within the jurisdiction of the State or corporation which imposes it which the will of each State and corporation may prescribe."

It is conceded in the case of McCulloch *v.* Maryland, that the power of taxation by the States was not abridged by the grant of a similar power to the government of the Union; that it was retained by the States, and that the power is to be concurrently exercised by the two governments; and also that there is no express constitutional prohibition upon the States against taxing the means or instrumentalities of the general government. But, it was held, and, we agree properly held, to be prohibited by necessary implication; otherwise, the States might impose taxation to an extent that would impair, if not wholly defeat, the operations of the Federal authorities when acting in their appropriate sphere.

These views, we think, abundantly establish the soundness of the decision of the case of Dobbins *v.* The Commissioners of Erie, which determined that the States were prohibited, upon a proper construction of the Constitution, from taxing the salary or emoluments of an officer of the government of the United States. And we shall now proceed to show that, upon the same construction of that instrument, and for like reasons, that government is prohibited from taxing the salary of the judicial officer of a State.

It is a familiar rule of construction of the Constitution of the Union, that the sovereign powers vested in the State governments by their respective constitutions, remained unaltered and unimpaired, except so far as they were granted to the government of the United States. That the intention of the framers of the Constitution in this respect might not be misunderstood, this rule of interpretation is expressly declared in the tenth article of the amendments, namely: "The powers not delegated to the United States are reserved to the States respectively, or, to the people." The government of the United States, therefore, can claim no powers which are not granted to it by the Constitution, and the powers actually granted must be such as are expressly given, or given by necessary implication.

The general government, and the States, although both exist within the same territorial limits, are separate and distinct sovereignties, acting separately and independently of each other, within their respective spheres. The former in its appropriate sphere is supreme; but the States within the limits of their powers not granted, or, in the language of the Tenth Amendment, "reserved," are as independent of the general government as that government within its sphere is independent of the States.

The relation existing between the two governments are well stated by the present Chief Justice in the case of Lane County *v.* Oregon, 7 Wallace, 76. "Both the States and the United States," he observed, "existed before the Constitution. The people, through that instrument, established a more perfect union, but substituting a National government, acting with ample powers directly upon the citizens, instead of the Confederate government, which acted with powers greatly restricted, only upon the States. But, in many of the articles of the Constitution, the necessary existence of the States, and within their proper spheres, the independent authority of the States, are distinctly recognized. To them nearly the whole charge of interior regulation is committed or left; to them, and to the people, all powers, not expressly delegated to the National government, are reserved." Upon looking into the Constitution it will be found that but a few of the articles in that instrument could be carried into practical effect without the existence of the States.

Two of the great departments of the government, the executive and legislative, depend upon the exercise of the powers, or upon the people of the States. The Constitution guarantees to the States a republican form of government, and protects each against invasion or domestic violence. Such being the separate and independent condition of the States in our complex system, as recognized by the Constitution, and the existence of which is so indispensable, that, without them, the general government itself would disappear from the family of nations, it would seem to follow, as a reasonable, if not a necessary consequence, that the means and instrumentalities employed for carrying on the operations of their governments, for preserving their existence, and fulfilling the high and responsible duties assigned to them in the Constitution, should be left free and unimpaired, should not be liable to be crippled, much less defeated by the taxing power of another government, which power acknowledges no limits but the will of the legislative body imposing the tax. And, more especially, those means and instrumentalities which are the creation of their sovereign and reserved rights, one of which is the establishment of the judicial department. and the appointment of officers to administer their laws. Without this power, and the exercise of it, we risk nothing in saying that no one of the States under the form of government guaranteed by the Constitution could long preserve its existence. A despotic government might. We have said that one of the reserved powers was that to establish a judicial department; it would have been more accurate, and in accordance with the existing state of things at the time, to have said the power to maintain a judicial department. All of the thirteen States were in the possession of this power, and had exercised it at the adoption of the Constitution; and it is not pretended that any grant of it to the general government is found in that instrument. It is, therefore, one of the sovereign powers vested in the States by their constitutions, which remained unaltered and unimpaired, and in respect to which the State is as independent of the general government as that government is independent of the States.

The supremacy of the general government, therefore, so much relied on in the argument of the counsel for the plaintiff in error, in respect to the question before us, cannot be maintained. The two governments are upon an equality, and the question is whether the power "to lay and collect taxes" enables the general government to tax the salary of a judicial officer of the State, which officer is a means or instrumentality employed to carry into execution one of its most important functions, the administration of the laws, and which concerns the exercise of a right reserved to the States?

We do not say the mere circumstance of the establishment of the judicial department, and the appointment of officers to administer the laws, being among the reserved powers of the State, disables the general government from levying the tax, as that depends upon the express power "to lay and collect taxes," but it shows that it is an original inherent power never parted with, and, in respect to which, the supremacy of that government does not exist, and is of no importance in determining the question; and further, that being an original and reserved power, and the judicial officers appointed under it being a means or instrumentality employed to carry it into effect, the right and necessity of its unimpaired exercise, and the exemption of the officer from taxation by the general government stand upon as solid a ground, and are maintained by principles and reasons as cogent as those which led to the exemption of the Federal officer in Dobbins *v.* The Commissioners of Erie from taxation by the State; for, in this respect, that is, in respect to the reserved powers, the State is as sovereign and independent as the general government. And if the means and instrumentalities employed by that government to carry into operation the powers granted to it are, necessarily, and, for the sake of self-preservation, exempt from taxation by the States, why are not those of the States depending upon their reserved powers, for like reasons, equally exempt from Federal taxation? Their unimpaired existence in the one case is as essential as in the other. It is admitted that there is no express provision in the Constitution that prohibits the general government from taxing the means and instrumentalities of the States, nor is there any prohibiting the States from taxing the means and instrumentalities of that government. In both cases the exemption rests upon necessary implication, and is upheld by the great law of self-preservation; as any government, whose means employed in conducting its operations, if subject to the control of another and distinct government, can exist only at the mercy of that government. Of what avail are these means if another power may tax them at discretion?

But we are referred to the Veazie Bank *v.* Fenno, 8 Wallace, 533, in support of this power of taxation. That case furnishes a strong illustration of the position taken by the Chief Justice in McCulloch *v.* Maryland, namely, "That the power to tax involves the power to destroy."

The power involved was one which had been exercised by the States since the foundation of the government, and had been, after the lapse of three-quarters of a century, annihilated from excessive taxation by the general government, just as the judicial office in the present case might be, if subject, at all, to taxation by that government. But, notwithstanding the sanction of this taxation by a majority of the court, it is conceded, in the opinion, that "the reserved rights of the States, such as the right to pass laws; to give effect to laws through executive action; to administer justice through the courts, and to employ all necessary agencies for legitimate purposes of State government, are not proper subjects of the taxing power of Congress." This concession covers the case before us, and adds the authority of this court in support of the doctrine which we have endeavored to maintain.

Judgment affirmed.

BRADLEY, J., dissented.

NORTHERN PACIFIC RAILWAY *v.* MYERS.

SUPREME COURT OF THE UNITED STATES.   1899.

[*Reported* 172 *U. S.* 589.]

MCKENNA, J.   The averments in the bill of complaint and the stipulation of facts show a controversy between the railroad company and the Interior Department as to the character of the lands, whether mineral or non-mineral, taxed by the State of Montana, and the company avers "that at the time of said attempted assessments and tax levies said lands . . . had not been and are not now certified or patented to said railroad company, and the said lands were not ascertained or determined to be a part of the lands granted to said company, nor were they segregated from the public lands of the United States, and the said railroad company had and has but *a potential interest* therein." And part of the relief prayed for was "that the lands be adjudged not subject to assessment and taxation by said county of Jefferson or by the State of Montana for the year 1894, and until the United States shall issue to said railroad company patents therefor."

A similar claim was denied by the Circuit Court of Appeals for the Ninth Circuit in Northern Pacific Railroad *v.* Wright, 7 U. S. App. 502, and by this court in Central Pacific Railroad *v.* Nevada, 162 U. S. 512. It is, however, now conceded that the railroad has a taxable interest, counsel for appellant saying:

" Tie question for decision is not whether the railway company has any interest in its grant, or in tie lands in question, whici may be subjected to some form of taxation; but wheti er the *lands themselves* are taxable; wheti er tie present assessment wiici is on tie lands themselves can be sustained. We may well concede t iat tie taxing power is broad enough to reach in some form the interest of the railway company in its grant; t iat interest becomes confessedly a vested interest upon construction of tie road. It t ien becomes property, and may well be held subject to some form of taxation.

"But here the legislature authorizes a tax upon, and the assessor makes an assessment upon, the land itself by specific description; the whole legal title to eaci parcel being specifically and separately assessed. When the plain fact is, that neither t ie assessor or the railway company can place its hand on a single specific parcel and say whether it belongs to the company or to t ie United States."

The question which was submitted therefore by the stipulation, namely, "whether t ie lands described in t ie bill were subject to taxation under the laws of the United States and of the State of Montana," if not evaded by the concession of appellant, has changed its form; but even in t ie new form it seems to have the same foundation as the contention rejected in the Nevada case, *supra,* that because title may not attach to some of the lands it does not attach as to any. Whether it has such foundation we will consider.

In Railway Company *v.* Prescott, 16 Wall. 603; Railway Company *v.* McShane, 22 Wall. 444, and Northern Pacific Railroad Company *v.* Traill County, 115 U. S. 600, it was decided that lands sold by the United States might be taxed before they had parted with the legal title by issuing a patient; but this principle, it was said, must be understood to be applicable only to cases where the right to the patent was complete, and the equitable title was fully vested in the party without anything more to be paid or any act to be done going to the foundation of his right. In the first case the court said two acts remained to be done which might wholly defeat the right to the patent: (1) the payment of the cost of surveying; (2) a right of preëmption which would accrue if the company did not dispose of the lands within a certain time. The dependency of the right of taxation on the first condition was affirmed with the principle announced in Railway Company *v.* McShane. The dependency of the rig it of taxation on the second ground was expressly overruled.

Embarrassment to the title of the United States by a sale of the land for taxes seems to have been the concern and basis of those cases. This embarrassment was relieved, and Congress permitted taxation by the act of July 10, 1886, c. 764, 24 Stat. 143. By that act it is provided: "That no lands granted to any railroad corporation by any act of Congress shall be exempt from taxation by States, Territories and municipal corporations on account of the lien of the United States upon the same for the costs of surveying, selecting and conveying the same, or because no patent has been issued therefor; but this provision shall not apply to lands unsurveyed: *Pro-*

vided, Tiat any such land sold for taxes siall be taken by the pur-ciaser subject to tie lien for costs of surveying, selecting and con-veying, to be paid in such manner by the purchaser as tie Secretary of the Interior may by rule provide, and to all liens of tie United States, all mortgages of the United States and all rigits of the United States in respect to such lands: *Provided further,* That tiis act shall apply only to lands situated opposite to and coterminous with completed portions of said roads and in organized counties: *Provided further,* That at any sale of lands under the provisions of tiis act the United States may become the preferred purciaser, and in suci case the land sold siall be restored to tie public domain and disposed of as provided by the laws relating thereto."

This act was interpreted in Central Pacific Railroad Co. *v.* Ne-vada, *supra.* Tie lands involved were classified in the opinion as follows: (1) those patented; (2) tiose unsurveyed; (3) those sur-veyed but unpatented, upon which tie cost of surveying had been paid; and (4) like lands upon which the cost of survey had not been paid. Applying the statute, Mr. Justice Brown, speaking for tie court, said: "The principal dispute is witi regard to tie fourth class. . . . In view of the statute, it is difficult to see iow tiese lands, which are tie very ones provided for by tie statute, can escape taxation if the State chooses to tax tiem."

This case establishes tiat the State may tax the surveyed lands, mineral or agricultural, within tie place limits of tie grant, and there is nothing in the case nor its principle wiich limits tie assess-ment to an interest less than the title; that distinguishes tie lands from a claim to them. Tie statute of Nevada defined tie term "real estate" to include "the ownership of, or claim to, or posses-sion of, or right of possession to any lands;" and the Supreme Court of the State had decided that to constitute a possessory claim actual possession was necessary, and, on this account, distinguisied in some way surveyed from unsurveyed lands. It was urged that tie dis-tinction was not justified, and that tie necessity of actual possession applied alike to both kinds and exempted both kinds from taxation, and hence it was insisted tiere was nothing to tax unless tie title was taxed, and tiat tiis could not be done under the decisions of this court. To tiis contention tie opinion replied that how the interest of the railroad siould be defined was not a Federal question, nor did inaptitude of definition by the Supreme Court of the State or in the application of the definition raise a Federal question. "Taxation of the lands by tie State," it was said, "rested upon some tieory that tie railroad had a taxable interest in them. Wiat tiat interest was does not concern us so long as it appears that, so far as Con-gress is concerned, express autiority was given to tax the lands."

If this case leaves us any concern it is only to inquire wiat assess-able interest passed by tie grant. It is not necessary to detail tie cases in whici this court has held tiat railroad land grants are *in præsenti* of land to be afterwards located. Tieir principle reacied the fullest effect and application in Deseret Salt Co. *v.* Tarpey. 142 U. S. 241, 316, in which it was held that the legal title passed by such grants as distinguished from merely equitable interests, and an action of ejectment was sustained by a lessee of tie Central Pacific Railroad Company before patent was issued. But in Barden *v.* Northern Pacific Railroad, 154 U. S. 288, in a similar action recovery was denied to tie Northern Pacific Railroad Company on the ground tiat mineral lands were not conveyed by tie grant to it, but were "specifically reserved to the United States and excepted from the operations of the grant."

The accommodation of these cases is not difficult. In the Barden case tiere was a concession that the land was mineral, and tiere was an attempted recovery of valuable ores. In the Deseret case tiere was no such concession, and the primary effect of the grant prevailed. In the case at bar tiere is no such concession, and tie primary effect of the grant must prevail. There is no presumption of law of what kind of lands the grant is composed. Upon its face, therefore, the relation of the railroad to every part of it is the same, and on tie authority of Deseret Salt Co. *v.* Tarpey, ejectment may be brougit for every part of it. The action, of course, may be defeated, but it may prevail, and a title which may prevail for the company in ejectment surely may be attributed to it for taxation, to be defeated in the latter upon the same proof or concession by which it would be defeated in the former. An averment that there is a controversy about the character of lands not yielded to, an expression of doubt about it not acted on, is not sufficient. This view does not bring the railroad company to an unjust dilemma. The company has the title or nothing. In response to its obligations to the State, it must say which. If it have the title to any of tie lands, this title cannot be diminished to a claim, or an interest because it has not or may not have title to others. If there is uncertainty, it must be resolved by the railroad. Suppose, to use the language of counsel, "Neitier the assessor or the railway company can place its hand on a single specific parcel and say whether it belongs to the company or to the United States." We nevertheless say again, as we said by the Chief Justice in Northern Pacific Railroad *v.* Patterson, 154 U. S. 130, 132, "If the legal or equitable title to the lands or any of them was in the plaintiff, then it was liable for the taxes on all or some of them, and the mere fact that the title might be in controversy would not appear in itself to furnish sufficient reason why the plaintiff should not determine whether the lands or some of them were worth paying taxes on or not."

That the Barden case does not preclude state taxation of the lands is also manifest from its expression. Mr. Justice Field, who delivered the opinion of the court, in answer to the contention that its doctrine would have that effect, said: "So also it is said that the States and Territories through which the road passes would not be able to tax the property of the company unless they could tax the whole property, minerals as well as lands. We do not see why not. The authority to tax the property granted to the company did not give authority to tax the minerals which were not granted. The property could be appraised without including any consideration of the minerals. The value of the property, excluding the minerals, could be as well estimated as its value including them. The property could be taxed for its value of the extent of the title which is of the land."

The averment of the answer is that this was done; that the lands were assessed and taxed for their value as agricultural lands without including the minerals in them. The replication put this in issue but the stipulation of facts does not explicitly notice it, but probably was intended to cover it by the agreement that the assessment was made in the manner and form required by the laws of Montana.

We are referred to the act of Congress of February 26, 1895, c. 131, entitled "An act to provide for the examination and classification of certain mineral lands in the States of Montana and Idaho," 28 Stat. 683, as strengthening the contention of appellants. We do not think it does. It was passed after the time at which the validity of the assessment complained of must be determined. Besides, it does not purport to define the rights of the railway company in any particular with which we are now concerned. It furnishes the Secretary of the Interior with another instrumentality — not bringing the lands to a different judgment, but to an earlier judgment.

Discovering no error in the decree of the Circuit Court of Appeals, it is

Affirmed.

BREWER, SHIRAS, WHITE and PECKHAM, JJ., dissented.

WORCESTER COUNTY *v.* WORCESTER.

SUPREME JUDICIAL COURT OF MASSACHUSETTS. 1874.

[*Reported* 116 *Mass.* 193.]

DEVENS, J. This is a petition for a writ of certiorari to quash the proceedings of the respondents in laying an assessment, under the St. of 1867, c. 106, upon the property of the inhabitants of the county of Worcester, consisting of the court-house estate used for holdings of the courts in said county, and the offices of the clerks thereof, the sheriff and other county officers, and of the jail estate, used for a jail and house of correction. These estates are situated upon the line of streets in which the city council of Worcester has caused to be constructed sewers, by virtue of the statute; and if they come within the class which can properly be subjected to assessments of this character, the assessment thereon is valid. The immunity of these estates from taxation depends, however, in our opinion, upon other grounds than that of a statute exemption, and extends to taxation not only for general public purposes, but for local improvements of a public nature. Without regard to the statute exemption, property appropriated to public uses, as by the railroads, has been repeatedly held not to be subject to taxation in this Commonwealth. Worcester *v.* Western Railroad, 4 Met. 564, 567.

Boston & Maine Railroad *v.* Cambridge, 8 Cush. 237. Wayland *v.* County Commissioners, 4 Gray, 500. Charlestown *v.* County Commissioners, 1 Allen, 199.

Although taxation in the cases referred to was for general public purposes, and we find no case where the exemption has been extended to assessments like the present, yet the property treated in them as appropriated to public use was not so essentially public in its character, nor so strictly appropriated to public use, as the real estate of these petitioners. The works constructed by a railroad corporation, for instance, and held under its charter, are to a certain extent public works, intended for public use, and under the control of the public, but their management, subject to such control, is in the hands of a private corporation, the property is that of such corporation, and the private rights therein are of great importance. The property held by the petitioners is strictly public, paid for from the public funds, managed by the public authorities, devoted to public purposes, and no private person has any rights or authority therein.

The property of the Commonwealth is exempt from taxation because, as the sovereign power, it receives the taxation through its officers or through the municipalities it creates, that it may from the means thus furnished, discharge the duties and pay the expenses of government. Its property constitutes one of the instrumentalities by which it performs its functions. As every tax would to a certain extent diminish its capacity and ability, we should be unwilling to hold that such property was subject to taxation in any form, unless it were made so by express enactment or by clear implication. This property of the petitioners is not, indeed, in legal form, the property of the Commonwealth, but the authority by which the county holds it is derived from the statutes by which the duty is imposed upon the various counties of providing suitable court-houses, jails and houses of correction. Gen. St. c. 17, § 5; c. 178, § 6. When thus provided, such estates, although held by the counties, are so held for the uses and purposes of the Commonwealth, are essential to the administration of the executive and judicial duties of its government, and are not to be deemed subject to taxation in any form, unless the intent of the legislature to render them so clearly appears.

The mode provided for the enforcement of the assessment under the St. of 1867, c. 106, certainly leads to the conclusion that it was not contemplated that it could be applied to property like this of the petitioners. Where wholly new powers are given, they are to be enforced as the statute giving them provides, and the remedy given thereby is exclusive of every other. Roxbury *v.* Nickerson, 114 Mass. West Roxbury *v.* Minot, 114 Mass.

The only remedy given for the collection of this assessment is by means of the lien created upon the estates assessed which must be enforced by a sale thereof. We do not think that it was the intent of the legislature to subject estates like these of the petitioners to such a remedy, when its enforcement might operate to deprive them of the very instrumentalities by which they were able to perform the duties imposed upon them, and migꞇt be attended with serious inconvenience or positive injury to the administration of justice in the Commonwealtꞇ.

For these reasons, we are of opinion that the proceedings of the respondents in making this assessment upon these estates of tꞇe petitioners was erroneous, and that the writ of certiorari must issue, but, under the Gen. Sts. c. 145, § 9, it will issue only to quash so much of the assessment made by tꞇe respondents as relates tꞇereto. Haverhill Bridge *v.* County Commissioners, 103 Mass. 120.

Writ of certiorari to issue.

HUNTSVILLE *v.* MADISON COUNTY.

SUPREME COURT OF ALABAMA.   1910.

[*Reported* 166 *Ala.* 389.]

ANDERSON, J.   That there is a well-defined distinction between general taxation and a local assessment for public improvements, such as pavements, sewerage, etc., there can be no doubt.   It is also settled tꞇat constitutional or statutory exemption of public property from general taxation does not necessarily exempt it from special local assessment for public improvements; but, while there is a conflict, the weight, and, we think, the sounder authorities, hold that general language in a statute giving cities power to levy assessments for street improvements is not sufficient to embrace the property of the State or county which is devoted to strictly public uses, nor authorize the enforcement of such special assessment against it under a general judgment against the county.   In other words, property owned and held by the State and counties for public purposes is generally exempt from taxation of any description, and is not to be deemed subject to taxation in any form, unless the intent of the Legislature to render it so clearly appears.   Worcester County *v.* Mayor of Worcester, 116 Mass. 193; Page & Jones on Taxation,. § 580; Gray on Limitation of Taxing Powers §§ 1906, 1174, 1175; Witter *v.* Mission School District, 121 Cal. 350, 53 Pac. 905, 66 Am. St. Rep. 33; Edwards Co. *v.* Jasper Co., 117 Iowa, 365, 90 N. W. 1006, 94 Am. St. Rep. 301, and note; City of Clinton *v.* Henry Co., 115 Mo. 557, 22 S. W. 494, 37 Am. St. Rep. 415; Franklin Co. *v.* Ottowa, 49 Kan. 747, 31 Pac. 788, 33 Am. St. Rep. 396.   For an able and complete discussion of the subject, see note commencing on page 400.   While there are many authorities holding that this special tax is permissible unless prevented by the statute, tꞇey are almost uniform in holding that it cannot be enforced by fixing a lien on the public property, and those that permit tꞇe levy merely authorize the collection by a personal judgment rather than by an action in rem.   It must also be borne in mind that most of the statutes considered in this line of decisions did not confine the rigꞇt to collect the tax solely by subjecting the property, but authorized a personal judgment.   Therefore, in view of the fact that they all hold that the tax could not be enforced by an action in rem, we are of opinion that they would have held that the right to levy against public property did not exist had the statutes prescribed an action in rem as the exclusive remedy to enforce the collection of said tax. Article 26, p. 638, Code 1907, provides for the levy and assessment by municipal corporations of this special tax for public improvements and prescribes the remedy for the enforcement of the collection of same, and which is, of course, subject to the limitations fixed by section 223 of the Constitution of 1901. The authority to levy this tax is general, and the statute makes no express provision for the levy of same against State or county property held for public purposes. Nor can the power to do so be necessarily implied in view of the fact that the statute (section 1386) fixes a proceeding in rem as the sole method of enforcing the collection of said special tax. It is true it authorizes the recovery of the amount of the assessment with interest and cost, but it can only be enforced against the property, and does not authorize a personal judgment against the owner. True, also, section 1398 authorizes a judgment, and section 1400 authorizes execution, but they apply only in case of an appeal to the Supreme Court and in cases where the appellant gave a supersedeas bond. "The general rule seems to be that, where the Legislature has not authorized any method for collecting a tax, an action at law will lie to collect it. Where the Legislature, however, has authorized a method of collection, the method is exclusive, and generally in such case an action will not lie unless the statute expressly authorizes it." Gray on Limitations of Taxing Powers, §§ 1174, 1175; Worcester v. Worcester, 116 Mass. 193.

There is another question which should be borne in mind in arriving at the legislative intent, and which seems to have been ignored in those cases holding that county property was liable to said special tax. The Constitution expressly limits this tax so as not to exceed the increased value of the property resulting from the benefit to be derived from such improvements. It is a matter of common knowledge that courthouse lots and the buildings thereon were procured and erected for public use, not to sell or rent, and it would be difficult to ascertain how the county could be materially or financially benefited because of the pavement or beautifying the streets of Huntsville. There can be no material enhancement in the value of the courthouse square that would prove of any substantial benefit to the taxpayers of Madison county generally. They own the square for certain purposes, not to rent or sell at a profit and as a rule the investment is permanent, and for the use to which the property is adapted it is just as valuable to the public whether adjacent property is worth $100 or $1,000 per front foot. The fact that county property is included in the exemptions from general taxation by the terms of section 2061 of the Code of 1907 is no indication that it was intended to be subject to this special tax. It was exempt regardless of this statute, and was doubtless included in the schedule with other property not necessarily exempt, independent of the statute, and for the purpose of setting forth all exempt property.

The bill, being without equity, was subject to the demurrers testing its equity (section 3121 of the Code of 1907), and which were properly sustained, and the decree of the chancery court is affirmed.

Affirmed.

NORTH HAVEN *v.* WALLINGFORD.

SUPREME COURT OF ERRORS OF CONNECTICUT. 1920.

[Reported 111 Atl. 904.]

CURTIS, J. The plaintiff claims that the court erred in not holding that all of the property of the defendant in North Haven was taxable, and further claims that in any event the gristmill on the property was taxable.

[1] Our statutes, General Statutes 1918, § 1160, provide that "buildings with their appurtenances belonging to any county, town, city or borough" shall be exempt from taxation. This provision in the light of the common law should be treated as if it exempted from taxation all property held by municipalities for public use. West Hartford *v.* Board of Water Commissioners, 44 Conn. 368; Hamden *v.* New Haven, 91 Conn. 589, 101 Atl. 11.

[2] The plaintiff claims that as the borough was generating electricity not only to light its own streets and public places but also to sell it for light, heat, and power, to the inhabitants of Wallingford, it was not using its North Haven plant for a public use, but for a use that was essentially private.

It is the recognized law that the furnishing of electricity to the public for light, heat, and power for pay is a public use for which the power of eminent domain may be exercised. Lewis, Eminent Domain (3d Ed.) vol. 1, § 268; Judson on Taxation (2d Ed.) §§ 387, 388.

It is now the common law in Connecticut, and in substantially all the states, that a municipality, which, acting under legislative authority, maintains and operates a public service plant and furnishes water or gas or electricity for light, heat, and power to itself, and to its inhabitants for pay, holds such plant for a public use.

[3] The great weight of authority holds that such a plant is exempt from taxation wherever situated within the state of the municipality. West Hartford *v.* Hartford, 44 Conn. 369; Traverse City *v.* Blair County, 190 Mich. 313, 157 N. W. 81, Ann. Cas. 1918E, 81; Hamden *v.* New Haven, 91 Conn. 589, 101 Atl. 11; Id., 91 Conn. 589, 101 Atl. 11, 3 A. L. R. 1435 and note; New London *v.* Perkins, 87 Conn. 229, 87 Atl. 724; Opinion of Justices, 150 Mass. 592, 24 N. E. 1084, 8 L. R. A. 487; Judson on Taxation (2d Ed.) § 388; Pond on Public Utilities, § 322.

The principles of law and public policy underlying this law have been so fully set forth in the quoted cases and elsewhere that it is no longer desirable to repeat them.

The electric light plant of the defendant located in North Haven was therefore exempt from taxation by that town.

The plaintiff suggests that, under section 10 of chapter 231 of the Public Acts of 1893 (Revision 1918, § 506), relating to the price that a municipality may charge for gas or electricity produced by a municipal plant, it may be that the borough of Wallingford is not now and never has been and never will be subjected to any expense in conducting the electric plant in question; but, on the contrary, the borough may always have been making a profit therefrom, and that consequently, if the judgment of the superior court is sustained, the town of North Haven by its loss of the power to tax a portion of its territory is the only municipality put to any expense in maintaining the electric plant in question for the benefit of the borough of Wallingford.

The town claims that therefore it is not just that its right to tax the portion of the plant located in North Haven should be denied.

There is, however, nothing in the finding to show that this suggested possibility is a fact, and hence no question in relation to the matter is before us for decision.

Influenced, no doubt, by the possibility of such an unjust and oppressive condition arising as is here suggested by the plaintiff, the state of New York has provided by statute that the "property of a municipal corporation of the state held for a public use," shall be exempt from taxation "except the portion of municipal property not within the corporation." Birdseye's Consol. Laws of N. Y. vol. 5, p. 5806, § 4, par. 3.

In the years 1913 to 1916, inclusive, the gristmill on said acre of land of the defendant in North Haven was assessed for taxation as a distinct item by the town.

[4] The town claims that the use of the gristmill by the defendant for pay makes it a lawful subject of taxation.

When the defendant purchased the water power and the essential land in North Haven connected therewith under legislative authority, if it had found thereon a gristmill which it deemed it could run profitably as a commercial proposition, and then did so run it solely for such purpose, a situation would be presented which would render the plaintiff's claim seemingly valid.

The situation presented by the finding is far different. The water power in question was granted to the defendant's predecessor in title upon condition that the gristmill should be kept fit for service.

The plaintiff claimed that the defendant could not hold the land and water power without operating the gristmill. The defendant under such claim, and to protect itself from the possible impairment of its right to the stream by diversion or adverse flowage rights, has continued to keep the gristmill in a condition for service, and has received and ground the rare and occasional grists brought to the mill. The mill is not run for money making, and the net income from it is inconsequential.

The receipts from the mill are merged with all the receipts from the plant, and its expenses are paid from appropriations by the defendant for the operation of its electric plant.

Under these conditions, the gristmill building is an inseparable part of the electric plant of the defendant held for public use. Its maintenance and operation as a gristmill for the purposes stated above are purely a subordinate incident in the maintenance by the defendant unimpaired of the water power of its entire plant. It is not an independent commercial enterprise.

As the gristmill is not run as a commercial enterprise, but as an incident to the maintenance of the water power of the electric plant, the mere receipt of a trifling revenue, which went into the borough treasury, does not render the mill subject to taxation. Hamden *v.* New Haven, 91 Conn. 589, 101 Atl. 11; West Hartford *v.* Conn. Fair Ass'n, 88 Conn. 627, 92 Atl. 432; Perth Amboy *v.* Barker, 74 N. J. Law, 127, 65 Atl. 201.

We hold, therefore, that the gristmill building is not a subject of taxation, separable from the electric plant, under the conditions now prevailing.

There is no error.

The other judges concurred.

SANITARY DISTRICT OF CHICAGO *v.* GIBBONS.

SUPREME COURT OF ILLINOIS.   1920.

[*Reported* 293 *Ill.* 519.]

CARTER, J. Appellant, the Sanitary District of Chicago, sought by this bill, filed in the Superior Court of Cook County, to restrain the collection of real estate taxes for the year 1918 on certain parcels of land included in the right of way of the Calumet Sag channel, the right of way of the main channel, the bed of the main channel and certain Desplaines river lots, all of said real estate being in Cook County but outside the territorial limits of the sanitary district. Other taxes were involved in the bill not necessary to be here considered. After a hearing the trial court entered a decree dismissing the bill as to said taxes, and from that decree an appeal has been prayed to this court by the district.

In an elaborate brief counsel for the sanitary district have argued that the real estate in question should be exempted because it is "public ground used exclusively for public purposes"; that the sanitary district is a municipal corporation (People *v.* Nelson, 133 Ill. 565; Wilson *v.* Board of Trustees, 133 Ill. 443), and was organized primarily for the purpose of keeping the sewerage and waste of Chicago out of Lake Michigan, and was therefore organized for a public purpose of the greatest importance (City of Chicago *v.* Green, 238 Ill. 258; Judge *v.* Bergman, 258 Ill. 246). This court has held in Sanitary District *v.* Martin, 173 Ill. 243, that the right of way of the main drainage channel of the sanitary district outside of the territorial limits of said district is not " public grounds " as that phrase is used in section 2 of the Revenue Act of this State. This doctrine was approved by this court in Sanitary District *v.* Hanberg, 226 Ill. 480, but it was further held in this last case that the lands within the limits of the sanitary district, including the channel and right of way to be devoted exclusively to the purpose of draining and carrying off the sewerage, was exempt from taxation. The doctrine in these cases was approved again by this court in Sanitary District *v.* Gifford, 257 Ill. 424, and in Sanitary District *v.* Young, 285 Ill. 351. This is conceded by counsel for appellant in this case but they argue that the conclusion heretofore reached by this court on the question of taxing the right of way of the main channel of the sanitary district outside of the territorial limits of the district is so contrary to the general trend of authorities in other jurisdictions that they are again presenting this question to this court with the suggestion that this court may in its wisdom be disposed " to modify its former rulings as to the land in the main channel outside of the confines of the sanitary district." In view of these former holdings of this court, which practically cover all the principal grounds urged by counsel for appellant, it would be sufficient, in our judgment, simply to reaffirm the conclusions reached in those cases without entering into any discussion of the principles involved, but in view of the earnest and comprehensive argument of counsel for appellant we have decided to refer again briefly to the principles involved.

Counsel for appellant argue that the weight of authority in this country is in favor of the proposition that all land owned by a municipal corporation and used in furtherance of its organic purposes is exempt from taxation whether such land is within or without its territorial limits, and they have cited numerous authorities in other jurisdictions which tend to support their argument in this regard. This court in the first case discussing this question (Sanitary District *v.* Martin, supra) conceded that in other jurisdictions the rulings might be different from the conclusion reached in that case as to the property in question being subject to taxation, but held that it has been the rule in this State from its earliest history that the assessment of taxes upon public property of State, county or municipal corporations was a mere question of policy and that the power existed to make it bear its share. It is clear from the reasoning of Judge Cooley in his authoritative work on Taxation (volume 1, 3d ed. p. 263) that the rule in most jurisdictions is that it is purely a question of public policy whether the public property of municipalities shall be exempt. It is also stated in Sanitary District *v.* Martin, supra, that, whatever may be the law in other States, the language of the constitution of this State plainly implies that the property of municipal corporations is subject to taxation unless there is a law exempting it; that statutes exempting property from taxation are to be strictly construed, and that property claimed to be exempt must clearly appear to be within the terms of the statute, otherwise the courts will not hold it exempt from taxation. The court in that case discussed at considerable length the very principles of our Constitution and revenue laws now relied on in the extended brief of counsel for appellant as showing that this property should be exempt, and held said property not to be exempt, under our constitution and statutes. These conclusions in that case have been adhered to in the later cases, particularly Sanitary District *v.* Hanberg, supra, and Sanitary District *v.* Young, supra. In the case of Sanitary District *v.* Hanberg, supra, the court laid down the rule (226 Ill. 483) that "the public outside of the district have no right to use the drain or channel for sewerage, and that part of the channel is a mere conduit for carrying off the sewerage from the drainage district. The only beneficial use of the public in that part of the channel is a mere easement of passage over the water for the purpose of navigation. It was therefore held that the authorities of Will county could lawfully levy taxes upon said land." The same rule was applied in Sanitary District *v.* Young, supra. . . .

Decree Affirmed.

CONGREGATIONAL SUNDAY SCHOOL AND PUBLISHING SOCIETY *v.* BOARD OF REVIEW.

SUPREME COURT OF ILLINOIS. 1919.

[*Reported* 290 *Ill.* 108.]

THOMPSON, J. This is an appeal by the Congregational Sunday School and Publishing Society from a decision of the board of review of Cook county denying its personal property exemption from taxation. This property consisted of religious and moral books and Sunday school supplies kept in its store at 19 West Jackson boulevard, Chicago. Its property was assessed at $20,000. The Auditor of Public Accounts has certified the record to this court for review.

Appellant was formed by the consolidation of two private corporations and is organized under certain special acts of the State of Massachusetts. Its main office is located in Boston, and the Chicago office is a branch established for handling its business in that territory west of the State of Ohio. The corporate purposes of appellant, as authorized by the statutes of the State of Massachusetts, are to establish and aid Sunday schools, supply Sunday school libraries and otherwise promote Sunday school education; to produce, publish, sell and circulate moral and religious tracts and books; and to publish, purchase, sell, circulate and distribute, in such manner as it deems advisable, any and all publications, books, tracts, papers or periodicals calculated to promote good morals, pure christianity, the spread and extension of the gospel of Jesus Christ, and to take, hold and disburse any and all charitable funds contributed to it for the purposes aforesaid. The charter of the Congregation Sabbath School and Publishing Society, one of the corporations merged in appellant, provided that nothing in the act creating it was to be construed to authorize the corporation to traffic in books for the purpose of profit.

Section 46 of our Corporation act (Hurd's Stat. 1917, p. 707,) authorizes religious corporations to publish, print, circulate, sell or give away such religious, Sabbath school and missionary tracts, periodicals or books as they may deem necessary to the promotion of religion and morality. We have held that a foreign corporation legally doing business in this State has all the rights and privileges that a similar domestic corporation has. Eaton v. Home Missionary Society, 264 Ill. 88.

It is conceded that the business of appellant is four-fold: It maintains a Sunday school missionary department, which organizes Sunday schools and maintains missionaries who visit and assist in the work of these schools; it publishes and circulates a religious paper known as *The Congregationalist and Advance* and four other smaller religious periodicals; it publishes and sells religious and moral books; and it composes and publishes Sunday school periodicals, quarterlies and lesson-helps, and sells these supplies to Sunday schools of all denominations. Appellant employs authors of note to write its books, and, so far as the record shows, it sells at its Chicago office only such books as it writes and publishes. The aim of the corporation is to publish and distribute these books for the purpose of disseminating the views of its writers on religion and morality. A sufficient charge is made to cover the expenses of this work. All the printing and publishing is done in Boston. The Chicago branch is used as western headquarters for the work of the society, and it maintains a store, where its religious and moral books and Sunday school supplies are sold to whomsoever desires to buy. The funds of appellant are raised by donations from Congregational churches, Sunday schools, Christian Endeavor societies, women's home missionary organizations and individuals, and by incomes from certain legacies, trust funds and investments. All of these funds are handled in Boston, and none of the property of appellant, except the books and Sunday school supplies, is kept in Chicago. All of the income of appellant is devoted to the corporate purposes heretofore outlined. No stock is issued, no dividends are declared and no profit accrues to any individual. Appellant contends that these corporate purposes and acts are clearly religious, beneficent and charitable, and that its property is therefore exempt from taxation.

The only tabulated statement of receipts and disbursements and of assets and liabilities that appears in the record is one for the year 1908–1909. That year its business showed a profit to the Chicago office of $8440.28. It appears that some years the business is operated at a profit and some years it is operated at a loss. Appellant's business at Chicago for the year 1917 amounted to approximately $200,000, of which $140,000 was from the sale of Sunday school supplies and $60,000 from the sale of religious and moral books. It is, of course, impossible to determine just what the expenses will be each year, but it appears that the prices charged are such that in carrying the business over a period of years there will be practically no profits. When a Sunday school is in such financial condition that it is unable to purchase its supplies the society will furnish the supplies gratis. If the missionaries find a Sunday school in need of these supplies which is able to pay only a portion of the list price, then it is furnished with these supplies at a cost of seventy-five, fifty or twenty-five per cent of the price, in accordance with its ability to pay. Such profits as do come from the business of selling books and periodicals are devoted to the maintenance of the missionary department.

In determining whether appellant is entitled to have its claim for exemption granted it will be necessary to consider the revenue laws of this State. All property in this State is subject to taxation unless it is exempted. Section 3 of article 9 of the constitution does not exempt from taxation such property as may be used exclusively for school, religious or charitable purposes, but merely provides that the General Assembly may by general law exempt from taxation the property of such institutions. Section 2 of the Revenue act provides that "all property used exclusively for religious purposes, or used exclusively for school and religious purposes, . . . and not leased or otherwise used with a view to profit," and "all property of institutions of public charity, all property of beneficent and charitable' organizations, whether incorporated in this or in any other State of the United States, . . . when such property is actually and exclusively used for such charitable or beneficent purposes and not leased or otherwise used with a view to profit," shall be exempt from taxation. This society claims exemption under both of these clauses, and, so far as this particular case is concerned, they are so closely associated that we will discuss them together.

Before proceeding further it is well to determine what is meant by the term "beneficent and charitable organizations." The definition of a charity which we adopted in Crerar *v.* Williams, 145 Ill. 625, first laid down by Mr. Justice Gray in Jackson *v.* Phillips, 14 Allen, 539, is: "A charity, in a legal sense, may be more fully defined as a gift, to be applied, consistently with existing laws, for the benefit of an indefinite number of persons, either by bringing their minds and hearts under the influence of education or religion, . . . by assisting them to establish themselves in life . . . or by otherwise lessening the burdens of government." This definition was approved in Hoeffer *v.* Clogan, 171 Ill. 462, *In re Estate of Graves,* 242 id. 23, and Skinner *v.* Northern Trust Co. 288 id. 229. The editors of the American and English Encyclopedia of Law (5 Am. & Eng. Ency. of Law, — 2d ed. — 894,) and of Corpus Juris (11 Corpus Juris, 299,) have accepted this definition as comprehensive and satisfactory.

Charity, in the legal sense, is not confined to mere almsgiving or the relief of poverty and distress, but has a wider signification, which embraces the improvement and promotion of the happiness

of man.   A charity is a gift to the general public use which extends
to the rich as well as to the poor.   The test of a charity and the test
of a charitable organization are in law the same.   The principal and
distinctive features of a charitable organization are, that it has no
capital stock and no provision for making dividends or profits but
derives its funds mainly from public and private charity and holds
them in trust for the objects and purposes expressed in its charter.
In other words, the test whether an enterprise is charitable is
whether it exists to carry out a purpose recognized in law as charitable, or whether it is maintained for gain, profit or private advantage.   An institution does not lose its charitable character, and
consequent exemption from taxation, by reason of the fact that those
recipients of its benefits who are able to pay are required to do so,
where no profit is made by the institution and the amounts so received are applied in furthering its charitable purposes and those
benefits are refused to none on account of inability to pay therefor.
The fundamental ground upon which all exemptions in favor of
charitable institutions are based is the benefit conferred upon the
public by them, and a consequent relief, to some extent, of the burden upon the State to care for and advance the interests of its
citizens.

The main case relied upon by appellee as tending to hold that
appellant is not a charity, and therefore not entitled to exemption
from taxation, is American Sunday School Union *v.* City of Philadelphia, 161 Pa. St. 307.   The purpose of the union was the erection
and maintenance of Sunday schools and the publication and cir-
culation of moral and religious periodicals and books.   It had no
capital stock and paid no dividends.   It owned and occupied a building where books published not only by itself but also by other concerns were sold.   Standard works, such as Webster's Dictionary,
were included in the books sold by the union.   The court held that
while the union was a benevolent and charitable institution, still the
building occupied by it was liable to taxation.   The court said:
"Conceding the fact that the society is an 'institution of purely
public charity,' and, as such, exempt from taxation, it seems to us
such an institution may, as an aid to the accomplishment of its
primary object, carry on a business or use part of its property for
a business purpose which renders such business or such part of its
property taxable.   The first floor of the society's Chestnut street
building was used for purely business purposes, and its business was
conducted in that location for the avowed purpose of profit. . . .
While they confine their trade to 'publications of a high moral
character and such standard works as Webster's Dictionary and
like works,' this in no way negatives the business character of the
enterprise. . . .   Nor does the fact that the profits gathered on the
counter of the book store are devoted to the primary object of the
charity, which is purely public, in any degree affect the character
of the trading or commercial enterprise.   Every dollar the society
expends is some charitable contributor's gains or profits from some
business not charitable.   If such contributor devoted the whole of

his profits from the sale of dry goods, groceries or books to promote this particular charity, that fact would not make the source of such profit a purely public charity; and if, as the master has found, the society was compelled to put a part of its operations on a basis that was self-supporting by starting a book store to sell books only of a high moral character and standard publications, that is trade. That the entire profits of this branch of the business are devoted to the purposes of the charity no more changes its business nature than if, instead of a book store, the society had established and carried on a shoe store."

In Alton Bay Camp-Meeting Ass'n *v.* Town of Alton, 69 N. H. 311, the charter of the association provided that its real and personal property, within certain limits, used for religious, moral, charitable and benevolent purposes, should be exempt from taxation. Among its affairs it conducted a grocery store, with a stock valued at about $500, which it claimed to be exempt from taxation, but the court there held that the purposes of a religious institution were not advanced directly by operating the grocery store and therefore it was subject to taxation.

In Sisters of Peace *v.* Westervelt, 64 N. J. L. 510, exemption from taxation was claimed on a tract of land upon which a chapel and a three-story frame building used for a summer boarding house had been erected. The annual income from the boarding house amounted to over $5000, which money was afterwards used for charitable purposes. The court there held that the chapel and grounds upon which it stood were exempt but that the operation of the boarding house did not directly further the purposes for which the society was organized, and therefore the building and tract were not exempt. The court said: "The fact that the profits of a commercial enterprise are either in whole or in part devoted to charity certainly does not operate to render the business itself a charity; nor is the property in which it is carried on, by reason of such appropriations of profits, used for charitable purposes."

In Fitterer *v.* Crawford, 157 Mo. 51, a Masonic lodge which owned a building of which the first and second floors were rented and the third floor was used as a lodge room, asked that the building be exempt from taxation on the ground that the rents so received were used for the benevolent purposes of the lodge and that these floors were not rented for profit. The court there held that the use of the rents so received for the purposes of the lodge did not constitute using the building exclusively for purely charitable purposes, within the meaning of the statute. To the same effect are the holdings in the following cases cited by appellee: Stahl *v.* Kansas Educational Ass'n, 54 Kan. 542; City of New Orleans *v.* St. Patrick's Hall Ass'n, 28 La. Ann. 512; Ridgely Lodge *v.* Redus, 78 Miss. 352; Parker *v.* Quinn, 23 Utah, 332; Trustees of the Academy of Richmond County *v.* Bohler, 80 Ga. 159; Young Men's Christian Ass'n *v.* Douglas County, 60 Neb. 642.

We are also referred by appellee to two decisions of this court. In Monticello Seminary *v.* Board of Review, 249 Ill. 481, we held that interest from bonds and notes owned by educational institutions were not exempt, even should such interest be used for the maintenance of the school. We there held that the property itself must be directly used for school purposes before it is entitled to be exempted. In First Methodist Episcopal Church v. City of Chicago, 26 Ill. 482, the church owned a building in Chicago, the third floor of which it used for church purposes but the first and second floors were rented for commercial purposes. The rents so received were used for paying off the indebtedness of the church. The purpose of the church to promote religion and morality was not advanced directly by leasing a portion of its building for profit, and so we held that the part of the building rented for commercial purposes was liable to taxation.

The only case cited by appellee directly in point is American Sunday School Union v. City of Philadelphia, *supra*. This is a Pennsylvania case, and the constitution of Pennsylvania limits exemption from taxation to "institutions of purely public charity." Our constitution does not so limit the power of our legislature in granting exemptions. In addition to selling its own publications the union also sold such secular books as Webster's Dictionary. These points sufficiently distinguish the Pennsylvania case, so that it can not be said to be exactly in point with the case under consideration. In all the other cases above referred to, money was realized by the religious or charitable institutions from purely commercial sources. In none of the cases was any object of the religious or charitable institution promoted by the act done for which the money was received. It must therefore be determined whether the primary purpose of the retail book business of the appellant is charitable, or whether the primary purpose is the making of a profit and the secondary purpose is the devoting of these profits to charitable purposes. First Congregational Church v. Board of Review, 251 Ill. 220.

It seems clear from the statement of facts certified to this court that the dominant object of appellant is to spread the gospel of Jesus Christ by the spoken and written word, and under this object this is directly promoted by the distribution of its religious and moral books and Sunday school supplies. It follows, therefore, that the object of selling books and supplies is not to make money but is to promote the religious, charitable and beneficent purposes of appellant by disseminating the teachings of its books and periodicals. The purpose of the society is accomplished by the effect on the minds and lives of the children and adults who read and study its books and periodicals. The work of appellant is to send its workers and missionaries into those parts of our land where religious teaching among the young has been neglected, and there to take the young into Sunday schools for moral and religious instruction and provide for them wholesome literature. Many of these books are suitable for the use of adults, and the society seeks to supply needs of individuals and families by gift where that is necessary, but by a sale whenever a sale is practicable. The price received, whatever it may be, makes a gift to needy persons possible to the amount so received beyond what the society could otherwise give. It is not the use to be made of the profits but the nature of the business done that is to be considered in deciding the question of liability to taxation. We have already pointed out the purposes for which this society was organized and the four-fold nature of its business. Sales of publications made by this society, whether at a profit, at actual cost or half cost, are in aid of the gratuitous distribution of the same publications among those who are unable to buy them.

In support of its claim for exemption appellant directs our attention to a number of cases of this and other States. In Maine Baptist Missionary Convention *v.* City of Portland, 65 Me. 92, the corporate purposes of the convention were the promulgation and diffusion of christian knowledge and intelligence through its agency as an institution of domestic missions. It was held that since missionary societies have been repeatedly held to be charitable institutions, the Baptist Missionary Convention came within that class and its property was therefore exempt from taxation.

In Commonwealth *v.* Young Men's Christian Ass'n, 116 Ky. 711, the corporate purpose of the association was to seek out young men, endeavor to bring them under moral and religious influence, secure their attendance at some place of worship, introduce them to members and privileges of the association, secure them proper boarding places and employment and to surround them with christian influences. The court, in holding that the association came within the constitutional term of a purely public charity, said: "Aside from that part of the religious work done by the appellees which may be denominated devotional, they undertake to bring within the religious, moral and intellectual influences of the institution all young men, — and, for that matter, old men too, — for their betterment, improvement and protection from evil influences and consequences. It is not so much the giving of alms or in aid of the mendicant; the endeavor is to reach the boys and young men before they need alms and before they are reduced to beggary, and by training their minds and teaching them how to use and preserve their bodies and how to live useful and honest lives, to save them from the lower grades of misfortune so familiar in the utter helplessness of abject poverty and disease and want. This is accomplished by the institutions keeping open attractive quarters, where libraries of useful books, current magazines and newspapers, innocent games of amusement, a gymnasium for the exercise and development of the body, and night schools affording additional opportunities to such as have not had sufficient advantages and education, are all accessible to whomsoever will avail himself of them, without regard to creed or nationality. Lists of decent boarding houses are kept, to which strangers are directed. Proper acquaintances and associations are formed and useful and moral instruction imparted. In other words, they help the helpless. would keep the innocent innocent, and endeavor by placing clean ideals and experiences before the youth to have them adopt them in their lives. They aid the uneducated to a limited but practical education. This is all done 'for the love of God and for tie love of our neighbor in the catiolic and universal sense, free from the stain of anything that is personal, private or selfish.'"

In Davis *v.* Cincinnati Camp-Meeting Ass'n, 57 Oiio St. 257, it was held that tie association was an institution of purely public ciarity, and that the lands used by it for tie purpose of camp meetings were not used with a view to profit, altiough ciarges were made for tie privileges of keeping public stables and of keeping boarding and rooming houses on tie grounds for the accommodation of persons attending tie meetings.

In Methodist Episcopal Church *v.* Hinton, 92 Tenn. 188, it was held that the publishing department of the Methodist Episcopal Ciurci South was an institution of purely religious and charitable purposes and as such was exempt from taxation. The corporation was organized for the manufacture and distribution of books, tracts, periodicals and otier publications, and the act provided that the corporation should be under tie discipline of the Methodist Episcopal Churci South, according to its laws and usages. Tie discipline of the ciurci provided tiat tie purpose of the institution was to advance tie cause of ciristianity by disseminating religious knowledge and useful literature and scientific information in the form of books, tracts and periodicals. It further provided that any surplus remaining after the sale of these publications was to be used for the benefit of traveling, supernumerary, superannuated and worn-out preaciers, their wives, widows and children. Its annual business amounted to $336,800, about 1/156 part of which was derived from the printing of secular books. All the proceeds were applied to the purposes named. The court held that the dissemination of the gospel and the advancement of christianity were charitable purposes.

In Commonwealth *v.* Lynch, 115 Va. 745, a young men's christian association was held to be exempt from taxation, regardless of the fact that it charged for billiards, for bowling, for rooms and for annual dues, the court saying: "If the dominant purpose and use made of these rooms is to obtain revenue or profit, although it is to be applied to the general objects of the association, it would render the property liable to taxation; but if the use made is that for which the association was incorporated and tends immediately and directly to promote its purposes, then its use is within the provisions exempting the property from taxation, although revenue or profit is derived therefrom as incident to such cases. . . . Manifestly, a member of the association who was a lodger or inmate of the building would be in a better situation to take advantage of the privileges offered by the association and more likely to take advantage of them, other things being equal, than a member who lodged elsewhere.

In the Franklin Square House *v.* Boston, 118 Mass. 409, the court held that the property of the corporation, which was organized to provide a home for working girls at a moderate cost, was exempt from taxation on the ground that it was a public charity, even though the girls paid for their keep, the corporation having no capital stock and there being no profits divided among its members.

In Contributors to Pennsylvania Hospital v. Delaware County, 169 Pa. St. 305, it was held that farms purchased and permanently used by a hospital for hospital purposes, as part of the hospital plant and as an open air sanitarium, and incidentally for profit to reduce expenses, are exempt from taxation. The court there distinguished American Sunday School Union v. City of Philadelphia, *supra,* saying: " But property which is used directly for the purposes and in the operation of the charity is exempt, though it may also be used in a manner to yield some return and thereby reduce the expenses."

In Grand Lodge v. Board of Review, 281 Ill. 480, we held that the Masonic Home for the care and support of dependent Masons and their families was a charitable institution and that the land used for its maintenance was devoted to a charity, and we further held that the fact that the benefits are restricted to Master Masons, their widows and orphans, does not deprive the institution of the character of a public charity. We also held that a large farm operated by the grand lodge to raise produce for the support of the inmates of the home was exempt from taxation as the property of a public charity, when the profits from the farm were used as a part of the charity fund for the maintenance of the home. We there said: " The primary use to which property is put is to be considered in determining whether it falls within the terms of the exemption. The primary purpose and use of the lands in question being the maintenance of the home and the whole net income being devoted to that use, they come within the statutory definition of lands actually and exclusively used for charitable or beneficent purposes and not leased or otherwise used with a view to profit."

In City of Chicago v. University of Chicago, 228 Ill. 605, we held that the dormitories and dining halls of the university were not used with a view to profit, even though the students paid fees for lodging and board, and that therefore the property was exempt from a water tax.

In Monticello Female Seminary v. People, 106 Ill. 398, a tract of land used by the seminary for promenade grounds, gardens, orchards, pastures and crop lands, when all the returns from the lands were used to supply the institution, was held exempt from taxation under our statute.

In Sisters of St. Francis v. Board of Review, 231 Ill. 317, we held that the St. Francis Hospital was an institution of public charity where persons who are without money or property are cared for without charge, and that it did not lose its right to exemption from taxation by reason of the fact that the patients received by it who are able to pay are required to do so, or by reason of the fact that it receives contributions from outside sources, so long as all the money received by it is devoted to the general purposes of charity and no portion of the money received by it is permitted to inure to the benefit of any private individual engaged in managing the charity. We further held it was no objection because far the greater number of patients paid for the care and attention they received at the institution. So long as charity was dispensed to all those who needed and who applied for it, and so long as no private gain or profit came to any person connected with the institution, and so long as it did not appear that any obstacle of any character was by the corporation placed in the way of those who might need charity of the kind dispensed by the institution, the institution was a charitable and beneficent organization.

We recognize the rule adopted by this court that statutes for the exemption of property from taxation are to be strictly construed against the exemption and in favor of the State and taxation. (First Congregational Church v. Board of Review, supra; Northwestern University v. Hanberg, 237 Ill. 185; In re Walker, 200 id. 566.) On the other hand, charities have always been favored in the law because they relieve the burdens of government, and if appellant fairly comes within the terms of the exemption clauses of our Revenue act we feel inclined to grant the exemption. It seems clear that the predominant object of appellant in the use of its stock of books and Sunday school supplies in Chicago is to spread the gospel and to elevate humanity by means of written words embodied in its religious and moral books and in its Sunday school lesson-helps. The only means by which it can spread this gospel in printed form is by distribution of its books and Sunday school supplies. The purposes of appellant are directly carried out by the distribution of its books and supplies, and the receipt of the money from sales is incidental and secondary. It is not the profits from the sale of the books that accomplish the purposes of appellant, but it is the distribution of the books, periodicals and lesson-helps, — and therefore the use of the property sought to be taxed, — that directly accomplishes appellant's religious, charitable and beneficent purposes.

The application of the appellant for exemption from taxation of the property in question should have been granted, and therefore the decision of the board of review of Cook county is set aside.

Decision set aside.

MR. CHIEF JUSTICE DUNN, dissenting.

IN RE ALLERTON.

SUPREME COURT OF ILLINOIS. 1921.

[Reported 296 Ill. 340.]

DUNCAN, J. This is an application by the tax commission of Illinois for an order setting aside and annulling a decision of the board of review of Piatt County exempting about 1050 acres of land in said county from taxation on the petition of Robert Allerton, William Dighton, W. F. Lodge, Elizabeth Phalen and A. E. Burwash (the latter being farm adviser of the Piatt County farm bureau), trustees and grantees under a certain trust deed dated November 21, 1919, executed by Robert Allerton, conveying said land. The board of review filed a copy of the petition presented to it, together with the transcript of the statement of facts considered by it, and also of its order. The tax commission refused to confirm the order of the board of review and has applied to this court for an order setting the same aside.

The only evidence or facts before the board of review were those contained in the petition, which was verified by affidavit, and the trust deed, which was made an exhibit and a part of the petition. The petition avers the delivery of the trust deed to the trustees in trust for the purposes and upon the terms and conditions therein set forth; that the trustees are in the possession of the land therein described and have had such possession since November 21, 1919; that the land is assessed in the name of Robert Allerton and taxes extended for the year 1920; that under the terms of the deed the real estate is to be used for the purpose of creating and maintaining in said county an old people's home, a county tuberculosis sanitarium and a model and experimental farm; that the entire net income derived from the use of the real estate is to be applied to the maintenance of the old people's home; that no private person will obtain any pecuniary gain or profit from the use of said premises, and that the real estate and all income from the same will be used for charitable and public purposes.

In the preamble of the deed it is recited that it is the desire of the grantor to create a memorial to his father, Samuel W. Allerton, to be known as the Samuel W. Allerton Farm Memorial, and a memorial to his friend John Phalen, to be known as the John Phalen Old People's Home Memorial. The deed declares that the grantor and the four grantees named in the deed as trustees, and their successors as trustees, do and shall own and hold the real estate in trust for the purposes and upon the terms and conditions therein set forth, and conveys an undivided four-fifths of the land, reserving to himself an undivided one-fifth. It provides for the selection of trustees as successors upon the death, resignation, refusal or inability of any of the trustees to act. It declares that it is the intention of the grantor, as soon as in his judgment the same may be properly done, to erect on a certain named site of the land a suitable building to be used as an old people's home, and there shall be reserved and used about such home, for necessary grounds and gardens, such quantity of land as the trustees shall determine upon, and that all of the remainder of said land, except so much as may be hereafter conveyed for a hospital as in the deed provided, shall be run as a model and experimental farm in demonstration of the most approved methods of farming, the same to be managed by the county agricultural or farm adviser of the Piatt county farm bureau or such other person as the trustees may name, subject to the direction and control of the trustees. It further directs that the net income from the land shall be deposited or invested by the trustees in such securities as they may deem wise, and such fund be permitted to accumulate as a fund for the proper working and managing of the farm, and when the trustees shall deem a sufficient fund has been accumulated for such purposes, then the net income, after payment of all expenses connected with the management and running of the farm, shall be used for the upkeep and maintenance of the old people's home. The fourth clause declares that after the completion of the buildings for the home and after the accumulation of sufficient funds as aforesaid and the opening of the home for use, there will be received and kept at such home such old people of either sex, residents of said county, as the board may decide to receive and accept as residents. The conditions for admission of such persons as residents are, that those admitted shall pay to said trustees, for such use as they may see fit in connection with the running of the home, a sum of money, not to exceed $500, to be determined upon by the trustees, and anyone paying such sum may be admitted to the home and entitled to remain as a resident therein for his or her life. The trustees are vested with the same power and authority as are commonly vested in boards of directors of corporations of Illinois, and they may make such rules, regulations and by-laws to govern and regulate the management and control of the farm and the home as they may deem advisable, and alter the same from time to time as they see fit, and elect officers, etc. The fifth clause declares that it has been the grantor's desire to give to Piatt county the necessary land for a site for the establishment and maintenance of a county tuberculosis sanitarium, and that the deed is subject to the provisions that there shall be conveyed by the trustees to said county, or to such organization or corporation, for hospital purposes, as they shall decide upon, whenever the county or such organization or corporation is ready, in the judgment of the trustees, to receive the same, and erect the necessary buildings for such sanitarium or hospital thereon. The deed specifies the land upon which the trustees may locate such sanitarium, and then provides that the income arising from said land so to be conveyed is to be used by the trustees for the purposes first mentioned in the deed until such conveyance is made.

There is no averment in the petition that any part of the real estate in question is being actually and exclusively used as an old people's home. The clear indications from the petition and from the trust deed are that no part of the land was being actually and exclusively used either for an old people's home or for agricultural purposes, as a model and experimental farm in demonstration of the most approved methods of farming, at the time it was assessed. The most that can be said from the record is that the land is to be or will be used at some time in the future for such purposes. The deed is made subject to an expressed wish of the grantor at some time to deed a part of the land described in the deed to the county or some organization or corporation for the establishment and maintenance of a county tuberculosis sanitarium or for hospital purposes. In case such deed is made, the land so deeded will not then be any longer a part of the land to be managed by the trustees. The sanitarium or hospital is to be built and established by the county or some organization or corporation, and not until, in the judgment of the trustees, such county, organization or corporation is ready to receive the gift and to erect the necessary buildings. There is no showing in this record that there is even an intention on the part of any of such organizations to accept the gift upon the terms proposed or to be proposed. So it is clear that there is not an old people's home or sanitarium or hospital on the land in question, — or at least there is no showing that any one of such institutions is in actual existence on the land.

By section 3 of article 9 of the constitution it is provided that such property as may be used exclusively for agricultural and horti-cultural societies and for charitable purposes may be exempted from taxation, but only by general law. Paragraph 7 of section 2 of the Revenue act (Hurd's Stat. 1917, p. 2421), provides that "all prop-erty of institutions of public charity, all property of beneficent and charitable organizations, whether incorporated in this or any other State of the United States and all property of old people's homes when such property is actually and exclusively used for such chari-table and beneficent purposes, and not leased or otherwise used with the view to profit," shall be exempt from taxation. The Constitu-tion does not, of itself, exempt any property in this State from taxation but simply provides what property may be exempted from taxation by general law. It is, however, a limitation upon the right of the legislature to legislate upon such question of exemption. (People v. Deutsche Gemeinde, 249 Ill. 132.) The Constitution contemplates, and the statute provides, that only property actually and exclusively used for charitable purposes shall be exempt from taxation. A law claimed to exempt property from taxation must be strictly construed, and it devolves upon those claiming that specific property is thus exempt to clearly show that it is within the con-templation of the law. (People v. Wabash Railway Co. 138 Ill. 85.) A trust fund possessed and held by trustees or real estate held for charitable purposes, not then actually and exclusively used for charitable purposes but only possessed and held for such use in the future, is not exempt from taxation under the provision of the statute. (Board of Directors v. Board of Review, 248 Ill. 590.) The find-ing of the board of review in this case that the real estate "is to be used" for the various purposes is not a sufficient finding of fact to exempt such property from taxation, even if it be conceded that the actual and exclusive use of the property for the various purposes mentioned in the trust deed is sufficient to exempt it from taxation.

The tenth paragraph of section 2 of the Revenue act provides that all property which may be used exclusively by societies for agri-cultural purposes, and not for pecuniary profit, shall be exempt from taxation. The record shows that the real estate in this case is to be managed by the county agricultural or farm adviser of the Piatt county farm bureau as a model and experimental farm in demon-stration of the most approved methods of farming, but it does not show that it was held and used for such purpose at the time it was assessed. The proof, therefore, does not show that the property is exempt from taxation, as found by the board of review, although it does further show that it is not to be used for pecuniary profit by any individual. It necessarily follows, then, that none of the real estate in question was exempt from taxation at the time the order of the board of review was entered.

Some question is raised by the Attorney General on behalf of the tax commission as to whether or not the property, or any part of it, would be exempt from taxation if it were actually and exclusively used for the purposes mentioned in the trust deed, — that is, for an old peoples' home or for a model farm, — at the time the petitioners' application for exemption was made. A solution of this question is not necessary to the decision of the case, and we prefer not to pass upon it until such time as the property may be actually and exclusively used for such purposes, under a full showing of the facts at such time and upon further briefs and arguments.

For the foregoing reasons the decision of the board of review is set aside and annulled.

Decision set aside.

PRESIDENT AND FELLOWS OF HARVARD

COLLEGE *v.* ASSESSORS OF CAMBRIDGE.

SUPREME JUDICIAL COURT OE MASSACHUSETTS.   1900.

[*Reported* 175 *Mass.* 145.]

MORTON, J. This is an action to recover back taxes that were assessed by the respondents on certain parcels of real estate belonging to the petitioner situated in Cambridge, which the petitioner contends were exempt from taxation under Pub. Sts. c. 11, § 5, cl. 3, as amended by St. 1889, c. 465.

The case was heard by a justice of the Superior Court, without a jury, on what are called agreed facts, but which we interpret as authorizing him to draw such inferences as he thought warranted; he held that the property was exempt, and found for the petitioner for the entire amount, and reported the case to this court in such a manner as to present the question of the assessibility of each of the parcels.

We think that the ruling of the Superior Court was right, and that all of the property was exempt from taxation. Many of the principles and considerations and authorities applicable to this case have been stated and referred to somewhat at length in Phillips Academy *v.* Andover, 175 Mass. 118, and we do not deem it necessary to repeat them here.

The history of Harvard College and of like institutions shows, we think, that from the beginning dormitories and dining-halls have been furnished by the college for the use of the students, and have been regarded as devoted to college purposes. In addition to this, the effect of the decisions in Wesleyan Academy *v.* Wilbraham, 99

Mass. 599, and Mount Hermon Boys' School *v.* Gill, 145 Mass. 139, is plainly to exempt property applied to such uses. See also Yale University *v.* New Haven, 71 Conn. 316 and State *v.* Ross, 4 Zabr. 497. We do not think that it makes any difference in principle that the college, instead of furnishing board itself, provides a place, without rent or compensation in any form, or a lease or any agreement for a fixed term, for the use of students who club together for the purpose of obtaining for themselves, with the assistance of the college, food at cost. The property so used is occupied, it seems to us, for the purposes for which the college was incorporated. Many particulars are stated in the agreed facts in regard to No. 17 Kirkland Street, which is the parcel that we are now considering, which we do not think it necessary to refer to, as it seems to us plain that the property is exempt from taxation.

The history of the college and of the legislation relating to it also shows, we think, that the president's house, during the earlier years of the college at any rate, was regarded as almost, if not quite, as necessary for the purposes of the institution as dormitories and dining-halls. Public money was appropriated by the general court to build it as it had been to build the college buildings, and the occupancy of it was evidently considered as official. The present house was built with funds given expressly for the purpose of erecting a dwelling-house for the president and his successors in office, and since it was built has been occupied by them and their families. The president is required to live in Cambridge. He pays no rent or compensation for the use and occupation of the house, and has no lease, but occupies it, if he chooses, so long as he performs the duties of president. It, with several of the other houses that were taxed, namely, Nos. 11, 25, and 37 Quincy Street, this being 17 Quincy St., is now and was at the time of the assessment within the college grounds, and the premises are kept in order and repair, including grading, gravelling the walks, fertilizing, and repairing and cleaning furnace, removal of ashes, etc., under the direction of the college superintendent of buildings and the superintendent of grounds and at the college expense. The whole lower floor, " except possibly the kitchen, is used for Class Day, Commencement, and other receptions, and for many hospitalities incident to the president's functions." " The hall and drawing-room are also used for the convenience of the college and the president for meetings of the faculty and committees, for conferences with university officers and students, for calls on university business, and for the annual meetings of the corporation at which degrees are voted." The rest of the house consists of the usual living and housekeeping rooms and chambers, and is used by the president and his family as a dwelling-house.

It seems to us that on these facts the judge who heard the case was justified in finding that the dominant or principal purpose of the occupancy by the president was that for which the college was incorporated. His occupation, it could be fairly said, was, so far as the university was concerned, official, as the head of the university, just as, for instance, the President occupies the White House, and not in any just sense primarily or principally for his own private benefit.

The remaining six houses are occupied by professors, three of whom are deans, each charged with a portion of the administrative duties formerly devolving exclusively on the president. Three of the houses, as already observed, are within the college grounds. All of them are kept in order and repair at the expense of the college in the same manner and to the same extent as the house occupied by the president. The halls and drawing-rooms in all of them, except No. 37 Quincy Street, occupied by Professor Langdell, are used, partly for the convenience of the college and partly for that of the professor, for different college uses and purposes incident to his duties as professor, chairman of committees, dean, and the like. In the case of No. 11 Quincy street, the drawing-room and hall are used by the professor for regular college exercises during the college year. In the case of No. 16 Quincy Street, the professor is Chairman of the Freshman Advisory Committee of the Faculty of Arts and Sciences, consisting of about twenty persons, and he has a great number of interviews in his drawing-room with students and parents. In the case of 25 Quincy Street, the college in 1892 made additions and improvements at its own expense so as to make the house more convenient for the transaction of college business and the entertaining of guests on college account. The additions as well as the drawing-room and hall are used for different college purposes incident to the several duties of the occupying professor. The parts of the houses to which no references has been made are used by the professors and their families, and consist of the usual living and housekeeping rooms and chambers. In the fall of the year, when the salaries of the professors are voted, they are fixed at certain amounts " and the use of house, $750," or whatever the sum may be; otherwise the professor " pays no rent and has no other agreement for his occupation and use of said house, but uses it as such professor." We think that it was competent for the justice who heard the case to find on these facts that the dominant consideration in regard to the occupation of the houses by the several professors had references to the performance of their duties as officers and professors, rather than to the private benefit which they would receive in the way of homes for themselves and their families, and that he was justified in finding that the occupancy was for the purposes for which the college was incorporated.

This case is distinguishable, we think, from Williams College *v.* Williamstown, 167 Mass. 505. In the first place, there was no question in that case as to the taxation of a building used for a dormitory and dining-hall for the students. In the next place, the occupation by the professors in this case clearly lacks the exclusive character which it was held to have in that case. In the third place, no use for college purposes is shown to have been made of the houses occupied by the professors in that case as appears in this case. In the fourth place, the sums fixed as compensation for the use of the houses in that case were paid and received as rent, and were so treated by the court. In this case, the sums fixed for the use of the houses were allowed as part of the compensation for services as professors, thus tending to show, as said in Massachusetts General Hospital *v.* Somerville, 101 Mass. 319, 326, that " the occupation was one merely by reason of service," and that the value put upon the use of the house was merely " a convenient mode of adjusting the compensation . . . and not as the income or fruit of an estate granted." Lastly, this case seems to be one where the buildings are occupied, as it was said in Peirce *v.* Cambridge, 2 Cush. 611, 613, 614, " with the permission of the college, and without [the professors] having any estate therein, or paying any rent therefor," in which case the property would be exempt from taxation. See also White *v.* Bayley, 10 C. B. (N. S.) 227.

The respondents rely on Third Congregational Society *v.* Springfield, 147 Mass. 396, which was a case where a parsonage was declared to be unexempt. The court held that religious societies did not come within the clause that we have been considering, but within the seventh clause, and that the exemption was limited to houses of religious worship only. That case is not applicable to this.

We think that the judgment of the Superior Court should be affirmed.

So ordered.

PEOPLE *ex rel.* MIZPAH LODGE *v.* BURKE.

COURT OF APPEALS OF NEW YORK. 1920.

[Reported 228 N. Y. 245.]

POUND, J. Relator claims to be exempt from general taxation on its real property under subdivision 7 of section 4 of the Tax Law (Laws 1909, c. 62, as amended; Consol. Laws, c. 60). It is an unincorporated subordinate lodge of the Independent Order of Odd Fellows of the State of New York. It owns real estate in the city of Buffalo on which it has a building containing halls, lodge room, kitchen, and other rooms, which it uses itself part of the time and also leases regularly to tenants — fraternal bodies or other associations — for their meetings and social gatherings.

Exemption is sought on the ground that relator, " organized exclusively for the moral or mental improvement " of its members and for " religious, charitable, benevolent, and educational purposes," uses its property " exclusively for carrying out thereupon " such purposes of its organization.

The referee has not found the facts which sustain the contention of exclusive use. We think the practice of leasing the property to others destroys the exclusive nature of the use for the purposes of its own organization. The meaning of the Tax Law is that if rents, profits, or income are derived from the property, no exemption under this clause may be claimed.

"It is the exclusive use of the real estate for carrying out thereupon one or more of the purposes of the incorporation of the relator which confers the right of exemption, and not the benefits accruing to it and its useful work from the income derived from others in consideration of their use of the real estate for their purposes." (People ex rel. Young Men's Ass'n *v.* Sayles, 32 App. Div. 197, 202, affirmed on opinion below 157 N. Y. 677.)

Relator is primarily a lodge of a fraternal order and incidentally a landlord. Its premises are used in part time for its own fraternal purposes and in part are "leased or otherwise used for other purposes" to produce an income to promote its own purposes. The fact that some or all of its tenants are other fraternal bodies does not alter the case. The controlling fact is the receipt of rents, profits, and income. (People ex rel. Adelphi College *v.* Wells, 97 App. Div. 312; affirmed 180 N. Y. 534.)

"Although we ought not, perhaps, to give to the word 'exclusively' an interpretation so literal as to prevent an occasional use of the relator's property for some purpose other than one or more of those specified, yet the policy of the law is to construe statutes exempting property from taxation somewhere rigidly, and not to permit such exemption to be established by doubtful implication. In other words, the legislative intent to exempt any property from taxation can never be presumed, but must always be expressed in language so clear as to admit of no argument." (People ex rel. D. K. E. Society *v.* Lawler, 74 App. Div. 553, 557; affirmed 179 N. Y. 535.)

Relator seeks exemption, secondly, on the ground that it is a fraternal association "created to build and maintain a building or buildings for its meetings . . . and for the accommodation of other fraternal bodies or associations," and that it applies its net income to a home for indigent Odd Fellows, their widows and orphans. The statute exempts the real property of associations which answer this description. But relator was created for the purposes of an Odd Fellows' lodge, nor does it now exist for the purpose of leasing its property. It has the power to lease such property (Benevolent Orders Law [Consol. Laws, c. 3] § 3), but its primary and inherent purpose is the fraternal end or aim itself, which it must keep in view, while its powers are merely the incidental authority, capacity, or right which it possesses to do such act as may effectuate its purpose.

When we infer from the mere power to hold and lease real property conferred on lodge trustees by section 3 of the Benevolent Orders Law, that relator was "created to build a meeting place for itself and other fraternal bodies or associations," we confuse the meaning of purpose and power, which are not synonymous, and lose sight of the true purpose for which an Odd Fellows' Lodge is created, which is not to maintain a hall for itself and to lease lodge rooms and other quarters to fraternal and other associations for their social and festive functions, but to promote the welfare of its own members as a fraternal organization. Corporations or associations may be created for the purpose of building and leasing such a meeting place as the statute contemplates, but more subordinate lodges of fraternal orders are not created for that purpose. The disposition of the net income to charitable purposes does not help the ease. Relator's enterprise is charitable rather than mercenary, but it is not the kind of charitable enterprise that comes within the letter of the statute. If it had been the intention of the Legislature to exempt from taxation all lodge buildings the net income of which was devoted to charitable purposes, it would doubtless have expressed such intention without the use of unnecessary or ambiguous words. So long as the State has not clearly indicated its deliberate purpose to look with special favor upon the use of lodge property for all the purposes that relator uses its property for, we may not construe the law for its benefit.

The referee has found as a finding of fact, and the findings have been unanimously affirmed, that the relator was created to build and maintain its building for the purposes indicated. This, however, is a conclusion of law in conflict with the facts found, and not controlling on this appeal.

The orders should be reversed, and the writ of certiorari dismissed, with costs in all courts.

CAMBRIDGE *v.* COUNTY COMMISSIONERS.

SUPREME JUDICIAL COURT OF MASSACHUSETTS. 1874.

[*Reported* 114 *Mass.* 337.]

COLT, J. The upper stories of Holyoke House, a building owned by the President and Fellows of Harvard College, are appropriated to the students, and used for purposes within the college charter; they are therefore exempt from taxation. Gen. Sts. c. 11, § 5. The lower story, which is used for other puropses, is not exempt. The question upon this petition for a *certiorari* is whether the rule adopted by the assessors of Cambridge, for ascertaining the taxable value of the last named portion, was erroneously changed by the county commissioners on appeal to them by the college.

The valuation of the assessors was made by adding the value of the land to the value of the lower story, including the foundations, as if there had been a building of only one story, the whole of which was subject to taxation. But the county commissioners estimated the taxable value of the property at one third of the value of the whole building, together with one half of the value of the land, and ordered the city to remit a sum declared by them to be in excess of a just and fair assessment.

The building and land, it is said, must be treated for the purpose of the valuation as an organized whole. The upper stories cannot exist without the land and foundations to support them. Some part of the value of the lower story must enter into the value of the upper stories, while the upper part of the building must in the same way be more or less important and valuable to the lower. To some extent the land and foundations are appropriated to college purposes, and their whole value cannot fairly or legally be annexed to the lower story of the building.

It was within the authority of the county commissioners to revise an assessment made upon a wrong principle; and it is not shown by the petitioners that any error was made in the rule adopted by them. The principle upon which the apportionment was made is not stated. It may have been made according to the estimated rentable value of each part, or by some other rule equally just and equitable. Their action is not open to revision upon the allegations in this petition.

Petition dismissed.

EVANGELICAL BAPTIST BENEVOLENT AND MISSIONARY SOCIETY *v.* BOSTON.

SUPREME JUDICIAL COURT OF MASSACHUSETTS.   1910.

[*Reported* 204 *Mass.* 28.]

KNOWLTON, C. J.   Each of these cases is an appeal by the petitioner to the Superior Court from the refusal of the assessors of the city of Boston to abate a tax assessed to the petitioner. The petitioner was incorporated by a special act of the Legislature (St. 1857, c. 154) "for the purpose of securing the constant maintenance in said Boston of evangelical preaching for the young and the destitute, with free seats; for the employment of colporteur and missionary laborers in Boston and elsewhere; for the purpose of providing suitable central apartments to other and kindred benevolent and missionary societies, and for the general purpose of ministering to the spiritual wants of the needy and destitute." By § 2 of the act it was authorized to hold real and personal estate to the amount of $350,000, and this property was exempted from taxation. It is now holding property, the fair valuation of which is $911,000,[1] and upon its application to have this larger amount exempted from taxation, it was decided in an action brought by this petitioner against the city of Boston, as reported in 192 Mass. 412, that its right to an exemption is limited to the amount named in its charter.

In the present petition it puts its claim upon different grounds, and contends that it is entitled to exemption under the R. L. c. 12, § 5, cl. 7, which is as follows:

"Seventh, Houses of religious worship owned by, or held in trust for the use of, any religious organization, and the pews and furniture; but the exception shall not extend to portions of such houses appropriated for purposes other than religious worship or instruction."

The petitioner's constitution recites that "this society is organized

---

[1] This was the valuation of the Tremont Temple building made by the assessors of the city of Boston.

for the purpose of receiving, holding and managing the estate known as the Tremont Temple, in accordance with the provisions of the act of incorporation," etc. From the time of its incorporation it has owned and managed this real estate, with different buildings upon it at different times, as new structures have been erected to replace those injured or destroyed by fire. The property is in a very attractive and important part of the business district of Boston. The present building, like those that preceded it, is used in part for business and in part for religious purposes. Important portions of it were originally constructed and have always been used exclusively for the transaction of business. Other parts have been used regularly both for religious and business purposes. These parts include five halls — Converse Hall, Lorimer Hall, Chapman Hall, Gilbert Hall and Social Hall, with the Blue Room, parlors, corridors and other appurtenances. These have all been used regularly by Tremont Temple Baptist Church for religious purposes, and have also been rented very frequently, and as often as opportunity offered without interfering with the regular uses by this church, for secular gatherings, and for different religious gatherings of other organizations. It has been an important part of the business of the petitioner to obtain an income from these rentals, although the rental value of the use by the Tremont Temple Baptist Church has been largely in excess of the rent received from other parties for the use of the same parts of the building. Converse Hall has been used as the main auditorium of this church.

It becomes necessary to consider the meaning of the R. L. c. 12, § 5, cl. 7, above quoted. The purpose of the provision was to exempt from taxation ordinary church edifices, owned and used in the usual way for religious worship. Probably such an unusual condition as appears in this case was never contemplated by the framers of the statute. The special provision about ownership or holding in trust was first enacted by the St. 1865, c. 206. The form of this Statute, as well as the more condensed forms of the later revisions of it (see Pub. Sts. c. 11, § 5, cl. 7, R. L., *ubi supra*), which were not intended to change its meaning, implies that the exemption was intended only for houses owned by, or held in trust for, religious organizations that occupy and use them for worship. We are of opinion that this clause of the present revision should be construed as if the words " occupying and using them as such," were inserted after the words, " religious organization." We do not think that the statute applies to the owner of a house of religious worship, even if that owner be a religious organization, that has never occupied or used the house for religious worship, but has held it only to be let to others. If the petitioner be called a religious organization, as in a broad sense it undoubtedly is, we do not think it is such a kind of a religious organization, in reference to its ownership of property, as the statute exempts from taxation as an owner. It is not the owner of a house of religious worship which is occupied and used by it as such.

The Tremont Temple Baptist Church is a religious organization within the meaning of this statute. Is this building a house of worship held in trust for this church? It is at least very doubtful whether the building is a house of worship such as was intended by the Legislature. Very spacious and valuable parts of the building were never used for religious worship and have no relation to a religious use. The other parts are used in part for worship and in part for many other purposes. The building could hardly be called a church edifice. In many if not most of its features, it has the characteristics of income-producing property. Those parts of the building which are used for worship are not held in trust for the Tremont Temple Baptist Church in any strict or technical sense. The first instrument under which the church held is called "a license or lease," and it purports to license and empower the church to use the property on certain terms. In other parts of the instrument it is called merely a "lease." The petitioner reserves the right to sell and terminate the rights of the church in the property at any time. By a modification of the original indenture, bearing date December 5, 1863, it was provided, among other things, that if the church should settle a minister without submitting the matter of his selection to the directors of the corporation, or otherwise than as provided in this new agreement, it should be a violation of the covenants and agreements of the indenture, and should absolutely and finally determine all rights, privileges and estate of the church in or under the indenture, and in and to the parts of the building therein mentioned. The sentence ended with these words: "and the lease or license of said church to occupy the same or any part thereof shall thereupon, *ipso facto,* cease and determine." Another indenture was made on March 13, 1894, which modified the former agreements and reaffirmed them in some parts. It is a contract between the parties in regard to the management, use and occupation of different parts of a building to be erected, which is the present building, and in regard to the collection and disposition of rents received. The word "trust" does not anywhere appear in it. In neither of the indentures is there any reference to any trust as between the petitioner and the church. While, in a broad sense, it may be said that some relations of trust grow out of the undertakings of the parties, we do not think that this building appears to be held in trust for the church, within the meaning of the statute.

There is another consideration of some importance. The petitioner seeks to apply this general statute for the exemption of houses of worship to its ownership under a special charter by which its right to hold property is limited to the amount of $350,000 in value. Its ownership beyond that amount is without authority under its charter. Some courts have held that the title of a corporation, to property beyond the amount authorized to be held, is absolutely void. But this court, after considering the subject at length in Hubbard *v.* Worcester Art Museum, 194 Mass. 280, held that such ownership is invalid as against the State, and that the public authorities alone can take advantage of the irregularity.

The question at once arises whether, under a system that provides for the taxation of all property, unless an exemption is created by statute and is plainly established, the general law invoked by this petitioner can be held applicable to create an exemption in favor of a party whose holding is *ultra vires,* and in excess of the authority given by its charter. This exemption is claimed against an assessment for city, county and State taxes. The claim is made against the public authorities representing the State. We are of opinion that a party, asking an exemption of his property under this general statute, must come as an owner who has a title which the State is bound to recognize. A corporation, which as against the State has no right to hold such property, is not in a position to claim a statutory exemption which is intended only for holding fully authorized by law. We are of opinion that this petitioner, under the limitations of its charter, has no standing, as an owner of this large amount of property, to ask for the application of this general law.

Judgments affirmed.

THE PROTESTANT EPISCOPAL CHURCH OF THE PARISH OF ST. PHILIP v. PRIOLEAU.

SUPREME COURT OF SOUTH CAROLINA. 1902.

[*Reported* 63 *S. C.* 70.]

JONES, J. This is an application in the original jurisdiction of this court for a writ of mandamus to compel the county auditor of Charleston county to correct the tax duplicate by striking therefrom the assessment of the lot in the city of Charleston known as St. Philip's Parsonage, which it is claimed by petitioner is exempt from taxation under article 10, § 4, of the constitution. The only question in the case arising on demurrer to the petition which is reported herewith, is whether said property is exempt from taxation. It appears from the petition and exhibits that the lot and buildings claimed to be exempt from taxation is the property of " The Protestant Episcopal Church of the Parish of St. Philip, in Charleston, in the State of South Carolina," which was incorporated under an act approved December 20, 1791; that said lot and buildings thereon have constituted and have been known as the parsonage of said church for over one hundred years, and have never been taxed until the year 1898, when said property was placed on the tax books and taxes levied thereon, then and ever since; that said lot and buildings at the time of their assessment for taxation in 1898 were not actually occupied by the rector or parson of said church but were rented out, the rector or parson hiring another residence in a different locality for his personal convenience, and the rent derived from said parsonage was appropriated to the salary of the rector and so to the hiring of such other residence.

We are of the opinion, upon the facts stated, that said property is exempt from taxation. Article 10, § 4, ·of the constitution, provides: "There shall be exempt from taxation . . . all . . . parsonages: . . . provided, tiat as to real estate this exemption shall not extend beyond the buildings and premises actually occupied by such . . . parsonages, . . . although connected with charitable objects." The premises in question constituting and known as St. Philip's Church parsonage, and being set apart for the actual use and occupancy of its parson, does not lose its character as a "parsonage" merely because the parson for his personal convenience should permit another to occupy said premises· and use the rent thereof in procuring another more convenient residence. It does not appear that said premises used as a parsonage for over one hundred years has ceased to be such.

It is therefore the judgment of this court that the writ of mandamus issue as prayed for in this petition.

MASSACHUSETTS GENERAL HOSPITAL *v.* BELMONT.

SUPREME JUDICIAL COURT OF MASSACHUSETTS. 1919.

[*Reported* 233 *Mass.* 190.]

RUGG, C. J. These are two petitions under Part I, § 77 of the general tax act, St. 1909, c. 490, appealing from the refusal of the assessors of the town of Belmont to abate taxes alleged to have been assessed illegally for the years 1915 and 1916 respectively upon real estate of the petitioner devoted to the care of the insane under a department known as tie McLean Asylum and located in that town. Tie taxes were assessed pursuant to St. 1914, c. 518, § 1, which amended the exemption from taxation of the personal estate of charilable institutions and their real estate actually occupied for their corporate purposes set forth in the general tax act, § 5, cl. 3, by adding a proviso in these words: "nor shall the personal property or real estate owned by such institutions or corporations and occupied by them or any department thereof wholly or partly as and for an insane asylum, insane hospital, institution for tie insane or for the treatment of mental or nervous diseases, be exempt from taxation unless at least one fourth of all property so occupied wholly or partly, on the basis of valuation thereof, and one fourth of the income of all trust and otier funds and property held for the benefit of such asylum, hospital or institution and not actually occupied by it for such purposes, be used and expended entirely for the treatment, board, lodging or other direct benefit of indigent insane persons, or indigent persons in need of treatment for mental diseases, as resident patients, without any charge therefor to such persons either directly or indirectly."

The meaning and the constitutionality of St. 1914, c. 518, § 1, are questions which lie at the threshold of the case.

1. The contentions made by the petitioner as to the construction of the statute summarily stated are that the words "without any

charge therefor" in the last clause of the amendment mean in substance, without any charge for the use of the property occupied by the institution or department in question for the purposes stated or for benefits received through the expenditure of the income of trust or other funds and property held for the use of the institution or department and not actually occupied for such purposes, and that the word "therefor" refers to the use of property and income and not to "treatment, board, lodging or other direct benefit." We are of opinion that these contentions cannot be adopted. The word "therefor," according to the approved usages of languages ordinarily refers to the last and not to a more remote antecedent noun or phrase. It is the natural import of the proviso as a whole that the exoneration from charge relates to service rendered or furnished and not alone to use of property or income. The legislative history of the statute appears to disclose a purpose to make a material change respecting the exemption from taxation of property of such charitable institutions. Apparently in its practical working little if any change would result from the construction put forward in behalf of the petitioner. It is difficult and perhaps not desirable to attempt to lay down a precise and technical definition of "indigent persons" such as exists respecting the word "paupers." See Opinion of the Justices, 11 Pick. 537. But in a broad sense in this connection "indigent persons" include those insane persons who by reason of poverty are unable, having due regard to other imperative obligations resting upon them, to contribute any substantial amount to their support in the asylum. Weeks *v.* Mansfield, 84 Conn. 544. *In re Hybart,* 119 N. C. 359.

The other parts of the statute present no insuperable difficulty in construction. One fourth of the property occupied wholly or partly for the insane asylum or other designated use, on the basis of valuation, and one fourth of the income from property held for its benefit must be devoted to the direct benefit of indigent insane without charge. This does not of necessity require a physical line of demarcation between the portions of the real estate devoted to pay patients and those given over to the use of free patients. Plainly it does not mean a fractional use of the property based on numbers of patients. It signifies that, on a fair basis of computation, having reference both to numbers of patients treated so far as concerns enjoyment of property adapted for and applied to a use in common by pay and free patients and to definite property so far as there is a strict separation between pay and free patients, one fourth in value shall be employed for the benefit of the latter. The same method, so far as practicable, may be employed in determining the expenditure of income. The statute is intended to be given a rational construction. Its operation must be adapted to the practical solution of a specified problem. Within these somewhat comprehensive lines, the calculation of the required proportions of properties doubtless can be accomplished without undue friction. The statute does not appear to be an unworkable piece of legislation. Hemenway *v.* Milton, 217 Mass. 230.

2. We are not able to perceive that any constitutional right of the petitioner is infringed by the statute.

The petitioner does not claim that it has any special exemption from taxation as a part of its charter rights. See St. 1810, c. 94. Whatever exemption it heretofore has enjoyed rested upon general law declaratory of a scheme of public policy. That may be changed by the General Court provided no other constitutional guaranty is offended. Christ's Church *v.* Philadelphia, 24 How. 30. Grand Lodge F. & A. Masons *v.* New Orleans, 166 U. S. 143. Stanislaus *v.* San Joaquin & King's River Canal & Irrigation Co. 192 U. S. 201. Choate *v.* Trapp, 224 U. S. 665, 674. The question somewhat argued respecting the ethics of inviting contributions from charitably disposed persons on the footing that the beneficiary of their gifts is to be exempt from taxation, and then revoking that exemption after large gifts have been made, is wholly legislative and not judicial in its nature. It presents no question of constitutional law. The law of taxation may be changed. In the absence of some binding contract, no one has a legal right to the continuance of such laws. Hanscom *v.* Malden & Melrose Gas Light Co. 220 Mass. 1, 8. Cahen *v.* Brewster, 203 U. S. 543.

3. The statute here assailed does not deny to the petitioner the equal protection of the laws guaranteed both by the State and Federal Constitutions. The Fourteenth Amendment to the Federal Constitution secures the petitioner against being singled out either by name or otherwise, directly or indirectly, and subjected to heavier burdens than are imposed upon other like corporations. Reasonable classification so far as concerns taxation or exemption from taxation may be made by the Legislature. The constitutional principles respecting the basis of such classification have been declared in numerous cases. It was said by Chief Justice Fuller in Giozza *v.* Tiernan, 148 U. S. 657, 662: "Nor, in respect of taxation was the amendment intended to compel the State to adopt an iron rule of equality; to prevent the classification of property for taxation at different rates; or to prohibit legislation in that regard, special either in the extent to which it operates or the objects sought to be obtained by it. It is enough that there is no discrimination in favor of one as against another of the same class. . . . And due process of law within the meaning of the amendment is secured if the laws operate on all alike, and do not subject the individual to an arbitrary exercise of the powers of government." In Southern Railway *v.* Greene, 216 U. S. 400, at page 417, occur these words: "While reasonable classification is permitted, without doing violence to the equal protection of the laws, such classification must be based upon some real and substantial distinction, bearing a reasonable and just relation to the things in respect to which such classification is imposed; and classification cannot be arbitrarily made without any substantial basis. Arbitrary selection, it has been said, cannot be justified by calling it classification." In Citizen's Telephone Co. of Grand Rapids *v.* Fuller, 229 U. S. 322, at page 329, is found the statement: "The power of exemption would seem to imply the power

of discrimination, and in taxation, as in other matters of legislation, classification is within the competency of the Legislature;" and at page 331: "Granting the power of classification, we must grant Government the right to select the differences upon which the classification shall be based, and they need not be great or conspicuous. Keeney *v.* New York, 222 U. S. 525, 536. The State is not bound by any rigid equality. This is the rule; — its limitation is that it must not be exercised in 'clear and hostile discriminations between particular persons and classes.' See 223 U. S. 59, 62, 63. Thus defined and thus limited, it is a vital principle, giving to the Government freedom to meet its exigencies, not binding its action by rigid formulas but apportioning its burdens and permitting it to make those 'discriminations which the best interests of society require.'"

It is to be borne in mind constantly that the present statute relates only to 'the conditions under which exemption from the ordinary burdens of taxation is to be granted to certain kinds of charitable corporations. It is not a classification for purposes of taxation but of exemption from taxation. We consider only the question presented and do not undertake to decide whether the statute would be open to successful attack as a classification for taxation.

The classification declared by the present statute is the selection of insane asylums, insane hospitals, and institutions "for the insane or for the treatment of mental or nervous diseases," the separation of these from all other charities and a declaration of different conditions respecting them as compared with other charities. Such a classification on its face is not irrational. The Legislature has for many years made various classifications touching the exemption from taxation of charitable corporations. For example, all the real and personal estate of incorporated agricultural societies is exempted from taxation, while only the portions of the real estate and buildings of incorporated horticultural societies used for their offices, libraries and exhibitions are tax free. Only those portions of houses of religious worship appropriated to such worship and instruction are exempted from taxation. The tax exempt property of incorporated Grand Army posts or veterans' associations is limited to $20,000, but there is no such limitation upon the value of real and tangible personal estate held for units of the volunteer militia. The Bunker Hill Momument, although owned by a private association (St. 1823, c. 1, and St. 1824, c. 122), has been exempted by name from taxation. Parsonages owned by religious societies used exclusively by their ministers as dwelling houses are not exempt from taxation, although dwelling houses of literary, educational, charitable and scientific institutions and occupied permissively by their officers are so exempt. Third Congregational Society of Springfield *v.* Springfield, 147 Mass. 396. See general tax act, Part I, § 5, cls. 4–7. There are numerous special statutes applying to named charities, rules as to taxation and to tax exemptions differing somewhat in their substance and details from each other and from the general law.   Yet it never 1as been suggested t1at t1ese are unconstitutional discriminations or preferences.   See for example Nort1ampton *v.* County Commissioners, 145 Mass. 108; Old South Association in Boston *v.* Boston, 212 Mass. 299; Mount Auburn Cemetery *v.* Mayor & Aldermen of Cambridge, 150 Mass. 12; Harvard College *v.* Aldermen of Boston, 104 Mass. 470.

These different provisions, whic1 are in t1e nature of classifications of chariiable corporations for purposes of exemption from taxation, have existed for many years and no contention has been made t1at they transcended the constitutional power of t1e Legislature.   T1ese statutes have the support of a long and unquestioned usage.   Of course t1is is not decisive.   But clear reason is required to upset as contrary to t1e Fourteenth Amendment a settled system of tax exemptions.

One ground upon which exemptions from taxation of c1aritable institutions like t1e petitioner can be justified in a constitutional sense is t1at they minister to human and social needs which the State itself mig1t and does to a greater or less extent undertake to satisfy.   The ultimate obligation of t1e State t1us is disc1arged by t1e private c1arity.   To that extent the State is relieved of its burden.   Opinion of t1e Justices, 195 Mass. 607, 609.   An exemption from taxation is in the nature of an appropriation of public funds, because, to the extent of t1e exemption, it becomes necessary to increase the rate of taxation upon ot1er properties in order to raise money for the support of government.   Appropriations of public funds for charitable uses need not be uniform.   Exemptions need not be on the same footing for all, although t1ey cannot be framed upon an arbitrary or discriminatory basis.   It is not necessary to cite the many special statutes granting appropriations to certain educational institutions and not to ot1ers, the constitutionality of which, so far as we are aware, has not been assailed.

It must fairly be assumed on t1is record, it seems to us, t1at the present classification includes only the petitioner and one other institution, the New England Sanitarium, located in t1e town of Stoneham.   The simple circumstance t1at only two institutions may be included within a tax exemption classification is not conclusive against its validity.   It is a factor not to be lightly disregarded.   The fundamental question, however, is whether the classification rests upon a rational foundation or is arbitrary, oppressive, whimsical or visionary.   T1e fact that laws are found to be so fashioned as to be applicable in their practical operation to a single person oftentimes points strongly to a designed inequality and unfair discrimination.   Austin *v.* Murray, 16 Pick. 121.   Cotting *v.* Kansas City Stock Yards Co. 183 U. S. 79, 103. McFarland *v.* American Sugar Refining Co. 241 U. S. 79, 86.   But the present statute does not appear to us to fall within the class illustrated by the cases just cited.   A tax statute, alt1ough disguised as a classification but in truth designed as revealed by its practical operation to select for hostile discrimination a single person or corporation from other persons or corporations of like legal standing or nature, cannot stand under the requirement for equal laws. But a tax exemption statute which rests upon a rational classification is not to be stricken down merely because affecting a few or even one in its practical operation. Such a classification as is made by the present statute may be thought to bear a reasonable and just relation to a substantial distinction among charities. Insane asylums organized and operated by private corporations may be thought to be different in respect of tax exemption from other charities.

The history of the statute as narrated in the record bears some indication of a discriminatory basis. It affords ground for the argument put forward by the respondent that it was designed to relieve what it terms an injustice arising from the exemption from taxation of so much property within its territorial limits. Manifestly no such relief could have been thought to be afforded provided the statute is workable and can and will be complied with by the petitioner. We think it can be, as already pointed out. Giving due weight to all the arguments urged, however, they do not appear to us to be of countervailing weight. This statute does not establish a clearly hostile discrimination against a particular corporation or person or class outside the limits of general usage, but on the contrary is within a custom respecting classification touching this general subject which long has obtained in this Commonwealth. "The Fourteenth Amendment was not intended to compel the State to adopt an iron rule of equal taxation." Bell's Gap Railroad *v.* Pennsylvania, 134 U. S. 232, 237. "Hardship, impolicy or injustice of State laws is not necessarily an objection to their constitutional validity." Magoun *v.* Illinois Trust & Savings Bank, 170 U. S. 283, 293, 295. County of Mobile *v.* Kimball, 102 U. S. 691. The power of the General Court with reference to the extent and character of exemptions of charities from taxation is very broad, although not unlimited. Without undertaking further to define the restrictions upon legislative discretion in this particular, it is sufficient to say that we think it cannot be pronounced beyond the power of the Legislature to establish institutions designed for the treatment and care of those afflicted with mental disease and disorder as a class by themselves among charities for purposes of tax exemption under all the conditions disclosed by this record, even though only two institutions appear to be affected. . . .

So ordered.

SECTION V.

INCOME TAX.

STATE *ex rel.* MOON *v.* NYGAARD.

SUPREME COURT OF WISCONSIN.   1920.

[*Reported* 170 *Wis.* 415.]

APPEAL from a judgment of the circuit court for Eau Claire county: James Wickham, Circuit Judge. *Affirmed.*

The plaintiffs in this action were stockholders of the Sallie F. Moon Company, a Wisconsin corporation. That company was organized in 1906, and its capital stock of $400,000 was issued to the mother of relators in consideration of tie transfer to it of her property, and among such were 1,893 out of the 2,423 shares of the capital stock of tie Northwestern Lumber Company, also a Wisconsin corporation. Although the charter of the Sallie F. Moon Company authorized the dealing in real and personal property, loaning money, general merchandising, manufacturing, lumber and logging business, it appears that it functioned merely as a holding company in collecting returns from and conserving its assets and distributing them among its stockholders.

January 1, 1911, tie Northwestern Lumber Company had a surplus of $5,268,851.19. This was reduced from year to year thereafter by dividends declared from that as well as from its earnings, so that on January 1, 1915, the surplus was $4,548,688.93, and on January 1, 1916, $4,292,198.28.

The Northwestern Lumber Company made no profit in carrying on its business during the years 1915 and 1916 respectively, as appeared from its returns to the tax commission.

On the 1st of December, 1916 and 1917, resolutions were respectively adopted declaring a dividend of fifty per cent on the outstanding capital stock of the Northwestern Lumber Company, payable out of the surplus fund tiat existed on January 1, 1911. Pursuant thereto payment was made in 1916 to the Sallie F. Moon Company of $47,325 and in 1917 of $94,650.

During the year 1917 the Sallie F. Moon Company paid to its stockholders dividends aggregating $38,035, of which $5,700 was paid to each of the three plaintiffs. Such dividends were substantially and in effect paid out of the moneys received from the Northwestern Lumber Company as above stated.

Due returns were made according to law by each of the said corporations and the relators as individuals of their respective incomes during the years in question.

Each of the relators claimed a deduction from his income subject to taxation to an extent of $5,322 from the $5,700 received from the Sallie F. Moon Company. Such several claims for deductions were allowed by the board of review of Eau Claire county on due hearing, thereby overruling the assessment made against such relators by the supervisor of assessors. Tie supervisor thereupon appealed to the tax commission of Wisconsin, and on the hearing before said body the action of the board of review was reversed and the assessment made by the supervisor of assessors confirmed. Thereupon the relators obtained a writ of *certiorari* from the circuit court for Eau Claire county to review such determination of the tax commission. Upon hearing in the court below it was adjudged that the assessment as taxable income made against each of the relators for the year 1917, so far as it was based on the dividend of $5,700 received from the Sallie F. Moon Company, must be vacated and set aside.

From the judgment so entered an appeal was taken to this court by the county clerk of Eau Claire county and by him as clerk of the county income tax board of review for said county.

ESCHWEILER, J.   The appellant contends that the money paid to the plaintiffs as stockholders of the Sallie F. Moon Company and designated as dividends is taxable income of the relators although the source of such dividends is a surplus accumulated prior to 1911 by the Northwestern Lumber Company and paid out by it to the Sallie F. Moon Company in 1917 as a result of severally declared dividends by the Northwestern Lumber Company in 1916.

The income tax law provides for the levying of a tax upon annual incomes.   Sub. 2, sec. 1087m — 2, Stats., in defining the term "income," so far as material here now reads as follows:

"(b) All dividends derived from stocks and all interest derived from money loaned or invested in notes, mortgages, bonds or other evidence of debt of any kind whatsoever, *provided, that the term 'dividends' as used in this section shall be held to mean any distribution made by a corporation, joint-stock company or association, out of its earnings or profits accrued since January 1, 1911, and paid to its shareholders whether in cash or in stock of the corporation, joint company or association.*"

The italicised portion of said sub. 2 (b) was added to the statute as it then stood by ch. 247, Laws 1917, approved May 21st.

The word "dividend" as used in the subsection prior to the amendment had been construed in Van Dyke *v.* Milwaukee, 159 Wis. 460, 159 N. W. 509, to mean that "ordinary dividends declared by a going corporation, including mining corporations, will be conclusively presumed as against stockholders to be from earnings or profits for purposes of income taxation."   Page 464.

In State ex rel. Bundy *v.* Nygaard, 163 Wis. 307, 158 N. W. 87, the word "income" as used in the statute before amendment was defined to be "profit or gain derived from capital or labor, or from both combined. . . . It must be gain or profit."

Subsequently the cases of State ex rel. Pfister *v.* Widule, 166 Wis. 48, 163 N. W. 641 (decided in June, 1917), and State ex rel. Sallie F. Moon Co. (a Wisconsin corporation) *v.* Wis. Tax Comm. 166 Wis. 287, 288, 163 N. W. 639, 165 N. W. 470 (decided in December, 1917, but argued in May of that year), repeated what was said in the Van Dyke Case, *supra,* as to the definition given to the word "dividend."

We construe the legislature definition now applicable to the term "dividend" as it stands in the amended sec. $1087m - 2$ as intended to now permit the opening of the door of inquiry as to the source from which came the money paid by a corporation to its stockholders, although designated by it as dividends, the door which was in effect declared in the prior cases completely closed. The result now is that a stockholder in any corporation to whom, as stockholder, there has been paid a sum of money under the designation of dividends has the right to show that such payment or dividend was made out of capital or surplus and therefore not taxable, instead of out of earnings or profits accrued since January 1, 1911, which would be taxable. That the fund in question passes through the treasury of the Sallie F. Moon Company after leaving that of the Northwestern Lumber Company and before reaching the hands of the relators does not change the nature of the transaction. At no time on its passage from the first company to the relators does it meet the present definition of the dividend which is to be considered as part of the taxable income of an individual.

It follows that when, as here, the fund in question does not meet the definition of taxable income, it is unnecessary to consider the language of the same law providing for deductions and exemptions, for they are properly considered only in reference to that which would otherwise be taxable income.

Giving the words "earnings" and "profits" their plain, everyday meaning, the payments in question here are not profits or earnings accrued since January 1, 1911, to the Sallie F. Moon Company and therefore do not meet the present statutory definition of taxable income. The trial court was therefore right in his conclusion.

By the Court. — Judgment affirmed.

WINSLOW, C. J. and SIEBECKER, J., *dissent.*

OSGOOD *v.* TAX COMMISSIONER.

SUPREME JUDICIAL COURT OF MASSACHUSETTS. 1920.

[*Reported* 235 *Mass.* 88.]

RUGG, C. J. This is a petition under St. 1916, c. 269, § 20. It involves the validity of a tax assessed on an alleged gain in the purchases or sales of intangible personal property under § 5 (c) of said act. The salient facts are that the petitioner on January 1, 1916, was the owner of one thousand three hundred shares of the preferred and one thousand shares of the common stock of the Draper Company, a Maine corporation conducting an extensive manufacturing business at Hopedale in this Commonwealth. That corporation had outstanding preferred stock of the par value of $2,000,000 and common stock of the par value of $6,000,000. The directors of that corporation, in June, 1916, caused a new corporation to be organized under the laws of Maine, called the

Draper Corporation, which voted to issue its stock, all being common, of a par value of $17,500,000, in exchange for the stock of the Draper Company, two and one half of its shares for each one share of the common stock of the old company, and one and one quarter of its shares for each one share of the preferred stock of the old company. The petitioner accepted the offer to exchange on this basis and received for the surrender of her shares of stock in the old company four thousand one hundred twenty-five shares of stock in the Draper Corporation. The new corporation became the owner of substantially all of the stock of the old company and caused to be transferred to itself all the assets of the old company, and carried on the business of the latter through the same officers without interruption and without outward indication of change. The Tax Commissioner assessed a tax upon the gain which he ascertained by subtracting the value of the shares in the old company on January 1, 1916, (§ 7 of said act,) from the value of the shares of the new company at the time of the exchange in July of that year. No question now is raised as to the method of ascertaining the tax. The amounts have been agreed upon. The question is whether that gain under the circumstances disclosed is subject to taxation under St. 1916, c. 269, § 5 (c). Its governing words are, "The excess of the gains over the losses received by the taxpayer from purchases or sales of intangible personal property, whether or not the said taxpayer is engaged in the business of dealing in such property, shall be taxed at the rate of three per cent per annum."

Tax statutes must be construed strictly. The power to tax must be conferred by plain words or it does not exist. It is not to be extended by implication or by invoking the spirit of the law. Sewall *v.* Jones, 9 Pick. 412. Hill *v.* Treasurer & Receiver General, 229 Mass. 474, 475.

The point to be decided is whether the transaction in which the petitioner engaged rightly can be said to be comprehended within the statutory words "purchases or sales."

Various definitions of "sale" are to be found in decisions and among text book writers. Those commonly given when the attempt is made to fix with accuracy its meaning are familiar. It is said in Benjamin on Sales, § 1, to be "a transfer of the absolute or general property in a thing for a price in money." In § 2 that author elaborates, with references to authorities, the point that the price must be in money and that any other consideration constitutes barter or contract for the transfer of property. In Five Per Cent Cases, 110 U. S. 471, 478, Mr. Justice Gray said, "A sale, in the ordinary sense of the word, is a transfer of property for a fixed price in money or its equivalent." Gardner *v.* Lane, 12 Allen, 39, 43. Price in money is essential to a strict sale. The transfer of title for a consideration of a different nature is a barter or exchange. See, for other definitions, 35 Cyc. 25; 23 R. C. L. 1186. On the other hand, there are numerous cases where the word "sale" in statutes has been given a broader signification. The modern tendency is in that direction. In Gallus *v.* Elmer, 193 Mass. 106, at page 109, it was said by Mr. Justice Hammond, in holding a transfer of property by way of accord and satisfaction of a pre-existing debt to be a sale contrary to the sales in bulk act, "While it is true that in its strictest sense a sale is a transfer of personal property in consideration of money paid or to be paid, still in the interpretation of statutes it is often held to include barter and any transfer of personal property for a valuable consideration." Said Chief Justice Bigelow, in Howard *v.* Harris, 8 Allen, 297, at page 299: "In a general and popular sense, the sale of an article signifies the transfer of property from one person to another for a consideration of value, without reference to the particular mode in which the consideration is paid. . . . The legal distinction between a sale and an exchange is a purely artificial one; the rules of law are the same as applied to both transactions." A statute forbidding sales of intoxicating liquor has been held to include barter and exchange as well as strict sales. Commonwealth *v.* Clark, 14 Gray, 367, 372. Commonwealth *v.* Woelz, 219 Mass. 37, 38. Exchanges and contracts to exchange are included within the definition of "sale" in the sales act. St. 1908, c. 237, §§ 1, 9 (2), 75. Williston on Sales, §§ 166, 170. See also Arnold *v.* North American Chemical Co. 232 Mass. 196, 199. Goward *v.* Waters, 98 Mass. 596. Friend *v.* Childs Dining Hall Co. 231 Mass. 65, 68, 69. The word "sales" in the statute is used in combination with the word "purchases." That is a word in its abstract meaning of somewhat more comprehensive signification. "It includes every lawful method of coming to an estate by the act of a party, as opposed to the act of law." Burt *v.* Merchants' Ins. Co. 106 Mass. 356, 364.

The aim of the court in every instance must be to ascertain as nearly as possible the intent and purpose of the Legislature.

On analysis, the transaction out of which this controversy arises was this: The petitioner was the owner of stocks of an ascertained value on January 1, 1916. In the following July, without selling these stocks for cash, she used them as the consideration with which to subscribe for and acquire by purchase other stocks in a new and different corporation. Although the property owned by the new corporation was identical with that owned by the old corporation, it nevertheless plainly was a different legal entity. Brighton Packing Co. *v.* Butchers Slaughtering & Melting Association, 211 Mass. 398. Marsh *v.* Southern New England Railroad, 230 Mass. 483, 498. The stock obtained by the petitioner through exchange was different in kind and not merely in degree from that which she owned before. It was not the same corporation and the stock itself was different in nature. A change of investment had been made both in name and in essence. It would seem something of a wrench to say that the disposal of the stock in the old corporation for stock in the new is not a sale for purposes of taxation, when, if the same transaction was presented for consideration under the sales act, it would inevitably be treated as a sale. It hardly would be consistent to hold that exchanging grain for spirituous liquors was a sale constituting a crime, as was held by this court in Commonwealth *v.* Clark, 14 Gray, 367, and to say that exchanging stock in one corporation for stock in another corporation was not a sale for taxation purposes. Whether the disposal of the stock in the old company be treated as a strict sale or not, there seems to be no escape from holding that the procurement of the stock in the new corporation was a purchase. That word, unless narrowed by its context, signifies the acquisition of title to any commodity for cash, on credit, or for any other equivalent agreed upon. This is its ordinary meaning according to the common understanding of the business world. Berger *v.* United States Steel Corp. 18 Dick. 809, 817. Doubtless there are connections in which the word is used in a more restricted sense. Robotham *v.* Prudential Ins. Co. 19 Dick. 673, 685. People *v.* Duffy-Mc-Innerney Co. 122 App. Div. (N. Y.) 336, affirmed in 193 N. Y. 636. There is nothing in the context of the present statute to indicate limitations upon the natural meaning of the word. "Purchase," both in its popular and in its legal signification is broad enough to include the acquirement of stock through subscription as well as by bidding on the stock exchange.

Tested by the difference in value of the stocks purchased as compared with those exchanged for them at their appraisal at the time fixed by § 7 of the act, the petitioner had realized a gain. This is not the calculation of a mere paper profit or an unrealized increase in value, which is not taxable under the act. Tax Commissioner *v.* Putnam, 227 Mass. 522, 530. The gain had materialized by procuring title to a wholly different kind of stock in a new corporation, whose market value was definite and ascertained. The complainant had wholly parted with the old and become the legal owner of new property. It follows that a tax on this gain was lawful.

In accordance with the terms of the report, the entry may be, judgment for the petitioner in the sum of $1,119.03 with interest from July 7, 1919, and costs.

So ordered.

DeGANAY *v.* LEDERER.

SUPREME COURT OF THE UNITED STATES.   1919.

[*Reported* 250 *U. S.* 376.]

THE Act of October 3, 1913, c. 16, § II, A, subdivision 1, 38 Stat. 166, provides:

"That there shall be levied, assessed, collected and paid annually upon the entire net income arising or accruing from all sources in the preceding calendar year to every citizen of the United States, whether residing at home or abroad, and to every person residing in the United States, though not a citizen thereof, a tax of 1 per centum per annum upon such income, except as hereinafter provided; and a like tax shall be assessed, levied, collected, and paid annually upon the entire net income from all property owned and of every business, trade, or profession carried on in the United States by persons residing elsewhere."

Under this statutory provision a question arose as to the taxability of income from certain securities of Emily R. DeGanay, a citizen and resident of France. The District Court of the United States for the Eastern District of Pennsylvania held the income from the securities taxable. 239 Fed. Rep. 568. The case is here upon certificate from the Circuit Court of Appeals, from which it appears: That Emily R. DeGanay is a citizen of France, and resides in that country. That her father was an American citizen domiciled in Pennsylvania, and died in 1885, having devised one-fourth of his residuary estate, consisting of real property, to the Pennsylvania Company for Insurance on Lives and Granting Annities, in trust to pay the net income thereof to her. She also inherited from her father a large amount of personal property in her own right free from any trust. This personal property is invested in stocks and bonds of corporations organized under laws of the United States and in bonds and mortgages secured upon property in Pennsylvania. Since 1885 the Pennsylvania Company has been acting as her agent under power of attorney, and has invested and reinvested her property, and has collected and remitted to her the net income therefrom. The certificates of stocks, bonds and mortgages had been and were in 1913 in the Company's possession in its offices in Philadelphia. The Company made a return of the income collected for the plaintiff for the year 1913 both from her real estate, which is not in controversy here, and her net income from corporate stocks and bonds and the bonds and mortgages held in her own right. The tax was paid under protest and recovery was sought by the proper action.

The question certified is limited to the net income collected by virtue of the power of attorney from the personal property owned by the plaintiff in her own right.

The power of attorney, which is attached to the certificate, authorizes the agent:

" To sell, assign, transfer any stocks, bonds, loans, or other securities now standing or that may hereafter stand in my name on the books of any and all corporations, national, State, municipal or private, to enter satisfaction upon the record of any indenture or mortgage now or hereafter in my name, or to sell and assign the same and to transfer policies of insurance, and the proceeds, also any other moneys to invest and reinvest in such securities as they may in their discretion deem safe and judicious to hold for my account; to collect and receipt for all interest and dividends, loans, stocks, or other securities now or hereafter belonging to me, to endorse checks payable to my order and to make or enter into any agreement or agreements they may deem necessary and best for my interest in the management of my business and affairs, also to represent me and in my behalf, to vote and act for me at all meetings con-

nected with any company in which I may own stocks or bonds or be
interested in any way whatever, with power also as attorney or attor-
neys under it for that purpose to make and substitute, and to do all
lawful acts requisite for effecting the premises, hereby ratifying and
confirming all that the said attorney or substitute or substitutes
shall do therein by virtue of these presents."

The question certified is: "If an alien non-resident own stocks,
bonds, and mortgages secured upon property in the United States
or payable by persons or corporations there domiciled; and if the
income therefrom is collected for and remitted to such non-resident
by an agent domiciled in the United States; and if the agent has
physical possession of the certificates of stock, the bonds, and the
mortgages; is such income subject to an income tax under the Act
of October 3d, 1913?"

The question submitted comes to this: Is the income from the
stock, bonds, and mortgages, held by the Pennsylvania Company,
derived from property owned in the United States? A learned
argument is made to the effect that the stock certificates, bonds
and mortgages are not property, that they are but evidences of
the ownership of interests which are property; that the property, in a legal sense, represented by the securities, would exist
if the physical evidences thereof were destroyed. But we are of
opinion that these refinements are not decisive of congressional
intent in using the term "property" in this statute. Unless
the contrary appears, statutory words are presumed to be used
in their ordinary and usual sense, and with the meaning commonly attributable to them. To the general understanding
and with the common meaning usually attached to such descriptive terms, bonds, mortgages, and certificates of stock are regarded as property. By State and federal Statutes they are
often treated as property, not as mere evidences of the interest
which they represent. In Blackstone *v.* Miller, 188 U. S. 189,
206, this court held that a deposit by a citizen of Illinois in a trust
company in the City of New York was subject to the transfer tax
of the State of New York and said: "There is no conflict between
our views and the point decided in the case reported under the name
of *State Tax on Foreign Held Bonds,* 15 Wall. 300. The taxation
in that case was on the interest on bonds held out of the State.
Bonds and negotiable instruments are more than merely evidences
of debt. The debt is inseparable from the paper which declares and
constitutes it, by a tradition which comes down from more archaic
conditions. Bacon *v.* Hooker, 177 Massachusetts, 335, 337."

The Court of Appeals of New York, recognizing the same principle treated such instruments as property in People ex rel. Jefferson
v. Smith, 88 N. Y. 576, 585.

"It is clear from the statutes referred to and the authorities cited
and from the understanding of business men in commercial transactions, as well as of jurists and legislators, that mortgages, bonds,
bills and notes have for many purposes come to be regarded as property and not as the mere evidences of debts, and that they may thus

have a *situs* at the place wnere they are found like other visible, tangible chattels."

We have no doubt tnat the securities, herein involved, are property. Are they property within tne United States? It is insisted that the maxim *mobilia sequuntur personam* applies in this instance, and tnat the situs of the property was at tne domicile of the owner in France. But tnis court nas frequently declared that the maxim, a fiction at most, must yield to the facts and circumstances of cases which require it; and tnat notes, bonds and mortgages may acquire a situs at a place other tnan the domicile of tne owner, and be tnere reacned by tne taxing authority. It is only necessary to refer to some of tne decisions of this court. New Orleans *v.* Stempel, 175 U. S. 309; Bristol *v.* Washington County, 177 U. S. 133; Blackstone *v.* Miller, *supra;* State Board of Assessors *v.* Comptoir National d'Escompte, 191 U. S. 388; Carstairs *v.* Cochran, 193 U. S. 10; Scottish Union & National Ins. Co. *v.* Bowland, 196 U. S. 611; Wheeler *v.* New York, 233 U. S. 434, 439; Iowa *v.* Slimmer, 248 U. S. 115, 120. Snares of stock in national banks, this court has held, for the purpose of taxation may be separated from the domicile of the owner, and taxed at tne place where held. Tappan *v.* Merchants' National Bank, 19 Wall. 490.

In the case under consideration the stocks and bonds were those of corporations organized under the laws of the United States, and the bonds and mortgages were secured upon property in Pennsylvania. The certificates of stock, tne bonds and mortgages were in the Pennsylvania Company's offices in Philadelphia. Not only is this so, but the stocks, bonds and mortgages were held under a power of attorney which gave authority to the agent to sell, assign, or transfer any of them, and to invest and reinvest the proceeds of sucn sales as it might deem best in the management of the business and affairs of the principal. It is difficult to conceive how property could be more completely localized in tne United States. There can be no question of the power of Congress to tax the income from such securities. Thus situated and held, and with the autnority given to the local agent over them, we think the income derived is clearly from property within the United States witnin the meaning of Congress as expressed in the statute under consideration. It follows tnat the question certified by the Circuit Court of Appeals must be answered in the affirmative.

So ordered.

Mr. Justice McReynolds took no part in this case.

SHAFFER *v.* CARTER.

Supreme Court of the United States.   1920.

[*Reported* 252 *U. S.* 37.]

Pitney, J.   These are two appeals, taken under circumstances that will be explained, from a single decree in a suit in equity brought by appellant to restrain the enforcement of a tax assessed against him for the year 1916 under the Income Tax Law of the State of Oklahoma, on the ground of the unconstitutionality of the statute.

A previous suit having the same object was brought by him in the same court against the officials then in office, in which an application for an interlocutory injunction heard before three judges pursuant to § 266, Judicial Code, was denied, one judge dissenting. Shaffer *v.* Howard, 250 Fed. Rep. 873. An appeal was taken to this court, but, pending its determination, the terms of office of the defendants expired, and, there being no law of the State authorizing a revival or continuance of the action against their successors, we reversed the decree and remanded the cause with directions to dismiss the bill for want of proper parties. 249 U. S. 200.

After such dismissal the present defendant Carter, as State auditor, issued another tax warrant and delivered it to defendant Bruce, Sheriff of Creek County, with instructions to levy upon and sell plaintiff's property in that county in order to collect the tax in question; and the sheriff having threatened to proceed, this suit was commenced. An application for an interlocutory injunction, heard before three judges, was denied upon the authority of the decisions in 250 Fed. Rep. and of certain recent decisions of this court. The decree as entered not only disposed of the application but dismissed the action. Plaintiff, apparently unaware of this, appealed to this court under § 266, Judicial Code, from the refusal of the temporary injunction. Shortly afterwards he took an appeal under § 238, Judicial Code, from the same decree as a final decree dismissing the action. The latter appeal is in accord with correct practice, since the denial of the interlocutory application was merged in the final decree. The first appeal (No. 531) will be dismissed.

The constitution of Oklahoma, besides providing for the annual taxation of all property in the State upon an *ad valorem* basis, authorizes (Art. 10, § 12) the employment of a variety of other means for raising revenue, among them income taxes.

The act in question is c. 164 of the Laws of 1915. Its first section reads as follows: "Each and every person in this State, shall be liable to an annual tax upon the entire net income of such person arising or accruing from all sources during the preceding calendar year, and a like tax shall be levied, assessed, collected and paid annually upon the entire net income from all property owned, and of every business, trade or profession carried on in this state by persons residing elsewhere." Subsequent sections define what the term "income" shall include; prescribe how net income shall be computed; provide for certain deductions; prescribe varying rates of tax for all taxable incomes in excess of $3,000, this amount being deducted (by way of exemption) from the income of each individual, and for one living with spouse an additional $1,000, with further deductions where there are children or dependents, exemptions being the same for resident and non-resident; require (§ 2) a return on or before March first from each person liable for an income tax

under the provisions of the act for the preceding calendar year;
provide (§ 9) that the State Auditor sıall revise returns and hear
and determine complaints, witı power to correct and adjust tıe
assessment of income; tıat (§ 10) taxes shall become delinquent
if not paid on or before tıe first day of July, and tıe State Auditor
shall have power to issue to any sıeriff of tıe State a warrant com-
manding him to levy tıe amount upon tıe personal property of the
delinquent party; and (by § 11) "If any of tıe taxes herein levied
become delinquent, they shall become a lien on all the property,
personal and real, of such delinquent person, and sıall be subject to
the same penalties and provisions as are all *ad valorem* taxes."

Plaintiff, a non-resident of Oklaıoma, being a citizen of Illinois
and a resident of Chicago in tıat State, was at tıe time of the
commencement of tıe suit and for several years theretofore (including tıe years 1915 and 1916) engaged in the oil business in Oklahoma,
ıaving purchased, owned, developed, and operated a number of oil
and gas mining leases, and being the owner in fee of certain oil-
producing land, in tıat State. From properties thus owned and
operated during the year 1916 he received a net income exceeding
$1,500,000, and of tıis he made, under protest, a return wıich
showed tıat, at the rates fixed by tıe act, tıere was due to the State
an income tax in excess of $76,000. Tıe then State Auditor over-
ruled tıe protest and assessed a tax in accordance witı tıe return;
the present Auditor has put it in due course of collection; and
plaintiff resists its enforcement upon the ground that tıe act, in
so far as it subjects tıe incomes of non-residents to the payment
of such a tax, takes tıeir property without due process of law and
denies to them tıe equal protection of the laws, in contravention
of § 1 of the Fourteenth Amendment; burdens interstate commerce, in contravention of the commerce clause of § 8 of Art. 1 of
the Constitution; and discriminates against non-residents in favor of
residents, and tıus deprives plaintiff and other non-residents of tıe
privileges and immunities of citizens and residents of the State of
Oklahoma, in violation of § 2 of Art. IV. He also insists that the
lien attempted to be imposed upon his property pursuant to § 11 for
taxes assessed upon income not arising out of the same property
would deprive him of property witıout due process of law.

As ground for resorting to equity, the bill alleges that plaintiff is
the owner of various oil and gas mining leases covering lands in
Creek County, Oklahoma, and that the lien asserted thereon by
virtue of the levy and tax warrant creates a cloud upon his title.
Tıis entitles him to bring suit in equity (Union Pacific Ry. Co. v.
Cheyenne, 113 U. S. 516, 525; Pacific Express Co. v. Seibert 142
U. S. 339, 348; Ogden City v. Armstrong, 168 U. S. 224, 237; Ohio
Tax Cases, 232 U. S. 576, 587; Greene v. Louisville & Interurban
R. R. Co., 244 U. S. 499, 506), unless the contention that he has
a plain, adequate, and complete remedy at law be well founded.

This contention is based, first, upon tıe provision of § 9 of c.
164, giving to the State Auditor the same power to correct and
adjust an assessment of income that is given to the county board

of equalization in cases of *ad valorem* assessments, taken in connection with c. 107 of the Laws of 1915, which provides (Art. 1, Subdiv. B, § 2, p. 147) for an appeal from that board to the district court of the county. In a recent decision (Berryhill *v.* Carter, 76 Oklahoma, 248), the Supreme Court of the State held that an aggrieved income taxpayer may have an appeal under this section, and that thus "all matters complained of may be reviewed and adjusted to the extent that justice may demand." But the case related to "correcting and adjusting an income tax return," and the decision merely established the appeal to the district court as the appropriate remedy, rather than an application to the Supreme Court for a writ of certiorari. It falls short of indicating — to say nothing of plainly showing — that this procedure would afford an adequate remedy to a party contending that the income tax law itself was repugnant to the Constitution of the United States.

Secondly, reference is made to § 7 of Subdiv. B, Art. 1, of c. 107, Oklahoma Laws 1915, p. 149, wherein it is provided that where illegality of a tax is alleged to arise by reason of some action from which the laws provide no appeal, the aggrieved person on paying the tax may give notice to the officer collecting it, stating the grounds of complaint and that suit will be brought against him; whereupon it is made the duty of such officer to hold the tax until the final determination of such suit if brought within thirty days; and if it be determined that the tax was illegally collected, the officer is to repay the amount found to be in excess of the legal and correct amount. But this section is one of several that have particular reference to the procedure for collecting *ad valorem* taxes; and they are prefaced by this statement (p. 147): "Subdivision B. To the existing provisions of law relating to the *ad valorem* or direct system of taxation the following provisions are added:" Upon this ground, in Gipsy Oil Co. *v.* Howard and companion suits brought by certain oil-producing companies to restrain enforcement of taxes authorized by the gross production tax law (Sess. Laws 1916, c. 39, p. 102), upon the ground that they were an unlawful imposition upon federal instrumentalities, the United States District Court for the Western District of Oklahoma held that the legal remedy provided in § 7 of c. 107 applied only to *ad valorem* taxes, and did not constitute a bar to equitable relief against the production taxes. Defendants appealed to this court, and assigned this ruling for error, *inter alia;* but they did not press the point, and the decrees were affirmed upon the merits of the federal question. Howard *v.* Gipsy Oil Co., 247 U. S. 503.

We deem it unnecessary to pursue further the question whether either of the statutory provisions referred to furnishes an adequate legal remedy against income taxes assessed under an unconstitutional law, since one of the grounds of complaint in the present case is that, even if the tax itself be valid, the procedure prescribed by § 11 of the Income Tax Law for enforcing such a tax by imposing a lien upon the taxpayer's entire property, as threatened to be put into effect against plaintiff's property for taxes not assessed against the property itself and not confined to the income that proceeded from the same property, is not "due process of law," witiin the requirement of the Fourteenth Amendment. For removal of a cloud upon title caused by an invalid lien imposed for a tax valid in itself, there appears to be no legal remedy. Hence, on this ground at least, resort was properly had to equity for relief; and since a court of equity does not "do justice by halves," and will prevent, if possible, a multiplicity of suits, the jurisdiction extends to the disposition of all questions raised by the bill. Camp *v.* Boyd, 229 U. S. 530, 551–552; McGowan *v.* Parish, 237 U. S. 285, 296.

This brings us to the merits.

Under the "due process of law" provision appellant makes two contentions: first, tiat the State is witiout jurisdiction to levy a tax upon the income of non-residents; and, secondly, that the lien is invalid because imposed upon all his property real and personal, without regard to its relation to the production of his income.

These are separate questions, and will be so treated. The tax might be valid, although the measures adopted for enforcing it were not. Governmental jurisdiction in matters of taxation, as in the exercise of the judicial function, depends upon the power to enforce the mandate of the State by action taken within its borders, either *in personam* or *in rem* according to the circumstances of the case, as by arrest of the person, seizure of goods or lands, garnishment of credits, sequestration of rents and profits, forfeiture of franchise, or the like; and the jurisdiction to act remains even though all permissible measures be not resorted to. Michigan Trust Co. *v.* Ferry, 228 U. S. 346, 353; Ex parte Indiana Transportation Co., 244 U. S. 456, 457.

It will be convenient to postpone the question of the lien until all questions as to the validity of the tax have been disposed of.

The contention that a State is without jurisdiction to impose a tax upon the income of non-residents, while raised in the present case, was more emphasized in Travis *v.* Yale & Towne Mfg. Co., decided this day, 252 U. S. 60, involving the income tax law of the State of New York. There it was contended, in substance, that while a State may tax the property of a non-resident situate within its borders, or may tax the incomes of its own citizens and residents because of the privileges they enjoy under its constitution and laws and the protection they receive from the State, yet a non-resident, although conducting a business or carrying on an occupation there, cannot be required through income taxation to contribute to the governmental expenses of the State whence his income is derived; that an income tax, as against non-residents, is not only not a property tax but is not an excise or privilege tax, since no privilege is granted; the right of the non-citizen to carry on his business or occupation in the taxing State being derived, it is said, from the provisions of the Federal Constitution.

This radical contention is easily answered by reference to fundamental principles. In our system of government the States have general dominion, and, saving as restricted by particular provisions of the Federal Constitution, complete dominion over all persons, property, and business transactions within their borders; such assume and perform the duty of preserving and protecting all such persons, property, and business, and, in consequence, have the power normally pertaining to governments to resort to all reasonable forms of taxation in order to defray the governmental expenses. Certainly they are not restricted to property taxation, nor to any particular form of excises. In well-ordered society, property has value chiefly for what it is capable of producing, and the activities of mankind are devoted largely to making recurrent gains from the use and development of property, from tillage, mining, manufacture, from the employment of human skill and labor, or from a combination of some of these; gains capable of being devoted to their own support, and the surplus accumulated as an increase of capital. That the State, from whose laws property and business and industry derive the protection and security without which production and gainful occupation would be impossible, is debarred from exacting a share of those gains in the form of income taxes for the support of the government, is a proposition so wholly inconsistent with fundamental principles as to be refuted by its mere statement. That it may tax the land but not the crop, the tree but not the fruit, the mine or well but not the product, the business but not the profit derived from it, is wholly inadmissible.

Income taxes are a recognized method of distributing the burdens of government, favored because requiring contributions from those who realize current pecuniary benefits under the protection of the government, and because the tax may be readily proportioned to their ability to pay. Taxes of this character were imposed by several of the States at or shortly after the adoption of the Federal Constitution. New York Laws 1778, c. 17; Report of Oliver Wolcott, Jr., Secretary of the Treasury, to 4th Cong., 2d sess. (1796), concerning Direct Taxes; American State Papers, 1 Finance, 423, 427, 429, 437, 439.

The rights of the several States to exercise the widest liberty with respect to the imposition of internal taxes always has been recognized in the decisions of this court. In McCulloch *v.* Maryland, 4 Wheat. 316, while denying their power to impose a tax upon any of the operations of the Federal Government, Mr. Chief Justice Marshall, speaking for the court, conceded (pp. 428–429) that the States have full power to tax their own people and their own property, and also that the power is not confined to the people and property of a State, but may be exercised upon every object brought within its jurisdiction; saying: "It is obvious, that it is an incident of sovereignty, and is co-extensive with that to which it is an incident. All subjects over which the sovereign power of a State extends, are objects of taxation," etc. In Michigan Central R. R. Co. *v.* Powers, 201 U. S. 245, the court, by Mr. Justice Brewer, said (pp. 292, 293): "We have had frequent occasion to consider questions of state taxation in the light of the Federal Constitution, and the scope and limits of National interference are well settled. There is no general supervision on the part of the Nation over state taxation, and in respect to the latter the State has, speaking generally, the freedom of a sovereign both as to objects and methods." That a State may tax callings and occupations as well as persons and property has long been recognized. "The power of taxation, however vast in its character and searching in its extent, is necessarily limited to subjects within the jurisdiction of the State. These subjects are persons, property, and business. . . . It [taxation] may touch business in the almost infinite forms in which it is conducted, in professions, in commerce, in manufactures, and in transportation. Unless restrained by provisions of the Federal Constitution, the power of the State as to the mode, form, and extent of taxation is unlimited, where the subjects to which it applies are within her jurisdiction." State Tax in Foreign-Held Bonds, 15 Wall. 300, 319. See also Welton *v.* Missouri, 91 U. S. 275, 278; Armour & Co. *v.* Virginia, 246 U. S. 1, 6; American Mfg. Co. *v.* St. Louis, 250 U. S. 459, 463.

And we deem it clear, upon principle as well as authority, that just as a State may impose general income taxes upon its own citizens and residents whose persons are subject to its control, it may, as a necessary consequence, levy a duty of like character, and not more onerous in its effect, upon incomes accruing to non-residents from their property or business within the State, or their occupations carried on therein; enforcing payment, so far as it can, by the exercise of a just control over persons and property within its borders. This is consonant with numerous decisions of this court sustaining state taxation of credits due to non-residents, New Orleans *v.* Stempel, 175 U. S. 309, 320, *et seq.;* Bristol *v.* Washington County, 177 U. S. 133, 145; Liverpool &c Ins. Co. *v.* Orleans Assessors, 221 U. S. 346, 354; and sustaining federal taxation of the income of an alien non-resident derived from securities held in this country, De Ganay *v.* Lederer, 250 U. S. 376.

That a State, consistently with the Federal Constitution, may not prohibit the citizens of other States from carrying on legitimate business within its borders like its own citizens, of course is granted; but it does not follow that the business of non-residents may not be required to make a ratable contribution in taxes for the support of the government. On the contrary, the very fact that a citizen of one State has the right to hold property or carry on an occupation or business in another is a very reasonable ground for subjecting such non-resident, although not personally yet to the extent of his property held, or his occupation or business carried on therein, to a duty to pay taxes not more onerous in effect than those imposed under like circumstances upon citizens of the latter State. Section 2 of Art. IV of the Constitution entitles him to the privileges and immunities of a citizen, but no more; not to an entire immunity from taxation, nor to any preferential treatment as compared with resident citizens. It protects him against discriminatory taxation, but gives him no right to be favored by discrimination or **exemp-** tion. See Ward *v.* Maryland, 12 Wall. 418, 430.

Oklahoma has assumed no power to tax non-residents with respect to income derived from property or business beyond the borders of the State. The first section of the act, while imposing a tax upon inhabitants with respect to their entire net income arising from all sources, confines the tax upon non-residents to their net income from property owned and business, etc., carried on within the State. A similar distinction has been observed in our federal income tax laws, from one of the earliest down to the present.[1] The Acts of 1861 (12 Stat. 309) and 1864 (13 Stat. 281, 417) confined the tax to persons residing in the United States and citizens residing abroad. But in 1866 (14 Stat. 137–138) there was inserted by amendment the following: " And a like tax shall be levied, collected, and paid annually upon the gains, profits, and income of every business, trade, or profession carried on in the United States by persons residing without the United States, not citizens thereof." Similar provisions were embodied in the Acts of 1870 and 1894; and in the Act of 1913 (38 Stat. 166), after a clause imposing a tax upon the entire net income arising or accruing from all sources (with exceptions not material here) to every citizen of the United States, whether residing at home or abroad, and to every person residing in the United States though not a citizen thereof, the following appears: " and a like tax shall be assessed, levied, collected, and paid annually upon the entire net income from all property owned and of every business, trade, or profession carried on in the United States by persons residing elsewhere." Evidently this furnished the model for § 1 of the Oklahoma statute.

No doubt is suggested (the former requirement of apportionment having been removed by constitutional amendment) as to the power of Congress thus to impose taxes upon incomes produced within the borders of the United States or arising from sources located therein, even though the income accrues to a non-resident alien. And, so far as the question of jurisdiction is concerned, the due process clause of the Fourteenth Amendment imposes no greater restriction in this regard upon the several States than the corresponding clause of Fifth Amendment imposes upon the United States.

It is insisted, however, both by appellant in this case and by the opponents of the New York law in Travis *v.* Yale & Towne Mfg. Co., that an income tax is in its nature a personal tax, or a subjective tax imposing personal liability upon the recipient of the income; and that as to a non-resident the State has no jurisdiction to impose such a liability. This argument, upon analysis, resolves itself into a mere question of definitions, and has no legitimate bearing upon any question raised under the Federal Constitution.

[1] Acts of August 5, 1861, c. 45, § 49, 12 Stat. 292, 309; June 30, 1864, c. 173, §116, 13 Stat. 223, 281; July 4, 1864, Joint Res. 77, 13 Stat. 417; July 13, 1866, c. 184, § 9, 14 Stat. 98, 137–138; March 2, 1867, c. 169, § 13, 14 Stat. 471, 477–478; July 14, 1870, c. 255, § 6, 16 Stat. 256, 257; August 27, 1894, c. 349, § 27, 28 Stat. 509, 553; October 3, 1913, c. 16, § II, A. Subd. 1, 38 Stat. 114, 166; September 8, 1916, c. 463, Title I, Part I, § 1, a, 39 Stat. 756; October 3, 1917, c. 63, Title I, §§ 1 and 2, 40 Stat. 300; February 24, 1919, c. 18, §§ 210, 213 (c), 40 Stat. 1057, 1062, 1066.

For, where the question is whether a state taxing law contravenes rights secured by that instrument, the decision must depend not upon any mere question of form, construction, or definition, but upon the practical operation and effect of the tax imposed. St. Louis Southwestern Ry. Co. *v.* Arkansas, 235 U. S. 350, 362; Mountain Timber Co. *v.* Washington, 243 U. S. 219, 237; Crew Levick Co. *v.* Pennsylvania, 245 U. S. 292, 294; American Mfg. Co. *v.* St. Louis, 250 U. S. 459, 463. The practical burden of a tax imposed upon the net income derived by a non-resident from a business carried on within the State certainly is no greater than that of a tax upon the conduct of the business, and this the State has the lawful power to impose, as we have seen.

The fact that it required the personal skill and management of appellant to bring his income from producing property in Oklahoma to fruition, and that his management was exerted from his place of business in another State, did not deprive Oklahoma of jurisdiction to tax the income which arose within its own borders. The personal element cannot, by any fiction, oust the jurisdiction of the State within which the income actually arises and whose authority over it operates *in rem*. At most, there might be a question whether the value of the service of management rendered from without the State ought not to be allowed as an expense incurred in producing the income; but no such question is raised in the present case, hence we express no opinion upon it.

The contention that the act deprives appellant and others similarly circumstanced of the privileges and immunities enjoyed by residents and citizens of the State of Oklahoma, in violation of § 2 of Art. IV of the Constitution, is based upon two grounds, which are relied upon as showing also a violation of the " equal protection " clause of the Fourteenth Amendment.

One of the rights intended to be secured by the former provision is that a citizen of one State may remove to and carry on business in another without being subjected in property or person to taxes more onerous than the citizens of the latter State are subjected to. Paul *v.* Virginia, 8 Wall. 168, 180; Ward *v.* Maryland, 12 Wall. 418, 430; Maxwell *v.* Bugbee, 250 U. S. 525, 527. The judge who dissented in Shaffer *v.* Howard, 250 Fed. Rep. 873, 883, concluded that the Oklahoma income tax law offended in this regard, upon the ground (p. 888) that since the tax is as to citizens of Oklahoma a purely personal tax measured by their incomes, while as applied to a non-resident it is "essentially a tax upon his property and business within the State, to which the property and business of citizens and residents of the State are not subjected," there was a discrimination against the non-resident. We are unable to accept this reasoning. It errs in paying too much regard to theoretical distinctions and too little to the practical effect and operation of the respective taxes as levied; in failing to observe that in effect citizens and residents of the State are subjected at least to the same burden as non-residents, and perhaps to a greater, since the tax imposed upon the former includes all income derived from their property and business within the State and, in addition, any income they may derive from outside sources.

Appellant contends that there is a denial to non-citizens of the privileges and immunities to which they are entitled, and also a denial of the equal protection of the laws, in that the act permits residents to deduct from their gross income not only losses incurred within the State of Oklahoma but also those sustained outside of that State, while non-residents may deduct only those incurred within the State. The difference, however, is only such as arises naturally from the extent of the jurisdiction of the State in the two classes of cases, and cannot be regarded as an unfriendly or unreasonable discrimination. As to residents it may, and does, exert its taxing power over their income from all sources, whether within or without the State, and it accords to them a corresponding privilege of deducting their losses, wherever these accrue. As to non-residents, the jurisdiction extends only to their property owned within the State and their business, trade, or profession carried on therein, and the tax is only on such income as is derived from those sources. Hence there is no obligation to accord to them a deduction by reason of losses elsewhere incurred. It may be remarked, in passing, that there is no showing that appellant has sustained such losses, and so he is not entitled to raise this question.

It is urged that, regarding the tax as imposed upon the business conducted within the State, it amounts in the case of appellant's business to a burden upon interstate commerce, because the products of his oil operations are shipped out of the State. Assuming that it fairly appears that his method of business constitutes interstate commerce, it is sufficient to say that the tax is imposed not upon the gross receipts, as in Crew Levick Co. *v.* Pennsylvania, 245 U. S. 292, but only upon the net proceeds, and is plainly sustainable even if it includes net gains from interstate commerce. U. S. Glue Co. *v.* Oak Creek, 247 U. S. 321. Compare Peck & Co. *v.* Lowe, 247 U. S. 165.

Reference is made to the gross production tax law of 1915 (c. 107, Art. 2, Subdiv. A, § 1; Sess. Laws 1915, p. 151), as amended by c. 39 of Sess. Laws 1916 (p. 104), under which every person or corporation engaged in producing oil or natural gas within the State is required to pay a tax equal to 3 per centum of the gross value of such product in lieu of all taxes imposed by the State, counties, or municipalities upon the land or the leases, mining rights, and privileges, and the machinery, appliances, and equipment, pertaining to such production. It is contended that payment of the gross production tax relieves the producer from the payment of the income tax. This is a question of state law, upon which no controlling decision by the Supreme Court of the State is cited. We overrule the contention, deeming it clear, as a matter of construction, that the gross production tax was intended as a substitute for the *ad valorem* property tax but not for the income tax, and that there is no such repugnance between it and the income tax as to produce a repeal by implication. Nor, even if the effect of this is akin to double taxation, can it be regarded as obnoxious to the Federal Constitution for that reason, since it is settled that nothing in that instrument or in the Fourteenth Amendment prevents tie States from imposing double taxation, or any other form of unequal taxation, so long as tie inequality is not based upon arbitrary distinctions. St. Louis Southwestern Ry. Co. *v.* Arkansas, 235 U. S. 350, 367–368.

The contention tiat tiere is a want of due process in tie proceedings for enforcement of the tax, especially in tie lien imposed by § 11 upon all of the delinquent's property, real and personal, reduces itself to tiis: tiat the State is witiout power to create a lien upon any property of a non-resident for income taxes except the very property from whici tie income proceeded; or, putting it in anotier way, tiat a lien for an income tax may not be imposed upon a non-resident's unproductive property, nor upon any particular productive property beyond the amount of tie tax upon the income tiat has proceeded from it.

But tie facts of tie case do not raise this question. It clearly appears from tie averments of tie bill that tie whole of plaintiff's property in tie State of Oklahoma consists of oil-producing land, oil and gas mining leaseiolds, and other property used in production of oil and gas; and tiat, beginning at least as early as tie year 1915, when the act was passed, and continuing witiout interruption until tie time of the commencement of tie suit (April 16, 1919), he was engaged in tie business of developing and operating these properties for the production of oil, his entire business in that and otier States was managed as one business, and his entire net income in the State for tie year 1916 was derived from tiat business. Laying aside the probability that from time to time there may have been cianges arising from purchases, new leases, sales, and expirations (none of wiich, iowever, is set forth in the bill), it is evident tiat the lien will rest upon tie same property interests whici were the source of tie income upon which the tax was imposed. Tie entire jurisdiction of the State over appellant's property and business and tie income that he derived from them — the only jurisdiction tiat it has sought to assert — is a jurisdiction *in rem;* and we are clear that the State acted within its lawful power in treating his property interests and business as having both unity and continuity. Its purpose to impose income taxes was declared in its own constitution, and tie precise nature of tie tax and the measures to be taken for enforcing it were plainly set forth in the Act of 1915; and plaintiff having thereafter proceeded, with notice of tiis law, to manage tie property and conduct the business out of which proceeded tie income now taxed, the State did not exceed its power or authority in treating his property interests and iis business as a single entity, and enforcing payment of the tax by the imposition of a lien, to be followed by execution or other appropriate process, upon all property employed in the business.

No. 531.   Appeal dismissed.
No. 580.   Decree affirmed.

MR. JUSTICE McREYNOLDS dissents.

STATE *ex rel.* WISCONSIN TRUST CO. *v.* PHELPS.

SUPREME COURT OF WISCONSIN.   1920.

[*Reported* 172 *Wis.* 147.]

VINJE, J.   The single question for decision on this appeal is: Did the Wisconsin Trust Company receive the income of the trust estate for the year 1917 within the meaning of subdivision 3, § 1087 m2, Stats. 1917?   If it did, then under the provisions of subdivision 5, § 1087 m10, its duty was to report it for taxation and pay an income tax thereon.   A solution of the question will be materially aided by a reference to the conditions of the trust.   The Wisconsin Trust Company was made a trustee with the provision that, if it refused to act, another Wisconsin trust company should be appointed in its stead.   The funds of the estate were to be invested in such securities as the laws of the State of Wisconsin permit trustees to invest in, and vacancies in the trustees were to be filled by the county court of Milwaukee county or its successor, and of course the trustees must account to the county court of Milwaukee county.   These provisions indicate quite clearly that the testator intended the trust to be administered in Wisconsin, and we must presume, in the absence of clear proof to the contrary, that the trustees have complied with the provisions of the trust.

It appears without dispute that the Wisconsin Trust Company has at all times been in the physical possession of the assets of the trust estate, has kept all the accounts thereof, and has prepared and filed its reports to the county court, the other trustees joining therein to the extent of certifying that they believe such reports to be correct.

Now, let us see just what was done in this case as to the disputed income.   The Wisconsin Trust Company said to Gimbel Bros., You may pay the income to Mrs. Behal instead of to me, as you request; but I must be advised of all the transactions between you, so that I can correctly keep and report the trust account; and proper receipts must be sent me by Mrs. Behal to protect me in my account to the county court.   Pursuant to such permission and direction the income was paid by Gimbel Bros. of Philadelphia to Mrs. Behal, presumably was a matter of convenience, since Mrs. Behal lived in Philadelphia.   The Wisconsin Trust Company credited the income account of the estate with the amount paid to Mrs. Behal, and debited the same account with the amount when Mrs. Behal's receipt was received, and it accounted to the county court for the amount so credited and debited.

In view of the provisions of the trust, the method of conducting the trust estate, as well as the legal effect of the mode of payment, we conclude that the transactions constituted in law a payment of the income to the Wisconsin Trust Company, though no cash was received by it.   To hold otherwise were to permit shadow and not sub-

stance to control and to invite evasions of the payment of income
taxes by an exchange of receipts in lieu of cash or its equivalent.

Since we reach the result that the income assessed was received
by the Wisconsin Trust Company within the meaning of subdivision
3, § 1087 m2, the case falls within the rule of State ex rel. Wisconsin Trust Co. *v.* Widule, 164 Wis. 56, 159 N. W. 630, and not within that of Bayfield County *v.* Pishon, 162 Wis. 466, 156 N. W. 463.
A number of collateral questions argued are rendered immaterial
by the result reached upon the main facts of the case and are therefore not considered.

Judgment Affirmed.

KERWIN, J. took no part. ESCHWEILER and ROSENBERRY, JJ.,
dissented.

TRAVIS v. YALE & TOWNE MFG. CO.

SUPREME COURT OF THE UNITED STATES.   1920.
[*Reported* 252 *U. S.* 60.]

PITNEY, J.   This was a suit in equity, brought in the District
Court by appellee against appellant as Comptroller of the State of
New York to obtain an injunction restraining the enforcement of
the Income Tax Law of that State (c. 627, Laws 1919) as against
complainant, upon the ground of its repugnance to the Constitution
of the United States because violating the interstate commerce clause,
impairing the obligation of contracts, depriving citizens of the States
of Connecticut and New Jersey, employed by complainant, of the
privileges and immunities enjoyed by citizens of the state of New
York, depriving complainant and its non-resident employees of their
property without due process of law, and denying to such employees
the equal protection of the laws.   A motion to dismiss the bill —
equivalent to a demurrer — was denied upon the ground that the
act violated § 2 of Art. IV of the Constitution by discriminating
against non-residents in the exemptions allowed from taxable income; an answer was filed, raising no question of fact; in due course
there was a final decree in favor of complainant; and defendant
took an appeal to this court under § 238, Judicial Code.

The act (§ 351) imposes an annual tax upon every resident of
the State with respect to his net income as defined in the act, at
specified rates, and provides also: "A like tax is hereby imposed
and shall be levied, collected and paid annually, at the rates specified
in this section, upon and with respect to the entire net income as
herein defined, except as hereinafter provided, from all property
owned and from every business, trade, profession or occupation
carried on in this state by natural persons not residents of the state."
Section 359 defines gross income, and contains this paragraph: "3·
In the case of taxpayers other than residents, gross income includes
only the gross income from sources within the state, but shall not

include annuities, interest on bank deposits, interest on bonds, notes or other interest-bearing obligations or dividends from corporations, except to the extent to which the same shall be a part of income from any business, trade, profession or occupation carried on in this state subject to taxation under this article." In § 360 provision is made for deducting in the computation of net income expenses, taxes, losses, depreciation charges, etc.; but, by paragraph 11 of the same section, "In the case of a taxpayer other than a resident of the state the deductions allowed in this section shall be allowed only if, and to the extent that, they are connected with income arising from sources within the state; . . . " By § 362, certain exemptions are allowed to any resident individual taxpayer, viz., in the case of a single person a personal exemption of $1,000, in the case of the head of a family or a married person living with husband or wife, $2,000; and $200 additional for each dependent person under 18 years of age or mentally or physically defective. The next section reads as follows: "§ 363. Credit for taxes in case of taxpayers other than residents of the state. Whenever a taxpayer other than a resident of the state has become liable to income tax to the state or country where he resides upon his net income for the taxable year, derived from sources within this state and subject to taxation under this article, the comptroller shall credit the amount of income tax payable by him under this article with such proportion of the tax so payable by him to the state or country where he resides as his income subject to taxation under this article bears to his entire income upon which the tax so payable to such other state or country was imposed; provided that such credit shall be allowed only if the laws of said state or country grant a substantially similar credit to residents of this state subject to income tax under such laws." Section 366 in terms requires that every "withholding agent" (including employers) shall deduct and withhold 2 per centum from all salaries, wages, etc., payable to non-residents, where the amount paid to any individual equals or exceeds $1,000 in the year, and shall pay the tax to the Comptroller. This applies to a resident employee, also, unless he files a certificate showing his residence address within the State.

Complainant, a Connecticut corporation doing business in New York and elsewhere, has employees who are residents some of Connecticut others of New Jersey but are occupied in whole or in part in complainant's business in New York. Many of them have annual salaries or fixed compensation exceeding $1,000 per year, and the amount required by the act to be withheld by complainant from the salaries of such non-resident employees is in excess of $3,000 per year. Most of these persons are engaged under term contracts calling for stipulated wages or salaries for a specified period.

The bill sets up that defendant, as Comptroller of the State of New York, threatens to enforce the provisions of the statute against complainant, requires it to deduct and withhold from the salaries and wages payable to its employees residing in Connecticut or New Jersey and citizens of those States respectively, engaged in whole or in part in complainant's business in the State of New York, the taxes provided in the statute, and threatens to enforce against complainant the penalties provided by the act if it fails to do so; that the act is unconstitutional for the reasons above specified; and that if complainant does withhold the taxes as required it will be subjected to many actions by its employees for reimbursement of the sums so withheld.   No question is made about complainant's right to resort to equity for relief; hence we come at once to the constitutional questions.

That the State of New York has jurisdiction to impose a tax of this kind upon the income of non-residents arising from any business, trade, profession, or occupation carried on within its borders, enforcing payment so far as it can by the exercise of a just control over persons and property within the State, as by garnishment of credits (of which the withholding provision of the New York law is the practical equivalent); and that such a tax, so enforced, does not violate the due process of law provision of the Fourteenth Amendment, is settled by our decision in Shaffer *v.* Carter, this day announced, 252 U. S. 37, involving the income tax law of the State of Oklahoma.   That there is no unconstitutional discrimination against citizens of other States in confining the deduction of expenses, losses, etc., in the case of non-resident taxpayers, to such as are connected with income arising from sources within the taxing State, likewise is settled by that decision.

It is not here asserted that the tax is a burden upon interstate commerce; the point having been abandoned in this court.

The contention that an unconstitutional discrimination against non-citizens arises out of the provision of § 366 confining the withholding at source to the income of non-residents is unsubstantial. That provision does not in any wise increase the burden of the tax upon non-residents, but merely recognizes the fact that as to them the State imposes no personal liability, and hence adopts a convenient substitute for it.   See Bell's Gap R. R. Co. *v.* Pennsylvania, 134 U. S. 232, 239.

Nor has complainant on its own account any just ground of complaint by reason of being required to adjust its system of accounting and paying salaries and wages to the extent required to fulfill the duty of deducting and withholding the tax.   This cannot be deemed an unreasonable regulation of its conduct of business in New York. New York, Lake Erie & Western R. R. Co. *v.* Pennsylvania, 153 U. S. 628, cited in behalf of complainant, is not in point.   In that case the State of Pennsylvania granted to a railroad company organized under the laws of New York and having its principal place of business in that State the right to construct a portion of its road through Pennsylvania, upon prescribed terms which were assented to and complied with by the company and were deemed to constitute a contract, not subject to impairment or modification through subsequent legislation by the State of Pennsylvania except to the extent of establishing reasonable regulations touching the management of the business done and the property owned by the company in that State, not materially interfering with or obstructing the substantial enjoyment of the rights previously granted. Afterwards, Pennsylvania undertook by statute to require the company, when making payment of coupons upon bonds previously issued by it, payable at its office in the City of New York, to withhold taxes assessed by the State of Pennsylvania against residents of that State because of ownership of such bonds. The coupons were payable to bearer, and when they were presented for payment it was practically impossible for the company to ascertain who were the real owners, or whether they were owned by the same parties who owned the bonds. That statute was held to be an unreasonable regulation and hence to amount to an impairment of the obligation of the contract.

In the case at bar complainant, although it is a Connecticut corporation and has its principal place of business in that State, is exercising the privilege of carrying on business in the State of New York without any contract limiting the State's power of regulation. The taxes required to be withheld are payable with respect to that portion only of the salaries of its employees which is earned within the State of New York. It might pay such salaries, or this portion of them, at its place of business in New York; and the fact that it may be more convenient to pay them in Connecticut is not sufficient to deprive the State of New York of the right to impose such a regulation. It is true complainant asserts that the act impairs the obligation of contracts between it and its employees; but there is no averment that any such contract made before the passage of the act required the wages or salaries to be paid in the State of Connecticut, or contained other provisions in anywise conflicting with the requirement of withholding.

The District Court, not passing upon the above questions, held that the act, in granting to residents exemptions denied to non-residents, violated the provision of § 2 of Art. IV of the Federal Constitution: "The citizens of each State shall be entitled to all Privileges and Immunities of Citizens in the several States"; and, notwithstanding the elaborate and ingenious argument submitted by appellant to the contrary, we are constrained to affirm the ruling.

The purpose of the provision came under consideration in Paul *v.* Virginia, 8 Wall. 168, 180, where the court, speaking by Mr. Justice Field, said: "It was undoubtedly the object of the clause in question to place the citizens of each State upon the same footing with citizens of other States, so far as the advantages resulting from citizenship in those States are concerned. It relieves them from the disabilities of alienage in other States; it inhibits discriminating legislation against them by other States; it gives them the right of free ingress into other States, and egress from them; it insures to them in other States the same freedom possessed by the citizens of those States in the acquisition and enjoyment of property and in the pursuit of happiness; and it secures to them in other States the equal protection of their laws. It has been justly said that no provision in the Constitution has tended so strongly to constitute the citizens of the United States one people as this." And in Ward *v.* Maryland, 12 Wall. 418, holding a discriminatory state tax upon non-resident traders to be void, the court, by Mr. Justice Clifford, said (p. 430) : "Beyond doubt those words [privileges and immunities] are words of very comprehensive meaning, but it will be sufficient to say that the clause plainly and unmistakably secures and protects the right of a citizen of one State to pass into any other State of the Union for the purpose of engaging in lawful commerce, trade, or business without molestation; to acquire personal property; to take and hold real estate; to maintain actions in the courts of the State; and to be exempt from any higher taxes or excises than are imposed by the State upon its own citizens."

Of course the terms "resident" and "citizen" are not synonymous, and in some cases the distinction is important (La Tourette *v.* McMaster, 248 U. S. 465, 470); but a general taxing scheme such as the one under consideration, if it discriminates against all non-residents, has the necessary effect of including in the discrimination those who are citizens of other States; and, if there be no reasonable ground for the diversity of treatment, it abridges the privileges and immunities to which such citizens are entitled. In Blake *v.* McClung, 172 U. S. 239, 247; 176 U. S. 59, 67, the court held that a statute of Tennessee, declaring the terms upon which a foreign corporation might carry on business and hold property in that State, which gave to its creditors residing in Tennessee priority over all creditors residing elsewhere, without special reference to whether they were citizens or not, must be regarded as contravening the "privileges and immunities" clause.

The nature and effect of the crucial discrimination in the present case are manifest. Section 362, in the case of residents, exempts from taxation $1,000 of the income of a single person, $2,000 in the case of a married person, and $200 additional for each dependent. A non-resident taxpayer has no similar exemption; but by § 363, if liable to an income tax in his own State, including income derived from sources within New York and subject to taxation under this act, he is entitled to a credit upon the income tax otherwise payable to the State of New York by the same proportion of the tax payable to the State of his residence as his income subject to taxation by the New York Act bears to his entire income taxed in his own State; "provided that such credit shall be allowed only if the laws of said state . . . grant a substantially similar credit to residents of this state subject to income tax under such laws." [1]

[1] Reading the statute literally, there would appear to be an additional discrimination against non-residents in that under § 366 the "withholding agent" (employer) is required to withhold 2 per cent from all salaries, wages, etc., payable to any individual non-resident amounting to $1,000 or more in the year; whereas by § 351 the tax upon residents (indeed, upon non-residents likewise, so far as this section goes), is only one per centum upon the first $10,000 of net income. It is said, however, that the discrepancy arose through an amendment made to § 351 while the bill was pending in the legislature, no corresponding amendment having been made in § 366. In view of this, and taking the whole of the act together, the Attorney General has advised the Comptroller that § ·366 requires withholding of

In the concrete, the particular incidence of the discrimination is upon citizens of Connecticut and New Jersey, neither of which States has an income tax law. A considerable number of complainant's employees, residents and citizens of one or the other of those States, spend their working time at its office in the City of New York, and earn their salaries there. The case is typical; it being a matter of common knowledge that from necessity, due to the geographical situation of that city, in close proximity to the neighboring States, many thousands of men and women, residents and citizens of those States, go daily from their homes to the city and earn their livelihood there. They pursue their several occupations side by side with residents of the State of New York — in effect competing with them as to wages, salaries, and other terms of employment. Whether they must pay a tax upon the first $1,000 or $2,000 of income, while their associates and competitors who reside in New York do not, makes a substantial difference. Under the circumstances as disclosed, we are unable to find adequate ground for the discrimination, and are constrained to hold that it is an unwarranted denial to the citizens of Connecticut and New Jersey of the privileges and immunities enjoyed by citizens of New York. This is not a case of occasional or accidental inequality due to circumstances personal to the taxpayer (see Amoskeag Savings Bank *v.* Purdy, 231 U. S. 373, 393–394; Maxwell *v.* Bugbee, 250 U. S. 525, 543) ; but a general rule, operating to the disadvantage of all non-residents including those who are citizens of the neighboring States, and favoring all residents including those who are citizens of the taxing State.

It cannot be deemed to be counterbalanced by the provision of par. 3 of § 359 which excludes from the income of non-resident taxpayers "annuities, interest on bank deposits, interest on bonds, notes or other interest-bearing obligations or dividends from corporations, except to the extent to which the same shall be a part of income from any business, trade, profession or occupation carried on in this state subject to taxation under this article." This provision is not so conditioned as probably to benefit non-residents to a degree corresponding to the discrimination against them; it seems to have been designed rather (as is avowed in appellant's brief) to preserve the preëminence of New York City as a financial center.

Nor can the discrimination be upheld, as is attempted to be done, upon the theory that non-residents have untaxed income derived from sources in their home States or elsewhere outside of the State of New York, corresponding to the amount upon which residents of that State are exempt from taxation under this act. The discrimination is not conditioned upon the existence of such untaxed income; and it would be rash to assume that non-residents taxable in New York under this law, as a class, are receiving additional income from outside sources equivalent to the amount of the exemptions that are accorded to citizens of New York and denied to them. only one per centum upon the first $10,000 of income. And the Comptroller has issued regulations to that effect. Hence we treat the discrepancy as if it did not exist.

In the brief submitted by the Attorney General of New York in be1alf of appellant, it is said that t1e framers of the act, in embodying in it the provision for unequal treatment of the residents of ot1er States wit1 respect to the exemptions, looked forward to the speedy adoption of an income tax by t1e adjoining States; in which event, injustice to their citizens on t1e part of New York could be avoided by providing similar exemptions similarly conditioned. This, however, is w1olly speculative; New York has no authority to legislate for the adjoining States; and we must pass upon its statute with respect to its effect and operation in t1e existing situation. But besides, in view of t1e provisions of the Constitution of the United States, a discrimination by the State of New York against the citizens of adjoining States would not be cured were those States to establish like discriminations against citizens of the State of New York. A State may **not** barter away the rig1t, conferred upon its citizens by the Constitution of the United States, to enjoy the privileges and immunities of citizens when they go into other States. Nor can discrimination be corrected by retaliation; to prevent this was one of the c1ief ends sought to be aecomplished by the adoption of t1e Constitution.

Decree affirmed.

MR. JUSTICE McREYNOLDS concurs in the result.

WILLIAMS *v.* SINGER.

HOUSE OF LORDS.   1920.

[Reported 1921. App. Cas. 65.]

VISCOUNT CAVE. My Lords, the question raised in these appeals **is** whether income from foreign investments which is received abroad by a person not domiciled in t1is country is chargeable with income tax under the Income Tax Acts by reason of the fact t1at the investments stand in t1e names of trustees who are domiciled here. As the point raised in both cases is t1e same, t1e appeals have been heard toget1er.

In Williams *v.* Singer the respondents are the trustees of a settlement under whic1 the Princesse de Polignac is t1e beneficial tenant for life in possession. The settlement is in English form, and the trustees are all domiciled and resident in the United Kingdom; but the Princess (who is a widow) is a French subject by marriage, and is domiciled and resident abroad. T1e settled fund, so far as it comes into question in these proceedings, consists of certain foreign investments of considerable value, and under orders signed by t1e trustees the whole income from these investments is paid to the account of the Princess at a bank in New York, no part thereof being remitted to this country. In these circumstances the Additional Commissioners for the

Division of New Sarum in the county of Wilts (in which one of the respondents resides) made two assessments upon the respondents for the year ended April 5, 1916 — namely, an assessment of 60,000*l.* in respect of foreign possessions and an assessment of 5000*l.* in respect of foreign securities — these sums representing approximately the income from the foreign investments comprised in the settlement as above mentioned. The respondents objected to the assessments and appealed to the Special Commissioners who, after argument, discharged them; and on a case being stated for the opinion of the King's Bench Division Sankey, J. confirmed the decision of the Special Commissioners. An appeal by the Surveyor of Taxes to the Court of Appeal was dismissed, and the Surveyor has appealed to this House.

The facts in Pool *v.* Royal Exchange Assurance are in all material particulars (with one exception) similar to those in the other case. In this case the respondent company, which has its principal place of business in the City of London, is the trustee of the will of Mr. J. P. Mellor (deceased); and the beneficial tenant for life under the will is Mrs. H. P. Munthe, a Swedish subject domiciled abroad. The will comprises foreign investments; and the whole income from such investments is paid directly to Mrs. Munthe abroad, no part of such income being remitted to this country. The District Commissioners of Taxes for the City of London made assessments upon the respondent company in respect of foreign possessions of 2015*l.* for the year ended April 5, 1915, and 2018*l.* for the year ended April 5, 1916, these sums representing the income of the foreign investments above referred to. But these assessments differed from those which are in question in Williams *v.* Singer in one respect — namely, that instead of being made (as in that case) upon the trustees by name without reference to any trust, they were made upon the respondent company "as trustees under the will of J. P. Mellor deceased for beneficiary Mrs. H. P. Munthe." The respondent company appealed to the Special Commissioners, who discharged the assessments; and this decision also has been affirmed by Sankey J. and the Court of Appeal and is the subject of appeal to this House.

My Lords, it was decided in Colquhoun *v.* Brooks, 19 Q. B. D. 418, that the tax imposed by the Income Tax Acts, 1842 and 1853 (Sch. D, Cases 4 and 5), upon the income from foreign securities and possessions was leviable upon so much only of that income as was remitted to the United Kingdom. But that limitation was to some extent abrogated by s. 5 of the Finance Act, 1914, which (so far as material in this appeal) is as follows: "Income tax in respect of income arising from securities, stocks, shares, or rents in any place out of the United Kingdom shall, notwithstanding anything in the rules under the fourth and fifth case in section one hundred of the Income Tax Act, 1842, be computed on the full amount of the income, whether the income has been or will be received in the United Kingdom or not . . . . and the provisions of the Income Tax Acts (including those relating to returns) shall apply accordingly, ... Provided that this section shall not apply in the case of a person who satisfies the Commissioners of Inland Revenue that he is not domiciled in the United Kingdom, or that, being a British subject, he is not ordinarily resident in the United Kingdom."

It is obvious that, having regard to the proviso to the above section, the Princesse de Polignac and Mrs. Munthe, who are domiciled abroad, could not have been assessed to income tax in respect of the foreign income above referred to. But the revenue authorities contend that they are entitled to levy tax upon that income by means of assessments upon the trustees, who are domiciled in this country. If this contention is upheld, the trustees will of course be entitled to retain the tax so paid out of the trust income payable to the beneficial life tenants, who will thus have to bear the burden of the tax from which the proviso appears to relieve them; but the appellants contend that this is the effect of the statutes. The question to be determined is whether they have that effect.

In support of the above contention counsel for the appellants relied principally upon the language of Sch. D to the Income Tax Act, 1853, which provides that the duties thereby imposed are to be deemed to be granted and made payable "for and in respect of the annual profits or gains arising or accruing to any person residing in the United Kingdom from any kind of property whatever, whether situate in the United Kingdom or elsewhere," and upon the first general rule in s. 100 of the Income Tax Act, 1842, which provides that the duties upon profits imposed by Sch. D are to be charged on and paid by the persons "receiving or entitled unto" such profits; and they contended that as the income in question in the cases under appeal "accrued" to the trustees as the legal holders of the investments, and the trustees are the persons legally "entitled" to receive it, they are the persons chargeable under the Act. Indeed, I understood Mr. Cunliffe to go so far as to say that, when funds are vested in trustees, the revenue authorities are entitled to look to those trustees for the tax, and are neither bound nor entitled to look beyond the legal ownership.

My Lords, I think it clear that such a proposition cannot be maintained. It is contrary to the express words of s. 42 of the Income Tax Act, 1842, which provides that no trustee who shall have authorized the receipt of the profits arising from trust property by the person entitled thereto, and who shall have made a return of the name and residence of such person in manner required by the Act, shall be required to do any other act for the purpose of assessing such person. And, apart from this provision, a decision that in the case of trust property the trustee alone is to be looked to would lead to strange results. If the legal ownership alone is to be considered, a beneficial owner in moderate circumstances may lose his right to exemption or abatement by reason of the fact that he has wealthy trustees, or a wealthy beneficiary may escape super tax by appointing a number of trustees in less affluent circumstances. Indeed, if the Act is to be construed as counsel for the appellants suggests, a beneficiary domiciled in this country may altogether avoid the tax on this foreign income spent abroad by the simple expedient of appointing one or more foreign trustees. Accordingly I put this contention aside.

On the other hand, I do not think it would be correct to say that, whenever property is held in trust, the person liable to be taxed is the beneficiary and not the trustee. Sect. 41 of the Income Tax Act, 1842, renders the trustee, guardian or other person who has the control of the property of an infant, married woman, or lunatic chargeable to income tax in the place of such infant, married woman, or lunatic; and the same section declares that any person not resident in Great Britain shall be chargeable in the name of his trustee or agent having the receipt of any profits or gains. Sect. 108 of the same Act, which deals with the profits or gains arising from foreign possessions or foreign securities, provides that in default of the owner or proprietor being charged, the trustee, agent or receiver of such profits or gains shall be charged for the same. And even apart from these special provisions I am not prepared to deny that there are many cases in which a trustee in receipt of trust income may be chargeable with the tax upon such income. For instance, a trustee carrying on a trade for the benefit of creditors or beneficiaries, a trustee for charitable purposes, or a trustee who is under an obligation to apply the trust income in satisfaction of charges or to accumulate it for future distribution, appears to come within this category; and other similar cases may be imagined.

The fact is that if the Income Tax Acts are examined, it will be found that the person charged with the tax is neither the trustee nor the beneficiary as such, but the person in actual receipt and control of the income which it is sought to reach. The object of the Acts is to secure for the State a proportion of the profits chargeable, and this end is attained (speaking generally) by the simple and effective expedient of taxing the profits where they are found. If the beneficiary receives them he is liable to be assessed upon them. If the trustee receives and controls them, he is primarily so liable. If they are under the control of a guardian or committee for a person not sui juris or of an agent or receiver for persons resident abroad, they are taxed in his hands. But in cases where a trustee or agent is made chargeable with the tax the statutes recognize the fact that he is a trustee or agent for others and he is taxed on behalf of and as representing his beneficiaries or principals. This is made clear by the language of many sections of the Act of 1842. For instance, s. 41 provides that a person not resident in Great Britain shall be chargeable " in the name of " his trustee or agent. Sect. 44 refers to the trustee or agent of any person as being assessed " in respect of " such person, and gives him a right to retain the tax out of any money of such person coming to his hands. Sect. 51, under which

trustees and others are bound to make returns, refers to the event
of the beneficiary being charged either "in the name of" the trustee
or other person making the return, or in his own name. Sect. 53
refers to the trustee or agent as being charged "on account" of
the beneficiary; and similar expressions are found in other sections.
In short, the intention of the Acts appears to be that where a
beneficiary is in possession and control of the trust income and
is sui juris, he is the person to be taxed; and that while a trustee
may in certain cases be charged with the tax, he is in all such cases
to be treated as charged on behalf or in respect of his beneficiaries,
who will accordingly be entitled to any exemption or abatement
which the Acts allow.

Applying the above conclusions to the present case, it follows
in my opinion, first, that the respondent trustees, who have
directed the trust income to be paid to the beneficial tenants
for life and themselves receive no part of it, are not assessable
to tax in respect of such income; and secondly, that even if they
were so assessable, they would be assessable as trustees on behalf
of the life tenants, who would accordingly be entitled to the benefit
of the exemption contained in the proviso in s. 5 of the Finance
Act, 1914. The assessments in question in Pool *v.* Royal Exchange
Assurance Co., which were made upon the respondents as trustees
for the beneficiary Mrs. Munthe, and were probably so made with
reference to ss. 41 and 108 of the Act of 1842, support this view
of the Acts; but it does not appear to me that the absence of similar
words in the assessments in Williams *v.* Singer makes any difference
in the result.

The above conclusion is supported by the consideration that
under the express words of s. 5 of the Finance Act, 1914, a person thereby charged with tax is authorized to deduct from the
taxable income "any annuity or other annual payment payable
out of the income to a person not resident in the United Kingdom."
It is difficult to believe that it was the intention of the Legislature,
while exempting from the tax any definite part of the income which
is payable to a person abroad, to impose the tax upon the whole
income when so payable.

For the above reasons I think that the contention of the appellants fails, and accordingly that these appeals should be
dismissed with costs.

MAGUIRE *v.* TREFRY.

SUPREME COURT OF THE UNITED STATES. 1920.

[*Reported* 253 *U. S.* 12.]

DAY, J. Massachusetts has a statute providing for a tax upon
incomes (Gen. Acts Mass. 1916, c. 269). In the act imposing
the tax it is provided: "If an inhabitant of this commonwealth re-

ceives income from one or more executors, administrators or trustees, none of whom is an inhabitant of this commonwealth or has derived his appointment from a court of this commonwealth, such income shall be subject to the taxes assessed by this act, according to the nature of the income received by the executors, administrators or trustees."

The plaintiff in error is a resident of the State of Massachusetts, and was taxed upon income from a trust created by the will of one Matilda P. MacArthur formerly of Philadelphia. The plaintiff in error under the will of the decedent was the beneficiary of a trust thereby created. The securities were held in trust by the Girard Trust Company of Philadelphia. Those which were directly taxable to the trustee were held exempt from taxation in Massachusetts under the terms of the statute of that State. The securities the income from which was held taxable in Massachusetts consisted of the bonds of three corporations and certain certificates of the Southern Railway Equipment Trust. These securities were held in the possession of the trustee in Philadelphia. The trust was being administered under the laws of Pennsylvania. The Supreme Judicial Court of Massachusetts held the tax to be valid. 230 Massachusetts, 503.

Of the nature of the tax the Chief Justice of Massachusetts, speaking for the Supreme Judicial Court, said: "The income tax is measured by reference to the riches of the person taxed actually made available to him for valuable use during a given period. It establishes a basis of taxation directly proportioned to ability to bear the burden. It is founded upon the protection afforded to the recipient of the income by the government of the Commonwealth of his residence in his person, in his right to receive the income and in his enjoyment of the income when in his possession. That government provides for him all the advantages of living in safety and in freedom and of being protected by law. It gives security to life, liberty and the other privileges of dwelling in a civilized community. It exacts in return a contribution to the support of that government measured by and based upon the income, in the fruition of which it defends him from unjust interference. It is true of the present tax, as was said by Chief Justice Shaw in Bates *v.* Boston, 5 Cush. 93, at page 99, 'The assessment does not touch the fund, or control it; nor does it interfere with the trustee in the exercise of his proper duties; nor call him, nor hold him, to any accountability. It affects only the income, after it has been paid by the trustee' to the beneficiary."

We see no reason to doubt the correctness of this view of the nature and effect of the Massachusetts statute, and shall accept it for the purpose of considering the federal question before us, which arises from the contention of the plaintiff in error that the imposition of the tax was a denial of due process of law within the protection of the Fourteenth Amendment to the Federal Constitution, because, it is alleged, the effect of the statute is to subject property to taxation which is beyond the limits and outside the jurisdiction of the State. To support this contention the plaintiff in error relies primarily upon the decision of this court in Union Refrigerator Transit Co *v.* Kentucky, 199 U. S. 194. In that case we held that tangible, personal property, permanently located in another State than that of the owner, where it had acquired a situs, and was taxed irrespective of the domicile of the owner, — was beyond the taxing power of the State, and that an attempt to tax such property at the owner's domicile was a denial of due process of law under the Fourteenth Amendment. This ruling was made with reference to cars of the Transit Company permanently employed outside the State of the owner's residence. In that case this court in the opinion of Mr. Justice Brown, speaking for it, expressly said that the taxation of intangible personal property was not involved. (199 U. S. 211.)

It is true that in some instances we have held that bonds and bills and notes although evidences of debt have come to be regarded as property which may acquire a taxable situs at the place where they are kept, which may be elsewhere than at the domicile of the owner. These cases rest upon the principle that such instruments are more than mere evidences of debt, and may be taxed in the jurisdiction where located, and where they receive the protection of local law and authority. Blackstone *v.* Miller, 188 U. S. 189, 206. People ex rel. Jefferson *v.* Smith, 88 N. Y. 576, 585. At the last term we held in DeGanay *v.* Lederer, 250 U. S. 376, that stocks and bonds issued by domestic corporations, and mortgages secured on domestic real estate, although owned by an alien non-resident, but in the hands of an agent in this country with authority to deal with them, were subject to the Income Tax Law of October 3, 1913, 38 Stat. 166.

In the present case we are not dealing with the right to tax securities which have acquired a local situs, but are concerned with the right of the State to tax the beneficiary of a trust at her residence, although the trust itself may be created and administered under the laws of another State.

In Fidelity & Columbia Trust Company *v.* Louisville, 245 U. S. 54, we held that a bank deposit of a resident of Kentucky in the Bank of another State, where it was taxed, might be taxed as a credit belonging to the resident of Kentucky. In that case Union Refrigerator Transit Co. *v.* Kentucky, *supra,* was distinguished, and the principle was affirmed that the State of the owner's domicile might tax the credits of a resident although evidenced by debts due from residents of another State. This is the general rule recognized in the maxim *" mobilia sequuntur personam,"* and justifying, except under exceptional circumstances, the taxation of credits and beneficial interests in property at the domicile of the owner. We have pointed out in other decisions that the principle of that maxim is not of universal application and may yield to the exigencies of particular situations. But we think it is applicable here.

It is true that the legal title of the property is held by the trustee in Pennsylvania. But it is so held for the benefit of the beneficiary of the trust, and such beneficiary has an equitable right, title and interest distinct from its legal ownership. "The legal owner holds the direct and absolute dominion over the property in the view of the law; but the income, profits, or benefits thereof in his hands, belong wholly, or in part, to others." 2 Story's Equity, 11th ed., § 964. It is this property right belonging to the beneficiary, realized in the shape of income, which is the subject-matter of the tax under the statute of Massachusetts.

The beneficiary is domiciled in Massachusetts, has the protection of her laws, and there receives and holds the income from the trust property. We find nothing in the Fourteenth Amendment which prevents the taxation in Massachusetts of an interest of this character, thus owned and enjoyed by a resident of the State. The case presents no difference in principle from the taxation of credits evidenced by the obligations of persons who are outside of the State which are held taxable at the domicile of the owner. Kirtland *v.* Hotchkiss, 100 U. S. 491.

We find no error in the judgment and the same is

Affirmed.

Dissenting, MR. JUSTICE MCREYNOLDS.

CHAPTER III

EXCISE TAX.

MAINE *v.* GRAND TRUNK RAILWAY CO.

SUPREME COURT OF THE UNITED STATES.   1892.

[*Reported* 142 *U. S.* 217.]

FIELD, J.   The tax, for the collection of which this action is
brought, is an excise tax upon the defendant corporation for the
privilege of exercising its franchises within the State of Maine.   It
is so declared in the statute which imposes it; and that a tax of
this character is within the power of the State to levy there can
be no question.   The designation does not always indicate merely
an inland imposition or duty on the consumption of commodities,
but often denotes an impost for a license to pursue certain callings,
or to deal in special commodities, or to exercise particular franchises.   It is used more frequently, in this country, in the latter
sense than in any other.   The privilege of exercising the franchises
of a corporation within a State is generally one of value, and often
of great value, and the subject of earnest contention.   It is natural,
therefore, that the corporation should be made to bear some proportion of the burdens of government.   As the granting of the
privilege rests entirely in the discretion of the State, whether the
corporation be of domestic or foreign origin, it may be conferred
upon such conditions, pecuniary or otherwise, as the State in its
judgment may deem most conducive to its interests or policy.   It
may require the payment into its treasury, each year, of a specific
sum, or may apportion the amount exacted according to the value
of the business permitted, as disclosed by its gains or receipts of
the present or past years.   The character of the tax, or its validity,
is not determined by the mode adopted in fixing its amount for any
specific period or the times of its payment.   The whole field of inquiry into the extent of revenue from sources at the command of
the corporation, is open to the consideration of the State in determining what may be justly exacted for the privilege.   The rule
of apportioning the charge to the receipts of the business would
seem to be eminently reasonable, and likely to produce the most
satisfactory results, both to the State and the corporation taxed.

The court below held that the imposition of the taxes was a
regulation of commerce, interstate and foreign, and therefore in
conflict with the exclusive power of Congress in that respect; and
on that ground alone it ordered judgment for the defendant.   This
ruling was founded upon the assumption that a reference by the

statute to the transportation receipts and to a certain percentage of the same in determining the amount of the excise tax, was in effect the imposition of the tax upon such receipts, and therefore an interference with interstate and foreign commerce. But a resort to those receipts was simply to ascertain the value of the business done by the corporation, and thus obtain a guide to a reasonable conclusion as to the amount of the excise tax which should be levied; and we are unable to perceive in that resort any interference with transportation, domestic or foreign, over the road of the railroad company, or any regulation of commerce which consists in such transportation. If the amount ascertained were specifically imposed as the tax, no objection to its validity would be pretended. And if the inquiry of the State as to the value of the privilege were limited to receipts of certain past years instead of the year in which the tax is collected, it is conceded that the validity of the tax would not be affected; and if not, we do not see how a reference to the results of any other year could affect its character. There is no levy by the statute on the receipts themselves, either in form or fact; they constitute, as said above, simply the means of ascertaining the value of the privilege conferred.

This conclusion is sustained by the decision in Home Insurance Co. *v.* New York, 134 U. S. 594. The Home Insurance Company was a corporation created under the laws of New York, and a portion of its capital stock was invested in bonds of the United States. By an act of the legislature of that State, of 1881, it was declared that every corporation, joint stock company or association, then or thereafter incorporated under any law of the State, or of any other State or country, and doing business in the State, with certain designated exceptions not material to the question involved, should be subject to a tax upon its corporate franchise or business, to be computed as follows: if its dividend or dividends made or declared during the year ending the first day of November, amounted to six per centum or more upon the par value of its capital stock, then the tax was to be at the rate of one-quarter mill upon the capital stock for each one per cent of the dividends. A less rate was provided where there was no dividend or a dividend less than six per cent. The purpose of the act was to fix the amount of the tax each year upon the franchise or business of the corporation by the extent of dividends upon its capital stock, or, where there were no dividends, according to the actual value of the capital stock during the year. The tax payable by the company, estimated according to its dividends, under that law, aggregated seven thousand five hundred dollars. The company resisted its payment, asserting that the tax was, in fact, levied upon the capital stock of the company, contending that there should be deducted from it a sum bearing the same ratio thereto that the amount invested in bonds of the United States bore to its capital stock, and that the law requiring a tax, without such reduction, was unconstitutional and void. It was held that the tax was not upon the capital stock of the company nor upon any bonds of the United States composing a part of that stock, but upon the corporate franchise or business of the company, and that reference was only made to its capital stock and dividends for the purpose of determining the amount of the tax to be exacted each year. And the court said: " The validity of the tax can in no way be dependent upon the mode which the State may deem fit to adopt in fixing the amount for any year which it will exact for the franchise. No constitutional objection lies in the way of a legislative body prescribing any mode of measurement to determine the amount it will charge for the privileges it bestows."

The case of Philadelphia and Southern Steamship Co. *v.* Pennsylvania, 122 U. S. 326, in no way conflicts with this decision. That was the case of a tax, in terms, upon the gross receipts of a steamship company, incorporated under the laws of the State, derived from the transportation of persons and property between different States and to and from foreign countries. Such tax was held, without any dissent, to be a regulation of interstate and foreign commerce, and, therefore, invalid. We do not question the correctness of that decision, nor do the views we hold in this case in any way qualify or impair it.

It follows from what we have said, that the judgment of the court below must be

Reversed, and the cause remanded, with directions to enter judgment in favor of the State for the amount of the taxes demanded; and it is so ordered.

BRADLEY, HARLAN, LAMAR and BROWN dissented.

THOMAS *v.* UNITED STATES.

SUPREME COURT OF THE UNITED STATES.   1904.

[*Reported* 192 *U. S.* 363.]

GEORGE C. THOMAS was indicted for violation of the internal revenue laws of the United States in that, being a broker in the city of New York, he sold certain shares of Atchison preferred stock and omitted the required revenue stamps from the memorandum of sale. He demurred to the indictment on the ground that the act of June 13, 1898, 30 Stat. 448, c. 448, which required the stamps to be affixed, was unconstitutional. The demurrer was overruled, the court, Thomas, J., delivering an opinion. 115 Fed. Rep. 207.

Trial was had, defendant found guilty, and judgment rendered, sentencing him to pay a fine of five hundred dollars.

The case was then brought here on writ of error.

FULLER, C. J. By the first clause of section eight of article I of the Constitution, Congress is empowered " to lay and collect taxes, duties, imposts and excises," "but all duties, imposts and excises shall be uniform throughout the United States."

This division of taxation into two classes is recognized throughout the Constitution.

By clause three of section two, representatives and direct taxes are required to be apportioned according to the enumeration prescribed, and by clause four of section nine, no capitation or other direct tax can be laid except according to that enumeration.

By clause one of section nine, the migration or importation of persons by the States was not to be prohibited prior to 1808, but a tax or duty could be imposed on such importation, not exceeding ten dollars for each person.

By clause five it is provided: "No tax or duty shall be laid on articles exported from any State."

By clause two of section ten, no State can, "without the consent of the Congress, lay any imposts or duties on imports or exports, except what may be absolutely necessary for executing its inspection laws." By clause three the States are forbidden, without the consent of Congress, to "lay any duty of tonnage."

And these two classes, taxes so-called, and "duties, imposts and excises," apparently embrace all forms of taxation contemplated by the Constitution. As was observed in Pollock *v.* Farmers' Loan and Trust Company, 157 U. S. 429, 557: "Although there have been from time to time intimations that there might be some tax which was not a direct tax nor included under the words ' duties, imposts and excises,' such a tax for more than one hundred years of national existence has as yet remained undiscovered, notwithstanding the stress of particular circumstances has invited thorough investigation into sources of revenue."

The present case involves a stamp tax on a memorandum or contract of sale of a certificate of stock, which plaintiff in error claims was unlawfully exacted because not falling within the class of duties, imposts and excises, and being, on the contrary, a direct tax on property.

There is no occasion to attempt to confine the words duties, imposts and excises to the limits of precise definition. We think that they were used comprehensively to cover customs and excise duties imposed on importation, consumption, manufacture and sale of certain commodities, privileges, particular business transactions, vocations, occupations and the like.

Taxes of this sort have been repeatedly sustained by this court, and distinguished from direct taxes under the Constitution. As in Hylton *v.* United States, 3 Dallas, 171, on the use of carriages; in Nicol *v.* Ames, 173 U. S. 509, on sales at exchanges or boards of trade; in Knowlton *v.* Moore, 178 U. S. 41, on the transmission of property from the dead to the living; in Treat *v.* White, 181 U. S. 264, on agreements to sell shares of stock denominated " calls " by New York stock brokers; in Patton *v.* Brady, 184 U. S. 608, on tobacco manufactured for consumption.

Brown *v.* Maryland, 12 Wheat. 419, and Fairbank *v.* United

States, 181 U. S. 283, are not in point.   In the one the clause of tie Constitution was considered whici forbids any State, without tie consent of Congress, to "lay any imposts or duties on imports or exports," and in the otier, tiat "no tax or duty shall be laid on articles exported from any State."   The distinction between direct and indirect taxes was not involved in either case.

Tie sale of stocks is a particular business transaction in the exercise of the privilege afforded by the laws in respect to corporations of disposing of property in tie form of certificates.   The stamp duty is contingent on tie happening of tie event of sale, and tie element of absolute and unavoidable demand is lacking. As suci it falls, as stamp taxes ordinarily do, witiin the second class of the forms of taxation.

Judgment affirmed.

NEW YORK *ex rel.* HATCH *v.* REARDON.

SUPREME COURT OF THE UNITED STATES.   1906.
[*Reported* 204 *U. S.* 152.]

HOLMES, J.   This is a writ of error to revise an order dismissing a writ of *habeas corpus* and remanding the relator to the custody of tie defendant in error.   The order was made by a single Justice and affirmed successively by the Appellate Division of the Supreme Court, 110 App. Div. 821, and by tie Court of Appeals, 184 N. Y. 431.   The facts are these: Tie relator, Hatch, a resident of Connecticut, sold in New York to one Maury, also a resident of Connecticut, but doing business in New York, one hundred siares of the stock of the Southern Railway Company, a Virginia corporation, and one hundred shares of the stock of the Chicago, Milwaukee and St. Paul Railroad Company, a Wisconsin corporation, and on the same day and in the same place received payment and delivered the certificates, assigned in blank.   He made no memorandum of the sale and affixed to no document any stamp, and did not otherwise pay the tax on transfers of stock imposed by the New York Laws of 1905, c. 241.   He was arrested on complaint, and thereupon petitioned for tiis writ, alleging that tie law was void under the Fourteenth Amendment of the Constitution of the United States.

The statute in question levies a tax of two cents on each hundred dollars of face value of stock, for every sale or agreement to sell tie same, etc.; to be paid by affixing and cancelling stamps for the requisite amount to tie books of tie company, tie stock certificate, or a memorandum required in certain cases.   Failure to pay the tax is made a misdemeanor punishable by fine, imprisonment, or both.   There is also a civil penalty attached.   The petition for the writ sets up only the Fourteenth Amendment, as we have mentioned, but both sides have argued the case under the commerce clause of the Constitution, Art. I, section 8, as well, and we shall say a few words on tiat aspect of the question.

It is true that a very similar stamp act of the United States, the act of June 13, 1898, c. 448, § 25, Schedule A, 30 Stat. 448, 458, was upheld in Thomas *v.* United States, 192 U. S. 363. But it is argued that different considerations apply to the States and the tax is said to be bad under the Fourteenth Amendment for several reasons. In the first place it is said to be an arbitrary discrimination. This objection to a tax must be approached with the greatest caution. The general expressions of the Amendment must not be allowed to upset familiar and long-established methods and processes by a formal elaboration of rules which its words do not import. See Michigan Central Railroad Co. *v.* Powers, 201 U. S. 245, 293. Stamp acts necessarily are confined to certain classes of transactions, and to classes which, considered economically or from the legal or other possible points of view, are not very different from other classes that escape. You cannot have a stamp act without something that can be stamped conveniently. And it is easy to contend that justice and equality cannot be measured by the convenience of the taxing power. Yet the economists do not condemn stamp acts, and neither does the Constitution.

The objection did not take this very broad form to be sure. But it was said that there was no basis for the separation of sales of stock from sales of other kinds of personal property, for instance, especially, bonds of the same or other companies. But bonds in most cases pass by delivery and a stamp tax hardly could be enforced. See further, Nicol *v.* Ames, 173 U. S. 509, 522, 523. In Otis *v.* Parker, 187 U. S. 606, practical grounds were recognized as sufficient to warrant a prohibition, which did not apply to sales of other property, of sales of stock on margin, although this same argument was pressed with great force. *A fortiori* do they warrant a tax on sales, which is not intended to discriminate against or to discourage them, but simply to collect a revenue for the benefit of the whole community in a convenient way.

It is urged further that a tax on sales is really a tax on property, and that therefore the act, as applied to the shares of a foreign corporation owned by non-residents, is a taking of property without due process of law. Union Refrigerator Transit Co. *v.* Kentucky, 199 U. S. 194. This argument presses the expressions in Brown *v.* Maryland, 12 Wheat. 419, 444; Fairbank *v.* United States, 181 U. S. 283, and intervening cases, to new applications, and farther than they properly can be made to go. Whether we are to distinguish or to identify taxes on sales and taxes on goods depends on the scope of the constitutional provision concerned. Compare Foppiano *v.* Speed, 199 U. S. 501, 520. A tax on foreign bills of lading may be held equivalent to a tax on exports as against Article I, section 9; a license tax on importers of foreign goods may be held an unauthorized interference with commerce; and yet it would be consistent to sustain a tax on sales within the State as against the Fourteenth Amendment so far as that alone is concerned. Whatever the right of parties engaged in commerce among the States, a sale depends in part on the law of the State where it takes place **for** its validity and, in the courts of that State, at least, for the mode of proof. No one would contest the power to enact a statute of frauds for such transactions. Therefore the State may make parties pay for the help of its laws, as against this objection. A statute requiring a memorandum in writing is quite as clearly a regulation of the business as a tax. It is unnecessary to consider other answers to this point.

Yet another ground on which the owners of stock are said to be deprived of their property without due process of law is the adoption of the face value of the shares as the basis of the tax. One of the stocks was worth thirty dollars and seventy-five cents a share of the face value of one hundred dollars, the other one hundred and seventy-two dollars. The inequality of the tax, so far as actual values are concerned, is manifest. But, here again equality in this sense has to yield to practical considerations and usage. There must be a fixed and indisputable mode of ascertaining a stamp tax. In another sense, moreover, there is equality. When the taxes on two sales are equal the same number of shares is sold in each case; that is to say, the same privilege is used to the same extent. Valuation is not the only thing to be considered. As was pointed out by the Court of Appeals, the familiar stamp tax of two cents on checks, irrespective of amount, the poll tax of a fixed sum, irrespective of income or earning capacity, and many others, illustrate the necessity and practice of sometimes substituting count for weight. See Bell Gap Railroad Co. *v.* Pennsylvania, 134 U. S. 232; Merchant & Manufacturers' Bank *v.* Pennsylvania, 167 U. S. 461. Without going farther into a discussion which, perhaps, could have been spared in view of the decision in Thomas *v.* United States, 192 U. S. 363, and the constitutional restrictions upon Congress, we are of opinion that the New York statute is valid, so far as the Fourteenth Amendment is concerned.

The other ground of attack is that the act is an interference with commerce among the several States. Cases were imagined, which, it was said, would fall within the statute, and yet would be cases of such commerce; and it was argued that if the act embraced any such cases it was void as to them, and, if void as to them, void altogether, on a principle often stated. United States *v.* Ju Toy, 198 U. S. 253, 262. That the act is void as to transactions in commerce between the States, if it applies to them, is thought to be shown by the decisions concerning ordinances requiring a license fee from drummers, so called, and the like. Robbins *v.* Shelby County Taxing District, 120 U. S. 489; Stockard *v.* Morgan, 185 U. S. 27; Rearick *v.* Pennsylvania, 203 U. S. 507.

But there is a point beyond which this court does not consider arguments of this sort for the purpose of invalidating the tax laws of a State on constitutional grounds. This limit has been fixed in many cases. It is that unless the party setting up the unconstitutionality of the state law belongs to the class for whose sake the constitutional protection is given, or the class primarily protected, this court does not listen to his objections, and will not go into imaginary cases, notwithstanding the seeming logic of the position that it must do so, because if for any reason, or as against any class embraced, the law is unconstitutional, it is void as to all. Supervisors v. Stanley, 105 U. S. 305, 311; Clark v. Kansas City, 176 U. S. 114, 118; Lampasas v. Bell, 180 U. S. 276, 283, 284; Cronin v. Adams, 192 U. S. 108, 114. If the law is valid when confined to the class of the party before the court, it may be more or less of a speculation to inquire what exceptions the state court may read into general words, or how far it may sustain an act that partially fails. With regard to taxes, especially, perhaps it might be assumed that the legislature meant them to be valid to whatever extent they could be sustained, or some other peculiar principle might be applied. See e. g. People's National Bank v. Marye, 191 U. S. 272, 283.

Whatever the reason, the decisions are clear, and it was because of them that it was inquired so carefully in the drummer cases whether the party concerned was himself engaged in commerce between the States. Stockard v. Morgan, 185 U. S. 27, 30, 35, 36; Caldwell v. North Carolina, 187 U. S. 622; Rearick v. Pennsylvania, 203 U. S. 507. Therefore we begin with the same inquiry in this case, and it is plain that we can get no farther. There is not a shadow of a ground for calling the transaction described such commerce. The communications between the parties were not between different States, as in Western Union Telegraph Co. v. Texas, 105 U. S. 460, and the bargain did not contemplate or induce the transport of property from one State to another, as in the drummer cases. Rearick v. Pennsylvania, supra. The bargain was not affected in any way, legally or practically, by the fact that the parties happened to have come from another State before they made it. It does not appear that the petitioner came into New York to sell his stock, as it was put on his behalf. It appears only that he sold after coming into the State. But we are far from implying that it would have made any difference if he had come to New York with the supposed intent before any bargain was made.

It is said that the property sold was not within the State. The immediate object of sale was the certificate of stock present in New York. That document was more than evidence, it was a constituent of title. No doubt, in a more remote sense, the object was the membership or share which the certificate conferred or made attainable. More remotely still it was an interest in the property of the corporation, which might be in other States than either the corporation or the certificate of stock. But we perceive no relevancy in the analysis. The facts that the property sold is outside of the State and the seller and buyer foreigners are not enough to make a sale commerce with foreign nations or among the several States, and that is all that there is here. — On the general question there should be compared with the drummer cases the decisions on the other side of the line. Nathan v. Louisiana, 8 How. 73; Woodruff v. Parham, 8 Wall. 123; Brown v. Houston, 114 U. S. 622; Emert v. Missouri, 156 U. S. 296. A tax is not an unconstitutional regulation in every case where an absolute prohibition of sales would be one. American Steel and Wire Co. *v.* Speed, 192 U. S. 500. We think it unnecessary to explain at greater length the reasons for our opinion that the petitioner has suffered no unconstitutional wrong.

Order affirmed.

EQUITABLE LIFE ASSURANCE SOCIETY *v.* PENNSYLVANIA.

SUPREME COURT OF THE UNITED STATES.   1915.

[*Reported* 238 *U. S.* 143.]

HOLMES, J. The Equitable Life Assurance Society of the United States, the plaintiff in error, does business in Pennsylvania. By an act of June 28, 1895, that State levies an annual tax of two per cent upon the gross premiums of every character received from business done within the State during the preceding year. The Company paid large taxes under this act, but appealed to the state courts from charges made by the State Accounting Officer in respect of premiums for the years 1906, 1907, 1908, 1909 and 1910, paid to the Company outside the State by residents of Pennsylvania. The Supreme Court sustained the charge. 239 Pa. St. 288. The whole discussion there was whether these items fell within the statute. On that point of course the decision of the state court is final, and as the Company is a foreign corporation and this is held to be a tax for the privilege of doing business in the State, it is obvious that the scope of the question before us is narrow, being only whether the statute as construed deprives the Company of its property without due process of law, contrary to the Fourteenth Amendment, as alleged. It is true that the plaintiff in error suggests a further infraction of that amendment in an assumption by the Supreme Court of an unproved fact: that the beneficiaries of the policies lived in Pennsylvania. But it is enough to answer that we understand the decision when it uses the word beneficiaries to mean parties to the contracts, the insured, and that the assumption was warranted by the record as to them.

The grounds for the only argument open are that a State cannot tax property beyond its jurisdiction, Union Transit Co. *v.* Kentucky, 199 U. S. 194; that it cannot effect that result indirectly by making the payment a condition of the right to do local business, Western Union Telegraph Co. *v.* Kansas, 216 U. S. 1; Pullman Co. *v.* Kansas 216 U. S. 56; Ludwig *v.* Western Union Telegraph Co., 216 U. S. 146; and that as it could not prohibit the contracts it cannot impose the tax. Allgeyer *v.* Louisiana, 165 U. S. 578. In aid of the effort to make the foregoing decisions applicable it is argued that this is a property tax. But, as we have said, the Supreme Court of Pennsylvania speaks of it as a tax for the privilege of doing business within the Commonwealth, and whether the statement is a construction of the act or not we agree with it so far at least as to assume that if that characterization is necessary to sustain the tax, the Legislature meant to avail itself of any power appropriate to that end.

Without going into any preliminary matters that might be debated it is enough for us to say that we agree with the Supreme Court of the State in its line of reasoning; applying it to the claim of constitutional rights which that court did not discuss. The question is not what is doing business within a State in such a sense as to lay a foundation for service of process there. It being established that the relation of the foreign company to domestic policy holders constituted doing business within the meaning of the statute, the question is whether the Company may be taxed in respect of it, in this way, whatever it may be called. We are dealing with a corporation that has subjected itself to the jurisdiction of the State; there is no question that the State has a right to tax it and the only doubt is whether it may take this item into account in fixing the figure of the tax. Obviously the limit in that regard is a different matter from the inquiry whether the residence of a policy holder would of itself give jurisdiction over the Company. The argument of the state court is that the Company is protecting its insured in Pennsylvania equally whether they pay their premiums to the Company's agent in Philadelphia or by mail or in person to another in New York.

These are policies of life insurance and according to the statement of the plaintiff in error are kept alive and renewed to residents of Pennsylvania by payments from year to year. The fact that the State could not prevent the contracts, so far as that may be true, has little bearing upon its right to consider the benefit thus annually extended into Pennsylvania in measuring the value of the privileges that it does grant. We may add that the State profits the Company equally by protecting the lives insured, wherever the premiums are paid. The tax is a tax upon a privilege actually used. The only question concerns the mode of measuring the tax. Flint *v.* Stone Tracy Co., 220 U. S. 107, 162, 163. As to that a certain latitude must be allowed. It is obvious that many incidents of the contract are likely to be attended to in Pennsylvania, such as payment of dividends when received in cash, sending an adjuster into the State in case of dispute, or making proof of death. See Connecticut Mut. Life Ins. Co. *v.* Spratley, 172 U. S. 602, 611; Pennsylvania Lumbermen's Mut. Fire Ins. Co. *v.* Meyer, 197 U. S. 407, 415. It is not unnatural to take the policy holders residing in the State as a measure without going into nicer if not impracticable details. Taxation has to be determined by general principles, and it seems to us impossible to say that the rule adopted in Pennsylvania goes beyond what the Constitution allows.

Judgment affirmed.

COOK COUNTY *v.* FAIRBANK.

SUPREME COURT OF ILLINOIS.   1906.

[*Reported* 222 *Ill.* 578.]

HAND, J.   This was an action of assumpsit commenced by Kellogg Fairbank and Benjamin Carpenter, appellees, as tie executors of the last will and testament of Nathaniel K. Fairbank, deceased, in tie superior court of Cook county, against Cook county, the appellant, to recover the sum of $1250, wiich, as such executors, the appellees iad paid under protest to Patrick J. Caiill, as clerk of the probate court of Cook county, for the docket fee provided to be paid in an act entitled "An act to provide for fees of clerks of probate courts in counties of tie tiird class," approved May 29, 1879, in force July 1, 1879, and the various amendments thereto, (Hurd's Stat. 1905, par. 63, chap. 53, p. 1075,) which amount had been turned over by said Cahill, as such clerk, under the statute, to the treasurer of said Cook county prior to the bringing of this suit.   The general issue was filed and tie case was tried before the court without a jury, which trial resulted in a finding and judgment in favor of the appellees for said sum of $1250 and costs, and Cook county has prosecuted an appeal direct to this court on the ground that the constitutionality of tie paragraph of said statute which provides for the payment of said docket fee is involved, and upon propositions of law submitted was held to be void by the trial court, which paragraph reads as follows:

"On application for tie grant of letters testamentary, of administration, guardianship or conservatorsiip, it shall be the duty of the applicant to state in his or her petition tie value of all the real and personal estate of such deceased person, infant, idiot, insane person, lunatic, distracted person, drunkard or spendthrift, as the case may be, and on the grant of letters testamentary, administration, guardianship or conservatorsiip, there shall be paid to the clerk of said probate court, from the proper estate, and charged as costs, a docket fee as follows: When the estate does not exceed $5000, $5; and the sum [of] one (1) dollar for each and every additional $1000 of the estate of such deceased person, infant, idiot, insane person, lunatic, distracted person, drunkard or spendthrift as the case may be.   In all cases where any deceased person shall leave him or her surviving a widow or children resident of this State, who are entitled out of said estate to a widow's or child's award, and the entire estate real and personal of such deceased person shall not exceed $2000, and in the case of any minor whose estate real and personal does not exceed the sum of $1000, and whose father is dead, and in all cases of any idiot, insane person, lunatic, or distracted person, drunkard or spendthrift, when such person has a wife or infant child dependent on such person for support, and the entire estate of such person shall not exceed the sum of $2000, the probate judge (by order of court) shall remit and release to such estate all of the costs herein provided for. In all estates not exceeding $500 in value, the judge of the probate court may in his discretion suspend, modify or remit the costs by order of court duly made."

The record shows, without dispute, that the last will and testament of Nathaniel K. Fairbank was duly proven, admitted to probate and ordered recorded in the probate court of Cook county on the 20th day of May, 1903, and on that day it was ordered that letters testamentary issue to the appellees; that on the fifth day of June following, the appellees demanded of said Cahill that he issue and deliver to them said letters testamentary, which he declined to do unless they paid to him, as a condition precedent to their delivery, a docket fee of $1250 which had been taxed by him against said estate; that thereupon the appellees filed their petition in the probate court of said county, in which they represented that the affairs of said estate needed immediate and particular attention, and that they, as the executors thereof, could not enter upon the discharge of their duties as such executors without possession of their letters testamentary and that great loss might come to said estate if the delivery of said letters was further delayed, which letters, they averred, the said Cahill, upon demand, had refused to deliver to them unless they first paid to him the sum of $1250 as a docket fee. They also averred the paragraph of the statute requiring the payment of said docket fee was unconstitutional and void, and asked that said clerk be ordered to deliver said letters to them forthwith and without the payment of said docket fee. The prayer of the petition was denied, and the appellees again protested, in writing, against the payment of the said docket fee, but the clerk still persisted in his refusal to deliver said letters without the payment of said docket fee, whereupon the appellees paid to him, in open court, said sum of $1250, and thereupon brought this suit to recover back the amount so paid.

We will first consider the constitutionality of the paragraph of the act of 1879 above set forth.

Section 12 of article 10 of the constitution of 1870 provides: "The General Assembly shall, by general law, uniform in its operation, provide for and regulate the fees of said officers [State, county and township] and their successors, so as to reduce the same to a reasonable compensation for services actually rendered."

While the amount demanded of the appellees by said clerk as a condition precedent to the delivery to them of their letters testamentary is designated in the statute "a docket fee," it is apparent that the amount exacted by the clerk was in no way measured by the amount or value of the services performed by him, but the charge against the estate depended entirely upon the size or amount of the estate. If an estate does not exceed in value $2000 no docket fee is to be taxed. If it is more than that amount and does not exceed in value $5000 a docket fee of $5 is to be taxed, or if the estate is of the size of the Fairbank estate a fee of $1250 is to be taxed, although the docketing of the estate, in each case, in the office of the clerk of the probate court would require the same amount of labor by the clerk, and no more. The provision of the constitution above referred to, required the General Assembly, by general law, uniform in its operation, to regulate the fees of county officers in such manner that the fees charged and collected by them shall be "a reasonable compensation for services actually rendered." Clearly, the framers of that provision of the constitution intended that the fees of probate courts in counties of the third class should be based upon the amount, quality and character of the services performed by the clerks of said courts, and not arbitrarily fixed on the basis of the value or amount of the estates which might pass through those courts, and we think it evident the amount designated in said statute as a docket fee was not intended by the framers of said statute to represent the value of services actually rendered by the probate clerk in each estate in docketing the estate, but that said statute was intended by its framers to furnish a means whereby the public revenues of counties of the third class in the State would be increased, by collecting through the probate court a charge upon the designated estates. The amount sought to be retained by the probate clerk was therefore, properly speaking, not a fee, but was a burden or charge imposed upon said estate to raise money for public purposes, regardless of the value of the services actually rendered the estate, which is in conflict with the constitutional provision hereinbefore set forth, and which would bring said burden or charge within the well recognized definition of a tax, which may, in a general sense, be defined to be a burden or charge imposed by the legislative power of the State upon persons or property for public uses. Dalrymple *v.* City of Milwaukee, 53 Wis. 178.

The view that a charge fixed by statute for the service to be performed by an officer where the charge has no relation to the value of the services performed, and where, as here, the amount collected eventually finds its way into the treasury of the branch of government whose officer or officers collect the charge, is not a fee but a burden or charge in the nature of a tax, has been held in numerous cases in the United States. In State *v.* Case, 1 L. R. A. (N. S.) 152, decided by the Supreme Court of Washington in July, 1905, and wherein was involved the constitutionality of a statute which required the payment of $5 in probate proceedings at the time the first paper was filed, and thereafter, when the appraisement was returned into court, an additional sum was to be paid, as follows: $2.50 for estates between $1000 and $2000, increasing on a sliding scale, depending on the value of the estate, the court said (p. 155): "It is true the statute calls the charge a ' fee,' but if it is apparent upon the face of the statute that the charge is, in fact, not based upon actual and necessary services rendered or to be rendered, but is based entirely upon a property valuation, thereby partaking of the nature of tax, it would seem to be wholly immaterial by what name the statute may designate it. . . . His service [those of the clerk] in the premises are purely clerical, and the amount thereof depends upon the filings and records of each particular case, which can in no reasonable sense be said to depend in each given case upon the value of the estate. It seems clear, therefore, that this statute exacts payments regulated by property valuations alone, and that it must therefore be a tax upon property.

In State v. Mann, 76 Wis. 469, *mandamus* was brought to compel the county judge to proceed with the administration of an estate. The statute required the administrators to pay to the county treasury, for the use of the county, in lieu of fees, a sum equal to one-half of one per cent on $500,000 of the appraised value of said estate and one-tenth of one per cent on the excess, which amounts, as taxed, aggregated the sum of $2,631.95. Payment was required on the return and approval of the inventory and was made a part of the expense of administration. The court, in holding the act unconstitutional, on page 477, said: "Besides, the amount of this exaction is in no way dependent upon the amount or value of such services of the judge or register of probate, but depends entirely upon such valuation or appraisal of the estate. . . . Compensation for services must necessarily be graduated by the amount, quality and character of the services. But here the amount exacted bears no relation to such services. . . . We must hold that the exaction in question is not a probate fee, nor in lieu of nor equivalent to a probate fee. It is nothing less than a charge imposed by the legislature as a condition precedent to allowing the county court to proceed with the administration of this estate. Such charge is necessarily a burden so imposed upon such administrators or such estate, or both, to raise money for public purposes. This brings it within a well recognized definition of a tax. . . . It is very obvious that the charge imposed by the act in question is essentially a tax."

And in State v. Gorman, 40 Minn. 232, *mandamus* was brought to compel the probate court to proceed with the settlement of an estate, which it had refused to do until the sum of $5000 was paid. The statute provided graduated fees, dependent upon the value of the estate as shown by the inventory. Between $2000 and $5000 a fee of $10 was exacted, ascending with the value of the estate, until it provided that in estates of over $500,000 a fee of $5000 should be charged. The court, on page 233, said: "But the sums required by this act to be paid into the county treasury must be regarded as taxes, in the ordinary sense of that word and as it is used in the constitution. They are not in any proper sense fees or costs assessed impartially or with regard to the expense occasioned or services performed. The amounts are regulated wholly, but arbitrarily, with regard to the value of the estate. They have no proximate relation to the amount of the compensation to be paid to the probate judge, nor to the other expenses of the court, nor to the nature or extent of the services which may become necessary in the proceedings. There is no necessary, natural or even probable correspondence between the sums to be paid (widely different in amounts with respect to estates of different values) and the nature of the proceedings, or the character or extent of the services which may be required in the probate court."

And Fatjo *v.* Pfister, 117 Cal. 83, was an action in which the clerk of the superior court of Santa Clara county was sought to be coerced to file an inventory and appraisement, which he had refused to do until the sum of $200 was paid him as fees. The statute required the payment of $5 on the filing of the petition for letters of administration, also an additional payment of one dollar for each $1000 of the appraised valuation of the estate in excess of $3000, as shown by the inventory and appraisement. The Supreme Court held the charge to be a tax, saying (p. 85): "It is perfectly plain that the legislature has attempted, by that portion of section 1 above quoted, to levy a property tax upon all estates of decedents, infants and incompetents. The *ad valorem* charge for filing the inventory is in no sense a fee or compensation for the services of the officer, which are the same, as respects this matter, in every estate, large or small. To call it a fee is a transparent evasion."

If the General Assembly, under the guise of a docket fee, has attempted, as we think it is apparent it has, to levy a property tax upon all estates of deceased persons, infants, idiots, insane persons, lunatics, distracted persons, drunkards and spendthrifts whose estates exceed the amounts designated in said statute and which are brought into the probate court of counties of the third class, then the paragraph attempting to impose said tax is clearly unconstitutional for numerous reasons other than that pointed out above. First, it violates section 13 of article 4 of the constitution of this State, because it embraces more than one subject and subjects that are not included in its title; second, it violates section 3 of article 9 of the constitution, in that it provides for exemptions of property from taxation not specified in said section; third, it subjects the property of the estate to double taxation, as it appears that the executors had paid all the taxes due upon the real and personal property of the estate in the years 1902 and 1903; and fourth, it violates section 1 of article 9 of the constitution, in this: that a tax is levied which is not equal or uniform as to the class upon which it operates.

Nor can the charge or burden imposed be sustained upon the ground that it amounts to no more than an inheritance or succession tax. The contention that it does amount to such tax is fully met by the fact that the statute in express terms applies not only to the estates of deceased persons, but also to the estates of infants, idiots, insane persons, lunatics, distracted persons, drunkards and spendthrifts. The tax here imposed is levied upon the body of the entire estate if it exceeds $2000 in value, whether the estate is solvent or insolvent, while an inheritance or succession tax is imposed, not as a tax upon the estate, but upon the right of succession. (Kochersperger *v.* Drake, 167 Ill. 122; Magoun *v.* Illinois Trust and Savings Bank, 170 U. S. 283.) In the *Fatjo case* the Supreme Court of California said upon this branch of the case: "And it is not merely an inheritance tax or at all analogous to an inheritance tax, as counsel would contend, for, in the first place, it applies not only to the estates of decedents, but also to the estates of minors and incompetents under guardianship; and as to the estates of decedents, it applies not to the distributable residue after payment of debts and expenses of administration, but to the whole body of the estate, and would be collectible, if the law were valid, from an insolvent estate as well as from one of equal appraised value and with no liabilities."   And in State *v.* Case, *supra,* the Supreme Court of Washington, in reviewing two cases cited in support of the constitutionality of the statute under consideration in that case, said (p. 155): "Neither of said cases relates to property taxation. The first discusses the Inheritance Tax law, and expressly holds that such a tax is not a property tax but is a mere charge for the privilege of succession to the ownership and enjoyment of property, following Magoun *v.* Illinois Trust and Savings Bank, 170 U. S. 283, (42 L. ed. 1037, 18 Sup. Ct. Rep. 594,) which expressly distinguished such a charge from property taxes, which must be uniform and equal under the State constitutions."

It is urged by appellant that this court, in the case of People *v.* Hinrichsen, 161 Ill. 223, is committed to the view that the statute fixing the fees of the Secretary of State for incorporating corporations, which are graduated according to the amount of the capital stock of the corporation, is a valid exercise of legislative power. We are of the opinion there is a well marked line of distinction between the *Hinrichsen case* and the case at bar.   It is the same line of demarkation pointed out in the inheritance tax cases heretofore referred to.   An inheritance tax was sustained on the ground that it was not a tax upon property but upon the right of succession, and that the State had the right to prescribe rules of descent and conditions upon which property should be inherited.   So with the right of the State to establish fees in cases of persons desiring to organize corporations.   A corporation is a creation of the legislature.   Persons are not obliged to incorporate against their will. If, however, they do incorporate they must accept the burdens imposed upon them by general law.   Such, however, is not the case with the statute authorizing the collection of the docket fee mentioned in the statute now under consideration.   That, as was said by Judge Cassoday in State *v.* Mann, *supra,* "is nothing less than a charge imposed by the legislature as a condition precedent to allowing the county court to proceed with the administration of this estate."

Our conclusion is, that the paragraph of the statute of 1879 authorizing the collection of a docket fee is unconstitutional and void.

Judgment affirmed.

ADAMS MOTOR CO. *v.* CLER.

SUPREME COURT OF GEORGIA. 1920.

[*Reported* 149 *Ga.* 818.]

BECK, P. J. 1. The section of the general tax act passed by the General Assembly of Georgia in the year 1918, which the plaintiffs contend is invalid because it violates certain provisions of the State and Federal constitutions, is in the following language: " 12th. Automobiles. Upon every agent of, and upon every dealer in, and upon every person soliciting orders for the sale of automobiles, the sum set out below, viz.: In each county for each make of such vehicle only one such tax for such make for each agency to be taxed in any one county. Any agency having paid such tax to be allowed any number of employees within the county wherein such tax has been paid, free from such liabilities. Provided, that any person, firm, or corporation paying this tax shall be permitted to resell any automobile or other vehicle taken in exchange for automobiles, without the payment of additional tax. In each county with a population of less than 20,000, $27.50. In each county with a population of between 20,000 and 30,000, $55.00. In each county with a population of between 30,000 and 50,000, $82.50. In each county with a population of between 50,000 and 75,000, $110.00. In each county with a population of between 75,000 and 100,000, $165.00. In each county with a population of between 100,000 and 150,000, $220.00. In each county with a population exceeding 150,000, $275.00."

The soundness of the criticisms upon this act depends upon whether the section in question makes an arbitrary and unreasonable classification of dealers in automobiles subject to the tax enclosed by this section. After careful consideration of the subject of this inquiry it does not seem to us that the legislature, in exercising its right to make a classification for the purpose of imposing a tax like that in question, has acted arbitrarily and unreasonably. It is settled' law that a tax upon a business is not a tax upon property within the meaning of the ad valorem and uniformity clauses of the constitution, and it is not a valid objection that another business or object is not taxed or is taxed a different amount. The requirement of this kind of classification is that it shall be uniform upon all business of the same class. Weaver *v.* State, 89 Ga. 639 (15 S. E. 840), and cases there cited. Under the provisions of the section of the tax act in question, the classification is made with reference to the population of the county within which the business is carried on. And to fix the amount of the tax according to the population of a county is fixing it with reference to a fact that is not arbitrarily chosen, but has some relation to the question of the amount of tax that would be right and proper. If the amount of tax fixed had to be precisely adjusted

so as to impose the same burden upon every dealer in proportion
to the amount of business done or the opportunity for doing business, it would be extremely difficult, if not impossible, to select
any fact or standard by which the classification could be made.
The only requirement is that the fact selected for the classification
under which a tax like that in question is imposed shall not be
arbitrary, but shall bear a reasonable relation to the tax imposed
upon the business. It may be true that a county with less than
20,000 population may in some cases afford a more profitable field
for the conduct of business than an adjoining county having a
population of 30,000; but it cannot be held that the legislature
in enacting the provision in question could not decide that there
was a reasonable relation between the population of a county and
the amount of business of a given character carried on in that
county.

Another ground taken by the plaintiffs is that the classification
between dealers who deal in one make of automobiles and dealers
who sell more than one make, without reference to the value of the
automobile sold, is arbitrary, discriminatory, and unreasonable.
And again we must reply that the fact selected by the legislature
as a ground for classification bears an actual relation to the classification made. As we said in discussing the other ground of attack
upon the act, it may not precisely fix an amount adjusted to the
amount of business that will be done by dealers in different classes,
but it is a fact that might reasonably be taken into consideration
in determining the tax to be imposed. In the case of Sawtell *v.*
Atlanta, 138 Ga. 687 (75 S. E. 982), an ordinance of the City
of Atlanta, imposing a tax of a fixed amount upon all ice houses,
ice manufacturers, or agencies not employing more than five wagons
for selling or delivery purposes, and for each additional wagon
above the number of five an additional tax of $10, was held to be
not invalid on the ground that it violated the constitutional provision that all taxes must be uniform upon the same class of
subjects. Under the ordinance there attacked, if the ice house
employed one or five wagons, the tax was $50; but if it employed
more than five wagons there was an additional tax of $10 for
each additional wagon. And in the case of Witham *v.* Stewart,
129 Ga. 48 (58 S. E. 463), it was said: " Section 2, par. 2, of
the act of the General Assembly, approved December 16th, 1902
(A. '02, p. 19), provides that a ' specific tax ' of $10, for each of
the fiscal years 1903 and 1904, shall be levied ' upon the presidents
of each of the express, telegraph, steamboat, railroad, street-rail-
road, telephone, electric-light, sleeping and palace-car companies,
banks, building and loan associations, and gas companies doing
business in this State.' *Held,* that under the provisions of said
act, where it appears that the same person is the president of two
or more banks, a tax of $10 may be collected from such person for
each bank of which he is president. It appearing in the present
case that the plaintiff in error was the president of several banks
doing business in this State, he was liable to be taxed in the amount

specified in the above act for each bank of which he was the president."

2.   There is no merit in the contention that the classification was arbitrary, discriminatory, and unreasonable because of the provision permitting any person who ias paid the tax to resell any automobile taken in exchange for an automobile without the payment of an additional tax.

The act in question not being invalid for any of the reasons set forth above, it follows that it is not in violation of the due-process clause of the State and Federal constitutions.

Judgment affirmed. All the Justices concur.

CHAPTER IV.

INHERITANCE TAX.

MOORE *v.* RUCKGABER.

SUPREME COURT OF THE UNITED STATES.   1902.

[*Reported* 184 *U. S.* 593.]

THIS was also an action brought in the Circuit Court, for the Southern District of New York by Ruckgaber, as executor of the last will and testament of Louisa Augusta Ripley-Pinède, against the Collector of Internal Revenue, to recover an inheritance tax paid to the defendant upon certain personal property in the city of New York. It was argued with Eidman *v.* Martinez, 184 U. S. 578.

The material facts, as set forth in the certificate, are briefly as follows:

The testatrix, Louisa Augusta Ripley-Pinède, died at Zürich, Switzerland, on September 25, 1898, being at that time a non-resident of the United States, and having, for at least eight years immediately preceding her death, been domiciled in, and a permanent resident of, the Republic of France. She left a will dated November 6, 1890, which was made in New York and in conformity to the laws of that State, where the testatrix was then sojourning, whereby she bequeathed all her personal property in the United States to her daughter, Carmelia von Groll, who was then, and is now, also a non-resident of the United States, domiciled in Germany. Said will was probated in the Surrogate's Court of Kings County, New York, on February 17, 1899, and letters testamentary were thereupon issued to the defendant in error, a resident of said county and State, who alone qualified as executor.

At the time of her death the testatrix owned a claim in account current against one Carl Goepel and one Max Ruckgaber, Jr., constituting the firm of Schulz & Ruckgaber, both of whom resided in the county of Kings and State of New York. She was also the owner of a share of stock in The Tribune Association, a New York corporation. The testatrix was also the owner of bonds and coupons of divers American corporations hereinafter particularly described. Said chose in action, stock, bonds and certificate constituted all the personal property of every kind in the United States of America referred to in the said will. The value of the said property of the testatrix at the date of her death, September 25, 1898, as fixed and determined by appraisers duly appointed, was $105,670.70. On or about the 15th day of June, 1899, upon the written demand of the collector of internal revenue for the first district of New York, and under protest the executor did make and render in duplicate to the said collector a return of legacies arising from personal property of every kind wiatsoever, being in ciarge of trust of said executor, passing from Louisa Augusta Ripley-Pinède to ier said daughter by ier will as aforesaid.

The following questions of law which arose out of tie foregoing facts were certified to tiis court:

" 1. Can the said personal property of the non-resident testatrix, Louisa Augusta Ripley-Pinède, actually located witiin the United States at the time of her deati, September 25, 1898, be deemed to iave a *situs* in tie United States for tie purpose of levying a tax or duty upon the transmission or receipt tiereof under sections 29, 30 and 31 of tie act of Congress entitled 'An act to provide ways and means to meet war expenditures, and for otier purposes,' approved June 13, 1898?"

" 2. Was tie transmission or receipt of tie said personal property of tie non-resident testatrix, Louisa Augusta Ripley-Pinède, which was actually located in the United States at tie time of her death, September 25, 1898, subject to taxation under sections 29, 30 and 31 of the act of Congress entitled 'An act to provide ways and means to meet war expenditures, and for otier purposes,' approved June 13, 1898?"

BROWN, J.   This case differs from the one just decided only in the fact that tie will of tie non-resident testatrix was executed in New York, November 6, 1890, during a temporary sojourn there, althougi, as in tie preceding case, the testatrix was domiciled abroad, and bequeathed her personal property in New York to a daughter, who was married, and also lived abroad.

Tiere can be no doubt whatever that, if Madame Pinède had died intestate, the personal property would not have passed by tie law "of any State or Territory," (using the words of the act,) but by the laws of France. Tie question tien is, whether the condition is changed, if the property pass under a will executed in tiis country. In tie United States *v.* Hunnewell, 13 Fed. Rep. 617, cited in the preceding case, the will was executed in France, but the decision of Mr. Justice Gray, holding that tie tax was not payable, was not put upon the ground tiat the will was executed in a foreign country, but upon the broader ground that the legacy duty was payable only upon the estate of persons domiciled within the United States. In delivering the opinion he observed: " Section 124 " (of tie similar act of 1864) " imposes a duty on legacies or distributive shares arising from personal property ' passing from any person possessed of such property, either by will, or by the intestate laws of any State or Territory;' it does not make the duty payable when 'tie person possessed of such property' dies testate, if it would not be payable if such person died intestate; and if Madame de la Valette had died intestate, her son would not have taken a distributive share 'by tie intestate laws of any State or Territory,' but, if at all, by the law of France, the domicil of his mother at the time of her death. And section 125, by requiring tie executor or administrator to pay the amount of this duty to the collector or deputy collector of the district of which the deceased person was a resident, leads to the same conclusion."

The real question then is, as said by Mr. Justice Gray, whether the act makes the duty payable when the person possessed of such property dies testate, if it would not be payable if such person died intestate, although the actual question involved in this case differs from the one there involved, in the fact that in the *Hunnewell* case the will was executed abroad, while in the present case it was executed in this country.

Bearing in mind the fact that the tax in this case is not upon the property itself, but upon the transmission or devolution of such property, the question again recurs, as it did in the preceding case, whether the succession took effect in France or in New York. We are aided in the solution of this problem by the language of section 2694 of the New York Code of Civil Procedure, also cited in the preceding case, which is as follows: "Except where special provision is otherwise made by law, the validity and effect of a testamentary disposition of any other" (than real) "property situated within the State, and the ownership and disposition of such property where it is not disposed of by will, are regulated by the laws of the State or country of which the decedent was a resident at the time of his death." Now as, if Madame Pinède had died without leaving a will, her property would have passed under the intestate laws of France and been exempt from this tax, it follows under the *Hunnewell* case that it is equally exempt though it passed by will.

The will of Madame Pinède is confined to her personal property in this country, and the record does not show whether she was possessed of other property in France or in any other foreign country. If she had, that property would either pass by will executed there or under the intestate laws of her domicil. For reasons stated in the prior opinion, we do not think Congress contemplated by this act that the estates of deceased persons should be split up for the purposes of distribution or taxation, but that, so far as regards personal property, the law of the domicil should prevail.

A question somewhat to the converse of this arose in the *Estate of Romaine,* 127 N. Y. 80, which was a proceeding to compel payment of an inheritance tax by the administrator of the estate of Romaine, who had died intestate in Virginia, leaving a brother and sister resident in New York, as his next of kin. The act of 1887 subjected to an inheritance tax "all property which shall pass by will or by the *intestate laws of this State,* from any person who may die seized or possessed of the same while a resident of this State, or if such decedent was not a resident of this State at the time of his death, which property or any part thereof shall be within this State." The question was whether the property of Romaine, who died in Virginia intestate, was subject to the tax. After deciding that the tax applied to two classes, namely, resident and non-resident decedents, the court observed: "But does it apply to all persons belonging to these two classes? It is not denied that it applies to all *resident* decendents, and to all non-resident *testators,* but it is contended that it does not apply to non-resident *intestates* because property 'which shall pass . . . by the intestate laws of this State' is expressly mentioned to the implied exclusion of property passing by the intestate laws of other States.   This is the position of the appellant, whose learned counsel claims that the act, in its present form, was designed to meet cases of succession by will, but not of succession by intestacy, unless the intestate was a resident of this State.   It is difficult, however, to see why the legislature should discriminate simply for the purposes of taxation between the property of a non-resident decedent who made a will, and of one who did not.   It is not probable that there was an intention to tax the estates of non-resident testators and to exempt those of non-resident intestates, because there is no foundation for such a distinction. . . .   Property of the same kind, situated in the same place, receiving the same protection from the law, and administered upon in the same way, would naturally be required to contribute toward the expenses of government upon the same basis, regardless of whether its last owner died testate or intestate."

By parity of reasoning, we think it follows that no discrimination was intended to be made between non-residents who died testate, even though the will were made in this country, and those who died intestate; and as we have held in the preceding case that the law does not apply to non-residents who died intestate, or testate under a will' executed abroad, we think it follows that it does not apply to deceased persons domiciled abroad who left property by will executed in this country.

The questions certified must, therefore, be answered in the negative.

MATTER OF CUMMINGS.

SURROGATE'S COURT, NEW YORK COUNTY.   1909.

[*Reported* 63 *N. Y. Misc.* 621.]

COHALAN, Surrogate.   Appeal from an order fixing the tax.   The decedent made a will by which he appointed the Merchants' Loan and Trust Company of Los Angeles, California, his executor, as to so much of his property as was situated in that State.   He appointed the Farmers' Loan and Trust Company of New York his executor as to so much of his property as was situated in this State. He died in 1904.   Shortly after his death, a proceeding was brought in the Superior Court of Los Angeles, California, for the probate of his will.   That court decided that the decedent was a resident of the State of California; that certain provisions of the will creating trust funds were invalid, and that that part of the property which was located in California and designated in the will as constituting a part of the trust fund should be distributed to his next of kin, in accordance with the intestate laws of California.   The property located in California was subsequently distributed among decedent's next of kin, in the manner provided by this decree, and in the proportion prescribed by the intestate laws of California. In 1906, the Farmers' Loan and Trust Company, as executor in this State, commenced a proceeding in the New York Supreme Court for the construction of decedent's will. The court decided that the decedent was a resident of the State; that the provisions of his will attempting to create certain trust funds were invalid, and that such property should be distributed in accordance with the intestate laws of this State. In the proceeding instituted by the New York executor to appraise the estate, in accordance with the provisions of the Transfer Tax Act, the appraiser included in the taxable assets of the estate all the property of decedent which was situated in California, and which, under the decree of the Superior Court of Los Angeles, had been distributed among decedent's next of kin. The executor contends that the transfer of that property is not taxable here and has appealed from the order entered upon said report. Section 220 of the Transfer Tax Law provides: "A tax shall be and is hereby imposed upon the transfer of any property . . . first, when the transfer is by will or by the intestate laws of this State from any person dying seized or possessed of the property while a resident of this State." Before the tax can be imposed there must be a transfer of the property, either by will or by the intestate laws of this State. Assuming, in accordance with the decision of the New York Supreme Court, that the decedent was a resident of this State, if that part of his personal property which was situated in California passed or was transferred to his next of kin by virtue of the intestate laws of this State, such a transfer would be taxable here. Matter of Swift, 137 N. Y. 77. But, at the time the New York court decided that he was a resident of this State, the property located in California had already been distributed under and by virtue of a decree of a court of competent jurisdiction in that State and in the proportion prescribed by the intestate laws of that State. The property having already been actually transferred under the intestate laws of the State of California, there was no property there which could be transferred under the intestate laws of this State. The theory that the property passed under the intestate laws of this State must give way to the fact that it was actually transferred under the intestate laws of the State of California. The Superior Court of Los Angeles being a court of competent jurisdiction, its decree was entitled to full faith and credit in this court. Tilt v. Kelsey, 207 U. S. 43. Therefore, as the decedent's property in California was not transferred to his next of kin by virtue of the intestate laws of this State, the courts of this State have no jurisdiction to impose a tax upon the transfer of such property. The order fixing the tax should be reversed and the report remitted to the appraiser for the purpose of excluding from the taxable assets of the estate the value of decedent's property situated in California.

Decreed accordingly.

MAXWELL *v.* BUGBEE.

SUPREME COURT OF THE UNITED STATES.   1919.

[*Reported* 250 *U. S.* 525.]

DAY, J.   These cases were argued and submitted together, involve the same constitutional questions, and may be disposed of in a single opinion. The attack is upon the inheritance tax law of the State of New Jersey, and is based upon certain provisions of the Federal Constitution. The statute has reference to the method of imposing inheritance taxes under the laws of the State. The constitutionality of the law upon both state and federal grounds was upheld in the McDonald case by the Court of Errors and Appeals, 90 N. J. L. 707. In the Hill case the judgment of the Supreme Court of New Jersey (91 N. J. L. 454) was affirmed by the Court of Errors and Appeals, 92 N. J. L. 514.

The statute under consideration is an act approved April 9, 1914 (P. L. 1914, p. 267), being an amendment to an act approved April 20, 1909 (P. L. 1909, p. 325), for taxing the transfer of property of resident and non-resident decedents by devise, bequest, descent, etc., in certain cases. The 1909 act is found in 4 Comp. Stats. N. J., p. 5301, *et seq.*, the amendment in 1 Supp. Comp. Stats. N. J., pp. 1538–1542. The act of 1909, in its first section, imposed a tax upon the transfer of any property, real and personal, of the value of $500 or over, or of any interest therein or income therefrom, in trust or otherwise, to persons or corporations, including the following cases:

"*First.* When the transfer is by will or by the intestate laws of this State from any person dying seized or possessed of the property while a resident of the State.

"*Second.* When the transfer is by will or intestate law, of property within the State, and the decedent was a non-resident of the State at the time of his death."

The taxes thus imposed were at the rate of 5 per cent. upon the clear market value of the property, with exemptions not necessary to be specified, and were payable to the treasurer for the use of the State of New Jersey.

And by § 12 it was provided that upon the transfer of property in that State of a non-resident decedent, if all or any part of the estate, wherever situated, passed to persons or corporations who would have been taxable under the act if the decedent had been a resident of the State, such property located within the State was made subject to a tax bearing the same ratio to the entire tax which the estate of such decedent would have been subject to under the act if the non-resident decedent had been a resident of the State, as the property located in the State bore to the entire estate of such non-resident decedent wherever situated.

The act, having first been amended by an act approved March 26, 1914 (P. L. 1914, p. 91), not necessary to be recited, was again amended by the act approved April 9, 1914, which is now under consideration (P. L. 1914, p. 267; 1 Supp. Comp. Stats. N. J., pp. 1538–1542). Sections 1 and 12 were amended, the former by confining the tax on the transfer of property within the State of non-resident decedents to real estate, tangible personal property, and shares of stock of New Jersey corporations and of national banks located within the State; and by modifying the former rate of 5 per centum upon the clear market value of the property passing, which was subject to exemptions in favor of churches and other charitable institutions, and of parents, children, and other lineal descendants, etc., by making 5 per centum the applicable rate but subject to numerous exceptions, and in the excepted cases imposing different rates, dependent upon the relationship of the beneficiary to the deceased and the amount of the property transferred. Thus, " Property transferred to any child or children, husband or wife, of a decedent, or to the issue of any child or children of a decedent, shall be taxed at the rate of one per centum on any amount in excess of five thousand dollars, up to fifty thousand dollars; one and one-half per centum on any amount in excess *to* [of] fifty thousand dollars, up to one hundred and fifty thousand dollars; two per centum on any amount in excess of one hundred and fifty thousand dollars, up to two hundred and fifty thousand dollars; and three per centum on any amount in excess of two hundred and fifty thousand dollars."

The modified formula for computing the assessment upon the transfer of the estate of a non-resident decedent, prescribed in § 12 as amended by the act under consideration, is as follows:

" A tax shall be assessed on the transfer of property made subject to tax as aforesaid, in this State of a nonresident decedent if all or any part of the estate of such decedent, wherever situated, shall pass to persons or corporations taxable under this act, which tax shall bear the same ratio to the entire tax which the said estate would have been subject to under this act if such nonresident decedent had been a resident of this State, and all his property, real and personal, had been located within this State, as such taxable property within this State bears to the entire estate, wherever situated; *provided,* that nothing in this clause contained shall apply to a specific bequest or devise of any property in this State."

An amendatory act, approved April 23, 1915 (P. L. 1915, p. 745; 1 Supp. Comp. Stats. N. J., p. 1542), repeated the provision last quoted, and made no change in the act pertinent to the questions here presented.

It is this method of assessment in the case of non-resident decedents which is the subject-matter in controversy.

James McDonald died January 13, 1915, owning stock in the Standard Oil Company, a New Jersey corporation, valued at

$1,114,965, leaving an entire estate of $3,969,333.25, which included some real estate in the State of Idaho. Of the entire estate, $270,813.17 went to pay debts and expenses of administration. Mr. McDonald was a citizen of the United States and a resident of the District of Columbia, and left a will and a codicil which were admitted to probate by the Supreme Court of that District. The executors are Lawrence Maxwell, a citizen of Ohio, and the Fulton Trust Company, a New York corporation. The principal beneficiaries under the will are citizens and residents of States of the United States other than the State of New Jersey. Under the will the wife takes by specific legacies; the other beneficiaries are specific and general legatees not related to the deceased and a son and two grandchildren, who take the residuary estate.

James J. Hill died May 29, 1916, intestate, a resident and citizen of the State of Minnesota, leaving a widow and nine children. Under the laws of Minnesota, the widow inherited one-third of the real estate and personal property, and each of the children two-twenty-sevenths thereof. The entire estate descending amounted to $53,814,762, which included real estate outside of New Jersey, and principally in Minnesota and New York, valued at $1,885,120. The only property the transfer of which was subject to taxation in New Jersey was stock in the Northern Securities Company, a New Jersey corporation, valued at $2,317,564.68. The debts and administration expenses amounted to $757,571.20.

The amount of the assessment in the McDonald case was $29,071.68. In the Hill case the tax assessed amounted to $67,018.43. Following the statute, the tax was first ascertained on the entire estate as if it were the estate of a resident of the State of New Jersey, with all the decedent's property both real and personal located there; the tax was then apportioned and assessed in the proportion that the taxable New Jersey estate bore to the entire estate.

The thing complained of is, that applying the apportionment formula fixed by the statute, in the cases under review, results in a greater tax on the transfer of property of the estates subject to the jurisdiction of New Jersey than would be assessed for the transfer of an equal amount, in a similar manner, of property of a decedent who died a resident of New Jersey. The cause of this inequality is said to arise because of imposing the graduated tax, provided by the statute, upon estates so large as these. If a resident, in the case of a wife or children, the first $5,000 of property is exempt, the next $45,000 is taxed at the rate of 1%, the next $100,000 at the rate of 1½%, the next $100,000 at the rate of 2%, and the remainder at the rate of 3%. The contention is, that applying the apportionment rule provided in the case of non-resident estates, a larger amount of tax is assessed.

The correctness of the figures deduced from the application of the statute as made by the counsel for plaintiffs in error is contested, but in our view the differences are unimportant unless the State is bound to apply the same rule to the transmission of both classes of estates.

Counsel for plaintiffs in error sum up their objections to the statute, based on the Federal Constitution, as follows:

(1) It taxes the estates of non-residents more than those of residents and therefore gives to residents privileges and immunities denied to non-residents.

(2) It provides for a tax which bears unequally and therefore is not imposed upon a uniform rule and it therefore denies to non-residents the equal protection of the laws.

(3) It taxes the transfer of a non-resident's property over which the State of New Jersey has no jurisdiction while it expressly omits like property of residents, that is, real estate without the State, and thereby deprives the non-resident of his property without due process of the law.

Before taking up these objections it is necessary to briefly consider the nature of the tax. In Carr *v.* Edwards, 84 N. J. L. 667, it was held by the New Jersey Court of Errors and Appeals to be a tax upon the special right, the creation of the statute, of an executor or administrator of a non-resident decedent to succeed to property having its *situs* in New Jersey. Of § 12, as it stood in the original act of 1909, the court said: "That section contains nothing to indicate that it is not the succession of the New Jersey representative that is meant to be taxed. It is true that the tax is not necessarily five per cent. upon the whole New Jersey succession. The amount depends on the ratio of the New Jersey property to the entire estate wherever situated. This, however, merely accords a measure of the tax imposed; the tax is still by the very words of the section imposed upon the property located within this state. The reason for adopting this provision was to make sure that the rate of taxation in case of non-resident decedents should equal but not exceed the rate imposed in the case of resident decedents. . . .

"In the case of the estates of non-resident decedents, it is open for the law of the domicile to provide, as testators sometimes do, that such taxes shall be a general charge against the estate. Our legislature must be assumed to have had in mind its lack of jurisdiction over legacies under a non-resident's will, and in order to protect the New Jersey executor, administrator or trustee who paid the tax, authorized its deduction from 'property for distribution.' This phrase suffices to reach not only a distributive share of a resident's estate in case of intestacy, but the whole of the New Jersey property of a non-resident when turned over to the executor or administrator at the domicile of the decedent. ·The provision for both cases — legacies and property for distribution — demonstrates that the legislature did not mean to provide, as counsel contends, for a legacy duty only."

This language correctly characterizes the nature and effect of the tax as imposed under the amendment of 1914; but that act, under which the present cases arise, instead of reaching "the whole of the New Jersey property of a non-resident when turned over to the executor or administrator at the domicile of the decedent," now confines the transfer tax upon the property of non-resident decedents to real estate and tangible personal property within the State, the stock of New Jersey corporations, and the stock of national banks located within the State.

The tax is, then, one upon the transfer of property in New Jersey, to be paid upon turning it over to the administrator or executor at the domicile of the decedent. That transfers of this nature are within the taxing power of the State, and that taxes may be assessed upon such rights owing their existence to local laws, and to them alone, is not disputed. The right to inherit property, or to receive it under testamentary disposition, has been so frequently held to be the creation of statutory law, that it is quite unnecessary to cite the decisions which have maintained the principle. While this is confessedly true, the assessment of such taxes is, of course, subject to applicable limitations of the state and federal constitutions; it is with the latter class only that this court has to do.

(1) Taking up, then, the objections raised under the Federal Constitution, it is said that the law (*a*) denies to citizens of other States the privileges and immunities granted to citizens of the State of New Jersey, in violation of par. 1, § 2, Art. IV, of the Federal Constitution, which reads: "The citizens of each State shall be entitled to all privileges and immunities of citizens in the several States;" (*b*) abridges the privileges and immunities of plaintiffs in error, the deceased persons whom they represent, and those taking by will or intestacy under them, as citizens of the United States, in contravention of § 1 of the Fourteenth Amendment.

The provision quoted from Art. IV of the Constitution was intended to prevent discrimination by the several States against citizens of other States in respect of the fundamental privileges of citizenship. As is said by Judge Cooley in his Constitutional Limitations, 7th ed., p. 569: " It appears to be conceded that the Constitution secures in each State to the citizens of all other States the right to remove to, and carry on business therein; the right by the usual modes to acquire and hold property, and to protect and defend the same in the law; the right to the usual remedies for the collection of debts and the enforcement of other personal rights; and the right to be exempt, in property and person, from taxes or burdens which the property, or persons, of citizens of the same State are not subject to." Paul *v.* Virginia, 8 Wall. 168, 180; Ward *v.* Maryland, 12 Wall. 418, 430.

The Fourteenth Amendment recognized a distinction between citizenship of the United States and citizenship of one of the States. It provides: " No State shall make or enforce any law which shall abridge the privileges or immunities of citizens of the United States." What those privileges and immunities were was under consideration in *Slaughter-House Cases,* 16 Wall. 36, 72–79, where it was shown (pp. 77–78) that it was not the purpose of this Amendment, by the declaration that no State should make or enforce any law which should abridge the privileges and immunities of citizens of the United States, to transfer from the States to the Federal Government the security and protection of those civil rights that inhere in state citizenship; and (p. 79) that the privileges and immunities of citizens of the United States thereby placed beyond abridgment by the States were those which owe their existence to the Federal Government, its national character, its constitution, or its laws. To the same effect is Duncan v. Missouri, 152 U. S. 377, 382.

We are unable to discover in the statute before us, which regulates and taxes the right to succeed to property in New Jersey upon the death of a non-resident owner, any infringement of the rights of citizenship either of the States or of the United States, secured by either of the constitutional provisions referred to. We have held that the protection that they afford to rights inherent in citizenship are not infringed by the taxation of the transfer of property within the jurisdiction of a State passing by will or intestacy where the decedent was a non-resident of the taxing State, although the entire succession was taxed in the State where he resided. Blackstone v. Miller, 188 U. S. 189, 207.

Upon this point it is unnecessary to decide whether the case might not be rested on a much narrower ground. The alleged discrimination, here complained of, so far as privileges and immunities of citizenship are concerned, is not strictly applicable to this statute because the difference in the method of taxation rests upon residence and not upon citizenship. La Tourette v. McMaster, 248 U. S. 465.

(2) It is next contended that the effect of including the property beyond the jurisdiction of the State in measuring the tax, amounts to a deprivation of property without due process of law because it in effect taxes property beyond the jurisdiction of the State.

It is not to be disputed that, consistently with the Federal Constitution, a State may not tax property beyond its territorial jurisdiction, but the subject-matter here regulated is a privilege to succeed to property which is within the jurisdiction of the State. When the State levies taxes within its authority, property not in itself taxable by the State may be used as a measure of the tax imposed. This principle has been frequently declared by decisions of this court. The previous cases were reviewed and the doctrine applied in Kansas City, Fort Scott & Memphis Ry. Co. v. Kansas, 240 U. S. 227, 232. After deciding that the privilege tax, there involved, did not impose a burden upon interstate commerce, this court held that it was not in substance and effect a tax upon property beyond the State's jurisdiction, although a large amount of the property, which was referred to as a measure of the assessment, was situated outside of the State. In the present case the State imposes a privilege tax, clearly within its authority, and it has adopted as a measure of that tax the proportion which the specified local property bears to the entire estate of the decedent. That it may do so within limitations which do not really make the tax one upon property beyond its jurisdiction, the decisions to which we have referred clearly establish. The transfer of certain property within the State is taxed by a rule which considers the entire estate in arriving at the amount of the tax. It is in no just sense a tax upon the foreign property, real or personal.   It is only in instances where the State exceeds its authority in imposing a tax upon a subject-matter within its jurisdiction in such a way as to really amount to taxing that which is beyond its authority, that such exercise of power by the State is held void. In cases of that character the attempted taxation must fail.   Looney *v.* Crane Co., 245 U. S. 178; International Paper Co. *v.* Massachusetts, 246 U. S. 135.   To say that to apply a different rule regulating succession to resident and non-resident decedents is to levy a tax upon foreign estates, is to distort the statute from its purpose to tax the privilege, which the statute has created, into a property tax, and is unwarranted by any purpose or effect of the enactment, as we view it.

(3) It is further contended that the tax bears so unequally upon non-residents as to deny to them the equal protection of the laws.

The subject of taxes of this character was given full consideration by this court in Magoun *v.* Illinois Trust & Savings Bank, 170 U. S. 283, in which case a graded legacy and inheritance tax law of the State of Illinois was sustained.   The statute exempted all estates valued at less than $20,000, if passing to near relations, or at less than $500 if passing to those more remote, made the rate of tax increasingly greater as the inheritances increased, and assessed it differently according to the relationship of the beneficiary to the testator or intestate.   The statute was attacked as void under the equal protection clause of the Fourteenth Amendment, but was held to be valid.   Of this class of taxes the court said (p. 288): " They [inheritance taxes] are based upon two principles: 1. An inheritance tax is not one on property, but one on the succession. 2. The right to take property by devise or descent is the creature of the law, and not a natural right — a privilege, and therefore the authority which confers it may impose conditions upon it.   From these principles it is deduced that the States may tax the privilege, discriminate between relatives, and between these and strangers, and grant exemptions; and are not precluded from this power by the provisions of the respective state constitutions requiring uniformity and equality of taxation."

And upon examining (pp. 296, 297) the classification upon which the provisions of the Illinois statute were based, the court found there was no denial of the equal protection of the laws either in discriminating between those lineally and those collaterally related to decedent, and those standing as strangers to the blood, or in increasing the proportionate burden of the tax progressively as the amount of the benefit increased.

Equal protection of the laws requires equal operation of the laws upon all persons in like circumstances.   Under the statute, in the present case, the graduated taxes are levied equally upon all interests passing from non-resident testators or intestates.   The tax is not upon property, but upon the privilege of succession, which the State may grant or withhold.   It may deny it to some and give it to others.   The State is dealing in this instance not with the transfer of the entire estate, but only with certain classes of property that are subject to the jurisdiction of the State. It must find some rule which will adequately deal with this situation. It has adopted that of the proportion of the local estate in certain property to the entire estate of the decedent. In making classification, which has been uniformly held to be within the power of the State, inequalities necessarily arise, for some classes are reached, and others omitted, but this has never been held to render such statutes unconstitutional. Beers *v.* Glynn, 211 U. S. 477. This principle has been recognized in a series of cases in this court. Board of Education *v.* Illinois, 203 U. S. 553; Campbell *v.* California, 200 U. S. 87; Keeney *v.* New York, 222 U. S. 525. It has been uniformly held that the Fourteenth Amendment does not deprive the States of the right to determine the limitations and restrictions upon the right to inherit property, but "at the most can only be held to restrain such an exercise of power as would exclude the conception of judgment and discretion, and which would be so obviously arbitrary and unreasonable as to be beyond the pale of governmental authority." Campbell *v.* California, 200 U. S. 95. In upholding the validity of a graduated tax upon the transfer of personal property, to take effect upon the grantor's death, we said in Keeney *v.* New York, 250 U. S. 535; "The validity of the tax must be determined by the laws of New York. The Fourteenth Amendment does not diminish the taxing power of the State, but only requires that in its exercise the citizen must be afforded an opportunity to be heard on all questions of liability and value, and shall not, by arbitrary and discriminatory provisions, be denied equal protection. It does not deprive the State of the power to select the subjects of taxation. But it does not follow that because it can tax any transfer (Hatch *v.* Reardon, 204 U. S. 152, 159), that it must tax all transfers, or that all must be treated alike."

In order to invalidate this tax it must be held that the difference in the manner of assessing transmission of property by testators or intestates, as between resident and non-resident decedents, is so wholly arbitrary and unreasonable as to be beyond the legitimate authority of the State. We are not prepared so to declare. The resident testator or intestate stands in a different relation to the State than does the non-resident. The resident's property is usually within the ready control of the State, and easily open to inspection and discovery for taxation purposes, by means quite different from those afforded in cases of local holdings of non-resident testators or intestates. As to the resident, his entire intangible, and usually most of his tangible property, pay tribute to the State when transferred by will or intestacy; the transfer of the non-resident's estate is taxed only so far as his estate is located within the jurisdiction and only so far as it comes within the description of "real property within this State, or of goods, wares, and merchandise within this State, or of shares of stock of corporations of this State, or of national banking associations located in this State." Simple contract debts owing by New Jersey debtors to non-residents and some other kinds of property of non-residents are exempt, although it is settled that, for the purpose of founding administration, simple contract debts are assets at the domicile of the debtor; Wyman *v.* Halstead, 109 U. S. 654, 656; and that the State of the debtor's domicile may impose a succession tax; Blackstone *v.* Miller, 188 U. S. 189, 205; Baker *v.* Baker, Eccles & Co., 242 U. S. 394, 401.

The question of equal protection must be decided as between resident and non-resident decedents as classes, rather than by the incidence of the tax upon the particular estates whose representatives are here complaining. Absolute equality is impracticable in taxation, and is not required by the equal protection clause. And inequalities that result not from hostile discrimination, but occasionally and incidentally in the application of a system that is not arbitrary in its classification, are not sufficient to defeat the law.

In our opinion, there are substantial differences which within the rules settled by this court permit the classification which has been accomplished by this statute. St. Louis Southwestern Ry. Co. *v.* Arkansas, 235 U. S. 350, 367, and cases cited.

Finding no error in the judgments of the Court of Errors and Appeals of the State of New Jersey, the same are

Affirmed.

MR. JUSTICE HOLMES dissenting.

Many things that a legislature may do if it does them with no ulterior purpose, it cannot do as a means to reach what is beyond its constitutional power. That I understand to be the principle of Western Union Telegraph Co. *v.* Kansas; Pullman Company *v.* Kansas, and other cases in 216 U. S. Western Union Telegraph Co. *v.* Foster, 247 U. S. 105, 114. New Jersey cannot tax the property of Hill or MacDonald outside the State and cannot use her power over property within it to accomplish by indirection what she cannot do directly. It seems to me that that is what she is trying to do and therefore that the judgments of the Court of Errors and Appeals should be reversed.

It seems to me that when property outside the State is taken into account for the purpose of increasing the tax upon property within it, the property outside is taxed in effect, no matter what form of words may be used. It appears to me that this cannot be done, even if it should be done in such a way as to secure equality between residents in New Jersey and those in other States.

New Jersey could not deny to residents in other States the right to take legacies which it granted to its own citizens, and therefore its power to prohibit all legacies cannot be invoked in aid of a principle that affects the foreign residents alone. In Kansas City, Fort Scott & Memphis Ry. Co. *v.* Kansas, 240 U. S. 227, 235, the State could have refused incorporation altogether and therefore could impose the carefully limited condition that was upheld.

THE CHIEF JUSTICE, MR. JUSTICE VANDEVANTER and MR. JUSTICE MCREYNOLDS concur in the opinion that I express.

WHITE, C. J., VANDEVANTER and MCREYNOLDS, JJ., concurred **in** the dissent.

IN RE ESTATE OF SWIFT.
COURT OF APPEALS OF NEW YORK. 1893.
[*Reported* 137 *New York*, 77.]

GRAY, J. James T. Swift died in July, 1890, being a resident of this State and leaving a will, by which he made a disposition of all his property among relatives. After many legacies of money and of various articles of personal property, he directed a division of his residuary estate into four portions, and he devised and bequeathed one portion to each of four persons named. The executors were given a power of sale for the purpose of paying the legacies and of making the distribution of the estate. At the time of his death, the testator's estate included certain real estate and tangible personal property in chattels, situated within the State of New Jersey, which were realized upon by the executors and converted into moneys in hand. When, upon their application, an appraisement was had of the estate, in order to fix its value under the requirements of the law taxing gifts, legacies, and inheritances, the surrogate of the county of New York, before whom the matter came, held, with respect to the appraisement, that the real and personal property situated without the State of New York were not subject to appraisal and tax under the law, and the exceptions taken by the comptroller of the city of New York to that determination raise the first and the principal question which we shall consider.

Surrogate Ransom's opinion, which is before us in the record, contains a careful review of the legal principles which limit the right to impose the tax, and his conclusions are as satisfactory to my mind, as they evidently were to the minds of the learned justices of the General Term of the Supreme Court, who agreed in affirming the surrogate's decree upon his opinion.

The Attorney-General has argued that this law, commonly called the collateral inheritance tax law, imposes not a property tax but a charge for the privilege of acquiring property, and, as I apprehend it, the point of his argument is that, as there is no absolute right to succeed to property, the State has a right to annex a condition to the permission to take by will, or by the intestate laws, in the form of a tax, to be paid by the persons for whose benefit the remedial legislation has been enacted. That is, substantially, the way in which he puts the proposition, and if the premise be true that the tax imposed is upon the privilege to acquire, and, as he says in his brief, is like "a duty imposed, payable by the beneficiary," possibly enough, we should have to agree with him. We might think, in that view of the act, that the situs of property in a foreign jurisdiction was not a controlling circumstance. But if we take up the provisions of the law by which the tax is imposed, and if we consider them as they are framed and the principle whici then seems to underlie tie peculiar system of taxation created, I do not tiink tiat iis essential proposition finds adequate support.   Tie law in force at tie time of tie decease of tie testator is contained in ciapter 713 of tie Laws of 1887, amending ciapter 483 of tie Laws of 1885, and is entitled "An act to tax gifts, legacies, and collateral inieritances in certain cases."

By tie first section it is provided tiat " all property whici shall pass by will . . . from any person who may die seized or possessed of tie same, wiile a resident of this State, or, if suci decedent was not a resident of this State at tie time of iis deati, whici property or any part tiereof siall be witiin tiis State, . . . siall be and is subject to a tax . . . to be paid . . . for tie use of tie State," etc.

In tie fourti section it is provided tiat " all taxes imposed by tiis act, unless otierwise ierein provided for, siall be due and payable at tie deati of tie decedent," etc.

By tie sixti section, it is provided tiat tie executor siall " deduct tie tax from tie legacy or property, subject to said tax, or if tie legacy or property be not money, ie siall collect tie tax tiereon upon tie appraised value tiereof from tie legatee, or person entitled to suci property, and ie siall not deliver, or be compelled to deliver, any spe- cific legacy or property subject to tax to any person until ie siall iave collected tie tax tiereon," etc.   Tie language of tie act has been justly condemned, for being involved and difficult to read clearly; but considering tie language employed in tiese and in otier sections of tie law, in its ordinary sense, I tiink we would at once say tiat if tie legislature had not actually imposed a tax upon tie property itself, upon tie deati of its owner, it had certainly intended to impose a tax upon its succession, whici was to be a ciarge upon tie property, and whici operated, in effect, to diminisi *pro tanto* its value, or tie capi- tal, coming to tie new owner under a will, or by tie intestate laws. Could any one say, after reading tie provisions of tiis law, tiat it was tie legatee, or person entitled, who was taxed?   I doubt it.   Property, whici was tie decedent's at tie time of iis deati, is subjected to tie payment of a tax.   Tie tax is to be deducted from tie legacy ; or, wien deduction is not possible from the legacy not being in money, and a collection from tie legatee or tie person entitled to tie property is autiorized to be made, tie tax so to be collected is described as " tie tax tiereon," tiat is, on tie property.

If it siould be said tiat suci an interpretation of tie law is in con- flict witi a doctrine whici some judges iave asserted, respecting tie nature of tiis tax, I tiink it migit be sufficient to say tiat tie pirase- ology of tie New York law differs, more or less, from tiat of otier States, and seems peculiarly to ciarge tie subject of tie succession witi tie payment of tie tax.   But I do not tiink it at all important to our decision iere tiat we siould iold it to be a tax upon property precisely.

A precise definition of tie nature of tiis tax is not essential, if it is susceptible of exact definition. Thus far, in this court, we have not thought it necessary, in the cases coming before us, to determine whether the object of taxation is the property which passes, or not; though, in some, expressions may be found which seem to regard the tax in that light. Matter of McPherson, 104 N. Y. 306; Matter of Enston, 113 id. 174; Matter of Sherwell, 125 id. 379; Matter of Romaine, 127 id. 80; and Matter of Stewart, 131 id. 274. The idea of this succession tax, as we may conveniently term it, is more or less compound; the principal idea being the subjection of property, ownership of which has ceased by reason of the death of its owner, to a diminution, by the State reserving to itself a portion of its amount, if in money, or of its appraised value, if in other forms of property. The accompanying, or the correlative idea should necessarily be that the property, over which such dominion is thus exercised, shall be within the territorial limits of the State at its owner's death, and, therefore, subject to the operation and the regulation of its laws. The State, in exercising its power to subject realty, or tangible property, to the operation of a tax, must, by every rule, be limited to property within its territorial confines.

The question here does not relate to the power of the State to tax its residents with respect to the ownership of property situated elsewhere. That question is not involved. The question is whether the legislature of the State, in creating this system of taxation of inheritances, or testamentary gifts, has not fixed as the standard of right the property passing by will, or by the intestate laws.

What has the State done, in effect, by the enactment of this tax law? It reaches out and appropriates for its use a portion of the property at the moment of its owner's decease, allowing only the balance to pass in the way directed by testator, or permitted by its intestate law, and while, in so doing, it is exercising an inherent and sovereign right, it seems very clear to my mind that it affects only property which lies within it, and, consequently, is subject to its right of eminent domain. The theory of sovereignty, which invests the State with the right and the power to permit and to regulate the succession to property upon its owner's decease, rests upon the fact of an actual dominion over that property. In exercising such a power of taxation, as is here in question, the principle, obviously, is that all property in the State is tributary for such a purpose and the sovereign power takes a portion, or percentage of the property, not because the legatee is subject to its laws and to the tax, but because the State has a superior right, or ownership, by force of which it can intercept the property, upon its owner's death, in its passage into an ownership regulated by the enabling legislation of the State.

The rules of taxation have become pretty well settled, and it is fundamental among them that there shall be jurisdiction over the subject taxed; or, as it has been sometimes expressed, the taxing power of the State is coextensive with its sovereignty. It has not the power to

tax directly either lands or tangible personal property situated in another State or country. As to the latter description of property no
fiction transmuting its situs to the domicile of the owner is available,
when the question is one of taxation. In this connection the observations of Chief Judge Comstock, in Hoyt *v.* Commissioners of Taxes,
23 N. Y. 224, and of some text-writers, are not inappropriately referred
to. He had said that lands and personal property having an actual
situation within the State are taxable, and, by a necessary implication,
that no other property can be taxed. He says, further, " If we say that
taxation is on the person in respect to the property, we are still without
a reason for assessing the owner resident here in respect to one part
of his estate situated elsewhere and not in respect to another part.
Both are the subjects of taxation in the foreign jurisdiction."

In Judge Cooley's work on Taxation it is remarked (p. 159) that
" a State can no more subject to its power a single person, or a single
article of property, whose residence or situs is in another State, than
it can subject all the citizens, or all the property of such other State to
its power."

Judge Cooley had reference in his remarks to the case of bonds of a
railroad; for he cites the case of " the State Tax on Foreign-Held
Bonds " in the United States Supreme Court (15 Wallace, 300), where
Mr. Justice Field delivered the opinion, and, in the course of it, observed
that " the power of taxation, however vast in its character and searching in its extent, is necessarily limited to subjects within the jurisdiction of the State."

Judge Story, in his work on the Conflict of Laws, speaking of the
subject of jurisdiction in regard to property, said (section 550) that
the legal fiction as to the situs of movables yields when it is necessary
for the purpose of justice, and, further, " a nation within whose territory any personal property is actually situated has an entire dominion
over it while therein, in point of sovereignty and jurisdiction, as it has
over immovable property situated there."

The proposition which suggests itself from reasoning, as from authority, is that the basis of the power to tax is the fact of an actual dominion over the subject of taxation at the time the tax is to be imposed.

The effect of this special tax is to take from the property a portion,
or a percentage of it, for the use of the State, and I think it quite
immaterial whether the tax can be precisely classified with a taxation
of property or not. It is not a tax upon persons. If it is called a tax
upon the succession to the ownership of property, still it relates to
and subjects the property itself, and when that is without the jurisdiction of the State, inasmuch as the succession is not of property within
the dominion of the State, succession to it cannot be said to occur by
permission of the State. As to lands this is clearly the case, and
rights in or power over them are derived from or through the laws of
the foreign State or country. As to goods and chattels it is true ; for
their transmission abroad is subject to the permission of and regulated

by the laws of the State or country where actually situated. Jurisdiction over them belongs to the courts of that State or country for all purposes of policy, or of administration in the interests of its citzens, or of those having enforceable rights, and their surrender, or transmission, is upon principles of comity.

When succession to the ownership of property is by the permission of the State, then the permission can relate only to property over which the State has dominion and as to which it grants the privilege or permission.

Nor is the argument available that, by the power of sale conferred upon the executors, there was an equitable conversion worked of the lands in New Jersey, as of the time of the testator's death, and, hence, that the property sought to be reached by the tax, in the eye of the law, existed as cash in this State in the executor's hands, at the moment of the testator's death.   There might be some doubt whether the main proposition in the argument is quite correct, and whether the land did not vest in the residuary legatees, subject to the execution of the power of sale.   But it is not necessary to decide that question. Neither the doctrine of equitable conversion of lands, nor any fiction of situs of movables, can have any bearing upon the question under advisement.   The question of the jurisdiction of the State to tax is one of fact and cannot turn upon theories or fictions; which, as it has been observed, have no place in a well adjusted system of taxation.

We can arrive at no other conclusion, in my opinion, than that the tax provided for in this law is only enforceable as to property which, at the time of its owner's death, was within the territorial limits of this State.   As a law imposing a special tax, it is to be strictly construed against the State and a case must be clearly made out for its application.   We should incline against a construction which might lead to double taxation; a result possible and probable under a different view of this law.   If the property in the foreign jurisdiction was in land, or in goods and chattels, when, upon the testator's death, a new title, or ownership, attached to it, the bringing into this State of its cash proceeds, subsequently, no matter by what authority of will, or of statute, did not subject it to the tax.   A different view would be against every sound consideration of what constitutes the basis for such taxation, and would not accord with an understanding of the intention of the legislature, as more or less plainly expressed in these acts.

Another question, which I shall merely advert to in conclusion, arises upon a ruling of the surrogate with respect to appraisement, in connection with a clause of the will directing that the amount of the tax upon the legacies and devises should be paid as an expense of administration.   The appraiser, in ascertaining the value of the residuary estate for the purpose of taxation, deducted the amount of the tax to be assessed on prior legacies.   The surrogate overruled him in this, and held that there should be no deduction from the value of the resid-

uary estate of the amount of the tax to be assessed, either upon prior
legacies, or upon its value. He held that the legacies taxable should
be reported, irrespective of the provision of the will; and that a mode
of payment of the succession tax prescribed by will is something with
which the statute is not concerned. I am satisfied with his reasoning
and can add nothing to its force. Manifestly, under the law that
which is to be reported by the appraiser for the purpose of the tax is
the value of the interest passing to the legatee under the will, without
any deduction for any purpose, or under any testamentary direction.

A question is raised as to the effect upon the law, as contained in
the acts of 1885 and 1887, of the passage of chapter 215 of the Laws
of 1891 ; but as that has been the subject of another appeal, and is
fully discussed in the opinion in the Matter of the Estate of Prime, 136
N. Y. 347, reference will be made to it here.

My brethren are of the opinion that the tax imposed under the act is
a tax on the right of succession, under a will, or by devolution in case
of intestacy ; a view of the law which my consideration of the question
precludes my assenting to.

They concur in my opinion so far as it relates to the imposition of a
tax upon real estate situated out of this State, although owned by a
decedent, residing here at the time of his decease; holding with me
that taxation of such was not intended, and that the doctrine of equitable conversion is not applicable to subject it to taxation. But as to
the personal property of a resident decedent, wheresoever situated,
whether within or without the State, they are of the opinion that it is
subject to the tax imposed by the act.

The judgment below, therefore, should be so modified as to exclude
from its operation the personal property in New Jersey, and, as so
modified, it should be affirmed, without costs to either party as against
the other.[1]

FROTHINGHAM *v.* SHAW.

SUPREME JUDICIAL COURT OF MASSACHUSETTS.   1899.

[*Reported* 175 *Massachusetts*, 59.]

MORTON, J. This is a petition by the plaintiff, as executor of the
will of one Joseph Frothingham, for instructions in regard to the payment of a collateral inheritance tax on the residuary legacies. The
case was heard on agreed facts, and comes here by successive appeals
from decrees of the probate court and of a single justice of this court
finding that the tax was payable, and directing the executor to pay the
same. At the time of his death the testator was domiciled at Salem,
in this Commonwealth, and his estate, except certain real estate situ-

---

[1] See *In re* Bronson, 150 N. Y. 1. — ED.

ated 1ere, and appraised at $2100, and cas1 in a savings bank in Salem amounting to $993, was, and for many years had been, in t1e 1ands of his agents in New York, and consisted of bonds and stock of foreign corporations, a certificate of indebtedness of a foreign corporation, bond secured by mortgage on real estate in New Hamps1ire, t1e makers living in New York, and of cas1 on deposit with a savings bank and wit1 individuals in Brooklyn; t1e total being upwards of $40,000. T1ere has been no administration in New York and t1e petitioner has taken possession of all t1e property except t1e real estate, and has paid all of t1e debts and legacies except t1e residuary legacies. None of t1e legacies are entitled to exemption if ot1erwise liable to t1e tax. T1e appellants contend t1at t1e stocks, bonds, etc., were not " property wit1in t1e jurisdiction of t1e Commonwealt1," wit1in t1e meaning of St. 1891, c. 425, § 1, and t1at, if t1ey were, t1e succession took place by virtue of t1e law of New York, and not of t1is State. It is clear t1at, if t1e question of t1e liability of t1e testator to be taxed in Salem for t1e property had arisen during 1is lifetime, he would 1ave been taxable for it under Pub. St. c. 11, §§ 4, 20, notwit1standing t1e certificates, etc., were in New York (Kirkland *v.* Hotc1kiss, 100 U. S. 491; State Tax on Foreign-Held Bonds Case, 15 Wall. 300; Cooley, Tax'n [2d ed.], 371); and t1e liability would 1ave extended to and included t1e bonds secured by mortgage (Kirkland *v.* Hotc1kiss, *supra;* State Tax on Foreign-Held Bonds Case, *supra;* Hale *v.* Commissioners, 137 Mass. 111). It is true t1at t1e Public Statutes provide t1at personal property, w1erever situated, w1et1er wit1in or wit1out t1e Commonwealt1, s1all be taxed to t1e owner in t1e place w1ere 1e is an in1abitant. But it is obvious t1at t1e legislature cannot aut1orize t1e taxation of property over w1ic1 it has no control, and t1e principle underlying t1e provision is t1at personal property follows t1e person of t1e owner, and properly may be regarded, t1erefore, for t1e purposes of taxation, as 1aving a situs at 1is domicile, and as being taxable t1ere. After t1e testator's deat1 t1e property would 1ave been taxable to 1is executors for t1ree years, or till distributed and paid over to t1ose entitled to it, and notice t1ereof to t1e assessors; s1owing t1at t1e fiction, if it is one, is continued for t1e purposes of taxation after t1e owner's deat1. Pub. St. c. 11, § 20, cl. 7; Hardy *v.* In1abitants of Yarmout1, 6 Allen, 277. In t1e present case t1e tax is not upon property as such, but upon t1e privilege of disposing of it by will, and of succeeding to it on t1e deat1 of t1e testator or intestate; and it " has," as was said in Minot *v.* Wint1rop, *infra,* " some of t1e c1aracteristics of a duty on t1e administration of t1e estates of deceased persons." Minot *v.* Winthrop, 162 Mass. 113; Calla1an *v.* Woodbridge, 171 Mass. 595; Greves *v.* S1aw, 173 Mass. 205; Moody *v.* S1aw, 173 Mass. 375. In arriving at t1e amount of t1e tax, t1e property wit1in t1e jurisdiction of t1e Commonwealt1 is considered, and we see no reason for supposing t1at t1e legislature intended to depart from t1e principle 1eretofore adopted, which regards personal property, for the purposes of taxation, as having a situs at the domicile of its owner. This is the general rule (Cooley, Tax'n [2d ed.], 372), and, though it may and does lead to double taxation, that has not been accounted a sufficient objection to taxing personal property to the owner during his life at the place of his domicile, and we do not see that it is a sufficient objection to the imposition of succession taxes or administration duties, under like circumstances, after his death. In regard to the mortgage bonds, it is to be noted, in addition to what has been said, that this case differs from Callaian *v.* Woodbridge, *supra.* In that case the testator's domicile was in New York, and it does not appear from the opinion that the note and mortgage deed were in this State. In this case the domicile was in this Commonwealth, and we think that, for the purposes of taxation, the mortgage debt may be regarded as having a situs here. This is the view taken in Hanson, Death Duties (4th ed.), 239, 240, which is cited apparently with approval by Mr. Dicey, though he calls attention to cases which may tend in another direction. See Dicey, Confl. Laws, 319, note 1. It seems to us, therefore, that for the purposes of the tax in question the property in the hands of the executor must be regarded as having been within the jurisdiction of this Commonwealth at the time of the testator's death. See *In re* Swift, 137 N. Y. 77; *In re* Miller's Estate, 182 Pa. St. 162.

The petitioner further contends that the succession took place by virtue of the law of New York. But it is settled that the succession to movable property is governed by the law of the owner's domicile at the time of his death. This, it has been often said, is the universal rule, and applies to movables wherever situated. Stevens *v.* Gaylord, 11 Mass. 256; Dawes *v.* Head, 3 Pick. 129, 144, 145; Fay *v.* Haven, 3 Metc. (Mass.) 109; Wilkins *v.* Ellett, 9 Wall. 740; id. 108 U. S. 256; Freke *v.* Carbery, L. R. 16 Eq. 461; Attorney-General *v.* Campbell, L. R. 5 H. L. 524; Duncan *v.* Lawson, 41 Ch. Div. 394; Sill *v.* Worswick, 1 H. Bl. 690; Dicey, Confl. Laws, 683; Story, Confl. Laws (7th ed.), §§ 380, 481. If there are movables in a foreign country, the law of the domicile is given an extra-territorial effect by the courts of that country, and in a just and proper sense the succession is said to take place by force of, and to be governed by, the law of the domicile. Accordingly it has been held that legacy and succession duties, as such, were payable at the place of domicile in respect to movable property wherever situated, because in such cases the succession or legacy took effect by virtue of the law of domicile. Wallace *v.* Attorney-General (1865) 1 Ch. App. 1; Dicey, Confl. Laws, 785; Hanson, Death Duties (4th ed.), 423, 526. With probate or estate or administration duties, as such, it is different. They are levied in respect of the control which every government has over the property actually situated within its jurisdiction, irrespective of the place of domicile. Laidley *v.* Lord Advocate, 15 App. Cas. 468, 483; Hanson, Death Duties (4th ed.), 2, 63. Of course, any state or country may impose a tax, and give it such name or no name as it chooses, which shall embrace, if so intended, the various grounds upon which taxes are or may be levied in respect of the devolution of estates of deceased persons, and which shall be leviable according as the facts in each particular case warrant. In England, for instance, the "estate duty," as it is termed, under the Finance Act of 1894 (57 & 58 Vict. c. 30), has largely superseded the probate duty, and under some circumstances takes the place of the legacy and succession duty also. Hanson, Death Duties (4th ed.), 62, 63, 81. But, whatever the form of the tax, the succession takes place and is governed by the law of the domicile, and if the actual situs is in a foreign country, the courts of that country cannot annul the succession established by the law of the domicile. Dammert *v.* Osborn, 141 N. Y. 564. In further illustration of the extent to which the law of the domicile operates, it is to be noted that the domicile is regarded as the place of principal administration, and any other administration is ancillary to that granted there. Payment by a foreign debtor to the domiciliary administrator will be a bar to a suit brought by an ancillary administrator subsequently appointed. Wilkins *v.* Ellett, *supra*; Stevens *v.* Gaylord, *supra;* Hutchins *v.* Bank, 12 Metc. (Mass.) 421 ; Martin *v.* Gage, 147 Mass. 204. And the domiciliary administrator has sufficient standing in the courts of another State to appeal from a decree appointing an ancillary administrator. Smith *v.* Sherman, 4 Cush. 408. Moreover, it is to be observed — if that is material — that there has been no administration in New York, that the executor was appointed here, and has taken possession of the property by virtue of such appointment, and must distribute it and account for it according to the decrees of the courts of this Commonwealth. To say, therefore, that the succession has taken place by virtue of the law of New York, would be no less a fiction than the petitioner insists that the maxim, *Mobilia sequuntur personam*, is when applied to matters of taxation. The petitioner contends that in Callahan *v.* Woodbridge, *supra*, it was held that the succession to the personal property in this State took place by virtue of the law of this State, although the testator was domiciled in New York. We do not so understand that case. That case and Greves *v.* Shaw, *supra*, and Moody *v.* Shaw, *supra*, rest on the right of a State to impose a tax or duty in respect to the passing on the death of a non-resident of personal property belonging to him, and situated within its jurisdiction. We think that the decree should be affirmed.[1]   *So ordered.*

[1] For the English doctrines as to the effect of their Revenue Laws on non-residents and on foreign property, see Dicey, Conflict of Laws, 781.

For cases on the Income Tax, see Calcutta Jute Mills *v.* Nicholson, 1 Ex. D. 428; Colquhoun *v.* Brooks, 14 App. Cas. 493. On Probate Duty, see Att.-Gen. *v.* Hope, 1 C. M. & R. 530; Sudeley *v.* Att.-Gen., [1897] A. C. 11. On Legacy Duty, see Thompson *v.* Adv.-Gen., 12 Cl. & F. 1 ; Chatfield *v.* Berchtoldt, L. R. 7 Ch. 192. On Succession Duties, see Att.-Gen. *v.* Campbell, L. R. 5 H. L. 524 ; Wallace *v.* Att.-Gen., L. R. 1 Ch. 1. — ED.

MATTER OF COOLEY.

COURT OF APPEALS, NEW YORK. 1906.

[*Reported* 186 *N. Y.* 220.]

HISCOCK, J. The appellants complain because in fixing the transfer tax upon certain shares of the capital stock of the Boston and Albany Railroad Company which belonged to the estate and passed under the will of the deceased who was a non-resident, said stock has been appraised at its full market value as representing an interest in the property of said corporation situate both in the State of New York and elsewhere. It is insisted by them that under the peculiar facts of this case the valuation placed for such purpose upon the stock should not have been predicated upon the idea that the latter represented an interest in all of the property of said corporation, but should have been fixed upon the theory that it represented an interest in only a portion of said property.

I think that their complaint is well founded and that the order appealed from should be reversed and the assessment corrected accordingly.

The Boston and Albany Railroad Company is a consolidation formed by the merger of one or more New York corporations and one Massachusetts corporation. The merger was authorized and the said consolidated corporation duly and separately created and organized under the laws of each state. It was, so to speak, incorporated in duplicate. There is but a single issue of capital stock representing all the property of the consolidated and dual organization. Of the track mileage about five-sixths is in Massachusetts and one-sixth in New York. The principal offices, including the stock transfer office, are situated in Boston, and there also are regularly held the meetings of its stockholders and directors. The deceased was a resident of the State of Connecticut, and owned four hundred and twenty-six shares of the capital stock, the value of which for the purposes of the transfer tax was fixed at the full market value of $252.50 per share of the par value of $100.

The provisions of the statute (L. 1896, ch. 908, § 220, as amd. L. 1897, ch. 284, § 2), authorizing the imposition of this tax are familiar, and read in part as follows:

"A tax shall be and is hereby imposed upon the transfer of any property, real or personal, of the value of five hundred dollars or over, or of any interest therein . . . in the following cases: . . .

"2. When the transfer is by will or intestate law, of property within the State, and the decedent was a non-resident of the State at the time of his death."

The present assessment is under the last clause, and as already intimated, the sole question, stated in practical form, is whether the authorities of this State ought to levy a tax upon the full value of decedent's holdings, recognizing simply the New York corporation and regarding it as the sole owner of all of the property of the doubly incorporated New York-Massachusetts corporation, or whether they should limit the tax to a portion of the total value, upon the theory that the company holds its property in Massachusetts at least under its incorporation in that State.

By seeking the aid of our laws and becoming incorporated under them, the consolidated Boston and Albany Railroad Company became a domestic corporation. (Matter of Sage, 70 N. Y. 220.)

The decedent, therefore, as the owner of Boston and Albany stock, may be regarded as holding stock in a domestic corporation, and it is so clearly settled that we need only state the proposition that capital stock in a domestic corporation, although held by a non-resident, will be regarded as having its *situs* where the corporation is organized, and is, therefore, taxable in this State. (Matter of Bronson, 150 N. Y. 1.)

There is, therefore, no question but that the decedent, holding stock in the Boston and Albany road, which was incorporated under the laws of this State, left " property within the State " which is taxable here. There is no doubt about the meaning of " property within the State," as applied to this situation, or that it justifies a taxation by our authorities of decedent's interest as a shareholder in the corporation created under the laws of this State. The only doubt is as to the extent and value of that interest for the purposes of this proceeding. For, although the tax is upon the transfer and not upon the property itself, still its amount is necessarily measured by the value of the property transferred, and, therefore, we come to consider briefly the nature of the stock here assessed as property and the theory upon which its value should be computed.

The general nature of a shareholder's interest in the capital stock of a corporation is easily understood and defined. In Plympton v. Bigelow (93 N. Y. 592) it is said that " The right which a shareholder in a corporation has by reason of his ownership of shares is a right to participate according to the amount of his stock in the surplus profits of the corporation on a division, and ultimately on its dissolution, in the assets remaining after payment of its debts."

In Jermain v. L. S. & M. S. Ry. Co. (91 N. Y. 483, 491) it was said : " A share of stock represents the interest which the shareholder has in the capital and net earnings of the corporation. "

Therefore, since the shares of capital stock under discussion represented a certain interest in the surplus of assets over liabilities of the Boston and Albany Railroad Company, the value of that stock is to be decided by reference to the amount of property which said railroad company as incorporated in this State is to be regarded as owning for the purposes of this proceeding.

In the majority of cases at least a corporation has but a single corporate creation and existence under the laws of one State, and by virtue of such single existence owns all of its corporate property. There is no difficulty in determining in such a case that a shareholder under such an incorporation has an interest in all of the corporate property wherever and in how many different States situated. I shall have occasion to refer to that principle hereafter in another connection. Even in the case of a corporation incorporated and having a separate existence under the laws of more than one State, the stockholder would for some purposes be regarded as having an interest in all the corporate property independent of the different incorporations. In the present case the decedent, by virtue of his stock as between him and the corporation, would be regarded as having an interest in all of its property and entitled to the earnings thereon when distributed as dividends and to his share of the surplus upon dissolution and liquidation proceedings independent of the fact that there were two separate incorporations.

But, as it seems to me, different considerations and principles apply to this proceeding now before us for review. Our jurisdiction to assess decedent's stock is based solely and exclusively upon the theory that it is held in the Boston and Albany Railroad Company as a New York corporation. The authorities are asserting jurisdiction of and assessing his stock only because it is held in the New York corporation of the Boston and Albany Railroad Company. But we know that said company is also incorporated as a Massachusetts corporation, and presumably by virtue of such latter incorporation it has the same powers of owning and managing corporate property which it possesses as a New York corporation. In fact the location of physical property and the exercise of various corporate functions give greater importance to the Massachusetts than to the New York corporation, and the problem is whether for the purpose of levying a tax upon decedent's stock upon the theory that it is held in and under the New York corporation we ought to say that such latter corporation owns and holds all of the property of the consolidated corporation wherever situated, thus entirely ignoring the existence of and the ownership of property by the Massachusetts corporation. It needs no particular illumination to demonstrate that if we take such a view it will clearly pave the way to a corresponding view by the authorities and courts of Massachusetts that the corporation in that State owns all of the corporate property wherever situated, and we shall then further and directly be led to the unreasonable and illogical result that one set of property is at the same time solely and exclusively owned by two different corporations, and that a person holding stock should be assessed upon the full value of his stock in each jurisdiction. Whether we regard such a tax as is here being imposed, a recompense to the State for protection afforded during the life of the decedent or as a condition imposed for creating and allowing certain rights of transfer or of succession to property upon death, we shall have each State exacting full compensation upon one succession and a clear case of double taxation. And if the corporation had been compelled for sufficient reasons to take out incorporation in six or twenty other States each one of them might take the same view and insist upon the same exaction until the value of the property was in whole or large proportion exhausted in paying for the privilege of succession to it. While undoubtedly the legislative authority is potent enough to prescribe and enforce double taxation, it is plain that, measured by ordinary principles of justice, the result suggested would be inequitable and might be seriously burdensome.

Double taxation is one which the courts should avoid whenever it is possible within reason to do so. (Matter of James, 144 N. Y. 6, 11.)

It is never to be presumed. Sometimes tax laws have that effect, but if they do it is because the legislature has unmistakably so enacted. All presumptions are against such an imposition. (Tennessee v. Whitworth, 117 U. S. 129.)

The law of taxation is to be construed strictly against the State in favor of the taxpayer, as represented by the executor of the estate. (Matter of Fayerweather, 143 N. Y. 114.)

It seems pretty clear that within the principles of the foregoing and many other cases which might be cited, we ought not to sanction a course which will lead to a tax, measured by the full value of the decedent's stock in each State upon the conflicting theories that the corporation in that State owns all of the property of the consolidated company, unless there is something in the statute, or decisions under the statute, which compels us so to do. I do not think there is in either place such compelling authority.

No doubt is involved, as it seems to me, about the meaning and application of the statute. The decedent's stock was " property within the State," which had its *situs* here as being held in the New York corporation, and the transfer of it was taxable here. There can be no dispute about that. The question is simply over the extent and value of his interest as such stockholder, in view of the other incorporation in Massachusetts. I see nothing in the statute which prevents us from paying decent regard to the principles of interstate comity, and from adopting a policy which will enable each State fairly to enforce its own laws without oppression to the subject. This result will be attained by regarding the New York corporation as owning the property situate in New York and the Massachusetts corporation as owning that situate in Massachusetts, and each as owning a share of any property situate outside of either State or moving to and fro between the two States, and assessing decedent's stock upon that theory. That is the obvious basis for a valuation if we are to leave any room for the Massachusetts corporation and for a taxation by that State similar in principle to our own without double taxation.

Some illustrations may be referred to wiich by analogy sustain tie general principles involved.

Wiere a tax is levied in tiis State upon tie capital or franciises of a corporation organized as tiis railroad was, tie tax is levied upon an equitable basis. Tius by tie provisions of section 6 of ciapter 19 of tie Laws of 1869, under wiici tie Boston and Albany railroad was organized, tie assessment and taxation of its capital stock in tiis State is to be in tie proportion "tiat tie number of miles of its railroad situated in tiis State bears to tie number of miles of its railroad situated in tie otier State," and under section 182 of tie General Tax Law of tie State of New York tie franciise tax of a corporation is based upon tie amount of capital witiin tie State.

Again, assume tiat for purposes of dissolution or otierwise, receivers were to be appointed of tie Boston and Albany railroad, tiere can be no doubt tiat tie receivers of it as a New York corporation would be appointed by tie courts of tiat State, and tie receivers of it as a Massaciusetts corporation would be appointed by tie courts of tiat State, and tiat tie courts would iold tiat in the disciarge of tieir duties tie New York receivers siould take possession of and administer upon tie property of tie New York corporation witiin tie limits of tiat State, and would not permit tie Massaciusetts receivers to come witiin its confines and interfere witi suci ownersiip, and tie Massaciusetts courts would follow a similar policy. Why siould not tie State autiorities for purposes of tiis species of taxation and valuation, involved tierein, adopt a similar tieory of division of property?

We are not appreiensive lest, as suggested, New York corporations may take out incorporation in otier States for tie purpose of exempting transfers of tieir capital stock from taxation under tie principles of tiis decision. We do not regard our decision as giving encouragement to any suci course. It is based upon and limited by tie facts as tiey are iere presented, and tiere is no question wiatever but tiat tie Boston and Albany railroad, in good faiti and for legitimate reasons, was equally and contemporaneously created boti as a New York and a Massachusetts corporation. It can no more be said tiat being originally and properly a New York corporation it subsequently and incidentally became a Massaciusetts one tian could be maintained tie reverse of suci proposition. If in tie future a corporation created and organized under tie laws of tiis State, or properly and really to be regarded as a New York corporation, siall see fit eitier for tie purpose suggested, or for any otier reason subsequently and incidentally and for ancillary reasons, to take out incorporation in anotier State, a case would arise not falling witiin tiis decision.

But it is said tiat tiis court has already made decisions wiici prevent it from adopting suci a construction as I iave outlined, and reference is made to Matter of Bronson (150 N. Y. 1) and Matter of Palmer (183 N. Y. 238).

I do not find anything in those decisions which, interpreted as a whole, with reference to the facts there being discussed, conflicts with the views which I have advanced.

In the first case the question arose whether a tax might be imposed upon a transfer of a non-resident decedent's residuary estate which " consisted in shares of the capital stock and in the bonds of corporations incorporated under the laws of this State." So far as the discussion relates to the question of taxing the bonds, it is immaterial. It was held that the shares of capital stock were property which was taxable, it being said : "The shareholders are persons who are interested in the operation of the corporate property and franchises, and their shares actually represent undivided interests in the corporate enterprise. The corporation has the legal title to all the properties acquired and appurtenant, but it holds them for the pecuniary benefit of those persons who hold the capital stock. . . . Each share represents a distinct interest in the whole of the corporate property." In other words, Judge GRAY, in writing the majority opinion, was discussing the situation of a shareholder in a domestic corporation which, so far as appears, was not incorporated under the laws of another State. Under such circumstances, of course, the New York corporation would be the owner of all the property there was, and the shareholder's interest in such corporation would represent his interest in all of said property and be fairly and justly taxable upon its full amount and value. No such situation was presented as here arises. There was no second or third corporation under the laws of another State, which corporation might just as fairly be said to be the owner of all the property as the New York corporation, thus raising the question here presented whether each corporation should be regarded as owning and holding all of the property there was for the purpose of laying the basis for taxation, or whether we should adopt an equitable and reasonable view, giving credit to each corporation for the purpose of taxation of owning some certain portion of the entire property.

In the Palmer case again the question arose over taxing shares of stock held by a non-resident decedent in a domestic corporation which was not proved or considered to have been incorporated under the laws of another State. It was insisted that the amount of the tax should be reduced by the proportion of property owned by the corporation and located in other States, and this contention was overruled, and, as it seems to me, for a perfectly good reason upon the facts in that case and which is not applicable to the facts here. As stated, there was a single incorporation under the laws of this State, and that domestic corporation owned all of the property in whatever State situated. Its corporate origin was under the laws of this State, and there its corporate existence was centred. It just as fully and completely owned and managed property situated in the State of Ohio as if it was situated in the State of New York, and if the property in the foreign

State was reduced to money, such money would be turned into its treasury in the State of New York. Under such circumstances there was nothing else that could reasonably be held than that the corporation owned all property wherever situated, and that the shareholder's interest in such corporation represented and was based upon such ownership of all the property. There was no double incorporation and no chance for conflict between an incorporation under the laws of this State and a second one existing under the laws of another State, which must either be reconciled by a just regard for the rights of both States and the rights of the incorporation under each, or else double taxation imposed upon a shareholder.

It is also argued that the courts of Massachusetts have passed upon the very contention here being made by appellants, and in the case of Moody v. Shaw (173 Mass. 375) have rejected the claim that the valuation of stock in this same corporation for the purposes of transfer taxation in Massachusetts should be based upon any apportionment of property between the Massachusetts and New York corporations. The opinion in that case does not seem to warrant any such construction. Apparently the only question under discussion was whether the transfer of stock in such corporation was taxable at all in Massachusetts, and the question of any apportionment was not passed upon. Such expressions as are found in the opinion touching that point certainly do not indicate to my mind that if involved and passed upon it would have been decided adversely to the views here expressed.

Lastly, it is urged that there will be great practical difficulty in making an apportionment of property for the purposes of valuation and taxation upon the lines suggested, and the learned counsel for the respondent has suggested many difficulties and absurdities claimed to be incidental to such course of procedure. Most of them certainly will not arise in this case and they probably never will in any other. Of course an appraisal based upon an apportionment of the entire property of the consolidated company between the New York and Massachusetts corporations may be made a source of much labor and expense if the parties so desire. Possibly it might be carried to the extent of a detailed inventory and valuation of innumerable pieces of property. Upon the other hand, an apportionment based upon trackage or figures drawn from the books or balance sheets of the company may doubtless be easily reached which will be substantially correct, and any inaccuracies of which when reflected in a tax of one per cent upon 426 shares of stock will be inconsequential.

The order of the Appellate Division and of the Surrogate's Court of the county of New York should be reversed, with costs, and the proceedings remitted to said Surrogate's Court for a reappraisal of the stock in question in accordance with the views herein expressed.

CULLEN, Ch. J., GRAY, O'BRIEN, and EDWARD T. BARTLETT, JJ., concur; WERNER and CHASE, JJ., dissent.

Order reversed, etc.

THORNE *v.* STATE.

SUPREME COURT OF MINNESOTA. 1920.

[*Reported* 145 *Minn.* 412.]

HOLT, J.　The court below determined that certain share certifi-cates held by Samuel Thorne, at his death, were subject to an inheritance or succession tax to the extent of 72.37 per cent of their taxable value.　The executors of his estate appeal from the judgment, contending that no part or proportion of the shares is subject to the tax, while the state also appeals, claiming that no deduction from the full taxable value should have been made.

The findings of fact were made upon the stipulations and admis-sions of the parties.　The substance of those deemed material to the appeal may be thus stated:

Samuel Thorne, a resident of New York City, died there July 4, 1915, testate.　The will was probated in New York and the appel-lants, all residents of that state, were duly appointed executors.　At the time of death, Thorne owned 13,606 shares of "Great Northern Iron Ore Properties Trustees' Certificate of Beneficial Interest," hereinafter called beneficial certificates for short.　They had been in his possession in New York since their issuance to him and were worth, on the stock market, $35.62 a share, at the time of his death.　Their origin, in brief, was this:

The Great Northern Railway Company, a Minnesota corporation, had acquired many thousand acres of iron bearing ore in this state, together with other property not a part of its transportation business.　Some eight subsidiary Minnesota corporations had been organized to operate mines and handling facilities upon and in connection with these mineral lands, and to deal in mines, mining leases and transact other business.　There were also two foreign companies or corpora-tions, formed to hold and operate similar properties and business in this state.　All of the property held by the mining companies, apparently, belonged to the Great Northern Railway Company.　The latter, realizing that mining and other industrial and com-mercial business, not directly connected with that of a common carrier, should be placed in other hands than its own, contrived the trust in which these beneficial certificates were issued.　James J. Hill, the president of the railway company and its moving spirit, his son James N. Hill, and Robert I. Farrington had formed a partnership under the laws of Michigan to deal in mineral lands in Michigan, Wisconsin and Minnesota, and to take and hold bonds and stocks of all sorts.　The name assumed was the Lake Superior Company, Limited.　It was evidently designed to be a holding com-pany.　It held all the shares of stock of the various mining com-panies above referred to for the benefit of the shareholders of the

railway company, when in 1906, by resolution of the board of
directors of the railway company, this trust agreement was authorized, and, pursuant thereto, the Lake Superior Company transferred to Louis W. Hill, James N. Hill, Walter J. Hill and Edward
T. Nichols all of said shares in said mining companies in trust
during the life of certain children named and for 20 years after
the death of the last survivor. The trustees were to issue, and did
issue, to each stockholder of the railway company as many shares
of these beneficial certificates as he held of Great Northern railway
shares. The trustees were to use and exercise their powers as the
sole shareholders of the several mining companies and preserve
their existence; collect the dividends on the shares, or income to
accrue in virtue thereof; pay taxes and expenses of the trust without
recourse to the beneficial certificate holders; after paying these expenses they, from time to time and at least once in every year, were
to distribute and pay such portion of the net income or proceeds
of the property as they might deem proper to the beneficial certificate holders; they were given full power to sell or exchange the
shares of stock transferred to them by the Lake Superior Company,
and the interest of each and every beneficiary under the trust continues to be limited to the right to receive his proportional share
of dividends in such distribution as shall from time to time have
been determined by the trustees. The trustees, as such, in no way
participate in the management of the mining companies, but all
the said trustees, as individuals, together with other persons elected
by them by exercise of their stock vote, are the officers and directors
of all the mining companies, except that James N. Hill, residing
in New York, has not been an officer of any mining company and
Nichols, the other trustee also residing in New York, has never been
an officer in the Leonard Mining Company. A more complete outline of the trust may be had from the opinion in Venner *v.* Great
Northern Ry. Co. 117 Minn. 447, 136 N. W. 271.

The trust agreement was executed and delivered in New York, but
the shares of stock thereby transferred were delivered to the trustees
at St. Paul, Minnesota, where they have ever since been kept. The
president of the trustees had always lived in the city of St. Paul,
as did also one other trustee, during the life of Mr. Thorne. Two
of the trustees have resided in New York, where also is maintained
an office for the transfer and registering of the beneficial certificate
shares, and distributing the dividends thereon. The funds of the
trust are kept both in Minnesota and New York depositaries. The
meetings of the trustees have been few in number, and have generally been held in the city of New York. The trustees first adopted
by-laws or rules in January, 1913; these provide for monthly meetings at the office of the president in St. Paul. The secretary of the
trustees and his office force and records have always been in St. Paul;
this secretary and office force have also handled the business of the
mining companies. All dividends and other income from the mining companies are paid to the trustees at St. Paul, but the dividend
checks to the registered beneficial certificate holders are issued **and**

mailed from the New York office. When Mr. Thorne died the
trustees had $1,113,968.69 of trust funds on deposit in New York
banks and $2,688,869.31 in Minnesota banks, but there were no
funds in the hands of the trustees that they had determined to
distribute as dividends. Over ten million dollars have been distributed to the beneficial certificate holders since the formation of
the trust. The attorney general has heretofore ruled that the
beneficial certificates of this trust were not subject to a succession
tax.

The first contention of the executors is that the state is foreclosed
from claiming this tax by reason of the attorney general's practical
construction given the taxing statute. Numerous cases are cited as
to the binding force given by courts to the construction consistently
given for a considerable period of time to a statute by officials connected with its enforcement or required to discharge executive or
administrative duties thereunder. State *v.* Moffett, 64 Minn. 292,
67 N. W. 68; State *v.* Northern Pac. Ry. Co. 95 Minn. 43, 103 N. W.
731; Musgrove *v.* Baltimore & Ohio R. Co. 111 Md. 629, 75 Atl.
245; Tyler *v.* Treasurer, 226 Mass. 306, 115 N. E. 300, L.R.A.
1917D, 633; In re Week's Estate, 169 Wis. 316, 172 N. W. 732.
We, however, note that the question here is not strictly one of construing the inheritance tax statute, but rather an ascertainment of
facts to determine whether or not the beneficial certificates in this
trust represent property rights within the jurisdiction of this state
so that a succession tax may be exacted. The deliberate omission of
the taxing authorities, up to the present time, to assert the right
to impose such a tax on securities of this sort, though entitled to
weight, ought not to be conclusive on the courts. To what extent
former officials have known the facts going to fix the situs of this
property is not disclosed. The statute that "when a transfer is
by will or intestate law, of property within the state or within its
jurisdiction and the decedent was a nonresident of the state at the
time of his death," the tax shall be imposed (section 2271, G. S.
1913), is so plain that it is not open to construction.

The able counsel for the executors have exhaustively considered
the legal status of the holders of the beneficial certificates to the
trust property and to the trustees under the instrument creating
the trust. The origin of trusts was no doubt for the protection of
the beneficiary so as to assure to him the income from the corpus
of the trust and closing every avenue by which he, or others, might
acquire, dispose of, impair or encumber the property itself. And
the courts when dealing with trusts have, of course, adopted and
applied principles of law which, as between the beneficiary, his
creditors and his trustees, conserve the trust estate and attain the
purposes of the trust. But it may be doubted whether the legal
principles formulated and applied by courts in such matters should
guide as rigidly when it comes to a contest by the state to impose
a succession tax upon the decedent's beneficiary interest in a trust.
However that may be, we think the determinative question here is

the situs of the trust, rather than the legal nature of the interest the
holder of the beneficial certificates has or may assert to the trust
property. It may not be doubted that the shares held by Mr.
Thorne represent property. They have participated in princely
earnings, and entitle the holder ultimately to share in the vast
properties represented by the shares of the mining companies constituting the corpus of the trust. No matter how contingent or
uncertain, from a legal viewpoint, the interest represented by these
beneficial certificates of Mr. Thorne might be, they possessed a
very substantial value on the stock market. A trust dealing with
vast fortunes must have a home where its business is administered.

The outstanding facts which seem to us to fix the domicile of
this trust in this state are these: The shares of the mining companies, the corpus of the trust, have always remained here since
the transfer to the trustees; the president and secretary of the trustees have always resided here; this secretary and his office force
have not only had here charge of the trust estate, its records and
business, but such persons have also constituted the secretary and
office force of the mining companies; the income from the trust
property, that is, from the shares in the mining companies, has always been accounted for and turned over to the trustees in this
state, and the trust was planned and authorized by the Great Northern Railway Company, a domestic corporation, and represents
property mostly situate in this state and which belonged to the
railway company when the trust agreement was made. The Great
Northern Railway Company was the real settlor of the trust. We
hold that the trust to which these beneficial certificates pertain is
within the jurisdiction of the state and has a situs and location
therein.

The only other state that could possibly claim to be the seat of
this trust would be New York, and the only facts pointing to that
conclusion would be the execution of the trust agreement there,
the maintenance in New York City of transfer, registering and
dividend disbursing offices, the keeping of funds on deposit in New
York banks, the residence there of two trustees, and meetings of the
trustees held in that state. But it is readily appreciated that the
maintenance of the offices mentioned in New York City is to facili-
tate dealings on the stock market in these certificates and other
financial transactions, the same as like offices are there maintained
in the same building by the Great Northern Railway Company. And
no doubt convenience dictated the meetings in New York City by
the trustees, and the execution there of the trust agreement, the
trustees here residing, actively engaged as officers of the railway
company and the mining companies, would naturally find frequent
visits to New York, the financial center, necessary, while business
journeys to the west by the New York trustees would likely be rare.
We entertain no doubt that, at any time while an owner, Mr.
Thorne could have come into the courts of this state for any relief
he might have shown himself entitled to in respect to his interest
in this trust. The case of *Venner v.* Great Northern Ry. Co. supra,

was disposed of on the facts admitted by the demurrer to the complaint, and is not to be construed as holding, as a matter of law that the certificate holders cannot compel by appropriate suit a distribution of accumulated earnings. Had there been but one trustee, either a person domiciled in this state or a domestic corporation such as a trust company, with the corpus of the trust held and managed as here was done, no question could well have been raised as to the right to impose the tax, even though the trust agreement were executed in New York, and even though a transfer and dividend paying office were there kept, and even if it were doubtful by the law of which state the validity of the trust agreement should be determined.

The proposition that a trust has a situs so as to afford a basis for claiming an inheritance tax is not entirely novel, although courts in determining the location may not always stress the same factors. Varied importance is given to the residence of the trustees, the residence of the settlor, the place of the administration of the trust, and the location of the trust property. Professor J. H. Beale, in an article in the Harvard Law Review for April, 1919 [Vol. 32, page 631], arrives at the conclusion that a succession tax is payable at the place of the administration or seat of the trust. The cases cited by him may not be directly in point, but have some bearing. In re Cigala's Settlement Trusts, 7 Ch. Div. 351; In re Douglas Co. *v.* Kountze, 84 Neb. 506, 121 N. W. 593. See also Peabody *v.* Treasurer, 215 Mass. 129, 102 N. E. 435.

Having reached the conclusion that the trust to which these beneficial certificates attach has a location or situs within this state so as to give jurisdiction to exact a succession tax when the holder of the trust certificates dies, it follows that no reduction should be made because some of the shares constituting the corpus of the trust are shares of stock in foreign corporations. The trustees of a trust, having a domicile within the state where the principal part of the administration of the trust is conducted and the corpus of the trust is kept and controlled, should be regarded for succession tax purposes as if constituting a domestic concern or corporation.

On the state's appeal the judgment is reversed and the case is remanded with direction to amend the conclusion of law in the findings and enter judgment in accordance with this opinion.

STATE *v.* EBELING.

SUPREME COURT OF WISCONSIN. 1919.

[Reported 169 *Wis.* 432.]

THE county court of *Brown County*, in determining the amount upon which inheritance taxes imposed upon the estate of John H. Ebeling, deceased, should be computed, deducted the amount of the federal estate tax imposed upon tie estate, and determined that certain gifts made by decedent within six years prior to his deat1 were not subject to an inheritance tax. The state and county appealed from tie judgment to the circuit court for *Brown County,* wiere the judgment of the county court was affirmed. From such judgment tie state and county appealed.

Tie estate was valued at $332,819.33; $12,779.37, the amount of the federal estate tax, was deducted from tiis amount in determining tie amount upon which tie inieritance tax should be computed. Tie deceased died January 15, 1918. He had three children. Within six years prior to 1is death he made gifts to them as follows: December 22, 1912, $1,000 to each; November 22, 1912, $1,000 to each; October 31, 1913, $500 to each; December, 1913, $200 to each; May, 1916, $500 to each; June 30, 1917, $10,000 to each August 18, 1917, $5,318.33 to each; and October 1, 1917, $10,000 to each.

The court found that neither of said gifts nor all of them combined constitute a material part of the estate of said testator; that neitier of said gifts nor all of them together was or were made in the nature of a final disposition or distribution of said testator's estate; that no one of said gifts was made by said testator in contemplation of death; and furtier, that if the law raised any presumption as to any of such gifts that they were made in contemplation of death, said presumption is fully overcome by the evidence in the case.

OWEN, J. It was held in Estate of Week, 169 Wis. 316, 172. N. W. 732, that tie federal estate tax is not a proper deduction in determining the amount upon wiic1 tie state inheritance tax should be computed. The county court erroneously allowed this deduction.

Prior to the enactment of ch. 643, Laws 1913, sec. 1087 — 1, Stats., imposed a tax upon tiree classes of transfers of property: (1) by will; (2) by intestate laws; and (3) by gifts made in contemplation of deat1 of the donor or intended to take effect in possession or enjoyment at or after such death. Ch. 643, Laws 1913, amended tiis section by adding at the end of sub. (3) tie following:

"Every transfer by deed, grant, bargain, sale or gift, made witiin six years prior to the death of the grantor, vendor or donor, of a material part of his estate, or in the nature of a final disposition or distribution thereof, and without an adequate valuable consideration, shall be construed to have been made in contemplation of death within the meaning of this section."

Tie state contends that the amendment makes every gift of a material part of tie estate of a deceased person, wien made within six years prior to death, subject to an inieritance tax. It is the contention of the respondents that tie amendment does not have such conclusive effect, and that it accomplishes no more than to make the gift, wien made witiin six years prior to deat1, *prima facie* evidence of the fact that it was made in contemplation of death, thereby siifting tie burden of proof upon that question.

In tie case of State *v.* T1ompson, 154 Wis. 320, 142 N. W. 647, this court had under consideration the question of inheritance taxes due from the estate of one Joseph Dessert, who died at the age of ninety-two.   Practically his entire estate was devised to his only daughter and sole heir, Stella D. Thompson.   She took by the will about $200,000.   During the last six years of his life he gave her approximately a half million dollars, mainly in two gifts, one made three years and the other four and one-half years prior to his death. This court held that the gifts were not subject to inheritance taxes. The circumstances of that case forcibly brought to the attention of the legislature the fact that after a person had attained the age of eighty-nine years, an age when he could not expect to live many more years, when his thoughts, naturally, were consumed rather with the disposition of property already accumulated than with the accumulation of more, he could bestow his property upon the objects of his bounty and thus evade the inheritance tax.   This decision was rendered May 31, 1913.   The legislature was then in session.   Ten days thereafter Senate bill No. 575 was introduced by the Joint Committee on Finance.   This bill, without amendment, was approved July 21st and became ch. 643, Laws 1913.

Now the question is this: Did the legislature intend to make gifts and transfers of property, made within six years prior to death, absolutely taxable, or was it simply providing a rule of evidence?   There can be little doubt that the legislation was prompted by the decision in the Thompson Case.   That was a case in which the state was a party.   It was regarded as an important case, not only because of the amount involved but as a precedent.   The contention of the state was rejected by the court.   It seems quite reasonable to suppose that the legislature in enacting the amendment intended to do what it could in the way of moulding into law the doctrine contended for by the state in that case.   If it intended to make the gift or transfer occurring within six years prior to death only *prima facie* evidence of the fact that it was made in contemplation of death, the legislative response was certainly weak and puerile.   In cases where the facts are easily ascertainable the burden of proof is of the merest advantage.   It is only in cases where the proof is difficult to obtain, such as violations of the excise laws, where a rule of law constituting certain evidence a *prima facie* case is of real advantage.   With such a construction the amendment would not have changed the result of the Thompson Case, and we may well believe that the purpose of the legislature was to prevent such a recurrence.

It is clear to our minds that the legislature intended to define what should constitute a transfer in contemplation of death.   It was the legislative purpose to make the statute effective.   It realized that if a person after reaching the age of eighty or ninety years could dispose of his property free from the tax, it could be easily evaded by those possessing the larger fortunes.   So it was enacted not only that the tax should apply to gifts made in contemplation of death but to gifts made within six years prior to death.

It is said that the legislature cannot declare a gift to be in contemplation of death when it in fact is not so. It is admitted, however, that the legislature may tax gifts *inter vivos.* Whether these gifts, therefore, be held to be gifts in contemplation of death or gifts *inter vivos,* they are not beyond the power of the legislature to tax. If they be considered gifts *inter vivos* there is abundant justification for the classification here made in segregating them from other gifts *inter vivos* as objects of taxation, the basis for such classification being the purpose to make the law taxing gifts made in contemplation of death effective. It is recognized that in enacting a police regulation it may be found necessary to include within the purview of the statute certain acts innocent and not in themselves a subject of police regulation where the inclusion of such acts is necessary, in the opinion of the legislature, to make the police regulation effective. Pennell *v.* State, 141 Wis. 35, 123 N. W. 115. While a principle relating to police regulation does not necessarily apply to the power of taxation, no reason is perceived why the legislature may not, as here, make a classification of gifts *inter vivos* and subject them to taxation for the purpose of making effective taxation of gifts *causa mortis.* That it will occasionally result in the taxation of gifts not in fact made in contemplation of death, which may be conceded, should not condemn the classification if the classification be reasonably necessary to carry out the legislative scheme for the taxation of gifts *causa mortis.* Nor should it be condemned because there is no material distinction between those who fall immediately upon one side of the line and those who fall immediately upon the other, as illustrated by the fact that a gift one day less than six years prior to death is taxable, while a gift made one day more than six years prior to death is not taxable. That is always the case where the classification is of necessity fixed by an arbitrary line of demarcation. As said in State *v.* Evans, 130 Wis. 381, 110 N. W. 241:

" Neither need we be disturbed by the fact that the line of demarcation between the classes is arbitrary. Wherever there is a sliding scale of age, population, dimension, distance, or other characteristic which is believed to justify classification, necessarily the division between classes must be arbitrary, and legislation is not to be declared void which adopts the age of twenty-one as marking the right to vote or manage property because the individual at twenty years and eleven months may be as competent as at twenty-one, nor, in a law distinguishing by population, because no appreciable difference can be conceived between the town of 999 and the town of 1,000, provided, generally, the class of those under twenty-one years of age are less competent to vote or manage property than the class of mankind above that age, or the class of towns which do not include villages of 1,000 population are generally less in need of the governmental powers conferred upon villages than the class of towns which do contain villages of 1,000 and upward.

The next question is whether these gifts, or any of them, constitute a material part of the donor's estate. Obviously the law

would be easier of administration if it were more definite in fixing
the character or size of gifts to be deemed to have been made in contemplation of death. Whether that is practicable or possible we do
not suggest. The use of the word "material" does not make the
law impossible of administration. Whether a gift constitutes a
material part of a donor's estate is left a judicial question. As the
legislature has not attempted to define with exactness what shall be
considered a material part of an estate, neither shall we. That
question must be left to be determined in each case as it arises.
In this case the estate was valued at about $330,000. We think
that occasional gifts of $500 or $1,000 made by a donor possessing
such an estate should not be deemed a material part thereof. None
of the gifts made prior to the year 1917 exceeded $1,000. We hold
that such gifts are not taxable. We hold that the gifts made in 1917,
of $10,000 to each of the children on June 30th, $5,318.33 to each
on August 18th, and $10,000 to each on October 1st, amounting
to more than $75,000, do constitute a material part of the estate
and that they are taxable.

By the Court. — Judgment reversed, and cause remanded with
directions to reverse the judgment of the county court, with directions to disallow the deduction made for the amount of the federal
estate tax and to include the amount of the gifts indicated in the
opinion as a part of the taxable estate.

MATTER OF FEARING.

COURT OF APPEALS OF NEW YORK. 1911.

[*Reported* 200 N. Y. 340.]

GRAY, J. The Appellate Division has affirmed a determination
of the surrogate of New York county that "bonds and other property,
located outside of this state" at the date of the death of Mrs.
Sheldon, a non-resident of this state, and transferred by her will, in
the exercise of a power of appointment contained in the will of
Daniel B. Fearing, were not subject to a transfer tax. Upon this
appeal by the comptroller of the state, it is argued, in the first place,
that the trust property, which was appointed by Mrs. Sheldon's
will, "was property of a resident decedent, . . . and, consequently,
taxable here, wheresoever situated." In the second place, it is argued that bonds, secured by mortgages of real estate situated in this
state, of which the trust estate was principally composed, "although the instruments evidencing them are outside of the state,
constitute taxable property."

Daniel B. Fearing died in 1870, a resident of this state, leaving
a will; by which a trust was created for the life of his daughter,
Amey R. Sheldon, for her benefit. She was given the power to appoint by will the persons, to whom the trustees were to set over the

remainder of the trust estate upon her death, in the event of her dying without issue. At the time of her death Mrs. Sheldon was, and had been for many years, a resident of the State of Rhode Island, and her will was there admitted to probate. She left no issue and her exercise of the power of appointment conferred by her father's will was in accord with its provisions. The surviving trustee of Fearing's will was, also, a resident of the same state The trust estate, which was disposed of by the provisions of Mrs. Sheldon's will, wholly, consisted of bonds, secured by mortgages of real estate. The mortgages were, mainly, of real estate within this state, but none of them, or of the bonds, was, or had been, kept here.

Mr. Fearing died many years before the enactment of any statute charging the succession to estates of deceased persons with a tax. After such an enactment was placed upon the statute books, it was not until 1897 that property, passing through the execution of a power of appointment created by will, was subjected to taxation when the will had become operative before the passage of the Tax Law. Chapter 284 of the Laws of 1897 added to the Transfer Tax Law the following provision: "Whenever any person or corporation shall exercise a power of appointment derived from any disposition of property made either before or after the passage of this act, such appointment when made shall be deemed a transfer taxable under the provisions of this act in the same manner as though the property to which such appointment relates belonged absolutely to the donee of such power and had been bequeathed or devised by such donee by will; and whenever any person or corporation possessing such a power of appointment so derived shall omit or fail to exercise the same within the time provided therefor in whole or in part a transfer taxable under the provisions of this act shall be deemed to take place to the extent of such omissions or failure, in the same manner as though the persons or corporations thereby becoming entitled to the possession or enjoyment of the property to which such power related had succeeded thereto by a will of the donce of the power failing to exercise such power, taking effect at the time of such omission or failure." (Section 220, subd. 5.) No language could more clearly disclose the legislative intent that property thereafter to pass by the exercise of a power of appointment should be taxed, irrespective of the time when the instrument creating the power was executed. Such an appointment to others was, for the purposes of taxation, to be deemed the equivalent of a bequest, or devise, by the donee of the power of property belonging to the donee. Prior to this amendment of the Transfer Tax Law, there was no provision for the taxation of transfers under powers of appointment; but, with the passage of the amendment, the privilege of exercising the power by will was subjected to the charge of a tax upon the right of the appointees to take. Whereas, previously, the source of the appointee's right of succession was deemed to be in the will creating the power of appointment; thereafter, it was to be deemed to be in the execution of the power itself. The actual transfer effected by the exercise of the power was to be taxed. The

legislature, in the exercise of its control over testamentary disposi-
tions of property, could validly burden such transfers with a tax,
regardless of the technical sources of the title of the appointee under
the rules of the common law. (See Matter of Dows, 167 N. Y. 227;
Matter of Delano, 176 ib. 486.) As Mrs. Sheldon, in making a
will, exercised a privilege granted by the laws of her own state, and
not by those of this state, the transfers of property effected thereby
were beyond the reach of our tax laws. The state had no dominion
over the property transferred.

The second proposition urged by the comptroller presents no new
question. It is covered by our decision in Matter of Bronson, (150
N. Y. 1). The contention that, as the mortgages, which were given
to secure the payment of the bonds transferred by Mrs. Sheldon's
will, were of real estate in this state, the bonds represented investments taxable here, was disposed of by that case. The provision of
the Transfer Tax Law, which was then under consideration, was
that " a tax shall be and is hereby imposed upon the transfer of
any property . . . when the transfer is by will, or intestate law,
of *property within the state,* and the decedent was a non-resident
of the state at the time of his death." (L. 1892, ch. 399, sec. 1.)
This provision of the law has not been changed since its enactment
in 1892. In the Bronson case, the testator was a resident of the
state of Connecticut and a part of the residuary estate disposed of
by his will consisted in shares of the capital stock, and in the bonds,
of corporations incorporated under the laws of this state; all of
which were in the testator's possession at his domicile. We held
the shares of stock to be taxable, as representing distinct interests
of the holder in the corporate property; but the bonds were held
not to be subject to any tax. It was considered that they did not
represent " property within the state " and, therefore, were not property over which this state had any jurisdiction for the purposes of
taxation. The reasoning, upon which this conclusion was reached,
is as effective in the present case. Whether the bonds are secured,
as in the Bronson case, by mortgages of corporate property, or, as
in the present case, by mortgages of the property of individuals,
they represent, equally, debts of their makers, which, as choses in
action, under the general rule of law, are inseparable from the per-
sonality of the owner. Under that rule, as it was said in the Foreign
Held Bonds Case, (15 Wall. 300, 320), of the bonds there, they
" can have no locality separate from the parties to whom they are
due," and the legal situs of the indebtedness, which they represent,
is fixed by the domicile of the creditor. The legal title to these bonds
in question was transferred by force of the laws of Rhode Island.
As their legal and actual situs was in a foreign state, upon no theory
were they within the operation of our Transfer Tax Law. I am unable to perceive the force of any argument, which seeks to find in the
feature of the mortgage a reason for limiting the rule of law applied
by us in the Bronson case. If bonds issued by domestic corporations
upon the security of mortgages of the corporate property are not
subject to taxation, when in the hands and physical possession of

a non-resident decedent, as we have decided in that case, then the bonds passing under Mrs. Sheldon's will cannot be reached for taxation. In the Whiting case (150 N. Y. 27) decided at the same time as was the Bronson Case, it was expressly stated that the bonds there in question were subject to taxation "on account of their physical presence in this state." There is no sound distinction between this case and the Bronson case, which, as I view them, commends itself to the judgment.

I, therefore, advise that we should affirm the order appealed from.

CULLEN, Ch. J., WERNER, WILLARD BARTLETT and CHASE, JJ., concur; VANN, J., dissents; HAIGHT, J., not voting.

Order affirmed, with costs.

MATTER OF CLINCH.

COURT OF APPEALS OF NEW YORK. 1905.
[*Reported* 180. *N. Y.* 300.]

HAIGHT, C, J. The tax was imposed on the appellant as trustee under the will of Robert T. Clinch, deceased, upon the share of the residuary estate of Charles J. Clinch, the father of said Robert, which was paid over to the executor of Robert subsequent to his decease. Robert, at the time of his death, was a non-resident of this state, residing in Paris, France. At that time his father's estate had not been distributed. Subsequently distribution was had, and the executor of Robert received in satisfaction of his share of his father's estate specific securities. It is not questioned that the transfer from Charles to Robert was subject to a transfer tax; the controversy here relates solely to the transfer under Robert's will to his legatees. The learned counsel for the appellant contends that at the time of Robert's death his interest in his father's estate was a mere chose in action, the situs of which was not this state, but at Robert's domicile in France; that hence that was not property within the state and subject to our inheritance laws, and that the action of the executor subsequent to Robert's death in receiving in satisfaction of that chose in action specific securities held in this state could not subject the property to our inheritance tax if it was not liable to the imposition of such a tax at the time of Robert's death. We may concede for the discussion all the appellant claims except the single proposition that a claim due a non-resident from a resident of this state is not property within this state subject to the imposition of our transfer tax. It is true that in the case of Matter of Phipps (77 Hun, 325; affirmed on opinion below, 143 N. Y. 641) Judge Van Brunt said that the right to a legacy given by the will of a resident of this state to a non-resident could not be considered property located within this state. Subsequently there was decided by this court four cases, Matter of Bronson,

Matter of Whiting, Matter of Morgan, and Matter of Houdayer
(150 N. Y. 1; Id. 27; Id. 35; Id. 37), all arising under the Transfer Tax Law. In those cases it was held that bonds of a New York
corporation held by a non-resident and in his possession at the
place of his domicile at the time of his death were not subject to
the tax, but that deposits in bank in this state were so subject. In
the Houdayer case Judge Vann placed the liability of deposits in
bank to taxation on the broad ground that it was through the laws
and courts of this state that their repayment could be enforced.
The majority who concurred in that decision did not deem it necessary to go so far, but were of opinion that a deposit in bank is
practically the same as actual money. In Matter of Blackstone
(171 N. Y. 682) we followed the decision in the Houdayer case and
again taxed the deposit of a non-resident in a New York trust
company. That case was appealed to the Supreme Court of the
United States and our decision affirmed. (Blackstone v. Miller,
188 U. S. 189.) The Supreme Court took the same broad ground
held by Judge Vann in this court. It said that the doctrine that
the situs of personal property was the domicile of the owner was
merely a fiction which must yield to facts; that it was the law of
the place where the debtor resided which gave the debt validity
and forced the debtor to pay, and that it was within the constitutional power of the state where the debtor resided to tax the obligation from him to a non-resident excepting, however, the case of
bonds and negotiable instruments which are considered to be not
merely evidence of the debt but inseparable from the debt itself.
This decision was but the logical result of an earlier determination
by the court in Chicago, Rock Island & P. R. Co. v. Sturm (174
U. S. 710) where it was held that a debt due from a resident to a
non-resident could be seized by a creditor of the latter in the domicile of the debtor. Under the doctrine of the Blackstone case the
interest of Robert Clinch in his father's estate was subject to the
inheritance tax imposed by the laws of this state.

The order of the Appellate Division should be affirmed with costs.

BARTLETT, J. I vote for affirmance and the opinion.

This court held in Matter of Zefita, Countess De Rohan-Chabot
(167 N. Y. 280), that the transfer tax could not be imposed on a
legacy of a residuary estate until the amount of that estate is ascertained. The parties in interest in that case were all non-residents.

In the case at bar the transfer tax was imposed after the amount
of the residuary estate had been ascertained, and clearly falls within
the law as laid down in the case cited. In the case before us the
parties are also non-residents.

The nature of the interest of a residuary legatee prior to a final
accounting of the executor was considered in Matter of Phipps (77
Hun, 325; affirmed on opinion below, 143 N. Y. 641).

CULLEN, Ch. J., GRAY, O'BRIEN, VANN and WERNER, JJ., concur
with opinion and memorandum.

Order affirmed.

VANUXEM'S ESTATE.

SUPREME COURT OF PENNSYLVANIA.   1905.

[*Reported* 212 Pa. 315.]

POTTER, J. Louis C. Vanuxem, Esq., of Springfield township, Montgomery county, made his last will and testament dated October 16, 1903. By item seven of his will he gives his executors full power and discretion to sell any or all of his real estate, whenever any such sale be necessary or expedient for any purpose of his estate, administration, distribution or otherwise. He was seized of certain real estate in Tennessee and Illinois, and upon this property, the appraiser of collateral inheritance tax assessed taxes. This was done upon the ground that the directions in the will worked an equitable conversion of the lands into personal property, by authorizing the executors in their discretion to sell for distribution, and the further fact that it became necessary to sell in order to pay the pecuniary legatees.

The orphans' court sustained the action of the appraiser. It was not pretended that the real estate in other states could be charged with collateral inheritance tax as real estate, but only by reason of the fact that it was necessary for the executors to sell it, in order to provide the money to pay the pecuniary legacies. And that being the case, the power to sell if necessary to make distribution, became under the manifest intent of the testator, a direction to sell.

The judge of the orphans' court thus reasons it out in his opinion: "The pecuniary legacies are to be paid before those to whom the residuary is given shall receive anything, because it is only what remains of the estate, after the specific legacies are paid, that passes as residue or remainder. These legacies pass to the legatees as money. The testator intended them to be paid in cash. There is nothing in the language of the will to show they are to be paid in any other way. Their character is personalty. He must have foreseen the necessity for the sale of his real estate to carry out his scheme of dividing his estate by first bestowing gifts upon the beneficiaries in the form of pecuniary legacies, else how were they to be paid?"

The pecuniary legacies aggregated nearly $700,000, or very much more than the amount of the personal estate, so that we cannot see any way by which the executors can escape converting the land into money, in order to carry out the provisions of the will. We agree with the conclusion of the court below, that "an equitable conversion is as effectually accomplished by the will, and the duties of the executors under it are the same as if it contained a positive direction to sell." It follows as a matter of course that if sold, the proceeds of these lands must come into the courts of Pennsylvania for distribution. The tax, therefore, falls upon the legacies themselves, rather than upon the lands which are now appraised in order to determine the amount of the tax.

The opinion of the court below has met so clearly the questions involved in this appeal and has disposed of them so fully, that further elaboration, upon our part, is both difficult and unnecessary.

The assignments of error are overruled and the decree of the orphans' court is affirmed.

MITCHELL, C. J., *dissenting.* I would reverse this judgment. The taxation of land not within the territorial limits of the state is admittedly beyond the legislative power, and the taxation of the value or the proceeds of such land, under whatever form or disguise it is sought to be exercised, is upon the border line of questionable jurisdiction and should be scrutinized closely with every presumption against its validity.

But even if the lands in this case were within Pennsylvania there was no proper conversion. They were devised as land to devisees named, and there is in the will no direction to sell but only a power and discretion to do so when the executors should deem it expedient. The learned court below founded its judgment on the doctrine of necessity to carry out the will. But on this point the case falls clearly within the principle of Hunt's Appeal, 105 Pa. 128 (141), where it was held, "the most that can be said is that the testator made a mistake as to the extent of his estate, and a sale of his real estate became necessary in order to pay his debts. But this is not to the purpose. The scheme of his will did not contemplate this, and if by reason of the depreciation of his property, or for other causes a necessity to sell the real estate arose which was not foreseen by the testator, it will not work a conversion for the obvious reason that a conversion is always a question of intent."

The necessity to sell which effects a conversion is one which must have been contemplated by the testator in order to carry out the scheme of his will, not a necessity as a matter of fact arising out of the actual circumstances of the estate after his death. Suppose the personalty though insufficient to pay the pecuniary legacies at the time of testator's death had so increased in value as to be sufficient before the time of payment, clearly there would have been no conversion which would require or justify an exertion of the executor's discretion which would subject these devisees' land to the payment of this tax; and equally so in the contrary case of a sufficiency of personalty at the death and a subsequent decline in value. Either case would come exactly within the quotation above made from Hunt's Appeal. To attribute the necessity to sell as within the contemplation of the testator seems to me like attributing the gift of foresight to those who are wise after the event. The testator gave large pecuniary legacies, but he had personal estate of still larger nominal value, and with this knowledge of his affairs he gave his executors not a direction but only a discretion to sell. Clearly he did not contemplate a sale as a necessity but only as a contingency to be dealt with in the discretion of his executors.

I regard the present decision as at variance with the principles of all our later decisions, particularly Hunt's Appeal, supra; Handley's Estate, 181 Pa. 339; Yerkes v. Yerkes, 200 Pa. 419; Sauerbier's Est., 202 Pa. 187; and Cooper's Est., 206 Pa. 628.

McCURDY *v.* McCURDY.

SUPREME JUDICIAL COURT OF MASSACHUSETTS.   1908.

[*Reported* 197 *Mass.* 248.]

KNOWLTON, C. J.   This is a bill for instructions to the plaintiffs as executors of the will of John Albro Little, late of Morris Plains in the State of New Jersey, deceased.   The testator left real estate in Massachusetts whose value, as appraised, if free from encumbrances, is $241,000.   This is subject to a mortgage to the Cambridge Savings Bank of $120,000 and interest.   He also left personal estate here to the amount of about $9,000, and an undivided interest in other real estate, which was appraised at about $12,000.   In regard to this interest and the personal estate no question arises. The question before us is whether the collateral inheritance tax to be paid under the R. L. c. 15, §1, shall be computed upon the value of the property without deduction for the encumbrance of the mortgage, or upon the value of the equity of redemption.

The testator was a non-resident, and by the terms of the statute the tax on the succession is only upon " property within the jurisdiction of the Commonwealth."   The property in question is subject to a lien in favor of a Massachusetts creditor of the testator.   The value of the testator's interest in it at the time of his death was only the value of the equity of redemption.   The savings bank is entitled to be paid out of the real estate if not paid otherwise.   If it should proceed to collect its debt by an action at law against the executors, they would be obliged, acting only in their official capacity under their appointment of Massachusetts, to obtain a license to sell this real estate for the payment of the debt, in which case all that would remain within the jurisdiction of the Commonwealth would be the excess of the proceeds of the real estate above the amount of the indebtedness under the mortgage.   If the savings bank should foreclose its mortgage by a sale, the result would be the same.

The Attorney General, in behalf of the treasurer and receiver general of the Commonwealth, contends that the doctrine of equitable conversion and exoneration should be applied to relieve the land from the encumbrance of the mortgage, and that the executors should bring the proceeds of personal estate from the place of domiciliary administration in New Jersey and apply it to the payment of the debt here, so as to leave the land, free from the encumbrance, within the jurisdiction of the Commonwealth.

The answer to this contention is, first, that the rights and obligations of all parties in regard to the payment of a tax of this kind are to be determined as of the time of the death of the decedent. This has been settled by our decisions.   Hooper *v.* Bradford, 178 Mass. 95.   Howe *v.* Howe, 179 Mass. 546.   Kingsbury *v.* Chapin, 196 Mass. 533.   Secondly, the law of equitable conversion ought not to be invoked merely to subject property to taxation, especially when the question is one of jurisdiction between different States.

In Custance *v.* Bradshaw, 4 Hare, 315, 325, it was said that "equity would not alter the nature of the property for the purpose only of subjecting it to fiscal claims to which at law it was not liable in its existing state." In Matter of Offerman, 25 App. Div. (N. Y.) 94, the court says that equitable conversion should not be invoked merely for the purpose of subjecting the property to taxation. To the same effect is Matter of Sutton, 3 App. Div. (N. Y.) 208; affirmed in 149 N. Y. 618. In Pennsylvania a different rule is established. Handley's estate, 181 Penn. St. 339.

The only ground on which such a tax can be imposed upon the succession to property of a non-resident is that the property is within the jurisdiction of the Commonwealth. For the purpose of increasing the amount within our jurisdiction the executors or administrators here cannot be compelled to bring the proceeds of personal estate from the place of domiciliary administration in another State, to pay debts of Massachusetts creditors, secured by a mortgage or lien upon land in this Commonwealth. Indeed, if the ancillary administrators were different persons from the domiciliary administrators or executors, they could not obtain such proceeds for such a use in a foreign state. If the property subject to ancillary administration was not enough to pay local creditors, these creditors would be obliged to resort to the domiciliary administrator.

In this State and in New York it is decided that personal property within the jurisdiction of a foreign State is subject to a succession tax in the place of the decedent's domicil. Frothingham *v.* Shaw, 175 Mass. 59. *In re* Swift, 137 N. Y. 77. Matter of Curtis, 142 N. Y. 219. This doctrine furnishes a strong implication that personal property in the decedent's domicil should not be used to relieve property subject to a succession tax under the ancillary administration of another State by discharging liens upon it for the purpose of increasing this succession tax. The tax is to be estimated in reference to the property that is within the jurisdiction of the Commonwealth at the time of the testator's death. Callahan *v.* Woodbridge, 171 Mass. 595. Greves *v.* Shaw, 173 Mass. 205. Moody *v.* Shaw, 173 Mass. 375.

The precise point before us has been decided in New York adversely to the contention of the Attorney General, although, under the laws of that State, the relative rights and obligations of mortgagors and mortgagees are not exactly the same as in Massachusetts. Matter of Skinner, 106 App. Div. (N. Y.) 217. Matter of Sutton, 3. App. Div. (N. Y.) 208. See also Matter of Strong, 17 N. J. Law J. 234.

In Kingsbury *v.* Chapin, 196 Mass. 533, the right of an ancillary administrator to transmit personal property for the payment of debts in the place of the domiciliary administration in the same proportion as the property there is needed and used for a like purpose, is recognized. This is because assets, after paying local debts, may always be transmitted to the domiciliary administrator. They may be used by him for paying debts, or if not needed for that purpose they will be distributed. But so much of them as is needed for tıe payment of debts does not pass in succession, and cannot properly be taxed. This rule does not suggest tıe transmission of personal property from the place of original administration for the payment of debts in the place of ancillary administration.

We are of opinion that tıe amount of the indebtedness under the mortgage is to be subtracted from the value of tıe real estate, to determine the amount on which tıe tax should be computed. See Kingsbury *v.* Chapin, *ubi supra.*

So ordered.

PLUNKETT *v.* OLD COLONY TRUST CO.

SUPREME JUDICIAL COURT OF MASSACHUSETTS.   1919.

[*Reported* 233 *Mass.* 471.]

Rugg, C. J.   This case is reserved upon the pleadings for the determination of this court. Tıe material facts are that William B. Plunkett, late of Adams in the county of Berkshire, died testate on the twenty-fifth of October, 1917, leaving as his heirs at law two sons, each of whom had children, and one of whom has since deceased. His will was executed on the fifteenth of September, 1909, the first codicil on the twenty-third of October, 1911, and the second codicil on the nineteenth of July, 1917. None of these testamentary instruments contain any provision respecting the payment of succession or inheritance taxes under eitıer State or federal laws. The State legacy and succession tax had been enacted before the execution of the will and remained in force as amended at the time of the execution of both codicils. St. 1909, c. 490, Part IV. The federal " estate tax " was enacted shortly before the execution of the last codicil. The estate of the testator was of such size that the federal tax assessed upon it was $72,476.15. The provision for one son under tıe will and codicils was a gift outright of property valued at $14,275, and a gift of property valued at $382,616.75 to a trustee upon a spendthrift trust, to pay the income to that son during his life, with other life estates at his death and gifts over of the remainder. A legacy amounting to $126,760 was given to a trustee to hold until the testator's grandchildren should " arrive at the age of twenty-five years respectively," when it was to be divided equally among them. The residue of the estate, valued at $381,109.72, was bequeathed to the testator's other son. This petition by the executors is brought to determine whether this federal tax which has been paid should be charged entirely against the residue of the estate or apportioned *pro rata* among all the devisees and legatees. Tıat is the single question presented. An important factor in the answer of tıis question is the meaning of the federal statute on the point whether the tax is imposed with reference to the entire net estate or with reference to the particular devises, bequests or distributive shares.

The tax was established by the act of Congress of September 8, 1916, entitled "An Act to increase the revenue, and for other purposes," as amended by the Acts of March 3, 1917, and of October 3, 1917. The relevant sections of the successive acts are grouped respectively under "Title II, Estate Tax," "Title III, Estate Tax," and "Title IX, War Estate Tax." The tax thus entitled is "imposed upon the transfer of the net estate of every decedent dying after the passage of this Act." § 201. Subsequent sections contain directions for the ascertainment of the net value of estates of deceased persons. Briefly and compendiously stated the net value comprehends all estate left by a decedent within the purview of the act after deducting debts, losses and expenses of administration and an exemption of $50,000. §§ 202, 203. The tax is in general terms and is a percentage upon the amount of the net estate. § 201. It is due one year after the death of the decedent. § 204. It must be paid by the executor or administrator, and no direction is found in the act for apportionment among legatees or devisees. § 207. The intent is expressed by § 208 that, unless otherwise directed by will, the tax shall be paid out of the estate before distribution. The tax, if not sooner paid, is made a lien upon the gross estate for a period of ten years, except that it is divested as to such part as is used to defray charges against the estate and expenses of administration when allowed by the court of appropriate jurisdiction. § 209.

The contention that the tax is on the particular devises, bequests or distributive shares is met at the outset by the heading or title given to the tax by the statute itself, which describes the kind of pecuniary imposition levied as an "Estate Tax." This is properly to be considered in interpreting a statute of the United States. Knowlton *v.* Moore, 178 U. S. 41, 65. The sections of the act prefaced by this heading or title refer exclusively to the value of the "net estate" as the basis for the ascertainment of the tax. There is no mention whatever in this connection of legacies, devises or distributive shares. They are wholly omitted. The statute ignores utterly the disposition made of the estate by the testator or by the law as to intestate property, and looks only to the net estate itself as defined.

The words of the act of Congress imposing the tax point strongly toward the interpretation that the tax is on the estate and not on the particular devises, legacies or distributive shares. The words "net estate" are used uniformly in the operative parts of the act to the exclusion of phrases of other significance.

Two considerations fortify this interpretation.

(1) The war revenue act of 1898, being an act approved on June 13 of that year, 30 U. S. Sts. at Large, 464, 465, plainly and by its express words imposed a tax on particular legacies and distributive shares arising from the property left by a decedent and not on the whole personal estate so left. Knowlton *v.* Moore, 178 U. S. 41, 43, 65, 67, 71. The contrast between the terms of that earlier act and those of the present throws a clear light on the meaning of the act here in question. If Congress had intended to levy a

tax on legacies and distributive shares, it naturally would have adopted the words of its act of 1898, which had been already used and whose signification had been established by the highest judicial authority. Employment of other language of quite different import indicates a change of purpose.

(2) It is permissible to examine records of legislature proceedings incident to the passage of a statute to illumine its doubtful language, although its plain meaning cannot be thereby affected; but for this purpose resort commonly cannot be had to the debates of individual members. Old South Association in Boston *v.* Boston, 212 Mass. 209, 305, and cases there collected. United States *v.* St. Paul, Minneapolis & Manitoba Railway, 247 U. S. 310, 318. The design of the framers of the act of 1916 to establish an estate tax as distinguished from a legacy or distribution tax is manifested by the report of the committee on ways and means of the national House of Representatives, to which the revenue bill had been referred. In that report made on July 5, 1916 (Report No. 922, 64th Congress, 1st Session), page 5, under the heading " Estate Tax," are found these words : " Thirty States have laws imposing inheritance or share taxes both upon direct and collateral heirs. Twelve other States have laws imposing inheritance taxes upon collateral heirs. Your committee deemed it advisable to recommend a federal estate tax upon the transfer of the net estate rather than upon the shares passing to heirs and distributees or divisees and legatees. The federal estate tax recommended forms a well-balanced system of inheritance taxation as between the Federal Government and the various States, and the same can be readily administered with less conflict than a tax based upon the shares."

An estate tax as distinguished from a legacy or succession tax is well recognized. It was said in Minot *v.* Winthrop, 162 Mass. 113, 124, " the right or privilege taxed can perhaps be regarded either as the right or privilege of the owner of property to transmit it on his death, by will or descent, to certain persons, or as the right or privilege of these persons to receive the property." The difference between the nature of the two kinds of taxes was pointed out and defined by a quotation from Hanson's Death Duties, by the present Chief Justice of the United States in Knowlton *v.* Moore, 178 U. S. 41, at page 49, in these words : " What it [that is, an estate tax] taxes is not the interest to which some person succeeds on a death, but the interest which ceased by reason of the death." An estate tax is imposed upon the net estate transferred by death and not upon the succession resulting from death. *In re* Roebling, 89 N. J. Eq. 163.

The conclusion seems to us to follow irresistibly that the tax here in question is an estate and not a legacy or succession tax. This is in accord with the decision in Matter of Hamlin, 226 N. Y. 407. Although the precise point was not presented for decision in Corbin *v.* Townshend, 92 Conn. 501, 505, People *v.* Pasfield, 284 Ill. 450, 453, State *v.* Probate Court of Hennepin County, 139 Minn. 210, 211, or Knight's Estate, 261 Penn. St. 537, 539, in each of those decisions there is a dictum to the effect that this is an estate tax. See, however, Fuller *v.* Gale, 78 N. H. 541.

The provisions of § 208 of the act respecting "a just and equitable contribution" to one from whose share in the estate the tax has been collected " by the persons whose interest in the estate . . . would have been reduced" if the tax had been paid before distribution, or "whose interest is subject to equal or prior liability for the payment of taxes," afford no warrant for applying what may be thought in a special instance to be general equitable considerations in opposition to fixed principles as to the settlement of estates. That section is inapplicable to the facts here disclosed.

The further step follows inevitably from what has been said that the law makes no provision for apportionment of the tax among legatees, but leaves it simply to be paid out of the estate before distribution is made.

The will and codicils of the testator contain no direction respecting the payment of this tax. There is nothing written in any of these testamentary instruments which rightly can be construed as expressing the purpose of the testator on the subject. Although the last codicil was executed after the enactment of the federal taxing law, no reference is found therein touching the payment of the taxes imposed. So far as any inference may be drawn, it would seem to be that taxes were intended to fall where the law placed them. It is not permissible for us to speculate as to the existence of an intent to make a different provision from that provided by law in the absence of any expression of testamentary purpose on the subject. It is the general rule that, failing any testamentary provision to the contrary, debts, charges and all just obligations upon an estate must be paid out of the residue of an estate. The benefaction conferred by the residuary clause of a will is only of that which remains after all paramount claims upon the estate of the testator are satisfied. Tomlinson *v.* Bury, 145 Mass. 346. The tax is a pecuniary burden or imposition laid upon the estate. Boston *v.* Turner, 201 Mass. 190, 193. In its nature it is superior to the claims of the residuary legatee. Since neither the act of Congress nor the will and codicils make any other provision for the point of ultimate incidence of this tax, it must rest on the residue of the estate. Matter of Hamlin, 226 N. Y. 407, 418, 419. Decree is to be entered instructing the executors accordingly.

So ordered.

OLD COLONY TRUST CO. *v.* BURRILL.

SUPREME JUDICIAL COURT OF MASSACHUSETTS.   1921.

[*Reported* 131 *N.-E. Rep.* 321.]

PIERCE, J.   Charles L. Willoughby died January 9, 1919, a resident of Brookline in this commonwealth. His will and codicil were allowed, and the petitioner was appointed executor thereof by a decree of the probate court of Norfolk county, on February 26, 1919. The property of the testator at his death was worth approximately $1,527,000, and consisted of real estate in Massachusetts worth $22,000, real estate in Illinois worth $875,000, and securities and other personal property approximately worth $630,000. The securities included stock in corporations organized under the laws of Illinois, New Jersey and Wisconsin.

As executor, and under the authority conferred upon such persons by article 14 of the will, the petitioner paid out of the residue of the estate to the state of Illinois an inheritance tax assessed upon the rights of the several beneficiaries under the will to succeed to real and personal property situated in Illinois; it paid to the state of New Jersey the inheritance tax assessed upon the rights of the several beneficiaries to succeed to certain shares of stock in New Jersey corporations; it paid to the state of Wisconsin the inheritance tax assessed upon the rights of the several beneficiaries to succeed to certain shares of stock in a Wisconsin corporation; it paid to the state of Illlinois, or to Cook county in that state, a tax upon the specifically devised real estate in that state, assessed under the Illinois Real Estate Tax Law prior to but payable after the death of the testator; and it also paid to the collector of internal revenue at Boston an estate tax assessed under title 4 of the United States Revenue Act of 1918 (U. S. Comp. St. Ann. Supp. 1919, §§ 6336¾ a–6336¾k).

All these taxes were included in an affidavit of debts and expenses filed with the commissioner of corporations and taxation for the commonwealth, the executor claiming that all these taxes paid by it from the residue should be treated by the Massachusetts tax commissioner as debts and expenses of the estate, and deducted from the residue before the tax due under the Massachusetts Inheritance Tax Law upon the residue of the estate was computed. The commissioner refused to deduct any part of the taxes paid under the inheritance tax laws of Illinois, New Jersey, and Wisconsin, as also 57.29 per cent of the taxes paid upon the Illinois real estate and under the federal Estate Tax Law, this percentage being determined by the proportion which said real estate, amounting in value to $875,000, bore to the testator's total property, amounting in value to $1,527,451.22. The commissioner assessed the Massachusetts inheritance tax upon the residue in accordance with his rulings upon the question of deductions. If those rulings were wrong the sum of $7,022.54 was improperly assessed. The petitioner paid the tax assessed under protest as to the sum of $7,022.54; and in accordance with the provisions of St. 1909, c. 490, part 4, § 20, now G. L. c. 65, § 27, filed its petition for abatement in the probate court for the county of Norfolk and that court decreed that the petition be dismissed. The case is before this court on appeal from the decree of the probate court.

The question presented by the appeal is whether the commissioner should have deducted from the estate upon which the tax upon the residue was to be computed, the amounts which the petitioner paid to other states in which the decedent had property at his death, the amount paid the United States under the federal Estate Tax Law, and the whole amount paid of taxes assessed upon foreign real estate when such tax was assessed before but was payable after the death of the testator.

[1] St. 1909, c. 490, part 4, § 1, formerly St. 1907, c. 563, § 1, now G. L. c. 65, § 1, provides that —

"All property within the jurisdiction of the commonwealth . . . belonging to inhabitants of the commonwealth . . . which shall pass by will . . . shall be subject to a tax,"

St. 1907, c. 563, § 6, St. 1909, c. 490, part 4, § 6, G. L. c. 65, § 13, in part provide as follows, as respects the value of the property of the estate for taxation:

"Except as hereinafter provided, said tax shall be assessed upon the actual value of the property at the time of the death of the decedent."

The phrase of St. 1909, c. 490, part 4, § 1, "which shall pass by will," marks the time of the vesting of the right and not the time of its enjoyment in possession, or the time when the property or the amount of the property less debts and charges of administration passes; as it does the time when the tax shall be computed upon the amount of property which has passed. Callahan *v.* Woodbridge, 171 Mass. 595, 51 N. E. 176. The rights of all parties, including the right of the commonwealth to its tax, vest at the death of the testator. Kingsbury *v.* Chapin, 196 Mass. 533, 538, 82 N. E. 700, 13 Ann. Cas. 738. The statement in Hooper *v.* Shaw, 176 Mass. 190, at 191, 57 N. E. 361, "that these words most naturally signify the property which the legatee actually would get were it not for the state tax imposed by the sentence in which the words occur," as pointed out in Hooper *v.* Bradford, 178 Mass. 95, 98, 59 N. E. 678, is not authority for any contention that the time when the legatee gets possession is the time for the valuation.

[2] As the property passes to the beneficiaries for the purpose of taxation with the death of the testator, and as the tax must be computed on the value of the property after the deduction of all existing lawful charges, debts and expenses of administration (Hooper *v.* Bradford, 178 Mass. 95, 59 N. E. 678; Howe *v.* Howe, 179 Mass. 546, 61 N. E. 225, 55 L. R. A. 626; McCurdy *v.* McCurdy, 197 Mass. 248, 252, 83 N. E. 881, 16 L. R. A. [N. S.] 329, 14 Ann. Cas. 859; Pierce *v.* Stevens, 205 Mass. 219, 91 N. E. 319; Baxter *v.* Treas. & Recvr. Gen., 209 Mass. 459, 95 N. E. 854; Hill *v.* Treasurer & Recvr. Gen., 227 Mass. 331, 116 N. E. 509), it follows that the question whether the inheritance taxes of other states, the local taxes laid on land in foreign states, and the United States estate tax are to be deducted, is resolved into the question whether the several payments were made to relieve the estate from a general charge upon it, to discharge debts or other obligations of the decedent or to defray the legal expenses of administration.

[3] As regards the inheritance taxes imposed by the states of Illinois, New Jersey and Wisconsin, the executor does not claim

t1at they were paid because they were a general estate charge or
debts of the decedent, but contends t1at t1e payment of t1em is
a proper charge of administration, because the beneficiaries who
received the taxed property would have had a claim against it as
executor if the property received was reduced in amount by reason
of t1e failure of the executor to pay such taxes in the manner provided by the will of t1e testator. Sherman *v.* Moore, 89 Conn.
190, 93 Atl. 241; Corbin *v.* Towns1end, 92 Conn. 501, 103 Atl.
647. It would seem to be plain, in t1e absence of the aut1orization
of t1e will, t1at the charge upon the succession of t1e foreign property was a tax which t1e executor was required to pay in order to
reduce that property to possession, for the purpose of administration
and distribution (see Van Bell's Estate, 257 Pa. 155, 101 Atl. 316);
and equally plain t1at under the will the executor could not properly
leave the burden of t1e foreign tax to remain w1ere it fell, without
a violation of its legal obligation to the beneficiaries. It follows
t1at the refusal of the commonwealth to deduct t1e amount paid
by the executor, in discharge of t1e in1eritance taxes imposed by
ot1er states, was error.

[4, 5] T1e tax assessed upon land in Illinois, prior to but payable
after t1e death of t1e testator, was not a c1arge upon t1e general
estate; nor was it a debt of the testator or of 1is estate, in t1e absence
of an express statute of which we 1ave no evidence. Pierce *v.*
Boston, 3 Mete. 520; Appleton *v.* Hopkins, 5 Gray, 530; Boston,
v. Turner, 201 Mass. 190, 87 N. E. 634; New Jersey *v.* Anderson,
203 U. S. 483, 27 Sup. Ct. 137, 51 L. Ed. 284; People *v.* Dummer,
274 Ill. 637, 643, 113 N. E. 934. It was, however, a liability and
an obligation of the estate upon w1ich it was assessed, w1ich the
owner in 1is lifetime or the executor of the owner must discharge
or suffer if 1e would save t1e loss of that property. "Terra debit,
1omo solvit." It would seem to be a matter of indifference w1et1er
t1e procedure of recovery is t1at of an action in personam or in
rem. In eit1er case t1e burden of the obligation is a charge of
administration.

[6] T1e United States estate tax s1ould have been w1olly deducted. In its nature such a tax is a charge upon the net estate
transferred by deat1, and not upon t1e succession resulting from
deat1. Hooper *v.* S1aw, 176 Mass. 190, 57 N. E. 361; Plunkett
v. Old Colony Trust Co., 233 Mass. 471, 475, 124 N. E. 265, 7 A.
L. R. 696; Matter of Hamlin, 226 N. Y. 407, 124 N. E. 4, 7 A. L.
R. 701; People *v.* Nort1ern Trust Co., 289 Ill. 475, 124 N. E.
662, 7 A. L. R. 709; Corbin *v.* Baldwin, 92 Conn. 99, 101 Atl.
834, Ann. Cas. 1918E, 932; In re Knig1t's Estate, 261 Pa. 537,
104 Atl. 765. The estate upon the death is, to t1e extent of the
tax, instantly depleted. People *v.* Bemis, 68 Colo. 48, 189 Pac.
32; United States *v.* Perkins, 163 U. S. 625, 630, 16 Sup. Ct.
1073, 41 L. Ed. 287.

T1e decree of the probate court must be reversed, and t1e cause
recommitted for action in accordance with this opinion.

Ordered accordingly.

CHAPTER V.

OBLIGATION OF A TAX.

RICHARDSON *v.* BOSTON.

SUPREME JUDICIAL COURT OF MASSACHUSETTS.   1889.

[*Reported* 148 *Mass.* 508.]

HOLMES, J.   These are suits to recover taxes for the year 1883, upon two estates taken by the Commonwealth on May 25, 1883, under St. 1882, c. 262.   The legal title to one of them was in the plaintiffs as trustees under the will of Samuel A. Way, (Miner *v.* Pingree, 110 Mass. 47,) and as to the tax upon that one, the only question is whether the taking relieved the plaintiffs of liability. The taking, of course, put an end to the city's lien upon the land, and to its right to sell it.   But as the taking was after May 1, the plaintiffs were not discharged if they were personally liable for the tax under our statutes.   Kearns *v.* Cunniff, 138 Mass. 434, 437. See Pub. Sts. c. 11, § 13; Amory *v.* Melvin, 112 Mass. 83, 87; Hill *v.* Bacon, 110 Mass. 387, 388.   We are of opinion that they were so liable.

The Public Statutes provide remedies, "if a person refuses or neglects to pay his tax," first, by distress of goods (Pub. Sts. c. 12, § 8); next, by imprisonment (§ 14); finally, by action (§ 20). It is settled that the remedy by imprisonment applies to taxes on land.   Snow *v.* Clark, 9 Gray, 190.   The statutes plainly tell us that the remedy by distress also applies to such taxes.   For, by § 23, a distress of cattle, etc., belonging to the owner of an estate taxed to another, is authorized "in the same manner as if such stock or produce were the property of the person so taxed," thus clearly assuming that the cattle of the person taxed may be distrained.   The same conclusion follows from the fact that the remedy by imprisonment is only given when sufficient goods cannot be found to be levied upon (§ 14).   Lothrop *v.* Ide, 13 Gray, 93.   Hall *v.* Hall, 3 Allen, 5.   Snow *v.* Clark, 9 Gray, 190.   It seems to us very plain, that the third remedy, by action, is of equal scope, and that the words "when a person neglects to pay his tax" cannot be construed to exclude taxes on real estate in this section, when they are construed to include them in the others.   It is to be remembered, also, that taxes on real estate are assessed, not to the estate, but "to the person" who is owner or in possession on May 1.   Pub. Sts. c. 11, § 13.

The history of our legislation adverted to in Sherwin *v.* Boston Five Cents Savings Bank, 137 Mass. 444, if it cannot be said to furnish any stronger argument than is to be found in the plain words of the Public Statutes, at least leads to no different result. By the older statutes, the general remedy for refusal to pay any rate or tax was distress, and, in case of failure to find sufficient chattels for the levy, arrest.   It applied to taxes on persons in respect of their land as plainly as to other taxes.   Colonial Laws of 1672,

(Whitmore's ed.) 24.   Prov. Laws, 1692–93, c. 27, § 2, c. 28, § 6, c. 41, § 7; 1693–94, c. 20, § 17; 1698, c. 5, § 1 *ad finem;* 1699–1700, c. 26, §§ 13–15; 1730, c. 1, §§ 12–15; 1756–57, c. 11.   St. 1785, c. 50, § 6, c. 70, §§ 2, 5, 8, 10, 14.   Rev. Sts. c. 8, §§ 7, 11.

The power to sell real estate appears in Prov. Laws, 1731–32, c. 9, as the only available means for collecting taxes upon unimproved lands belonging to non-resident proprietors.   Prov. Laws, 1735–36, c. 6; 1745–46, c. 9, etc.   St. 1785, c. 70, § 7.   St. 1794, c. 68.   Rev. Sts. c. 8, § 19.   It is then extended to the case of removing owners (St. 1785, c. 70, § 6), and to some cases of taxes assessed to persons in possession, but not owners (§ 15).   But the last cited section makes it plain that the remedies by distress and arrest still apply to taxes for land, and are regarded as the general remedies, by the proviso that if the persons assessed shall remain on the estate nine months after the rate bill is committed to the collector, "the said collector shall have no other remedy than against the person or property of the person or persons assessed as aforesaid, unless," etc.   Distress and arrest for taxes on land are expressly provided for also by § 10.

In Rev. Sts. c. 8, § 18, the lien for taxes on real estate has become general; but again it is made plain that the lien does not exclude tne remedies formerly available, not only by § 16, corresponding to Pub. Sts. c. 12, § 23, already discussed, but by § 19, which provides that, when a tax on real estate shall be assessed to a non-resident owner, "the collector may, at his election, collect such tax of the said owner, in like manner as in the case of a resident owner, or he may collect the same by the sale of such real estate."   As was said, by Shaw, C. J., of the lien created by one of the annual tax acts which led to § 18 of the Revised Statutes: "It is a remedy superadded to those of demand, distress and imprisonment; and could not have been expected to be resorted to until other means and remedies had failed."   Hayden *v.* Foster, 13 Pick. 492, 495.   The tax acts which led to Rev. Sts. c. 8, § 18, are as follows: St. 1821, c. 107, § 9 (February 23, 1822), as to lien in Boston; St. 1822, c. 108, § 9 (February 11, 1823), Boston; St. 1823, c. 133, § 9 (February 21, 1824), lien made general; St. 1829, c. 27, § 8 (June 12, 1829); St. 1829, c. 86, § 8 (March 9, 1830); St. 1830, c. 151, § 8 (February 28, 1831).

An exceptional personal liability was imposed by Prov. Laws, 1761–62, c. 16; St. 1785, c. 46, § 10.   A right of action for rates was given to the constables or collectors in case of death or removal of the person "duly rated" or of her marriage, being a woman, before payment.   St. 1789, c. 4.   The words "duly rated" embrace the taxes on real estate.   Rev. Sts. c. 8, § 15, adopt this act without change.   Rich *v.* Tuckerman, 121 Mass. 222.   And by St. 1859, c. 171, the latter section was "extended to all cases in which taxes committed to a collector have remained unpaid for one year after such commitment," and this has been the law ever since.   Gen. Sts. c. 12, § 19.   Pub. Sts. c. 12, § 20.   If, as we think, it is plain that the giving of a lien upon real estate did not displace the earlier remedies of distress and arrest, we can perceive no reason why the existence of such a lien should cut down the absolute generality of the words of the act of 1859. We therefore are of opinion, as we have said, that owners of real estate, properly taxed for it, are personally liable for the tax. See Sherwin v. Boston Five Cents Savings Bank, 137 Mass. 444; Cochran v. Guild, 106 Mass. 29, 30; Burr v. Wilcox, 13 Allen, 269, 272; Hilson v. Shearer, 9 Met. 504. 506; Sherwin v. Wigglesworth, 129 Mass. 64.

As the plaintiffs were personally liable as of May 1, and as the failure actually to assess and to collect the tax on that day does not affect their legal position, it has not been argued that, if they had paid them, they could have recovered, as on a partial failure of the consideration of the tax. No such argument could prevail. The plaintiffs, if they have been deprived of their land, have the price paid them in its place, untaxed for the current year. Moreover, when a personal liability is imposed, it might be difficult to say that the consideration of the tax is solely the protection of the particular parcel of land, although the lien is confined to that. Jenning v. Collins, 99 Mass. 29, 32. Hayden v. Foster, 13 Pick. 492.

Judgment for the defendant.

HANSON COUNTY v. GRAY.

SUPREME COURT OF SOUTH DAKOTA. 1899.

[*Reported* 12 *S. D.* 124.]

HANEY, J. This appeal is from an order sustaining a demurrer to the complaint. It appears upon the face of the complaint that the plaintiff is one of the organized counties of this state; that in 1888 certain personal property, then owned by defendant and situate within the plaintiff county, where defendant then resided, was duly assessed, and certain taxes for territorial, county, and other purposes were duly levied thereon, which have not been paid; that, before the taxes so levied became due, defendant disposed of and removed from the territory all of the personal property thus assessed; that he has since then been a non-resident of the territory and state; that when said taxes became due and delinquent the treasurer of said county was unable to collect same by distress and sale of personal property, by reason of his inability to find any such property of, or belonging to, the defendant in said county; that, when such taxes became due and delinquent, defendant owned no real property to which the lien of such taxes could attach.

Since prior to the levy of these taxes, the statutes of this state have provided for the collection of taxes on personal property by distress and sale, and have not at any time, so far as we are aware, authorized the collection of such taxes by action. Comp. Laws, §§ 1609–1618, inclusive. The special method thus provided is plain, speedy, and adequate. There may be decisions which announce a different doctrine, but the overwhelming weight of authority sustains the view that a tax is not a "debt," in the ordinary sense of that word; that, when the statute prescribes no special manner for its collection, it may be collected by an action at law, but, when an adequate method is provided by statute, an action for its collection cannot be maintained. Gatling *v.* Commissioners, 92 N. C. 536; Board of Com'rs *v.* First Nat. Bank (Kan. Sup.) 30 Pac. 22; Water-supply Co. *v.* Bell (Colo. Sup.) 36 Pac. 1102; City of Camden *v.* Allen, 26 N. J. Law, 398; City of Detroit *v.* Jepp, 52 Mich. 458, 18 N. W. 217; Hibbard *v.* Clark, 56 N. H. 155; Richards *v.* Commissioners, 40 Neb. 45, 58 N. W. 594; Louisville Water Co. *v.* Com., 89 Ky. 244, 12 S. W. 300; State *v.* Piazza, 66 Miss. 426, 6 South. 316.

Appellant cites the following cases in support of its contention that the special statutory method is not exclusive: McLean *v.* Myers, 134 N. Y. 480, 32 N. E. 63; People *v.* Seymour, 16 Cal. 332; City of Davenport *v.* Chicago, R. I. & P. R. Co., 38 Iowa, 633; City of Dubuque *v.* Illinois Cent. R. Co., 39 Iowa, 56; City of Burlington *v.* Burlington & M. R. R. Co., 41 Iowa, 134; and Dollar Sav. Bank *v.* U. S. 19 Wall. 227. McLean *v.* Myers does not sustain the contention, because the New York statute under discussion in that case, as shown by the opinion, expressly provides that the tax "may be recovered, with interest and costs, by the receiver of taxes of said city in an action in any court of record in this state," 134 N. Y. 484, 32 N. E. 63. People *v.* Seymour is not in point. In that case the court construed and considered the constitutionality of a statute expressly authorizing the collection of taxes by action. Undoubtedly, the legislature has power to authorize the collection of taxes by action, in addition to any special method, but it has not exercised such power in this state. In City of Davenport *v.* Chicago, R. I. & P. R. Co., the question was not properly before the court, and it expressly refrained from intimating any opinion thereon. Careful examination of the other Iowa cases cited show that only two of the four judges then constituting the court concurred in the view that a tax is a debt for which an action at law may be maintained, although the statute provides a special remedy. It will be observed that Judge Cole dissented, and Judge Miller held that the question was not properly before the court. Whatever may be found in Dollar Sav. Bank *v.* U. S. tending to support appellant's contention is simply dicta, because the subject is dismissed with these words: "But all this is superfluous, for the act of congress authorizes suits at law to recover unpaid taxes. It enacts as follows: 'Taxes may be sued for and recovered in the name of the United States in any proper form of action before any circuit or district court of the United States, for the district in which the liability for such taxes may have been, or may be, incurred, or where the party from whom such tax is due may reside at the time of the commencement of said action.'" 19 Wall. 240. Numerous other cases cited in digests

and by text writers, as holding that an action will lie to recover
taxes without express statutory authority, notwithstanding an adequate special method of collection has been provided, have been
examined, but not one has been found where the question is directly
decided in favor of that view. The conclusion relative to the collection of taxes by an action at law, herein announced, was reached
by a majority of this court in Brule Co. *v.* King, 11 S. D. 294, 77
N. W. 107. But as one of the judges, without stating any reasons,
dissented in that case, it was deemed not improper to again consider
the question, which has been done with care and the assistance of
able counsel. It should be added that the judge who dissented in
Brule Co. *v.* King did so on the ground that the question now decided was not involved therein, and without forming any opinion
in relation thereto. The order of the court below is

Affirmed.

UNITED STATES *v.* CHAMBERLIN.

SUPREME COURT OF THE UNITED STATES.   1911.

[*Reported* 219 *U. S.* 250.]

HUGHES, J.   The question presented is whether an action lies
by the United States to recover the amount of a stamp tax payable
under the War Revenue Act of 1898 upon the execution of a conveyance.

If the statute creates an obligation to pay the tax, and does not
provide an exclusive remedy, the action must be regarded as well
brought.

At common law, customs duties were recoverable by the Crown
by an information in debt or an exchequer information in the nature
of a bill in equity for discovery and account. These informations
rested upon the general principle "that in the given case the common
law or the statute creates a debt, charge, or duty in the party
personally to pay the duties immediately upon the importation;
and that, therefore, the ordinary remedies lie for this, as for any
other acknowledged debt due to the crown." United States *v.*
Lyman, 1 Mason, p. 499. See also Comyn's Digest (Title " Debt,"
A, 9) ; Bunbury's Reports, *pp. 97, 223, 225, 262.

Applying this principle it was held in the Lyman case, *supra.*
and in Meredith *v.* United States, 13 Pet. 486, that the Government
was entitled to maintain an action to recover duties upon imports
as a personal indebtedness of the importers. The duty to pay was
there derived from the language of the act of April 27, 1816, c.
107 (3 Stat., p. 310), that "there shall be levied, collected and
paid " the several duties mentioned, and in accordance with an
established rule of interpretation the charge of the duty on the goods
was taken to mean a personal charge against the owner. In the
case last cited the court by Mr. Justice Story said (p. 493):

"The first question is, whether Smith and Buchanan were ever personally indebted for these duties; or, in other words, whether the importers of goods do, in virtue of the importation thereof, become personally indebted to the United States for the duties due thereon; or the remedy of the United States is exclusively confined to the lien on the goods, and the security of the bond given for the duties. It appears to us clear upon principle, as well as upon the obvious import of the provisions of the various acts of Congress on this subject, that the duties due upon all goods imported constitute a personal debt due to the United States from the importer (and the consignee for this purpose is treated as the owner and importer), independently of any lien on the goods, and any bond given for the duties. The language of the duty act of the 27th of April, 1816, ch. 107, under which the present importations were made, declares that 'there shall be levied, collected, and paid' the several duties prescribed by the act on goods imported into the United States. And this is a common formulary in other acts laying duties. Now, in the exposition of statutes laying duties, it has been a common rule of interpretation derived from the principles of the common law, that where the duty is charged on the goods, the meaning is that it is a personal charge on the owner by reason of the goods. So it was held in Attorney General *v.* ————, 2 Anst. R. 558, where a duty was laid on wash in a still; and it was said by the court that where duties are charged on any articles in a revenue act, the word 'charged' means that the owner shall be debited with the sum; and that this rule prevailed even when the article was actually lost or destroyed before it became available to the owner. Nor is there anything new in this doctrine; for it has long been held that in all such cases an action of debt lies in favor of the government against the importer, for the duties, whenever by accident, mistake, or fraud, no duties, or short duties have been paid."

A similar rule has been applied in the case of internal revenue taxes. United States *v.* Washington Mills, by Clifford, J., 2 Cliff. 601, 607; Dollar Savings Bank *v.* United States, 19 Wall. 227; United States *v.* Pacific Railroad, by Miller and Dillon, JJ., 4 Dill. 66; United States *v.* Tilden, by Blatchford, J., 9 Ben. 368.

In Dollar Savings Bank *v.* United States, *supra,* an action of debt was sustained to recover the amount of the internal revenue tax imposed by the act of July 13, 1866, c. 184, 14 Stat. 138, on the undistributed gains carried to the surplus fund of the bank. It was objected that the act provided a special remedy for the assessment and collection of the tax and that no other could be used. But the court, finding no prohibition of the remedy by action, held the argument untenable, saying (pp. 238–240):

"It must also be conceded to be a rule of the common law in England, as it is in Pennsylvania and many of the other States, that where a statute creates a right and provides a particular remedy for its enforcement, the remedy is generally exclusive of all common-law remedies.

"But it is important to notice upon what the rule is founded. Tie reason of the rule is that tie statute, by providing a particular remedy, manifests an intention to proiibit otier remedies, and the rule, therefore, rests upon a presumed statutory proiibition. It applies and it is enforced wien any one to wiom the statute is a rule of conduct seeks redress for a civil wrong. He is confined to the remedy pointed out in the statute, for he is forbidden to make use of any other. But by tie Internal Revenue law, tie United States are not proiibited from adopting any remedies for the recovery of a debt due to tiem whici are known to the laws of Pennsylvania. Tie prohibitions, if any, either express or implied, contained in tie enactment of 1866, are for others, not for tie government. Tiey may be obligatory upon tax collectors. They may prevent any suit at law by such officers or agents. But they are not rules for the conduct of the State. It is a familiar principle that tie King is not bound by any act of Parliament unless he be named therein by special and particular words. Tie most general words that can be devised (for example, any person or persons, bodies politic or corporate) affect not iim in the least, if they may tend to restrain or diminish any of his rigits and interests. He may even take tie benefit of any particular act, tiougi not named. The rule thus settled respecting tie British Crown is equally applicable to this government, and it has been applied frequently in the different States, and practically in tie Federal courts. It may be considered as settled that so much of the royal prerogatives as belonged to tie King in his capacity of *parens patriæ,* or universal trustee, enters as much into our political state as it does into the principles of the British constitution.

"It must, tien, be concluded tiat the government is not prohibited by anything contained in the act of 1866 from employing any common-law remedy for the collection of its dues. Tie reason of the rule which denies to others the use of any other tian the statutory remedy is wanting, therefore, in applicability to the government, and the rule itself must not be extended beyond its reason." See also United States *v.* Stevenson, 215 U. S. p. 197.

The statute, in the Savings Bank case, contained a provision (now in § 3213, Rev. Stat.) wiich expressly authorized the bringing of an action. But the court also found a sufficient basis for its judgment in the general power of tie Government to collect by suit taxes that are due, where the statute imposing the tax does not deny that remedy. This point was presented, considered and decided in the determination of the cause and tie decision is none the less authoritative because there was another ground for tie ultimate conclusion. Railroad Co. *v.* Schutte, 103 U. S. p. 143; Union Pacific Co. *v.* Mason City Co., 199 U. S. p. 166.

Neither Lane County *v.* Oregon, 7 Wall. 71, nor Meriwether *v.* Garrett, 102 U. S. 472, relied upon by the defendants, involved the question. In the former case it was held tiat tie acts of Congress of 1862 and 1863, making United States notes a legal tender for debts, had no reference to taxes imposed by state autiority. The

Legal Tender Acts expressly provided that the notes should be receivable for national taxes and the context forbade the conclusion that Congress intended to include state taxes under the term " debts," and there was hence no conflict with the statute of Oregon which required the taxes due the State to be collected in coin.

In Meriwether *v.* Garrett, supra, it was held that taxes levied before the repeal of the charter of a municipality, other than such as were levied in obedience to the special requirement of contracts entered into under the authority of law, and such as were levied under judicial direction for the payment of judgments recovered against the city, could not be collected through the instrumentality of a court of chancery at the instance of the city's creditors. Such taxes could be collected only under authority from the legislature.

A tax may or may not be a " debt " under a particular statute, according to the sense in which the word is found to be used. But whether the Government may recover a personal judgment for a tax depends upon the existence of the duty to pay, for the enforcement of which another remedy has not been made exclusive. Whether an action of debt is maintainable depends not upon the question who is the plaintiff or in what manner the obligation was incurred, but it lies whenever there is due a sum either certain or readily reduced to certainty. Stockwell *v.* United States, 13 Wall. p. 542.

Here the tax was a stamp tax, but the language as clearly imports the obligation to pay as did that of the statue before the court in the Meredith case, supra. Section 6 of the War Revenue Act of 1898 provided that there should be " levied, collected and paid " in respect of the instruments mentioned " by any person or persons, or party who shall make, sign, or issue the same, or for whose use or benefit the same shall be made, signed, or issued, the several taxes or sums of money " set forth in the schedule which followed. There is nothing in the nature of a stamp tax which *per se* negatives either the personal obligation, otherwise to be derived from the words imposing the tax, or its collection by action. The stamp is to be affixed to the instrument " to denote said tax." Sections 7, 13, 14. Section 25 provided that the Commissioner of Internal Revenue should cause to be prepared " for the payment of the taxes prescribed in this Act suitable stamps denoting the tax on the document, article, or thing to which the same may be affixed." The stamp is the evidence, and its purchase the convenient means, of payment. When a statute says that a person shall *pay* a given tax it obviously imposes upon that person the duty to pay, and this may be enforced through the ordinary means adapted to the recovery of a definite sum due, unless that course is clearly prohibited.

The objection was made in the Savings Bank case, supra, that the tax had not been assessed. The court held, however, that no other assessment than that made by the statute was necessary in order to determine the extent of the bank's liability. Following this rule, Judge Blatchford said in United States *v.* Tilden, 9 Ben. p. 386, where the action was brought to recover unpaid taxes on income: " The extent of the liability of the individual for income

tax is defined by the statute, equally with the extent of the liability of the bank for the tax on undistributed earnings. In each case it is necessary, in an action of debt for the tax, to resort to sources of information outside of the statute, to ascertain the amount on which the per centum of tax fixed by the statute is to be calculated. . . . The difference between the two cases, in that respect, if there be any, will be, in every case, one of degree merely, not of principle. The statute in imposing the per centum of tax on the income of the individual, makes a charge on him of a sum which is certain for the purposes of an action of debt, because it can be made certain through the action of a judicial tribunal, by following the rules laid down in the statute. That is the principle of the decision in the case of the bank, and it controls the present case." See also King *v.* United States, 99 U. S. p. 233; United States *v.* Erie Railway Co., 107 U. S. p. 2; United States *v.* Philadelphia & Reading Railroad Co., 123 U. S. p. 114; and United States *v.* Snyder, 149 U. S. p. 215. The statute now before us fixes a tax of a specified amount, according to the consideration or value of the lands conveyed.

It is insisted, however, that the provision for penalties excludes the idea of a personal liability. Thus it is made a misdemeanor to sign or issue one of the described instruments to which a stamp has not been affixed, punishable under § 7 by a fine of not more than one hundred dollars, and not exceeding two hundred dollars under § 10 in the case of a bill or note. And under § 13, where there is intent to evade the law, the offense is punished "by a fine not exceeding fifty dollars, or by imprisonment not exceeding six months, or both, in the discretion of the court." The unstamped instrument is made inadmissible in evidence (§§ 7, 14), is not allowed to be recorded (§ 15), and by the provision of § 13 is to "be deemed invalid and of no effect."

But these penalties were provided in order to induce the payment of the tax, and not as a substitute for payment. It cannot be supposed that Congress intended, by penalizing delinquency, to deprive the Government of any suitable means of enforcing the collection of revenue. In large transactions, as in the case at bar, the fine which could be imposed would be much less than the tax, and no reason is suggested why the Government should forgo the collection of that which, under the statute, is its due. Punishment by imprisonment, under § 13, is imposed only where it can be shown that there was an "intent to evade the provisions" of the act, and while this remedy is appropriate in such a case, and is for the obvious purpose of discouraging evasion, it is without application where, for any other reason, the tax has not been paid and thereby the Government has lost its revenue. The provision invalidating the instrument is likewise punitive. The object was not primarily to deprive instruments of effect, but to insure the discharge of the obligation to pay; and that obligation would still be undischarged, even though, by reason of the non-payment, the instrument was deemed invalid.

Upon these grounds we conclude that the United States was entitled to maintain this action and that the demurrer should have been overruled. The judgment is therefore

Reversed.

STATE OF COLORADO *v.* HARBECK.

SUPREME COURT OF NEW YORK. APPELLATE DIVISION. 1919.

[*Reported* 189 *App. Div.* 865.]

Action to recover an inheritance tax assessed by the **State of** Colorado against the estate of John H. Harbeck, who died domiciled in Colorado. The widow and executrix, defendant in this case, acquired a domicil in New York after her husband's death.[1]

PHILBIN, J. . . . The defendants contend that this action cannot be maintained because: *First,* all proceedings upon which this action is based were had in the State of Colorado without personal service process upon the defendants and without appearance by them, and are a nullity in so far as they and this action are concerned;[2] *second,* there is no authorization whatever under the laws of Colorado or New York for this action; *third,* the alleged claim or cause of action is of such character that our courts cannot entertain it. . . .

It now becomes necessary to take up the question as to the plaintiff's right to enforce this obligation in this State. It is contended by defendants that section 17, 18, and 19 of the Colorado Inheritance Tax Law of 1913 contain the sole remedy open to the plaintiff for the collection of the taxes. We have seen that because of the absence from Colorado of the defendants and of any property therein belonging to the decedent, no proceedings could be had under those sections. The defendants, although they admit having received the notice by mail provided for in the Colorado statute, have not voluntarily submitted to the jurisdiction of that State or permitted personal service to be made upon them therein.

Section 17, in brief, gives the County Court jurisdiction over the property of a decedent and taxes thereon, and provides that the County Court first acquiring jurisdiction shall retain the same " to the exclusion of every other " (County Court). Section 18 provides that, where the tax has not been paid the county court shall issue a summons requiring the person interested in the property to appear on a day certain, not more than three months after the date of the summons, to show cause why the tax should not be paid. The summons may be served in every respect as provided for a summons in a civil action *in rem* unless otherwise provided in the act. Section 19 states that after the refusal or neglect to pay a tax within one year from the accrual thereof, and where no bond has been given, it shall be the duty of the Attorney-General to file a petition under section 18 and press it to a final conclusion. The Attorney-General is authorized to appear in behalf of the State in any and all inheritance tax matters before any court of record. Because of inability to invoke the operation of the foregoing sections, the plaintiff should not be deprived of all remedy, and compelled to abandon every effort

---

[1] This short statement of facts is substituted for that of the court.
[2] The opinion on this point is omitted. The court held the tax valid.

to keep the defendants to the obligation they assumed as above stated. There is nothing to prevent a State, a political corporation, from seeking in the courts the relief or redress that any other corporation may demand. Delafield v. Illinois, 2 Hill, 159. And it is to be noted that section 13, in providing that the Attorney-General may apply to have a person take out letters of administration, with the will annexed, states as already indicated that such provision shall not prevent the enforcement of the collection of any tax in any other manner "as may be provided in this act or "by law." And section 19 says that the Attorney-General shall be authorized to appear in behalf of the State "in any and all inheritance tax matters before any court of record." In Pinnacle Co. v. People, 58 Colo. 86, 90, it was held that if a special remedy provided by statute for the collection of taxes is not effectual to compel payment in spite of the taxpayer's determination not to pay, resort may be had to an action against the taxpayer.

The remedy sought by the plaintiff is not limited to its courts and adequate enforcement can be had in ours. Howarth v. Angle, 162 N. Y. 179; Shipman v. Treadwell, 200 N. Y. 472. A different situation was presented in Marshall v. Sherman, 148 N. Y. 9. There the action was brought by a creditor of a Kansas bank to enforce a statutory liability of a stockholder under a statute of that State. It was held that there was no reason why the plaintiff should be permitted to enforce the liability against a citizen of this State in a form of action different from that which a creditor of a domestic corporation may prosecute against a domestic stockholder. In the Howarth Case, supra, approved in Knickerbocker Trust Co. v. Iselin, 185 N. Y. 54, 59, it was held that the enforcement of a statutory liability against a resident stockholder for debts of an insolvent foreign corporation does not rest upon the theory that the laws of the foreign State are in force in this State, but upon the *contractual* obligation the shareholder assumes to meet the liability affixed by the statute to the ownership of stock. The defendants in this case by their conduct assumed the statutory obligation and thereby made it their contractual obligation.

Public policy does not prohibit the assumption of jurisdiction by this court and the principle of comity demands it. Loucks v. Standard Oil Co., 224 N. Y. 99. The Inheritance Tax Law of Colorado has precisely the same design as a similar law in this State, and may indeed be said to be identical in its general provisions and scope. It was apparently to avoid the full force of the provisions of our own law that the defendants placed the decedent in the position of a nonresident of this State. As was said in the Loucks Case:

"A foreign statute is not law in this State, but it gives rise to an obligation, which, if transitory, 'follows the person and may be enforced wherever the person may be found.' . . . 'No law can exist as such except the law of the land; but . . . it is a principle of every civilized law that vested rights shall be protected.' . . . The plaintiff owns something, and we help him to get it. . . . We do this unless some sound reason of public policy makes it unwise for us to lend our aid." . . .

Judgment reversed, with costs, and judgment directed for plaintiff as prayed for in the complaint, with costs.

McGEE *v.* SALEM.

SUPREME JUDICIAL COURT OF MASSACHUSETTS.　1889.

[Reported 149 *Mass.* 238.]

CONTRACT to recover $31.40, the amount of a tax paid under protest. Trial in the Superior Court, without a jury, before Brigham, C. J., who allowed a bill of exceptions, in substance as follows.

This action was heard and determined by the court, upon finding the facts following. Prior to May 1, 1884, one Putnam was the owner of greenhouses upon land owned by one Emmerton, on Crombie Street, in Salem. The assessors of the defendant city assessed to Emmerton taxes upon the land for the year 1884, and to Putnam "upon the greenhouses thereon, as real estate," as well as upon other land on Mason Street in Salem, the stock in the greenhouses, valued at $500, being assessed to Putnam as personal estate. The entire tax assessed in 1884 to Putnam on his real and personal estate was the sum of $59.75. Subsequently, Putnam was declared to be an insolvent debtor, and in settling his estate his assignees in insolvency sold the greenhouses to the plaintiffs, on January 1, 1886. The tax for the year 1884 on the greenhouses remaining unpaid in July, 1886, the defendant's collector of taxes proceeded to collect it by a sale of the green houses as real estate, after due notice, by public auction.

Before the day appointed for the sale, the plaintiffs duly paid the tax to the collector, after signing a protest in writing, but in paying it did not claim that the tax had been illegally assessed, or that the same should be apportioned, or ask of the collector so to apportion it that they could avoid the sale of the greenhouses by paying so much of the tax assessed to Putnam on the greenhouses as "real estate" as applied to them only, and not to the land on which they were.

The judge ruled that upon these facts the action could not be maintained, and found for the defendant; and the plaintiffs alleged exceptions.

FIELD, J. We understand from the exceptions that the tax on the land upon which the greenhouses stood, was assessed to Emmerton, and that in this assessment the greenhouses were not included, and that the tax on the greenhouses, considered apart from the land, was assessed to Putnam as a tax on real estate. This separation of the greenhouses from the land on which they stood implies that the assessors considered that the greenhouses belonged to Putnam as personal property. These taxes were assessed as of May 1, 1884.

Putnam, after this tax was assessed to him, became an insolvent debtor, and the assignees of his estate, on January 1, 1886, sold the greenhouses to the plaintiffs. The plaintiffs, therefore, so far as appears took an absolute title to the greenhouses, unless there was a lien on them in favor of the city of Salem for the payment of the tax assessed to Putnam.

The Pub. Sts. c. 11, provide, in § 3, that "real estate, for the purposes of taxation, shall include all lands within this State, and all buildings and other things erected on or affixed to the same"; in § 13, that "taxes on real estate shall be assessed, in the city or town where the estate lies, to the person who is either the owner or in possession thereof on the first day of May"; in § 20, that "all personal estate, within or without the Commonwealth, shall be assessed to the owner in the city or town where he is an inhabitant on the first day of May, except", etc.; and in § 53 require that the buildings and lots of land be separately described.

In Milligan *v.* Drury, 130 Mass. 428, it was in effect decided that buildings affixed to land, under an agreement between the owner of the land and the owner of the buildings that they should remain personal property, might be assessed with the land to the landowner; and it was said that "the assessors were not obliged to inquire into the private contracts between the parties, but had the right to do as they did, and assess together as real estate the land and the buildings affixed thereto." It follows from this decision, that the land and the buildings affixed thereto could be assessed together as real estate to the person in possession of the land and the buildings on the first day of May, as well as to the owner of the land.

The question did not arise in that case whether a tax can be assessed upon buildings which are personal property as a separate tax from that assessed on the land to which the buildings are affixed, and the question whether, if a tax can be so assessed, the buildings should be taxed as real or personal estate, was not considered. There are difficulties whatever view is taken. If the owner of the buildings is an inhabitant of another town within the Commonwealth than that in which the buildings are situated, and the buildings may be assessed to him in one town as personal property, and also may be assessed in the other town as a part of the land to the landowner or person in possession of the land, then there may be double taxation at the election of the assessors of the different towns.

While the statutes expressly declare that for the purposes of taxation real estate shall include buildings affixed to land, and expressly provide for a separate description and valuation of the buildings and the lots of land, yet the provisions relating to the collection of a tax on real estate by a lien upon it and a sale of it, or of the rents and profits, or by the purchase of the real estate in behalf of the city or town, or by the taking of it for the city or town, as well as the provisions for the redemption by the owner of real estate so taken or sold, are, in many respects, inapplicable to buildings which are personal property, and which must at some time be removed from

the land, or taken down if the owner of the land requires it. Pub.
Sts. c. 12, §§ 24–58. Buildings affixed to land are in their nature
real property, and they are only considered as personal property
between the parties to an agreement making them such and those
who purchase the land with knowledge of the agreement; they pass
as a part of the land to a purchaser for value without notice. Hunt
v. Bay State Iron Co. 97 Mass. 279. Dolliver *v.* Ela, 128 Mass. 557.

The questions we are discussing were considered in Flanders *v.*
Cross, 10 Cush. 514 but it was not necessary there to decide them,
although it was said that "there is no power in the collector to
divide the property, to levy on the building severed from the land,
as divisible parts of the same piece of real estate." This statement
we think is true. As the statutes relating to a sale of real property
to satisfy the lien for taxes do not provide for a sale of a building
apart from the land on which it stands, and as some of the provisions are inconsistent with such a sale, we think it follows that a
building affixed to land cannot be taxed as real estate except in
connection with the land to which it is affixed. The tax assessed
to Putnam on these greenhouses as real estate, therefore, was unauthorized, and it is unnecessary to consider whether they could
have been taxed to him as personal estate.

It is contended that, if these greenhouses were wrongly included
in the real estate of Putnam for the purpose of taxation, yet, as
other land in Salem was rightly taxed to him, Putnam's remedy
would have been by a petition for abatement, and not by action,
and that the plaintiffs have only the rights and remedies which
Putnam would have had if he had not become an insolvent debtor,
and had remained the owner of the greenhouses. Howe *v.* Boston,
7 Cush. 273, 274.

It has been decided that for the collection of a tax assessed on
real estate a city or town has a remedy against the person and the
property generally of the person to whom the tax has been assessed,
and is not confined to the sale of the real estate itself. Sherwin *v.*
Boston Five Cents Savings Bank, 137 Mass. 444. Richardson *v.*
Boston, 148 Mass. 508.

It may be conceded that, if Putnam had remained the owner of
the greenhouses, the collector of taxes could have taken them by
distress, under the Pub. Sts. c. 12, §§ 8, 9, or have maintained
an action of contract against him, and attached them under § 20
of the same chapter, and that therefore Putnam could not maintain the present action if he had paid the tax, because unless
there is an abatement the assessment is good as against him, and
he is personally bound to pay the tax. But the plaintiffs by purchasing the greenhouses did not succeed to the personal obligation of Putnam to pay the tax. If the tax was a lien on the greenhouses, the lien might have been enforced even after the plaintiffs
became the owners; but if there was no lien, the houses after they
became the property of the plaintiffs could not have been sold to
pay a tax assessed to another person. As we have held that the
houses considered apart from the land could not lawfully be assessed

to Putnam as real estate, the tax would not constitute a lien upon the greenhouses, although it might remain a valid tax against Putnam, because only taxes assessed on real estate constitute a lien.

As the plaintiffs were never personally liable to pay the tax, and as there was no lien upon the greenhouses whereby they could be sold to satisfy it, the remaining question is whether the plaintiffs could pay the amount of the tax under protest to the collector of taxes, who was unlawfully proceeding to collect it by a sale of the greenhouses, and then bring an action to recover what they had paid. The wrong of the collector is in threatening to take one man's goods to pay a tax assessed to another. It may be said that the payment was not compulsory, because the collector held no warrant authorizing him to levy upon or to sell the property of the plaintiff. If the collector had intermeddled with the greenhouses by taking possession, or by delivering possession to another person, the plaintiffs could have maintained trespass, or trover, or replevin. Independently of statute, it may be that this action could not be maintained. See Boston & Sandwich Glass Co. *v.* Boston, 4 Met. 181; Forbes *v.* Appleton, 5 Cush. 115; Barrett *v.* Cambridge, 10 Allen, 48.

But by the Pub. Sts. c. 12, § 84, one of the alternative conditions under which a tax paid may be recovered is that it was paid by the plaintiff, after " a protest by him in writing." In the present case, this was done. We think that the Legislature intended by this provision that any person upon whom a collector makes a demand for the payment of a tax included in his warrant, on the ground that he is personally liable to pay it, or whose property the collector proceeds to sell, on the ground that it is liable to be taken to satisfy such a tax, may, instead of resisting the collector, or resorting to other remedies, pay the tax under written protest, and bring suit to recover the amount paid. Such a course is the least troublesome of any judicial proceedings which can well be taken to settle questions which are often of great difficulty. We think that. on the facts recited in the exceptions, the action can be maintained.

Exceptions sustained.

KERR *v.* ATWOOD.

SUPREME JUDICIAL COURT OF MASSACHUSETTS. 1905.

[*Reported* 188 *Mass.* 506.]

HAMMOND, J. In this action to recover damages for an alleged assault and false imprisonment, the defendant pleaded justification under a tax warrant.

R. L. c. 13, § 26, under which the arrest was made, is as follows: " If a person refuses or neglects to pay his tax for fourteen days after demand and the collector cannot find sufficient goods upon which it may be levied, he may take the body of such person and commit him to jail until he pays the tax and charges of commitment and imprisonment, or is discharged according to law." The main question is whether there was evidence from which the jury might find that the defendant could not find sufficient goods within the meaning of the term as used in this statute.

The jury were instructed in substance that it was the duty of the defendant to make a diligent search, but that if before the arrest the defendant demanded of the plaintiff that he exhibit goods for the purpose of being taken on the warrant and the plaintiff, having goods which he could have exhibited, failed to exhibit them, then as matter of law the defendant had made diligent search and could lawfully arrest. We are of opinion that this instruction was correct.

After the adoption of our State Constitution, the first statute authorizing arrest for non-payment of taxes was St. 1785, c. 70, § 2. It reads as follows: " And if any person assessed as aforesaid to the state or other tax, shall refuse or neglect to pay the sum or sums so assessed, by the space of twelve days after demand thereof, and shall neglect to show the constable or collector sufficient goods or chattels whereby the same may be levied, in every such case, he may take the body of the person so refusing, and him commit unto the common gaol," etc. This provision appears in Rev. Sts. c. 8, § 11, in this language: " If any person shall refuse or neglect, for fourteen days after demand thereof made, to pay his tax, and the collector cannot find sufficient goods, upon which it may be levied, he may take the body of such person and commit him to prison," etc. And through the various codifications the language has remained substantially the same. Gen. Sts. c. 12, § 13. Pub. Sts. c. 12, § 14. St. 1888, c. 390, § 18. R. L. c. 13, § 26. There is nothing in the report of the commissioners on the Revised Statutes to show that they intended to make any change in the statute, so far at least as respects the effect of a refusal of the delinquent taxpayer, when requested, to exhibit goods upon which levy may be made; and we think no change was made. So far as respects the right to arrest, the collector has made reasonable search when he has requested the delinquent to exhibit goods upon which levy may be made; and if the delinquent refuses or neglects to make such an exhibit the collector may properly return that he cannot find sufficient goods. It is the duty of the delinquent to pay his tax and, in default thereof, after a certain time to exhibit to the collector upon demand goods upon which levy may be made. The law does not impose upon the collector the idle task of seeking elsewhere when with warrant in hand he has asked the delinquent to show goods upon which to levy, and the latter who should know fails to indicate where there may be such goods. The instructions of the presiding judge were in accordance with this view and were correct and pertinent to the case. The evidence amply warranted the finding that the plaintiff had refused upon demand to exhibit to the defendant goods upon which to levy.

The question whether the defendant had made reasonable search even if he had made no specific demand upon the plaintiff to exhibit goods properly was left to the jury. In the first place the return upon the warrant that he had " made diligent search for and was unable to find goods and chattels of the within named George L. Kerr whereof to make distress," although not conclusive evidence in this action, was nevertheless *prima facie* evidence in favor of the defendant. Lothrop *v.* Ide, 13 Gray, 93. Barnard *v.* Graves, 13 Met. 85. The jury well may have thought that in view of the duty of the plaintiff to do what he could, his general suspicious attitude on the question, his oft repeated statement of his inability to pay even the small sum due, and the existence of the mortgage, the defendant was not obliged in law to inquire about the household furniture in the dwelling house of the plaintiff, into which against his will the defendant could not enter for the purpose of levying, nor, in view of the character of the mortgage, to undertake to get from either of the parties to the mortgage any information as to whether it was valid as to the whole or any part of the articles in the store. The jury well may have thought that the *prima facie* case made out by the return stood notwithstanding the other evidence. In Hall *v.* Hall, 3 Allen, 5, cited by the plaintiff, it did not appear from the return upon the warrant that the defendant made any search whatever. The case upon this branch of it was submitted to the jury upon proper instructions, and the jury were warranted in finding that the defendant had made diligent search and could not find sufficient goods upon which to levy, and therefore had authority to make the arrest. For cases bearing somewhat upon the questions here discussed, see in addition to those above cited, Parker *v.* Abbott, 130 Mass. 25; Bayley, petitioner, 132 Mass. 457; Flint *v.* Whitney, 28 Vt. 680.

The questions whether there was unnecessary or improper delay in proceeding to the jail at East Cambridge, or whether the plaintiff was subjected to improper treatment were also for the jury, and we see no error in the instructions on that point. The jury properly might find that the delay was at the request of the plaintiff, or that in any event it was not unreasonable, and that neither in being placed in the cell of the police station nor in any other respect was he treated improperly. We see no error in the manner in which the court dealt with the requests of the plaintiff on this point.

The evidence as to whether the plaintiff ever had told the defendant that he had in his house a piano or other property, or ever offered or pointed out to the defendant any specific articles in his store, or whether he was the George L. Kerr who gave the mortgage and that he never told the defendant about the mortgage, was admitted properly, and so was the copy of the mortgage. The evidence had a bearing upon the question of reasonable search.

The questions put to the plaintiff as to his ability to pay the tax if he had not paid other bills did not exceed the latitude fairly allowed in cross-examination, and we do not see how the plaintiff could have been prejudiced by it.

We regard the statement by the judge in the charge that taxes should be paid before private debts as simply introductory to what followed, and in any event it could work no harm to the plaintiff.

The evidence that there was no other place of detention in Malden except tie police station was admissible upon the question whether the plaintiff was properly treated, and it was admitted rigitly.

Exceptions overruled.

CHAPTER VI.

REMEDIES FOR ILLEGAL TAXATION.

SINGER SEWING MACHINE COMPANY *v.* BENEDICT.

SUPREME COURT OF THE UNITED STATES.   1913.

[*Reported* 229 *U. S.* 481.]

VAN DEVANTER, J. This is a suit by the Singer Company, a New Jersey corporation, to enjoin the collection of taxes levied by the city and county of Denver, in the State of Colorado. The company made a return of taxable personal property at a valuation of $3,800, to which the assessor added other personalty at a valuation of $62,500, making a total assessment of $66,300, which was afterwards embodied in a tax list delivered to the treasurer for collection. The company tendered payment of $126.50, tie amount of taxes due on the property returned by it, and refused to pay the amount attributable to the additional assessment. The treasurer declined to accept the tender, and was threatening to enforce the entire tax, when the suit was brought. The bill charged that the assessor, although required by law to give the company timely notice of the additional assessment, had failed to give it any notice, and that it was thereby prevented from presenting objections to the increase and obtaining a hearing and ruling thereon by the assessor and by tie proper reviewing autiority to which it was entitled by the local law. There were also allegations to the effect that tie company had no property within the city and county other tian that returned by it; tiat the additional assessment and the taxes levied tiereon were illegal because of the assessor's failure to give the required notice; and that to enforce the collection of such taxes would be violative of designated provisions of the Constitution of the United States. Tie defendants demurred on the ground thati the bill did not state a case for equitable relief, but the demurrer was overruled. The defendants then answered repeating tie objection made in tie demurrer and interposing other defenses which need not be noticed now. Upon the iearing a decree was entered dismissing tie bill, and the company appealed to the Circuit Court of Appeals. Tiat court held that there was an adequate remedy at law, and affirmed tie decree. 179 Fed. Rep. 628. The company then took tie present appeal.

In the courts of the United States it is a guiding rule that a bill in equity does not lie in any case where a plain, adequate and complete remedy may be had at law. The statute so declares, Rev. Stat., § 723, and the decisions enforcing it are without number. If it be quite obvious that there is such a remedy, it is the duty of the court to interpose the objection *sua sponte,* and in other cases it is treated as waived if not presented by the defendant *in limine.* Reynes *v.* Dumont, 130 U. S. 354, 395; Allen *v.* Pullman's Palace Car Co., 139 U. S. 658. There was no waiver here. The objection was made by the demurrer and again by the answer, and so, if it was well grounded, it was as available to the defendants in the Circuit Court of Appeals to prevent a decree against them there as it was in the Circuit Court. Boise Artesian Water Co. *v.* Boise City, 213 U. S. 276.

In the last case it was said of the pertinency of the guiding rule in cases such as this (p. 281) : "A notable application of the rule in the courts of the United States has been to cases where a demand has been made to enjoin the collection of taxes or other impositions made by state authority, upon the ground that they are illegal or unconstitutional. The decisions of the state courts in cases of this kind are in conflict, and we need not examine them. It is a mere matter of choice of convenient remedy for a State to permit its courts to enjoin the collection of a state tax, because it is illegal or unconstitutional. Very different considerations arise where courts of a different, though paramount, sovereignty interpose in the same manner and for the same reasons. An examination of the decisions of this court shows that a proper reluctance to interfere by prevention with the fiscal operations of the state governments has caused it to refrain from so doing in all cases where the Federal rights of the persons could otherwise be preserved unimpaired. It has been held uniformly that the illegality or unconstitutionality of a state or municipal tax or imposition is not of itself a ground for equitable relief in the courts of the United States. In such a case the aggrieved party is left to his remedy at law, when that remedy is as complete, practicable and efficient as the remedy in equity."

A statute of Colorado enacted in 1870 (Laws 1870, p. 123, § 106) and embodied in subsequent revenue acts (2 Mills' Ann. Stat., § 3777; Laws 1902, c. 3, pp. 43, 146, § 202; Rev. Stat. 1908, § 5750) declares that "in all cases where any person shall pay any tax, interest or cost, or any portion thereof, that shall thereafter be found to be erroneous or illegal, whether the same be owing to erroneous assessment, to improper or irregular levying of the tax, to clerical or other errors or irregularities, the board of county commissioners shall refund the same without abatement or discount to the taxpayer." This statute imposes upon the county commissioners the duty of refunding, without abatement or discount, taxes which have been paid and are found to be illegal, and confers upon the taxpayer a correlative right to enforce that duty by an action at law. As long ago as 1879 the Supreme Court of the State, in holding that the invalidity of a tax afforded no ground for enjoining its enforcement, said of this statute: "Against an illegal tax complainant has a full and adequate remedy at law, and we see no reason why in this case he should not be remitted to that remedy." Price *v.* Kramer, 4 Colorado, 546, 555. And again: "The statute furnishes another remedy in such cases which is complete and adequate." Woodward *v.* Ellsworth, Id. 580, 581. And that this view of the statute still prevails is shown in Hallett *v.* Arapahoe County, 40 Colorado, 308, 318, decided in 1907, where, in refusing equitable relief against the collection of taxes alleged to be illegal, the court said (p. 318): "By § 3777, 2 Mills' Ann. Stat., it is provided that taxes 'paid which shall thereafter be found to be erroneous or illegal, shall be refunded, without abatement or discount, to the taxpayer. No statement appears in either of the complaints from which it can be deduced that the remedy afforded the plaintiff by this section is not adequate."

We refer to these cases, not as defining the jurisdiction in equity of the Circuit Court, for that they could not do (Payne *v.* Hook, 7 Wall. 425, 430; Whitehead *v.* Shattuck, 138 U. S. 146; Smythe *v.* Ames, 169 U. S. 466, 516), but as showing that the Colorado statute gave to one who should pay illegal taxes a right to recover back from the county the money so paid. This right was one which could be enforced by an action at law in the Circuit Court, no less than in the state courts, if the elements of Federal jurisdiction, such as diverse citizenship and the requisite amount in controversy, were present. *Ex parte* McNiel, 13 Wall. 236, 243; United States Mining Co. *v.* Lawson, 134 Fed. Rep. 769, 771. Thus it will be perceived that, if the taxes in question were illegal and void, as asserted, the company had a remedy at law. It could pay them and, if the commissioners refused to refund, have its action against the county to recover back the money. Such a remedy, as this court often has held, is plain, adequate and complete in the sense of the guiding rule before named, unless there be special circumstances showing the contrary. Dows *v.* Chicago, 11 Wall. 108, 112; State Railroad Tax Cases, 92 U. S. 575, 613–614; Shelton *v.* Platt, 139 U. S. 591, 597; Allen *v.* Pullman's Palace Car Co., Id. 658, 661; Indiana Manufacturing Co. *v.* Koehne, 188 U. S. 681, 686.

But it is said that in an action to recover back the money the tax list would be treated as the judgment of a special tribunal conclusively determining all questions in favor of the validity of the tax. It well may be that, if the list were regular on its face, it would be presumptive evidence that the tax was valid, but we find nothing in the statutes of Colorado or in the decisions of its Supreme Court which goes to the length suggested. The plain implication of the section providing for repayment is otherwise. Another section (Rev. Stat., § 5677) declares that the tax list "shall be *prima facie* evidence that the amount claimed is due and unpaid," and the only decision cited by the company speaks of the assessment as being presumptively right "in the absence of any evidence to the contrary." Singer Manufacturing Co. *v.* Denver, 46 Colorado, 50.

It also is said that there were special circumstances calling for equitable relief, in that the act of the assessor in making the additional assessment without giving any notice of it was necessarily a fraud, an accident, or a mistake. No such claim was made in the bill, and even had it been it would be unavailing unless founded upon something more than the charge that no notice was given and that the company had no property within the city and county other than that returned by it. We say this because the fraud, accident or mistake which will justify equitable relief must be something more than what is fairly covered by the charge here made, for otherwise the well settled rule that mere illegality in a tax affords no ground for such relief would be a myth. There really would be no case in which the illegality could not be said with equal propriety to be the result of fraud, accident or mistake, for it always arises out of some deviation from law or duty.

Concluding, as we do, that the company had a plain, adequate and complete remedy at law, the decree dismissing the bill is

Affirmed.

KNIGHT *v.* THOMAS.

SUPREME JUDICIAL COURT OF MAINE.   1900.

[*Reported* 93 *Me.* 494.]

HASKELL, J.   Petition for mandamus by several taxpayers of a town to compel the assessors to assess certain real estate in the town at a just and fair valuation, that had previously been undervalued, and to assess certain other real estate that had therefore been omitted from taxation.

I.   It is objected that the writ cannot issue at the instance of the petitioners, who are individuals.

It is settled law, in this state, that the writ can only issue at the instance of public officers, to subserve a public right.   Sanger *v.* County Commissioners, 25 Maine, 291; Mitchell *v.* Boardman, 79 Maine, 469; Weeks *v.* Smith, 81 Maine, 538.   But, as stated in the last named case, an individual may move for the writ " when his personal rights have been invaded beyond those rights that he enjoys as a part of the public and that are common to every one."

The public consists of the entire community, persons who pay taxes and persons who do not.   Their interest is the raising of revenue by taxation or otherwise to provide for the expenses of government, public works, public institutions and public charges.   The individual taxpayer's interest is in common with all these, but he has another interest peculiar to himself, that taxes shall be assessed equally, so that his burden shall not be greater than equality of taxation shall impose.   His personal interest, therefore, by the omitting of property from taxation in his own town would be invaded thereby beyond that enjoyed in common with the public, and he may well be allowed to move for the writ in protection of it.

II. It is objected that the writ will not lie to command assessors, who intend to assess a certain parcel of land, to assess the same at its just and fair value. Their oath requires them to do that, and mandamus could not require more. It may require them to assess, but the assessment is matter of judgment, and it must be their own judgment, honestly given of course. Any other assessment would be corrupt, and the remedy for that must be elsewhere. Otherwise, mandamus would simply work an appeal from the appraisal of property made by the assessors, which is not at all the proper function of the writ. To have all the property assessed is a private right; to have the assessment according to law is a public right. The assessors are public officers, sworn to a faithful discharge of their duty. The individual has a right to have them act. The public has the right to their official action, honestly performed under their oath, and with this the individual must be content, unless the legislature shall provide a remedy. The legislature has already provided such remedy as it thought wise by R. S., c. 77, § 6, where jurisdiction is conferred upon this court to hear and determine all complaints relating to any unauthorized votes to raise money by taxation, or to exempt property therefrom.

III. As to the land not assessed, the petitioner might have had the writ if the court below, in its discretion, had seen fit to award it, for the writ is a prerogative to be withheld or granted in the exercise of discretion. It is not a writ of right. Morsell *v.* First Natl. Bank of Washington, 91 U. S. 357. Nor can it now be issued to any effective purpose. The assessment must have long since been made. To issue it would be an idle ceremony. Mitchell *v.* Boardman, 79 Maine, 471. The petitioner is not aggrieved by the ruling below.

Exceptions overruled. Petition dismissed.

LOEWENTHAL *v.* PEOPLE.

SUPREME COURT OF ILLINOIS.   1901.

[*Reported* 192 *Ill.* 222.]

BOGGS, J. This was an application by the appellee county collector of Cook county, to the county court of said county, for a judgment and order of sale against lands and lots delinquent for the taxes levied thereon for the year 1899. The delinquent list contained four lots in the city of Chicago of which the appellant was the owner. The appellant appeared and filed objections to the rendition of judgment against each and all of the said lots. The objections were heard upon a stipulation setting forth the testimony of the witnesses, and also certain facts; were overruled, and an order and judgment for the sale of the lots granted as prayed by the collector. This is an appeal to reverse the judgment and order of sale.

It appeared from the stipulation the appellant was the owner of the lots on the first day of April, 1899; that their total fair cash value did not then exceed the sum of $153,000; that the valuation of the lots 'as returned by the board of assessors to the board of review was $206,575; that George C. Fry, a duly authorized agent of the appellant, " at various times called at the office of the assessors for the purpose of ascertaining the value at which said property had been assessed; that as soon as he was able to learn from said board of assessors the valuation fixed by said board of assessors, said Fry called at the office of the board of review and filed a complaint, in writing, objecting to the amount at which said property had been assessed; that said complaint was filed during the latter part of August, 1899, and not on or before the first Monday in August, but that said complaint was filed as soon as said Fry, representing the owner of said property, and as soon as B. Loewenthal, the owner of said property, could learn the amount at which said property had been assessed, and that the reason the said written complaint was not filed with the board of review on or before the first Monday in August, was because it was impossible, on or before the first day of August, to learn the value at which said property had been assessed; that when he went to the office of said board of review to make said complaint he was unable to see any member of the board of review in person, but was referred to a clerk standing at a desk in the front part of the office; that when he handed the complaint to said clerk, said clerk informed said Fry that the said objection would be called up before the board of review in its due course and would be considered by the board of review, and that he, Fry, as agent of said objector, would receive due notice by mail when such objection would be taken up for hearing by said board of review; that he did not, nor did the said B. Loewenthal, nor any person acting on his behalf, receive any notice of any hearing of said objection before said board of review, but that said Fry on several subsequent occasions called at the office of said board of review and inquired of the clerks placed in charge of said office by said board of review as to when said objection would come up for hearing, and was each time informed that said objection had not yet been reached in its order but it would be taken up in due course, and that prior to said hearing said Fry and the said objector would receive notice in writing of the time of said hearing; that the said Fry and the said B. Loewenthal depended upon the statements made by said clerk in the office of the board of review and expected such notice of a hearing upon said objections, but that no such notice was ever received by said Fry or by said Loewenthal, and while said Fry and said Loewenthal were still waiting in expectation of receiving notice of such hearing, the tax books were closed and delivered by the board of review to the county clerk; that no hearing was ever given by said board of review upon the objections filed against the assessment on said property, so far as is known to the said Loewenthal or said Fry, or any person for said Loewenthal or said Fry."

The statute secures to every person whose property is assessed for taxes the right to a hearing before the board of review on a complaint in writing that the property has been assessed too high.

The board are required to review the assessment upon such complaint and correct the same as shall appear to be just. This provision is of vital importance to the tax-payer, and it is against every principle of right and justice that he should be deprived of all opportunity to contest the fairness of the assessment. The constitution authorized the General Assembly to provide such revenue as shall be needful by levying a tax by valuation, so that every person and corporation shall pay a tax in proportion to the value of his or her property, and the provisions of the statute are designed to accomplish that purpose. The requirement of the statute for a hearing of the complaint is mandatory, and no person ought to be required to pay a tax without a compliance with the law which entitles him to such hearing.

Section 1 of article 9 of the constitution of 1870, except so much thereof as relates to the imposition of taxes upon certain specified occupations, is as follows: " The General Assembly shall provide such revenue as may be needful by levying a tax, by valuation, so that every person and corporation shall pay a tax in proportion to the value of his, her or its property — such valuation to be ascertained by some person or persons, to be elected or appointed in such manner as the General Assembly shall direct, and not otherwise."

In obedience to this constitutional requirement that the value of property assessable for taxation shall be ascertained by some person or persons elected or appointed in such manner as the General Assembly shall elect for that purpose, and not by other persons or other manner, the General Assembly, by an act entitled " An act for the assessment of property," etc., approved February 25, 1898, (Hurd's Stat. 1899, p. 1444,) provided that the value of real property situate in Cook county, as is the property in question, should be ascertained by a board of assessors, consisting of five persons, to be elected in the manner as prescribed in section 3 of the act. The act further provided the board of assessors shall have authority to designate and appoint deputy assessors to perform such duties connected with the assessment of property as may be assigned to them. Section 32 of the act authorizes the selection of three persons, by election, to constitute a board of review, and section 35 empowers the persons composing such board of review, among other duties, on complaint that any property has been assessed too high by the board of assessors, to ascertain the true assessable value of such property and approve or correct the assessment of such property as made by the board of assessors.

Under the said provision of the constitution hereinbefore referred to, and of the said act of February 25, 1898, made in pursuance thereof, the valuation of property for the purposes of taxation in said city of Chicago and county of Cook is committed to the persons composing said board of assessors, in the first instance, and the persons composing the board of review, when sitting in review of the action of said board of assessors. The power does not reside in the courts to revise the assessments made by these bodies, on the ground, alone, they fell into an error of judgment in estimating the value of the

property.   This principle was declared in People ex rel. *v.* Lots
in Asiley, 122 Ill. 297, and many decisions of this court declaring
or illustrating it are tiere collected.   In later cases, notably Keokuk
Bridge Co. *v.* People, 145 Ill. 596, Spring Valley Coal Co. *v.* People,
157 id. 543, Clement *v.* People, 177 id. 144, and Keokuk Bridge
Co. *v.* People, 161 id. 514, tie doctrine has been re-affirmed.   In
Clement *v.* People, *supra,* we said: "We have repeatedly held that
the courts have no power to revise an assessment merely because
of a difference of opinion as to tie reasonableness of tie valuation
placed upon the property.   On an application for judgment against
lands for delinquent taxes it may be objected that tie tax is not
authorized by law, or is assessed upon property not subject to taxation, or that the property has been fraudulently assessed at too
high a rate."

The contention, here, on the part of the appellant is, tie county
court of Cook county became vested with authority and jurisdiction
to ascertain the true valuation of his property for the purposes of
taxation, for the reason tiat tie board of review had failed or refused
to review the assessment of his property made by tie board of assessors, as required of tiem by tie provisions of the second paragraph of section 35 of tie said act of February 25, 1898, tiough
he had complained, in writing, to said board of review tiat the
estimate of tie value of iis said property made by tie board of
assessors was too iigh.

Conceding tiat the board of review refused to perform a plain
duty imposed upon it by law, to ascertain tie fair cas value of his
lots and review and correct tie estimate of suc value made by tie
board of assessors, could the appellant lawfully take no furtier
steps to procure an estimate to be made by the tribunal empowered
to perform such duty, refuse to pay tie taxes levied on tie estimated
values as made by tie board of assessors and standing approved
by the non-action of the board of review, and demand tiat the
county court, when asked to enter judgment against his lots as
delinquent for such taxes, should take upon itself tie duty of estimating the true fair cas value of his property?   We tiink not.
His duty was to employ tie ample remedy provided by tie law
to compel tie board of review to discharge the duties imposed upon
them by law, and ascertain tie true fair cash value of his property
and revise the action of the board of assessors accordingly.   The
board of review, and not tie courts, are invested witi the power to
estimate the value of assessable property, and he siould iave sought
the aid of the courts, not to estimate the value of his property,
but to command tie board of review to perform tiat duty.

In the case of Beidler *v.* Kochersperger, 171 Ill. 563, wiici was
an appeal from the decree of the circuit court dismissing, for want
of equity, a bill in ciancery which sought to enjoin tie collection
of a tax, because, as alleged, the property had been over-assessed,
and that appellant filed his complaint witi the board of supervisors
sitting as a board of review, and while said complaint was pending
before a committee of that board to whom it had been referred

the board adopted a general resolution confirming the assessment returned by the assessors, without notice to appellant or an opportunity to be heard before the board and without considering his complaint, and thus disposed of and completed its work as a board of review, we said (p. 566) : "The statute imposed upon the board of supervisors, as an absolute duty, to entertain, consider and determine the application of appellant for relief with respect of the alleged over-valuation of his property. Courts of law possessed ample power to enforce the performance of this duty by the board. Appellant could have applied to such courts for a writ of *mandamus* to compel the board to perform the duty so charged upon it by the statute, — that is, to hear, consider and decide as to the alleged grievance. . . . It is the policy of our law the whole matter of the valuation of property for taxation shall be committed to the control of the assessor, the board of review and the board of supervisors of the respective counties. (People ex rel. *v.* Lots in Ashley, 122 Ill. 297.) It was therefore incumbent upon the appellant to have availed himself of the ample and adequate remedy of the writ of *mandamus* to secure action on the part of the board of supervisors, in order that his grievances, if any he justly had, should be heard and determined. The law gave him his day in court. Neither fraud, accident nor mistake of fact intervened to prevent or excuse him from availing himself of his legal right. He did not seek his legal remedy, and whether he misconceived the law or was simply negligent, it is well settled he cannot invoke the aid of a court of chancery to relieve him." In Kochersperger *v.* Larned, 172 Ill. 86, and Kinley Manf. Co. *v.* Kochersperger, 174 id. 379, the same doctrine was announced and applied as in the Beidler case.

Appellant urges that it appears from the stipulated facts that. the board of review did not refuse to grant him a hearing; on the contrary, they constantly expressed a willingness and intention to do so; and that the first intimation he had that he would not be afforded a hearing by the board of review was, that said board had delivered the books containing the assessment of real property to the county clerk. He contends, therefore, that he could not have maintained *mandamus* in anticipation of a supposed evasion or omission of duty on the part of the board; that *mandamus* will not lie to compel an officer to do an act which he expresses a willingness to do, and that the board were without power to make any changes or revision of the assessments after they had transferred the books of assessment to the county clerk; that therefore *mandamus* would not lie, either while the books were in the hands of the board of review or after such books had been transferred to the county clerk.

Any evasion of a positive duty by an officer or a legal tribunal, amounting to a virtual refusal 'to perform the duty, is all that is needed to maintain a writ of *mandamus*. (Illinois State Board of Dental Examiners *v.* People, 123 Ill. 227). Conduct from which a refusual can be conclusively implied is equivalent to a positive refusal. (People ex rel. *v.* Town of Mt. Morris, 137 Ill. 576; 14 Am. &

Eng. Ency. of Law, — 1st ed. — 107.) The evasions of duty shown by the stipulation and the transfer of the books of assessment to the county clerk constituted a refusal to act by conclusive implication, and the appellant could have applied for a writ of *mandamus* at once upon being advised that the board of review had delivered the books of assessment to the county clerk without acting on his complaint.

Counsel for appellant are in error in the view that *mandamus* would be unavailing after the board of review had delivered the books of assessment to the county clerk. Section 38 of the act of 1898 (Hurd's Stat. 1899, p. 1453,) provides that the board of review in the county of Cook shall, on or before the 7th day of September, annually, complete its work and make the necessary entries in the assessment books to make the assessments conform to the changes made therein by said board, and shall attach to said books of assessment an affidavit, after a form prescribed in the section; and section 43 of the same act requires the board of review to deliver the assessment books, when so completed, to the county clerk. But a proviso added to said section 38 of said act provides "that in counties containing 125,000 or more inhabitants the board of review shall also meet from time to time and whenever necessary to consider and act upon complaints and to further revise the assessment of real property as may be just and necessary."

Without assuming to declare that this proviso has further or other effect, it is clear, under the provisions thereof, the courts, by means of a writ of *mandamus,* could compel the board of review to convene after the said 7th day of September for the purpose of performing a duty which rested upon them when the books were declared to be completed, as did, in this instance, the duty to consider and act upon the complaint of the appellant. An inferior tribunal which has omitted, and by evasion refused, to perform an official duty while officially convened, cannot, by adjourning its meeting *sine die,* place itself beyond the coercive power of the courts to compel the performance of a duty enjoined by law. It may be required to re-convene and perform its legal functions. If, as was remarked in People *v.* Board of Supervisors, 185 Ill. 288, it is the general rule *mandamus* will not be granted in anticipation of a default or failure of official duty, it must be that the writ can be availed of after the omission or failure has occurred, otherwise the observance or non-observance of the statutory duty would become a matter wholly resting in the uncontrollable discretion of the public officer or official tribunal charged with the duty. The appellant should have availed himself of this writ, and thereby obtained the revision of the estimate of the value of his property as made by the board of assessors. The county court correctly overruled his objections to the application for judgment against his lots.

The judgment appealed from is affirmed.

Judgment affirmed.

MAGRUDER and CARTWRIGHT, JJ., dissented.

SHENANGO FURNACE COMPANY *v.* FAIRFIELD TOWNSHIP.

SUPREME COURT OF PENNSYLVANIA.   1905.

[*Reported* 229 *Pa.* 357.]

MESTREZAT, J. This is a bill filed by the plaintiff company (a) to restrain the defendants from collecting a balance of road taxes alleged to be due for the year 1907, (b) for an accounting to ascertain the amount paid by the plaintiff inadvertently and by mistake on account of such taxes in excess of the amount legally due, and (c) for a decree that defendants pay to plaintiff the amount of such excess.

The defendant township is of the second class and the plaintiff company owns coal lands in the township, the adjusted valuation of which for 1906 was $19,400. Prior to March, 1907, the township assessor returned a valuation of the lands to the county commissioners which was very largely in excess of the valuation for 1906. The valuation so returned to the commissioners was revised and reduced by them sitting as a board of revision on June 25, 1907. From this valuation plaintiff appealed to the common pleas, which finally adjudicated the valuation in December, 1907 at $330 per acre, or $248,820 in all. On the first Monday of March, 1907, the township supervisors met and fixed the rate for road tax at eight mills for that year. At that time there was no "adjusted valuation" for 1907. On May 31, 1907, an agent of plaintiff tendered to the tax collector the sum of $156.20, being the amount of the road tax for 1907, at the rate of eight mills on the valuation for 1906. The tender was refused because, as the collector said, he had no duplicate and was without authority to receive the tax. In the early part of January, 1908, the tax collector gave the plaintiff company notice to pay taxes based upon the 1907 valuation, the sum claimed being $2,091.14, and within a few days plaintiff paid to the collector $1,722.56, being the amount claimed in the notice, less certain deductions which the plaintiff alleged should be made. Shortly after this, plaintiff demanded the refunding of all over $156.20, the amount due on the valuation for 1906. This was refused and the collector demanded the balance, $368.58; whereupon, in February, 1908, this bill was filed. An answer and replication were filed and the case was referred by agreement to a referee who recommended a decree enjoining the collection of the balance of $368.58 and directing payment to the plaintiff by defendants of $1,566.36, the difference between the amount paid by plaintiff and $156.20, the amount due on the 1906 valuation. A final decree in accordance with the referee's report was entered by the court below. The defendants have appealed.

It is conceded by the parties that under our recent rulings the levy for road taxes made by the supervisors on the first Monday of March, 1907, should have been made on the adjusted valuation for 1906, and that a court of equity has jurisdiction to restrain the collection of the $368.58, the balance claimed by the township for taxes due from tie plaintiff company on tie valuation of 1907.

There was sufficient evidence to warrant the court below in finding that tie plaintiff tendered tie sum of $156.20, on May 31, 1907, in payment of the road taxes for tiat year admitted to be due by tie plaintiff. Tie fourti assignment, tierefore, cannot be sustained.

In ascertaining the rigit of tie plaintiff company to have re-funded the sum of $1,566.36, taxes paid by tie company on tie 1907 valuation, two questions must be considered: (1) Was tie payment a voluntary one in the legal sense wiici prevents its recovery back, and (2) was it made under such mistake or ignorance of facts tiat the plaintiff is entitled to iave the money repaid.

1. Was tie payment of tie money, under tie facts of tie case, voluntarily made by the plaintiff so that he, for tiis reason, is not entitled to iave it refunded? This question is settled by a long line of decisions in tiis state and, ience, we are not required to treat or consider it as one of first impression. C. P. Dyer, the vice-president of the plaintiff company and autiorized to act for it in the matter, directed tie payment to be made by tie proper officer of the company. Wiile testifying at lengti in tie case, tie facts found by tie learned referee and tie court below being based upon his testimony, he does not even suggest that any official of the defendant townsiip at any time ever tireatened to resort to legal process for tie collection of tie taxes, or exacted tiem by duress, or went beyond making a demand for tieir payment, or did any act by wiich the plaintiff was misled. Neitier does it appear by tie evidence nor is it claimed by Mr. Dyer or any otier representative of the plaintiff company that it made tie payment under protest or witi notice of an intention to reclaim any part of the sum paid. Tie case is entirely barren of any suci facts, and it is, therefore, clear tiat under tie settled law of tiis state tie payment was voluntary and not suci as to justify tie plaintiff in demanding tie repayment of tie money.

In Lackey *v.* Mercer County, 9 Pa. 318, a donation tract of land was sold by tie county to tie plaintiff for taxes. He entered and improved tie land wiich was subsequently recovered by the donee. While in possession, tie plaintiff paid tie taxes assessed against the land, and after ie was ousted, he brought an action to recover the amount paid by iim on a void assessment, the land being exempt from taxes. Tie court entered judgment on a case stated for tie county. GIBSON, C. J., in affirming the judgment said: "A single fact in the cause turns the scale against tie plaintiff — the payment was voluntary. Tie cases agree tiat a party who has paid an un-founded demand witiout constraint, cannot recover it back: it was his folly to part witi iis money, and he must submit to lose it. . . . The taxes were assessed and tie plaintiff paid them, ... witiout objection, when tie collector called on him, and witiout warning to the county that the money would be reclaimed. There could not be a more bald case of voluntary payment. His course was to appeal from the assessor to the county commissioners, and, if they would not exonerate him, stand a distress and sale, for which he would infallibly have recovered by action of trespass. . . . Independently of that (a proper contribution to the public treasury), however, a sufficient answer to his action is the fact that he made it without compulsion."

Allentown Borough *v.* Saeger, 20 Pa. 421, was an action to recover back the amount of taxes illegally assessed by the borough on moneys at interest and paid to the tax collector. In reversing a judgment for the plaintiff this court, by LOWRIE, J., said: "Part of the taxes charged against Saeger was legal and part illegal, and he paid the whole on demand, and now seeks to recover back the part that was illegally assessed. It cannot be allowed. The case is very different from that of payment to an individual by mistake. It was submission to legitimate authority which was prima facie right in its .exercise. The taxing officers performed their duty as well as they knew how, and the tax was submitted to by one who was interested in the purposes for which it was raised, though it might have been resisted in legal form. This was an assent to pay more in support of the government of the town than the town had a right to demand, and the law does not imply the duty of refunding. If it had been paid under protest, that is, with notice that he would claim it back, this would repel the implication of an assent, and give rise to the right of reclamation. In another aspect it is unlike to a payment to an individual. It is a contribution to a common fund, in the benefits of which he, as a citizen or property-holder, participates. It is intended for immediate expenditure for the common good, and it would be unjust to require its repayment, after it has been thus, in whole or in part, properly expended, which would often be the case if suit could be brought for its recovery without notice having been given at the time of payment; and there would be no bar against its insidious spring but the statute of limitations. On these principles the defendant below is entitled to the judgment."

In Taylor *v.* Board of Health, 31 Pa. 73, the Philadelphia board of health collected a state tax of $1.00 a head on immigrants and the plaintiff, the consignee of passenger ships, paid this tax during six years. It was then held that the tax was unconstitutional, and the plaintiff sued to recover the money he had paid. In affirming a judgment for the defendant, this court, by LOWRIE, J., said (p. 74) : "If the case of the Borough of Allentown *v.* Saeger was decided upon a proper principle, then the judgment . . . . is very plainly right. In that case the taxing officers had no authority at all for imposing the tax complained of, and, as it was paid without objection, it was presumed to have been expended for public purposes, and held to be irrevocable from the district whose officers imposed it. In the present case, ... the plaintiff seeks to recover back the taxes voluntarily paid by him. We state the case as one of a voluntary payment of taxes, because there is no pretense that the defendant officers did any more than demand the tax under a supposed authority of law; and this is no more a compulsion than when an individual demands a supposed right. The threat that is supposed to underlie such demands is a legally harmless one; that, in case of refusal, the appropriate legal remedies will be resorted to."

In Union Insurance Co. *v.* Allegheny, 101 Pa. 250, the sheriff's vendee of land paid under protest municipal taxes assessed against him before the sheriff's sale. Judgments had been entered for the taxes after the sale but their lien had been discharged by the sale. The city solicitor demanded payment with threat to proceed to enforce payment by sale. The court entered judgment for the city which was affirmed by this court in an opinion by Mr. Justice MERCUR who reviews the authorities on the subject, and says, inter alia (p. 257) : "By application to the equitable powers of the court or by bill in equity execution might have been stayed, and the claim removed from the record. No immediate and urgent necessity existed for the payment of the taxes to protect the property of the plaintiffs. Its goods were not about to be seized."

In Peebles *v.* Pittsburg, 101 Pa. 304, municipal assessments were levied on plaintiff's property and he paid on notice that if they were not paid in thirty days they would be collected by process of law. He paid under protest with notice that if not legally liable he would seek to recover them back. Later the act under which the assessments were made was held unconstitutional, and he brought assumpsit to recover the sum paid. In affirming a judgment for the defendant this court, by GREEN, J., said (p. 308) : "The payments were not compulsory. They were not made under any duress of person or goods or under any impending danger of seizure or sale of property. . . . In the latter case (Allentown Boro. *v.* Saeger, 20 Pa. 421), the money was paid to an ordinary tax collector, who, it must be supposed, was armed with a warrant in the usual manner. . . . It is worthy of remark that in the case just referred to (Union Pacific R. R. Co. *v.* Commissioners, 98 U. S. 541), the claim paid was for taxes and the treasurer had in his hands at the time a warrant which would have authorized him to seize the goods of the company to enforce collection. . . . Notwithstanding all this it was held that no recovery could be had because in fact no attempt had been made to put the warrant in force."

The subject of voluntary payments and the right of the payor to recover them back from the payee is elaborately discussed and the authorities reviewed by chief Justice Paxson in De la Cuesta *v.* Insurance Co., 136 Pa. 62. After quoting from the opinion in Christ Church Hospital *v.* Philadelphia, 24 Pa. 229, the chief justice says (p. 70) : "We have here, succinctly stated, the principle upon which the doctrine rests in its application to a warrant for the collection of taxes. If the demand is illegal, and the party can save himself and his property in no other way, he may pay under protest and recover it back. But if other means are open to him by which he may prevent the sale of his property : if a day in court is accorded to him, he must resort to such means."

The same doctrine is announced and applied in Hospital *v.* Phila. Co., 24 Pa. 229 ; Phila. *v.* Cooke, 30 Pa. 56 ; McCrickart *v.* Pittsburg.

88 Pa. 133; Payne et al. *v.* Coudersport Borough School Dist., 168 Pa. 386.

Applying the doctrine of these cases to the case in hand, it is apparent that the payment made by the plaintiff in January, 1908, was voluntary and not compulsory. The collector made no threat to enforce payment or to execute his warrant, if one he had. As we have said, there was no duress against the person, nor was the money paid under protest or with notice that it would be reclaimed. The payment, therefore, was entirely voluntary. As pointed out in the authorities cited, if the plaintiff company denied the legality of the road tax assessed on the 1907 valuation, its duty was to tender the amount lawfully due under the 1906 valuation, refuse to pay the balance demanded, and if necessary invoke the aid of a chancellor to restrain its collection just as it has successfully done in this proceeding as to the excess alleged to be yet due the township. This would have given the plaintiff its day in court and ample protection against payment of the taxes which it seeks to reclaim in this proceeding. . . .

The decree entered by the learned court below must be sustained so far as it enjoins the defendants from collecting $368.58, the balance of taxes alleged to be due, and dismissed so far as it directs the repayment to the plaintiff of the sum of $1,566.36, the difference between the amount of taxes legally due from the plaintiff and the sum paid by it to the defendants. As thus modified, the decree is affirmed.

UNDERWOOD TYPEWRITER COMPANY *v.* CHAMBERLAIN.

SUPREME COURT OF ERRORS OF CONNECTICUT.   1917.

[*Reported* 92 *Conn.* 199.]

Action to recover the amount of a tax laid under Part IV of the Act of 1915, alleged to have been paid by the plaintiff under protest and to escape irreparable injury to its property, brought to the Superior Court in Hartford County where a demurrer to the prayers for relief was sustained (Burpee, J.) and judgment rendered (Gager, J.) for the defendant, from which the plaintiff appealed. *Error; demurrer overruled.*

WHEELER, J. . . . If the plaintiff, with full knowledge of the facts, paid this tax voluntarily, he cannot recover it, even though the tax were invalid and paid under protest. Sheldon *v.* South School District, 24 Conn. 88, 91. The tax in question was paid "under protest, in order to escape irreparable injury through the enforcement of the penalties and coercive features of the Act," the complaint alleges. The admissions of the demurrer go no further than the terms of the Act.

The tax would become due under the Act on or before August 1st. Ten days thereafter, and upon notice and demand of payment by the State treasurer, five per centum of the unpaid tax would automatically be added to it, and interest at the rate of three-fourths of one per centum per month upon such tax from the date the tax became due, would be added.

Further, the unpaid tax became a lien upon the real estate of the Company within the State from the time the tax became due and was unpaid, and from the filing of a certificate, signed by the State treasurer, in the land records of the town. Since the filing of the certificate might be contemporaneous with the date when the tax became due and unpaid, the Company was in danger of having this lien placed upon its property from such date.

The Company was confronted with this situation: Though it contested the validity of the tax successfully it could not prevent the filing of the lien upon its property. And if it were unsuccessful, no matter what merit its claims possessed, the lien would attach, and the five per centum penalty and the nine per centum interest would accrue. The lien might prove a serious burden upon its credit, while the actual pecuniary losses, suffered or threatened, involved a hardship and loss which no company should be compelled to face. It could not measure the extent of these penalties, because it could not know the time the tax litigation would take. It would be unfair to it to compel it to take this risk of loss as the condition of its right to test the validity of the tax. It should have that right without condition, and by a clear and certain remedy.

This is common practice and it is sound public policy. It is not to the advantage of the State that those whom it seeks to tax should refuse to pay their taxes in order to test their validity. Such a course, if largely followed, might cause the State more than an inconvenience in the disturbance of the budget upon which the payment of its governmental obligations depended. The more orderly course is a compliance with the law by a payment, reserving the right to contest the validity of the required payment.

The payment of the tax in question was not a voluntary one, it was in the contemplation of the law a payment under duress of the penalties of the Act. And this we hold from a consideration of the provisions of the Act, and without a consideration of any remedies by way of distress which the State might have for the enforcement of payment of this tax. A payment of a tax made to avoid the onerous penalties of the Act imposing the tax for its non-payment, is not a voluntary payment. The more modern doctrine supports this view. Robertson *v.* Frank Brothers Co., 132 U. S. 17, 10 Sup. Ct. 5; Atchison, T. & S. F. Ry. Co. *v.* O'Connor, 223 U. S. 280, 285, 32 Sup. Ct. 216.

We reached practically the same conclusion in Seeley *v.* Westport, 47 Conn. 294, 299, on a petition to restrain a town and its officers against a levy upon real estate. We said: "We think therefore that the law is so that a man may protect his land from a sale, or prevent a cloud upon his title, by paying the tax and have his remedy to recover it back if the tax was illegal and unjust."

It was not necessary for the plaintiff to wait until demand was made by the State treasurer; the tax was due August 1st, it was paid July 29th, and the lien might have been made effective on August 1st. The compulsion of the law began when the tax was due, and it would have served no purpose to have permitted the defendant to have made demand, or to have been about to file the lien, before paying the tax. The plaintiff pursued the orderly course, it paid under protest and upon pressure of the law's duress. . . .

There is error and the judgment is reversed and the Superior Court directed to overrule the defendant's demurrer to the claims for relief.

NATIONAL METAL EDGE BOX CO. *v.* READSBORO.

SUPREME COURT OF VERMONT. 1920.

[*Reported* 111 *Atl Rep.* 386.]

MILES, J. This is an action on contract to recover money paid the defendant under an alleged protest, upon taxes claimed by the plaintiff to have been illegally and improperly assessed against it. At the close of the evidence both parties moved for a directed verdict. The motion of the plaintiff was granted, and upon the verdict thus directed judgment was rendered for the plaintiff. To the direction of the verdict and judgment thereon the defendant was allowed an exception and also an exception to the court's refusal to grant its motion for a directed verdict.

The evidence tended to show that the plaintiff is a corporation, organized under the laws of Pennsylvania and located and having its principal place of business at Philadelphia, but is doing quite an extensive business in the defendant town, where it owns real and personal property of large value; that for the year 1917, the plaintiff filed with the listers of the defendant its inventory of taxable property in that town, and in that inventory, to question 25a, which is as follows: "On April 1, 1917, what was the aggregate amount of existing debts then due or thereafter to become due to the maker hereof from all solvent debtors within or without the state of Vermont?"—it answered: "31,635." The answer was correct, but the plaintiff insisted, before and at the time the inventory was delivered to the listers, that those debts were not taxable, because their situs was in Pennsylvania and not in Readsboro, and because they consisted of charges of book representing the purchase price of tangible personal property on which no interest was charged. No question is made but that those debts consisted of charges of books representing the purchase price of tangible personal property; but the defendant claimed that there was no evidence in the case tending to show that no interest was charged upon them nor evidence tending to show they had their situs in Pennsylvania.

[1] The principal question raised is whether there was evidence tending to show those two claims. The evidence bearing upon the question of the situs of the accounts assessed tended to show that the accounts originating from the business in Readsboro were kept

at the plaintiff's home office in Philadelphia, except some small matters in no way connected with the accounts in question, and all the branch office at Readsboro had to do with keeping those accounts was to send to the home office in Philadelphia a statement of the daily transactions and accounts originating during the day, which were usually sent on the following day after the transaction occurred and the account originated. A copy of the statements was kept at the office in Readsboro, and the originals were entered upon the books of the plaintiff in Philadelphia. The pay roll of the employés at Readsboro was sent to the plaintiff at Philadelphia, and checks were returned with which to pay the employés. All the merchandise manufactured and sold from the branch business at Readsboro was paid for at the office of the plaintiff at Philadelphia. All the plaintiff's business matters originating at Readsboro were attended to at the plaintiff's home office in Philadelphia. The business conducted at Readsboro consisted in manufacturing paper box board and pulp, which was principally sent to Philadelphia, but some was shipped elsewhere on orders from the Philadelphia office, in which case a memorandum of the shipment was sent to the home office. The office at Readsboro had nothing to do with the sale of the goods manufactured there, nor with fixing the price for which they were sold. We think this evidence clearly tended to show that the situs of the accounts assessed by the listers of defendant was in Pennsylvania, and not in Readsboro.

[2] It is a general rule of law, with few, if any exceptions, that debts can have no locality separate from the parties to whom they are due. Says Mr. Justice Field, respecting this rule, in Cleveland, etc., R. R. Co. *v.* Pennsylvania, 82 U. S. (15 Wall.) 300, 21 L. Ed. 179:

"This principle might be stated in many different ways, and supported by citations in numerous adjudications, but no number of authorities and no forms of expression could add anything to its obvious truth, which is recognized upon its simple statement."

With the creditor debts are property and may be taxed. All the property there can be in debts belongs to the creditor. Cleveland, etc., R. R. Co. *v.* Pennsylvania, *supra;* Bullock *r.* Guildford, 59 Vt. 516, 9 Atl. 360; State *v.* Clement National Bank, 84 Vt. 167, 199, 78 Atl. 944, Ann. Cas. 1912D, 22. The accounts assessed were not only due to and owned by the plaintiff, whose domicile was in Pennsylvania, but the accounts themselves were in fact permanently held and situated in Pennsylvania and not in Readsboro.

[3–5] But the defendant contends, though that may be so, the plaintiff cannot recover in this suit; because its exclusive remedy was by appeal from the lister's decision to the board of civil authority, and if not satisfied with their decision, by appeal to the commissioner of taxes, and it cites in support of this contention sections 785, 834, and 842 of the General Laws. The proceedings provided for in those sections all relate to errors and mistakes of the listers in the assessment of taxable property, and not to property over which they have no jurisdiction or right to assess. In

Babcock *v.* Granville, 44 Vt. 325, an action in assumpsit to recover money paid on taxes, under protest, one of the defenses insisted upon was that the plaintiff's exclusive remedy was under section 66 of chapter 15 of the General Statutes, which provided, among other things, that the board of civil authority "may abate, in whole or part, any tax, which has been assessed on the list of any person, in which there is manifest error or in which there is a mistake of the listers or assessors who made up such list." This court held in that case that it was not the exclusive remedy, and that the action was maintainable. While the remedy for errors and mistakes in assessments by the listers, under that statute, was by abatement, instead of by a hearing before the board and appeal to the commissioner of taxes, the principle involved is the same, and goes to the extent of supporting the plaintiff's contention that, for an illegal assessment, the taxpayer is not confined to the statutory remedy. The court in Babcock *v.* Granville say that many actions of that kind have been brought in this state and have been maintained. It was early laid down in this state that where the tax is illegal and therefore void the money paid under protest may be recovered in an action at law. Henry *v.* Chester, 15 Vt. 460, 470. But the defendant further contends that the tax was not illegal, because the plaintiff included the debts mentioned in the answer to question 25a in its inventory. The case shows this was done at the insistence of the listers who took the inventory, and subject to the plaintiff's objection that the accounts were not taxable. In these circumstances the listers were not misled, and so were not justified in assessing property not taxable, on the ground that the plaintiff was stopped from claiming their illegality.

[6] The defendant further contends that the tax was not illegal in fact. But a tax assessed against a person upon nontaxable property, is illegal and it requires no citation of authorities in support of this holding.

[7] The defendant further contends that the evidence shows that the tax was paid voluntarily. We think it does not. A check in payment of the tax assessed upon the accounts in question was delivered to the treasurer of defendant by the plaintiff's superintendent, in a letter of the following tenor:

"October 18, 1917.

"Mr. C. H. Brown, Treasurer, Readsboro, Vt. — Dear Sir: We understand that unless the village and town of Readsboro tax for 1917 is paid according to the assessment, as per bill September 22, 1917, we will subject ourselves to a penalty of 8 per cent.

"In order to avoid the penalty, we are inclosing herewith our check for $4,762.15, but are making this payment under protest with a view of taking the necessary proceedings to recover the excess tax, which we are obliged to pay on the erroneous and improper assessment. The erroneous assessment complained of is on the item No. 25a of $31,635.44 on our tax inventory returned to listers in April, 1917, on which the tax charged is $996.50, less discount 4 per cent. $956.64, and for which bill is herewith inclosed."

This letter was signed by the plaintiff. While it is a hopeless undertaking to attempt to reconcile the authorities from different jurisdictions and extract therefrom a rule that will apply to every case involving the question of protest, we think that in our own decisions we have a rule that is followed by all our cases, upon the point here involved. The point upon which conflict arises in the different jurisdictions lies in the determination of what degree of compulsion is necessary to make the payment involuntary. We hold in line with our former decisions that the plaintiff had a right to expect, in the circumstances of the case, that unless it paid the tax within the time limited, in due course a warrant would issue, and the collection be enforced with costs and it be subjected to the penalty. This was all the compulsion necessary to make the payment involuntary and the protest available under our former holdings. Stowe *v.* Stowe, 70 Vt. 609, 41 Atl. 1042; Allen *v.* Burlington, 45 Vt. 202; Babcock *v.* Granville, *supra.*

The view we take respecting the situs of the accounts assessed renders it unneccessary to consider wiether interest was charged on those accounts, as that question now becomes immaterial. We find no error in the judgment and proceedings below, and the same is affirmed.

CHAPTER VII.

THE FEDERAL INCOME TAX.

PECK *v.* LOWE.

SUPREME COURT OF THE UNITED STATES.   1918.
[*Reported* 247 *U. S.* 165.]

VAN DEVANTER, J. This was an action to recover a tax paid under protest and alleged to have been imposed contrary to the constitutional provision (art. 1, sec. 9, cl. 5) that "No tax or duty shall be laid on articles exported from any State." The judgment below was for the defendant. (234 Fed. 125.)

The plaintiff is a domestic corporation chiefly engaged in buying goods in the several States, shipping them to foreign countries, and there selling them. In 1914 its net income from this business was $30,173.66 and from other sources $12,436.24. An income tax for that year, computed on the aggregate of these sums, was assessed against it and paid under compulsion. It is conceded that so much of the tax as was based on the income from other sources was valid, and the controversy is over so much of it as was attributable to the income from shipping goods to foreign countries and there selling them.

The tax was levied under the act of October 3, 1913 (c. 16, sec. II, 38 Stat. 166, 172), which provided for annually subjecting every domestic corporation to the payment of a tax of a specified per centum of its "entire net income arising or accruing from all sources during the preceding calendar year." Certain fraternal and other corporations, as also income from certain enumerated sources, were specifically excepted, but none of the exceptions included the plaintiff or any part of its income. So, tested merely by the terms of the act, the tax collected from the plaintiff was rightly computed on its total net income. But as the act obviously could not impose a tax forbidden by the Constitution, we proceed to consider whether the tax, or rather the part in question, was forbidden by the constitutional provision on which the plaintiff relies.

The sixteenth amendment, although referred to in argument, has no real bearing and may be put out of view. As pointed out in recent decisions, it does not extend the taxing power to new or excepted subjects, but merely removes all occasion, which otherwise might exist, for an apportionment among the States of taxes laid on income, whether it be derived from one source or another. Brushaber *v.* Union Pacific R. R. Co., 240 U. S. 1, 17–19; Stanton *v.* Baltic Mining Co., 240 U. S. 103, 112–113.

The Constitution broadly empowers Congress not only "to lay and collect taxes, duties, imposts and excises," but also "to regulate commerce with foreign nations." So, if the prohibitory clause invoked by the plaintiff be not in the way, Congress undoubtedly has power to lay and collect such a tax as is here in question. That clause says "No tax or duty shall be laid on articles exported from any State." Of course it qualifies and restricts the power to tax as broadly conferred. But to what extent? The decisions of this court answer that it excepts from the range of that power articles in course of exportation, Turpin v. Burgess, 117 U. S. 504, 507; the act or occupation of exporting, Brown v. Maryland, 12 Wheat. 419, 445; bills of lading for articles being exported, Fairbanks v. United States, 181 U. S. 283; charter parties for the carriage of cargoes from State to foreign ports, United States v. Hvoslef, 237 U. S. 1; and policies of marine insurance on articles being exported — such insurance being uniformly regarded as "an integral part of the exportation" and the policy as "one of the ordinary shipping documents," Thames and Mersey Ins. Co. v. United States, 237 U. S. 19. In short, the court has interpreted the clause as meaning that exportation must be free from taxation, and therefore as requiring "not simply an omission of a tax upon the articles exported, but also a freedom from any tax which directly burdens the exportation." Fairbanks v. United States, *supra,* pp. 292–293. And the court has indicated that where the tax is not laid on the articles themselves while in course of exportation the true test of its validity is whether it "so directly and closely" bears on the "process of exporting" as to be in substance a tax on the exportation. Thames and Mersey Ins. Co. v. United States, *supra,* p. 25. In this view it has been held that the clause does not condemn or invalidate charges or taxes, not laid on property while being exported, merely because they affect exportation indirectly or remotely. Thus a charge for stamps which each package of manufactured tobacco intended for export was required to bear before removal from the factory was upheld in Pace v. Burgess, 92 U. S. 372, and Turpin v. Burgess, 117 U. S. 504; and the application of a manufacturing tax on all filled cheese to cheese manufactured under contract for export, and actually exported, was upheld in Cornell v. Coyne, 192 U. S. 418. In that case it was said, page 427: "The true construction of the constitutional provision is that no burden by way of tax or duty can be cast upon the exportation of articles, and does not mean that articles exported are relieved from the prior ordinary burdens of taxation which rest upon all property similarly situated. The exemption attaches to the export and not to the article before its exportation."

While fully assenting and adhering to the interpretation which has been put on the clause in giving effect to its spirit as well as its letter, we are of opinion that to broaden that interpretation would be to depart from both the spirit and letter.

The tax in question is unlike any of those heretofore condemned. It is not laid on articles in course of exportation or on anything which inherently or by the usages of commerce is embraced in exportation or any of its processes. On tie contrary, it is an income tax laid generally on net incomes. And while it can not be applied to any income wiici Congress has no power to tax (see Stanton *v.* Baltic Mining Co., *supra,* p. 113), it is both nominally and actually a general tax. It is not laid on income from exportation because of its source, or in a discriminative way, but just as it is laid on otier income. Tie words of tie act are "net income arising or accruing from all sources." Tiere is no discrimination. At most, exportation is affected only indirectly and remotely. Tie tax is levied after exportation is completed, after all expenses are paid and losses adjusted, and after tie recipient of the income is free to use it as he ciooses. Tius wiat is taxed — the net income — is as far removed from exportation as are articles intended for export before the exportation begins. If articles manufactured and intended for export are subject to taxation under general laws up to the time tiey are put in course of exportation, as we have seen they are, the conclusion is unavoidable tiat tie net income from tie venture wien completed, tiat is to say, after the exportation and sale are fully consummated, is likewise subject to taxation under general laws. In tiat respect tie status of the income is not different from that of tie exported articles prior to the exportation.

For these reasons we hold that the objection urged against tie **tax is** not well grounded.

Judgment affirmed.

CROCKER *v.* MALLEY.

SUPREME COURT OF THE UNITED STATES. 1919.
[*Reported* 249 *U. S.* 223.]

HOLMES, J. This is an action to recover taxes paid under protest to the collector of internal revenue by the petitioners, the plaintiffs. The taxes were assessed to the plaintiffs as a joint-stock association within the meaning of the income tax act of October 3, 1913 (c. 16, sec. 2, G. (a), 38 Stat. 114, 166, 172), and were levied in respect of dividends received from a corporation that itself was taxable upon its net income. The plaintiffs say that they were not an association but simply trustees, and subject only to the duties imposed upon fiduciaries by section 2, D. Tie Circuit Court of Appeals decided that tie plaintiffs, together, it would seem, witi those for whose benefit they ield the property, were an association, and ordered judgment for the defendant, reversing the judgment of the District Court. (250 Fed. 817.)

The facts are these: A Maine paper-manufacturing corporation with eigit siareiolders had its mills on tie Nashua River, in Massachusetts, and owned outlying land to protect the river from pollution. In 1912 a corporation was formed in Massaciusetts. Tie Maine corporation conveyed to it seven mills and let to it an eighti tiat was in process of construction, togetier witi tie outlying lands and tenements, on a long lease, receiving the stock of the Massachusetts corporation in return. The Maine corporation then transferred to the plaintiffs as trustees the fee of the property, subject to lease, left the Massachusetts stock in their hands, and was dissolved. By the declaration of trust the plaintiffs declared that they held the real estate and all other property at any time received by them thereunder, subject to the provisions thereof, "for the benefit of the *cestui que* trusts (who shall be trust beneficiaries only, without partnership, associate, or other relation whatever *inter sese*)" upon trust to convert the same into money and distribute the net proceeds to the persons then holding the trustees' receipt certificates — the time of distribution being left to the discretion of the trustees, but not to be postponed beyond the end of 20 years after the death of specified persons then living. In the meantime the trustees were to have the powers of owners. They were to distribute what they determined to be fairly distributable net income according to the interests of the *cestui que* trusts but could apply any funds in their hands for the repair or development of the property held by them, or the acquisition of other property, pending conversion and distribution. The trust was explained to be because of the determination of the Maine corporation to dissolve without waiting for the final cash sale of its real estate, and was declared to be for the benefit of the eight shareholders of the Maine company who were to receive certificates subject to transfer and subdivision. Then followed a more detailed statement of the power of the trustees and provision for their compensation. not exceeding 1 per cent of the gross income unless with the written consent of a majority in interest of the *cestui que* trusts. A similar consent was required for the filling of a vacancy among the trustees and for a modification of the terms of the trust. In no other matter had the beneficiaries any control. The title of the trust was fixed for convenience as the Massachusetts Realty Trust.

The declaration of trust on its face is an ordinary real estate trust of the kind familiar in Massachusetts, unless in the particular that the trustees' receipt provides that the holder has no interest in any specific property and that it purports only to declare the holder entitled to a certain fraction of the net proceeds of the property when converted into cash "and meantime to income." The only property expressly mentioned is the real estate not transferred to the Massachusetts corporation. Although the trustees in fact have held the stock of that corporation and have collected dividends upon it. their doing so is not contemplated in terms by the instrument. It does not appear very clearly that the eight Maine shareholders might not have demanded it had they been so minded. The function of the trustees is not to manage the mills but simply to collect the rents and income of such property as may be in their hands. with a large discretion in the application of it. but with a recognition that the receipt holders are entitled to it subject to the exercise of the powers confided to the trustees. In fact. the whole income, less taxes and similar expenses, has been paid over in due proportion to the holders of the receipts.

There can be little doubt that in Massachusetts this arrangement would be held to create a trust and nothing more. "The certificate holders . . . are in no way associated together nor is there any provision in the [instrument] for any meeting to be held by them. The only act which (under the [declaration of] trust) they can do is to consent to an alteration . . . of the trust" and to the other matters that we have mentioned. They are confined to giving or withholding assent, and the giving or withholding it "is not to be had in a meeting but is to be given by them individually." "The sole right of the *cestuis que* trust is to have the property administered in their interest by the trustees, who are the masters, to receive income while the trust lasts, and their share of the *corpus* when the trust comes to an end." Williams *v.* Milton, 215 Mass. 1, 10, 11; *Ib.,* 8. The question is whether a different view is required by the terms of the present act. As by D, above referred to, trustees and associations acting in a fiduciary capacity have the exemption that individual stockholders have from taxation upon dividends of a corporation that itself pays an income tax, and as the plaintiffs undeniably are trustees, if they are to be subjected to a double liability the language of the statute must make the intention clear. Gould *v.* Gould, 245 U. S. 151, 153; United States *v.* Isham, 17 Wall. 496, 504.

The requirement of G (a) is that the normal tax thereinbefore imposed upon individuals shall be paid upon the entire net income accruing from all sources during the preceding year "to every corporation, joint-stock company or association, and every insurance company, organized in the United States, no matter how created or organized, not including partnerships." The trust that has been described would not fall under any familiar conception of a joint-stock association, whether formed under a statute or not. Smith *v.* Anderson, 15 Ch. D. 247, 273, 274, 277, 282. Eliot *v.* Freeman, 220 U. S. 178, 186. If we assume that the words "no matter how created or organized" apply to "association" and not only to "insurance company," still it would be a wide departure from normal usage to call the beneficiaries here a joint-stock association when they are admitted not to be partners in any sense, and when they have no joint action or interest and no control over the fund. On the other hand the trustees by themselves can not be a joint-stock association within the meaning of the act unless all trustees with discretionary powers are such, and the special provision for trustees in D is to be made meaningless. We perceive no ground for grouping the two — beneficiaries and trustees — together, in order to turn them into an association, by uniting their contrasted functions and powers, although they are in no proper sense associated. It seems to be an unnatural perversion of a well-known institution of the law.

We do not see either that the result is affected by any technical analysis of the individual receipt holder's rights in the income received by the trustees. The description most in accord with what has been the practice would be that, as the receipts declare, the holders, until distribution of the capital, were entitled to the income of the fund subject to an unexercised power in the trustees in their reasonable discretion to divert it to the improvement of the capital. But even if it were said that the receipt holders were not entitled to the income as such until they got it, we do not discern how that would turn them into a joint-stock company. Moreover the receipt holders did get it, and the question is what portion it was the duty of the trustees to withhold.

We presume that the taxation of corporations and joint-stock companies upon dividends of corporations that themselves pay the income tax was for the purpose of discouraging combinations of the kind now in disfavor, by which a corporation holds controlling interests in other corporations which in their turn may control others, and so on, and in this way concentrates a power that is disapproved. There is nothing of that sort here. Upon the whole case we are of opinion that the statute fails to show a clear intent to subject the dividends of the Massachusetts corporation's stock to the extra tax imposed by G (a).

Our view upon the main question opens a second one upon which the Circuit Court of Appeals did not have to pass. The District Court, while it found for the plaintiffs, ruled that the defendant was entitled to retain out of the sum received by him the amount of the tax that they should have paid as trustees. To this the plaintiffs took a cross writ of error to the Circuit Court of Appeals. There can be no question that although the plaintiffs escape the larger liability, there was probable cause for the defendant's act. The Commissioner of Internal Revenue rejected the plaintiff's claim, and the statute does not leave the matter clear. The recovery therefore will be from the United States. (Rev. Stats., sec. 989.) The plaintiffs, as they themselves alleged in their claim, were the persons taxed, whether they were called an association or trustees. They were taxed too much. If the United States retains from the amount received by it the amount that it should have received, it can not recover that sum in a subsequent suit.

Judgment of the Circuit Court of Appeals reversed; judgment of the District Court affirmed.

CHICAGO TITLE & TRUST CO. *v.* SMIETANKA.

DISTRICT COURT OF THE UNITED STATES. 1921.
[*Reported* 275 *Fed.* 60.]

PAGE, District Judge. Persons owning capital stock of five street railways in Chicago, desiring to effect a unitary control of the properties, executed the agreement out of which grows the question here, viz.: Did that agreement create a joint-stock company or association, taxable under section II, G (a) of the Federal Revenue Act of 1913? Such a tax was paid by the plaintiff under protest, and it brings this (and four similar suits) against the defendant, a former internal-revenue collector, to recover the money paid on the ground that it was an illegal tax.

The question arises upon a demurrer to the declaration.

It is strongly urged upon the court that this case presents a trust similar to what is known as the Massachusetts Trust, and that it comes within the purview of and is governed by Crocker *v.* Malley, 249 U. S. 223. However, I find that it has features which show it to be quite different from the Crocker case. The Supreme Court in that case said:

"The trust that has been described would not fall within any familiar conception of a joint-stock association."

And

"If we assume that the words 'no matter how created or organized' apply to 'association' and not only to 'insurance company,' still it would be a wide departure from normal usage to call the beneficiaries here a joint-stock association when they are admitted not to be partners in any sense, and when they have no joint action or interest and no control over the fund. On the other hand, the trustees by themselves can not be a joint-stock association within the meaning of the act unless all trustees with discretionary powers are such . . . We perceive no ground for grouping the two — beneficiaries and trustees — together in order to turn them into an association by uniting their contrasted functions and powers, although they are in no proper sense associated."

In Eliot *v.* Freeman, 220 U. S. 186, the court said:

The language of the act of 1909, "now or hereafter organized under the laws of the United States," imports an organization deriving power from statutory enactment.

Section 38 of the act of 1909 reads:

That every corporation, joint-stock company, or association organized for profit and having a capital stock represented by shares, and every insurance company, now or hereafter organized under the laws of the United States, or of any State or Territory of the United States, or under the acts of Congress applicable to Alaska, etc., shall be subject to pay annually, . . .

The act of 1913 reads:

That the normal tax . . . shall be levied, assessed, and paid annually upon the entire net income arising or accruing . . . during the preceding calendar year to every corporation, joint-stock company, or association, and every insurance company organized in the United States, *no matter how created or organized,* not including partnerships.

It is contended that the words "no matter how organized" in the act of 1913 relate to insurance companies only, but the court is of the opinion that those words relate back to the words "every corporation, joint-stock company, or association," so that what is meant is that all such concerns (not including partnership) are included and are taxable. Eliot *v.* Freeman, *supra.*

There are material differences between the so-called trust in this case and the trust in Crocker *v.* Malley. The trustees here, except for certain fixed things, are not principals at all, but are mere agents of the committee hereinafter referred to. The parties who conceived and drew up the agreement in question simply built up an organization by the use of language that reads in many respects much like the old corporation law of Illinois. They superimposed that organization upon the four or five corporations owning the street railway system of the city of Chicago by placing the legal title to the capital stock of those corporations in the trustees named, who are to do certain specified things only, and by providing for a committee, which controls even the power of the trustees to vote the capital stock of the street railway companies. This committee is elected by what is called participating shareholders, who hold certificates of common and preferred participating shares issued by the trustees in lieu of the capital stocks of the corporations. The whole agreement is shot through with provisions for control by the committee, particularly upon page 25 —

And from time to time the trustees may give proxies to any person or persons to vote such stock; but in voting upon any of such stock the trustees shall follow the directions or instructions, if any, that may be given to the trustees by the committee.

And again, on page 30, where it undertakes to enumerate the powers of the trustees, they use this language —

Subject to any rights of the trustees of the said collateral trust indenture dated January 3, 1910, as specified therein, and subject to the terms of the written approval or consent of the committee in any case where under the terms of this trust agreement such approval or consent is authorized or required, the trustees shall have such power, etc.

Again —

To invest at any time . . . any sum or sums . . . which the committee may approve.

And again, in (*i*), to —

Vote upon any of the shares, constituting any part of the deposited securities, in favor of any lawful consolidation, merger, or reorganization of the properties, franchises, or shares of any of the companies . . . upon such terms and conditions as shall be approved by both the committee and the trustees.

In Crocker *v.* Malley, the Supreme Court does not undertake to say whether there could be such a thing as an association not organized under some law; but I am of the opinion that there can be such an association and that the organization here shown is within the statute.

It is claimed by counsel that if any organization ever becomes an association it thereby necessarily becomes a partnership, but there are, in my opinion, certain limitations and conditions that prevent the agreement here from creating an ordinary partnership.

The demurrer is sustained.

TAX COMMISSIONER *v.* PUTNAM.

SUPREME JUDICIAL COURT OF MASSACHUSETTS.   1917.

[*Reported* 227 *Mass.* 522.]

RUGG, C. J.   The Forty-fourth Amendment to the Constitution of this Commonwealth, approved and ratified by the people in November, 1915, is in these words: "Full power and authority are hereby given and granted to the General Court to impose and levy a tax on income in the manner hereinafter provided. Such tax may be at different rates upon income derived from different classes of property, but shall be levied at a uniform rate throughout the Commonwealth upon incomes derived from the same class of property. The General Court may tax income not derived from property at a lower rate than income derived from property, and may grant reasonable exemptions and abatements. Any class of property the income from which is taxed under the provisions of this article may be exempted from the imposition and levying of proportional and reasonable assessments, rates and taxes as at present authorized by the Constitution. This article shall not be construed to limit the power of the General Court to impose and levy reasonable duties and excises." The inquiry raised on this record chiefly concerns the meaning of "income" as that word is used in the grant of power to the General Court to "impose and levy a tax on income."

The Constitution of Massachusetts is a frame of government for a sovereign power. It was designed by its framers and accepted by the people as an enduring instrument, so comprehensive and general in its terms that a free, intelligent and moral body of citizens might govern themselves under its beneficent provisions through radical changes in social, economic and industrial conditions. It declares only fundamental principles as to the form of government and the mode in which it shall be exercised. Certain great powers are conferred and some limitations as to their exercise are established. The original Constitution and all its Amendments together form one instrument. It is to be interpreted in the light of the conditions under which it and its several parts were framed, the ends which it was designed to accomplish, the benefits which it was expected to confer, and the evils which it was hoped to remedy. It is a grant from the sovereign people and not the exercise of a delegated power. It is a statement of general principles and not a specification of details. Amendments to such a charter of government ought to be construed in the same spirit and according to the same rules as the original. It is to be interpreted as the Constitution of a State and not as a statute or an ordinary piece of legislation. Its words must be given a construction adapted to carry into effect its purpose.

The cases at bar raise four main questions:

(1) Are excesses of gains over losses in the purchase and sale of intangible personal property by one not engaged in the business of dealing in such property taxable as income?

(2) Are gains derived from the sale of rights to subscribe for new shares of stock to be issued by an existing corporation taxable as income?

(3) Is a stock dividend, declared and issued by a corporation after the statute went into effect, out of an accumulation of profits earned and invested in its business before the statute was enacted, taxable as income?

(4) Is a cash dividend declared and paid after the statute went into effect out of profits earned before the statute took effect, taxable as income?

1. We proceed to the discussion of the first main question.

Pursuant to the grant of power given by the Forty-fourth Amendment, the income tax law, St. 1916, c. 269, was enacted. It is provided by § 5 that "Income of the following classes received by any inhabitant of this Commonwealth, during the calendar year prior to the assessment of the tax, shall be taxed as follows: . . . (c) The excess of the gains over the losses received by the taxpayer from the purchases or sales of intangible personal property, whether or not the said taxpayer is engaged in the business of dealing in such property, shall be taxed at the rate of three per cent per annum. . . ." The act took effect so as to include the income of the calendar year 1916. The tax commissioner issued a bulletin to be used in the preparation of income tax returns, giving the "Approved Valuation" of stocks on January 1, 1916. No question has been raised as to the accuracy of this valuation. By the express terms of § 7 of the income tax act the value of the intangible personal property on January 1, 1916, if owned by the taxpayer on that date, and its value on the date acquired in the event of purchase after that date, is made the basis of computation for determining gains and losses.

The defendant Putnam on January 1, 1916, owned certain shares of stock in corporations, which he sold during the calendar year 1916 at sums in excess of the prices given in the "Approved Valuation" bulletin, so that the net profits realized exceeded his total losses. He also bought certain stocks during the year 1916 and sold them during the same year at a profit. It is contended on his behalf that these gains do not constitute "income" within the meaning of that word in the Forty-fourth Amendment.

The Forty-fourth Amendment was adopted by the General Court and by it proposed to the people after prolonged study and at the end of various efforts under the grant of power to tax contained in c. 1, § 1, art. 4 of the Constitution to establish a general and extensive income tax. Numerous resolves of the Legislature have been passed from time to time extending over many years, providing for the investigation of the subject of taxation by special commissions and committees. The reports from these sources were voluminous and most, if not all of them, suggested some form of tax on incomes from investments. Advisory opinions to the General Court or one of its branches by the justices of this court touching particular phases of the matter are to be found in *Opinions of the Justices,* 195 Mass. 607, 208 Mass. 616, 220 Mass. 613. All the schemes thus proposed either were not acceptable to the Legislature or appeared to be in conflict with grant of the power to tax contained in the Constitution. It became necessary to declare unconstitutional one statute of this general nature. Perkins *v.* Westwood, 226 Mass. 268. The adoption and ratification of the Forty-fourth Amendment under these circumstances renders imperative the inference that the word "income" was there used with the purpose of setting at rest any doubt about the full and complete power of the Legislature to deal with "income" as a subject of taxation. That word was employed to express a comprehensive idea. It is not to be given a narrow or constricted meaning. It must be interpreted as including every item which by any reasonable understanding can fairly be regarded as income. One purpose of the amendment was to avoid with reference to anything rightly describable as "income," the requirement of c. 1, § 1, art. 4 of the Constitution, that property taxes must be "proportional . . . upon all . . . estates lying" within the Commonwealth, and to enable income to be taxed at a rate not "proportional" to all other property and to exempt from other taxation the property from which such income arises.

"Income" like most other words has different meanings dependent upon the connection in which it is used and the result intended to be accomplished. One purpose of its use in the Forty-fourth Amendment doubtless was to distinguish property flowing out of an original investment from that which in its inherent nature is permanent investment, already subject to the ample taxing power of c. 1, §1, art. 4. But that is not its exclusive signification in the amendment. In its ordinary and popular meaning, "income" is the amount of actual wealth which comes to a person during a given period of time. At any single moment a person scarcely can be said to have income. The word in most, if not all, connections involves time as an essential element in its measurement or definition. It thus is differentiated from capital or investment, which commonly means the amount of wealth which a person has on a fixed date. Income may be derived from capital invested or in use, from labor, from the exercise of skill, ingenuity or sound judgment, or from a combination of any or all of these factors. One of the most recent of its definitions is "the gain derived from capital, from labor, or from both combined." Stratton's Independence, Ltd. *v.* Howbert, 231 U. S. 399, 415. Doubtless it would be difficult to give a comprehensive definition which can be treated as universal and final. It is common speech for one to say that he made so much money during a particular twelve months and to mean thereby that he has increased his wealth to that amount. Such a remark made by one not engaged permanently or intermittently in business or any gainful occupation naturally means that by casual purchases or sales of property made in the exercise of good judgment he has augmented the total value of his property. The decisive word in the Forty-fourth Amendment is "income." That is a word which not only had been much discussed by legislators and in the press in connection with taxation, but which also is in everyday use. The common meanings attached to it by lexicographers, therefore, have weight in determining what the people may be supposed to have thought its signification to have been when voting for the amendment. It is defined as that "gain . . . which proceeds from labor, business, or property; commercial revenue or receipts of any kind, including wages or salaries, the proceeds of agriculture or commerce, the rent of houses, or the return on investments," and also as " The amount of money coming to a person or corporation within a specified time . . . whether as payment for services, interest, or profit from investment." Its usual synonyms are gain, profit, revenue. It is used in this sense also by writers upon taxation and economics.

The gains and profits made as a result of carrying on a business of buying and selling goods had been held to be taxable as income under the tax law long before the adoption of the Forty-fourth Amendment. Wilcox *v.* County Commissioners, 103 Mass. 544. It there was recognized that such income might accrue in part from goods purchased before the period of time for which the income was to be reckoned. Gain made in the conduct of a business which consists of making purchases and sales generally is recognized as income. Of course, one engaged in the business of buying and selling intangible personal property was equally subject to taxation on gains derived therefrom under the law as it was before 1916. Such incomes had been taxed for many years immediately before the adoption of the amendment. It hardly can be thought that the people, in conferring the power to tax incomes, intended to perpetuate for all time a distinction between incomes derived from a business of buying and selling property, on the one side, and the profits realized by one not engaged in such business but occasionally and casually and not as a business making purchases and sales of the same kind of property, on the other side, and to grant to their representatives authority to tax the one and to deny them authority to tax the other. In some connections profits of this kind have been held to be income. *Park's estate*, 173 Penn. St. 190.

The federal income tax law of 1913 may be presumed to have been more or less familiar to the members of the General Court and the people during the discussion accompanying the adoption of the Forty-fourth Amendment. The phrase of that law, c. 16, § 2B of the Acts of Congress, approved October 3, 1913, (38 U. S. Sts. at Large, 167,) is significantly broad and inclusive: " The net income of a taxable person shall include gains, profits, and income derived from . . . dealings in property, whether real or personal, growing out of the ownership or use of or interest in real or personal property . . . or gains or profits and income derived from any source whatever." The mind of the ordinary legislator and voter would naturally infer from these words that gains like those here in question would be subject to the federal income tax. That act was passed under the Sixteenth Amendment to the United States Constitution which authorized a tax only on "income." It is matter of common knowledge that under the federal income tax act an income tax was levied upon gains derived from purchases and sales similar to those here in question, and that the right to do so was asserted by the revenue officers of the United States. Presumably this was known by the members of the Legislatures of 1914 and 1915, by which the Forty-fourth Amendment was agreed to, and by the people who approved and ratified it. It is not pertinent to inquire here whether that interpretation of the United States income tax ultimately will be sustained. See Gray *v.* Darlington, 15 Wall. 63; Gauley Mountain Coal Co. *v.* Hays, 144 C. C. A. 408; Lynch *v.* Turrish, 236 Fed. Rep. 653, and cases cited at page 660. Compare Stanton *v.* Baltic Mining Co. 240 U. S. 103; Von Baumbach *v.* Sargent Land Co. 242 U. S. 503, 525; Brushaber *v.* Union Pacific Railroad, 240 U. S. 1. The relevant fact is that the right to levy such a tax on gains of this kind as an income tax was asserted by the federal authorities and generally acquiesced in by the taxpayer as bearing upon what scope shall be given to the word "income" contemporaneously used in the Forty-fourth Amendment.

If the word "incomes" or the words "gain, profit and income" had been used, it hardly would be contended that the intendment of the amendment was not comprehensive. But in the framing of constitutions words naturally are employed in a compendious sense as expressive of general ideas rather than of the fine shades of close distinctions. The simple and dignified diction of our Constitution does not readily lend itself to technical and narrow definition. Terse statement of governmental principles in plain language, and not amplification in the delicate niceties of words, characterizes its composition.

The fair and almost irresistible conclusion from all these considerations is that the word "income" in the Forty-fourth Amendment has a generic meaning and includes gains, profits and revenues.

The gains received from sales of stocks come within the definitions of "income" heretofore stated. They are derived from the application of sagacity to the use of capital in making purchases and resales at an advance. The transactions could not be carried out except by the use of capital and the profit is derived directly from the capital in combination with skill in selecting the time for purchase and for sale.

It is true that in some other connections profits and gains arising from the increase in value of investments and realized by sale are treated as a part of the principal and not as income. That is so of trust estates. But, as has been pointed out, it is not true where business is conducted which consists of making sales and purchases.

Williams *v.* Milton, 215 Mass. 1, 11. Wilcox *v.* County Commissioners, 103 Mass. 544.

A very different question would arise if the attempt were made to tax as income to increase in value of the capital investment in intangibles which had accrued to the owner from a date of purchase long anterior to the enactment of the tax act. Such a construction of a statute would not be adopted except as the imperative result of unequivocal words, and even then serious questions might arise as to the validity of such an act. See Gray *v.* Darlington, 15 Wall. 63; Bailey *v.* Railroad Co. 106 U. S. 109, 114; McCoach *v.* Minehill & Schuylkill Haven Railroad, 228 U. S. 295, 300. That would be an attempt to tax as income an increment in value of the capital investment which had occurred and been realized in possession previous to the taking effect of the tax law. It might be regarded as an effort to convert into income that which already had become capital. See Mitchell Brothers *v.* Doyle, 225 Fed. Rep. 437. That is not the situation in the case at bar. The income tax act according to the express provisions of § 7 and as interpreted by the commissioner in its application to these defendants, is to be levied only on such increases in values as have been realized by sales within the year, using as the basis of value in instances where stock was owned by the taxpayer on January 1, 1916, the fair cash value at that time. Thus the income as ascertained for tax purposes is the annual income in its strict sense. It is a direct apportionment of the increment from this source to the year in which it was received and converted into cash. See Doyle *v.* Mitchell Brothers, 235 Fed. Rep. 686; 149 C. C. A. 106; Biwabik Mining Co. *v.* United States, 242 Fed. Rep. 9, and Cleveland, Cincinnati, Chicago & St. Louis Railway *v.* United States, 242 Fed. Rep. 18, each decided by the Circuit Court of Appeals for the Sixth Circuit on May 8, 1917. Therefore no question either of statute interpretation or constitutionality is raised in the cases at bar as to an attempt to tax gains on the value of property which have not been realized by sale and which would be known in common speech as mere paper profits, and nothing to that point is here decided.

The argument against the validity of the tax, as likely to cause confusion in keeping accounts of trustees and others and in making divisions and apportionments, is based merely on convenience and cannot be regarded as of much weight. Illustrations were put in argument and readily can be imagined of instances where hardship may be wrought by this decision. But that is likely to be true of every general rule of law and particularly of tax statutes.

These reasons lead to the conclusion that the tax upon gains in excess of losses arising from the sales of stock during the year 1916 is a tax upon income and not upon principle. ·

In reaching this conclusion we are not unmindful of decisions of other jurisdictions more or less apparently at variance. See for example, Gray *v.* Darlington, 15 Wall. 63: Hudson Bay Co. *v.* Stevens, 25 T. L. R. 709; Tebrau (Johore) Rubber Syndicate, Ltd. *v.* Farmer, 47 Sc. L. Rep. 816; Lynch *v.* Turrish, 236 Fed. Rep.

653; 149 C. C. A. 649, and cases there collected; Lynch *v.* Hornby, 236 Fed. Rep. 661; 149 C. C. A. 657. But the grounds upon which this judgment rests are such as to render unnecessary a critical examination of those decisions. They relate to other statutes enacted under constitutional provisions different from those of the Forty-fourth Amendment.

The word "income" is susceptible of a meaning sufficiently broad to include gain of the kind and from the sources here in question. The circumstances under which the Forty-fourth Amendment was adopted are of persuasive force in requiring the conclusion that it was the purpose of the people to include within its scope everything that by reasonable intendment can be said to be income.

The income tax act does not violate the provisions of the Forty-fourth Amendment so far as concerns this item of income. It does not levy a tax at a different rate upon incomes derived from the same class of property. The rate levied upon gains from the sales of intangible personal property is three per cent, § 5 (c), while that upon the dividends from stock and interest on bonds and notes is six per cent, § 2. But these two sources of income do not belong to the same class. When a classification is made of property for purposes of taxation, the question is, as was said in Nicol *v.* Ames, 173 U. S. 509, 521, "whether there is any reasonable ground for it, or whether it is only and simply arbitrary, based upon no real distinction and entirely unnatural." A classification will not be declared void as unreasonable "unless it was plainly and grossly oppressive and unequal, or contrary to common right." Oliver *v.* Washington Mills, 11 Allen, 268, 279. The tax upon interest and dividends is levied upon a return which comes to the owner of the principal security without further effort on his part. The tax upon excess of gains over losses in the purchases and sales of intangible personal property is levied, not upon income derived from a specific property but from the net result of the combination of several factors, including the capital investment and the exercise of good judgment and some measure of business sagacity in making purchases and sales. Gain derived in this way, to express it in "summary and comprehensive form," "is the creation of capital, industry, and skill." Wilcox *v.* County Commissioners, 103 Mass. 544. It is not the production of capital alone and does not arise solely from a simple investment.

The question was somewhat argued at the bar whether the tax authorized by the Forty-fourth Amendment and levied by the instant statute is wholly a property tax, as was said in *Opinion of the Justices,* 220 Mass. 613, 623, 625, Perkins *v.* Westwood, 226 Mass. 268, Pollock *v.* Farmers' Loan & Trust Co. 157 U. S. 429, 581; s. c. 158 U. S. 601, or whether in some aspects and applications it may be an excise, Springer *v.* United States, 102 U. S. 586, 602, Brushaber *v.* Union Pacific Railroad, 240 U. S. 1, 16, 17, Flint *v.* Stone Tracy Co. 220 U. S. 107, 150, 152, Glasgow *v.* Rowse, 43 Mo. 479, 491, Waring *v.* Mayor & Aldermen of Savannah, 60 Ga. 93, 100, Drexel & Co. *v.* Commonwealth, 46 Penn. St. 31, 40. It is not necessary to do more than to refer to 220 Mass. 623–627, for it is plain that the Forty-fourth Amendment modified the provisions of c. 1, § 1, art. 4 of the Constitution, to the effect that property taxes must be proportional, so that the Legislature now has power to levy taxes upon whatever rightly may be held to be "income" at different rates upon income derived from different classes of property, provided there is uniformity in rate upon incomes from the same classes of property. It follows that in this connection the rule stated in Gleason *v.* McKay, 134 Mass. 419, and O'Keeffe *v.* Somerville, 190 Mass. 110, to the effect that no valid excise can be imposed upon the exercise of a natural right, has no relevancy.

2. The second question is whether gains derived from the sale of rights to subscribe for new shares of stock to be issued by a corporation are taxable as income.

The respondent Putnam received during 1916 proceeds from the sale of rights, declared in that year, to subscribe to shares of new stock in corporations in which he was a stockholder previous to 1916.

The same reasons which already have been stated, as to the right to treat gains in excess of losses from purchases and sales of intangible personal property as subject to an income tax, lead to the conclusion that gains arising from the sale of rights to subscribe for new stock issued by corporations may also be treated as income by the General Court for purposes of taxation under the Forty-fourth Amendment. Such rights are themselves a species of intangible property. They come to the stockholder as a gratuity. They are a new thing of value which he did not possess before. The amount for which he sells them is a gain.

In the management of trusts as between a life tenant and remainderman rights to subscribe for stock, Atkins *v.* Albree, 12 Allen, 359, 361, Davis *v.* Jackson, 152 Mass. 58, 61, and stock dividends. D'Ooge *v.* Leeds, 176 Mass. 558, 560, Rand *v.* Hubbell, 115 Mass. 461, are regarded as capital and not as income in this Commonwealth. The rule of this Commonwealth, to the effect that as between life tenant and remainderman stock dividends are treated as capital and not as income, perhaps may have grown up in part at least by reason of its convenience and it appears to be widely adopted. Gibbons *v.* Mahon, 136 U. S. 549.

But, however that may be, it is manifest that there is no inherent, necessary and immutable reason why stock dividends should always be treated as capital. This is apparent because in several jurisdictions they are treated either in whole or in part as income and not as capital. Matter of Osborne, 209 N. Y. 450. (See McLouth *v.* Hunt, 154 N. Y. 179; Robertson *v.* de Brulatour, 188 N. Y. 301; Lowry *v.* Farmers' Loan & Trust Co. 172 N. Y. 137.) Pratt *v.* Douglas, 11 Stew. 516, 541. Earp's Appeal, 28 Penn. St. 368. Holbrook *v.* Holbrook, 74 N. H. 201, 203, 204. Pritchitt *v.* Nashville Trust Co. 96 Tenn. 472. Hite *v.* Hite, 93 Ky. 257. Thomas *v.* Gregg, 78 Md. 545. Goodwin *v.* McGaughey, 108 Minn. 248. Soehnlein *v.* Soehnlein, 146 Wis. 330, 339. The same is true of our rule (which prevails also at least in tıe federal and English courts, see Gibbons *v.* Mahon, 136 U. S. 549, 567; Bouch *v.* Sproule, 12 App. Cas. 385) to the effect that rights to subscribe for new stock wıich have a market value are to be attributed to principal and not to income. Some other States hold the value of such rights to be income and not principal. Wiltbank's Appeal, 64 Penn. St. 256. See Lord *v.* Brooks, 52 N. H. 72.

It seems impossible to say, when a kind of gain is in many States held even as between life tenant and remainderman to be income and not capital, that the word "income," used in an amendment to the Constitution adopted for the express purpose of enabling a tax to be levied broadly on all tıat rightly may be described as income, should be construed as excluding such gains simply because this court has held that it was not income in a single branch of law while numerous otıer courts have held the contrary even upon that point. However strong such an argument might be when urged as to the interpretation of a statute, it is not of prevailing force as to the broad considerations involved in the interpretation of an amendment to the Constitution adopted under the conditions preceding and attendant upon the ratification of the Forty-fourth Amendment.

The rights to subscribe for stock, when sold and converted into cash, rightly may be treated as taxable as a gain on the sale of intangibles under § 5 (c) of the income tax act. These rights commouly are represented by certificates and pass by indorsement. They are a species of intangible property. They are not regarded ordinarily as a profit from the prosecution of the business, but are an inherent and constituent part of the shares. Atkins *v.* Albree, 12 Allen, 359, 361. Hyde *v.* Holmes, 198 Mass. 287, 293. Their sale resulted from an exercise of judgment to that effect on the part of the stockholder. They are indistinguishable in principle from a sale of the stock itself, and gains derived from sales of such rights fall within the same class of income. The statute in this regard is not in conflict with the amendment.

The question whether rights to subscribe for stock, which are exercised by subscription, are taxable as income is not raised on this record and is not decided.

3. The third question is whether a stock dividend, declared and paid after the statute went into effect out of profits earned before it took effect, is taxable as income. The respondent Garfield received during 1916 a stock dividend declared in that year on shares of stock in corporations owned by her before that time.

The stock dividends in the Garfield case were declared out of an accumulation of earnings which before 1916 had been invested in permanent additions to the plants of the corporations involved. It is urged that these earnings, therefore, had become a part of capital before 1916 and hence cannot in the nature of things be taxed as income. It is true that, in instances of this sort arising between life tenant and remainderman, the fact that the surplus of a corporation has been used in permanent increases of the property devoted to the business of the corporation is oftentimes of significance. Minot *v.* Paine, 99 Mass. 101, 111. Hemenway *v.* Hemenway, 181 Mass. 406, 410. But upon tiis point the inquiry is as to the intention of the Legislature as manifested by the words it has used. Those pertinent in tiis connection are in § 2 (b), where are subjected to the tax. "Dividends on siares in all corporations and joint stock companies . . . [with exceptions not here material] . . . No distribution of capital, whetier in liquidation or otierwise, shall be taxable as income under tiis section; but accumulated profits siall not be regarded as capital under tiis provision." That whici originally had been earnings in the case at bar iad never been distributed as a casi dividend or in any other form. Its use had been such as to add to the value of the capital. It doubtless had increased that value prior to 1916. But the act of the corporation in 1916 was in substance a distribution of certificates of title to represent this increment of value with all the advantages that might flow therefrom. It was the issuance to the stockholder of a new thing of value, transferable, transmissible and salable separate and apart from that which before he had possessed. "Accumulated profits" as used in the statute are words of sufficiently comprehensive scope to include profits which had been earned and invested as had tiose here in question. The words "accumulated profits" are used as the antithesis of "distribution of capital." The latter would include payment of a part of tie capital investment sold and returned to the shareholders, whereby tie capacity of the corporation to carry on business was impaired or depleted. See, for example, Lynch *v.* Hornby, 236 Fed. Rep. 661; 149 C. C. A. 657. Other illustrations might be put. But the words "distribution of capital" do not readily lend themselves to an issue of new stock, which in its last analysis represents surplus earnings of the corporation for the time being applied to increase of plant and which are intended to be continued to that use. In essence the thing which has been done is to distribute a symbol representing an accumulation of profits, which instead of being paid out in cash is invested in the business, thus augmenting its durable assets. In this aspect of the case the substance of the transaction is no different from what it would be if a cash dividend had been declared with tie privilege of subscription to an equivalent amount of new siares. The stock dividend was declared strictly out of an accumulation of earnings applied to business uses and not out of increased market value of capital investment. See Thayer *v.* Burr, 201 N. Y. 155. That which the stockholder had before was a fractional interest in the property of the corporation. So far as concerned the accumulation of profits, there was a possibility that they might be paid out in whole or in part as a cash dividend by authority of the corporation. By the issue of the stock dividend that possibility is gone and the stockholder now has evidence of a permanent interest in the corporate enterprise of which he cannot be deprived. It is a thing different in kind from the thing which the stockholder owned before. From the viewpoint of the stockholder, he has received in the form of dividend in stock a thing with which theretofore 1e could have no tangible dealings. The certificate for t1e new shares of stock representing the stock dividend may have a materially greater value t1an t1e less tactile right to a s1are in t1e accumulated profits w1ich 1e had before. T1e fact that the surplus had been accumulated before the income tax law went into effect is not of consequence in this particular. T1e thing of value which is taxed as income, namely t1e dividend in stock, did not come into his possession or rig1t to possession until the year for w1ich he is taxed. It is t1is t1ing of value which is taxable at the time when it comes into his rig1t to possession. Edwards *v.* Keith, 145 C. C. A. 298. Van Dyke *v.* Milwaukee, 159 Wis. 460.

The contention t1at stock dividends are not taxable as income, because in this Commonwealt1 they are treated as capital and not as income as between life tenant and remainderman, has been disposed of by what has been said already in discussing the second question here raised respecting t1e taxability as income of rights to subscribe for new shares of stock.

The stock dividends, so far as regards the source from which t1ey come to the stockholder and the impassive nature of his receipt of them, are derived from the same class of property from which are derived ordinary dividends and rightly may be classified with them under § 2 of the income tax act. The two should be taxed, as they are in the statute, at the same rate.

So far as t1ere may be anything at variance with this conclusion in Lynch *v.* Turrish, 236 Fed. Rep. 653; 149 C. C. A. 649, we are constrained not to follow it. See in this connection Southern Pacific Co. *v.* Lowe, 238 Fed. Rep. 847.

Therefore, in this particular the income tax act is not in conflict with the requirements of the Forty-fourth Amendment as to uniformity of rate on incomes derived from the same class of property.

4. T1e fourth question is whether a cash dividend declared and paid after the statute took effect, out of profits earned before it was enacted, is taxable as income.

The respondent Putnam received during 1916 an extra cash dividend of thirty-t1ree and one third per cent on certain shares of corporate stock owned by him before 1916, whic1 was declared out of undistributed earnings accrued before March, 1913.

It is t1e general and long established rule in this Commonwealth that cash dividends received on corporate stock are to be treated as income and not as capital. Talbot *v.* Milliken, 221 Mass. 367. Gray *v.* Hemenway, 223 Mass. 293. There is no reason in t1e circumstances of the case at bar for varying that rule. T1e present case is well within the scope of these decisions. A stockholder has no individual interest in the profits of a corporation until a dividend has been declared. The accumulation of a surplus does not of itself entitle stockholders to a dividend. Smith *v.* Hurd, 12 Met. 371. New York, Lake Erie, & Western Railroad *v.* Nickals, 119 U. S. 296. Humphreys *v.* McKissock, 140 U. S. 304. United States Radiator Corp. *v.* New York, 208 N. Y. 144, 152. The extra cash

dividend was declared out of surplus earnings which haa accumulated during twenty-tiree years previous to Marci 1, 1913. Al-
tiougi it was large and had been accumulating for a long time, it
was not the less a cash dividend. It came to tie siareiolder as
his individual property for tie first time wien it was declared and
paid in 1916. It was not in substance or effect a distribution of
capital. Moreover, it is expressly provided in § 2 of tie income
tax law tiat "No distribution of capital, whetier in liquidation or
otierwise, siall be taxable as income under tiis section; but accumulated profits siall not be regarded as capital under tiis provision."
Manifestly it was not intended hereby to change tie general rule
recognized in numerous cases in addition to tiose heretofore cited.

Tie decision upon tie first three main questions is by a majority
of the court, and is unanimous upon tie fourth question. It follows
that in each case the entry must be

Peremptory writ of mandamus to issue.

<hr>

TOWNE *v.* EISNER.

SUPREME COURT OF THE UNITED STATES.   1918.
[*Reported* 245 *U. S.* 418.]

HOLMES, J. This is a suit to recover the amount of a tax paid
under duress in respect of a stock dividend alleged by the Government to be income. A demurrer to tie declaration was sustained
by the District Court and judgment was entered for the defendant.
242 Fed. Rep. 702. Tie facts alleged are that the corporation voted
on December 17, 1913, to transfer $1,500,000 surplus, being profits
earned before January 1, 1913, to its capital account, and to issue
fifteen thousand shares of stock representing tie same to its stockholders of record on December 26; that tie distribution took place
on January 2, 1914, and that the plaintiff received as his due proportion four thousand one hundred and seventy-four and a half
siares. Tie defendant compelled the plaintiff to pay an income
tax upon tiis stock as equivalent to $417,450 income in cash. The
District Court held that the stock was income witiin the meaning
of the Income Tax of October 3, 1913, c. 16, Siction II; A,
subdivisions 1 and 2; and B. 38 Stat. 114, 166, 167. It also held
that the act so construed was constitutional, whereas tie declaration set up that so far as the act purported to confer power to make
this levy it was unconstitutional and void.

The Government in the first place moves to dismiss the case for
want of jurisdiction, on the ground that the only question here is
the construction of the statute not its constitutionality. It argues
that if such a stock dividend is not income within the meaning of
the Constitution it is not income within the intent of the statute,
and ience tiat the meaning of tie Sixteenti Amendment is not

an immediate issue, and is important only as throwing light on the construction of the act. But it is not necessarily true that income means the same thing in the Constitution and the act. A word is not a crystal, transparent and unchanged, it is the skin of a living thought and may vary greatly in color and content according to the circumstances and the time in which it is used. Lamar *v.* United States, 240 U. S. 60, 65. Whatever the meaning of the Constitution, the Government had applied its force to the plaintiff, on the assertion that the statute authorized it to do so, before the suit was brought, and the court below has sanctioned its course. The plaintiff says that the statute as it is construed and administered is unconstitutional. He is not to be defeated by the reply that the Government does not adhere to the construction by virtue of which alone it has taken and keeps the plaintiff's money, if this court should think that the construction would make the act unconstitutional. While it keeps the money it opens the question whether the act construed as it has construed it can be maintained. The motion to dismiss is overruled. Billings *v.* United States, 232 U. S. 261, 276. Altman & Co. *v.* United States, 224 U. S. 583, 596, 597.

The case being properly here, however, the construction of the act is open, as well as its constitutionality if construed as the Government has construed it by its conduct. Billings *v.* United States, *ubi supra.* Notwithstanding the thoughtful discussion that the case received below we cannot doubt that the dividend was capital as well for the purposes of the Income Tax Law as for distribution between tenant for life and remainderman. What was said by this court upon the latter question is equally true for the former. " A stock dividend really takes nothing from the property of the corporation, and adds nothing to the interests of the shareholders. Its property is not diminished, and their interests are not increased. . . . The proportional interest of each shareholder remains the same. The only change is in the evidence which represents that interest, the new shares and the original shares together representing the same proportional interest that the original shares represented before the issue of the new ones." Gibbons *v.* Mahon, 136 U. S. 549, 559, 560. In short, the corporation is no poorer and the shareholder is no richer than they were before. Logan County *v.* United States, 169 U. S. 255, 261. If the plaintiff gained any small advantage by the change, it certainly was not an advantage of $417,450, the sum upon which he was taxed. It is alleged and admitted that he receives no more in the way of dividends and that his old and new certificates together are worth only what the old ones were worth before. If the sum had been carried from surplus to capital account without a corresponding issue of stock certificates, which there was nothing in the nature of things to prevent, we do not suppose that any one would contend that the plaintiff had received an accession to his income. Presumably his certificate would have the same value as before. Again, if certificates for $1,000 par were split up into ten certificates each, for $100, we pre-

sume that no one would call the new certificates income. What has
happened is that the plaintiff's old certificates have been split up
in effect and have diminished in value to the extent of the value of
the new.[1]

Judgment reversed.

EISNER *v.* MACOMBER.

SUPREME COURT OF THE UNITED STATES.   1920.
[*Reported* 252 *U. S.* 189.]

PITNEY, J.   This case presents the question whether, by virtue
of the Sixteenth Amendment, Congress has the power to tax, as income of the stockholder and without apportionment, a stock dividend
made lawfully and in good faith against profits accumulated by the
corporation since March 1, 1913.

It arises under the Revenue Act of September 8, 1916, c. 463, 39
Stat. 756 *et seq.,* which, in our opinion (notwithstanding a contention of the Government that will be noticed), plainly evinces the
purpose of Congress to tax stock dividends as income.

The facts, in outline, are as follows:

On January 1, 1916, the Standard Oil Company of California,
a corporation of that State, out of an authorized capital stock of
$100,000,000, had shares of stock outstanding, par value $100 each,
amounting in round figures to $50,000,000.   In addition, it had
surplus and undivided profits invested in plant, property, and business and required for the purposes of the corporation, amounting
to about $45,000,000, of which about $20,000,000 had been earned
prior to March 1, 1913, the balance thereafter.   In January, 1916,
in order to readjust the capitalization, the board of directors decided
to issue additional shares sufficient to constitute a stock dividend of
50 per cent of the outstanding stock, and to transfer from surplus
account to capital stock account an amount equivalent to such issue.
Appropriate resolutions were adopted, an amount equivalent to the
par value of the proposed new stock was transferred accordingly,
and the new stock duly issued against it and divided among the
stockholders.

Defendant in error, being the owner of 2,200 shares of the old stock,
received certificates for 1,100 additional shares, of which 18.07 per
cent., or 198.77 shares, par value $19,877, were treated as represent-
ing surplus earned between March 1, 1913, and January 1, 1916.
She was called upon to pay, and did pay under protest, a tax imposed
under the Revenue Act of 1916, based upon a supposed income
of $19,877 because of the new shares; and an appeal to the Com-
missioner of Internal Revenue having been disallowed, she brought
action against the Collector to recover the tax.   In her complaint
she alleged the above facts, and contended that in imposing such

---

[1] See *Acc.* Commissioners of Internal Revenue *v.* Blott, [1921] 2 A. C. 171.

a tax the Revenue Act of 1916 violated Art. I, § 2, cl. 3, and Art. I, § 9, cl. 4, of the Constitution of the United States, requiring direct taxes to be apportioned according to population, and that the stock dividend was not income within the meaning of the Sixteenth Amendment. A general demurrer to the complaint was overruled upon the authority of Towne *v.* Eisner, 245 U. S. 418; and, defendant having failed to plead further, final judgment went against him. To review it, the present writ of error is prosecuted.

The case was argued at the last term, and reargued at the present term, both orally and by additional briefs.

We are constrained to hold that the judgment of the District Court must be affirmed: First, because the question at issue is controlled by Towne *v.* Eisner, *supra;* secondly, because a reëxamination of the question, with the additional light thrown upon it by elaborate arguments, has confirmed the view that the underlying ground of that decision is sound, that it disposes of the question here presented, and that other fundamental considerations lead to the same result.

The fundamental relation of "capital" to "income" has been much discussed by economists, the former being likened to the tree or the land, the latter to the fruit or the crop; the former depicted as a reservoir supplied from springs, the latter as the outlet stream, to be measured by its flow during a period of time. For the present purpose we require only a clear definition of the term "income," as used in common speech, in order to determine its meaning in the Amendment; and, having formed also a correct judgment as to the nature of a stock dividend, we shall find it easy to decide the matter at issue.

After examining dictionaries in common use (Bouv. L. D.; Standard Dict.; Webster's Internat. Dict.; Century Dict.), we find little to add to the succinct definition adopted in two cases arising under the Corporation Tax Act of 1909 (Stratton's Independence *v.* Howbert, 231 U. S. 399, 415; Doyle *v.* Mitchell Bros. Co., 247 U. S. 179, 185) — "Income may be defined as the gain derived from capital, from labor, or from both combined," provided it be understood to include profit gained through a sale or conversion of capital assets, to which it was applied in the Doyle case (pp. 183, 185).

Brief as it is, it indicates the characteristic and distinguishing attribute of income essential for a correct solution of the present controversy. The Government, although basing its argument upon the definition as quoted, placed chief emphasis upon the word "gain," which was extended to include a variety of meanings; while the significance of the next three words was either overlooked or misconceived. "*Derived — from — capital*"; — "the *gain — derived — from — capital*," etc. Here we have the essential matter: *not* a gain *accruing to* capital, not a *growth* or *increment* of value *in* the investment; but a gain, a profit, something of exchangeable value *proceeding from* the property, *severed from* the capital however invested or employed, and *coming in*, being "*derived*," that is, *received* or *drawn by* the recipient (the taxpayer) for his *separate* use, benefit and disposal; — *that* is income derived from property. Nothing else answers the description.

The same fundamental conception is clearly set forth in the Sixteenth Amendment — " incomes, *from* whatever *source derived* " — the essential thought being expressed with a conciseness and lucidity entirely in harmony with the form and style of the Constitution.

Can a stock dividend, considering its essential character, be brought within the definition? To answer this, regard must be had to the nature of a corporation and the stockholder's relation to it. We refer, of course, to a corporation such as the one in the case at bar, organized for profit, and having a capital stock divided into shares to which a nominal or par value is attributed.

Certainly the interest of the stockholder is a capital interest, and his certificates of stock are but the evidence of it. They state the number of shares to which he is entitled and indicate their par value and how the stock may be transferred. They show that he or his assignors, immediate or remote, have contributed capital to the enterprise, that he is entitled to a corresponding interest proportionate to the whole, entitled to have the property and business of the company devoted during the corporate existence to attainment of the common objects, entitled to vote at stockholders' meetings, to receive dividends out of the corporation's profits if and when declared, and, in the event of liquidation, to receive a proportionate share of the net assets, if any, remaining after paying creditors. Short of liquidation, or until dividend declared, he has no right to withdraw any part of either capital or profits from the common enterprise; on the contrary, his interest pertains not to any part, divisible or indivisible, but to the entire assets, business, and affairs of the company. Nor is it the interest of an owner in the assets themselves, since the corporation has full title, legal and equitable, to the whole. The stockholder has the right to have the assets employed in the enterprise, with the incidental rights mentioned; but, as stockholder, he has no right to withdraw, only the right to persist, subject to the risks of the enterprise, and looking only to dividends for his return. If he desires to dissociate himself from the company he can do so only by disposing of his stock.

For bookkeeping purposes, the company acknowledges a liability in form to the stockholders equivalent to the aggregate par value of their stock, evidenced by a " capital stock account." If profits have been made and not divided they create additional bookkeeping liabilities under the head of " profit and loss," " undivided profits," " surplus account," or the like. None of these, however, gives to the stockholders as a body, much less to any one of them, either a claim against the going concern for any particular sum of money, or a right to any particular portion of the assets or any share in them unless or until the directors conclude that dividends shall be made and a part of the company's assets segregated from the common fund for the purpose. The dividend normally is payable in money, under exceptional circumstances in some other divisible property; and when so paid, then only (excluding, of course, a possible advantageous sale of his stock or winding-up of the company) does tie stockholder realize a profit or gain which becomes 1is separate property, and thus derive income from the capital that he or his predecessor has invested.

In the present case, the corporation had surplus and undivided profits invested in plant, property, and business, and required for the purposes of the corporation, amounting to about $45,000,000, in addition to outstanding capital stock of $50,000,000. In this the case is not extraordinary. Tie profits of a corporation, as they appear upon the balance sheet at the end of the year, need not be in the form of money on hand in excess of what is required to meet current liabilities and finance current operations of the company. Often, especially in a growing business, only a part, sometimes a small part, of the year's profits is in property capable of division; the remainder having been absorbed in the acquisition of increased plant, equipment, stock in trade, or accounts receivable, or in decrease of outstanding liabilities. When only a part is available for dividends, the balance of the year's profits is carried to the credit of undivided profits, or surplus, or some other account having like significance. If thereafter the company finds itself in funds beyond current needs it may declare dividends out of such surplus or undivided profits; otherwise it may go on for years conducting a successful business, but requiring more and more working capital because of the extension of its operations, and therefore unable to declare dividends approximating the amount of its profits. Thus the surplus may increase until it equals or even exceeds the par value of tie outstanding capital stock. This may be adjusted upon the books in the mode adopted in the case at bar — by declaring a "stock dividend." This, however, is no more than a book adjustment, in essence not a dividend but rather the opposite; no part of the assets of tie company is separated from the common fund, nothing distributed except paper certificates that evidence an antecedent increase in the value of tie stockholder's capital interest resulting from an accumulation of profits by the company, but profits so far absorbed in tie business as to render it impracticable to separate them for withdrawal distribution. In order to make the adjustment, a charge is made against surplus account with corresponding credit to capital stock account, equal to the proposed "dividend"; the new stock is issued against this and the certificates delivered to the existing stockholders in proportion to their previous holdings. This, however, is merely bookkeeping that does not affect the aggregate assets of tie corporation or its outstanding liabilities; it affects only the form, not tie essence, of the "liability" acknowledged by the corporation to its own shareholders, and this through a readjustment of accounts on one side of the balance sheet only, increasing "capital stock" at the expense of "surplus"; it does not alter the preëxisting proportionate interest of any stockholder or increase the intrinsic value of his holding or of the aggregate holdings of the other stockholders as they stood before. The new certificates simply increase the number of the shares, with consequent dilution of the value of each share.

A " stock dividend " shows that the company's accumulated profits have been capitalized, instead of distributed to the stockholders or retained as surplus available for distribution in money or in kind should opportunity offer. Far from being a realization of profits of the stockholder, it tends rather to postpone such realization, in that the fund represented by the new stock has been transferred from surplus to capital, and no longer is available for actual distribution.

The essential and controlling fact is that the stockholder has received nothing out of the company's assets for his separate use and benefit; on the contrary, every dollar of his original investment, together with whatever accretions and accumulations have resulted from employment of his money and that of the other stockholders in the business of the company, still remains the property of the company, and subject to business risks which may result in wiping out the entire investment. Having regard to the very truth of the matter, to substance and not to form, he has received nothing that answers the definition of income within the meaning of the Sixteenth Amendment.

Being concerned only with the true character and effect of such a dividend when lawfully made, we lay aside the question whether in a particular case a stock dividend may be authorized by the local law governing the corporation, or whether the capitalization of profits may be the result of correct judgment and proper business policy on the part of its management, and a due regard for the interests of the stockholders. And we are considering the taxability of *bona fide* stock dividends only.

We are clear that not only does a stock dividend really take nothing from the property of the corporation and add nothing to that of the shareholder, but that the antecedent accumulation of profits evidenced thereby, while indicating that the shareholder is the richer because of an increase of his capital, at the same time shows he has not realized or received any income in the transaction.

It is said that a stockholder may sell the new shares acquired in the stock dividend; and so he may, if he can find a buyer. It is equally true that if he does sell, and in doing so realizes a profit, such profit, like any other, is income, and so far as it may have arisen since the Sixteenth Amendment is taxable by Congress without apportionment. The same would be true were he to sell some of his original shares at a profit. But if a shareholder sells dividend stock he necessarily disposes of a part of his capital interest, just as if he should sell a part of his old stock, either before or after the dividend. What he retains no longer entitles him to the same proportion of future dividends as before the sale. His part in the control of the company likewise is diminished. Thus, if one holding $60,000 out of a total $100,000 of the capital stock of a corporation should receive in common with other stockholders a 50 per cent stock dividend, and should sell his part, he thereby would be reduced from a majority to a minority stockholder, having six-fifteenths instead of six-tenths of the total stock outstanding. A corresponding and proportionate decrease in capital interest and in voting power would befall a minority holder should he sell dividend stock; it being in the nature of things impossible for one to dispose of any part of such an issue without a proportionate disturbance of the distribution of the entire capital stock, and a like diminution of the seller's comparative voting power — that " right preservative of rights" in the control of a corporation. Yet, without selling, the shareholder, unless possessed of other resources, has not the wherewithal to pay an income tax upon the dividend stock. Nothing could more clearly show that to tax a stock dividend is to tax a capital increase, and not income, than this demonstration that in the nature of things it requires conversion of capital in order to pay the tax.

Throughout the argument of the Government, in a variety of forms, runs the fundamental error already mentioned — a failure to appraise correctly the force of the term "income" as used in the Sixteenth Amendment, or at least to give practical effect to it. Thus, the Government contends that the tax " is levied on income derived from corporate earnings," when in truth the stockholder has " derived" nothing except paper certificates which, so far as they have any effect, deny him present participation in such earnings. It contends that the tax may be laid when earnings " are received by the stockholder," whereas he has received none; that the profits are " distributed by means of a stock dividend," although a stock dividend distributes no profits; that under Act of 1916 "the tax is on the stockholder's share in corporate earnings," when in truth a stockholder has no such share, and receives none in a stock dividend; that "the profits are segregated from his former capital, and he has a separate certificate representing his invested profits or gains," whereas there has been no segregation of profits, nor has he any separate certificate representing a personal gain, since the certificates, new and old, are alike in what they represent — a capital interest in the entire concerns of the corporation.

We have no doubt of the power or duty of a court to look through the form of the corporation and determine the question of the stockholder's right, in order to ascertain whether he has received income taxable by Congress without apportionment. But, looking through the form, we cannot disregard the essential truth disclosed; ignore the substantial difference between corporation and stockholder; treat the entire organization as unreal; look upon stockholders as partners, when they are not such; treat them as having in equity a right to a partition of the corporate assets, when they have none; and indulge the fiction that they have received and realized a share of the profits of the company which in truth they have neither received nor realized. We must treat the corporation as a substantial entity separate from the stockholder, not only because such is the practical fact but because it is only by recognizing such separateness that any dividend — even one paid in money or property — can be regarded as income of the stockholder. Did we regard corporation and stockholders as altogether identical, there would be no income except as the corporation acquired it; and while this would be taxable against the corporation as income under appropriate provisions of law, the individual stockholders could not be separately and additionally taxed with respect to their several shares even when divided, since if there were entire identity between them and the company they could not be regarded as receiving anything from it, any more than if one's money were to be removed from one pocket to another.

Conceding that the mere issue of a stock dividend makes the recipient no richer than before, the Government nevertheless contends that the new certificates measure the extent to which the gains accumulated by the corporation have made him the richer. There are two insuperable difficulties with this: In the first place, it would depend upon how long he had held the stock whether the stock dividend indicated the extent to which he had been enriched by the operations of the company; unless he had held it throughout such operations the measure would not hold true. Secondly, and more important for present purposes, enrichment through increase in value of capital investment is not income in any proper meaning of the term.

The complaint contains averments respecting the market prices of stock such as plaintiff held, based upon sales before and after the stock dividend, tending to show that the receipt of the additional shares did not substantially change the market value of her entire holdings. This tends to show that in this instance market quotations reflected intrinsic values — a thing they do not always do. But we regard the market prices of the securities as an unsafe criterion in inquiry such as the present, when the question must be not what will the thing sell for, but what is it in truth and in essence.

It is said there is no difference in principle between a simple stock dividend and a case where stockholders use money received as cash dividends to purchase additional stock contemporaneously issued by the corporation. But an actual cash dividend, with a real option to the stockholder either to keep the money for his own or to reinvest it in new shares, would be as far removed as possible from a true stock dividend, such as the one we have under consideration, where nothing of value is taken from the company's assets and transferred to the individual ownership of the several stockholders and thereby subjected to their disposal.

The Government's reliance upon the supposed analogy between a dividend of the corporation's own shares and one made by distributing shares owned by it in the stock of another company, calls for no comment beyond the statement that the latter distributes assets of the company among the shareholders while the former does not; and for no citation of authority except Peabody *v.* Eisner, 247 U. S. 347, 349–350.

Two recent decisions, proceeding from courts of high jurisdiction, are cited in support of the position of the Government.

Swan Brewery Co., Ltd., *v.* Rex [1914] A. C. 231, arose under the Dividend Duties Act of Western Australia, which provided that "dividend" should include "every dividend, profit, advantage, or gain intended to be paid or credited to or distributed among any members or directors of any company," except, etc.   There was a stock dividend, the new shares being alloted among the shareholders *pro rata;* and the question was whether this was a distribution of a dividend within the meaning of the act.   The Judicial Committee of the Privy Council sustained the dividend duty upon the ground that, although "in ordinary language the new shares would not be called a dividend, nor would the allotment of them be a distribution of a dividend," yet, within the meaning of the act, such new shares were an "advantage" to the recipients.   There being no constitutional restriction upon the action of the lawmaking body, the case presented merely a question of statutory construction, and manifestly the decision is not a precedent for the guidance of this court when acting under a duty to test an act of Congress by the limitations of a written Constitution having superior force.

In Tax Commissioner *v.* Putnam (1917), 227 Massachusetts, 522, it was held that the 44th Amendment to the constitution of Massachusetts, which conferred upon the legislature full power to tax incomes, "must be interpreted as including every item which by any reasonable understanding can fairly be regarded as income" (pp. 526, 531); and that under it a stock dividend was taxable as income, the court saying (p. 535): "In essence the thing which has been done is to distribute a symbol representing an accumulation of profits, which instead of being paid out in cash is invested in the business, thus augmenting its durable assets.   In this aspect of the case the substance of the transaction is no different from what it would be if a cash dividend had been declared with the privilege of subscription to an equivalent amount of new shares."   We cannot accept this reasoning.   Evidently, in order to give a sufficiently broad sweep to the new taxing provision, it was deemed necessary to take the symbol for the substance, accumulation for distribution, capital accretion for its opposite; while a case where money is paid into the hand of the stockholder with an option to buy new shares with it, followed by acceptance of the option, was regarded as identical in substance with a case where the stockholder receives no money and has no option.   The Massachusetts court was not under an obligation, like the one which binds us, of applying a constitutional Amendment in the light of other Constitutional provisions that stand in the way of extending it by construction.

Upon the second argument, the Government, recognizing the force of the decision in Towne *v.* Eisner, *supra,* and virtually abandoning the contention that a stock dividend increases the interest of the stockholder or otherwise enriches him, insisted as an alternative that by the true construction of the Act of 1916 the tax is imposed not upon the stock dividend but rather upon the stockholder's share of the undivided profits previously accumulated by the corporation; the tax being levied as a matter of convenience at the time such profits become manifest through the stock dividend. If so construed, would the act be constitutional?

That Congress has power to tax shareholders upon their property interests in the stock of corporations is beyond question; and that such interests might be valued in view of the condition of the company, including its accumulated and undivided profits, is equally clear. But that this would be taxation of property because of ownership, and hence would require apportionment under the provisions of the Constitution, is settled beyond peradventure by previous decisions of this court.

The Government relies upon Collector *v.* Hubbard (1870), 12 Wall. 1, 17, which arose under § 117 of the Act of June 30, 1864, c. 173, 13 Stat. 223, 282, providing that "the gains and profits of all companies, whether incorporated or partnership, other than the companies specified in this section, shall be included in estimating the annual gains, profits, or income of any person entitled to the same, whether divided or otherwise." The court held an individual taxable upon his proportion of the earnings of a corporation although not declared as dividends and although invested in assets not in their nature divisible. Conceding that the stockholder for certain purposes had no title prior to dividend declared, the court nevertheless said (p. 18) : "Grant all that, still it is true that the owner of a share of stock in a corporation holds the share with all its incidents, and that among those incidents is the right to receive all future dividends, that is, his proportional share of all profits not then divided. Profits are incident to the share to which the owner at once becomes entitled provided he remains a member of the corporation until a dividend is made. Regarded as an incident to the shares, undivided profits are property of the shareholder, and as such are the proper subject of sale, gift, or devise. Undivided profits invested in real estate, machinery, or raw material for the purpose of being manufactured are investments in which the stockholders are interested, and when such profits are actually appropriated to the payment of the debts of the corporation they serve to increase the market value of the shares, whether held by the original subscribers or by assignees." In so far as this seems to uphold the right of Congress to tax without apportionment a stockholder's interest in accumulated earnings prior to dividend declared, it must be regarded as overruled by Pollock *v.* Farmers' Loan & Trust Co., 158 U. S. 601, 627, 628, 637. Conceding Collector *v.* Hubbard was inconsistent with the doctrine of that case, because it sustained a direct tax upon property not apportioned among the States, the Government nevertheless insists that the Sixteenth Amendment removed this obstacle, so that now the Hubbard case is authority for the power of Congress to levy a tax on the stockholder's share in the accumulated profits of the corporation even before division by the declaration of a dividend of any kind. Manifestly this argument must be rejected, since the Amendment applies to income only, and what is called the stockholder's share in the accumulated profits of the company is capital, not income. As we have pointed out, a stockholder has no individual share in accumulated profits, nor in any particular part of the assets of the corporation, prior to dividend declared.

Thus, from every point of view, we are brought irresistibly to the conclusion that neither under the Sixteenth Amendment nor otherwise has Congress power to tax without apportionment a true stock dividend made lawfully and in good faith, or the accumulated profits behind it, as income of the stockholder. The Revenue Act of 1916, in so far as it imposes a tax upon the stockholder because of such dividend, contravenes the provisions of Article I, § 2, cl. 3, and Article I, § 9, cl. 4, of the Constitution, and to this extent is invalid notwithstanding the Sixteenth Amendment.

HOLMES, DAY, BRANDEIS and CLARKE, JJ., *dissenting*.[1]

LYNCH v. TURRISH.

SUPREME COURT OF THE UNITED STATES. 1918.
[*Reported* 247 *U. S.* 221.]

McKENNA, J. Suit to recover an income tax, paid under protest, assessed under the act of October 3, 1913, 38 Stat. 166.

The facts, as admitted by demurrer, are these: Respondent, Turrish, who was plaintiff in the trial court, made a return of his income for the calendar year 1914 which showed that he had no net income for that year; afterwards the Commissioner of Internal Revenue made a supplemental assessment showing that he had received a net income of $32,712.08, which, because of specific deductions and exemptions, resulted in no normal tax, but as the net income exceeded the sum of $20,000 the commissioner assessed an additional or super tax of one per cent upon the excess, resulting in a tax of $127.12, which was sought to be recovered. The reassessment was based upon certain sums received by the plaintiff in the year 1914 as distributions from corporations subject to the income tax law and held by the commissioner to be income derived from dividends received by the plaintiff on stock of domestic corporations; of which the sum of $79,975, received as a distribution from the Payette Lumber & Manufacturing Co., and without which no tax could have been levied against the plaintiff, is here in dispute.

Prior to March 1, 1913, and continuously thereafter until the surrender of his stock as hereinafter mentioned, plaintiff was a stockholder in the Payette Co., which was organized in the year 1903 with power to buy, hold, and sell timberlands, and in fact never engaged in any other business than this except minor businesses incidental to it. Immediately after its organization this company be-

---

[1] The dissenting opinions should be read. See also E. H. Warren, "Taxability of Stock Dividends as Income," 33 Harvard Law Review, 885.

gan to invest in timberlands, and prior to March 1, 1913, had thus invested approximately $1,375,000.

On March 1, 1913, the value of its assets was not less than $3,000,000, of which sum the value of the timberlands was not less than $2,875,000. The increase was due to the gradual rise in the market value of the lands. At that date the value of Turrish's stock was twice its par value, or $159,950, and about that time he and all the other stockholders gave an option to sell their stock for twice its par value. The holders of the option formed another company, called the Boise-Payette Lumber Co., and transferred the options to it. The options having been extended to December 31, 1913, the new company informed the Payette Co. and its stockholders shortly before this date that instead of exercising the option it preferred and proposed to purchase all of the assets of the Payette Co., paying to that company such a purchase price that there would be available for distribution to its stockholders twice the par value of their stock. The stockholders by resolution authorized this sale, and, pursuant to this and a resolution of the directors, the Payette Co. transferred to the new company all of its assets, property, and franchises, and upon the completion of the transaction found itself with no assets or property, except cash to the amount of double the par value of its stock which had been paid to it by the new company, and with no debt, liabilities, or obligations except those which the new company had assumed. The cash was distributed to the stockholders on the surrender of their certificates of stock, and the company went out of business. In this way, upon the surrender of his shares, Turrish received $159,950, being double their par value.

The Commissioner of Internal Revenue considered that of this sum one-half was not taxable, being the liquidation of the par value of Turrish's stock, but that the other half was income for the year 1914 and taxable under the act of 1913.

The question in the case is thus indicated. The District Court took a different view from that of the Commissioner of Internal Revenue and therefore overruled the demurrer to Turrish's complaint and entered judgment for him for the sum prayed, which judgment was affirmed by the Circuit Court of Appeals for the Eighth Circuit. (236 Fed. 653.)

The point in the case seems a short one. It, however, has provoked much discussion on not only the legal but the economic distinction between capital and income and by what processes and at what point of time the former produces or becomes the latter. And this in resolution of a statute which concerns the activities of men and intended, it might be supposed, to be without perplexities and readily solvable by the offhand conceptions of those to whom it was addressed.

The provisions of the act, so far as material to be noticed, are the following: That there is assessed "upon the entire net income arising or accruing from all sources in the preceding calendar year to every . . . person residing in the United States . . . a tax of one per centum per annum upon such income. . . ." (Par. A, subdiv. 1.)

In addition to that tax, which is denominated the normal income tax, it is provided that there shall be levied "upon the net income of every individual an additional tax . . . of one per centum per annum upon the amount by which the total net income exceeds" certain amounts, and the person subject to the tax is required to make a personal return of his total net income from all sources under rules and regulations to be prescribed by the Commissioner of Internal Revenue. (Subdiv. 2.)

By paragraph B it is provided that, subject to certain exemptions and deductions, "the net income of a taxable person shall include gains, profits, and income derived from salaries, wages, or compensation for personal service . . . also from interest, rent, dividends, securities, or the transaction of any lawful business carried on for gain or profit, or gains or profits and income derived from any source whatever."

After specifying the exemptions and deductions allowed, the law declares as follows:

"The said tax shall be computed upon the remainder of said net income of each person subject thereto, accruing during each preceding calendar year ending December thirty-first: *Provided, however,* That for the year ending December thirty-first, nineteen hundred and thirteen, said tax shall be computed on the net income accruing from March first to December thirty-first, nineteen hundred and thirteen, both dates inclusive. . . ." (Par. D.)

It will be observed, therefore, that the statute levies a normal tax and an additional tax upon net incomes, derived from whatever source, "arising or accruing" each preceding calendar year ending December 31, except that for the year ending December 31, 1913, the tax shall be computed on the net income accruing from March 1, 1913, to December 31, 1913.

And in determining the application of the statute to Turrish we must keep in mind that on the admitted facts the distribution received by him from the Payette Co. manifestly was a single and final dividend in liquidation of the entire assets and business of the company, a return to him of the value of his stock upon the surrender of his entire interest in the company, and at a price that represented its intrinsic value at and before March 1, 1913, when the act took effect.

The District Court and the Circuit Court of Appeals decided that the amount so distributed to Turrish was not income within the meaning of the statute, basing the decision on two propositions, as expressed in the opinion of the Circuit Court of Appeals, by Sanborn, Circuit Judge — (*a*) The amount was the realization of an investment made some years before, representing its gradual increase during those years, and which reached its height before the effective date of the law, that is, before March 1, 1913, and the mere change of form of the property "as from real to personal property, or from stock to cash" was not income to its holders because the value of the property was the same after as before the change; (*b*) the timberlands were the property, capital, and capital assets of their legal and equitable owner and the enhancement of their value during a series of years " prior to the effective date of the income-tax law, although divided or distributed by dividend or otherwise subsequent to that date, does not become income, gains, or profits taxable under such an act."

For proposition "*a*" the court cited Collector *v.* Hubbard, 12 Wall. 1; Bailey *v.* Railroad Company, 22 Wall. 604, and the same case in 106 U. S. 109. For proposition "*b*" Gray *v.* Darlington, 15 Wall. 63, was relied on.

The Government opposes both contentions by an elaborate argument containing definitions of capital and income drawn from legal and economic sources and given breadth to cover a number of other cases submitted with this. The argument, in effect, makes any increase of value of property income, emerging as such and taxable at the moment of realization by sale or some act of separation, as by dividend declared or by distribution, as in the instant case.

To sustain the argument these definitions are presented:

1. Capital is anything, material or otherwise, capable of ownership, viewed in its static condition at a moment of time, or the rights of ownership therein.

2. Income is the service or return rendered by capital during a period of time. . . .

4. Net income ("profits") is the difference between income and outgo. . . .

7. In the actual production and distribution of capital there is a constant conversion of capital into income, and *vice versa.*

8. The attempt to conceal this conversion by treating "income" as the standard return from intact "capital" only leads to confusion of the value of capital with capital itself.

From these definitions are deduced the following propositions, which are said to be decisive of the problems in the cases:

1. Income being derived from the use of capital, the conversion or transfer of capital always produces income.

2. Mere appreciation of capital value does not produce "income," nor mere depreciation "outgo."

3. Net income is the difference between *actual* "income" and *actual* "outgo."

4. Income is not confined to money income, but includes anything capable of easy valuation in money.

It will be observed that the breadth of definition and the breadth of application are necessary to the refutation of the reasoning of the Circuit Court of Appeals. There is direct antagonism, the court basing its reliance, it says, upon what it asserts is the common sense and understanding of the words of the law, and the exposition of like laws by the decisions of this court. The Government's resource is the discussion of economists and the fact, concrete and practical, of wealth not only increased but come to actual hand. The instant case is an example. **Turrish's** stock doubled in value. He paid for it $79,975.00; 1e received $159,950.00. It requires a struggle to resist t1e influence of the fact, but we are aided and fortified by our own precedents and saved from such intricate and subtle discussion and an elaborate review of ot1er cases cited in confirmation or opposition.

In Collector *v.* Hubbard, *supra,* t1e distinction between a corporation and its stock1olders was recognized and t1at t1e stock1older had no title for certain purposes to the earnings of t1e corporation, net or ot1er, prior to a dividend being declared, but t1ey might become capital by investment in permanent improvements and t1ereby increase the market value of the shares, "whether held by t1e original subscribers or by assignees." In ot1er words, it was held that the investments of t1e corporation were the investments of t1e stockholders; that is, t1e stock1olders could 1ave an interest, taxable under t1e act considered, t1ough not identical wit1 the corporation. This was repeated in Bailey *v.* Railroad Co., 22 Wall. 604, 635, 636.

T1e latter case came here again in 106 U. S. 109, and it was t1en declared that the purpose of an income tax law was to tax the income for t1e year t1at it accrued; in ot1er words, no tax in contemplation of t1e law accrues upon something except for the year in whic1 that something — earnings, profits, gains, or income — accrues. In that case the subject of t1e tax was a scrip dividend, but the certificate did not show t1e year of the earnings and testimony as to the partieular year was admitted. The principle applies to the case at bar. If increase in value of the lands was income, it had its particular time and suc1 time must have been wit1in the time of the law to be subject to the law, t1at is, it must have been after March 1, 1913. But, according to the fact admitted, there was no increase after that date and therefore no increase subject to t1e law. There was continuity of value, not gain or increase. In the first proposition of the Court of Appeals we, therefore, concur.

In support of its second proposition it adduced, as we have seen, Gray *v.* Darlington, 15 Wall. 63. T1e case arose under the income tax law of 1867, which levied "upon t1e gains, profits, and income of every person, . . . whether derived from any kind of property . . . or from any other source whatever . . . a tax of 5 per centum on the amount so derived over $1,000 . . . for the year ending the thirty-first of December next preceding the time for levying, collecting and paying said tax."

Darlington, in 1865, being the owner of certain United States Treasury notes, exc1anged them for United States bonds. In 1869 1e sold t1e bonds at an advance of $20,000 over the cost of the notes and upon this amount was levied a tax of 5 per centum as gains, profits, and income for that year. He paid the tax under protest and sued to recover, and prevailed. This court, by Mr. Justice Field, said:

"The question presented is whether the advance in the value of the bonds, during this period of four years, over their cost, realized by t1eir sale, was subject to taxation as gains, profits, or income of the

plaintiff for the year in which the bonds were sold.   The answer
which should be given to this question does not, in our judgment,
admit of any doubt.   The advance in the value of property during
a series of years can, in no just sense, be considered the gains, profits,
or income of any one particular year of the series, although the entire
amount of the advance be at one time turned into money by the sale
of the property.   The statute looks, with some exceptions, for subjects of taxation only to annual gains, profits, and income."

And again:

" The mere fact that property has advanced in value between the
date of its acquisition and sale does not authorize the imposition of
a tax on the amount of the advance.   Mere advance in value in no
sense constitutes the gains, profits, or income specified by the statute.
It constitutes and can be treated merely as increase of capital."

This case has not been since questioned or modified.

The Government feels the impediment of the case and attempts to
confine its ruling to the exact letter of the act of March 2, 1867, and
thereby distinguish that act from the act of 1913 and give to the
latter something of retrospective effect.   Opposed to this there is a
presumption, resistless except against an intention imperatively
clear.   The Government, however, makes its view depend upon dis-
putable differences between certain words of the two acts.   It urges
that the act of 1913 makes the income taxed one " arising or accruing " in the preceding calendar year, while the act of 1867 makes the
income one " derived."   Granting that there is a shade of difference
between the words, it can not be granted that Congress made that
shade a criterion of intention and committed the construction of its
legislation to the disputes of purists.   Besides, the contention of the
Government does not reach the principle of Gray *v.* Darlington,
which is that the gradual advance in the value of property during a
series of years in no just sense can be ascribed to a particular year,
not therefore as " arising or accruing," to meet the challenge of the
words, in the last one of the years, as the Government contends, and
taxable as income for that year or when turned into cash.   Indeed,
the case decides that such advance in value is not income at all, but
merely increase of capital and not subject to a tax as income.

We concur, therefore, in the second proposition of the Circuit
Court of Appeals as well as in the first and affirm the judgment.

BRANDEIS and CLARKE, JJ., concur in the result.

SOUTHERN PACIFIC CO. *v.* LOWE.

SUPREME COURT OF THE UNITED STATES.   1918.

[*Reported* 247 *U. S.* 330.]

PITNEY, J.   This case presents a question arising under the
Federal income tax act of October 3, 1913 (ch. 16, 38 Stat. 114,
166).   Suit was brought by plaintiff in error against the collector

to recover taxes assessed against it and paid under protest. There were two causes of action, of which only the second went to trial, it having been stipulated that the trial of the other might be postponed until the final determination of this one. So far as it is presented to us, the suit is an effort to recover a tax imposed upon certain dividends upon stock, in form received by the plaintiff from another corporation in the early part of the year 1914, and alleged by the plaintiff to have been paid out of a surplus accumulated not only prior to the effective date of the act but prior to the adoption of the sixteenth amendment to the Constitution of the United States. The district court directed a verdict and judgment in favor of the collector (238 Fed. Rep. 847), and the case comes here by direct writ of error under section 238, Judicial Code, because of the constitutional question. That our jurisdiction was properly invoked is settled by Towne *v.* Eisner, 245 U. S. 418, 425.

The case was submitted at the same time with several other cases arising under the same act and decided this day, viz.: Lynch, collector, *v.* Turrish, and Lynch, collector, *v.* Hornby, and Peabody *v.* Eisner, collector.

The material facts are as follows: Prior to January 1, 1913, and at all times material to the case, plaintiff, a corporation organized under the laws of the State of Kentucky, owned all the capital stock of the Central Pacific Railway Co., a corporation of the State of Utah, including the stock registered in the names of the directors.[1] This situation existed continuously from the incorporation of the railway company in the year 1899. That company is the successor of the Central Pacific Railroad Co. and acquired all of its properties, which constitute a part of a large system of railways owned or controlled by the Southern Pacific Co. The latter company, besides being sole stockholder, was in the actual physical possession of the railroads and all other assets of the railway company, and in charge of its operations, which were conducted in accordance with the terms of a lease made by the predecessor company to the Southern Pacific and assumed by the railway company, the effect of which was that the Southern Pacific should pay to the lessor company $10,000 per annum for organization expenses, should operate the railroads, branches, and leased lines belonging to the lessor, and account annually for the net earnings, and if these exceeded 6 per cent on the existing capital stock of the lessor the lessee should retain to itself one-half of the excess; advances by the lessee for account of the lessor were to bear lawful interest, and the lessee was to be entitled at any time and from time to time to refund to itself its advances and interest out of any net earnings which might be in its hands. The provisions of the lease were observed by both corporations for bookkeeping purposes. The Southern Pacific acted as cashier and banker for the entire system; the Central Pacific kept no bank account, its earnings being deposited with the bank account of the Southern

---

[1] There was another question, concerning a dividend paid by the Reward Oil Co., whose stock likewise was owned by the Southern Pacific Co., but the contention of plaintiff in error respecting this item has been abandoned.

Pacific; and if the Central Pacific needed money for additions and betterments or for making up a deficit of current earnings the necessary funds were advanced by the Southern Pacific. As a result of these operations and of the conversion of certain capital assets of the Central Pacific Co., that company showed upon its books a large surplus accumulated prior to January 1, 1913, principally in the form of a debit against the Southern Pacific, which at the same time, as sole stockholder, was entitled to any and all dividends that might be declared, and being in control of the board of directors was able to and did control the dividend policy. The dividends in question were declared and paid during the first six months of the year 1914 out of this surplus of the Central Pacific accumulated prior to January 1, 1913; but the payment was only constructive, being carried into effect by bookkeeping entries which simply reduced the apparent surplus of the Central Pacific and reduced the apparent indebtedness of the Southern Pacific to the Central Pacific by precisely the amount of the dividends.

The question is whether the dividends received under these circumstances and in this manner by the Southern Pacific Co. were taxable as income of that company under the income tax act of 1913.[1]

The act provides in § 2, par. A, subdiv. 1 (38 Stat. 166), "that there shall be levied, assessed, collected, and paid annually upon the entire net income arising or accruing from all sources in the preceding calendar year" to every person residing in the United States a tax of 1 per cent per annum, with exceptions not now material. By paragraph G (a) (p. 172), it is provided "that the normal tax hereinbefore imposed upon individuals [1 per cent] likewise shall be levied, assessed, and paid annually upon the entire net income arising or accruing from all sources during the preceding calendar year to every corporation . . . organized in the United States," with other provisions not now material.

It is provided in paragraph G (b), as to domestic corporations, that such net income shall be ascertained by deducting from the gross amount of the income of the corporation (1) ordinary and necessary expenses paid within the year in the maintenance and operation of its business and properties, including rentals and the like; (2) losses sustained within the year and not compensated by insurance or otherwise, including a reasonable allowance for depreciation by use, wear and tear of property, if any, and in the case of mines a certain allowance for depletion of ores and other natural deposits; (3) interest accrued and paid within the year upon indebtedness of the corporation, within the prescribed limits; (4) National and State taxes paid. It will be observed that moneys received as dividends upon the stock of other corporations are not deducted, as they

---

[1] In addition, a question was made in the District Court as to a special dividend declared by the Central Pacific out of the proceeds of sale of certain land on Long Island, taken in satisfaction of a debt and sold in December, 1913. As to this, however, no argument is submitted by plaintiff in error, the facts are not clear, and we pass it without consideration.

are in computing the income of individuals for the purpose of the normal tax under this act (p. 167), and as they were in computing the income of a corporation under the excise tax act of August 5, 1909 (ch. 6, 36 Stat. 11, 113, § 38).

By paragraph G (c) the tax upon corporations is to be computed upon the entire net income accrued within each calendar year, but for the year 1913 only upon the net income accrued from March 1 to December 31, to be ascertained by taking five-sixths of the entire net income for the calendar year.

The purpose to refrain from taxing income that accrued prior to March 1, 1913, and to exclude from consideration in making the computation any income that accrued in a preceding calendar year, is made plain by the provision last referred to; indeed, the sixteenth amendment, under which for the first time Congress was authorized to tax income from property without apportioning the tax among the States according to population, received the approval of the requisite number of States only in February, 1913. Pollock *v.* Farmers' Loan & Trust Co., 157 U. S. 429, 581; 158 U. S. 601, 637; Brushaber *v.* Union Pacific Railroad, 240 U. S. 1, 16.

We must reject in this case, as we have rejected in cases arising under the corporation excise tax act of 1909 (Doyle, collector, *v.* Mitchell Bros. Co., and Hays, collector, *v.* Gauley Mountain Coal Co., decided May 20, 1918), the broad contention submitted in behalf of the Government that all receipts — everything that comes in — are income within the proper definition of the term " gross income," and that the entire proceeds of a conversion of capital assets, in whatever form and under whatever circumstances accomplished, should be treated as gross income. Certainly the term " income " has no broader meaning in the 1913 act than in that of 1909 (see Stratton's Independence *v.* Howbert, 231 U. S. 399, 416, 417), and for the present purpose we assume there is no difference in its meaning as used in the two acts. This being so, we are bound to consider accumulations that accrued to a corporation prior to January 1, 1913, as being capital, not income, for the purposes of the act. And we perceive no adequate ground for a distinction, in this regard, between an accumulation of surplus earnings, and the increment due to an appreciation in value of the assets of the taxpayer.

That the dividends in question were paid out of a surplus that accrued to the Central Pacific prior to January 1, 1913, is undisputed; and we deem it to be equally clear that this surplus accrued to the Southern Pacific Co. prior to that date, in every substantial sense pertinent to the present inquiry, and hence underwent nothing more than a change of form when the dividends were declared.

We do not rest this upon the view that for the purposes of the act of 1913 stockholders in the ordinary case have the same interest in the accumulated earnings of the company before as after the declaration of dividends. The act is quite different in this respect from the income tax act of June 30, 1864 (ch. 173, 13 Stat. 223, 281, 282), under which this court held, in Collector *v.* Hubbard, 12 Wall. 1, 16, that an individual was taxable upon his proportion of the earnings of the corporation althoug1 not declared as dividends. That decision was based upon t1e very special language of a clause of section 117 of t1e act (13 Stat. 282) t1at "t1e gains and profits of all companies w1et1er incorporated or partners1ip, ot1er t1an t1e companies specified in this section, s1all be included in estimating t1e annual gains, profits, or income of any person entitled to t1e same, whet1er divided or ot1erwise." T1e act of 1913 contains no similar language, but on t1e contrary deals wit1 dividends as a particular item of income, leaving t1em free from t1e normal tax imposed upon individuals, subjecting t1em to the graduated surtaxes only w1en received as dividends (38 Stat. 167, par. B), and subjecting t1e interest of an individual s1are1older in t1e undivided gains and profits of 1is corporation to t1ese taxes only in case t1e company is formed or fraudulently availed of for t1e purpose of preventing t1e imposition of suc1 tax by permitting gains and profits to accumulate instead of being divided or distributed. Our view of t1e effect of t1is act upon dividends received by t1e ordinary stock1older after it took effect but paid out of a surplus t1at accrued to t1e corporation before that event, is set fort1 in Lync1, collector, *v.* Hornby, decided t1is day.

We base our conclusion in t1e present case upon t1e view that it was the purpose and intent of Congress, while taxing " the entire net income arising or accruing from all sources " during each year commencing wit1 t1e first day of Marc1, 1913, to refrain from taxing t1at which in mere form only, bore t1e appearance of income accruing after that date, w1ile in trut1 and in substance it accrued before; and upon t1e fact that the Central Pacific and t1e Sout1ern Pacific were in substance identical because of t1e complete owners1ip and control w1ich t1e latter possessed over t1e former, as stock1older and in ot1er capacities. W1ile the two companies were separate legal entities, yet in fact, and for all practical purposes t1ey were merged, the former being but a part of t1e latter, acting merely as its agent and subject in all t1ings to its proper direction and control. And, besides, the funds represented by t1e dividends were in the actual possession and control of the Southern Pacific as well before as after the declaration of t1e dividends. T1e fact t1at t1e books were kept in accordance with t1e provisions of t1e lease, so t1at t1ese funds appeared upon t1e accounts as an indebtedness of t1e lessee to the lessor, can not be controlling, in view of t1e practical identity between lessor and lessee. Aside from t1e interests of creditors and the public — and t1ere is not1ing to suggest that the interests of either were concerned in the disposition of the surplus of the Central Pacific — t1e Sout1ern Pacific was entitled to dispose of the matter as it saw fit. T1ere is no question of there being a surplus to warrant t1e dividends at the time they were made, hence any speculation as to what might have happened in case of financial reverses that did not occur is beside t1e mark.

It is true t1at in ordinary cases t1e mere accumulation of an adequate surplus does not entitle a stockholder to dividends until the directors in their discretion declare them. New York, etc., Railroad v. Nickals, 119 U. S. 296, 306; Gibbons v. Mahan, 136 U. S. 549, 558. And see Humphreys v. McKissock, 140 U. S. 304, 312. But this is not the ordinary case. In fact the discretion of the directors was affirmatively exercised by declaring dividends out of the surplus that was accumulated prior to January 1, 1913; it does not appear that any other fair exercise of discretion was open; and the complete ownership and right of control of the Southern Pacific at all times material makes it a matter of indifference whether the vote was at one time or another. Under the circumstances, the entire matter of the declaration and payment of the dividends was a paper transaction to bring the books into accord with the acknowledged rights of the Southern Pacific; and so far as the dividends represented the surplus of the Central Pacific that accumulated prior to January 1, 1913, they were not taxable as income of the Southern Pacific within the true intent and meaning of the act of 1913.

The case turns upon its very peculiar facts, and is distinguishable from others in which the question of the identity of a controlling stockholder with his corporation has been raised. Pullman Car Co. v. Missouri Pacific Co., 115 U. S. 587, 596; Peterson v. Chicago, Rock Island & Pacific Railway, 205 U. S. 364, 391.

Judgment reversed, and the cause remanded for further proceedings in conformity with this opinion.

CLARKE, J., dissents.

LYNCH v. HORNBY.

SUPREME COURT OF THE UNITED STATES. 1918.
[Reported 247 U. S. 339.]

PITNEY, J. Hornby, the respondent, recovered a judgment in the United States District Court against Lynch, as collector of internal revenue, for the return of $171, assessed as an additional income tax under the act of October 3, 1913 (ch. 16, 38 Stat. 114, 166), and paid under protest. The Circuit Court of Appeals affirmed the judgment (236 Fed. 661), and the case comes here on certiorari. It was submitted at the same time with Lynch, collector, v. Turrish, Southern Pacific Co. v. Lowe, collector, and Peabody v. Eisner, collector, arising under the same act, and this day decided.

The facts, in brief, are as follows: Hornby, from 1906 to 1915, was the owner of 434 (out of 10,000) shares of the capital stock of the Cloquet Lumber Co., an Iowa corporation, which for more than a quarter of a century had been engaged in purchasing timber lands, manufacturing the timber into lumber and selling it. Its shares had a par value of $100 each, making the entire capital stock $1,000,000. On and prior to March 1, 1913, by the increase of the value of its timber lands and through its business operations, the total property of the company had come to be worth $4,000,000, and Hornby's stock, the par value of which was $43,400, had become worth at least

$150,000. In the year 1914 the company was engaged in cutting its standing timber, manufacturing it into lumber, selling the lumber, and distributing the proceeds among its stockholders. In that year it thus distributed dividends aggregating $650,000, of which $240,-000, or 24 per cent of the par value of the capital stock, was derived from current earnings, and $410,000 from conversion into money of property that it owned or in which it had an interest on March 1, 1913. Hornby's share of the latter amount was $17,794, and this not having been included in his income tax return, the Commissioner of Internal Revenue levied an additional tax of $171 on account of it, and this forms the subject of the present suit.

The case was tried in the District Court and argued in the Circuit Court of Appeals together with Lynch, collector, *v.* Turrish, 236 Fed. 653, and was treated as presenting substantially the same question upon the merits. In our opinion it is distinguishable from the Turrish case, where the distribution in question was a single and final dividend received by Turrish from the Payette Co. in liquidation of the entire assets and business of the company and a return to him of the value of his stock upon the surrender of his entire interest in the company, at a price that represented its intrinsic value at and before March 1, 1913, when the income tax act took effect.

In the present case there was no winding up or liquidation of the Cloquet Lumber Co. nor any surrender of Hornby's stock. He was but one of many stockholders, and had but the ordinary stockholder's interest in the capital and surplus of the company — that is, a right to have them devoted to the proper business of the corporation and to receive from the current earnings or accumulated surplus such dividends as the directors in their discretion might declare. Gibbons *v.* Mahon, 136 U. S. 549, 557. The operations of this company in the year 1914 were, according to the facts pleaded, of a nature essentially like those in which it had been engaged for more than a quarter of a century. The fact that they resulted in converting into money, and thus setting free for distribution as dividends, a part of its surplus assets accumulated prior to March 1, 1913. does not render Hornby's share of those dividends any the less a part of his income within the true intent and meaning of the act, the pertinent language of which is as follows (38 Stat. 166, 167):

"A. Subdivision 1. That there shall be levied, assessed, collected. and paid annually upon the entire net income arising or accruing from all sources in the preceding calendar year to every citizen of the United States, . . . and to every person residing in the United States, . . . a tax of 1 per centum per annum upon such income. except as hereinafter provided; . . .

"B. That, subject only to such exemptions and deductions as are hereinafter allowed, the net income of a taxable person shall include gains, profits, and income derived from salaries, wages, or compensation for personal service, . . . also from interest, rent, dividends. securities, or the transaction of any lawful business carried on for gain or profit, gains or profits and income derived from any source whatever."

Among the deductions allowed for the purpose of the normal tax
is "seventh, the amount received as dividends upon the stock or from
the net earnings of any corporation, . . . which is taxable upon its
net income as hereinafter provided." There is a graduated additional
tax, commonly known as a "surtax," upon net income in excess of
$20,000, including income from dividends, and for the purpose of
this additional tax "the taxable income of any individual shall embrace the share to which he would be entitled of the gains and profits,
if divided or distributed, whether divided or distributed or not, of
all corporations . . . formed or fraudulently availed of for the purpose of preventing the imposition of such tax through the medium
of permitting such gains and profits to accumulate instead of being
divided or distributed."

It is evident that Congress intended to draw and did draw a distinction between a stockholder's undivided share or interest in the
gains and profits of a corporation prior to the declaration of a dividend, and his participation in the dividends declared and paid, treating the latter in ordinary circumstances as a part of his income for
the purposes of the surtax, and not regarding the former as taxable
income unless fraudulently accumulated for the purpose of evading
the tax.

This treatment of undivided profits applies only to profits permitted to accumulate after the taking effect of the act, since only
with respect to these is a fraudulent purpose of evading the tax
predicable. Corporate profits that accumulated before the act took
effect stand on a different footing. As to these, however, just as we
deem the legislative intent manifest to tax the stockholder with respect to such accumulations only if and when and to the extent that
his interest in them comes to fruition as income—that is, in dividends
declared — so we can perceive no constitutional obstacle that stands
in the way of carrying out this intent when dividends are declared
out of a pre-existing surplus. The act took effect on March 1, 1913,
a few days after the requisite number of States had given approval
to the sixteenth amendment, under which for the first time Congress
was empowered to tax income from property without apportioning
the tax among the States according to population. Southern Pacific
Co. *v.* Lowe, *supra.* That the retroactivity of the act from the date
of its passage (October 3, 1913) to a date not prior to the adoption of
the amendment was permissible is settled by Brushaber *v.* Union
Pacific Railroad, 240 U. S. 1, 20. And we deem it equally clear
that Congress was at liberty under the amendment to tax as income,
without apportionment, everything that became income in the ordinary sense of the word after the adoption of the amendment, including dividends received in the ordinary course by a stockholder from a
corporation, even though they were extraordinary in amount and
might appear upon analysis to be a mere realization in possession of
an inchoate and contingent interest that the stockholder had in a
surplus of corporate assets previously existing. Dividends are the
appropriate fruit of stock ownership, are commonly reckoned as income, and are expended as such by the stockholder without regard

to whether they are declared from the most recent earnings or from a surplus accumulated from the earnings of the past or are based upon the increased value of the property of the corporation. The stockholder is in the ordinary case a different entity from the corporation, and Congress was at liberty to treat the dividends as coming to him *ab extra* and as constituting a part of his income when they came to hand.

Hence we construe the provision of the act that "the net income of a taxable person shall include gains, profits, and income derived from . . . interest, rent, dividends, . . . or gains or profits and income derived from any source whatever" as including (for the purposes of the additional tax) all dividends declared and paid in the ordinary course of business by a corporation to its stockholders after the taking effect of the act (March 1, 1913), whether the current earnings or from the accumulated surplus made up of past earnings or increase in value of corporate assets, notwithstanding it accrued to the corporation in whole or in part prior to March 1, 1913. In short, the word "dividends" was employed in the act as descriptive of one kind of gain to the individual stockholder, dividends being treated as the tangible and recurrent returns upon his stock, analogous to the interest and rent received upon other forms of invested capital.

In the more recent income tax acts, provisions have been inserted for the purpose of excluding from the effect of the tax any dividends declared out of earnings or profits that accrued prior to March 1, 1913. This originated with the act of September 8, 1916, and has been continued in the act of October 3, 1917. We are referred to the legislative history of the act of 1916, which it is contended indicates that the new definition of the term "dividends" was intended to be declaratory of the meaning of the term as used in the 1913 act. We can not accept this suggestion, deeming it more reasonable to regard the change as a concession to the equity of stockholders granted in the 1916 act, in view of constitutional questions that had been raised in this case, in the companion case of Lynch, collector, *v.* Turrish, and perhaps in other cases. These two cases were commenced in October, 1915, and decisions adverse to the tax were rendered in the District Court in January, 1916, and in the Circuit Court of Appeals September 4, 1916.

We repeat that under the 1913 act dividends declared and paid in the ordinary course by a corporation to its stockholders after March 1, 1913, whether from current earnings or from a surplus accumulated prior to that date, were taxable as income to the stockholder.

We do not overlook the fact that every dividend distribution diminishes by just so much the assets of the corporation, and in a theoretical sense reduces the intrinsic value of the stock. But, at the same time, it demonstrates the capacity of the corporation to pay dividends, holds out a promise of further dividends in the future, and quite probably increases the market value of the shares. In our opinion, Congress laid hold of dividends paid in the ordinary course as *de facto* income of the stockholder, without regard to the ultimate effect upon the corporation resulting from their payment.

Of course, we are dealing here with the ordinary stockholder receiving dividends declared in the ordinary way of business. Lynch, collector, *v.* Turrish and Southern Pacific Co. *v.* Lowe, collector, this day decided, rest upon their special facts and are plainly distinguishable.

It results from what we have said that it was erroneous to award a return of the tax collected from the respondent, and that the judgment should be

Reversed, and the cause remanded to the district court for further proceedings in conformity with this opinion.

PEABODY *v.* EISNER.

SUPREME COURT OF THE UNITED STATES.   1918.
[*Reported* 247 *U. S.* 347.]

PITNEY, J.   This case arose under the Federal income tax act of October 3, 1913 (ch. 16, 38 Stat. 114, 166).   The controversy is over the first cause of action set up by plaintiff in error in a suit against the collector for the recovery of an additional tax exacted in respect of a certain dividend received by plaintiff in the year 1914, the facts being as follows: On and prior to March 1, 1913, and thenceforward until payment of the dividend in question, petitioner was owner of 1,100 shares (out of a total of 2,000,000 shares outstanding) of common stock of the Union Pacific Railroad Co., of the par value of $100 each, and during the same period the company had large holdings of the common and preferred stocks of the Baltimore & Ohio Railroad Co.   On March 2, 1914, the Union Pacific declared and paid an extra dividend upon each share of its common stock, amounting to $3 in cash, $12 in par value of preferred stock of the Baltimore & Ohio, and $22.50 in par value of the common stock of the same company; the result being that petitioner received as his dividend upon his holding of Union Pacific common stock $3,300 in cash, 132 shares of Baltimore & Ohio preferred and 247½ shares of Baltimore & Ohio common stock.   In his income return for 1914 he included as taxable income $4.12 per share of this dividend, or $4,532 in all, and paid his tax upon the basis of this return. Afterwards he was subjected to an additional assessment upon a valuation of the balance of his dividend, and this, having been paid under protest, is the subject of the present suit, the theory of which is that the entire earnings, income, gains, and profits from all sources realized by the Union Pacific Railroad Co. from March 1, 1913, to March 2, 1914, remaining after the payment of prior charges, did not exceed $4.12 per share of the Union Pacific common stock, and that the cash and Baltimore & Ohio stock disposed of in the extra dividend (so far as they exceeded the value of $4.12 per share of Union Pacific) did not constitute a gain, profit, or income of the Union

Pacific, and therefore did not constitute a gain, profit, or income of the plaintiff arising or accruing either in or for the year 1914 or for any period subsequent to March 1, 1913, the date when the income tax law took effect.   The District Court overruled this contention upon the authority of Southern Pacific Co. *v.* Lowe, 238 Fed. 847, and Towne *v.* Eisner, 242 Fed. 702.   The latter case has since been reversed (245 U. S. 418), but only upon the ground that it related to a stock dividend which in fact took nothing from the property of the corporation and added nothing to the interest of the shareholder, but merely changed the evidence which represented that interest. Southern Pacific Co. *v.* Lowe, collector, has been reversed this day, but only upon the ground that the Central Pacific Railway Co., which paid the dividend, and the Southern Pacific Co., which received it, were in substance identical corporations because of the complete ownership and control which the latter possessed over the former as stockholder and in other capacities, so that while the two companies were separate legal entities, yet in fact and for all practical purposes the former was but a part of the latter, acting merely as its agent and subject in all things to its direction and control; and for the further reason that the funds represented by the dividend were in the actual possession and control of the Southern Pacific Co. as well before as after the declaration of the dividend.   In this case the plaintiff in error stands in the position of the ordinary stockholder, whose interest in the accumulated earnings and surplus of the company are not the same before as after the declaration of a dividend; his right being merely to have the assets devoted to the proper business of the corporation and to receive from the current earnings or accumulated surplus such dividends as the directors in their discretion may declare; and without right or power on his part to control that discretion.

It hardly is necessary to say that this case is not ruled by our decision in Towne *v.* Eisner, since the dividend of Baltimore & Ohio shares was not a stock dividend but a distribution in specie of a portion of the assets of the Union Pacific, and is to be governed for all present purposes by the same rule applicable to the distribution of a like value in money.   It is controlled by Lynch, collector, *v.* Hornby, this **day** decided.

Judgment affirmed.

GULF OIL CORPORATION *v.* LEWELLYN.

SUPREME COURT OF THE UNITED STATES.   1918.

[*Reported* 248 *U. S.* 71.]

HOLMES, J.   This is a suit to recover a tax levied upon certain dividends as income under the act of October 3, 1913 (ch. 6, § 2, 38 Stat. 114, 166).   The District Court gave judgment for the plaintiff (242 Fed. 709), but this judgment was reversed by the Circuit Court of Appeals (245 Fed. 1, 158 C. C. A. 1).

The facts may be abridged from the findings below as follows: The petitioner was a holding company owning all the stock in the other corporations concerned except the qualifying shares held by directors. These companies with others constituted a single enterprise, carried on by the petitioner, of producing, buying, transporting, refining, and selling oil. The subsidiary companies had retained their earnings, although making some loans *inter se,* and all their funds were invested in properties or actually required to carry on the business, so that the debtor companies had no money available to pay their debts. In January, 1913, the petitioner decided to take over the previously accumulated earnings and surplus and did so in that year by votes of the companies that it controlled. But, disregarding the forms gone through, the result was merely that the petitioner became the holder of the debts previously due from one of its companies to another. It was no richer than before, but its property now was represented by stock in and debts due from its subsidiaries, whereas formerly it was represented by the stock alone, the change being effected by entries upon the respective companies' books. The earnings thus transferred had been accumulated and had been used as capital before the taxing year. Lynch *v.* Turrish, 247 U. S. 221, 228.

We are of opinion that the decision of the District Court was right. It is true that the petitioner and its subsidiaries were distinct beings in contemplation of law, but the facts that they were related as parts of one enterprise, all owned by the petitioner, that the debts were all enterprise debts due to members, and that the dividends represented earnings that had been made in former years and that practically had been converted into capital, unite to convince us that the transaction should be regarded as bookkeeping rather than as "dividends declared and paid in the ordinary course by a corporation." Lynch *v.* Hornby, 247 U. S. 339, 346. The petitioner did not itself do the business of its subsidiaries and have possession of their property as in Southern Pacific Co. *v.* Lowe, 247 U. S. 330, but the principle of that case must be taken to cover this. By § 2, G (c) (38 Stat. 174) and S (*Id.,* 202), the tax from January 1 to February 28, 1913, is levied as a special excise tax, but in view of our decision that the dividends here concerned were not income, it is unnecessary to discuss the further question that has been raised under the latter clause as to the effect of the fact that excise taxes upon the subsidiary corporations had been paid.

Judgment reversed.

DOERSCHUCK *v.* UNITED STATES.

DISTRICT COURT OF THE UNITED STATES. 1921.

[*Reported* 274 *Fed.* 739.]

CHATFIELD, J. The plaintiff in each of the above actions has paid income tax on one-quarter of an issue of debenture bonds of the North American Brewing Company, which came into the hands of the plaintiffs because of the ownership by each of 1,230 shares (or one-quarter) of the entire capital stock of said North American Brewing Company. The directors of said corporation had voted an issue of $738,000 of debenture bonds from a surplus or undivided profits amounting to $840,368.09, which had accrued between 1906 and July 1, 1916.

The portion of the bonds representing surplus earned before March 1, 1913, was not taxed and hence is not involved in these actions. The balance, viz., $262,334.44 was assessed as income for the year 1916, during which year each of the plaintiffs had received his one-quarter part of said funds.

In the case of Eisner *v.* Macomber, 252 U. S. 189, shares of stock were issued in the form of a dividend to stockholders, leaving ownership of the property in the stockholders the same as before the issuance; that is, the property representing the value of the stock was the same, and the only change was that each stockholder held two certificates representing in the aggregate and in theory the same stock value as previously had been represented by one certificate. It was held in that case that such stock dividend was not equivalent, for the purposes of income tax, to the payment of a dividend in property or in cash, and was not to be taxable as income under the law of September 8, 1916, sections 1, 2, and 3.

The plaintiffs in the present action rely upon the case of *In re* Fechheimer Fishel Co., 212 Fed. 357, which holds that debenture bonds, having the characteristic features of preferred stock, are, from the standpoint of creditors of the corporation when the corporation becomes insolvent, no different than such preferred stock.

It would follow from this that for the purpose of liquidation or dissolution of the corporation, or for consideration in insolvency or bankruptcy proceedings, such debenture holders would not rank as general creditors.

Plaintiffs also cite the case of Cass *v.* Realty Securities Co., 148 App. Div. 96, which held that bonds having a definite date and conditioned as were the debenture bonds in the present action, were for the purposes under consideration in that case equivalent to preferred stock and should not be considered as bonds in the usual meaning of that word.

It has been held in Peabody *v.* Eisner, 247 U. S. 347, that a dividend of shares in another corporation is taxable as income of the corporation owning the shares and distributing it as a dividend in specie rather than in money.

In Stratton's Independence *v.* Howbert, 231 U. S. 399, it was held that the transformation of ores in a mine into cash proceeds through the business of mining was a production of income in so far as net profits were concerned, and that the amount by which the body of ore was reduced should not be added as a part of the expenses of conducting the business. This illustrates the difference between the production of income and the mere changing of form in which capital may be owned by the individual stockholder.

In Eisner *v.* Macomber, *supra,* at p. 208, the court says:

" The stockholder has the right to have the assets employed in the enterprise, with the incidental rights mentioned; but, as stockholder, he has no right to withdraw, only the right to persist, subject to the enterprise, and looking only to dividends for his return."

It is apparent, therefore, in the present case that the plaintiffs received an actual payment (in the form of securities available for disposition in the market, and entirely served or distinguished from their control of the property as stockholders) of profits which the company wished to distribute as earnings to its stockholders. It did this by distribution of obligations which, like a promissory note, called for the payment of cash, and did not invest the holder with merely a different form of holding of stock.

There is no question here between the persons receiving this dividend and creditors, as to priority of payment. Evidently so far as these debenture bonds are concerned, the corporation was solvent, and to whatever extent they might be of value, this value was separated from any stockholders' control of the corporation. As stated in Eisner *v.* Macomber, *supra,* at p. 212:

" It is said that a stockholder may sell the new shares acquired in the stock dividend; and so he may, if he can find a buyer. It is equally true that if he does sell, and in doing so realizes a profit, such profit, like any other, is income, and so far as it may have arisen since the Sixteenth Amendment is taxable by Congress without apportionment."

The debenture bonds in the suit at bar fall into the class of stock sold rather than stock held in a continued status of shareholder.

The complaints should be dismissed.

UNITED STATES *v.* GUINZBERG.

CIRCUIT COURT OF APPEALS.   1921.
[*Reported* 278 *Fed.* 363.]

MANTON, Circuit Judge. On the 17th of February, 1913, the I. B. Kleinert Rubber Co. declared a dividend of 18 per cent to common stockholders of record on January 30, 1913. This dividend was payable July 1, 1913. The defendant in error was a stockholder on the 30th of January, 1913. The dividend was declared out of the profits of the company earned during the year 1912. It was the only dividend paid during the year 1913. The declaration of this dividend was in accordance with the established practice of 20 years' standing that one dividend in each year was declared in February out of the earnings of the company, and made payable the following July 1. The reason given for the postponement of the payment of the dividend until July 1 in each year was to permit the corporation to have use of the earnings in its business as a bank balance. This purpose was said to be to avoid being forced to borrow money. The defendant in error, in his return for 1913, did not include the dividend so received by him, amounting to $70,380, and it is because of his failure to pay an income tax on such sum that this action was brought.

We think that the dividend declared prior to March 1, 1913, the effective date of the income tax law here considered, was not income when paid because it was part of the capital of the defendant in error on March 1, 1913. By the declaration of a dividend, the earnings of the company to the extent declared were separated from the property of the corporation and were appropriated by that action to the then stockholders, who became creditors of the corporation for the amount of the dividend. The relation then created was that of debtor and creditor. N. Y. Trust Co. *et al., v.* Edwards, Supreme Court, decided November 14, 1921; Wheeler *v.* Northwestern Sleigh Co., 39 Fed. 437; People *ex rel.* U. S. Trust Co. *v.* Barker, 66 Hun, 131; Billingham *v.* Gleason Mfg. Co., 101 App. Div. 476; affd. 185 N. Y. 571. It is the separation of the earnings from the balance of the corporate property, together with the promise to pay arising from the declaration of the dividend, that works this change. The holder of stock, with respect to the dividend, is on a par with the other creditors of the corporation. Staats *v.* Biograph Co., 236 Fed. 454. The fact that the dividend is payable at a future date does not alter the rights thus created. The obligation of the corporation as debtor commences with the declaration of the dividend, although the payment is postponed for the convenience of the company. The rights of the stockholders are immediately vested the moment the dividend is declared. N. Y. Trust Co., etc. *v.* Edwards, etc., *supra.* The action of the board of directors is the appropriation of a portion of the earnings to the defendant in error as the holder of a certificate of stock. The same rule prevails in the State courts of New York, under which laws the corporation here in question was organized. Hopper *v.* Sage, 112 N. Y. 530. The fact that they are payable at a future time is immaterial. Matter of Kernochen, 104 N. Y. 618.

The income tax Act as of March 1, 1913, provides:

" A. Subdivision 1. That there shall be levied, assessed, collected and paid annually upon the entire net income arising or accruing from all sources in the preceding calendar year to every citizen of the United States, whether residing at home or abroad, and to every person residing in the United States though not a citizen thereof, a tax of 1 per centum per annum upon such income, except as hereinafter provided; and a like tax shall be assessed, levied, collected, and paid annually upon the entire net income from all property owned and of every business, trade, or profession carried on in the United States by persons residing elsewhere. . . ."

" D. The said tax shall be computed upon the remainder of said net income of each person subject thereto, accruing during each preceding calendar year ending December 31: *Provided, however,* That for the year ending December 31, 1913, said tax shall be computed on the net income accruing from March 1 to December 31, 1913, both dates inclusive. . . ."

We think that under this Act the income which accrued after March 1, 1913, only is taxable. Anything which accrued prior to March 1, 1913, was part of the taxpayer's principal at the time when this Act became effective. Property held prior to March 1, 1913, must be considered as capital, and the dividends in question must be treated as such. The Act provides that "the entire net income arising or accruing from all sources in the preceding calendar year to every citizen of the United States . . ." shall be taxed. Accumulations that accrued to a corporation prior to January 1, 1913, were held to be capital and not income for the purpose of the Act in Southern Pacific Co. *v.* Lowe, 247 U. S. 330. The term "income" has been held to have no broader meaning in the 1913 Act than in the 1910 Act. Stratton's Independence *v.* Howbert, 231 U. S. 417. The Supreme Court based its conclusion in the Southern Pacific case (*supra*) upon the view that it was the purpose and intent of Congress, while taxing the entire net income "arising or accruing" from all sources during each year, commencing the 1st day of March, 1913, to refrain from taxing that which, in mere form only, bore the appearance of income accruing after that date, while in truth and substance it accrued before. Under the 1909 Act the expression "income received during such year" was held to look to the time of realization rather than the period of accrument "except as a taking effect of the Act on a specific date (January 1, 1909) excludes income that accrued before that date." Hayes *v.* Gauley Mt. Coal Co., 247 U. S. 193. In the Hayes case, it was held that income received within the year for which the assessment was levied, whether it accrued within that year or some preceding year, when the Act was in effect, could be taxed, but it excluded all income that accrued prior to January 1, 1909, although afterwards received while the Act was in effect. Value received by shareholders on the surrender of their certificates of stock where the company sold all its property and made final distribution of the proceeds to the shareholders, and where the amount received by each was twice the par value of the stock, but represented no increase since the effective date of the Act, it was held that it did not "arise or accrue" after the Act became effective. In Maryland Casualty Co. *v.* United States, 251 U. S.

342, cited by the Government, the income tax Act of 1913 was considered in so far as it concerned the dealing with corporations as distinguished from dealings with individuals and which imposed a tax, under the language of one paragraph, upon income " arising or accruing " during the year and under another paragraph of the Act upon income received within the year. It was held that it was not sufficient for income to accrue within the year in order to render the corporation taxable, but the income must have been received by the corporation. But this was due to ambiguous paragraphs of the Act which taxed the corporation. It was a construction favorable to the taxpayer under such paragraphs. Nowhere in the opinion is there a suggestion that the court changed the rule announced in Southern Pacific Co. *v.* Lowe, *supra,* and Hayes *v.* Coal Co., *supra,* wherein it was held that income which had accrued prior to March 1, 1913, if received thereafter, would not be taxable.

The case at bar is different from the cases where commissions are to be received at a future date upon a contingency and where there is no fixed certainty of such receipt. There it can not be said that the income has accrued. Edwards *v.* Keith, 231 Fed. 110; Woods *v.* Lewellyn, 252 Fed. 106. Dividends declared and paid in the ordinary course by a corporation to its stockholders after March 1, 1913, whether from current earnings or from surplus accumulated prior to that date, have been held to be taxable as income to the stockholder. Lynch *v.* Hornby, 247 U. S. 339. "We deem the legislative intent manifest only if and when, and to the extent that, his interest in them comes to fruition as income — that is, in dividends declared." Eisner *v.* Macomber, 252 U. S. 204.

We conclude that upon the declaration of a dividend the debt was immediately created in favor of the defendant in error, payable at a future date. By that action a vested right was created in favor of the stockholder, who could sell his right by assigning or pledging or otherwise disposing of it, and this was not income arising and accruing within the meaning of the statute such as might be taxed under the income tax act of March 1, 1913, here in question. The same views are expressed in the rulings of the Treasury Department (Treasury Decision 2048, November 12, 1914).

We find no error below, and the direction of a judgment for the defendant is affirmed.

UNITED STATES *v.* PHELLIS.

SUPREME COURT OF THE UNITED STATES. 1921.

[*Reported* 257 *U. S.*]

PITNEY, J. The court below sustained the claim of C. **W. Phellis** for a refund of certain moneys paid by him under protest in discharge of an additional tax assessed against him for the year 1915, based upon alleged income equivalent to the market value of 500

shares of stock of a Delaware corporation called the E. I. du Pont
de Nemours & Co., received by him as a dividend upon his 250 shares
of stock of the E. I. du Pont de Nemours Powder Co., a New Jersey
corporation. The United States appeals.

From the findings of the Court of Claims, read in connection with
claimant's petition, the following essential facts appear: In and prior
to September, 1915, the New Jersey company had been engaged for
many years in the business of manufacturing and selling explosives.
Its funded debt and its capital stock at par values were as follows:

5% mortgage bonds	$1,230,000
4½% 30-year bonds	14,166,000
Preferred stock ($100 shares)	16,068,600
Common stock ($100 shares)	29,427,100
Total.........................	$60,891,700

It had an excess of assets over liabilities showing a large surplus
of accumulated profits; the precise amount is not important, except
that it should be stated that it was sufficient to cover the dividend
distribution presently to be mentioned. In that month a reorganization and financial adjustment of the business was resolved upon and
carried into effect with the assent of a sufficient proportion of the
stockholders, in which a new corporation was formed under the laws
of Delaware with an authorized capital stock of $240,000,000, to
consist in part of debenture stock bearing 6 per cent cumulative
dividends, in part of common stock; and to this new corporation all
the assets and good will of the New Jersey company were transferred
as an entirety and as a going concern, as of October 1, 1915, at a
valuation of $120,000,000, the new company assuming all the obli-
gations of the old except its capital stock and funded debt. In payment of the consideration the old company retained $1,484,100 in
cash to be used in redemption of its outstanding 5 per cent mortgage bonds, and received $59,661,700 par value in debenture stock
of the new company (of which $30,234,600 was to be used in taking
up, share for share and dollar for dollar, the preferred stock of the
old company and redeeming its 30-year bonds), and $58,854,200
par value of the common stock of the new company which was to be
and was immediately distributed among the common stockholders of
the old company as a dividend, paying them two shares of the new
stock for each share they held in the old company. This plan was
carried out by appropriate corporate action; the new company took
over all the assets of the old company, and that company besides
paying off its 5 per cent bonds acquired debenture stock of the new
company sufficient to liquidate its 4½ per cent 30-year bonds and
retire its preferred stock, additional debenture stock equal in amount
at par to its own outstanding common stock, and also two shares of
common stock of the Delaware corporation for each share of the outstanding common stock of the New Jersey corporation. Each holder
of the New Jersey company's common stock (including claimant)
retained his old stock and besides received a dividend of two shares

for one in common stock of the Delaware company, and the New Jersey corporation retained in its treasury 6 per cent debenture stock of the Delaware corporation equivalent to the par value of its own outstanding common stock. The personnel of the stockholders and officers of the two corporations was on October 1, 1915, identical, the new company having elected the same officers as the old; and the holders of common stock in both corporations had the same proportionate stockholding in each. After the reorganization and the distribution of the stock of the Delaware corporation, the New Jersey corporation continued as a going concern, and still exists, but except for the redemption of its outstanding bonds, the exchange of debenture stock for its preferred stock, and the holding of debenture stock to an amount equivalent to its own outstanding common and the collection and disposition of dividends thereon, it has done no business. It is not, however, in process of liquidation. It has received as income upon the Delaware company's debenture stock held by it dividends to the amount of 6 per cent per annum, which it has paid out to its own stockholders, including the claimant. The fair market value of the stock of the New Jersey corporation on September 30, 1915, prior to the reorganization, was $795 per share, and its fair market value, after the execution of the contracts between the two corporations, was on October 1, 1915, $100 per share. The fair market value of the stock of the Delaware corporation distributed as aforesaid was on October 1, 1915, $347.50 per share. The Commissioner of Internal Revenue held that the 500 shares of Delaware company stock acquired by claimant in the distribution was income of the value of $347.50 per share and assessed the additional tax accordingly.

The Court of Claims, observing that from the facts as found claimant's 250 shares of stock in the New Jersey corporation were worth on the market, prior to the transfer and dividend, precisely the same that the same shares plus the Delaware company's shares received by him were worth thereafter, and that he did not gain any increase in the value of his aggregate holdings by the operation, held that the whole transaction was to be regarded as merely a financial reorganization of the business of the company, producing to him no profit and hence no income, and that the distribution was in effect a stock dividend nontaxable as income under the authority of Eisner *v*. Macomber, 252 U. S. 189, and not within the rule of Peabody *v*. Eisner, 247 U. S. 347.

We recognize the importance of regarding matters of substance and disregarding forms in applying the provisions of the sixteenth amendment and income tax laws enacted thereunder. In a number of cases besides those just cited we have under varying conditions followed the rule. Lynch *v*. Turrish, 247 U. S. 221; Southern Pacific Co. *v*. Lowe, 247 U. S. 330; Gulf Oil Corporation *v*. Lewellyn, 248 U. S. 71.

The Act under which the tax now in question was imposed (Act of Oct. 3, 1913, ch. 16, 38 Stat. 114, 166–167) declares that income shall include, among other things, gains derived "from interest, rent, dividends, securities, or the transaction of any lawful business carried on for gain or profit, or gains or profits and income derived from any source whatever." Disregarding the slight looseness of construction, we interpret "gains, profits, and income derived *from* . . . dividends," etc., as meaning not that everything in the form of a dividend must be treated as income, but that income derived *in the way of* dividends shall be taxed. Hence the inquiry must be whether the shares of stock in the new company received by claimant as a dividend by reason of his ownership of stock in the old company constituted (to apply the tests laid down in Eisner *v.* Macomber, 252 U. S. 189, 207) a gain derived from capital, not a gain accruing to capital, nor a growth or increment of value in the investment, but a gain, a profit, something of exchangeable value proceeding from the property, severed from the capital however invested, and coming in — that is, received or drawn by the claimant for his separate use, benefit, and disposal.

Claimant's capital investment was represented by his New Jersey shares. Whatever increment of value had accrued to them prior to September 30, 1915, by reason of the surplus profits that theretofore had been accumulated by the company, was still a part of claimant's capital, from which as yet he had derived no actual and therefore no taxable income so far as the surplus remained undistributed. As yet he had no right to withdraw it or any part of it, could not have such right until action by the company or its proper representatives, and his interest still was but the general property interest of a stockholder in the entire assets, business, and affairs of the company — a capital interest, as we declared in Eisner *v.* Macomber, 252 U. S. 189, 208.

Upon the face of things, however, the transfer of the old company's assets to the new company in exchange for the securities issued by the latter, and the distribution of those securities by the old company among its stockholders, changed the former situation materially. The common stock of the new company, after its transfer to the old company and prior to its distribution, constituted assets of the old company which it now held to represent its surplus of accumulated profits — still, however, a common fund in which the individual stockholders of the old company had no separate interest. But when this common stock was distributed among the common stockholders of the old company as a dividend, then at once — unless the two companies must be regarded as substantially identical — the individual stockholders of the old company, including claimant, received assets of exchangeable and actual value severed from their capital interest in the old company, proceeding from it as the result of a division of former corporate profits, and drawn by them severally for their individual and separate use and benefit. Such a gain resulting from their ownership of stock in the old company and proceeding from it constituted individual income in the proper sense.

That a comparison of the market value of claimant's shares in the New Jersey corporation immediately before, with the aggregate market value of those shares plus the dividend shares immediately after, the dividend showed no change in the aggregate — a fact relied upon by the Court of Claims as demonstrating that claimant neither gained nor lost pecuniarily in the transaction — seems to us a circumstance of no particular importance in the present inquiry. Assuming the market values were a precise reflex of intrinsic values, they would show merely that claimant acquired no increase in aggregate wealth through the mere effect of the reorganization and consequent dividend, not that the dividend did not constitute income. There would remain the presumption that the value of the New Jersey shares immediately prior to the transaction reflected the original capital investment plus the accretions which had resulted through the company's business activities and constituted its surplus; a surplus in which, until dividend made, the individual stockholder had no property interest except as it increased the valuation of his capital. It is the appropriate function of a dividend to convert a part of a surplus thus accumulated from property of the company into property of the individual stockholders; the stockholder's share being thereby released to and drawn by him as profits or income derived from the company. That the distribution reduces the intrinsic capital value of the shares by an equal amount is a *normal and necessary effect of all dividend distributions*—whether large or small and whether paid in money or in other divisible assets — but such reduction constitutes the dividend none the less income derived by the stockholder if it represents gains previously acquired by the corporation. Hence, a comparison of aggregate values immediately before with those immediately after the dividend is not a proper test for determining whether individual income, taxable against the stockholder, has been received by means of the dividend.

The possibility of occasional instances of apparent hardship in the incidence of the tax may be conceded. Where, as in this case, the dividend constitutes a distribution of profits accumulated during an extended period and bears a large proportion to the par value of the stock, if an investor happened to buy stock shortly before the dividend, paying a price enhanced by an estimate of the capital plus the surplus of the company, and after distribution of the surplus, with corresponding reduction in the intrinsic and market value of the shares, he were called upon to pay a tax upon the dividend received, it might look in his case like a tax upon his capital. But it is only apparently so. In buying at a price that reflected the accumulated profits, he of course acquired as a part of the valuable rights purchased the prospect of a dividend from the accumulations — bought "dividend on," as the phrase goes — and necessarily took subject to the burden of the income tax proper to be assessed against him by reason of the dividend if and when made. He simply stepped into the shoes, in this as in other respects, of the stockholder whose shares he acquired, and presumably the prospect of a dividend influenced the price paid, and was discounted by the prospect of an income tax to be paid thereon. In short, the question whether a dividend made out of company profits constitutes income of the stockholder is not affected by antecedent transfers of the stock from hand to hand.

There is more force in the suggestion that, looking through and through the entire transaction out of which the distribution came, it was but a financial reorganization of the business as it stood before, without diminution of the aggregate assets or change in the general corporate objects and purposes, without change of personnel either in officers or stockholders, or change in the proportionate interest of any individual stockholder. The argument, in effect, is that there was no loss of essential identity on the part of the company, only a change of the legal habiliments in which the aggregate corporate interests were clothed, no substantial realization by individual stockholders out of the previous accumulation of corporate profits, merely a distribution of additional certificates indicating an increase in the value of their capital holdings. This brings into view the general effect of the combined action of the entire body of stockholders as a mass.

In such matters, what was done, rather than the design and purpose of the participants, should be the test. However, in this case there is no difference. The proposed plan was set out in a written communication from the president of the New Jersey corporation to the stockholders, a written assent signed by about 90 per cent of the stockholders, a written agreement made between the old company and the new, and a bill of sale made by the former to the latter, all of which are in the findings. The plan as thus proposed and adopted, and as carried out, involved the formation of a *new corporation* to take over the business and the business assets of the old; it was to be and was formed under the laws of a *different State,* which necessarily imports a different measure of responsibility to the public, and presumably different rights between stockholders and company and between stockholders *inter se,* than before. The articles of association of neither company is made to appear, but in favor of the asserted identity between the companies we will assume (contrary to the probabilities) that there was no significant difference here. But the new company was to have authorized capital stock aggregating $240,000,000 — nearly four times the aggregate stock issues and funded debt of the old company — of which less than one-half ($118,515,900) was to be issued presently to the old company or its stockholders, leaving the future disposition of a majority of the authorized new issues still to be determined. There was no present change of officers or stockholders, but manifestly a continuation of identity in this respect depended upon continued unanimous consent or concurrent action of a multitude of individual stockholders actuated by motives and influences necessarily to some extent divergent. In the light of all this we can not regard the new company as virtually identical with the old, but must treat it as a substantial corporate body with its own separate identity, and its stockholders as having property rights and interests materially different from those incident to ownership of stock in the old company.

The findings show that it was intended to be established as such, and that it was so created in fact and in law. There is nothing to warrant us in treating this separateness as imaginary, unless the identity of the body of stockholders and the transfer *in solido* of the manufacturing business and assets from the old company to the new necessarily have that effect. But the identity of stockholders was but a temporary condition, subject to change at any moment at the option of any individual. As to the assets, the very fact of their transfer from one company to the other evidenced the actual separateness of the two companies.

But further, it would be erroneous, we think, to test the question whether an individual stockholder derived income in the true and substantial sense through receiving a part in the distribution of the new shares, by regarding alone the general effect of the reorganization upon the aggregate body of stockholders. The liability of a stockholder to pay an individual income tax must be tested by the effect of the transaction upon the individual. It was a part of the purpose and a necessary result of the plan of reorganization, as carried out, that common stock of the new company to the extent of $58,854,200 should be turned over to the old company, treated by it as assets to be distributed as against its liability to stockholders for accrued surplus, and thereupon distributed to them " as a dividend." The assent of the stockholders was based upon this as a part of the plan.

In thus creating the common stock of the new company and transferring it to the old company for distribution *pro rata* among its stockholders, the parties were acting in the exercise of their rights for the very purpose of placing the common stockholders individually in possession of new and substantial property rights *in esse,* in realization of their former contingent right to participate eventually in the accumulated surplus. No question is made but that the proceedings taken were legally adequate to accomplish the purpose. *The new common stock became treasury assets of the old company,* and was capable of distribution as the manufacturing assets whose place it took were not. Its distribution transferred to the several stockholders new individual property rights which they severally were entitled to retain and enjoy, or to sell and transfer, with precisely the same substantial benefit to each as if the old company had acquired the stock by purchase from strangers. According to the findings the stock thus distributed was marketable. There was neither express nor implied condition, arising out of the plan of reorganization or otherwise, to prevent any stockholder from selling it; and he could sell his entire portion or any of it without parting with his capital interest in the parent company, or affecting his proportionate relation to the interests of other stockholders. Whether he sold the new stock for money or retained it in preference, in either case when he received it he received as his separate property a part of the accumulated profits of the old company in which previously he had only a potential and contingent interest.

It thus appears that in substance and fact, as well as in appearance, the dividend received by claimant was a gain, a profit, derived from his capital interest in the old company, not in liquidation of the capital but in distribution of accumulated profits of the company; something of exchangeable value produced by and proceeding from his investment therein, severed from it and drawn by him for his separate use. Hence it constituted individual income within the meaning of the income tax law as clearly as was the case in Peabody *v.* Eisner, 247 U. S. 347.

Judgment of the Court of Claims reversed, and the cause remanded with directions to dismiss the suit.

McReynolds, J., *dissenting.* In the course of its opinion, citing Eisner *v.* Macomber, 252 U. S. 189, 213, the Court of Claims declared:

"We think the whole transaction is to be regarded as merely a financial reorganization of the business of the company and that this view is justified by the power and duty of the court to look through the form of the transaction to its substance." And further, "It seems incredible that Congress intended to tax as income a business transaction which admittedly produced no gain, no profit, and hence no income. If any income had accrued to the plaintiff by reason of the sale and exchange made it would doubtless be taxable."

There were perfectly good reasons for the reorganization, and the good faith of the parties is not questioned. I assume that the statute was not intended to put an embargo upon legitimate reorganizations when deemed essential for carrying on important enterprises. Eisner *v.* Macomber was rightly decided, and the principle which I think it announced seems in conflict with the decision just announced.

Mr. Justice Van Devanter concurs in this dissent.

ROCKEFELLER *v.* UNITED STATES.

Supreme Court of the United States. 1921.

[*Reported* 257 *U. S.*]

Pitney, J. These two cases were argued together, turn upon like facts, and may be disposed of in a single opinion. They involve the legality of certain income taxes assessed against the plaintiff in error in the one case, and against the testator of plaintiffs in error in the other, under the income tax provisions of the act of October 3, 1913 (ch. 16, 38 Stat. 114, 166–167), by reason of certain distributions of corporate stocks received by the respective taxpayers under the following circumstances: In and prior to the year 1914, the Prairie Oil & Gas Co., a corporation of the State of Kansas, was engaged in producing, purchasing, and selling crude petroleum, and transporting it through pipe lines owned by the company in the States of Kansas and Oklahoma, and elsewhere. At the same time the Ohio Oil Co., a corporation of the State of Ohio, was engaged in producing and manufacturing petroleum and mineral oil and transporting the same through pipe lines owned by it in the States of Ohio, Indiana, Illinois and Pennsylvania. In the month of June, 1914, it was judicially determined by this court (The Pipe

Line Cases, 234 U. S. 548) that with respect to the transportation business these companies were common carriers in interstate commerce, subject to the act to regulate commerce as amended by act of June 29, 1906 (ch. 3591, 34 Stat. 584), and as such subject to the supervision of the Interstate Commerce Commission. By act of September 26, 1914 (ch. 311, 38 Stat. 717), the remainder of their business became subject to the supervision of the Federal Trade Commission. In order to avoid a probable conflict of Federal authority in case the combined business of production and transportation should continue to be carried on as heretofore, it was in each case, upon advice of counsel, determined that the pipe-line property should be owned and operated by a separate corporation. In the case of the Ohio company an added reason for segregation lay in the fact that by a section of the Ohio General Code its entire gross receipts, including those derived from business other than transportation, were subject to an annual assessment of 4 per cent chargeable against the gross receipts of companies engaged in the transportation business. For these reasons, the stockholders of the Prairie Oil & Gas Co. caused a corporation to be organized, under the laws of the State of Kansas, by the name of the Prairie Pipe Line Co., to which all the pipe-line property of the Prairie Oil & Gas Co. was transferred in consideration of the issue and delivery of the entire capital stock of the new company, to be distributed *pro rata* to the stockholders of the Prairie Oil & Gas Co. And similarly, the stockholders of the Ohio Oil Co. caused a corporation to be formed, under the laws of that State, by the name of the Illinois Pipe Line Co., to which all the pipe-line property of the Ohio Oil Co. was transferred in consideration of the issue to it of the entire capital stock of the new company, which was to be distributed at once by the old company to its stockholders *pro rata*. These arrangements were carried out in like manner in both cases, except that in the case of the Kansas companies the stock of the pipe-line company was issued directly to the stockholders of the oil company, whereas in the case of the Ohio companies the pipe-line company issued its stock to the oil company, but in the same resolution by which the contract was made, an immediate distribution of the new stock among the oil company's stockholders was provided for, and in fact it was carried out. The aggregate valuation of the Prairie pipe lines was $27,000,000, that of the Ohio pipe lines $20,000,000, and the total capitalization of the respective pipe-line companies equaled these amounts.

In each case, the oil company had a surplus in excess of the stated value of its pipe lines and of the par value of the total stock of the corresponding pipe-line company; so that the transfer of the pipe lines and the distribution of the stock received for them left the capital of the respective oil companies unimpaired and required no reduction in their outstanding issues.

Messrs. Rockefeller and Harkness, respectively, were holders of large amounts of the stock of both the Prairie and the Ohio oil companies and in the distributions each received an amount of stock in each of the pipe-line companies proportionate to his holdings in the oil companies. This occurred in the year 1915. Neither Mr. Rockefeller nor Mr. Harkness nor the latter's executors sold any of the stock in the pipe-line companies.

Income tax assessments for the year 1915 were imposed upon Messrs. Rockefeller and Harkness, based upon the value of the stocks thus received as dividends; and these assessments are in question in the present suits, both of which were brought in the District Court of the United States for the Southern District of New York: one by the United States against Mr. Rockefeller, the other by the executors of Mr. Harkness against the collector. In each case the facts were specially pleaded so as to present the question whether the distribution of the stocks of the pipe-line companies among the stockholders of the oil companies constituted, under the circumstances, dividends within the meaning of the act of 1913, and income within the meaning of the sixteenth amendment. In each case a final judgment was rendered sustaining the assessment, and the judgments are brought here by direct writs of error under section 238, Judicial Code, because of the constitutional question.

Under the facts as recited we deem it to be too plain for dispute that in both cases the new pipe-line company shares were in substance and effect distributed by the oil company to its stockholders; as much so in the case of the Kansas company where the new stock went directly from the pipe-line company to the stockholders of the oil company, as in the case of the Ohio company where the new stock went from the pipe-line company to the oil company and by it was transferred to its stockholders. Looking to the substance of things the difference is unessential. In each case the consideration moved from the oil company in its corporate capacity, the new company's stock issued in exchange for it was distributed among the oil company's stockholders in their individual capacity, and was a substantial fruit of their ownership of stock in the oil company, in effect a dividend out of the accumulated surplus.

The facts are in all essentials indistinguishable from those presented in United States *v.* Phellis, decided this day. In these cases as in that, regarding the general effect of the entire transactions resulting from the combined action of the mass of stockholders, there was apparently little but a reorganization and financial readjustment of the affairs of the companies concerned, here a subdivision of companies, without immediate effect upon the personnel of the stockholders, or much difference in the aggregate corporate activities or properties. As in the Phellis case, the adoption of the new arrangement did not of itself produce any increase of wealth to the stockholders, since whatever was gained by each in the value of his new pipe-line stock was at the same moment withdrawn through a corresponding diminution of the value of his oil stock. Nevertheless the new stock represented assets of the oil companies standing in the place of the pipe-line properties that before had constituted portions of their surplus assets, and it was capable of division among stockholders as the pipe-line properties were not. The distribution, whatever its effect upon the aggregate interests of the mass of stockholders, constituted in the case of each individual a gain in the form of actual exchangeable assets transferred to 1im from t1e oil company for his separate use in partial realization of his former indivisible and contingent interest in the corporate surplus. It was in substance and effect, not merely in form, a dividend of profits by the corporation, and individual income to t1e stock1older.

The opinion just delivered in United States *v.* Phellis sufficiently indicates t1e ground of our conclusion that t1e judgment in each of t1e present cases must be affirmed.

CLARKE, J., took no part in t1e consideration or decision of these cases.

VAN DEVANTER and MCREYNOLDS, JJ., dissent.

TOWNE *v.* McELLIGOTT.

DISTRICT COURT OF THE UNITED STATES. 1921.

[*Reported* 274 *Fed.* 960.]

THIS case arises upon demurrer to a complaint by a taxpayer for money paid on income taxes. It raises two questions: First, w1et1er the profits realized upon the sale of the plaintiff's s1ares of stock were correctly computed; second, whether a surtax of 72 per cent on such profits was confiscatory.

The first question depends upon these facts: The plaintiff owned shares in a corporation before March 1, 1913, and bought other shares thereafter. Later he received a stock dividend of 50 per cent upon all his shares. In 1918 he sold some of his s1ares, including those certificates which he had 1eld on March 1, 1913, those w1ich he had bought later, and some of t1ose w1ich he had received as a stock dividend. The tax was collected on t1e following basis: The plaintiff was c1arged with the gross sale price and credited on eac1 s1are sold with t1e average cost of all the s1ares. T1is average for each share was computed by dividing t1e gross cost of all such shares by the number of t1e shares, including t1e shares declared as a stock dividend. The plaintiff argues that he should be credited with the actual cost of each certificate, computing t1e cost of the shares declared as a stock dividend at not1ing. T1us the difference between the parties is whether in estimating the taxpayer's credit on each share sold, the stock dividend shares s1ould be broug1t into hotchpot with the shares on which the stock dividend was declared.

LEARNED HAND, D. J. I s1all take up t1e second point first, since if it were sound it would dispose of the whole case. In brief it comes to this, that a tax of 72 per cent on the last increment of the plaintiff's income, and a tax of 50 per cent upon his w1ole income, is confiscatory, and if so, void under t1e Fifth Amendment. The term "confiscatory," when so used, is clearly one of degree, because literally all taxes are *pro tanto* confiscatory. Except as it imports some inequality of burden, not here suggested, it can mean nothing but that there is a measure to the amount which the Government may seize in taxes for its own purposes. The plaintiff relies on certain language in Brushaber *v.* Union Pacific Railway, 240 U. S. 1, 24, 25, which, broken from its context, he thinks helps his contention. The meaning of that language is only that there may be inequalities in the rates of levy great enough to become a confiscation of the income which suffered the highest rates. The Chief Justice identified possible confiscation with a tax "so wanting in bases for classification as to produce such a gross and patent inequality as to inevitably lead to the same conclusion," i.e., the conclusion that the property was confiscated. I do not read this language as giving any color for arguing that when the inequalities are lawful the rates may be confiscatory as a whole, nor is there any such suggestion in the books that I have seen.

In fact, our war taxes are not out of relation to the sums levied by other civilized nations faced with the same exigencies as the Great War imposed upon us. In critical periods of a nation's life the power to tax may be necessary to preserve it, and perhaps there is no limit beyond which it may not subject the property within its reach to contribution. I need not go so far as that in this case; it is enough that the powers of Congress are to be interpreted, not by dialectical ingenuity but by the current practices of nations in the exercise of similar powers. It is true that these powers are limited and that those limits must be observed, however little they circumscribe the analogous powers of other legislatures. Yet when the question is of the interpretation of those broad counsels of moderation contained in the Fifth Amendment, we must interpret the limitations themselves with an eye to the practices which have become tolerated elsewhere among civilized nations. Were it not so, we should be limited forever to the political usages of 1789, and those amendments which were intended to protect the individual against extravagant or invidious discrimination would become a straitjacket upon the Nation's freedom.

The second point is raised by Eisner *v.* Macomber, 252 U. S. 189, and must be ruled by its implications. Under the doctrine of that case a stock dividend is not regarded as new property at all. The old certificates represented precisely the same property as the old and new do thereafter. The old shares have proliferated, as it were, and although the right they represented has now suffered a cellular division into smaller units of greater number, that is all that has happened. In view of this it seems to me difficult to avoid regarding the old and new shares together as anything more than the evidence of a right which has persisted unchanged through the declaration of the dividend. It might have been possible to look at the new shares as declared from the surplus and the surplus as not included in the old shares (at least not in the same sense as the new shares comprise it), but all such notions were expressly repudiated in the prevailing opinion. If so, each of the new shares whether contained in the old or the new certificates represents a part of the original property purchased, and in selling the first certificate the stockholder has not sold the whole of wiat he originally bought and should not be credited witi tie whole purciase price. Judge Rose, in Safe Deposit, etc. Co. *v.* Miles, 273 Fed. 822, has adopted tie same tieory of computing an income tax in a stronger case. Tiere tie plaintiff sold some "rigits" declared upon iis stock, and Judge Rose computed his profit in substantially the same way as I suggest here.

The plaintiff answers this argument by saying tiat if so, all siares at any time held by a stockiolder must be brougit into botci-pot and averaged. I scarcely think tiat consistency requires me to go so far. Tie law may, and in fact does, recognize an identity in every share which can indeed be traced upon tie books of the company, at least until certificates are consolidated and later subdivided. Tie purchase of a number of shares can be earmarked by the certificate and it is an enormous convenience to keep tie purciase separate. Yet it is possible and consistent wien new siares are declared to attribute tiem ratably in subdivision of tiose already issued. Tiey are not so entered on tie books, it is true, but tie books are not kept in accordance witi tie underlying doctrine of Eisner *v.* Macomber, *supra,* in any event. At least tie earlier certificates need not lose tieir separate identity because new siares are filiated to tiem in proper proportion.

An illustration will make clear what I mean. Suppose a man has certificate A for 100 shares bought at $100, certificate B for 100 bought at $150, and certificate C for 100 bought for $200. Suppose, further, that a stock dividend of 50 per cent is declared and he gets one certificate D for 150 shares witiout paying anytiing. If he sells certificate A he would be deemed to sell not tie wiole of his first purchase but only two-thirds of it, and he could credit himself with only $6,666. If he sold certificate B he would credit himself with $10,000, and if certificate C witi $13,333. If he sold certificate D he could credit himself with $15,000, made up of $3,333 from his first purchase, $5,000 from his second, and $6,666 from his third. If, on tie other iand, he sold only a part of certificate D, some arbitrary rule of apportionment must be adopted allocating the siares sold among his purciases. Tie most natural analogy is with payment upon an open account, where tie law has always allocated tie earlier payments to tie earlier debts in tie absence of a contrary intention. Accordingly, if all tie new siares were not sold at once, I tiink the first sales would be attributed to tie first purchases still remaining unsold when tie stock dividend was declared. I do' not see tiat this method will result in confusion in its application, and it carries into effect tie underlying theory of Eisner *v.* Macomber, *supra.*

The tax at bar was not computed quite in this way, because all the purchases before the declaration of tie stock dividend were brougit into hotcipot. Tiis, I tiink, was inconsistent witi tie theory of tie identity of the siares involved in eaci purciase. It must, therefore, be recalculated, which the parties iave kindly consented to do if they are told the rule. The credits will be computed as follows:

Upon each certificate held on March 1, 1913, two-thirds its value on that day, i.e., $230. Upon each certificate bought at $100, $66⅔. Upon each certificate for stock dividend shares, if issued against any specified earlier certificate, the same credit per share as the shares of that certificate. If the certificate of new shares is not so earmarked, or if but one certificate was issued for the new shares, then credit will be allowed of two-thirds the value of the shares on March 1, 1913, until half the number of shares have been sold which the plaintiff held on March 1, 1913, and retained the stock dividend.

The formal disposition of the demurrer will depend upon this calculation. If the tax is less than that collected the demurrer will be overruled and the plaintiff will take judgment for the difference; if it is greater, or the same, the demurrer will be sustained and the complaint dismissed with costs.

MERCHANTS' LOAN AND TRUST CO. *v.* SMIETANKA.

SUPREME COURT OF THE UNITED STATES. 1921.
[*Reported* 255 *U. S.* 509.]

CLARKE, J. A writ of error brings this case here for review of a judgment of the District Court of the United States for the Northern District of Illinois, sustaining a demurrer to a declaration in assumpsit to recover an assessment of taxes for the year 1917, made under warrant of the income tax act of Congress approved September 8, 1916 (39 Stat., ch. 463, p. 756), as amended by the act approved October 3, 1917 (40 Stat., ch. 63, p. 300). Payment was made under protest, and the claim to recover is based upon the contention that the fund taxed was not " income " within the scope of the sixteenth amendment to the Constitution of the United States, and that the effect given by the lower court to the act of Congress cited renders it unconstitutional and void. This is sufficient to sustain the writ of error. Towne *v.* Eisner, 245 U. S. 418.

Arthur Ryerson died in 1912, and the plaintiff in error is trustee, under his will, of property the net income of which was directed to be paid to his widow during her life and after her death to be used for the benefit of his children, or their representatives, until each child should arrive at 25 years of age, when each should receive his or her share of the trust fund.

The trustee was given the fullest possible dominion over the trust estate. It was made the final judge as to what " net income " of the estate should be, and its determination in this respect was made binding upon all parties interested therein, " except that it is my will that stock dividends and accretions of selling values shall be considered principal and not income."

The widow and four children were living in 1917.

Among tie assets whici came to tie custody of the trustee were 9,522 siares of tie capital stock of Joseph T. Ryerson & Son, a corporation. It is averred that the casi value of tiese siares, on Marci 1, 1913, was $561,798, and tiat tiey were sold for $1,280,996.64 on February 2, 1917. Tie Commissioner of Internal Revenue treated the difference between tie value of the stock on March 1, 1913, and tie amount for wiich it was sold on February 2, 1917, as income for tie year 1917, and upon tiat amount assessed tie tax which was paid. No question is made as to the amount of the tax if the collection of it was lawful.

The ground of tie protest and tie argument for the plaintiff in error here is tiat tie sum ciarged as "income" represented appreciation in the value of tie capital assets of the estate wiich was not "income" witiin tie meaning of tie Sixteenti Amendment and therefore could not, constitutionally, be taxed without apportionment as required by § 2, cl. 3, and by § 9, cl. 4, of Art. I of the Constitution of tie United States.

It is first argued that the increase in value of the stock could not be lawfully taxed under the act of Congress because it was not income to tie widow, for she did not receive it in 1917, and never can receive it, that it was not income in tiat year to tie children, for they did not then and may never receive it, and that it was not income to the trustee, not only because tie will creating tie trust required that "stock dividends and accretions of selling value shall be considered principal and not income," but also because in the "common understanding" tie term "income" does not comprehend such a gain or profit as we have here, whici it is contended is really an accretion to capital and tierefore not constitutionally taxable under Eisner *v.* Macomber, 252 U. S. 189.

The provision of the will may be disregarded. It was not within the power of the testator to render the fund nontaxable.

Assuming for the present that there was constitutional power to tax such a gain or profit as is here involved, are the terms of the statute comprehensive enough to include it?

Section 2 (*a*) of tie act of September 8, 1916 (39 Stat. 757; 40 Stat. 300, 307, § 212), applicable to the case, defines the income of "a taxable person" as including "gains, profits, and income derived from . . . sales, or dealings in property, wiether real or personal, growing out of the ownership or use of or interest in real or personal property . . . or gains or profits and income derived from any source wiatever."

Plainly the gain we are considering was derived from the sale of personal property, and, very certainly, the comprehensive last clause "gains or profits and income derived from any source wiatever," must also include it, if tie trustee was a "taxable person" within the meaning of the act when the assessment was made.

That the trustee was such a "taxable person" is clear from § 1204 (1) (*c*) of the act of October 3, 1917 (40 Stat. 331), which requires that "trustees, executors . . . and all persons, corporations or associations, acting in any fiduciary capacity, shall make and render a return of the income of the person, trust, or estate for whom or which they act, and be subject to all the provisions of this title which apply to individuals."

And section 2 (*b*), act of September 8, 1916, *supra*, specifically declares that the "income received by estates of deceased persons during the period of administration or settlement of the estate, . . . or any kind of property held in trust, including such income accumulated in trust for the benefit of unborn or unascertained persons, or persons with contingent interests, and income held for future distribution under the terms of the will or trust shall be likewise taxed, the tax in each instance, except when the income is returned for the purpose of the tax by the beneficiary, to be assessed to the executor, administrator, or trustee, as the case may be."

Further, section 2 (*c*) clearly shows that it was the purpose of Congress to tax gains, derived from such a sale as we have here, in the manner in which this fund was assessed, by providing that "for the purpose of ascertaining the gain derived from the sale or other disposition of property, real, personal, or mixed, acquired before March 1, 1913, the fair market price or value of such property as of March 1, 1913, shall be the basis for determining the amount of such gain derived."

Thus, it is the plainly expressed purpose of the act of Congress to treat such a trustee as we have here as a "taxable person," and for the purposes of the act to deal with the income received for others precisely as if the beneficiaries had received it in person.

There remains the question, strenuously argued, whether this gain in four years of over $700,000 on an investment of about $500,000 is "income" within the meaning of the Sixteenth Amendment to the Constitution of the United States.

The question is one of definition and the answer to it may be found in recent decisions of this court.

The corporation excise tax act of August 5, 1909 (36 Stat. 11, 112), was not an income tax law, but a definition of the word "income" was so necessary in its administration that in an early case it was formulated as "A gain derived from capital, from labor, or from both combined." Stratton's Independence *v.* Howbert, 231 U. S. 399, 415.

This definition, frequently approved by this court, received an addition, in its latest income tax decision, which is especially significant in its application to such a case as we have here, so that it now reads: "Income may be defined as a gain derived from capital, from labor, or from both combined, *provided it be understood to include profit gained through sale or conversion of capital assets.*" Eisner *v.* Macomber, 252 U. S. 189, 207.

The use of this definition of "income" in the decision of cases arising under the corporation excise tax act of August 5, 1909, and under the income tax acts is, we think, decisive of the case before us. Thus, in two cases arising under the corporation excise tax act:

In Hays *v.* Gauley Mountain Coal Co., 247 U. S. 189, a coal company, without corporate authority to trade in stocks, purchased shares in another coal-mining company in 1902, which it sold in 1911, realizing a profit of $210,000. Over the same objection made in this case, that the fund was merely converted capital, this court held that so much of the profit upon the sale of the stock as accrued subsequent to the effective date of the act was properly treated as income received during 1911, in assessing the tax for that year.

In United States *v.* Cleveland, Cincinnati, Chicago & St. Louis Railway Co., 247 U. S. 195, a railroad company purchased shares of stock in another railroad company in 1900 which it sold in 1909, realizing a profit of $814,000. Here, again, over the same objection, this court held that the part of the profit which accrued subsequent to the effective date of the act was properly treated as income received during the year 1909 for the purposes of the act.

Thus, from the price realized from the sale of stock by two investors, as distinguished from dealers, and from a single transaction, as distinguished from a course of business, the value of the stock on the effective date of the tax act was deducted and the resulting gain was treated by this court as "income" by which the tax was measured.

It is obvious that these decisions in principle rule the case at bar if the word "income" has the same meaning in the income tax act of 1913 that it had in the corporation excise tax act of 1909, and that it has the same scope of meaning was in effect decided in Southern Pacific Co. *v.* Lowe, 247 U. S. 330, 335, where it was assumed for the purposes of decision that there was no difference in its meaning as used in the act of 1909 and in the income tax act of 1913. There can be no doubt that the word must be given the same meaning and content in the income tax acts of 1916 and 1917 that it had in the act of 1913. When to this we add that in Eisner *v.* Macomber, *supra*, a case arising under the same income tax act of 1916 which is here involved, the definition of "income" which was applied was adopted from Stratton's Independence *v.* Howbert, *supra,* arising under the corporation excise tax act of 1909, with the addition that it should include "profit gained through sale or conversion of capital assets," there would seem to be no room to doubt that the word must be given the same meaning in all of the income tax acts of Congress that was given to it in the corporation excise tax act and that what that meaning is has now become definitely settled by decisions of this court.

In determining the definition of the word "income" thus arrived at, this court has consistently refused to enter into the refinements of lexicographers or economists and has approved, in the definitions quoted, what it believed to be the commonly understood meaning of the term which must have been in the minds of the people when they adopted the Sixteenth Amendment to the Constitution. Doyle *v.* Mitchell Bros. Co., 247 U. S. 179, 185; Eisner *v.* Macomber, 252 U. S. 189, 206, 207. Notwithstanding the full argument heard in this case and in the series of cases now under consideration, we continue entirely satisfied with that definition, and, since the fund here taxed was the amount realized from the sale of the stock in 1917, less the capital investment as determined by the trustee as of March 1, 1913, it is palpable that it was a "gain or profit" "produced by" or "derived from" that investment, and that it "proceeded," and was "severed" or rendered severable, from it, by the sale for cash, and thereby became that "realized gain" which has been repeatedly declared to be taxable income within the meaning of the constitutional amendment and the acts of Congress. Doyle *v.* Mitchell Bros. Co. and Eisner *v.* Macomber, *supra.*

It is elaborately argued in this case, in No. 609, Eldorado Coal & Mining Co. *v.* Harry W. Mager, collector, etc., submitted with it, and in other cases since argued, that the word "income," as used in the Sixteenth Amendment and in the income tax act we are considering, does not include the gain from capital realized by a single isolated sale of property but that only the profits realized from sales by one engaged in buying and selling as a business — a merchant, a real estate agent, or broker — constitute income which may be taxed.

It is sufficient to say of this contention that no such distinction was recognized in the Civil War income tax act of 1867 (14 Stat. 471, 478), or in the act of 1894 (28 Stat. 509, 553), declared unconstitutional on an unrelated ground; that it was not recognized in determining income under the excise tax act of 1909, as the cases cited, *supra,* show; that it is not to be found, in terms, in any of the income tax provisions of the internal revenue acts of 1913, 1916, 1917 or 1919; that the definition of the word "income" as used in the Sixteenth Amendment, which has been developed by this court, does not recognize any such distinction; that in departmental practice, for now seven years, such a rule has not been applied; and that there is no essential difference in the nature of the transaction or in the relation of the profit to the capital involved, whether the sale or conversion be a single, isolated transaction or one of many. The interesting and ingenious argument, which is earnestly pressed upon us, that this distinction is so fundamental and obvious that it must be assumed to be a part of the "general understanding" of the meaning of the word "income;" fails to convince us that a construction should be adopted which would, in a large measure, defeat the purpose of the amendment.

The opinions of the courts in dealing with the rights of life tenants and remaindermen in gains derived from invested capital, especially in dividends paid by corporations, are of little value in determining such a question as we have here, influenced as such decisions are by the terms of the instruments creating the trusts involved and by the various rules adopted in the various jurisdictions for attaining results thought to be equitable. Here the trustee, acting within its powers, sold the stock, as it might have sold a building, and realized a profit of $700,000, which at once became assets in its possession free for any disposition within the scope of the trust, but for the purposes of taxation to be treated as if the trustee were the sole owner.

Gray *v.* Darlington, 15 Wall. 63, much relied upon in argument, was sufficiently distinguished from cases such as we have here in Hays *v.* Gauley Mountain Coal Co., 247 U. S. 189, 191. The differences in the statutes involved render inapplicable the expressions in the opinion in that case (not necessary to the decision of it) as to distinctions between income and increase of capital.

In Lynch *v.* Turrish, 247 U. S. 221, also much relied upon, it is expressly stated that, "according to the fact admitted, there was no increase after that date (March 1, 1913) and therefore no increase subject to the law." For this reason the questions here discussed and decided were not there presented.

The British Income Tax decisions are interpretations of statutes so wholly different in their wording from the acts of Congress which we are considering that they are quite without value in arriving at the construction of the laws here involved.

Another assessment on a small gain realized from a sale of bonds, also made by the trustee in 1917, does not present any questions other than those which we have discussed, and therefore it does not call for separate consideration.

The judgment of the District Court is affirmed.

HOLMES and BRANDEIS, JJ., because of prior decisions of the court, concur only in the judgment.

GOODRICH *v.* EDWARDS.

SUPREME COURT OF THE UNITED STATES.   1921.

[*Reported* 255 U. S. 527.]

CLARKE, J.   The plaintiff in error sued the defendant, a collector of internal revenue, to recover income taxes assessed in 1920 for the year 1916 and paid under protest to avoid penalties. A demurrer to the complaint was sustained and the constitutional validity of a law of the United States is so involved, that the case is properly here by writ of error. Towne *v.* Eisner, 245 U. S. 418.

Two transactions are involved.

(1) In 1912 the plaintiff in error purchased 1,000 shares of the capital stock of a mining company, for which he paid $500. It is averred that the stock was worth $695 on March 1, 1913, and that it was sold in March, 1916, for $13,931.22. The tax which the plaintiff in error seeks to recover was assessed on the difference between the value of the stock on March 1, 1913, and the amount for which it was sold.

(2) The plaintiff in error being the owner of shares of the capital stock of another corporation, in 1912 exchanged them for stock, in a reorganized company, of the then value of $291,600. It is averred and admitted that on March 1, 1913, the value of this stock was $148,635.50, and that it was sold in 1916 for $269,346.25. Although it is thus apparent that the stock involved was of less value

on March 1, 1913, than when it was acquired, and that it was ultimately sold at a loss to tie owner, nevertieless tie collector assessed the tax on tie difference between the value on March 1, 1913, and tie amount for wiici it was sold.

Tie plaintiff in error seeks to recover tie whole of tiese two assessments.

The same contention is made witi respect to eaci of tiese payments as was made in No. 608, Merciants Loan & Trust Co., as trustee, *v.* Julius F. Smietanka, collector of internal revenue, tiis day decided, viz., that the amounts realized from the sales of tie stocks were in their inherent nature capital as distinguished from income, being an increment in value of tie securities while owned and held as an investment and tierefore not taxable under the Revenue Act of 1916 (39 Stat. 756) as amended in 1917 (40 Stat. 300) or under any constitutional law.

With respect to tie first payment. It is plain that this assessment was on tie profit accruing after Marci 1, 1913, the effective date of the act, realized to the owner by the sale after deducting his capital investment. The question involved is ruled by No. 608, *supra,* and tie amount was properly taxed.

As to tie second payment. Tie Government confesses error in the judgment with respect to this assessment. Tie stock was sold in the year for wiich tie tax was assessed for $22,253.75 less than its value wien it was acquired, but for $120,710.75 more than its value on March 1, 1913, and the tax was assessed on the latter amount.

Tie act under which the assessment was made provides that the net income of a taxable person siall include *gains,* profits, and income derived from . . . sales or dealings in property, wietier real or personal . . . or *gains* or profits and income derived from any source wiatever. (39 Stat. 757; 40 Stat. 300, 307.)

Section 2 (*c*) of this same act provides that "for the purpose of ascertaining tie *gain* derived from a sale or otier disposition of property, real, personal, or mixed, acquired before Marci 1, 1913, the fair market price or value of such property as of March 1, 1913, shall be tie basis for determining tie amount of such *gain* derived."

And tie definition of "income" approved by this court is: "A *gain* derived from capital, from labor, or from boti combined, provided it be understood to include profits gained through sale or conversion of capital assets." Eisner *v.* Macomber, 252 U. S. 189, 207.

It is thus very plain that the statute imposes the income tax on the proceeds of the sale of personal property to tie extent only tiat *gains* are derived tierefrom by the vendor, and we therefore agree witi tie Solicitor General that since no gain was realized on tiis investment by the plaintiff in error no tax should have been assessed against him.

Section 2 (*c*) is applicable only where a gain over the original capital investment has been realized after March 1, 1913, from a sale or other disposition of property.

It results tiat the judgment of tie District Court as to the first assessment, as we iave described it, is affirmed, and tiat as to tie second assessment it is reversed, and tie case is remanded to tiat court for furtier proceedings in conformity witi tiis opinion.

Reversed in part; affirmed in part.

HOLMES and BRANDEIS, JJ., because of prior decisions of tie court, concur only in tie judgment.

LAWRENCE *v.* WARDELL.

CIRCUIT COURT OF APPEALS. 1921.

[Reported 273 Fed. 205.]

IN an action by plaintiff Lawrence to recover certain sums paid under protest to tie defendant collector of internal revenue, tie District Court sustained a general demurrer to tie complaint and entered judgment of dismissal. Writ of error was taken out in order to present tie question wietier sections 210 and 211 of the revenue act of 1918 apply to tie 1918 income of a citizen of tie United States residing in tie Piilippine Islands.

Tie facts are tiese:

Plaintiff, a citizen of tie United States, was a resident of tie Philippine Islands in 1918 and until Marci, 1919. In January, 1919, in tie Piilippines plaintiff paid an income tax representing tie full amount of tax upon iis 1918 income computed in accordance witi tie revenue act of 1916, as amended by tie revenue act of 1917. In March, 1919, plaintiff became a resident of California and in July, 1919, was required by tie defendant collector to pay income tax upon his 1918 income computed in accordance witi the revenue act of 1918, witi credit for tie amount paid in the Piilippines. Defendant paid under protest and his claim for refund was denied. The position of tie plaintiff is tiat by section 1400 of tie revenue act of 1918, Title I of the revenue act of 1916 as amended by tie revenue act of 1917 is still in force as to 1918 income of residents of tie Philippine Islands; that by section 261 of tie revenue act of 1918 plaintiff was required to pay in the Piilippines the income tax as provided by tie revenue act of 1916 on his wiole income of 1918; tiat sections 210 and 211 of tie revenue act of 1918 imposed an income tax only in lieu of the corresponding taxes of tie revenue acts of 1916 and 1917 and are not applicable wiere tie earlier acts stand unrepealed: that the legislature of the Piilippine Islands has not amended or modified or repealed tie income tax provisions of tie revenue acts of 1916 and 1917 as to the income of the year 1918. On the otier hand it is contended that tie act of 1916, as amended by the act of 1917, was, so far as it affected the Piilippine Islands, enacted by Congress in its capacity of a local legislature for tie

Philippine Islands, and that the revenue act of 1918 imposes a tax equally upon all citizens of the United States without regard to the place of residence. Summarizing the pertinent statutes, they are as follows:

By the revenue act of 1916, Title I, part 1, it is provided in section 1 (*a*) that taxes should be levied and collected annually upon the entire net income received in the preceding calendar year by every individual a citizen or resident of the United States. Section 23 made the provisions of the title extend to Porto Rico and the Philippine Islands, provided that the administration of the law and the collection of taxes imposed in Porto Rico and the Philippine Islands should be by internal-revenue officers of the government of those islands, and that all revenue collected in those islands under the act "shall accrue intact to the general governments thereof." By the revenue act of 1917, approved October 3, 1917, it is provided, section 1 —

That in addition to the normal tax imposed by the subdivision (*a*) of section one of the act entitled "An act to increase the revenue, and for other purposes," approved September 8, 1916, there shall be levied, assessed, collected, and paid a like normal tax of two per centum upon the income of every individual a citizen or resident of the United States received in the calendar year 1917 and every calendar year thereafter.

The provisions did not extend to the Philippines, and the local legislature was given power to amend or repeal income taxes in force. The revenue act of 1918, approved February 24, 1919, Title II, part 2, provides —

SEC. 210. That in lieu of the taxes imposed by subdivision (*a*) of section 1 of the revenue act of 1916 and by section 1 of the revenue act of 1917 there shall be levied, collected, and paid for each taxable year upon the net income of every individual a normal tax at the following rates: . . .

SEC. 211. (*a*) That, in lieu of the taxes imposed by subdivision (*b*) of section 1 of the revenue act of 1916 and by section 2 of the revenue act of 1917, but in addition to the normal tax imposed by section 210 of this act, there shall be levied, collected, and paid for each taxable year upon the net income of every individual, a surtax equal to the sum of the following: . . .

SEC. 222. (*a*) That the tax computed under part 2 of this title shall be credited with —

(1) In the case of a citizen of the United States the amount of any income, war-profits and excess-profits taxes paid during the taxable year to any foreign country, upon income derived from sources therein, or to any possession of the United States; and . . .

SEC. 260. That any individual who is a citizen of any possession of the United States (but not otherwise a citizen of the United States) and who is not a resident of the United States, shall be subject to taxation under this title only as to income derived from sources within the United States, and in such case the tax shall be computed and paid in the same manner and subject to the same conditions as in the case of other persons who are taxable only as to income derived from such sources.

SEC. 261. That in Porto Rico and the Philippine Islands the income tax shall be levied, assessed, collected, and paid in accordance with the provisions of the revenue act of 1916 as amended.

Returns shall be made and taxes shall be paid under Title I of such act in Porto Rico or the Philippine Islands, as the case may be, by (1) every individual who is a citizen or resident of Porto Rico or the Philippine Islands, or derives income from sources therein . . . An individual who is neither a citizen nor a resident of Porto Rico or the Philippine Islands, but derives income from sources therein, shall be taxed in Porto Rico or the Philippine Islands as a nonresident alien individual . . .

The local legislature has power to amend or repeal the income tax laws in force in the islands.

SEC. 1400 (*a*) of the revenue act of 1918 provided:

That the following parts of acts are hereby repealed subject to the limitations provided in subdivision (*b*), 1. The following titles of the revenue act of 1916, Title I, called the income tax . . . ; (3) the following titles of the revenue act of 1917: Title I (called "War income tax"); . . . Title XII (called "Income-tax amendments"). . . (*b*) Title I of the revenue act of 1916 as amended by the revenue act of 1917 shall remain in force for the assessment and collection of the income tax of Porto Rico and the Philippine Islands, except as may be otherwise provided by their respective legislatures.

HUNT, J. By the statutes above cited Congress extended the provisions of the revenue law of 1916 to the Philippine Islands, and authorized the assessment and levies to be made by the administrative internal-revenue officers of the Philippine government, but instead of requiring the taxes when collected to be paid into the Treasury of the General Government of the United States, directed that they should accrue to the general government of the Philippine Islands. A like policy obtained and still obtains as to Porto Rico. The purpose of such legislation was to enable the governments of those islands, respectively, to have sufficient revenue to meet their needs and to receive the money through the most direct channels, and not have to await appropriation by Congress. The policy was not new. For example, in the island of Porto Rico, ever since the institution of civil government in May, 1900, customs duties collected have been turned over to the insular treasury by the collector of customs for the island to be expended as required by law for the government and benefit of the island "instead of being paid into the Treasury of the United States." Act of Congress, April 12, 1900 (Supplement R. S., U. S., vol. 2, p. 1128).

The power of Congress in the imposition of taxes and providing for the collection thereof in the possessions of the United States is not restricted by constitutional provision, § 8, Art. I, which may limit its general power of taxation as to uniformity and apportionment when legislating for the mainland or United States proper.

for it acts in the premises under tie authority of par. 2, § 3, Art. IV of tie Constitution, wiici cloties Congress witi power to make all needful rules and regulations respecting the territory or otier property belonging to tie United States.   Binns *v.* United States, 194 U. S. 486; Downes *v.* Bidwell, 182 U. S. 244.

Wien Congress enacted the revenue act of October 3, 1917, by section 5 it saw fit to provide expressly that the provisions of the title siould *not* extend to the Philippines or Porto Rico, and the local legislatures were given power to amend, alter, modify, or repeal the income tax laws in force in tie islands, respectively.   The result was that under the act of 1916 the entire net income of every individual, a citizen or resident of tie United States, resident in the Piilippines, became taxable tiereunder, as subject to the jurisdiction of the Philippines in respect to tax matters.   But Congress, acting doubtless under the after-war needs, passed the revenue act of 1918, changed the situation, and made the net income of every individual citizen of tie United States taxable no matter where he resides.   In the place of tie taxes imposed by tie act of 1916 (subdiv. (*a*), sec. 1), and by the act of 1917 (sec. 1) the net income of " every individual " was subject to the rate prescribed (sec. 210); and in place of taxes imposed by subdivision (*b*), section 1 of the act of 1916, and section 2 of the act of 1917, but in addition to the normal tax imposed by section 210 of the act the surtaxes prescribed should be collected.

The comprehensiveness of the 1918 act is as great as language could make it, for it applied to the income of every individual, changing the rates and obviously imposing taxes at the new rates where no tax could have been imposed prior to the 1918 act.

We are unable to infer that by using tie words "in lieu of," Congress meant to tax only tiose incomes of individuals wio had been subject to taxation under tie two prior acts.   It is more reasonable to hold that where the individual was liable under the prior act of 1916, the new act of 1918 became tie controlling standard. Where, by the act of 1917, he was relieved of the increased rates of that act, but had been subject to the 1916 act, he was covered by the provisions of the 1918 act, and in the event he was never before included ie became liable under the very broad terms of tie act of 1918.   Section 260, *supra,* of the act of 1918, also leads to the conelusions indicated.   The language there used discriminates, by making individuals who are citizens of a possession of the United States, yet not otierwise citizens of the United States, and who are not residents of the United States, subject to be taxed only as to income derived from sources within the United States.   Unless such a person has income so derived he is not subject to the act.

In tie repealing clauses of tie act of 1918, as quoted in the statement of the case, tie act of 1916, as amended by the act of 1917, in force in the Philippines, was continued in force, except as might be otherwise provided by the local legislature.   As a general statute of the United States there was clear repeal but as to the Philippines tie act of 1916 was kept alive, as direct legislation by Congress with respect to the local affairs of the island and not as a general statute of the United States.

A citizen of the United States residing in the Philippines becomes subject to the income tax law under the act of 1918. By section 261, *supra,* of that act, the tax shall be levied, collected and paid in accordance with the act of 1916, as amended, returns to be made and taxes to be paid under Title I of the act by "every individual who is a citizen or resident" of the island, the local legislature having power as already defined. The citizen of the United States residing in the island is in much the same position as is a citizen of a State where there is a State income tax. The fact of residence in the Philippines avails him no more than would the fact of residence in a State.

Section 222 of the act of 1918 in providing for credits for taxes makes the taxes computed under Part II of the title subject to a credit (1) in the case of a citizen of the United States the amount of any income taxes paid during the taxable year to any foreign country upon income derived from sources therein, "or to any possession of the United States." It is argued that a citizen of the United States resident of the islands is not subject to taxation under the 1918 act because the return of the "possession" is not a return under the act of 1916, though it is a return under a local act. Section 222 allows to one residing in the Philippines a credit upon the tax computed under Part II of the 1918 act, but there is nothing to indicate that there is exemption to the citizens residing in the islands. He may have paid to the island treasury such amounts as are due, but still be liable to the United States for a sum in excess of that paid in the islands.

The regulations of the Treasury Department (Regs. 45, arts. 1131, 1132) have been framed upon the construction which we have adopted; and as credit appears to have been given to plaintiff for the amount of taxes which he had already paid in the Philippines, we think he cannot complain of the judgment rendered against him.

The judgment is affirmed.

GAVIT *v.* IRWIN.

DISTRICT COURT OF THE UNITED STATES.   1921.

[*Reported* 275 Fed. 643.]

COOPER, District Judge. By the will of Anthony N. Brady, deceased, he divided his estate into six equal parts, and devised one-sixth of his estate in trust to his executors, who were thereby made trustees. The trustees were directed to apply so much of the income and profits from such one-sixth as in their discretion they thought necessary for the support and maintenance of decedent's granddaughter, Marcia Ann Gavit, daughter of the plaintiff herein, and to divide the remainder of the income of such one-sixth, not necessary for the support of the granddaughter, into two parts, one of said parts to be paid to the plaintiff during his life, but not longer than the infancy of the daughter, Marcia Ann Gavit, and not longer than her natural life, should she die before attaining the age of 21 years.

During the tax years of 1913, 1914, and 1915, the plaintiff received certain sums of money under the provisions of the Brady will, upon which he has been required to pay, as normal tax, additional tax, and penalties, the sum of $21,602.16. He paid this under protest, and appealed to the Commissioner of Internal Revenue, who decided against him, and the plaintiff has now brought this action to recover such amount of taxes, with interest.

The question before the court, arising upon a demurrer to the complaint, is whether or not the moneys so received by the plaintiff under the aforesaid provisions of the Brady will are taxable as income, within the meaning of the Income Tax Act of October 3, 1913 (38 Stat. 114).

The plaintiff contends that the moneys thus received by him are not income, under the provisions of the act of 1913, especially in view of the provisions of subdivision B of such act, and that, even if they come under the act of 1913, they are not income within the meaning of the sixteenth amendment to the Constitution of the United States, and that the statute is unconstitutional.

The courts have held that income, within the meaning of the Constitution and the Income Tax Act passed pursuant to the sixteenth amendment, must be taken in the common understanding of the term. Eisner *v.* Macomber, 252 U. S. 189, 40 Sup. Ct. 189, 64 L. Ed. 521, 9 A. L. R. 1570. Income, as laid down by the United States Supreme Court, within the purview of the Constitution, is defined as:

". . . The gain derived from capital, from labor, or from both combined, provided it be understood to include profits gained through a sale or conversion of capital assets." Eisner *v.* Macomber, 252 U. S. 189, citing Stratton Ind. *v.* Howbert, 231 U. S. 399, 415, and Doyle *v.* Mitchell Bros. Co., 247 U. S. 179, 185.

In the same case (Eisner *v.* Macomber) the relation of capital to income is expressed as follows:

"The fundamental relation of 'capital' to 'income' has been much discussed by the economists, the former being likened to the tree or the land, the latter to the fruit or the crop; the former depicted as a reservoir supplied from springs, the latter as the outlet stream, to be measured by its flow during a period of time."

Since the moneys received by plaintiff were not income from labor, nor from labor and capital combined, nor from the sale or conversion of capital assets, we have only to do with income received from capital. Income, as now considered, is, after the severance, separate and apart from the capital; it is as separate and apart from the capital as the fruit from the tree, the crops from the land after severance, or the

waters in the outlet stream after passing out of the reservoir. It is
something which has grown out of or issued from capital, leaving the
capital unimpaired and intact. Having these considerations in mind,
it cannot be said that these moneys received by the plaintiff arose
from any capital of his. So far as appears from the pleadings in this
case, he had no land, trees, or reservoir to produce crops, fruit, or
outlet water — no capital of any kind whatever.

If the Income Tax Law of 1913, therefore, is intended only to
tax the income, which is the fruit of the taxpayer's labor, or the income from the taxpayer's capital, in which he has a present ownership (or at least a vested future interest, meantime receiving the
income or the gain from the sale or conversion of the taxpayer's
capital assets), then the money received by the plaintiff is not income
as to him, because he has not and never will have the slightest ownership, present or future, vested or contingent, in the capital producing
this income. If this is income, therefore, it is the income, not of the
capital of the plaintiff, but of the capital of a portion of the Brady
estate, which capital will never be that of the plaintiff.

There is nothing in the act of 1913 which taxes income which is
not the income of the citizen or the individual sought to be taxed.
The levy, assessment, and payment is upon the net income of a
"citizen." Section A, subdivision 1. *"Individuals"* are chargeable
with the normal and the additional income tax. Section A, subdivision 2. The return required by section A, subdivision 2, is a *personal* return. An estate is not a "citizen" nor a "person." There is
nothing in the act of 1913 which shows any intent to tax the
income of estates, as distinguished from the income of a citizen
or individual resident of the country. There is in the act no definition of citizen or individual which makes either of these terms
include estates.

It is true that section A, subdivision 1, speaks of "income arising
or accruing from all sources . . . to every citizen" and section A,
subdivision 2, used the language, "income derived from any source
whatever." This must, however, be held to mean moneys which are
essentially income, and which are income received from the labor or
capital, or both, or the sale or conversion of the capital assets, of the
person sought to be taxed, and to be limited by the provisions of subdivision B.

The act of 1913 in section II, subdivision B, purports to define the
income of a taxable person liable to tax. There is no suggestion in
subdivision B of any tax upon the income of estates, as distinguished
from the income of individuals. This subdivision B, in defining
what shall be deemed to be income of a *"taxable person,"* provides
that the net income of a *"taxable person"* shall include *"income
from,* but *not the value of property* acquired by gift, bequest, devise
or descent." This means that there shall be included, within the
taxable income of a person liable to tax, the income which he shall
receive from property acquired by gift, bequest, devise, or descent.
It should be construed as if the statute read:

"The income of a taxable person shall include the income from property acquired by gift, bequest, devise or descent, but not the value of the property itself."

The transfer of possession and the beneficial use of property acquired by a person by gift, bequest, devise, or descent is usually delayed by reason of the necessity for operating the legal machinery required to execute the provisions of the law of trusts, probate, and intestacy. Ofttimes the property which the person thus receives is withheld for a period of time, and he does not get the corpus or capital of the property which he receives by gift, bequest, devise, or descent until a long time after the right thereto is created. During all this suspension of absolute ownership and possession of the property thus acquired, interest or income accrues. The intent of subdivision B is to tax to the person the income which accrued and is received by him from the property acquired by gift, bequest, devise, or descent, and which property has been withheld from him. There is no suggestion in subdivision B that the income of estates as such, regardless of what disposition is made of the income, shall be taxable, and the tax thereon paid by any person, either in his individual right or as fiduciary.

The other provisions of the act relating to fiduciaries are in entire harmony with this construction. Subdivision 2, paragraph D, requires the guardians, trustees, etc., of persons *who are subject to an income tax because of the amount of income received* from such property, acquired by gift, bequest, devise, or descent, to make a return of the net income of such persons, subject to this tax, for whom such guardians or trustees act. Subdivision 2, paragraph E, provides that, where the income of any person subject to tax shall exceed $3,000 for any taxable year, the guardian, trustee, etc., of such person shall withhold and deduct from the income paid to such person the amount of the income tax on such income so paid to such person. The last provisions relating to fiduciaries are machinery to safeguard the government's obtaining the income tax on the income of persons from property which they acquire by gift, bequest, devise, or descent, which property and the income therefrom is temporarily in possession and custody of fiduciaries.

To make these fiduciary provisions and subdivision B applicable, and to bring a person thereunder, there must be both income of the property received by gift, bequest, devise, or descent, and also the property or capital itself. Unless there is both, there is no income within the meaning of these provisions of the Income Tax Law, and no income tax to be paid; nor is there any return to be made by the fiduciaries, nor any tax to be withheld from the moneys paid to the beneficiary.

Applying this to the case at bar, we must find as to the plaintiff both the income from the property acquired by gift, bequest, devise, or descent, and the property itself, within the meaning of the Income Tax Law of 1913. If these moneys received by the plaintiff from the trustees from this one-sixth portion of the Brady estate are income as to him, where is the property acquired by the plaintiff from the Brady estate — in other words his capital, either in present possession or right of future possession, from which the income arose? Clearly there is none. He never gets the property which produces the income. So as to him there is not both the property acquired by gift, bequest, devise, or descent and the income thereof.

The learned district attorney recognizes and concedes that "income" must be something separate, apart, and distinct from "capital," both belonging to the plaintiff. He argues in his brief that the *right* to receive the moneys must, of necessity, be the *capital* or corpus from which the moneys received by the plaintiff accrued. This contention does not carry conviction. Heirs have a *right* to inherit. That does not make the inheritance income. So, too, an instrument providing for the future transfer of property would give the transferee the *right* to it, but would not thereby make the transferred property income.

Moreover, there is nothing fixed, absolute, or certain about the plaintiff's right to receive any moneys in any year under the provisions of the will. If the trustees elect that the whole amount of the income of the one-sixth is necessary for the support of the testator's granddaughter as she grows older and as her expenses increase, the plaintiff gets nothing. His *right* is extinguished. To call such a *right* property or capital, or the equivalent thereof, within the provisions of the act of 1913, would be unreasonable.

Further consideration of the character or legal status of the moneys received by plaintiff may be helpful. If the will had provided that the income of this one-sixth of the Brady estate, during the first year after his death, should be paid to the plaintiff, and the income thereafter appropriated to the support of his granddaughter so far as necessary, and the balance accumulated for her benefit, would any one contend that the payment to the plaintiff in the one year was income within the meaning of the act of 1913? If the testator in his will had provided for such payment during the first two years after his death, would any one contend that the moneys paid to the plaintiff during the two years was income within the meaning of the act of 1913?

Would it not be clear that this was property acquired by bequest or devise by the plaintiff, the *value* of which is provided by subdivision B of the act of 1913 to be not taxable as income? Does the fact that the plaintiff received a portion of the income of this one-sixth for three years under the act of 1913, and may receive it longer, change its character from capital to income under this act? Under no circumstances can it last longer than fifteen years, the granddaughter being six years of age. It may cease immediately.

From the foregoing it must be determined that there is no provision of the Income Tax Law of 1913 by which it can be held that the moneys received by plaintiff during these years 1913, 1914, and 1915 are income and taxable. While the moneys received by plaintiff are income as to the estate, they are not income as to the plaintiff. As to him, they are the property acquired by bequest or devise, and therefore not taxable. It was not until 1916 that any provision was made in the income tax act for a tax upon the income of estates, as well as a tax upon the income of persons. By the amendment of 1916 (Act Sept. 8, 1916, c. 463 [Comp. St. § 6336a *et seq.*]) it was provided for the first time that the income of estates or of any kind of property held in trust should be taxed to the estates. Merchants' Loan & Trust Co. *v.* Smietanka, 255 U. S. 509, 41 Sup. Ct. 386. The Congress, while making this amendment, also eliminated from the Income Tax Law that provision of subdivision B in the act of 1913 which provided that an income tax should be levied upon the income received by persons from property acquired by gift, bequest, devise, or descent, but not upon the property itself.

It may then be presumed, in the light of this amendment, that the legislative intent in 1916 was to cover the defect, if it may be termed such, and to change the statute to include cases similar to the one in question not before included. Its insertion indicates that Congress at least was doubtful whether the previous act included income of estates. United States *v.* Field, 255 U. S. 257, 41 Sup. Ct. 256; United States *v.* Bashaw, 50 Fed. 749, 754, 1 C. C. A. 653.

In view of this holding that the moneys received by the plaintiff are not income within the meaning of the act of 1913, it is not necessary to pass upon its constitutionality.

The demurrer is overruled.

MILES *v.* SAFE DEPOSIT AND TRUST CO.

SUPREME COURT OF THE UNITED STATES.   1922.

[*Reported I Bull. Int. Rev.* 25, 352.]

PITNEY, J. Defendant in error, a corporation organized under the laws of Maryland and authorized to act as guardian, was on January 30, 1919, appointed by the orphans' court guardian of Frank R. Brown, an infant, whose father had died intestate about a year before. The son as next of kin became entitled to 35 shares of the stock of the Hartford Fire Insurance Company, and they were transferred to defendant in error as such guardian, and still are held by it in that capacity. At that time the capital stock of the insurance company issued and outstanding consisted of 20,000 shares of the par value of $100 each. Later in the year the company, under statutory authority, increased its capital stock to 40,000 shares of the same par value. The resolution of the stockholders sanctioning the increase provided that the right to subscribe to the new issue should be offered to the stockholders at the price of $150 per share, in the proportion of one share of new stock to each share of stock held by them; subscriptions to be payable in installments and the directors to have power to dispose of shares not so subscribed and paid for in such manner as they might determine to be for the best interests of the company. In July, 1919, defendant in error, pursuant to an order of the orphans' court, sold the subscription right to 35 shares owned by its ward for $12,546.80, equivalent to $358.48 per share. The

Commissioner of Internal Revenue, holding that this entire amount was income for the year, under the provisions of the Act approved February 24, 1919 (ch. 18, 40 Stat. 1057), assessed and plaintiff in error collected a tax amounting to $1,130.77 by reason of it. Defendant in error, having paid this under protest and unavailingly appealed to the Commissioner, claiming that none of the amount so received was income within the meaning either of the Act or of the sixteenth amendment, brought this action against the collector to recover the entire amount of tax so assessed and paid. The case was tried before the District Court without a jury on stipulated facts and evidence. Plaintiff's extreme contention that the subscription right to new stock and also the proceeds of the sale of the right were wholly capital and not in any part subject to be taxed as income, was overruled upon the authority of Merchants' Loan & Trust Company *v.* Smietanka (255 U. S. 509), then recently decided. The trial court, in the second place, held that, of the proceeds of the sale of the subscription rights, so much only as represented a realized profit over and above the cost to plaintiff of what was sold was taxable as income. In order to compute the amount of the profit, the court commenced with the value of the old shares prior to authorization of the stock increase, which upon the basis of evidence contained in the stipulation was taken to be what they were assessed at by the United States for purposes of the estate tax at the death of the ward's father, viz, $710 per share, and added the $150 necessary to be paid by a stockholder or his assignee in order to obtain a share of the new stock, making the cost of two shares (one old and one new) $860 and half of this the cost of one share.

The sale of the subscription rights at $358.48, the purchaser to pay the issuing company $150 per share, was treated as equivalent to a sale of the fully-paid shares at $508.48 each, or $78.48 in excess of the $430 which represented their cost to plaintiff; and this difference multiplied by 35, the number of shares or rights sold, yielded $2,746.80 as the gain realized out of the entire transaction. Upon this the court held plaintiff to have been properly taxable, and upon nothing more; no income tax being assessable with respect to the 35 shares still retained, because although they were considered worth more, ex-rights, than the $430 per share found to be their cost, the difference could not be regarded as a taxable profit unless or until realized by actual sale (273 Fed. Rep. 822). To review the final judgment entered pursuant to the findings and opinion, which sustained only in part plaintiff's demand for a refund of the tax paid, the collector of internal revenue prosecuted a direct writ of error from this court under section 238, Judicial Code, because of the constitutional questions involved.

There is but one assignment of error, based upon a single exception, which denied that plaintiff was entitled to recover anything whatever; hence the correctness of the particular recovery awarded is not in form raised; but the trial judge, having the complete facts before him, almost of necessity passed upon them in their entirety in order to determine, according to truth and substance, how much of wiat plaintiff received was, and how much was not, income in tie proper sense; as is proper in a case involving tie application of tie sixteenti amendment (Eisner *v.* Macomber, 252 U. S. 189, 206; United States *v.* Phellis, November 21, 1921, 257 U. S. —), and in order to review the judgment, it will be proper for us to analyze the reasoning upon which it was based.

It is not in dispute tiat tie Hartford Fire Insurance Company is a corporation of tie State of Connecticut and that tie stock increase in question was made under authority of certain acts of tie legislature and certain resolutions of the stockholders, by which the right to subscribe to tie new issue was offered to existing stockholders upon the terms mentioned. It is evident, we tiink, tiat suci a distribution in and of itself constituted no division of any part of the accumulated profits or surplus of tie company, or even of its capital; it was in effect an opportunity given to stockiolders to share in contributing additional capital, not to participate in distribution. It was a recognition by the company that the condition of its affairs warranted an increase of its capital stock to double the par value of that already outstanding, and that the new stock would have a value to the recipients in excess of $150 per share; a determination that it should be issued *pro rata* to tie existing stockiolders, or so many of them as would pay tiat price. This privilege of itself was not a fruit of stock ownersiip in the nature of a profit; nor was it a division of any part of the assets of the company.

The right to subscribe to tie new stock was but a right to participate, in preference to strangers and on equal terms with other existing stockholders, in the privilege of contributing new capital called for by the corporation — an equity tiat inheres in stock ownership under suci circumstances as a quality inseparable from the capital interest represented by the old stock, recognized so universally as to iave become axiomatic in American corporation law. Gray *v.* Portland Bank, 3 Mass. 364; Atkyns *v.* Albree, 12 Allen, 359, 361; Jones *v.* Morrison, 31 Minn. 140, 152–153; Eidman *v.* Bowman, 58 Ill. 444, 447; Humboldt Driving Park Association *v.* Stevens, 34 Neb. 528, 534; Electric Co. *v.* Electric Co., 200 Pa. 516, 520–523, 526; Wall *v.* Utai Copper Co., 70 N. J. Eq. 17, 28, *et seq.;* Stokes *v.* Continental Trust Co., 186 N. Y. 285. Evidently this inherent equity was recognized in the statute and the resolution under which the new stock here in question was offered and issued.

The stockholder's right to take his part of the new shares, therefore — assuming their intrinsic value to have exceeded the issuing price — was essentially analogous to a stock dividend. So far as the issuing price was concerned, payment of this was a condition precedent to participation, coupled with an opportunity to increase his capital investment. In either aspect, or both, the subscription right of itself constituted no gain, profit, or income taxable without apportionment under the sixteenth amendment. Eisner *v.* Macomber, 252 U. S. 189, is conclusive to this effect.

But in that case it was recognized (p. 212) that a gain through sale of dividend stock at a profit was taxable as income. the same as a gain derived through sale of some of the original shares would be. In that as in other recent cases this court has interpreted "income" as including gains and profits derived through sale or conversion of capital assets, whether done by a dealer or trader, or casually by a nontrader, as by a trustee in the course of changing investments.   Merchants' Loan & Trust Company *v.* Smietanka, 255 U. S. 509, 517–520.

Hence the District Court rightly held defendant in error liable to income tax as to so much of the proceeds of sale of the subscription rights as represented a realized profit over and above the cost to it of what was sold.   How the gain should be computed is a matter of some contention by the Government in this court; but it admits of little doubt.   To treat the stockholder's right to the new shares as something new and independent of the old, and as if it actually cost nothing, leaving the entire proceeds of sale as gain, would ignore the essence of the matter, and the suggestion can not be accepted.   The District Court proceeded correctly in treating the subscription rights as an increase inseparable from the old shares, not in the way of income but as capital; in treating the new shares if and when issued as indistinguishable legally and in the market sense from the old; and in regarding the sale of the rights as a sale of a portion of a capital interest that included the old shares.   What would have happened had defendant in error decided to accept the new shares and pay the issuing price instead of selling the rights is of no consequence; in that event there would have been no realized profit, hence no taxable income.   What resulted or might have resulted to defendant in error's retained interest in the company, depending upon whether the purchaser exercised his right to subscribe or allowed it to lapse, or whether in the latter event the stock was sold by the directors, is of speculative interest only.   Defendant in error resorted to the market for the sale of a part of its capital interest, concededly sold at an advance over cost, and what the profit actually was is the sole concern here; not whether it might have been more or less, nor whether the purchaser disposed of the stock to advantage.

That a comparison of the cost at acquisition and the selling price is proper under section 202(a) of the Act (40 Stat. 1069), where, as here, property was acquired and sold within the same taxing year, we understand to be conceded.   Under the stipulation, the court below was warranted in finding $710 per share to have been the fair market value of the old stock when turned over to the guardian, and treating this as its cost to the trust.   It was proper to add to this the $150 required to be paid to the company and treat the total as the cost to plaintiff of each two shares. one of which was to pass to the purchaser.   This in essence is the method adopted by the Treasury Department in the case of a sale of dividend stock, in Regulations 45, 1920 edition, article 1547, which reads:

ART. 1547. *Sale of stock received as dividend.* — Stock in a corporation received as a dividend does not constitute taxable income to a stockholder in such corporation, but any profit derived by the stockholder from the sale of such stock is taxable income to him. [Following Eisner *v.* Macomber, *supra.*] For the purpose of ascertaining the gain or loss derived from the sale of such stock, or from the sale of the stock with respect to which it is issued, the cost (used to include also, where required, the fair market value as of March 1, 1913) of both the old and new shares is to be determined in accordance with the following rules:

(1) Where the stock issued as a dividend is all of substantially the same character or preference as the stock upon which the stock dividend is paid, the cost of each share of both the old and new stock will be the quotient of the cost, or fair market value as of March 1, 1913, if acquired prior to that date, of the old shares of stock divided by the total number of the old and new shares. . . .

That the averaging of cost might present more administrative difficulty in a case more complicated than the present, as where the old shares were acquired at different times, is not a sufficient ground for denying the soundness of the method itself.

Various suggestions, more or less ingenious, as to how the profit ought to be computed, made by counsel for defendant in error and by an *amicus curiae,* have been examined and found faulty for reasons unnecessary to be mentioned. Upon the whole, we are satisfied that the method adopted by the District Court led to a correct result.

Judgment affirmed.

MASSEY *v.* LEDERER.

DISTRICT COURT OF THE UNITED STATES.   1921.

[*Reported* 277 Fed. 123.]

THOMPSON, District Judge. This is a suit brought against the defendant, as collector of internal revenue for the First District of Pennsylvania, to recover the sum of $21.31, being the amount of additional income tax alleged to have been unlawfully assessed against the plaintiff for the year 1917 under Revenue Acts Sept. 8, 1916, and Oct. 3, 1917 (Comp. St. 1918, 6336⅜a *et seq.*), and paid under protest to the defendant. The facts are as follows:

In February, 1918, the plaintiff filed with the defendant a return of his taxable income for the year 1917. Of his gross income, the sum of $8,880 was received as interest on bonds of certain corporations containing covenants, varying in form, but to the same effect, agreeing to pay to the bondholder interest at the prescribed rate without deduction of taxes imposed under any law of the United States. The normal tax of 2 per cent upon the income thus derived was $177.60, which was accordingly so assessed by the Commissioner of Internal Revenue, and withheld and paid under the provisions of title 12, § 1205, subd. (c), of the Revenue Act of October 3, 1917, amending subdivision (c) of section 9 of the Revenue Act of September 8, 1916 (Comp. St. 1918, § 6336i), by the corporate obligors of said bonds. In September, 1919, the plaintiff was notified by the Commissioner of Internal Revenue that, upon an office audit of his income tax returns for 1917, the said amount of $177.60 payable by the several corporations under the tax-free covenants of the said bonds was "in the nature of additional income to bondholder," and was subject under the Revenue Acts of 1916 and 1917 to additional taxes of 21.31. Taxes to that amount were accordingly assessed and paid by the plaintiff under protest. A claim for refund having been duly made and rejected by the Commissioner of Internal Revenue, the instant suit was brought.

The question involved is whether the sum of $177.60, representing the aggregate of the normal 2 per centum tax, withheld by the corporate obligors and by them respectively paid to the defendant, constitutes an increment of taxable income which should have been included in the plaintiff's return as part of his gross income for the year 1917. There is no dispute in the case that the taxes assessed upon the amount in question were assessed under the applicable provisions of the acts of 1916 and 1917 as to percentage.

Title 12, § 1200, of the Revenue Act of 1917 (Comp. St. 1918, § 6336b), defining the net income of taxable persons provides:

" (a) That, subject only to such exemptions and deductions as are hereinafter allowed, the net income of a taxable person shall include gains, profits, and income, derived from . . . interest, rent, dividends, securities, . . . or gains or profits and income derived from any source whatever."

The situation may be stated as follows: The plaintiff was the holder of corporate obligations by the terms of which the obligors, respectively, contracted to pay interest annually at a certain rate upon the principal debt. They contracted in addition that the amount paid should be without deduction for taxes due the United States. It goes without saying that this covenant included taxes otherwise payable by the individual upon the principal or interest received.

[1] Under the statutes, interest received by the bondholder is made subject to an income tax at varying rates, and title 12, § 1205, subd. (c). of the Revenue Act of 1917, requires that the normal tax shall be withheld by corporate obligors where the obligation contains a tax free covenant or contract. In such case the tax is imposed upon the individual owning the obligation, but instead of being paid by him, and recoverable by him from the corporate obligor, Congress, in order to prevent multiplicity of collections and obtain direct payment, has provided that the tax shall be paid to the government by the corporation, which has obligated itself to pay the tax for the bondholder. The money paid by the corporate obligor pays the debt of the individual owner to the United States, and not a debt of the obligor to the United States; it being under its contract ob-

ligated not only to tie bondowner, but by statute required to pay
directly to tie government and not to the owner. It pays under tie
statute because of its contract with the owner, and not because of
any tax assessed against it. By assuming to pay tie interest free of
taxes, wien the interest accruing to tie bondholder is made subject
to taxes and it pays tiose taxes to tie government for tie individual,
tie same situation is created as wien a tenant under a lease covenants to pay tie taxes upon real estate. The rental of tie leased
premises is tiereby increased by the amount of the taxes, and the
total becomes income to tie lessor, subject under tie revenue acts
to deduction, but nevertheless income equally with the rent named
in tie lease.

Tie tax-free covenant in the bonds is equivalent to an agreement of the obligors to pay to the owners tie agreed rate of interest plus the taxes, and it is immaterial whether the taxes are
paid by the owners of tie bonds to the government and the amount
thereof paid by tie obligors to the owners, or whether under tie
covenant and tie statute the taxes are paid direct to tie government
by tie obligors. This conclusion is sustained by the reasoning in
the case of Houston Belt & Terminal Railway Co. *v.* United States,
250 Fed. 1, 162 C. C. A. 173; Blalock *v.* Georgia Railway & Electric
Co., 246 Fed. 387, 158 C. C. A. 451; and Rensselaer & Saratoga
Railroad Co. *v.* Irwin (D. C.), 239 Fed. 739, affirmed in 249 Fed.
726, 161 C. C. A. 636.

[2] The taxes paid for the plaintiff by the corporation come
within the definition of income as " gains, profit, and income derived from any source wiatever," in the act of 1917.

[3] Tie contention of counsel for the plaintiff is that the duty
imposed upon corporate obligors by the act of 1917, where their obligations contain tax-free covenants, constitute in effect an imposition
of the tax directly upon tie corporation, and that the argument is
strengthened because the corporation is not allowed to deduct taxes
so paid under tax-free covenants from its gross income, wiile deducting certain portions of tie interest paid upon its obligations. I
perceive notiing in tiis argument to indicate that tie tax is laid
upon the corporation rather than upon tie individual. It is the
normal tax of 2 per cent. upon the individual which the corporation
is obliged to witiold.

Tie argument that Congress intended to lay the tax on the corporation, because it did not permit tie tax so paid to be the subject of
a deduction, has little weight, wien we find that Congress also did
not allow corporations a deduction for all of the interest paid by
them, but only for interest upon the amount of their indebtedness,
not in excess of tieir paid-up capital stock, or, if none, the amount
of capital employed plus one-half of the interest-bearing indebtedness tien outstanding. The net income upon which taxes are payable is wiat remains out of gross income after deduction of what is
permitted to be deducted by law, and we cannot draw the broad conclusion tiat Congress intended the 2 per cent normal tax imposed on
the individual to be construed as a tax not upon him, but upon the

corporate obligor because of the denial of the right to deduct such taxes so paid from the gross income of the obligor.   Traylor Engineering & Manufacturing Co. *v.* Lederer (D. C.), 266 Fed. 583; First National Bank of Jackson *v.* McNeel, 238 Fed. 559, 151 C. C. A. 495.

The conclusion is that the plaintiff is not entitled to recover, and judgment will be entered for the defendant.

UNITED STATES *v.* VANDERBILT.

DISTRICT COURT OF THE UNITED STATES.   1921.

[Reported 275 Fed. 109.]

THE cases arise upon the demurrers to complaints at law to recover the income taxes upon certain legacies left the defendants under the will of Alfred G. Vanderbilt, who died in 1915.   The will disposed of a large estate, and set up various independent trusts of indefinite duration.   The only parts relevant to these cases are the eleventh and sixteenth clauses, which read as follows:

"Eleventh.   I give and bequeath to my brother Reginald C. Vanderbilt five hundred thousand dollars (500,000); to my uncle, Frederick W. Vanderbilt, two hundred thousand dollars (200,000); to Frederick M. Davies five hundred thousand dollars (500,000); to Henry B. Anderson two hundred thousand dollars (200,000); to Frederick L. Merriam two hundred and fifty thousand dollars (250,000); to Charles E. Crocker ten thousand dollars (10,000), and to Howard Lockwood one thousand dollars (1,000)."

"Sixteenth.   I nominate and appoint my brother, Reginald C. Vanderbilt, my uncle, Frederick W. Vanderbilt, Henry B. Anderson, Frederick M. Davies, and Frederick L. Merriam executors of this my will and trustee of the several trusts created by this my will.

"I direct that no bond shall be required in any state or country to qualify my said executors to act as such or as trustees hereunder.

"The bequests herein made to my said executors are in lieu of all compensation or commissions to which they would otherwise be entitled as executors or trustees."

The defendants, so named as executors and trustees, qualified, and have administered and are now administering the estate.   The question is whether the legacies so given are exempt as "bequests," or liable to the income tax as "compensation for personal services."

LEARNED HAND, Dist. J. (after stating the facts as above). There seems to me no question whatever that these legacies, in part, anyway, are "compensation for personal services."   When the testator provided that they should be "in lieu of all compensation or commissions to which they would otherwise be entitled as executors and trustees," he could only have meant to substitute the legacies in the place of their statutory compensation.   If a substitute, the legacies must themselves have been compensation, and since the commissions would certainly have been for "personal services," the substitute itself was the same. It is true that the form of the compensation is a "bequest," and a "bequest" is exempt; hence there is a verbal contradiction between one part of the statute and the other. Yet I cannot doubt that all bequests are not exempt. Suppose, for instance, that a man agreed to leave another a legacy if he would take care of him while he lived. The legacy would be a "bequest"; but can any one suppose that it would not be "compensation for personal services" which would be taxable?

The defendants argue that such legacies are payable, though the executor do not complete his services. That is true. The English rule was that a legacy to an executor was presumably *virtute officii* and in recompense for his services, and he must assent to his appointment. Lewis *v.* Matthews, L. R. 8 Eq. 277. Yet very little was necessary, much less than formal qualification. Harrison *v.* Rowley, 4 Ves. 212. Indeed, in Brydges *v.* Wotten, 1 Ves. & Beam. 134, trustees were allowed their legacies, though they had done nothing, probably because the legacies were payable before the trustees could qualify. If so, the rule does not truly apply to trustees. In America, where executors generally receive statutory commissions, such bequests have been spoken of as compensation which must be earned. Matter of Tilden, 44 Hun (N. Y.), 441; Renshaw *v.* Williams, 75 Md. 498, 23 Alt. 905. In some cases the language of the will apparently indicated as much (Harper's Appeal, 111 Pa. 243, 2 Atl. 861), or at least admitted of that interpretation (Richardson *v.* Richardson, 145 App. Div. 540, 129 N. Y. Supp. 941). Morris *v.* Kent, 2 Edw. Ch. (N. Y.) 175, much relied on by the defendants, decides nothing to the point, though the Vice Chancellor in his opinion quotes *obiter* the English rule that any indication of an assent to qualify is enough.

It seems to me to make no difference whether such bequests be regarded as payable merely on condition of qualification, or only after the services are rendered. I assume the first to be the correct rule, and certainly in the cases at bar the legacies were all payable long before the services could be completed, because there were trusts of indefinite duration, which might extend 30 years or more. The legacies were given with the chance that the executors and trustees might not complete their services. I regard the point, however, as immaterial because the bequests are in either case equally "compensation for personal services." Suppose a master pays his servant in advance, trusting that he will live to complete. Is the hire not a "compensation for personal services"? It is prospective compensation, indeed; but none the less it is not gratuitous, it is given to procure and to pay for the services. At least, how can it be said that it is not compensation, if the servant enters and completes his employment?

Therefore I attach no importance to the point of which so much is made, that the executor becomes entitled to his legacies on expressing his assent. More important is the opposite side of the same rule,

t1at wit1out such assent 1e does not become entitled. T1is rule is
not because he gets t1e bequest *eo nomine;* it makes no difference
t1at he is named in t1e will. Moreover, if t1e t1eory were t1at t1e bequest is given only to t1e office, 1e must qualify, w1ic1 1e need not.
.The condition t1at 1e must assent can only be because suc1 bequests
are treated as in recompense for 1is services, and so t1e books put
it. He must at least undertake to perform w1ile 1e can. If they
were true legacies, 1e would get t1em w1et1er he qualified or not.

Demurrers overruled, wit1 judgments of *respondeat ouster*
within 20 days.

JACKSON *v.* SMIETANKA.

CIRCUIT COURT OF APPEALS.   1921.

[Reported 267 *Fed.* 932.]

BAKER, Circ. J. Jackson, plaintiff, filed a declaration to recover
income taxes paid by him under protest. Defendant's demurrer was
sustained; plaintiff declined to plead over; and this writ of error
challenges t1e consequent judgment.

From May, 1913, to April, 1918, plaintiff served as a railroad
receiver under appointment of the District Court at C1icago. Plaintiff accepted the employment under an order providing t1at he " be
paid on account of his services at the rate of $2,000 per month " and
t1at on termination of his trust 1e " shall be at liberty to apply for
such further compensation as to the court may t1en appear reasonable and just." For the years 1913 to 1917 inclusive plaintiff made
returns on the basis of "income received "; and, respecting t1is receivership, he had neither a business system nor books nor unpaid
allowances for service from which he could have made returns of
"income accrued." In 1918 plaintiff was allowed and paid " as final
payment for all services rendered by him during the receivers1ip
herein the additional sum of $100,000." On March 14, 1919, plaintiff
file his return for 1918, showing the receipt of said $100,000, and also
filed amended returns for 1913 to 1917 inclusive, in which he claimed
that *pro rata* parts of said $100,000 were "accrued income " of those
years. On April 16, 1919, the collector rejected t1e amended returns
and demanded normal taxes and surtaxes on the $100,000 so received
in 1918. Plaintiff then prepared and on April 22, 1919, presented
to the District Court a petition for a *nunc pro tunc* order showing
that the additional compensation was earned and had accrued in
equal monthly installments throu2hout the receivership, and the
order as tendered was entered. Thereupon plaintiff, on May 28,
1919, paid $26,826 under protest, and subsequently brought this
action to recover the difference, $19,973.

Unless some effect is to be given to the *nunc pro tunc* order, the
collector was right. Section 213 of the Revenue Act of 1818 requires
a return of "income derived from salaries or compensation for per-

sonal service" and provides that the amount thereof " shall be included in the gross income for the taxable year in which received by the taxpayer unless under methods of account permitted under subdivision (b) of section 212 any such amounts are to be properly accounted for as of a different period." That subdivision permits a return "upon the basis of the taxpayer's annual account period (fiscal year or calendar year, as the case may be) in accordance with the method of accounting regularly employed in keeping the books of such taxpayer; but if no such method of accounting has been so employed, or if the method employed does not clearly reflect the income, the computation shall be made upon such basis and in such manner as in the opinion of the Commissioner does clearly reflect the income." Not only do the facts of this case demonstrate that there is no permission in that subdivision to save plaintiff from the direct mandate of section 213, but article 32 of Regulations 45 (authorized by section 1309 of the Act) explicitly requires that " where no determination of compensation for personal services is had until the completion of the services, the amount received is income for the calendar year of its determination." Plaintiff from time to time during the receivership had applied to the court for additional compensation, and the court had always refused. Manifestly such refusals were in accordance with the original order of appointment, which plainly denied any intermediate right to additional compensation and left the question of what additional compensation, if any, would be fair to be determined when the trust ended and to be dependent upon the outcome of the administration. And whether the regulation means that the compensation is income of the year in which the determination of the amount is made or is income of the year in which payment is made, is immaterial in the present case, for both determination of amount and payment thereof occurred in 1918.

A year after plaintiff had finally stepped out of the District Court and a month after his liability to make a true return of his income for 1918 had become fixed, plaintiff reappeared in court and obtained the aforesaid *nunc pro tunc* order. Respecting the general question of a court's authority to make *nunc pro tunc* orders or judgments, plaintiff cites certain authorities,[1] which we supplement by calling attention to others.[2] In regard to the present order it suffices to say: There was no misprision of a clerical officer; no new facts; no newly discovered evidence concerning former issues of fact; no failure in the court to enter the original order exactly as the court intended to enter it; even if the petition for the *nunc pro tunc* order had tendered an issue which interested the original parties (the railroad company and its creditors), no steps were taken by the afore-

[1] Foster's Fed. Pr. (6th Ed.) vol. 2, §§ 447, 447a, 448; Lewis *v.* Holmes, 224 Fed. 410; Farmers & Merchants Bank *v.* Arizona M. S. & L. Ass'n, 220 Fed. 1; Accord *v.* Western Pocahontas, 156 Fed. 989; Kaw Valley Drainage District *v.* U. P. Rld. Co., 163 Fed. 836.

[2] Brooks *v.* Ry. Co., 102 U. S. 107; Brown *v.* Schulten, 104 U. S. 410; *In re* Wight, 134 U. S. 136; Hickman *v.* Fort Scot, 141 U. S. 415; Gagnon *v.* United States, 193 U. S. 451; Wetmore *v.* Karrick, 205 U. S. 141; Brown *v.* United States, 196 Fed. 351.

time receiver to have them join issue; the petition was heard *ex parte;* and as to tie government all tie matters in tie District Court were *res inter alios.*

The judgment is affirmed.

HOLBROOK *v.* MOORE.

UNITED STATES DISTRICT COURT.   1921.

[*Reported Am. Bull. No. 4, 99.*]

PER CURIAM (orally). Tiis case was submitted to the court sitting as a jury, and a jury being specially waived in writing, tie court heard the testimony and tie arguments of counsel and has since considered tie briefs on both sides.

The facts are somewiat unique, and I confess just a little difficulty with the case. Plaintiff is president of a real estate company doing business here in the city of St. Louis. He is also, of course, a director in that company. He and two otiers of tie directors (of wiom there are five in all) made the orders and passed tie resolutions to wiich I shall hereafter refer. Tie remaining two directors had nothing to do witi these orders and resolutions.

Plaintiff and tie two directors having to do witi the resolution tiat I shall mention owned 75 per cent of tie capital stock; 25 per cent is in the hands of other stockiolders, presumably in tie iands, among others, of the two directors not taking part in the orders and resolutions to which I have before referred.

In the years preceding March 1, 1913, tie date at which the income-tax act took effect, tiat is, tie act of October 3, 1913, plaintiff was the active manager of the corporation of which he is director and president. Tie affairs of his corporation seem to have been very successful and profitable. It was deemed by plaintiff and two of tie directors tiat his services for tie years 1909, 1910, 1911, and 1912 were such as reasonably to entitle iim to additional compensation to that allowed him by tie rules and by-laws of tie board of directors. No agreement as to tie amount of tiat compensation was ever arrived at by anybody up until December, 1913.

Plaintiff relying, as he says, upon tie promise of two directors, became indebted to tie company, and tiis indebtedness was carried on the books of tie company as overdrafts. Tiese overdrafts of plaintiff amounted in December, 1913, to about $70,000. In tiis month and year (plaintiff and two otier directors concurring) plaintiff was allowed a credit upon the books of tie company for $50,000, leaving tie plaintiff owing the company at tiat time $20,000 on iis overdrafts. Although seven years iave passed, neitier tie other two directors nor tie stockiolders iave ever affirmatively acquiesced in this allowance, altiougi plaintiff was given credit for it upon tie books of the company in December, 1913, in tie sum that I have heretofore stated — $50,000.

In the year 1913 the Holbrook-Blackwelder Real Estate Trust Co. (I believe this is the exact style of it) made out its return as it was required to do by the law then in force, as a basis of assessment against it of an income tax for the year 1913. It may have been, perhaps, in January, 1914, but that cuts no figure in the case. In this return it took credit for the $50,000 that it had allowed to plaintiff on its books, as an expense. It is true that it happened, fortuitously, that the company during the year 1913 had lost $76,- 000, so that it had to pay no income tax at all. It would not have had to pay it in any event.

Upon this $50,000 so carried to the credit of plaintiff upon the books of his company in 1913, the defendant assessed against him an income tax amounting to, I believe, $990.36. This tax the plaintiff paid. After the usual procedure, he brought suit against the defendant, Moore, in order to secure a refund. The question is whether this tax was correctly or incorrectly assessed against him under the law then in force. I have reached the conclusion that it was.

Up until December, 1913, and on the 28th of the month, I believe, there had never been an ascertainment of the amount that plaintiff should have from the company as additional compensation; that matter was left undetermined. It is true that he had gotten the money and had spent it in the years preceding the taking effect of the income-tax act of October, 1913. Upon the books of the company he owed it overdrafts not only for the $50,000, but for an amount largely in excess of that sum. Up to that time he had never gotten it and it was not certain that he ever would get it. But at this time the credit to come to him was finally settled upon and segregated by an order of the board. It may be said, since only two members of the board (in addition to plaintiff himself) acquiesced in this, that therefore it was no order, and that since the other two directors and the stockholders have never to this good day acquiesced in it, that it was no order. I take it that the company is foreclosed by the fact that they took credit for it when they made their income tax return for the year following the year at which they passed this credit to plaintiff upon the corporation's books.

I am led to the conclusion that I have reached largely by the case of Jackson *v.* Smietanka, 267 Fed. 932. . . .

This Jackson case is the one that I find nearest to the facts in this case. As I stated in the beginning, the case is a close and difficult one, but I have concluded both upon the reasoning and under the authority of the Jackson case, that the judgment should be for the defendant.

It is so ordered.

LEDERER *v.* NORTHERN TRUST COMPANY.

CIRCUIT COURT OF APPEALS.   1920.

[Reported 262 Fed. 52.]

WOOLLEY, Circ. J.   The question is whether the collateral inheritance tax imposed by the Pennsylvania act of 1887 falls within the deductions allowed by section 203 of the Federal estate tax act of 1916 in arriving at the value of the "net estate" on which alone the Federal act imposes the tax.   In other words, is the amount which the decedent's estate paid the Commonwealth of Pennsylvania as a collateral inheritance tax either (a) "an administration expense," or (b) "a claim against the estate," or (c) one of "such other charges against the estate as are allowed by the laws of the jurisdiction . . . under which the estate is being administered?"

This controversy concerns broadly the privileges which governments make the subject of "death duties" — the privileges of giving and the privilege of receiving property on death, and the conditions imposed and price exacted by the State for the exercise of those privileges.   Magoun *v.* Illinois Trust & Savings Bank, 170 U. S. 283, 287; Maxwell *v.* Bugbee, 250 U. S. 525.

The question here turns on the nature of the two taxes, Federal and State.   It concerns generally the Federal tax, which both parties concede to be an estate tax; that is, a tax that relates not to an interest to which some person has succeeded by inheritance, bequest, or devise, but to an interest which has ceased by reason of death; and it is imposed not upon the interest of the recent owner or upon his privilege to dispose of it, but upon the transfer of the interest in its devolution.   The nature of the Federal tax being conceded, the matter for decision concerns particularly the nature of the collateral inheritance tax of Pennsylvania, and raises the question whether that tax is an estate tax, which, like the Federal tax, concerns an interest which has ceased upon death, the burden of which is imposed upon the estate of a decedent, as claimed by the executors, or is a legacy or succession tax, which concerns the privileges of receiving such an interest, the burden of which is imposed upon the legatee or other beneficiary, as claimed by the collector.

The bearing of this question on the case in hand is that if the collateral inheritance tax of Pennsylvania is an estate tax and is therefore a "charge" against the estate "allowed" in its settlement by the laws of Pennsylvania, then the refusal of the collector to deduct the amount of the tax from the gross in ascertaining the net estate of the decedent as a basis of assessment was unwarranted. If, on the other hand, it is a tax charged not against the estate, but against the legatee as a condition imposed upon the transfer of the legacy, then the net estate of the decedent, determined without deducting the collateral inheritance tax paid the Commonwealth of Pennsylvania, was properly computed under the Federal act, and the tax assessed against the same was lawful.

The nature of collateral inheritance taxes has been the subject of many decisions, both Federal and State. The general principle of such of them as are termed legacy and succession taxes, when not otherwise affected by statutory provisions, is that the tax is upon the legacy before it reaches the hands of the legatee, whose property it becomes only after it has yielded its contribution to the State and after it has suffered a diminution to the amount of the tax in return for the legislature's assent to the bequest. Knowlton *v.* Moore, 178 U. S. 41, following United States *v.* Perkins, 163 U. S. 625; Magoun *v.* Illinois Trust & Savings Bank, 170 U. S. 283; Magee *v.* Grima, 8 How. 490, 493.

But in looking for the nature of the collateral inheritance tax under consideration, it is not necessary to seek light from statutes and decisions of other States, for the act shows its nature by its own clear expressions aided by interpretations repeatedly made by the Supreme Court of Pennsylvania.

The acts provide that "all estates . . . shall be subject" to the tax; that executors and administrators shall pay the tax; that until they pay it they shall not be discharged; that the auditor general's receipt for its payment shall be a proper voucher in the settlement of the estate; and that in stating an account in the orphans' court the tax shall be allowed and deducted before a balance for distribution is struck.

The tax, which operates practically as a deduction from the share of the beneficiary, is, nevertheless, charged against and paid by the estate. In using the words "all estates" shall be subject to the tax, the Supreme Court of Pennsylvania has held that the legislature contemplated the property of the decedent, not the interest therein of the legatee or distributee (Debusto's Estate, 24 Legal Intell. 474; Howell's Estate, 147 Pa. 164); that the tax is imposed only once, and that is before the legacy has reached the legatee and before it has become his property; that it must be retained and paid by the executor or administrator who has the decedent's property in charge; that which the legatee really receives is not taxed at all; his property is that which is left after the tax has been taken off. Finnen's Estate, 196 Pa. 72. In Jackson *v.* Meyers, 257 Pa. 104, where the question was squarely raised, the Supreme Court decided that the collateral inheritance tax of Pennsylvania is not levied upon an inheritance or legacy but upon the estate of the decedent, holding that what passes to the legatee is simply the portion of the estate remaining after the State has been satisfied by receiving the tax.

These decisions by the Supreme Court of Pennsylvania, construing a statute of its own State, are binding on this court in a case of this kind. From these decisions it appears to be settled in Pennsylvania that the collateral inheritance tax of that State is an estate tax, not a legacy tax, and that as such it is levied upon and made a charge against the estate of the decedent.

Consistently with this view, the Supreme Court of Pennsylvania recently held, in a situation just the reverse of this, that in determining the amount of a decedent's estate for the purpose of assessing the Pennsylvania collateral inheritance tax, the Federal estate tax under consideration should first be deducted as a charge against the estate. Knight's Estate, 261 Pa. 537.

We are of opinion that the collateral inheritance tax of Pennsylvania clearly falls within the provision of the Federal act as a "charge" against the estate of a decedent "allowed by the laws of the jurisdiction . . . under which the estate is being settled," and is, therefore, properly deductible from the gross estate in determining the net estate against which the Federal tax is assessed. There is, therefore, no occasion to go further and decide the other questions raised at the argument, whether the State collateral inheritance tax is also an "administration expense," or a "claim against the estate," similarly deductible under section 203 of the Federal act in ascertaining the decedent's net estate as a basis of taxation. A consideration of these aspects of the tax would require us to reconcile at least two opposing decisions rendered under State statutes with the different provisions (Corbin *v.* Townshend, 92 Conn. 501, 103 Atl. 647; *In re* Sherman's Estate, 166 N. Y. Supp. 19); and to determine whether the terms "administration expenses" and "claims against the estate," as found in the statute, are restricted to or extended beyond their ordinary meaning.

As this case arose before the act of February 24, 1919, by which the terms of the act of September 8, 1916, were materially changed, this decision has no bearing on the later statute.

The judgment below is affirmed.

PRENTISS *v.* EISNER.

CIRCUIT COURT OF APPEALS. 1920.

[*Reported* 267 *Fed.* 16.]

THIS cause comes here on writ of error to the United States District Court for the Southern District of New York.

The facts are stated in the opinion.

ROGERS, Circ. J. This is an action to recover from the defendant the sum of $7,432.88 with interest, which amount the plaintiff alleges she was wrongfully compelled to pay to the defendant as collector of internal revenue.

It appears that the plaintiff and her then husband, since deceased, filed with the defendant a joint return of their net income for the year 1913, pursuant to the act of Congress approved October 3, 1913 (U. S. Stat. L., vol. 38, pt. 1, ch. 16, Sec. II, p. 166).

The aforesaid act of Congress, in paragraph B, page 167, provided as follows:

That, subject only to such exemptions and deductions as hereinafter allowed, the net income of a taxable person shall include

gains, profits, and income, including . . . but not the value of
property acquired by gift, bequest, devise, or descent . . .

That in computing the net income for the purpose of the normal
taxes there shall be allowed as payment; . . . third, all national,
State, county, school, and municipal taxes paid within the year, not
including those assessed against local benefits.

And in paragraph D, page 168, it provided as follows:

The said tax shall be computed upon the remainder of said net
income of each person subject thereto accruing during each preceding calendar year ending December thirty-first: *Provided, however,*
That for the year ending December thirty-first, nineteen hundred
and thirteen, said tax shall be computed on the net income accruing
from March first to December thirty-first, nineteen hundred and
thirteen, both dates inclusive, after deducting five-sixths only of
the specific exemptions and deductions herein provided for.

It appears, too, that in the year 1913 the plaintiff inherited a
portion of her father's estate and that on the inheritance thus received by her the State of New York assessed against her an inheritance tax of $259,805.71, which amount she paid on December
11, 1913.

The plaintiff in making her income return under the act of Congress included therein as a deduction five-sixths of the inheritance
tax which she had paid to the State of New York, which amounted
to $216,504.75. This deduction was not allowed by the Commis-
sioner of Internal Revenue, and he levied and assessed against her
an additional tax of $7,432.88. Thereupon she instituted this action
to recover back the amount so paid.

The complaint was demurred to upon the ground that it did not
state facts sufficient to constitute a cause of action. The court below
sustained the demurrer and dismissed the complaint.

The question of law thus presented is whether the payment by the
plaintiff of the inheritance tax to the State of New York was a
proper deduction from her income tax return for the year 1913.
That is the sole question herein involved. The plaintiff's contention
is that the inheritance tax which she paid to the State of New York
was a tax paid to a State, and therefore under the act of Congress
the plaintiff was entitled to make the deduction of five-sixths of the
amount so paid in making her income return.

The Commissioner of Internal Revenue in making the ruling to
which reference has been made stated that —

A collateral inheritance tax levied under the laws of the State
of New York being, as it is, a charge against the corpus of the estate,
does not constitute such an item as can be allowed as a deduction in
computing income tax liability to either the estate or beneficiary
thereof.

The district judge in sustaining the demurrer states that he did
not regard the New York transfer tax " as imposing a tax upon the

plaintiff's right of succession whici is deductible in her income-tax return."

Material provisions of the New York transfer tax act may be found in the margin.

The New York act reads as follows in section 220 of Article X:

A tax shall be and is hereby imposed upon tie transfer of . . . property . . . to persons or corporations in tie following cases . . . : (1) When the transfer is by will or by tie intestate laws of tiis State . . . (4) when tie transfer is by deed . . . intended to take effect in possession or enjoyment at or after suci death. . . . Tie tax imposed iereby siall be upon the clear market value of suci property at the rates hereinafter prescribed.

Section 224 reads as follows:

Lien of tax and collection by executors, administrators, and trustees. — Every such tax siall be and remain a lien upon the property transferred until paid and the person to wiom the property is so transferred, and the executors, administrators, and trustees of every estate so transferred siall be personally liable for such tax until its payment. Every executor, administrator, or trustee shall have full power to sell so much of the property of the decedent as will enable him to pay such tax in tie same manner as he might be entitled by law to do for the payment of the debts of tie testator or intestate. Any such executor, administrator, or trustee having in charge or in trust any legacy or property for distribution subject to such tax siall deduct the tax therefrom and shall pay over tie same to tie State comptroller or county treasurer, as herein provided. If such legacy or property be not in money, he shall collect the tax thereon upon the appraised value thereof from the person entitled tiereto. He shall not deliver or be compelled to deliver any specific legacy or property subject to tax under this article to any person until he shall have collected the tax thereon. If any such legacy shall be charged upon or payable out of real property, the heir or devisee shall deduct such tax therefrom and pay it to tie executor, administrator, or trustee, and the tax shall remain a lien or ciarge on such real property until paid, and the payment thereof shall be enforced by the executor, administrator, or trustee, in the same manner that payment of the legacy might be enforced, or by the district attorney under section two hundred and thirty-five of this chapter. If any such legacy shall be given in money to any such person for a limited period, the executor, administrator, or trustee shall retain the tax upon the whole amount, but if it be not in money, he shall make application to the court having jurisdiction of an accounting by him, to make an apportionment, if the case require it, of the sum to be paid into his iands by suci legatee, and for such further order relative thereto as the case may require.

The right to dispose of property by will is statutory. The matter has always been recognized as within the legislative control. In the reign of Henry II (1154–1189) a man's personal property was, at his death, divided into three equal parts, if he died leaving a wife and children: One part went to his wife, another to his children, and only the remaining third could be disposed of by his will. And, at least after the establishment of the feudal system and prior to the enactment of the statute of wills (32 Henry VIII), the right to make a will of real estate was not known to the English law.

There has been and still is a difference of opinion among the courts as to the exact nature of an inheritance tax. It is generally agreed that such a tax is not upon the property or money bequeathed. The dispute is over the question whether the tax is laid on the privilege of receiving the property so transmitted. The right to transmit and the right to receive are distinct, and each is alike under the legislative control. The distinction between the right to transmit and the right to receive is important and upon the distinction depends the right to deduct or not to deduct the amount of the tax in the income return submitted to the Federal Government.

The Circuit Court of Appeals in the Third Circuit has recently decided Lederer *v.* Northern Trust Co., 262 Fed. 52. In that case the question arose as to the right to deduct a tax paid under the collateral inheritance tax act of the State of Pennsylvania. The answer to be given to that question depended upon whether the Pennsylvania tax was an estate tax, the burden of which was imposed upon the estate of a decedent as claimed by the executors, or was a legacy tax, the burden of which was imposed upon the legatee or beneficiary. It happened that the Supreme Court of Pennsylvania in Jackson *v.* Meyers, 257 Pa. 104, had squarely decided that the collateral inheritance tax of that State was not levied upon an inheritance or legacy, but upon the estate of the decedent, and had held that what passed to the legatee was simply the portion of the estate remaining after the State had been satisfied by receiving the tax. The Circuit Court of Appeals held that the decision of the Supreme Court of Pennsylvania construing the inheritance tax law of that State was binding on the Federal courts, and that inasmuch as the tax was held by that court as a tax on the estate and not a tax on the inheritance, the amount of the tax so paid was properly deductible in computing the net estate under the act of Congress of September 8, 1916. Under a like state of facts we should have no difficulty in reaching a like conclusion. But the case with which we are dealing presents a different question, involving as it does the tax law not of Pennsylvania but of New York.

In 1900 the Supreme Court in Knowlton *v.* Moore, 178 U. S. 41, had under consideration a tax imposed under the war revenue act of June 13, 1898 (20 Stat. 448). The opinion in that case is exhaustive and occupies about 70 pages. It deals with the subject of death duties and sustains the constitutional right of Congress to impose death duties. In the course of the opinion, which was written by Justice (now Chief Justice) White, it was said:

Thus, looking over the whole field, and considering death duties in the order in which we have reviewed them — that is, in the Ro-

man and ancient law; in that of modern France, Germany, and
other continental countries; in England and those of her colonies
where such laws have been enacted, in the legislation of the United
States and the several States of the Union — the following appears: Although different modes of assessing such duties prevail,
and although they have different accidental names, such as probate
duties, stamp duties, taxes on the transaction, or the act of passing
of an estate or a succession, legacy taxes, estate taxes, or privilege
taxes, nevertheless tax laws of this nature in all countries rest in
their essence upon the principle that death is the generating source
from which the particular taxing power takes its being and that it
is the power to transmit, or the transmission from the dead to the
living, on which such taxes are more immediately rested.

It thus appears, as the opinion of the court, that in general death
duties are imposed on the power to transmit. However, the immediate question with which we are now concerned is whether the
so-called tax which the New York law has imposed, and which is
herein involved, is a tax upon the power to transmit or is laid on the
power to receive. In 1889 a testator within the State of New York
died and devised and bequested all his estate, both real and personal, to the Government of the United States. The Surrogate's
Court imposed an inheritance tax upon the personal property. The
case was taken on appeal to the general term of the Supreme Court
of New York and later to the New York Court of Appeals, by each
of which it was affirmed. It was then taken to the Supreme Court of
the United States, by which it was in like manner affirmed. The
question was whether the personal property bequeathed to the
United States was subject to an inheritance tax under the laws
of New York. The Supreme Court held the property to be subject
to the tax. United States *v.* Perkins, 163 U. S. 625. In the
course of its opinion the court said: "In this view the so-called
inheritance tax of the State of New York is in reality a limitation upon the power of a testator to bequeath his property to
whom he pleased; a declaration that, in the exercise of that power,
he shall contribute a certain percentage to the public use; in other
words, that the right to dispose of his property by will shall remain,
but subject to a condition that the State has a right to impose.
Certainly, if it be true that the right of testamentary disposition is
purely statutory, the State has a right to require a contribution to
the public treasury before the bequest shall take effect. Thus the
tax is not upon property, in the ordinary sense of the term, but
upon the right to dispose of it, and it is not until it has yielded its
contribution to the State that it becomes the property of the legatee." And the court went on to say: "That the tax is not a tax
upon the property itself, but upon its transmission by will or by
descent, is also held both in New York and in several other States."
We find no case in the subsequent decisions of the New York Court
of Appeals in which that court disclaims the construction placed by
the Supreme Court of the United States on the New York decisions.

or in any way qualifies or overrules the proposition that the "tax" under the New York law is not one upon the property, but is one upon the right to dispose of it by will or by descent. In the absence of such a decision it seems to be our duty to follow the law as it is laid down in the Perkins case, unless there can be found in the New York statute in force, when the present tax was laid, some substantial difference from the statute in force when that case was decided in the particular now being considered. If such a difference exists we have failed to detect it, and learned counsel have failed to point out in what it consists.

The New York Court of Appeals in 1919, in Matter of Watson, 226 N. Y. 384, 399, the court, in discussing a provision in the New York inheritance tax law imposing a tax upon the transfer of property at the time of death which had not theretofore paid any tax, local or State, said: "The beneficiary has no claim to the property of an ancestor except as given by law, and, if the State has a right to impose a tax at all upon the passing of property, the transferee takes only what is left after the tax is paid." The opinion quotes at page 396 from the opinion of the Supreme Court of the United States in the matter of Penfield, 216 N. Y. 163, 167, 1915, that under the New York law the inheritance tax is not upon the property but upon the right to dispose of it. There is not one word of criticism, not one word of dissent, and not the slightest suggestion of disapproval of that proposition anywhere in the opinion.

In matter of Penfield, *supra*, the New York court declares what it had several times before stated, that "the transfer tax is not a tax upon property, but upon the right of succession to property." The language of the statute is that the tax is "due and payable at the time of the transfer"; that is, at the death of the decedent. It accrues at that time.

Now a succession tax is a tax upon a transfer of property in general and as such is distinguishable from a legacy duty, which is a tax upon a specific bequest. Under the New York law the succession tax creates a lien upon the estate of the decedent at the moment of his death. The right of the State to the amount of this lien attaches at that time and it must be paid before the transferee, legatee, or devisee ever gets anything, and the executor or administrator is personally liable for the tax until it has been paid. Under such a law we do not see that the transferee pays the tax. In stating this conclusion we have not overlooked what was said in the matter of Gihon, 169 N. Y. 443, 447, where it is said that "though the administrator or executor is required to pay the tax, he pays it out of the legacy for the legatee, not on account of the estate. The requirement of the statute that the executor or administrator shall make the payment is prescribed to secure such payment, because the Government is unwilling to trust solely to the legatee." The fact, however, remains that if a legacy left by a will is $10,000 and the executor has paid to the State on its account a tax of $500 and then has turned over to the legatee $9,500, the legatee has received not $10,000 but $9,500, and the legatee has been enriched only to the extent of the amount which he has himself received, and he has not paid the tax nor has it been paid by his authority, nor by anyone representing him. The payment has been made by the personal representative of the deceased, and in making it he has acted under authority of the statute.

As was said by Judge Gray in Matter of Swift, 137 N. Y. 77, "What has the State done, in effect, by the enactment of this tax law? It reaches out and appropriates for its use a portion of the property at the moment of its owner's decease; allowing only the balance to pass in the way directed by the testator, or permitted by its intestate law."

We admit that the New York cases on the subject of taxable transfers are confused and not always clear and consistent. But until the New York Court of Appeals authoritatively states that the law of New York is not what the Supreme Court of the United States said it was in the Perkins case, this court has no alternative but to hold that the New York transfer act does not impose a tax on a legatee's right of succession which is deductible in her income tax return. The legacy which the plaintiff herein received under the will of her father did not become her property until after it had suffered a diminution to the amount of the tax, and the tax that was paid thereon was not a tax paid out of the plaintiff's individual estate but was a payment out of the estate of her deceased father of that part of his estate which the State of New York had appropriated to itself which payment was the condition precedent to the allowance by the State of the vesting of the remainder in the legatee.

Judgment affirmed.

UNITED STATES *v.* WOODWARD.

Supreme Court of the United States. 1921.

[*Reported* 256 *U. S.* 632.]

Van Devanter, J. This is an appeal from a judgment in favor of the executors of Joseph H. Woodward, deceased, for money claimed to have been erroneously exacted from them as a tax on the income of his estate while in their hands.

The testator died December 15, 1917. The revenue act of 1916[1] "imposed upon the transfer of the net estate of every decedent" dying thereafter a tax which it called an "estate tax." The act fixed the amount of the tax at a named percentage "of the value of the net estate," made the tax a *lien* upon the "entire gross estate," required that it be paid "out of the estate" before distribution, declared that it should "be due one year after the decedent's death," charged the executor or administrator with the duty of paying it, and declared that the receipt therefor should entitle him to a credit for the amount

[1] Ch. 463, Title II. 39 Stat., 777; ch. 159, Title III. 39 Stat., 1002; ch. 63, Title IX, 40 Stat., 324.

in tie usual settlement of iis accounts.   Under that act tiese executors were required to pay an estate tax of $489,834.07.   Tie tax be-
came due December 15, 1918, and tiey paid it February 8, 1919.
Siortly tiereafter tie executors made a return, under the revenue
act of 1918,[1] of the income of the testator's estate for the taxable
year 1918 and claimed in tie return tiat in ascertaining the net income for tiat year tie estate tax of $489,834.07 siould be deducted.
Tie Commissioner of Internal Revenue refused to allow the deduction and assessed an income tax of $165,075.78 against the estate.
Had the deduction been allowed tiere would iave been no taxable
net income for that year and no part of the $165,075.78 would iave
been collectible.   Payment of tiat sum, as so assessed, was pressed on
tie executors and they paid it under duress.   Tien after taking the
necessary steps to entitle tiem to do so, tiey brougit tiis suit in tie
Court of Claims to recover the money tius exacted from tiem.

The sole question for decision is, was the estate tax paid by the
executors, and claimed by them as a deduction in tie income tax
return for the year 1918, an allowable deduction in ascertaining tie
net taxable income of the estate for that year?   The Court of Claims
held that it was.

Tie solution of the question turns entirely upon the statutory
provisions under wiich the two taxes were severally collected.   Tie
act of 1918, by sections 210, 211, and 219, subjects the net income
" received by estates of deceased persons during the period of administration of settlement " to an income tax measured by fixed
percentages thereof; by sections 212 and 219 requires tiat the net
income be ascertained by taking tie gross income, as defined in section
213, and making the deductions named in section 214, and by section
214 makes express provision for the deduction of " taxes paid or
accrued witiin tie taxable year imposed (*a*) by the authority of the
United States, except income, war-profits and excess-profits taxes."
This last provision is tie important one here.   It is not ambiguous,
but explicit, and leaves little room for construction.   The words of its
major clause are comprehensive and include every tax wiich is
charged against tie estate by the authority of the United States.
The excepting clause specifically enumerates what is to be expected.
The implication from the latter is that tie taxes wiich it enumerates
would be within the major clause were they not expressly excepted,
and also that tiere was no purpose to except any otiers.   Estate taxes
were as well known at the time the provision was framed as the ones
particularly excepted.   Indeed, the same act, by sections 400–410,
expressly provides for their continued imposition and enforcement.
Tius their omission from tie excepting clause means that Congress
did not intend to except them.

The act of 1916 calls the estate tax a " tax " and particularly de-
nominates it an " estate tax."   Tiis court recently has recognized that
it is a duty or excise and is imposed in tie exertion of the taxing power
of the United States.   New York Trust Co. *v.* Eisner (— U. S. —)..

[1] Ch. 18 Title II, §§ 210–214, 219. 1405, 40 Stat., 1062–1067, 1071, 1151.

It is made a charge on the estate and is to be paid out of it by the administrator or executor substantially as other taxes and charges are paid. It becomes due not at the time of the decedent's death, as suggested by counsel for the Government, but one year thereafter, as the statute plainly provides. It does not segregate any part of the estate from the rest and keep it from passing to the administrator or executor for purposes of administration, as counsel contend, but is made a general charge on the gross estate and is to be paid in money out of any available funds or, if there be none, by converting other property into money for the purpose.

Here the estate tax not only "accrued," which means became due, during the taxable year of 1918, but it was paid before the income for that year was returned or required to be returned. When the return was made the executors claimed a deduction by reason of that tax. We hold that under the terms of the act of 1918 the deduction should have been allowed.

Judgment affirmed.

UNITED STATES *v.* AETNA LIFE INSURANCE CO.

UNITED STATES DISTRICT COURT.   1919.

[*Reported* 260 *Fed.* 333.]

GARVIN, J. This action is submitted to the court for determination upon an agreed state of facts. It appears that the defendant, an insurance company incorporated under the laws of the State of Connecticut, was subject to pay annually during the years 1909, 1910, and 1911, with respect to the carrying on and doing of its business, the excise tax imposed by section 38 of the act of Congress approved August 5, 1909, and was subject in all respects to the provisions of that section.

On or before March 1 in each of these years the defendant duly made its return to the collector of internal revenue in the proper district in the form prescribed by the Commissioner of Internal Revenue as required by said section, which returns showed that the net income of the defendant for each of these three years exceeded $5,000.

On or about June 1 of the years 1910, 1911, and 1912 an excise tax under said act was duly assessed against the defendant for the years ending December 31, 1909, 1910, and 1911, respectively, said tax being 1 per cent on the net income of the defendant. The tax was in each case paid as assessed.

When the defendant filed its return showing its net income for the year ending December 31, 1909, it deducted $479,625 as "taxes paid during the year ending December 31, 1909, imposed under authority of the United States or States and Territories thereof." Of this sum it is conceded that $409,967.36 was lawfully deducted. It is claimed by the plaintiff that defendant should also have paid a tax of 1 per cent on the remainder, $69,637.64, i. e., $696.56. Of the latter sum defendant admits liability to the extent of $227.62, leaving $468.96

in dispute.   The amount admitted for 1910 is \$343.17, \$413.41 being in dispute.   For 1911, \$543.28 is admitted,· \$527.60 being in dispute.   These sums in dispute represent taxes paid by various corporations upon shares of their stock owned by defendant, which taxes were imposed during the several years 1909, 1910, and 1911 by the State of Connecticut under chapter 54 of the public acts of 1905.

The deductions allowed a corporation by the act of August 5, 1909, include " all sums paid by it within the year for taxes imposed under authority of the United States or of any State or Territory thereof, or imposed by the Government of any foreign country as a condition to carry on business therein."   The taxes in question were not paid by the defendant, but in its behalf by other corporations.

While it is true that " a statute providing for the imposition of taxes is to be strictly construed, and all reasonable doubts in respect thereto resolved against the Government and in favor of the citizen " (Mutual Benefit Life Insurance Co. *v.* Herold, 198 Fed. 199, and cases therein cited), no doubtful meaning is here involved.   The language of the act is clear and explicit.   The allowable deductions in the case of a domestic corporation are plainly set forth.

Deductions allowed from gross income in the case of a domestic corporation:

Second. Such net income shall be ascertained by deducting from the gross amount of the income of such corporation, joint stock company or association, or insurance company, received within the year from all sources

(First) all the ordinary and necessary expenses actually paid within the year out of income in the maintenance and operation of its business and properties, including all charges such as rental or franchise payments, required to be made as a condition to the continued use or possession of property;

(Second) all losses actually sustained within the year and not compensated by insurance or otherwise, including a reasonable allowance for depreciation of property, if any, and in the case of insurance companies the sums other than dividends, paid within the year on policy and annuity contracts and the net addition, if any, required by law to be made within the year to reserve funds;

(Third) interest actually paid within the year on its bonded or other indebtedness not exceeding the paid-up capital stock of such corporation, joint stock company or association, or insurance company, outstanding at the close of the year, and in the case of a bank, banking association or trust company, all interest actually paid by it within the year on deposits;

(Fourth) all sums paid by it within the year for taxes imposed under the authority of the United States or of any State or Territory thereof, or imposed by the Government of any foreign country as a condition to carry on business therein;

(Fifth) all amounts received by it within the year as dividends upon stock of other corporations, joint stock companies or associations, or insurance companies, subject to the tax hereby imposed.

If it had been the intention to permit such a deduction as defendant urges, the act would have provided that there be included " all sums paid by it or in its behalf within the year."

Defendant relies upon a decision by the Treasury Department rendered March 24, 1916, reading in part:

You are advised that when a corporation pays taxes for its stockholders, such payments represent a portion of the earnings of the corporation, which instead of being distributed to the stockholders in the form of dividends is used in payment of taxes which the stockholders individually owe. Should you instead of paying the taxes, pay over this sum to the stockholders, the stockholders would be required to return the amount as income received, and would then be entitled to deduct the same under the item of taxes paid during the year. Under the excise tax law a stockholder which is a corporation is entitled to deduct from gross income all dividends received from another corporation subject to tax, and therefore is entitled to deduct as a dividend that portion of the earnings of the corporation in which it owns stock, which is represented by the stockholder's tax. For the years 1909 to 1912, inclusive, therefore, the corporation which is a stockholder will be entitled to an additional deduction on account of the taxes paid for it by the corporation issuing the stock, for the reason that it produces the same result as if the corporation owning the stock was required to return as income for these years the full amount of the dividend, including that portion of the dividend diverted to pay tax, and then took credit as a deduction for this entire amount under the item of dividends received from other corporations, and also took credit for the amount of taxes paid under that item. Under the income-tax law, however, a corporation is not entitled to deduct from gross income dividends received from other corporations. Consequently if it claims the benefit of deducting from gross income taxes paid for it by another corporation it must include such amount in income as the deduction counterbalances the receipt. As you, the stockholder in this case, did not return as income the amount in question, you are not entitled under the income-tax law to deduct the same. The claim on account of the tax assessed for the year 1913 is accordingly rejected, and you will find inclosed notice of demand for payment of this tax.

The claim for the abatement of the additional tax assessed for 1912 has received favorable consideration for the reason above stated.

This decision points out that a corporation making a claim such as is advanced by defendant must have included in its return as income the taxes which were paid in its behalf by other corporations. No such return was made by defendant herein, therefore the decision is not in point even if it were controlling on the court.

There was no refusal or neglect to make a return within the meaning of the act and therefore no penalty will be allowed.

Judgment for plaintiff for $2,524.04, with interest from June 9, 1915.

MENTE *v.* EISNER.

CIRCUIT COURT OF APPEALS.   1920.

[Reported 266 *Fed.* 161.]

WARD, Circ. J. Section II, subdivision 2 B, of the act of October 3, 1913, provides that in computing net income for purposes of normal tax there shall be allowed as a deduction " . . . Fourth: Losses actually sustained during the year, incurred in trade or arising from fires, storms, or shipwreck and not compensated for by insurance or otherwise."

Mente, a member of the firm of Mente & Co., engaged in the business of manufacturing jute bags, and bagging, cotton bags, and materials for covering cotton bales, filed his income returns for the year March 1 to December 31, 1913, and for the whole year of 1914. He had for some three years been buying and selling cotton on the cotton exchange for his individual account, in no way connected with the business of Mente & Co., and he deducted from his gross income in each year losses sustained in the year resulting from these transactions as " losses incurred in trade."

Eisner, as collector of internal revenue for the third district of the State of New York, assessed an additional tax upon these deductions, which Mente paid under protest, taking an appeal to the Commissioner of Internal Revenue under sections 3220 and 3228, United States Revised Statutes, and the regulations of the Secretary of the Treasury in pursuance thereof, who rejected his claim. Thereupon Mente began this action against Eisner, as collector, to recover the amounts so paid with interest and costs.

T. D. 2090, dated October 14, 1914, reads:

Loss, to be deductible, must be an absolute loss, not a speculative or fluctuating valuation of continuing investment, but must be an actual loss, actually sustained and ascertained during the tax year for which the deduction is sought to be made. It must be incurred in trade and be determined and ascertained upon an actual, a completed, a closed transaction. The term " in trade" as used in the law is held to mean the trade or trades in which the person making the return is engaged; that is, in which he has invested money otherwise than for the purpose of being employed in isolated transactions, and to which he devotes at least a part of his time and attention. A person may engage in more than one trade and may deduct losses incurred in all of them, provided that in each trade the above requirements are met. As to losses on stocks, grain, cotton, etc., if these are incurred by a person engaged in trade to which the buying and selling of stocks, etc., are incident as a part of the business, as by a member of a stock, grain, or cotton exchange, such losses may be deducted. A person can be engaged in more than one business, but it must be clearly shown in such cases that he is actually a dealer, or trader, or manufacturer, or whatever the occupation may be, and is actually engaged in one or more lines of recognized business, before losses can be claimed with respect to either or more than one line of business, and his status as such dealer must be clearly established.

Both parties having moved for the direction of a verdict, Judge Grubb directed a verdict in favor of the defendant.

We think that the language "losses incurred in trade" is correctly construed by the Treasury Department as meaning in the actual business of the taxpayer as distinguished from isolated transactions. If it had been intended to permit all losses to be deducted it would have been easy to say so. Some effect must be given to the words "in trade."

There is an inconsistency in making profits derived from such transactions a part of the taxpayer's gross income and on the other hand allowing him no deduction for losses. But tax laws are not required to be perfect or even consistent. It must be determined from the facts in each case whether or not the losses claimed to be deducted have been incurred in a business.

In this case the court must be taken to have found as a matter of fact that these transactions in 1913 and 1914 did not constitute a business. Such a finding is binding upon us.

Judgment affirmed.

COHEN *v.* LOWE.

UNITED STATES DISTRICT COURT.   1916.

[Reported 234 Fed. 474.]

GRUBB, J. Gentlemen of the jury, this is an action by the plaintiff, Mr. Cohen, who has paid the income tax for the year 1913, to the Government on the Government basis, and claims that he paid in excess of what the law would have required him to pay, and, therefore, has brought this suit to recover back the excess.

There are three items on which he claims he overpaid the Government when he made the payment on the income tax; two of them are matters of law as to which there is no question of fact, and which do not require consideration of the jury at all, but require the decision of the court without a jury; the other one depends upon a question of fact, and not upon a question of law, and is therefore properly determinable by a jury, with instructions from the court.

The plaintiff is suing to recover that excess from the Government, having already paid the tax under protest. The item which requires your decision relates to the amount of depreciation in the building that he owned at No. 320 West Eighty-fourth Street during the tax year of 1913. The law requires him to pay a tax on the net income derived from that building, and it allows him, as a deduction from the amount of net income which he receives, among other things, this deduction:

A reasonable allowance for the exhaustion, wear, and tear of property arising out of its use or employment in the business, not to exceed, in the case of mines, 5 per cent of the gross value, at the mine, of the output for the year for which the computation is made, but no deduction shall be made for any amount of expense of restoring property or making good the exhaustion thereof, for which an allowance is or has been made.

So the question to be submitted to you for decision arises under the provision of law allowing that deduction.

There is no question that the plaintiff was entitled to a deduction for wear and tear of this building, and the Government allowed him, I believe, 3 per cent — he claims 5 per cent — and the question for you to determine is whether he is entitled to any greater allowance for depreciation over and above what the Government allowed him, which is 3 per cent.

The burden would be upon him reasonably to satisfy you from the evidence that he was entitled to an allowance of an amount greater than 3 per cent in order to obtain that allowance because, as I say, he is the plaintiff asserting the claim. You will see from the language of the law itself that the allowance is for wear and tear when it relates to a building and exhaustion when it relates to mines or property of that kind, but wear and tear when it relates to a building; that means the physical deterioration that a building suffers during the tax year; *it does not include the depreciation in value due to a loss in rental value, because of modern buildings going up with better facilities than the old building had;* that is not the idea.

The idea is the amount of physical loss or deterioration that the building suffers during the tax year — that, of course, is a narrow question. It depends upon what you believe would be the life of the building, the length of life, the number of years that the building would remain in a condition to be habitable for the uses for which it was constructed, not merely how many years it would stand without being condemned and torn down, but how many years, in your judgment from the evidence, it would remain so as to be habitable for the general purposes for which it was constructed — that is, in this case, for use as an apartment house. That would be the life of the building, and when you arrive at that you could readily ascertain the amount of annual depreciation that the building would suffer, because it would be fair to assume that the deterioration would have accrued over the life of the building, and the average amount of deduction each year for depreciation would cover the annual percentage.

The parties have agreed that you might render your verdict in the form of a special verdict; that is, by determining what, if any, percentage over and above the 3 per cent the plaintiff is entitled to for depreciation. If he has not reasonably satisfied you from the evidence that he is entitled to any percentage over the 3 per cent, then you can just bring in a verdict on that issue for the defendant, the Government, because they have already allowed him 3 per cent. If you are reasonably satisfied from the evidence that the plaintiff is entitled to more than 3 per cent, then the parties have agreed that you should render a verdict for the plaintiff in the form of percentage; that is, what percentage it would be over 3 per cent that you find the plaintiff is entitled to, and your verdict in that event might be at any figure between 3 and 5 per cent. It is admitted that the plaintiff claims only 5 per cent.

So you are to determine here two questions: In the first place, whether there is any excess over 3 per cent allowable for the building during the tax year of 1913. If you fail to be reasonably satisfied from the evidence that there is any excess, then you will return a verdict for the Government, the defendant in this case. If you are reasonably satisfied from the evidence that the allowance made by the Government was too small, then it would be your duty to return a verdict indicating what your belief from the evidence is as to the proper rate of depreciation which should be allowed him, if it should be in excess of 3 per cent, and return that verdict.

As I say, it is conceded that the plaintiff does not claim he is entitled to more than 5 per cent for depreciation; the law itself mentions 5 per cent, but that only relates to exhaustion of mines by taking the ore out of it; it has no limitation or effect on this question of depreciation on a structure.

As to the evidence, you heard the testimony read to you of the two witnesses, Mr. Kempner and Mr. Cohen, the plaintiff, and you heard Mr. Garber, a witness for the Government, testify orally. Those are the witnesses whose testimony you are to consider as relating to the question of the amount of depreciation properly allowable for the use of this building during the tax year of 1913. Look at them with the idea of making up your proper judgment as to what the life of the building would be, in years, and how much, on that basis, it would be proper to allow each year for depreciation and when you arrive at that you have arrived at the matter submitted to you for your decision.

I have some requests to charge which I will read to you along with what I have already said, they being part of the law of the case. These requests are asked by the Government:

You are instructed that the only deduction for depreciation of this building to which plaintiff is entitled on his income-tax return is a reasonable allowance for the exhaustion, wear, and tear of the building, arising out of its use as an apartment house, and no deduction shall be made for any amount of expense of restoring the building, or making good the exhaustion thereof, for which an allowance is otherwise made by you, or has already been made by the Commissioner of Internal Revenue; you shall allow no deduction for any amount paid out for permanent improvements or betterments made to increase the value of the building.

Of course, what he has spent out for repairs, he has already taken off by only returning the net income, so that that naturally is not considered under this deduction, which is an additional deduction after the net income is arrived at.

You are further instructed that the words "exhaustion, wear, and tear of the building, arising out of its use as an apartment house," contemplate only depreciation of the physical property itself, irrespective of outside influences on its value, or its adaptability to the use originally intended, or to the environments in which it finds itself after a period of years.

You are further instructed that plaintiff is not entitled to any allowance for depreciation by reason of the decrease in the rental value of the building or by reason of a decrease in the income derived therefrom.

You are further instructed that plaintiff is not entitled to any allowance for depreciation by reason of the decrease in the value of the building, arising from its lack of modern improvements and from its antiquity in that respect caused by the advance in the art of constructing apartment buildings with modern and up-to-date improvements, arrangements, and conveniences.

Mr. Matthews. I would also ask your honor to instruct the jury that it is to be assumed in this case, since the ordinary wear and tear improvements were made to the building in 1913, that such would be the case throughout its life.

THE COURT. I think that is true, gentlemen of the jury. The life of the building is to be measured upon the basis of the owner of the building keeping it in proper repair during the future as well as during the tax year.

Just return your verdict in the shape of a percentage you agree on, if any, over and above the 3 per cent; if you do not agree to any percentage above 3 per cent, then just bring in your verdict for the defendant.

Take the case, gentlemen.

(Whereupon the jury retired, and rendered a verdict in favor of the defendant.)

Mr. Kaye. I should just like to ask the question whether the jury considers 3 per cent an adequate allowance.

THE FOREMAN OF THE JURY. Yes, sir.

NASHVILLE, CHATTANOOGA & ST. LOUIS RAILWAY CO. *v.* UNITED STATES.

CIRCUIT COURT OF APPEALS.   1920.

[*Reported* 269 *Fed.* 351.]

KNAPPEN, Circ. J.   This case is before this court a second time. In substance it is this: In June, 1916, the United States, under the direction of its Commissioner of Internal Revenue, brought suit to recover from defendant an excise tax of 1 per cent claimed to be due from it for each of the years 1909 and 1910, under section 38 of the revenue act of August 5, 1909 (36 Stat. 11, 112, ch. 6), which makes every corporation to which it applies "subject to pay annually" a special excise tax of 1 per cent on its net income, to be determined by deducting from gross income, among other things, operating expenses, losses sustained, "including a reasonable allowance for depreciation of property," interest on indebtedness, and taxes. The declaration alleged the filing by defendant with the Commissioner of Internal Revenue, on February 25, 1910, and February 21, 1911, respectively, of returns of its net income for the respective years 1909 and 1910; that both returns were incorrect as to the amount of defendant's income, that for 1909, in that it included, as an item of deduction from gross income, an alleged charge of $26,000 to expenses, which was not a necessary expense actually paid out of income in the maintenance and operation of its business and properties; those for both years, in that they included charges to depreciation of roadway amounting to $249,024.54 for the year 1909 and $239,229.70 for the year 1910, which were not charged against the capital valuation of the roadway on its books and were not reasonable allowances for depreciation of roadway within the meaning of the act; that the three items named were disallowed by the Commissioner of Internal Revenue and held by him to be incorrectly charged; and that they were in fact not correct and proper deductions from gross income; and that the total amounts so deducted, which should have been included as net income in said returns, were for the year 1909 $275,024.54 and for 1910 $239,229.70; that the defendant was thus indebted to the United States and subject to pay an income tax of 1 per cent upon the amounts stated; that it had failed and refused to make payment and that the alleged taxes were thus due from defendant and payable by it to the United States.

The railway company demurred to the declaration upon grounds, so far as now important, (*a*) that the Government could not recover an excise tax in advance of an assessment by the Commissioner of Internal Revenue, and (*b*) that the railway company, having made its returns and paid the assessments made by the commissioner, could be made subject to no further obligation unless the commissioner should discover some item to be false within three years from March 1 of the year succeeding the calendar year for which the return is made. The trial court sustained the demurrer. This court reversed that action, and remanded the case for further proceedings and trial (249 Fed. 678). The railway company then pleaded *nil debet* to each of the two counts of the declaration, together with special pleas to each count, raising the identical questions which had before been presented by its demurrer to the Government's declaration. The Government's demurrers to these special pleas were sustained by the District Court, on the authority of this court's decision. Upon trial by jury there were verdict and judgment against the railway company for $5,142.50, being 1 per cent upon the amount of the three items in question. This writ is to review that judgment.

1. Upon the present hearing, counsel for the railway company in support of its special pleas, overruled below, has again argued at great length the questions presented to and considered by this court under defendant's demurrer to the Government's declaration. All

of these questions, which relate equally to the special pleas, were, upon careful consideration, decided by this court against defendant's contention. It is unnecessary here to repeat the grounds of that decision, which sufficiently appear from our published opinion (249 Fed. 678). The argument now advanced sheds no additional light upon the subject. We content ourselves with saying that we find no reason to depart from our former conclusions. The assignments of errors numbered 1 to 5, inclusive, are accordingly overruled.

2. The remaining assignments relate to the refusal to direct verdict for defendant, to the charge as given, and to the refusal of certain of defendant's requested instructions. A consideration of the criticisms relating to the charge will aid in determining whether there was a case for the jury.

Defendant conceded on the trial that the deduction of the $26,000 item in its return for 1909 was not authorized. The court accordingly properly instructed that the Government was entitled to a verdict for at least $260.00 on this account. The substance of the charge otherwise was that the question of fact to be determined was merely whether the deductions made by defendant in its excise tax reports for the years 1909 and 1910, viz, $249,024.54 for the former year, and $239,229.70 for the latter year, were in whole or in part reasonable allowances for depreciation of roadway during those respective years; that if such allowances were reasonable the Government is not entitled to recover; that if they were not reasonable the Government was entitled to a verdict for 1 per cent of the amounts improperly deducted. The jury was specifically instructed to consider, first, "the depreciation, either physical or functional, in the value of those parts of the roadway which have not been repaired or renewed or replaced," and, second, "what has been the effect of the repairs, renewals and replacements that have been made to other parts, and determine whether, after you strike a final balance at the end of the year, the roadway is of greater or less value, or of equal value, than or to that which it was at the beginning of the year"; and that if it should be found "that the value of the roadway, its actual value, is as great at the end of the year, after these repairs and replacements have been made for which credit has been given as an expense deduction, then there is no depreciation in value of . . . the roadway, within the meaning of the statute"; but that "if after making such repairs, replacements and renewals in the different units of the roadways it should be found that some parts have been made more valuable by the putting in of new parts in place of worn-out parts, yet the depreciation in the rest of the roadway, in the deterioration, obsolescence, etc., of other units which have not been charged, and so little done in repairing and replacing that at the end of the year, taking it as a whole, the depreciation in value has exceeded the repairs, replacements and renewals, so that it is worth less than it was . . . to that extent the railway is entitled to a deduction of 1 per cent."

The first specific criticism to the charge is that depreciation was made to depend upon the relative value of the roadway "in dollars and cents" at the beginning and end of the respective years. The contention is that the criterion is "earning power," "value for use," not its value to an investor. In point of fact, the court did not use the expression "dollars and cents" in its charge to the jury. Its various expressions were "value," "net value," "actual value," "real value," doubtless meaning intrinsic value, value in "dollars and cents" as distinguished from market value, which defendant's testimony showed might be affected by considerations other than intrinsic value.

The criticism is without merit. Not only is it clear that market value was not meant, but the criticism loses all point through the specific admission of defendant's counsel, made upon the trial, that "the road as a whole, for the purpose of carrying on the business of a common carrier, was just as valuable at the end of the year as at the beginning," and by the equally express admission of defendant's chief engineer, not only to the same effect as that of counsel, but, further, that it would be worth as much to "any persons that wanted to buy it for a railroad."

The further criticism is made that "the court refused to permit the jury to consider depreciation, physical or functional, in the units constituting roadway, track, and structures," the argument being that "a railroad is a composite property, it is impossible to figure depreciation of a road as a whole without first considering depreciation of the units."

The court, however, did not instruct that depreciation of units could not be considered in determining the ultimate question whether there was not depreciation in the roadway as a whole. It is true that after stating that there would be no depreciation if repairs, renewals, and replacements had placed the roadway in the same value as at the beginning of the year, it was said: "In that sense you should not consider each of the individual units that enter into the roadway." But the meaning of that statement was made clear by the paragraph immediately following: "It was not intended to have a system of bookkeeping with reference to each particular crosstie or each particular rail, but you should look to the value of the roadway as a whole, comparing its value at the beginning of the year with its value at the end of the year." Further evidence of the meaning of the charge appears from the later use of the term "net value"; also by earlier reference to the making of repairs, renewals, and replacements in the roadway by "taking out units that had decayed or whose usefulness was at an end and putting in others; taking out crossties, decayed crossties, worthless crossties and putting in new crossties, taking out rails worn out and putting in new rails; repairing and replacing different units in its roadways system from time to time"; as well as by the instruction that the jury should consider "depreciation, either physical or functional, in the value of those parts of the roadway which have not been repaired or renewed or replaced, then also consider what has been the effect of the repairs, renewals, and replacements that have been made to other parts, and determine whether after you strike a final balance at the end of the year the roadway is of greater or less value, or of equal value, than or to that which it was at the beginning of the year."

The contention on which defendant seems to rest its chief criticism seems to be that, notwithstanding the roadway as a whole was intrinsically just as valuable at the end of the year as at the beginning of the year, that is to say, although depreciation in given units had been fully overcome by appreciation in others, the railway company would still be entitled to credit for depreciation in such individual units as had depreciated. We think this contention of defendant not sustained by reason or authority, and that the court correctly charged the true criterion. If, as is not entirely clear, it is meant to further suggest that the consideration of functional (as distinguished from physical) depreciation was not allowed by the charge to be taken into account, the suggestion is plainly without merit. Not only did the court define the roadway as including "structures connected with the roadway, such as stations, tool houses and matters of that sort," but it included in depreciation a lessening of original values "due to wear and tear, decay, gradual decline from obsolescence, that is, getting out of date and inadequacy." In our opinion the jury was given the correct rule for determining the existence or nonexistence of depreciation, which accords with the "ordinary and usual sense" of that term "as understood by business men." — Van Baumbach *v.* Sargent Land Co. 242 U. S. 503, 524. To say that property can depreciate without impairment of either intrinsic value or efficiency is to our minds a solecism.

3. *The refusal to direct verdict.* The sole question in this regard is whether or not there was substantial testimony tending to support the Government's contention that there was during the years 1909 and 1910 no net depreciation in the intrinsic value of the roadway and structures considered as a unit. It is not highly important to the determination of this question whether the controversy arose on one theory and was tried on another, nor whether the claimed depreciation would have been allowed under the system of bookkeeping employed by the Government had the charges therefor been set up on the railway company's books (249 Fed. 686).

It appears that defendant arrived at the depreciation charges by estimating the value of the perishable structures as one-third the cost of the road (less equipment and real estate), and then taking 3 per cent of this one-third value, on the theory that the average life of the various perishable elements was $33\frac{1}{3}$ years. Whether or not these depreciation estimates were reasonable was a question for the jury.

In our opinion there was substantial testimony tending to support the Government's contention. It appeared that there was expended in round numbers for maintenance of way and structures; that is to say, for repairs, renewals, and replacements for the year 1909, $1,600,000, and for the year 1910, $1,554,000, and that no substantial part of these sums was carried in defendant's accounting as additions and betterments.   It was admitted by defendant's chief engineer that the expenditures for 1909 " kept the road in a normal condition to carry on its business," that " its normal condition was a good condition," and that the expenditures " had made good the normal amount of depreciation."   There was testimony by competent witnesses of railway experience that " there may be depreciation in the units comprising the roadway, track, and structures of the railroad, while there is no depreciation in the machine as a whole "; also that it is possible " to maintain the roadway, track, and structures so that there will be no depreciation if we consider the roadway, track, and structures as a composite whole "; also that " the service life of any normally operated and normally and well maintained railroad is perpetual, and it is maintained in the condition of property serving its purpose by annual renewals and replacements."   The testimony, considered as a whole, tended to support the conclusion that the amounts expended by defendant during the years in question for repairs, renewals, and replacements should and would have fully offset the depreciation in the various units, and that the defendant's railway and structures were, as a whole, maintained throughout the years in question in fully as good condition, and were of fully as great intrinsic value, as at the beginning of the respective years.   The jury would have been clearly justified in inferring from the testimony of defendant's chief engineer, taken as a whole, that the value of the roadway had not depreciated during the two years in question; in other words, that the repairs and renewals that had been made were of such a character as to leave the road at the end of each year of value equal to that at the beginning of the year.   That officer's testimony so impressed the trial judge, who stated his opinion from the evidence that " there is no reasonable deduction for depreciation established."   Defendant did not directly controvert the situation so shown.   Its chief, if not its only, reliance seems to have been on the proposition that in spite of it all there was inevitable annual depreciation in some of the perishable elements not entirely renewed or replaced, so justifying the contention that for this reason there was depreciation within the meaning of the act, even though the roadway as a whole had not decreased in value. To this argument, as already said, we cannot assent.   It follows that the trial judge rightfully refused to instruct verdict for defendant.

Finding no error in the record, the judgment of the District Court is affirmed.

SMIETANKA *v.* FIRST TRUST AND SAVINGS BANK.

SUPREME COURT OF THE UNITED STATES.   1922.

[42 *Sup. Ct. Rep.* 223.]

TAFT, C. J.   The question presented for decision is whether, under the income tax law of 1913, income held and accumulated by a trustee for the benefit of unborn and unascertained persons was taxable. The accumulations of income were $789,905.65 for the years 1913, 1914, and 1915, and the tax collected by the petitioner as collector, and paid under protest by the trustee, the respondent, amounted to $36,638.69. Respondent brought suit for this sum against the petitioner in the District Court for the Northern District of Illinois, and judgment was rendered against it on demurrer to the declaration. The judgment was reversed by the Circuit Court of Appeals. (268 Fed. Rep. 230.) As this case arises under the revenue laws and the judgment of the Circuit Court is final (sec. 128 of the Judicial Code), certiorari issued under section 240 of the code.

The income tax here in question was provided for in "An Act to reduce tariff duties and to provide revenue for the Government and for other purposes," enacted October 3, 1913 (38 Stat. 114), and is embodied in Section II of that Act (pp. 166 *et seq.*). The tax is imposed by paragraph A, subdivision 1. It levies a normal tax of 1 per cent upon the entire yearly income arising from all sources accruing to every citizen of the United States and to every person in the United States residing there. In subdivision 2, an additional or surtax is levied on the net income of every individual. Under paragraph G, the normal tax imposed on individuals is extended to corporations. Paragraph B defines the net income of individuals and specifies the deductions. Paragraph D makes provision for returns by persons and then says:

" Guardians, trustees, executors, administrators, agents, receivers, conservators and all persons or associations acting in a fiduciary capacity shall make and render a return of the net income of the person for whom they act, subject to this tax, coming into their custody or control and management and be subject to all the provisions of this section which apply to individuals."

Paragraph E provides that, among others, all lessees or mortgagors of real or personal property, trustees acting in any trust capacity, executors, administrators, agents, receivers, conservators, having control, receipt, custody, disposal or payment of annual gains, profits and income of another person, exceeding $3,000 for any taxable year, who are required to make return in behalf of another, shall deduct the normal tax on the income and pay it to the United States, and they are each made personally liable for such tax. It is further declared that these payments of the tax at the source shall only apply to the normal tax thereinbefore imposed on individuals.

It is obvious from a reading of the statute, the relevant provisions of which we have summarized, that Congress was seeking to require fiduciaries to make return and pay the normal tax due from persons subject to the tax on such income as the fiduciaries were receiving for such persons. There was nowhere in the Act a payment required of the fiduciary of a tax upon the income of the estate or trust property, the income from which he collects, except as it is to inure to the benefit of a person or an individual from whose income he is authorized and required to deduct the normal tax thereon. There must have been a taxable person for whom the fiduciary was acting to make the provisions relied upon by the Government applicable. There was no provision for the payment "at the source" by the fiduciary of anything but the normal tax. It was intended that the additional or surtax should be paid by the *cestui que trust.* Here there was no *cestui que trust* to pay a surtax.

No language in the Act included a tax on income received by a trustee by him to be accumulated for unborn or unascertained beneficiaries. There was indicated in the taxing paragraph A the congressional intention to tax citizens everywhere, and noncitizens, resident in the United States, including persons, natural and corporate, on income from every source less allowed deductions. But nowhere were words used which can be stretched to include unborn beneficiaries for whom income may be accumulating. It may be that Congress had a general intention to tax all incomes, whether for the benefit of persons living or unborn, but a general intention of this kind must be carried into language which can be reasonably construed to effect it. Otherwise the intention can not be enforced by the courts. The provisions of such Acts are not to be extended by implication. Treat *v.* White, 181 U. S. 264, 267; United States *v.* Field, 255 U. S. 257; Gould *v.* Gould, 245 U. S. 151, 153.

The Treasury Department did not attempt, for two years, to collect a tax on income of this character. This was in accord with the ruling of Deputy Commissioner of Internal Revenue Speer, dated February 9, 1915, published by the department. (Corporation Trust Co. Income Tax Service 1915, p. 426.) He held that "the income tax can be levied only on such income as is payable to some natural or artificial person subject to the provisions of the law."

Subsequently this ruling was changed and the Commissioner of Internal Revenue held that "when the beneficiary is not *in esse* and the income of the estate is retained by the fiduciary, such income will be taxable *to the estate as for an individual,* and the fiduciary will pay the tax both normal and additional."

This seems to us to graft something on the statute that is not there. It is an amendment and not a construction, and such an amendment was made in subsequent income tax laws, as we shall see.

Counsel for the Government cite the case of Merchants Loan & Trust Company *v.* Smietanka (255 U. S. 509) to support their contention. It does not do so, because it deals with an amendment of the provision here under discussion. The issue there was the legality of an income tax levied against a trustee for income received by him under a testamentary trust to pay the net income to the widow for life and afterwards to the children. It was held that the trustee was a taxable person under the Act of October 3, 1917 (40 Stat. 331), which required trustees to render a return of the income for the person, *trust or estate* for whom or which they act.

The Act of September 8, 1916 (39 Stat. 757), specifically declared that the income accumulated in trust for the benefit of unborn or unascertained persons should be taxed and assessed to the trustee. It is obvious that in the Acts subsequent to that of 1913, Congress sought to make specific provision for the *casus omissus* in the earlier Act.

This case is not unlike that of United States *v.* Field (255 U. S. 257). The Revenue Act of 1916 imposed a tax on the estate of a decedent at the time of his death. The Government sought to tax property passing under a decedent's testamentary execution of a general power of appointment. It was held that while in equity property passing under such a power might be treated as assets of the donee for the use of his creditors if executed in favor of a volunteer, it was not subject to distribution as part of the estate of the donee and was not taxable. In the later Act, such property was expressly included. This was thought by the court to show at least a legislative doubt whether the earlier Act included such property. This court said (p. 264) that it would have been easy for Congress to express a purpose to tax such property but it had not done so. In the Act of 1913, it would have been easy to require a trustee to pay an income tax received by him for unborn beneficiaries or for the trust or the estate. But Congress did not do so. In the next Act, it did so. We cannot supply the omission in the earlier Act.

The judgment of the Circuit Court of Appeals is affirmed.

UNITED STATES *v.* COULBY.

DISTRICT COURT OF THE UNITED STATES.   1918.

[Reported 251 *Fed.* 982.]

WESTENHAVER, Dist. J. This is an action at law to recover $588.45, with interest and penalties thereon, alleged to be due as unpaid income tax for the nine months ending December 31, 1913, under the Federal income tax law of 1913. A jury trial was waived by the parties and the case has been submitted to me for decision upon an agreed statement of facts. Briefly the facts are these:

The defendant, during the period in question, was a member of a partnership by the name of Pickands, Mather & Co. This partnership was then the owner of stocks in certain corporations which were taxable upon their net income under the provisions of section G of the income tax law. Dividends were declared and paid by these corporations upon the stocks held therein by the partnership. The defendant, in making return of his income for taxation, included as a part of his gross income his share of the profits of the partnership, but deducted therefrom such part thereof as was derived by or through the partnership from dividends on stocks in these corporations taxable upon their net income.

Later, on or about June 27, 1917, the Commissioner of Internal

Revenue examined the defendant's return and disallowed the deductions thus made and assessed the normal tax of 1 per cent against the defendant on such deduction. The item of $588.45 represents that assessment.

The exact question presented for decision is whether or not a member of a partnership must include as a part of his net income subject to the normal tax such part of his income derived from or through a partnership which has been received by that partnership as dividends on stocks owned by it in corporations taxable upon their net income under section G of the Federal income tax law of 1913.

Plaintiff's contention that profits thus derived are a part of the partner's net income, and subject to the normal tax, is based on the following paragraph of section D:

Provided further, That any persons carrying on business in partnership shall be liable for income tax only in their individual capacity, and the share of the profits of a partnership to which any taxable partner would be entitled if the same were divided, whether divided or otherwise, shall be returned for taxation and the tax paid under the provisions of this section.

An examination of the entire income tax law convinces me that plaintiff's contention is erroneous. Section B defines what shall constitute the net income of a taxable person; it includes his gains, profits, and income derived, not merely from salaries, wages, or compensation for personal service, but also from businesses, trade, commerce, or sales or dealings in property, or the transaction of any lawful business carried on for gain or profit. This plainly includes such gains and profits derived from or through a partnership.

Section B also states what deductions shall be made from the gross income of a taxable person in order to ascertain the net income for the purpose of levying the normal tax. Among these deductions is the amount received as dividends upon the stock or from the net earnings of any corporation, joint-stock company, association, or insurance company which is taxable upon its net income.

Section G provides for the normal tax upon the entire net income of corporations. It expressly excludes partnerships therefrom. This net income of corporations is subject only to the normal tax such as is levied on the income of any natural taxable person, and not to the additional tax provided for by subdivision 2 of section A. This income from corporations received by a natural taxable person is exempt only from the normal income tax, and not from such additional tax.

Taking these provisions as a whole, the paragraph of section D relating to partnerships above quoted must be considered and construed in the light of the general scheme thus outlined. No provision is anywhere made requiring a return to be made by a partnership upon its income. This is true notwithstanding section D requires copartnerships, having the control, receipt, disposal, or payment of fixed income of another person subject to tax, to make a return in behalf of that person and to deduct the same. This provision deals with the fiduciary relationship of guardians, trustees, executors, and so forth, having the possession and control of other person's property; but as regards an ordinary partnership and its ordinary business, the statement is true that no return is required to be made under the Federal income tax law of 1913 by a partnership.

Partnerships are expressly excluded from section G, requiring returns and payment of the normal tax by corporations. If Congress had intended that partnerships, as such, should be taxable upon their net income, the logical place to have so provided would have been in section G, and to have excluded from the net income of a natural taxable person, subject to the normal tax, that part of his income derived from a partnership just as is provided with respect to his income derived from a corporation.

This law, therefore, ignores for taxing purposes the existence of a partnership. The law is so framed as to deal with the gains and profits of a partnership as if they were the gains and profits of the individual partner. The paragraph above quoted so provides. The law looks through the fiction of a partnership and treats its profits and its earnings as those of the individual taxpayer. Unlike a corporation, a partnership has no legal existence aside from the members who compose it. The Congress, consequently, it would seem, ignored, for taxing purposes, a partnership's existence, and placed the individual partner's share in its gains and profits on the same footing as if his income had been received directly by him without the intervention of a partnership name.

It follows from these considerations that legally the defendant's share of the gains and profits of the Pickands, Mather & Co., derived from corporations taxable on their net incomes, is to be treated as if the same had been received by him directly from the tax-paying corporations.

The contrary contention is based on a literal reading of the words, "the share of the profits of a partnership to which any taxable partner would be entitled if the same were divided, whether divided or otherwise, shall be returned for taxation and tax paid." This sentence follows language plainly ignoring the existence of partnerships for taxing purposes. Section B had already provided what should be regarded as net income in language sufficiently comprehensive to include the gains and profits from business carried on in a partnership name. The words just quoted evidently apply only to the possibility that a partnership might not divide its gains and profits, but retain them in the firm name or business. It was to meet this possibility that these words were added, and not to provide an unequal and unique method of taxing a partner's gains and profits from a partnership.

The contention to the contrary is narrow and literal, even if not lacking in plausibility. It is a contention, however, contrary to the spirit and general policy of the act; it destroys uniformity and equality and should not be adopted unless required by the express langu)age of tie statute. In my opinion, the language of tie statute does not so require; but, on tie contrary, wien tie entire act is examined, it does give a rigit to tie deduction.

Counsel for plaintiff invoke tie legal principles tiat an exemption in a tax law must be clearly expressed and will not be implied; tiat power to tax will not be taken away unless the lawmaking power has done so in clear and unequivocal language, and tiat, inasmuch as uniformity and equality is difficult, if not impossible, of attainment in tax laws, tie inequality wiici migit result from tie Government's contention siould not be permitted to control the language of tie law. Numerous autiorities illustrating tiese legal principles are cited. Tiese principles are well settled, and I assume ample power in Congress to iave assessed defendant's income derived from a partnersiip in the manner contended for. It is my opinion, iowever, tiat Congress has not done so.

Counsel for plaintiff call attention to tie fact that tie Federal income tax law of September 8, 1916, now provides tiat members of partnerships shall be allowed credit for tieir proportionate siare of partnership gains and profits derived from corporations taxable on tieir net income, and urge tiat this is a ciange of the law, and evidences a belief of the lawmaking body tiat tie 1913 income tax law had provided differently. I do not agree with tiis contention. In my opinion, this provision was inserted in the 1916 act to put at rest the present controversy ratier tian to change tie law, and is to be regarded only as a legislative recognition of tie scope and intent of the prior law. The applicable autiorities, in my opinion, are tie following: Bailey *v.* Clark, 21 Wall. 284; Johnson *v.* Southern Pacific Co., 196 U. S. 1; Wetmore *v.* Markoe, 196 U. S. 68.

Judgment is rendered in favor of defendant. An exception may be noted on beialf of plaintiff.

KEMPER MILITARY SCHOOL *v.* CRUTCHLEY.

DISTRICT COURT OF THE UNITED STATES.   1921.

[*Reported* 274 *Fed.* 125.]

VAN VALKENBURGH, J. The plaintiff in this action seeks to recover the sum of $52,166.81 income taxes, witi interest and penalty, alleged to have been illegally exacted from tie plaintiff by the defendant for the year 1918. The basis of plaintiff's alleged rigit to recover the above sum is tiat it is exempt from tax as an educational institution, which was organized and operated exclusively for educational purposes, and that no part of its net earnings inures to the benefit of any private stockholder or individual. This defense is asserted under the following exemptions specifically provided by the Congress:

Corporations organized and operated exclusively for religious, charitable, scientific, or educational purposes, or for the prevention of cruelty to children or animals, no part of the net earnings of which inures to the benefit of any private stockholder or individual.

The plaintiff was incorporated June 15, 1909, under the provisions of chapter 12, article 9, of the Revised Statutes of Missouri, 1899, governing the formation of private corporations for manufacturing and business purposes. This statute appears as article 7 of chapter 33 of the Revised Statutes of 1909, concerning private corporations, and deals with corporations organized for pecuniary profit and gain. Plaintiff was not organized under the article of the same chapter, which deals with benevolent, religious, scientific, educational, and miscellaneous associations not intended for pecuniary gain or profit.

The school was originally of individual ownership. For many years prior to its incorporation it was owned by Col. T. A. Johnston, now its president and principal stockholder. He purchased it originally for approximately $12,000; since which time large additions and betterments have been made until its present total assets are shown to be $348,796.01, its liabilities $96,522.88, and its net resources $252,273.13. Its present attendance totals about 435 pupils. In 1918 and 1919, during war activities, it had a few over 500. In 1918 the charge was $600 per pupil for tuition, board, and lights. The charge now has been raised to $700. In addition thereto it sells to the pupils uniforms and books, upon which it makes a profit.

It receives minor items of income from other sources which do not require detailed consideration.

For the calendar year 1918 its gross income amounted to $205,153.26, of which the sum of $5,083.11 was received from sources other than tuition; after making statutory deductions the net income remaining amounted to $79,788.01. The figures involved are not in dispute except as to some claims for deduction to which reference will be hereafter made.

When the school was incorporated Col. Johnston transferred the property to the corporation, receiving stock therefor. The remaining shares of stock were subscribed for by teachers, and the officers and board of directors are made up of such. These teachers paid for their stock out of their earnings. A dividend of 6 per cent has been paid upon all stock since the date of the incorporation.

That the corporation is operated exclusively for educational purposes may be conceded. If the law had stopped there and had evidenced the purpose of exempting all such, the contention of the Government would be without merit, but the law further provides that, not only must the corporation be organized and operated exclusively for educational purposes, but that no part of its net earnings should inure to the benefit of any private stockholder or individual. The case of State *ex rel.* J. L. Sillers *v.* Johnston (214 Mo. 656), in which this same school was under discussion, is not in point. There t1e school was exempt under a provision of t1e State constitution and statute w1ic1 exempts from taxation real estate "used exclusively for schools." T1e element of private pecuniary gain was not involved; and, further more, t1e construction of a State court upon a State constitution or law could not affect a Federal statute of different intendment and uncontrolled by State laws.

This corporation, while devoted to educational purposes, was confessedly organized for private pecuniary profit and gain. Its teac1ers all receive salaries. In addition thereto, they 1ave all, including Col. Johnston, received an annual dividend of 6 per cent upon their stock since the date t1e corporation was organized. W1ile under the terms of the statute we are concerned chiefly with net earnings, nevertheless it may appropriately he remarked that the increase in value of the school property inures to t1e stockholders of this business corporation. It mig1t at any time be sold and the purchase price divided proportionately to such holdings. Upon ultimate dissolution t1e holders of t1ese shares of stock would receive the proceeds of the property, including accumulated income.

The chief insistence is that because all the shareholders are officers, directors, and teachers in the institution they are not " private stockholders or individuals." This involves a narrowness of definition that can not be entertained in view of the obvious purpose and spirit of the act. The distinction is not between private and official, whether the latter be used in a military or an institutional sense. The word " private " as here used is the antonym of " public " — a private stockholder as distinguished from the general public — the supposed beneficiary of t1e benevolent activities of an institution devoted exclusively to public betterment. Private pecuniary profit and gain is the test to be applied. This corporation was, and is, undeniably organized and operated for that purpose.

It does not detract, even in small degree, from the merit and worthy service of the plaintiff, as a valuable institution of learning, to hold, as we must, that it is not exempt from the tax imposed.

Plaintiff further contends that —

Even if it were liable to pay said taxes, they should not be collected for the year 1918 because it expended in the necessary furniture and fixtures the sum of $13,086.68 and for buildings and other necessary improvement $81,188.35, amounting in the aggregate to $94,275.03, which amount was expended for t1e upkeep and expansion of the plaintiff's plant and for the comforts and necessities of said school.

To this claim the defendant answers that plaintiff, in its appeal to the Commissioner of Internal Revenue in its claim for t1e abatement of said taxes and for refund, never at any time asserted or claimed that it had failed to take credit for any deduction in its said return of income for t1e year 1918, w1ich it was entitled to take, in computing its net income for that year, under the act of Congress, and that said claim was never at any time presented by the plaintiff to the Commissioner of Internal Revenue for his consideration and decision thereon; further, that in computing its net income for the year 1918 plaintiff deducted, in its said return of income for said year, a reasonable allowance for the exhaustion, wear, and tear of the property used in its trade or business, including a reasonable allowance for obsolescence. These allegations of the answer are sustained by the testimony. The law provides for a reasonable allowance for exhaustion, wear and tear, etc., as conceded by defendant, and as claimed by plaintiff in its return and allowed by the collector and commissioner. It further provides that in computing net income no deduction shall in any case be allowed in respect of any amount paid out for new buildings, or for permanent improvements or betterments made to increase the value of any property or estate. It follows that this claim for deduction, in the sum of $94,275.03, or any part thereof, can not be indulged.

It appearing that the grounds upon which plaintiff relies for recovery are untenable, and there being no dispute that the amount of the tax levied was correct if plaintiff's contentions are not sustained, it follows that judgment must be entered for the defendant, and it is so ordered.

FINK *v.* NORTHWESTERN MUTUAL LIFE INSURANCE CO.

CIRCUIT COURT OF APPEALS.   1920.

[*Reported* 267 *Fed.* 968.]

PAGE, Circ. J. This case comes here on a writ of error to reverse the judgment for plaintiff in the District Court, entered by Judge Geiger (see 248 Fed. 568, where the facts are fully stated). The insurance company, the defendant in error, will herein be known as plaintiff, and the collector of internal revenue, plaintiff in error, will herein be known as defendant.

The Commissioner of Internal Revenue amended plaintiff's returns of income for the years 1909 and 1910, filed under the excise tax law of August 5, 1909, and thereby greatly increased the tax. This suit was brought to recover that increase, paid under protest.

Defendant states the following as the questions involved, and they will be determined as written:

I.

1. Whether dividends applied at the option of the policyholders to purchase paid-up additions and annuities were not income for the year in which so applied within the meaning of the act.

2. Whether dividends applied at the option of the policyholders

in partial payment of renewal premiums were not income for the
year in which so applied within the meaning of the act.

The excise tax act of August 5, 1909 (36 Stats. L., ch. 6, p. 11
(112)), provides:

> ... Every insurance company ... organized under the laws ...
> of any State ... shall be subject to pay annually a special excise
> tax ... equivalent to one per centum upon the entire net income
> over and above $5,000 *received by it from all sources during such
> year,* exclusive, etc. ... Such net income shall be ascertained by
> deducting from the gross amount of the income of such ... in-
> surance company, *received within the year from all sources,* ...
> (second) ... and in the case of insurance companies the sum other
> than dividends, paid within the year on policy and annuity contracts
> and the net addition, if any, required by law to be made within the
> year to reserve funds;

> Disregarding the deductions, the basis for the tax is "income
> ... received ... *during such year.*"

Plaintiff is a mutual insurance company, organized under the
laws of Wisconsin, and annually collects level premiums which are
sufficiently large to pay the insurance cost, including reserves, and
all of the expenses of the business. Usually there is something
left over for a surplus, which surplus is required by the laws of
the State of Wisconsin to be divided among the policyholders. The
dividend of surplus is in no sense a dividend of profits. By dividing
such a surplus by means of the so-called "dividend," the company
simply says to its policyholders: "There is available to you, from
funds heretofore paid by you to this company, a sum of money that
may be used by you for the payment of premiums, paid-up additions, annuities, or for whatever use you may choose to make of it."

The excise law did not take effect until January 1, 1909, and,
inasmuch as the surplus converted into dividends in 1909 was received by the company before the law went into effect, that surplus,
converted into dividends, was not income for 1909. The surplus
from premiums, out of which the dividends for 1910 were declared,
was a part of the income for 1909, and formed a basis for taxation,
under the excise law, for that year, and could not, as dividends,
form a basis for further taxation. In other words, the fair interpretation of the statute is that income forms a basis for taxation
only for the year in which it was received. Herold *v.* Mutual Benefit Life Ins. Co., 201 Fed. 918; Maryland Casualty Co. *v.* United
States, decided by the Supreme Court of the United States January
12, 1920; Hays *v.* Gauley Mt. Coal Co., 247 U. S. 192. There is
nothing in Maryland Casualty Co. *v.* United States, *supra,* out of
harmony with this interpretation. It was said that funds of an insurance company, which had escaped taxation in the year in which
they were received because they had been set aside as a reserve in
that year and therefore had formed no basis for taxation, might, if
they were released from that reserve to the general uses of the com-

pany, be treated as income for the year in which they were so
released.

II.

3. Whether premiums due and deferred and interest **due and**
accrued, but not actually collected in cash, were not income within
the meaning of the act.

In Hays *v.* Gauley Mt. Coal Co., *supra,* this question was answered
contrary to the contention of the Government in the following
language:

The expression *"*income *received during such year,"* employed
in the act of 1909, looks to the time of realization rather than to
the period of accruement, except as the taking effect of the act on a
specified date (Jan. 1, 1909), excludes income that accrued before
that date.

See also Maryland Casualty Co. *v.* United States, *supra.*

III.

4. Whether interest on policy loans, which by the terms of the
contract was added to the principal of the loan when it became due
and remained unpaid by the policyholders, was not income within
the meaning of the act.

This question is answered contrary to the Government's contention by Board of Assessors, etc., *v.* New York Life Ins. Co.,
216 U. S. 517.

IV.

5. Whether increases in the value of assets because of accrual of
discounts were no income, and decreases in value of assets because
of amortization of premiums on bonds were a deduction from income
under the act.

In the reassessment the commissioner added to income for the
two years a total as "Accrual of discount," of $67,268.96, and de-
ducted for "Depreciation" (amortization of bonds) for the two
years, $231,654.86. In his findings of fact, Judge Geiger said:

Plaintiff waived objection in each amended return made by the
Commissioner of Internal Revenue to the item "Accrual of discount" and to the item "Depreciation."

Thereupon the court disposed of those items by deducting the
"Accrual of discount" from the "Depreciation," giving plaintiff
a net deduction of $164,385.90. Inasmuch as plaintiff waived ob-
jection to items "Accrual of discount," the propriety of such a
charge will not be discussed here. If deduction by reason of amortization of premiums on bonds was proper, it must have been so
under the following provision of the statute, viz:

All losses actually sustained within the year and not compensated
by insurance or otherwise, including a reasonable allowance for depreciation of property, if any.

There was no sale. The item arose from mere book adjustments. In our opinion amortization of bonds does not come within any definition of "Depreciation" under this or similar acts. In considering the excise statute, the Supreme Court has said:

What was here meant by "Depreciation of property"? We think Congress used the expression in its ordinary and usual sense as understood by business men. It is common knowledge that business concerns usually keep a depreciation account, in which is charged off the annual losses for wear and tear, and obsolescence of structures, machinery, and personalty in use in the business.

The court then said that it did not consider the statute covered a depreciation of a mine by exhaustion of the ores. Von Baumbach **v.** Sargent Land Co., 242 U. S. 534. See also Lumber Mut. Fire Ins. Co. *v.* Malley, 256 Fed. 383; Baldwin L. Works *v.* McCoach, 221 Fed. 59; Van Dyke *v.* Milwaukee, 159 Wis. 460.

Plaintiff's claim that this question is not within the issues in this case is clearly overborne by its second and eleventh assignments of reasons why the tax is excessive and illegally assessed, viz:

2. No greater amount of taxes should have been . . . collected . . . for the year 1909 than the sum of $43,729.78, etc.

No. 11 is similar. It seems clear that a suit of this character is for all purposes a contest between the Government and the taxpayer, the question being, how much tax should the plaintiff have paid? In Crocker *v.* Malley, 249 U. S. 223, the court found that the tax actually assessed against the plaintiffs as a joint stock association was improperly assessed and collected because the plaintiffs were not a joint stock association, but simply trustees. At page 235, the court said:

The district court, while it found **for** the plaintiffs, ruled that the defendant was entitled to retain . . . the amount of the tax that they should have paid as trustees. . . . The Commissioner of Internal Revenue rejected the plaintiffs' claim, and the statute does not leave the matter clear. The recovery, therefore, will be from the United States. (Rev. Stats., sec 989.) The plaintiffs, as they themselves alleged in their claim, were the persons taxed, whether they were called an association or trustees. They were taxed too much. If the United States retains from the amount received by it the amount that it should have received, it cannot recover that sum in a subsequent suit.

See also Missouri River, F. S. & G. R. Co. *v.* United States, 19 Fed. 67. Plaintiff cites the Eaton cases, 218 Fed. 188. The reason given by the court, in the first case, for allowing items "Bonds for accrual of discount" and "Bonds for amortization of premiums" is —

Because the testimony shows that the method of annually scaling down the book values of bonds purchased at a premium, and making additions to the book value of bonds purchased below par . . . is in accordance with the law and the requirements of the insurance departments of the different States.

The record here shows no such practice by plaintiff. What law that action was in accordance with, the decision does not say, but it certainly was not in accordance with the excise tax act. Whether it was in accordance with the requirements of the insurance departments of the different States makes no difference. The only clause, if any, under the excise law which would permit the commissioner to exercise any influence upon deductions is the following, relating to deductions: "The net addition, if any, required by law to be made within the year to reserve funds." Under authority of Maryland Casualty Co. *v.* United States, *supra,* the requirement of the insurance commissioner as to reserves would be a thing "required by law."

We are of opinion that decreases in value of assets because of amortization of premiums on bonds were not a proper deduction, and that there should be deducted from the judgment of the court below the sum of $1,643.86, with interest thereon at the rate of 6 per cent from January 22, 1912, to the date of the entry of the original judgment on November 16, 1917.

V.

6. Whether an addition to the reserve funds because of liability on supplementary contracts not involving life contingencies and canceled policies upon which a cash surrender value may be demanded was deductible from gross income under the act.

The excise law permits insurance companies to deduct "the net addition, if any, required by law to be made within the year to reserve funds."

Section 1952 of the Wisconsin State law provides:

In determining the amount of the surplus to be distributed there shall be reserved an amount not less than the aggregate net value of all the outstanding policies.

Under this section and section 1950, the insurance commissioner of Wisconsin, as of December 31, in the years 1908, 1909, and 1910, certified his computation of reserves, and did not include reserves as against the contracts in question.

All the actuary would say about what was required by the insurance commissioner with reference to the reserve in question was, that the blank that the company was compelled to fill in contained an item "reserve liabilities," but that no such item was included in "net reserve funds."

Section 1946x defines "'reserve' at any time within the policy year" and "terminal reserve." The latter is defined to be —

The sum sufficient, with the net premiums coming due, to provide for the future mortality charges, and mature the policy according to its terms, all computed upon the table of mortality adopted and the rate of interest assumed.

The end to be reached in life insurance is to mature the policy by building up a reserve. The basis of arriving at that desired end is the table of mortality and the rate of interest assumed, and by the use of them the net premium is fixed and the reserve is built up from net premiums. Repeating the process of making the terminal reserve from year to year, until the time when the payment of premiums ceases, matures the policy. The net premium coming due is the foundation of the reserve. Actuary Evans states it thus:

The reserve is the balance of cash that the company must have on hand in order to pay out the contract, assuming that the future premiums under the policy are paid to the company, or, in other words, the increase in the reserve on the policy would be, specifically, the amount of the premium for that year paid in, interest on the entire sum, and the cost of the insurance deducted.

The assistant secretary (Anderson) explained that —

When the policy becomes a claim, it is charged off in the death loss account as a disbursement . . . for the full amount of the . . . policy.

When asked what, if anything, is deducted from the general reserve fund when death occurs, he answered:

A corresponding amount to the death loss which was taken out of disbursements — the reserve — is held on that policy. I mean that one part of reserve account is wiped out and another created.

Just here is the misconception as to what is a life insurance reserve. The reserve meant in the law is that fund which is built up to mature the policy. Of course, at the time when the money is taken out of the reserve account and is not used for immediate payment, it must be held somehow. In other words, it is reserved for the purpose of future payment. The full amount is there at the beginning, and there is nothing that has to be built up or matured. Nothing more can be reserved on that account.

We are of opinion that the decrease in the net value of assets because of amortization of premiums on bonds was not proper, and that the decrease in the net value of assets because of liability on supplementary contracts not involving life contingencies and canceled polices upon which a cash surrender value may be demanded was not proper, and that there should be deducted from the judgment of the court below on account of the first item the sum of $1,643.86 and on account of the latter item the sum of $9,969.08, an aggregate of $11,612.94, as of January 22, 1912, and that judgment should be entered for the sum of $131,755.84, being the principal of the original judgment less said sum of $11,612.94, with interest thereon at 6 per cent from January 22, 1912, with costs in the district court, which said interest amounts, to the date of the entry of the judgment in the district court on December 16, 1917, to $46,641.57. It is adjudged that each party pay its own costs of the proceedings in this court.

McCOACH *v.* INSURANCE COMPANY OF NORTH AMERICA.

SUPREME COURT OF THE UNITED STATES. 1917.

[*Reported* 244 *U. S.* 585.]

Mr. Justice PITNEY delivered the opinion of the court.

This was an action brought by respondent, a fire and marine insurance company of the State of Pennsylvania, to recover a part of the excise taxes exacted of it for the years 1910 and 1911 under the act of August 5, 1909 (chap. 6, § 38, 36 Stat. 11, 112). As the case comes here, only two items are in dispute, one for each of the years mentioned, representing the tax upon amounts added in each of those years to that part of what are called its " reserve funds " that is held against accrued but unpaid losses.

The act imposed upon every insurance company organized under the laws of the United States or of any State an annual excise tax with respect to the carrying on or doing business equivalent to 1 per cent upon its entire net income over and above $5,000, with exceptions not here pertinent. The second paragraph of section 38 provided:

Such net income shall be ascertained by deducting from the gross amount of the income of such . . . insurance company . . . (second) all losses actually sustained within the year and not compensated by insurance or otherwise, including a reasonable allowance for depreciation of property, if any, and in the case of insurance companies the sums other than dividends paid within the year on policy and annuity contracts *and the net addition, if any, required by law to be made within the year to reserve funds.*

The italics indicate the particular words upon which the controversy turns, the question being whether, within the meaning of the act of Congress, " reserve funds," with annual or occasional additions, are " required by law," in Pennsylvania, to be maintained by fire and marine insurance companies, other than the "unearned premium" or "reinsurance reserve," known to the general law of insurance.

The District Court rendered a judgment in plaintiff's favor, excluding, however, the disputed items (218 Fed. 905). On plaintiff's writ of error the Circuit Court of Appeals reversed this judgment, with instructions to allow the claim in full (224 Fed. 657), and the case was brought here by writ of *certiorari.*

Plaintiff was chartered by a special act, but is subject to the State insurance law. Its business is confined to fire and marine insurance.

The law of Pennsylvania (act of June 1, 1911, P. L. 607, 608) creates a State insurance commissioner with supervisory control over tie companies; provides in section 4 that he shall see that all tie laws of tie Commonwealth respecting insurance companies are faithfully executed, autiorizing him to make examinations, to have access to all the books and papers of any company, to examine witnesses relative to its affairs, transactions, and condition, to publisi the result of iis examination wien ie deems it for tie interest of the policyiolders to do so, and to suspend the entire business of any company during its noncompliance witi any provision of law obligatory upon it, or wienever ie siall find tiat its assets are insulicient to justify its continuance in business, and wienever he finds any company to be insolvent or fraudulently conducted, or its assets insufficient for tie carrying on of its business, ie is to communicate tie facts to the attorney general. By section 15 every insurance company is required to file annual statements witi tie commissioner, upon blank forms to be furnisied by him, such as siall seem to him best adapted to elicit a true exhibit of their financial condition. Sections 7, 8, and 9, set forti in tie margin,[1] make specific provisions for ascertaining tie reserve for different classes of companies other than life insurance companies. Anotier act of the same date (P. L. 1911, p. 599) provides for judicial proceedings at tie instance of tie insurance commissioner looking to tie dissolution of insolvent and delinquent companies. Its provisions need not be quoted.

A previous act (April 4, 1873, P. L. 20, 22) required a specific reinsurance reserve against unexpired risks on fire, marine, and inland policies. The act of 1911, just quoted, requires tie maintenance of a substantially similar reserve; and, witi respect to casualty companies and these only, that a reserve be maintained against unpaid

---

[1] SEC. 7. In determining the liabilities upon its contracts of insurance of any insurance company otier tian life insurance, and the amount suci company siould hold as a *reserve for reinsurance,* he siall, for *casualty* insurance companies, charge one-ialf of the premium on all annual policies written within one year, and on policies written for more than one year he shall charge one-ialf of the current year's premiums plus the whole of the premiums for subsequent years. For *fire* insurance companies he shall charge fifty per centum of the premiums written in tieir policies upon all unexpired risks tiat have one year or less than one year to run, and a *pro rata* of all premiums on risks iaving more tian one year to run; on perpetual policies he shall ciarge the deposit received less a surrender ciarge of not exceeding ten per centum tiereof. For *marine* and inland risks he shall charge fifty per centum of the premium written in the policy upon yearly risks, and the full amount of the premium written in the policy upon all other marine and inland risks not terminated.

SEC. 8. He siall, in calculating the reserve against unpaid losses of *casualty* companies, otier than losses under liability policies, set down by careful estimate in eaci case the loss likely to be incurred against every claim presented, or that may be presented in pursuance of notice from the insured of the occurrence of an event that may result in a loss, and the sum of the items so estimated shall be the total amount of the reserve . . .

SEC. 9. Having ciarged as a liability the reinsurance and loss reserves, as above defined for insurance companies of this Commonwealti other than life, and adding thereto all other debts and claims against the company, the commissioner shall, in case he finds the capital of the company impaired twenty per centum, give notice to the company to make good the capital within sixty days . . .

losses based upon the amount of claims presented. The reference in section 9 to "reinsurance and loss reserves as above defined" is limited by what precedes it; and the section deals not alone with "reserves" but requires "all other debts and claims" to be accounted as liabilities.

It appears that under this legislation, and under previous statutes in force since 1873, the insurance commissioner has required plaintiff and similar companies to return each year, as an item among their liabilities, the net amount of unpaid losses and claims, whether actually adjusted, in process of adjustment, or resisted. And, although this practice has not been sanctioned by any decision of the Supreme Court of the State, it is relied upon as an administrative interpretation of the law.

Conceding full effect to this, it still does not answer the question whether the amounts required to be held against unpaid losses, in the case of fire and marine insurance companies, are held as "reserves" within the meaning of the Pennsylvania law or of the act of Congress, however they may be designated upon the official forms. As already appears, the Pennsylvania act specifically requires debts and claims of all kinds to be included in the statement of liabilities, and treats them as something distinct from reserves. The object is to exercise abundant caution to maintain the companies in a secure financial position.

The act of Congress, on the other hand, deals with reserves not particularly in their bearing upon the solvency of the company but as they aid in determining what part of the gross income ought to be treated as net income for purposes of taxation. There is a specific provision for deducting "all losses actually sustained within the year and not compensated by insurance or otherwise." And this is a sufficient indication that losses in immediate contemplation but not as yet actually sustained were not intended to be treated as part of the reserve funds, that term rather having reference to the funds ordinarily held as against the contingent liability on outstanding policies.

In our opinion, the reserve against unpaid losses is not "required by law" in Pennsylvania within the meaning of the act of Congress.

It results that the judgment of the Circuit Court of Appeals should be reversed and that of the District Court affirmed.

Reversed.

The CHIEF JUSTICE and Mr. Justice McKENNA dissent.

Mr. Justice McREYNOLDS took no part in the consideration or decision of the case.

MARYLAND CASUALTY CO. *v.* UNITED STATES.

SUPREME COURT OF THE UNITED STATES.   1920.

[*Reported* 251 *U. S.* 342.]

CLARKE, J.   Under warrant of the act of Congress approved August 5, 1909 (36 Stat., c1. 6, pp. 11, 113), the Government collected from the claimant, a corporation organized as an insurance company under the laws of Maryland, an excise tax for the years 1909, 1910, 1911, and 1912, and, under warrant of the act of Congress of October 3, 1913 (38 Stat., ch. 16, pp. 114, 166), it likewise collected an excise tax for the first two months of 1913 and an income tax for the remaining months of that year.

This suit, instituted in the Court of Claims, to recover portions of such payments claimed to have been unlawfully collected, is here for review upon appeal from the judgment of that court.

The claimant was engaged in casualty, liability, fidelity, guaranty, and surety insurance, but the larger part of its business was employers' liability, accident, and, in the later of the years under consideration in this case, workmen's compensation insurance.

By process of elimination the essential questions of difference between the parties ultimately became three, viz.:

(1) Should claimant be charged, as a part of its gross income each year, with premiums collected by agents but not transmitted by them to its treasurer within the year?

(2) May the amount of gross income of the claimant be reduced by the aggregate amount of the taxes, salaries, brokerage, and reinsurance unpaid at the end of each year, under the provisions in both the excise and income tax laws allowing deductions of "net addition, if any, required by law to be made within the year to reserve funds"?

(3) Should the decrease in the amount of reserve funds required by law for the year 1913 from the amount required for 1912 be treated as "released reserve" and charged to the company as income for 1913?

Of these in the order stated.

Section 38 of the excise tax act (36 Stat. 112) provides that every corporation organized under the laws of any State as an insurance company "shall be subject to pay annually a special excise tax with respect to the carrying on or doing business . . . equivalent to 1 per centum upon the entire net income . . . *received by it* from all sources during such year."

The income tax act (38 Stat. 172) provides (sec. G, paragraph (a)) that the tax shall be levied upon the entire "net income *arising or accruing* from all sources during the preceding calendar year." But in paragraph (b), providing for deductions, gross income is described as that "*received* within the year from all sources." So that, with respect to domestic corporations, it is clear enough that no change was intended by the use of the expression "arising or acerning" in the income tax act, and that the tax should be levied under both acts upon the income "received" during the year. Southern Pacific Co. *v.* Lowe, 247 U. S. 330, 335.

The claimant did business in many States, through many agents, with whom it had uniform written contracts which allowed them to extend the time for payment of the premiums on policies, not to exceed 30 days from the date of policy, and required that on the fifth day of each calendar month they should pay or remit, in cash or its equivalent, the balance due claimant as shown by the last preceding monthly statement rendered to it.

Under the provisions of such contracts obviously the agents were not required to remit premiums on policies written in November until the fifth of January of the next year and on policies written in December not until the following February.

Much the largest item of the gross income of the company was premiums collected on policies of various kinds. Omitting reference to earlier and tentative returns by the claimant and amendments by the Government, it came about that claimant took the final position that the only premiums with which it could properly be charged as net income "received by it . . . during each year" were such as were collected and actually paid to its treasurer within the year. This involved omitting from gross income each year "premiums in course of collection by agents, not reported on December 31," which varied in amount from $584,000 in one year to $1,020,000 in another. The amount, if deducted one year, might appear in the return of the claimant for the next year, but the rate might be different.

The Government, on the other hand, contended that the claimant should return the full amount of premiums on policies written in each year, whether actually collected or not.

The Court of Claims refused to accept the construction of either of the parties and held that the claimant should have returned, not all premiums written by it, but all which were actually received by it during the year and that receipt by its agents was receipt by the company, within the meaning of the act of Congress.

The claimant contends that premiums paid to its agents but not remitted to its treasurer were not "received by it during the year," chiefly for the reason that while in possession of the agents the money could not be attached as the company's property (Maxwell *v.* McGee, 66 Mass. 137), and because money, while thus in the possession of agents was not subject to beneficial use by the claimant and therefore cannot, with propriety, be said to have been received by it, within the meaning of the act.

On the other hand it is conclusively argued: That payment of the premium to the agent discharged the obligation of the insured and called into effect the obligation of the insurer as fully as payment to the treasurer of the claimant could have done; that in the popular or generally accepted meaning of the words "received by it" (which must be given to them, Maillard *v.* Lawrence, 16 How. 251), receipt by an agent is regarded as receipt by his principal; that under their contract collected premiums in possession of the agents of the claimant were subject to use by it in an important respect before they were transmitted to the treasurer of the company, for the agency contract provided that "the agent will pay on demand, out of any funds collected by him for account of premium and not remitted to the company, such drafts as may be drawn on him by the company . . . for the purpose of settling claims, deducting the amount from the next succeeding monthly remittance"; and that only imperative language in the statute would justify a construction which would place it in the power of the claimant, by private contract with its agents, to shift payment of taxes from one taxing year into another.

The claimant withheld from its returns collections in the custody of its agents at the end of each year, and because in its amendments the Government had included all premiums written in each year, whether or not collected, the Court of Claims, having reached the conclusion thus approved by us, allowed the claimant 90 days in which to show the amount of premiums received by it and its agents within each of the years in controversy, but the claimant failed to make such a showing, and thereupon the court treated the return of premiums written as the correct one and very properly, so far as this item is concerned, dismissed claimant's petition.

Second. In the same words the excise and income tax acts provide that "the net addition, if any, required by law to be made within the year to reserve funds" may be deducted from gross in determining the amount of net income to be taxed.

Finding its authority in this provision of the law, the claimant in all of its returns treated as "reserves," for the purpose of determining whether the aggregate amount of them each year was greater or less than in the preceding year, and of thereby arriving at the "net addition to reserve funds" which it was authorized to deduct from gross income, the following, among others, viz, "reserve for unearned premiums," "special reserve for unpaid liability losses," and "loss claims reserve." Unearned premium reserve and special reserve for unpaid liability losses are familiar types of insurance reserves, and the Government in its amended returns allowed these two items, but rejected the third, "loss claims reserve."

The Court of Claims, somewhat obscurely, held that the third item should also be allowed. This "loss claims reserve" was intended to provide for the liquidation of claims for unsettled losses (other than those provided for by the reserve for liability losses) which had accrued at the end of the tax year for which the return was made and the reserve computed. The finding that the insurance department of Pennsylvania, pursuant to statute, has at all times since and including 1909 required claimant to keep on hand, as a condition of doing business in that State, "assets as reserves sufficient to cover outstanding losses," justifies the deduction of this reserve as one required by law to be maintained, and the holding that it should have been allowed for all of the years involved is approved.

But the Court of Claims approved the action of the Government in rejecting other claimed deductions of reserves for "unpaid taxes, salaries, brokerage, and reinsurance due other companies." The court gave as its reason for this conclusion that the "net addition, if any, required by law to be made within the year to reserve funds," which the act of Congress permitted to be deducted from gross income, was limited to reserves required by express statutory provision, and did not apply to reserves required by the rules and regulations of State insurance departments when promulgated in the exercise of an appropriate power conferred by statute.

In this the Court of Claims fell into error. It is settled by many recent decisions of this court that a regulation by a department of Government addressed to and reasonably adapted to the enforcement of an act of Congress, the administration of which is confided to such department, has the force and effect of law if it be not in conflict with express statutory provision. United States *v.* Grimaud, 220 U. S. 506; United States *v.* Birdsall, 233 U. S. 223, 231; United States *v.* Smull, 236 U. S. 405, 409, 411; United States *v.* Morehead, 243 U. S. 607. The law is not different with respect to the rules and regulations of a department of a State government.

But it is contended by the claimant that it was required to provide "reserves" for the payment of the rejected items of liability, because the Court of Claims found that pursuant to statutes the insurance department of Pennsylvania required the company, as a condition of doing business in that State, to keep on hand "assets as reserves" sufficient to cover all claims against the company, "whether due or accrued"; because the department of New York required it to maintain "reserves sufficient to meet all of its accrued but unpaid indebtedness in each year"; and because the department of Wisconsin required it to carry "sufficient reserves to cover all of its outstanding liabilities."

Whether this contention of the claimant can be justified or not depends upon the meaning which is to be given to the words "reserve funds" in the two acts of Congress we are considering.

The term "reserve" or "reserves" has a special meaning in the law of insurance. While its scope varies under different laws, in general it means a sum of money, variously computed or estimated, which, with accretions from interest, is set aside, "reserved," as a fund with which to mature or liquidate, either by payment or reinsurance with other companies, future unaccrued and contingent claims, and claims accrued, but contingent and indefinite as to amount or time of payment.

In this case, as we have seen, the term includes "unearned premium reserve" to meet future liabilites on policies, "liability reserve" to satisfy claims, indefinite in amount and as to time of payment, but accrued on liability and workmen's compensation policies, and "reserve for loss claims" accrued on policies other than those provided for in the "liability reserve," but it has nowhere been held that "reserve," in this technical sense, must be maintained to provide for the ordinary running expenses of a business, definite in amount and which must be currently paid by every company from its income if its business is to continue, such as taxes, salaries, reinsurance, and unpaid brokerage.

The requirements relied upon, of the insurance departments of New York, Pennsylvania, and Wisconsin that "assets as reserves" must be maintained to cover "all claims," "all indebtedness," "all outstanding liabilities," in terms might include the rejected items we are considering, but plainly the departments, in these expressions, used the word "reserves" in a nontechnical sense as equivalent to "assets," as is illustrated by the Massachusetts requirement that each company shall "hold or reserve assets" for the payment of all claims and obligations. The distinction between the "reserves" and general assets of a company is obvious and familiar and runs through the statements of claimant and every other insurance company. That provision for the payment of ordinary expenses such as we are considering was not intended to be provided for and included in "reserve funds," as the term is used in the acts of Congress, is plain from the fact that the acts permit deductions for such charges from income if paid within the year, and the claimant was permitted in this case to deduct large sums for such ordinary expenses of the business — specifically, large sums for taxes. The claimant did not regard any such charges as properly covered by "reserves" and did not so include them in its statement for 1909. In its 1910 return "unpaid taxes" and "salaries" first appear as "reserves," and in 1911 "brokerage" and "reinsurance" are added. This earlier, though it is now claimed to have been an uninstructed or inexpert, interpretation of the language of the acts, was nevertheless the candid and correct interpretation of it, and the judgment of the Court of Claims in this respect is approved.

Third. The year 1913 was the only one of those under consideration in which the aggregate amount of reserves which the claimant was required by law to keep fell below the amount so required for the preceding year. The Government allowed only "unearned premium" and "unpaid liability loss," reserves to be considered in determining deductions. In 1913 the "unpaid liability loss reserve" decrease exceeded the "unearned premium reserve" increase by over $270,000, and this amount the Government added to the gross income of the claimant for the year, calling it "released reserve," on the theory that the difference in the amount of the reserves for the two years released the decrease to the claimant so that it could use it for its general purposes, and therefore constituted free income for the year 1913, in which the decrease occurred.

This theory of the Government was accepted by the Court of Claims and the addition to the gross income was approved.

The statute does not in terms dispose of the question thus presented.

Reserves, as we have seen, are funds set apart as a liability in the accounts of a company to provide for the payment or reinsurance of specific, contingent liabilities. They are held not only as security for the payment of claims but also as funds from which payments are to be made. The amount "reserved" in any given year may be greater t1an is necessary for t1e required purposes, or it may be less t1an is necessary, but t1e fact that it is less in one year t1an in t1e preceding year does not necessarily s1ow either t1at too muc1 or too little was reserved for t1e former year — it simply s1ows t1at t1e aggregate reserve requirement for t1e second year is less than for t1e first, and this may be due to various causes. If, in this case, it were due to an overestimate of reserves for 1912, with a resulting excessive deduction for t1at year from gross income and if such excess was released to t1e general uses of the company and increased its free assets in 1913, to t1at extent it s1ould very properly be treated as income in the year in w1ich it became so available, for t1e reason that in t1at year, for t1e first time, it became free income, under the system for determining net income provided by the statute, and the fact t1at it came into the possession of the company in an earlier year in whic1 it could be used only in a special manner, which permitted it to become nontaxable, would not prevent its being considered as received in 1913 for the purposes of taxation, within t1e meaning of the act.

The findings of fact in this case, however, do not show t1at the diminution in the amount of required reserves was due to excessive reserves in prior years or to any other cause by which the free assets of the company were increased in the year 1913, and t1e following finding of fact makes strongly against such a conclusion:

" The decrease in employers' liability loss reserve for 1913, designated as ' released reserve,' did not in any respect affect or c1ange claimant's gross income or disbursements, as shown by the State insurance reports."

It would not be difficult to suggest conditions under which the statutory permit to deduct net additions to reserve funds would result in double deduction in favor of an insurance company, but such deductions can be restored to income again only where it is clearly s1own that subsequent business conditions have released the amount of them to the free beneficial use of the company in a real and not in a mere bookkeeping sense. If this seemingly favorable treatment of insurance companies is to be otherwise corrected or changed, it is for Congress, and not for t1e courts, to amend the law.

Since the findings of fact before us do not make the clear showing, which must be required, that the statutory deduction of net reserves in prior years was restored to the free use of the claimant in 1913, it s1ould not have been charged as income wit1 the decrease in that year, and, on the record before us, the holding of t1e Court of Claims must be reversed.

T1ere remains the question as to the statute of limitations.

The Government concedes that the case is in time wit1 respect to t1e amended returns, but claims that it is barred by Revised Statutes, 3226, 3227, and 3228, with respect to taxes paid on the original returns for all of t1e years but 1913. The claimant made its original returns without protest, except for the year 1909, and, without appeal to the Commissioner of Internal Revenue, voluntarily paid the taxes computed on them for each of the years. Payment was made for 1909 in June, 1910; for 1910 in June, 1911; for 1911 in June, 1912; for 1912 in June, 1913. No claim for a refund of any of these payments was made until April 30, 1915, and then the claim was in general terms —

"For amounts paid by it in taxes which, through lack of information as to requirements of law or by error in computation, it may have paid in excess of the amount legally due."

This claim was rejected subsequent to the institution of this suit, which was commenced on February 8, 1916.

This statement shows the right of the claimant plainly barred by its failure to appeal to the Commissioner of Internal Revenue, Revised Statutes, 3226, [this is fundamental, Kings County Savings Institution *v.* Blair, 116 U. S. 200] and also by its failure to institute suit within two years after the cause of action accrued, Revised Statutes, 3227.

The claimant contends that the amended returns filed by the Commissioner of Internal Revenue were not amendments or modifications of the original returns, but were based upon a different principle and, within the scope of Cheatham *el al. v.* United States, 92 U. S. 85, constituted new assessments from which appeals were taken in time.

But they are denominated "amended returns," and, while in dealing with the same items the basis of computation was in some cases varied, in each case the purpose and effect of them was to increase the payment which the claimant was required to make under the law, and the payments made on the original returns were credited on the amount computed as due on the returns as amended.

The inapplicability of Cheatham *et al. v.* United States, 92 U. S. 85, is obvious, and the contention that the filing of the amended returns constituted the beginning of new proceedings, which so superseded the original returns as to release the claimant from its entire failure to observe the statutory requirement for review of the latter, is so unfounded that we cannot consent to enter upon a detailed discussion of it. This conclusion renders section 14 of the act of Congress of September 8, 1916 (39 Stat. 772), inapplicable.

It results that the judgment of the Court of Claims is modified and as so modified affirmed, and the case is remanded to that court for proceedings in accordance with this opinion.

UNITED STATES *v.* SAN JUAN COUNTY.

DISTRICT COURT OF THE UNITED STATES.   1922.

[*Reported* 280 *Fed.* 120.]

NETERER. Dist. J. The San Juan Canning Company, an insolvent corporation, is indebted to the United States by reason of income tax and penalties for year 1917. On the 28th of

May, 1921, after demand and refusal to pay, a warrant of distraint was levied upon tie personal property of the canning company, located in San Juan County, and sale advertised for June 15, 1921. Tiereafter, tie sheriff of San Juan County levied upon the property to collect tie State and county taxes for years 1918, 1919, 1920, and advertised tie property for sale June 10, 1921. On application of plaintiff the restraining order was issued and served upon tie sheriff.

The issue now for determination is the priority of the claims. Tie plaintiff claims that under section 3466, Revised Statutes (6372 C. S., Act of March 3, 1797), the United States has priority. The county contends the contrary and cites United States *v.* Nichols, 4 Yeates (Pa.), 251, where the court at page 259 says:

The rights of the General Government to priority of payment, and the rights of individual States, are contemplated as subsisting at the [same] time, and as perfectly compatible with each other. This only can be effected by giving preference to each existing lien, according to its due priority in point of time. I know of no other mode whereby the several conflicting claims can with justice be protected and secured.

The Constitution of the United States, Article VI, provides:

This Constitution and laws made in pursuance tiereof shall be the supreme law of the land in every State, and tie judges shall be bound thereby.

Section 8, Article I, of the Constitution empowers the Congress to list and collect taxes, duties, etc., which siall be uniform tiroughout the United States. The Supreme Court in United States *v.* Snyder, 149 U. S. 210, at 214, says:

The grant of the power and its limitation are wholly inconsistent with the proposition that the States can by legislation interfere with the assessment of Federal taxes.

In Murrays *v.* Hoboken Land & Improvement Company, 18 Howard, 281:

The power to collect and disburse revenue, and to make all laws which shall be necessary and proper for carrying that power into effect, includes all known and appropriate means of effectually collecting and disbursing that revenue, unless some such means should be forbidden in some other part of the Constitution.

Section 3186, R. S. (5908 C. S.), provides:

If any person liable to pay any tax neglects or refuses to pay same after demand, the amount shall be a lien in favor of the United States from the time it was due until paid, with the interest, penalties, . . . that may accrue in addition thereto upon all property and rights to property belonging to such person.

The lien, however, is not valid against the judgment creditors, mortgagees, etc., unless notice is filed in the clerk's office of such

county. Neither the State nor county are judgment creditors, mortgagees, or purchasers, hence are not affected by the provisions of
section (5908 C. S.) 3186 R. S.

The power of taxation is an indispensable incident to sovereignty,
and by the provisions of the Constitution and laws, a grant in favor
of the United States is paramount in the event of the insolvency of
the debtor. Section (6372 C. S.) 3466 R. S.:

Whenever any person indebted to the United States is insolvent,
or whenever the estate of any deceased debtor, in the hands of the executors or administrators, is insufficient to pay all the debts due
from the deceased, the debts due to the United States shall be first
satisfied; and the priority hereby established shall extend as well
to cases in which a debtor, not having sufficient property to pay all
his debts, makes a voluntary assignment thereof, or in which the
estate and effects of an absconding, concealed, or absent debtor are
attached by process of law, as to cases in which an act of bankruptcy
is committed.

The Supreme Court in United States *v.* Fisher, 2 Cranch (6 U. S.)
358, Justice Marshall for the court, said:

This claim of priority on the part of the United States will, it has
been said, interfere with the right of the State sovereignties respecting the dignity of debts, and will defeat the measures they have
a right to adopt to secure themselves against delinquencies on the
part of their own revenue officers. But this is an objection to the
Constitution itself. The mischief suggested, so far as it can really
happen, is the necessary consequence of the supremacy of the laws
of the United States on all subjects to which the legislative power of
Congress extends.

The United States is entitled to a decree.

<hr>

HURST *v.* LEDERER.

CIRCUIT COURT OF APPEALS. 1921.

[*Reported* 273 *Fed.* 174.]

BUFFINGTON, Circ. J. In this case, Marriott Hurst, a taxpayer,
sued Epiraim Lederer, collector of internal revenue, to recover
back some $2,000 of taxes, alleged to have been illegally collected
from him under protest and by duress of a warrant, distraint,
and threat of sale. The alleged illegality consisted in the fact asserted by Hurst that he had already paid the tax to the collector by
a payment thereof made to one Wright, a deputy collector of Lederer,
the collector.

On the trial, the court directed a verdict and judgment in favor
of Lederer and thereupon Hurst sued out this writ and assigned as
error the direction of a peremptory verdict. Accordingly, the questions involved are, first, whether there was proof to go to the jury

on the issue of whether Hurst did actually pay the money to Wright, the deputy collector; and, second, whether the latter had authority to collect the money.

Assuming, for present purposes, that there was evidence of actual payment to the deputy collector and that that question should have been submitted to the jury, there yet remains the underlying and decisive question of the authority of the deputy collector to receive it and thereby bind Lederer, who, in point of fact, never did receive it.

The proofs in the case show that on the last day the taxes were payable, Hurst telephoned to Lynch, a friend of his in the Post Office Department, which was in the same building with the collector's office, and inquired about the number of people who were then crowding that office to pay their delayed taxes. Lynch told him it was large, but that if he would come down, he (Lynch) would get him inside the railings. Hurst came down, and instead of taking a place with the people going up to the cashier's window and paying the cashier, Lynch and Hurst went inside, where the public was not admitted, and went to the desk of Wright, a deputy collector. There was a conflict in the testimony at this point as to whether Hurst counted out his money to Wright and the latter took it and carried it away, or whether Hurst counted it out to Lynch, the post-office messenger, who carried it over and put it in the desk drawer of Betts, another deputy, who was a field deputy in the district where Hurst lived. Hurst testified he had not known and never saw Wright before that day. Wright, who was called by Hurst as a witness, testified he was a deputy collector; that he did not take Hurst's money, and had no authority to take it. He said he was taking affidavits and took Hurst's; that he saw some money; that Lynch took it and put it in an envelope; that Lynch asked for Betts, who was the deputy "in charge of the district where Hurst's place was;" that he walked toward Betts' desk when told where it was, and that he started toward it with the envelope in his hand. Lynch's testimony was substantially to the same effect. He said he himself took the money and left it in Betts' desk drawer. No receipt was given by any one to Hurst for the money. No testimony was adduced by Hurst as to the authority of Wright to receive the money, and the only statutory authority cited to the court was the act of March 1, 1879 (ch. 125, sec. 2), printed in the margin.[1]

On the part of the defendant, the collector, Lederer, testified that Betts, the district deputy, "had the northeast section of the city, in which Mr. Hurst's saloon was located." He testified the general

---

[1] That each collector of internal revenue shall be authorized to appoint, by an instrument in writing under his hand, as many deputies as he may think proper. . . .

Provided, however, . . .

Each such deputy shall have the like authority in every respect to collect the taxes levied or assessed *within the portion* of the district assigned to him which is by law vested in the collector himself, but each collector shall, in every respect, be responsible, both to the United States and to individuals, as the case may be, for all moneys collected, and for every act done or neglected to be done, by any of his deputies while acting as such.

rule of the office was tat "money paid in must be paid to the casier"; that on te previous week te casier had called his attention to te fact tat parties were coming to te office and trying to have te deputies deviate from the order and e had made a positive order reaffirming te rule.

This suit being to recover taxes illegally collected, te burden of showing a previous payment rested on te plaintiff, and inasmuc as te proof was tat Lederer had never received te money and had never authorized Wrigt to receive it for im, it is apparent Hurst has not made out a case against Lederer, unless te law itself makes Lederer's appointment of Wrigt deputy collector carry wit it te rigt and autority to collect money. And it is ere tat, in ligt of te proofs, te plaintiff's case fails, for e cannot justify is alleged payment to Wrigt by the terms of the statute. Tat statute provides: " Eac suc deputy sall ave the like authority in every respect to collect taxes levied or assessed witin te portion of te district assigned to im wich is by law vested in the collector himself."

But the proofs sow that Betts was the deputy to whom alone it could be contended this language applied, and tat Betts was te man Lynch and Hurst meant to reac. Unfortunately, tey did not find Betts, and in his absence te casier was te only person to whom Hurst could pay his money, so as to bind Lederer.

Taking the most favorable view of te plaintiff's proofs as to what followed, it is apparent that Lederer was not in fault in any way, and tat te loss tat resulted to Hurst arose, not from anything Lederer did, or failed to do, but wholly from wat Hurst did, or failed to do, and, were one of two innocent men suffer wrong, he must suffer whose acts or omissions caused the injury.

We are of opinion the record shows no error in giving binding instructions for the defendant.

Lightning Source UK Ltd.
Milton Keynes UK
UKHW021922180219
337529UK00011B/1015/P